Westminster Abbey

WESTMINSTER ABBEY

A Church in History

Edited by

DAVID CANNADINE

Paul Mellon Centre for Studies in British Art
In association with
The Dean and Chapter of the Collegiate Church of St Peter Westminster (Westminster Abbey)
Distributed by
Yale University Press, New Haven and London

First published in 2019 by the Paul Mellon Centre for Studies in British Art

First published in paperback 2024

16 Bedford Square, London, WC1B 3JA

paul-mellon-centre.ac.uk

ISBN 978-1-913107-47-5 PB

Library of Congress Control Number: 2019936789

British Library Cataloguing-in-Publication Data
A catalogue record for this book is available from the British Library

Project management and design by Gillian Malpass
Editing by Rosemary Roberts
Picture research by Cecilia Mackay
Index by Jane Horton
Origination by Evergreen Colour Management Ltd
Printed in China through Worldprint

Endpapers: The Cosmati pavement in front of the high altar, laid in 1268.

Pages i and iii: Tiles from the pavement of the mid-13th-century chapter house.

Page ii: View of the west front of Westminster Abbey from across Broad Sanctuary.

Contents

Acknowledgements

THIS BOOK WAS COMMISSIONED TO MARK THE 750th anniversary of the consecration of the third abbey church, constructed by Henry III and dedicated on 13 October 1269. My first and heartfelt thanks go to the Dean and Chapter for having commissioned and supported this collective venture with great generosity and imagination. On behalf of my fellow contributors, I am especially grateful to the Dean himself, the Very Revd Dr John Hall, and to Sir Stephen Lamport, then the Receiver General, for their wisdom and constancy, and their steadfast practical assistance. I am eager to make plain that the Dean and Chapter have never sought to interfere with, or to exert influence over, our findings and interpretations contained in the chapters that follow. All of us are also hugely indebted to the abbey staff, especially to Dr Tony Trowles, the Head of the Abbey Collections and Librarian, and Matthew Payne, the Keeper of the Muniments, who preside over and cherish one of the great archival accumulations of the Western world, and to Christine Reynolds, Assistant Keeper.

The preparation of this book for publication has been a complex matter of logistics and coordination, and it has been overseen with characteristic brilliance and efficiency by Gillian Malpass. The illustrations are an essential part of this wide-ranging history, not just optional extras, and the picture research has been undertaken by Cecilia Mackay, with her customary flair and expertise. The copy-editing of this multi-authored text has been meticulously carried out by Rosemary Roberts, and the index has been skilfully compiled by Jane Horton. The Director of the Paul Mellon Centre in London, Professor Mark Hallett, has been unfailingly helpful, and we are all much indebted and beholden to him and to his staff, as also to their colleagues at Yale University Press. Beyond these specific and essential expressions of gratitude, my own thanks also go to my fellow contributors to this volume, for their forbearance, collegiality and professionalism. It has been a pleasure and a privilege to have worked with them.

David Cannadine
Norfolk
5 March 2019

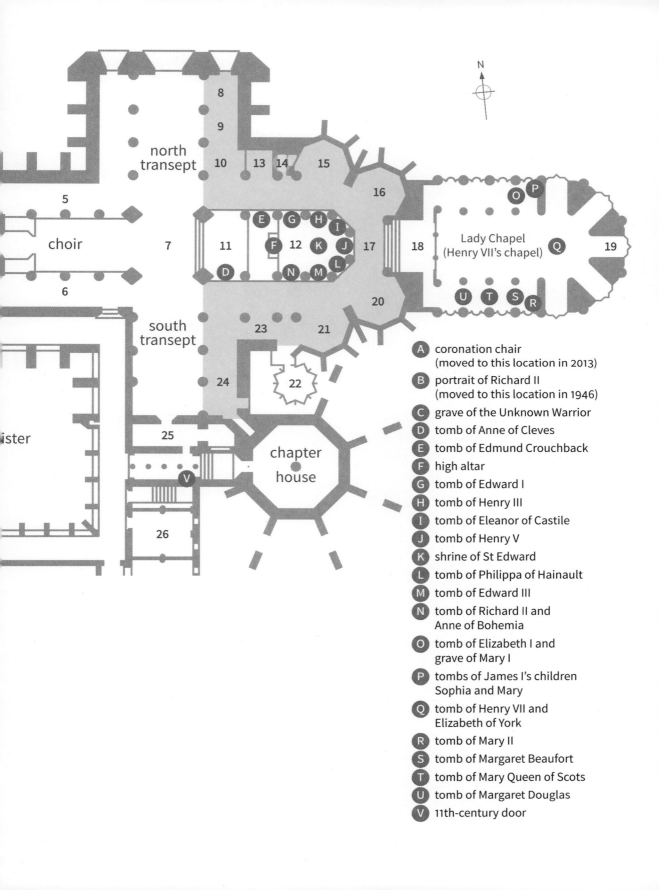

N

north
transept

choir

south
transept

ister

5

6

7

8

9

10   13 14   15

16

11   12   17   18

20

23   21

24   22

25

26

chapter
house

Lady Chapel
(Henry VII's chapel)

19

E   G   H

F   K   J

D   N   M   L

I

O   P

Q

U   T   S   R

A   coronation chair
     (moved to this location in 2013)
B   portrait of Richard II
     (moved to this location in 1946)
C   grave of the Unknown Warrior
D   tomb of Anne of Cleves
E   tomb of Edmund Crouchback
F   high altar
G   tomb of Edward I
H   tomb of Henry III
I   tomb of Eleanor of Castile
J   tomb of Henry V
K   shrine of St Edward
L   tomb of Philippa of Hainault
M   tomb of Edward III
N   tomb of Richard II and
     Anne of Bohemia
O   tomb of Elizabeth I and
     grave of Mary I
P   tombs of James I's children
     Sophia and Mary
Q   tomb of Henry VII and
     Elizabeth of York
R   tomb of Mary II
S   tomb of Margaret Beaufort
T   tomb of Mary Queen of Scots
U   tomb of Margaret Douglas
V   11th-century door

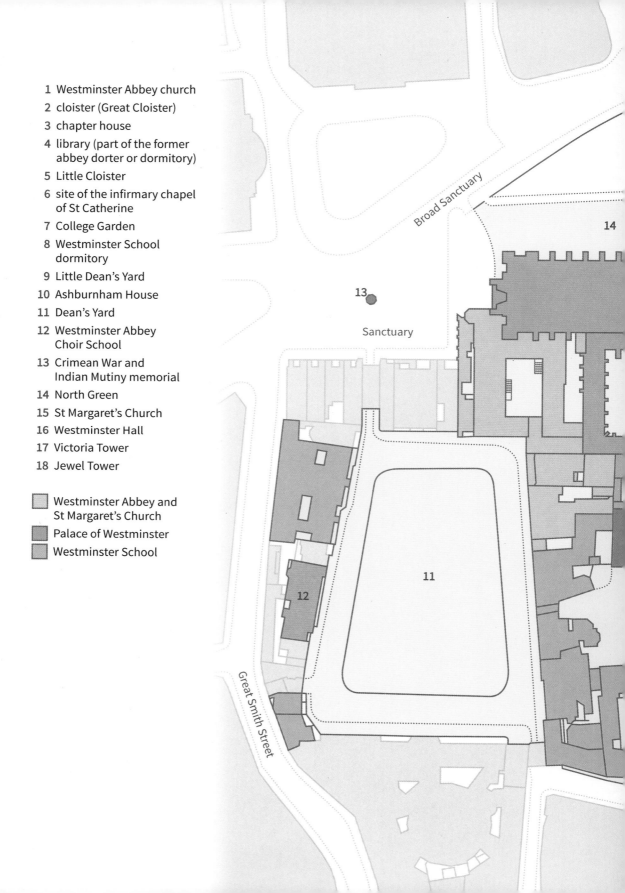

1 Westminster Abbey church
2 cloister (Great Cloister)
3 chapter house
4 library (part of the former
   abbey dorter or dormitory)
5 Little Cloister
6 site of the infirmary chapel
   of St Catherine
7 College Garden
8 Westminster School
   dormitory
9 Little Dean's Yard
10 Ashburnham House
11 Dean's Yard
12 Westminster Abbey
   Choir School
13 Crimean War and
   Indian Mutiny memorial
14 North Green
15 St Margaret's Church
16 Westminster Hall
17 Victoria Tower
18 Jewel Tower

Westminster Abbey and
St Margaret's Church
Palace of Westminster
Westminster School

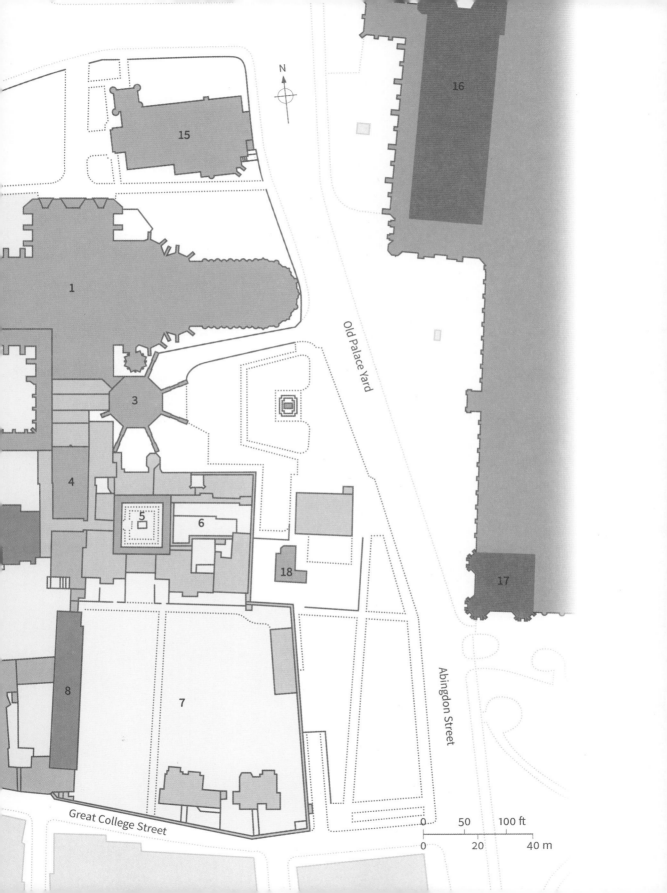

N

15

16

1

Old Palace Yard

3

4

5

6

18

17

7

8

Abingdon Street

Great College Street

0   50   100 ft

0   20   40 m

Prologue

The Abbey Now

JOHN HALL, DEAN OF WESTMINSTER

WHAT IS THE ABBEY'S LIFE, ITS MINISTRY AND MISSION, almost a fifth of the way into the twenty-first century? The story this book tells is, above all, of the abbey's engagement with the community around it, with the nation as a whole, and with the wider world. As the book describes, this is a story of constant change and varying fortune, and of unforeseen new directions. The abbey's place in the life of the nation is probably more central today than it has been for many centuries. And that engagement is not always comfortable. In the middle of the afternoon on 22 March 2017, a terrorist drove a car at speed onto the pavement of Westminster Bridge, heading towards Parliament Square and the Palace of Westminster. He injured fifty people on the bridge, four of whom subsequently died. He then abandoned the car and ran to the carriage gates at the House of Commons end of the Palace of Westminster and stabbed and killed Police Constable Keith Palmer, one of the police guarding the gates. He was shot and killed by another police officer. Those responsible for the security of the Houses of Parliament invoked a procedure that suspended parliament itself, protected people within the building and brought into the security cordon potential witnesses of the incident.

Less than two hours after the attack, at about 4.30 p.m., the abbey was asked to offer temporary refuge to a number of people from within the Palace of Westminster. Some 1,400 people, including senior government ministers and members of both Houses of Parliament, as well as many people who support the infrastructure there, arrived at the abbey just before 5 p.m. and stayed for more than four hours, by which time they had been interviewed briefly by a large number of detectives. The abbey staff and our catering staff served well beyond their duty in caring for this large number of people, who waited patiently for things to be resolved. I led a prayer from the abbey's

1 (FACING PAGE)   Located in the heart of London, beside the seat of government, Westminster Abbey (*bottom left*) is seen, and sees itself, as standing for faith at the heart of the nation.

great pulpit, and a little later a commander of the Metropolitan Police addressed the people from the same pulpit about what would happen next. It seems unlikely that any similar event has ever taken place within the hallowed walls of the abbey. Leaving their contact details with the police, the patient parliamentarians finally filed out at about 9 p.m.; others, who had witness statements to make, stayed longer.

In the meantime, the abbey was planning to hold a service of Evening Prayer at 5 p.m.; had it not been a Wednesday, the service would have been Evensong with the abbey choir and a congregation of 400 or 500 people. As security was tight, Evening Prayer was said quietly in St Faith's Chapel by a handful of the abbey clergy and people. The daily round of prayer – Morning Prayer, the early morning Eucharist, the midday Eucharist and then Evensong, or, once a week, Evening Prayer, twenty-eight services a week, week in and week out – forms the indispensable foundation of the life of the abbey.

Two weeks later, in a plan that had been drawn up only a few months earlier in consultation with the Metropolitan Police and key faith leaders from across London, we held a Service of Hope in the abbey, attended by 2,000 or more of those who had been most closely involved in events on the day: the first responders – police, ambulance crews and doctors and nurses, fire officers and many others – the families of those who had died, and the injured. The Duke and Duchess of Cambridge and Prince Harry attended the service, which was televised by the BBC. The service included those of all faiths and none. Prayers were said by a Muslim commander of the Metropolitan Police, by a Jewish rabbi and by a Sikh, as well as by Christians. The mayor of London, Sadiq Khan, read a familiar Christian prayer that begins 'Lord, make me an instrument of thy peace'. Afterwards, the victims' families, the injured and the members of the emergency services met the Duke and Duchess and Prince Harry in the Deanery.

What does this tell us about the essence of the modern abbey, and why would it agree to conduct an interfaith service, planned at short notice and disrupting the even stream of its daily life? In truth, there is nothing unfamiliar or strange about such a service, though the particular context was unique. The abbey welcomes leaders of the Christian denominations and leaders of other faiths to take part in special services from time to time, as occasion seems right, since the abbey itself occupies a particularly privileged and special place within the heart of our national life, surrounded as it is by all the senior institutions dedicated to the public service. Thus uniquely located, the abbey is seen, and sees itself, as standing for faith at the heart of the nation. In the twenty-first century, religious faith takes many forms. The Christian Churches include our near neighbours, the Methodists at Central Hall Westminster and the Roman Catholics at Westminster Cathedral at the other end of Victoria Street. We often work with their leaders. And we have held services in the abbey to mark the special anniversaries of Christian communities and of other faiths.

Within recent years, for example, we have marked with a special service the centenary of the Armenian genocide, working closely with representatives of the Armenian Church in this country, the twentieth anniversary of the Srebrenica massacres, working with our Muslim neighbours, and the anniversaries of Kristallnacht and of the liberation of Auschwitz, working with the representatives of synagogues in London; we also held a service to mark the twentieth anniversary of the National Holocaust Centre and Museum. On all these occasions the abbey has been filled largely with members of those particular communities. It seems entirely right and fitting to welcome representatives of other faith communities into the precious place the abbey occupies at the heart of our democracy. It also seems right, in consequence, to invite them to pray from within their own faith traditions. The Church of England does not formally allow prayers to be said publicly in acts of worship by people of different religions. The abbey, however, as a royal peculiar, is not subject to the restrictions imposed within the Church of England, and has for many years welcomed prayers from other faiths.

This practice has ceased to be seen as controversial, and – indeed – is central to a particular annual ceremony in the abbey, attended by the Queen, at one time known as the Commonwealth Day Observance to distinguish it from a formal Christian service, though now we call it a 'service'. Every year on the second Monday of March, we welcome to this occasion people from every country in the Commonwealth and every known faith. On 12 March 2018 a congregation of 2,200 people included 700 children and young people from schools across the United Kingdom, together with the high commissioners, flag-bearers and other representatives of every Commonwealth country, the prime minister, who read a lesson, and the leader of the opposition. With the Queen, in her role as head of the Commonwealth, were ten members of the royal family. Prayers were said by representatives of the Methodist Church and the Coptic Orthodox Church, the Baha'i community, Liberal Judaism, the Zoroastrian community and the Sunni Muslim community. The long-standing representative of the Jain community, Dr Natubhai Shah, was among those presented at the end of the service to the Queen. Earlier in the day, I had attended a breakfast meeting with students of Westminster School, focusing on the Commonwealth, and a lunch with eighteen faith leaders, Christian, Jewish, Muslim, Hindu, Sikh, Buddhist, Jain, Zoroastrian and Baha'i, to discuss our collaboration. After the service, the Duke and Duchess of Cambridge and Prince Harry and his fiancée Meghan Markle attended a reception in the Deanery.

Some of the special services that take place annually in the abbey date back further. The first service held in London to commemorate the landings by the Australian

2   Every year on the second Monday of March, people from every country in the
Commonwealth and every known faith are welcomed to the abbey in a service organized by the
Royal Commonwealth Society; here, flagbearers participate in the Commonwealth Day service
on 12 March 2018.

and New Zealand Army Corps (Anzac) and other allied forces at Gallipoli in the
Dardanelles took place in the abbey in 1916. It was attended by George V and other
members of the royal family, and great crowds lined the streets of London to welcome
the troops marching through the city. On the centenary of the landings, 25 April 2015,
the Queen and the Duke of Edinburgh attended the annual Anzac Day service in the
abbey, together with more than 2,000 Australians and New Zealanders. Another annual
service, on the second Sunday of September, commemorates the Battle of Britain. A
memorial book with the names of all the allied airmen who died, which is usually
kept in the Royal Air Force Chapel at the far east end of the abbey, is carried to the
altar by representatives of the RAF, including an ever dwindling but inspiring number
of 'the Few' who took part in the battle. In May every year, we hold a service to
commemorate Florence Nightingale and to celebrate nursing. In October, we mark
the beginning of the legal year in the company of the lord chancellor and lord chief
justice, the justices of the Supreme Court, lords and ladies justice of appeal, high
court judges and representatives of the circuit and district judges and Queen's counsel,
together with representatives of Commonwealth and European legal jurisdictions. In

3   An annual service, on the second Sunday of September, commemorates the Battle of Britain, fought in the skies over southern England in the summer and autumn of 1940; among those attending are RAF veterans, including an ever smaller number of 'the Few' who served in the battle (seen here in 2017).

November, the abbey welcomes volunteer Scout and Guide leaders from throughout the United Kingdom, all of them with long service, to celebrate their remarkable work with great numbers of young people.

In 2018, besides these annual events, the abbey held a service to mark the fiftieth anniversary of the death of Martin Luther King Jr, commemorated among the twentieth-century martyrs on the abbey's west front. On 10 July, 100 years and 100 days after its inauguration, a service celebrated the work of the Royal Air Force. And services were held to give thanks for the life and work of Professor Stephen Hawking in June, with the burial of his ashes beside the remains of Isaac Newton, and, in September, a year after his death, to celebrate Sir Peter Hall, the doyen of theatre directors. At a special Evensong in November, we gave thanks for Archbishop Oscar Romero (also commemorated on the west front), martyred at the altar of a hospital chapel in San Salvador in 1980 and recently canonized by Pope Francis. Four years of centenary commemoration of the First World War marked, notably, in 2014, the outbreak of the conflict and, in 2016, the beginning of the Battle of the Somme, observed by an all-night vigil. On Sunday 11 November 2018, the hundredth anniversary of Armistice

173

4

10

4   The abbey has a unique role as Britain's national mausoleum; in June 2018 a service was held
to give thanks for the life and work of Professor Stephen Hawking, at which his ashes were
buried beside the remains of Isaac Newton, in Scientists' Corner in the nave.

Day, in addition to the annual service of Remembrance, a special service, attended by
representatives of all the countries involved in the First World War, was held as the
culmination of the commemorations.

Other twenty-first-century events that stand out in the memory include the service
of Evening Prayer with Pope Benedict XVI on 17 September 2010, and the visit of the
abbey choir to sing with the Sistine Chapel choir in St Peter's basilica in Rome on 29
June 2012; the wedding of Prince William and Catherine Middleton, now the Duke
and Duchess of Cambridge, on 29 April 2011, watched by 2.4 billion people – a third
of the world's population; and the visit of President Barack Obama and the First Lady
on 24 May 2011. The American president laid a wreath at the grave of the Unknown
Warrior, following a solemn observance performed by almost every head of state who
comes to Britain on a state visit. After the ceremony at the grave, the visitors and
their entourage make a circuit of the abbey. The King and Queen of Spain, visiting
in 2017, were shown the grave of Eleanor of Castile, the queen of Edward I, and that
of Mary I, who married Philip II of Spain, with Elizabeth I. The kings and queens
of Belgium and of the Netherlands have also recently been among our distinguished

visitors. The visit of the Emir of Qatar did not include prayers at the grave of the Unknown Warrior, but a discussion was held, in which the Anglican Bishop of Cyprus and the Gulf took part, about permitting diversity of faith within his emirate.

The abbey has an ancient commitment to education, having founded within its precincts a monastic school, which was re-founded by Henry VIII after the dissolution of the monastery in 1540 and again by Elizabeth I in 1560, after the dissolution of Mary I's monastery in 1559. Westminster School remains on its original site and, although it became a separate charity in 1868, it retains strong links with the abbey. The dean has always chaired the school's governing body and inducts new Queen's Scholars into membership of the wider abbey community. The school worships in the abbey twice a week. When the Queen visited for a thanksgiving service marking the 450th anniversary in 2010 of Elizabeth I's re-foundation of the abbey as the Collegiate Church of St Peter in Westminster, she unveiled a statue of Elizabeth I in Little Dean's Yard, within the school grounds, and opened in Dean's Yard the abbey's Education Centre, which now welcomes many thousands of children, students and other young people making organized visits to the abbey each year. In 2014 Westminster School, working with the Harris Federation, opened in Tothill Street, within two minutes' walk of the abbey, Harris Westminster Sixth Form, a government-funded college to educate, in a highly selective academic environment, 600 16- to 18-year-olds, with an absolute preference for young people from disadvantaged backgrounds. Another abbey establishment is the Westminster Abbey Choir School, a small boarding-school in Dean's Yard that offers a strong academic and musical education to the thirty or so boys in the abbey choir.

In the centuries before international tourism, the abbey always welcomed a small number of visitors during the day, who paid one of the staff for a tour. One visitor in the early nineteenth century described the sepulchral gloom and the birds nesting in the eaves of the Henry VII chapel. Things have changed. In the past year, 1.3 million people visited the abbey as tourists. Our aim is to welcome them as visitors and pilgrims, and to offer them a spiritual experience and an insight into history, while our responsibility is to ensure their safety and security. A duty chaplain leads prayers regularly throughout the day and offers ministries of word and sacrament. The welcome team serves the visitors, processing tickets and managing our audioguide operation. The caretaking and service-support team prepares the abbey for services and keeps the abbey and its precincts clean and tidy. Red-gowned marshals give people directions and keep an eye on security, supported by the yard beadles who check bags and manage queues. Blue-gowned volunteer abbey guides offer advice and information.

Behind the scenes, the abbey collection team maintains the library and extensive archives; precious holdings include the document that granted land for the original

5   A display of royal funeral effigies in The Queen's Diamond Jubilee Galleries, opened by Her Majesty the Queen in June 2018. Situated high above the abbey floor in the medieval triforium, the gallery and exhibition space provide permanent public access to over 300 treasures and artefacts, as well as a breathtaking view down the nave

abbey, authorized by King Edgar (r. 959–75). The conservation team protects the fabric of the abbey and precinct buildings and the many precious artefacts they contain. In June 2018, the Queen, with the Prince of Wales, opened The Queen's Diamond Jubilee Galleries in the eastern section of the triforium, high above the floor of the abbey, financed by a successful £23 million appeal, including generous contributions from the American Fund for Westminster Abbey, launched in 2012. The seven-storey Weston Tower, tucked behind flying buttresses, with a lift and a beautiful oak staircase, gives easy access to the galleries, which afford fine views of the abbey and its surroundings, and display rich and rare objects from the historic abbey collection, including wooden and wax figures, many in their own clothes, of kings and queens buried here.

6 (FACING PAGE)   The most significant addition to the fabric of the abbey church since the completion of Nicholas Hawksmoor's west towers in 1745, the Weston Tower gives access to The Queen's Diamond Jubilee Galleries. As visitors ascend, captivating details of stained glass and the exterior ornament of the Lady Chapel and chapter house are revealed, at close hand.

Near the entrance to the abbey's Great Cloister, fitted into existing buildings, the Cellarium café and restaurant, opened by the Duke of Edinburgh in October 2012, can seat 130 people at a time, for breakfast, morning coffee, lunch, afternoon tea and on some days an evening meal. The Cellarium, mostly for our visitors but also open to the general public and well used, is part of the abbey's commitment to hospitality, one of the principles of the Benedictine community that inhabited the abbey for 600 years until the mid-sixteenth century and whose spirit lives on. Continuing to prize the monastic tradition of prayer, work and study, we have recently commissioned a number of novice oblates and oblates, committed to be associated with the abbey community in prayer and regular worship – our foundational purpose.

The tenth-century abbey, raised before any other significant building took place in the area, was built on an island, Thorney (Thorn Island), a mile and a half from the city of London, surrounded by the Thames and one of its tributaries. The very name Westminster identifies the abbey's location, pointing up the distinction between the abbey church to the south-west of the city – the west minster – and another great church, St Paul's Cathedral – the east minster within the city of London. The Palace of Westminster arrived in the eleventh century, and for many centuries thereafter was simply one of the king's palaces, as the developing parliament met within the abbey precincts until 1540; at that date parliament removed to the palace, where it has resided ever since. The government offices in Whitehall arrived centuries later and the Supreme Court only in 2009. These are our nearest neighbours, alongside the headquarters of the Metropolitan Police, the London District of the British army and the royal households centred on Buckingham Palace.

In 2013 the abbey established an institute to focus the relationship with these neighbours. Lectures, symposia and dialogues take place at the abbey, involving a whole host of people working within these institutions. The Westminster Abbey Institute was founded to foster faith in public life, among those working around Parliament Square and beyond. It draws on the abbey's resources of spirituality and scholarship, rooted in its Benedictine tradition, to provide a public forum for debate on issues of faith, ethics, politics and public policy making. Part of the programme supports intensive work each year with a group of fellows, people in mid-career, each of whom has a mentor from among the very senior public servants who constitute a Council of Reference for the institute.

When I became Dean of Westminster in December 2006, I was told that the life of the abbey was relentless. So it is: full of vigour and endeavour and welcome and worship, still developing, still imagining a better future, working with all who will work with us, representing at the heart of our nation the faith that formed us. The Church's year and the great Christian festivals of Christmas, Easter and Pentecost maintain the rhythm of the abbey's life. Maundy Thursday and Good Friday we mark with particular solemnity as we look forward to the Church's transformation from sorrow to glory at the Paschal Vigil and Easter. These great observances allow us to focus on the heart of our purpose and mission as a church: the worship of God and the celebration of the Life, Death and Resurrection of our Lord Jesus Christ, revealing God's abiding and transforming love. On Easter day, as at Christmas, we are joined by 2,000 or more worshippers at each of the great services – people from all over the world who gather with us to worship Almighty God.

The abbey's contribution over the centuries to national life is a prominent and fascinating element of the country's story, which deserves to be better understood. As this history of the abbey is published, we look forward to marking joyfully the 750th anniversary of the consecration in 1269 of the current – third – abbey church building. In the midst of much change over the centuries, there is continuity. Although the manner of our life now is radically different from the earliest days of the monastery in 960, the foundation of our community life is unchanged. The daily round of prayer and worship still keep the abbey rooted and focused, and they provide us with our purpose, our calling and our work.

March 2019

Introduction

DAVID CANNADINE

'WE ARE', W. S. GILBERT BOASTED TO HIS COLLABORATOR Sir Arthur Sullivan in 1887, 'world-known, and as much an institution as Westminster Abbey', the very church where the service to mark Queen Victoria's golden jubilee was held in that same year.[1] Gilbert's comparison was distinctly self-aggrandizing in regard to the Savoy Operas, but he was undeniably correct in describing the abbey as an extraordinary national institution with a remarkable global resonance, and since then that extraordinariness and that resonance have only further increased. To be sure, there are many other great Western churches, among them St Paul's Cathedral and Canterbury cathedral in England, Notre-Dame, Reims and Chartres in France, St Peter's in Rome and the National Cathedral in Washington, D.C. All have their claims – in terms of their ecclesiastical importance, their architectural significance, their historical associations, their links with the secular powers of government, and their national and global reach – to be considered as charismatic places of worship and as iconic ecclesiastical buildings. But Westminster Abbey might well be regarded as the most charismatic and iconic of them all. It has been a house of prayer and devotion for much more than a millennium. It is a building of outstanding architectural significance, and an unrivalled national mausoleum. Its close and lengthy relations with the parliaments and the governments of this country are unequalled by any other church in any other nation and, with only two exceptions, every English and subsequently British monarch has been crowned in the abbey since 1066.

Yet this is no simple, linear, predictable, one-way story. On the contrary, the abbey's long history abounds with paradoxes, contradictions, unexpected turns, disruptive

7 (FACING PAGE)   A detail from the Westminster Retable, showing St Peter, the patron saint of the abbey, holding the key of heaven. Designed for the high altar of Henry III's church, the retable (see pages 62–3) is acknowledged to be one of the most important surviving examples of 13th-century English panel painting.

redirections and unforeseen outcomes. It came into being as one monastery among
the many that were founded in the cosmopolitan world of early medieval Catholic
Christendom, yet it was later repurposed as a powerful symbol of a more localized and
specific Protestant national identity. Much of its architecture, especially its apsidal east
end, is quintessentially French in origin and inspiration, but for several centuries the
abbey has been widely regarded as a no less quintessentially English (or British) building.
There is no church in Europe where the royal connection has been so sustained and
so strong, but there was nothing preordained about that before 1066, and during the
Republic and Cromwellian Protectorate of the 1650s the abbey was invested with a
very different purpose and identity, as the place where the parliamentary enemies of
the monarchy were admiringly interred and enthusiastically commemorated. Uniquely
among our great churches, the abbey has had no bishop (except briefly during the
1540s), because it was previously presided over by an abbot, and, on its re-founding
by Elizabeth I in 1560, it was established as a royal peculiar, and has ever since been
outside the hierarchy and jurisdiction of the Church of England. Although its royal
tombs and heroic monuments are unsurpassed by any other church in Europe, it is
the grave of an ordinary man, the Unknown Warrior, that in modern times has
become its most resonant burial place and tourist attraction. And while Westminster
Abbey has been, in turn, a Catholic monastery and a bastion of Anglicanism, it has
also been in the forefront of multi-faith dialogue and ecumenicalism since the Second
World War.

There are, then, many histories of Westminster Abbey, leading in many different
directions, some of them concerned with the building and the internal workings of the
church itself as a great religious house, others exploring broader contexts and supplying
wider perspectives, and this means that no single volume, even when multi-authored,
can realistically hope to encompass or do justice to them all. Accordingly, it is the aim
of this book to situate the abbey in the life of the Church (Roman Catholic, then
Protestant), in the history of the nation (England, then Great Britain, then the United
Kingdom), and in the geographies of the wider world (first continental Europe, later
the British Empire, then the Commonwealth, then the global Anglican communion,
and in more recent times, other faiths, too). For much of its history, the religious role
of the abbey has been shaped, defined and sometimes abruptly changed by political
events in London and beyond, even as it has also helped to shape and influence some
of those events. This, in turn, means that since the Norman Conquest, there has often
been a tension between the abbey as a house of God, a place of prayer, worship and
contemplation, and the abbey as a 'house of kings', where the connection between
Church and state has been the closest. This tension is most elaborately articulated in
the unrivalled proliferation of tombs and monuments (beginning with Edward the

8   The wedding of
Prince William and
Catherine Middleton
took place in the abbey
in 2011; upon their
marriage they became
the Duke and Duchess
of Cambridge. The
pre-eminent royal and
state church, Westminster
Abbey has witnessed the
evolving ceremonials of
coronations, royal burials
and royal weddings
since 1066.

Confessor), and in the evolving ceremonials of coronations (almost continuously since
1066), of royal burials and funerals (the former ended in 1760, the latter more recently
revived) and of royal weddings (occasionally in medieval times and again more recently).   8
From one perspective, the abbey is a deeply sacred building; from another, it is the
most secular church in the country, with the Dean and Chapter subordinate to the
sovereign, but recognizing no higher ecclesiastical power or authority.

There are only meagre sources for the abbey's early history, which cannot be fully
relied on, and its possible founding date of AD 604 must remain a matter of conjecture, as
indeed must the architectural details of the first monastic building. Its continuous history
begins more than three hundred years later, with its re-founding by Bishop Dunstan
of London and King Edgar, probably in 959. But it was the subsequent interventions
of two very different kings that transformed the abbey's status and fortunes. The first
was Edward the Confessor (r. 1042–66), who began to rebuild the abbey in the 1050s
on an exceptionally lavish scale, and endowed it with corresponding generosity; he was
buried there, he was canonized in 1161, and he was later magnificently entombed and
enshrined. The second was William the Conqueror (r. 1066–87), who defeated King
Harold (r. 1066) at the Battle of Hastings, but who followed him in being crowned
at Westminster Abbey, on Christmas day 1066. Thus was the tradition invented and
established, enduring into our own time, that the coronation of our monarchs, which
had previously happened elsewhere in England, takes place in the abbey. The Confessor
and the Conqueror were the first sovereigns to associate themselves so closely with
the abbey, and they also made Westminster their place of residence and the seat of
government, thereby connecting Church and state in a bond that has lasted and evolved
across the subsequent millennium. The Confessor's splendid Romanesque church was
replaced by an even more magnificent Gothic building, constructed by Henry III (r.
1216–72), the abbey's greatest architectural patron, and although the west front would
long remain uncompleted, Henry's church was dedicated on 13 October 1269. Richard
II (r. 1377–99) oversaw the construction of the northern entrance and several bays of
the nave, and Henry VII (r. 1485–1509) created the extraordinary Lady Chapel at the
east end which is more popularly known by his name than the Virgin Mary's.

These energetic and expensive royal interventions transformed the original monastic
foundation that had been established on Thorn Island into one of the most significant
churches in Catholic Christendom, partly on account of its size and scale, and its
innovatively cosmopolitan architecture and decoration, and partly because of the
uniquely close connection that was established between the English monarchy and
the abbey, which from the time of Henry III became the established burial place for
sovereigns, their consorts and often their children as well. But the fourteenth and
fifteenth centuries also witnessed lengthy intervals of royal indifference and neglect,
especially during the Wars of the Roses towards the end of this period, when the
English crown and throne were themselves subjects of violent contention. Yet even
during these troubled and uncertain times, the monastic life of the abbey, which since
the tenth century had been regulated according to the rule of St Benedict, went on
and endured. Indeed, it was as a monastery, presided over by an abbot, rather than
as a royal church, where the sovereign was crowned, that the abbey had obtained its

9 The coronation of William the Conqueror, on Christmas day in 1066, established Westminster as the place where kings and queens are anointed and receive their crowns; this miniature comes from Matthew Paris's 13th-century annal of the abbey's recent past, *Flores historiarum* ('Flowers of history').

freedom from the jurisdiction of the Bishop of London in 1222, and was thereafter answerable only to the pope himself. That independence was successively redefined, rescinded and eventually reasserted during the turbulent and traumatic sixteenth century: Henry VIII (r. 1509–47) converted the abbey into a cathedral, no longer under papal jurisdiction, and replaced the abbot and the monks with a Dean and Chapter (and, briefly, with a bishop); Edward VI (r. 1547–53) re-founded Westminster as a subordinate cathedral to neighbouring St Paul's; Queen Mary (r. 1553–8) reversed these changes and temporarily restored the Benedictine monastic community; and Elizabeth I (r. 1558–1603) re-established the abbey as a Protestant church, and as a royal peculiar directly under the monarch's control, governed once more by a Dean and Chapter.

The sixteenth century was indeed the hinge era for the abbey, but the eventual, late Tudor outcome was no foregone conclusion.

No one, looking forward in the 1500s, could have predicted that all this would happen to the abbey during the remainder of the century, and no one, looking forward in the 1600s, could have been sure what would happen next. The burial of Queen Elizabeth (1603), the reburial of Mary, Queen of Scots (1612), the coronation and burial of James I (r. 1603–25) and the coronation of Charles I (r. 1625–49) deliberately linked together the abbey, the old Tudor and the new Stuart dynasties and the recent Protestant settlement. But during the 1640s and 1650s, there was another abrupt break point and change of direction: the execution of Charles I, the abolition of the monarchy, the disestablishment of the Church of England, and the replacement of the abbey's Dean and Chapter as its governing body by a parliamentary committee ushered in a new and completely different world. The 'house of kings' had been superseded by the 'house of regicides', as the abbey was again repurposed, this time as a republican temple of fame, in which were interred such parliamentary paragons and military heroes as John Pym and Oliver Cromwell. But with the Restoration of the monarchy and the Church of England in 1660, the 'Glorious Revolution' of 1688 and the Hanoverian succession in 1714 the abbey resumed its role as the pre-eminent royal and state church, as if the Cromwellian Interregnum had never happened. Purcell and Handel composed notable coronation anthems, and the west front was belatedly completed, with the construction of two towers designed by Nicholas Hawksmoor. They would furnish the abbey with its most famous image, as recorded in Canaletto's painting of the knights of the Bath in procession in 1749.

George II (r. 1727–60) would be the last monarch to be buried in the abbey, and the ensuing decades were a time of religious and institutional torpor, contrasting strongly with the wrenching and turbulent changes of Tudor and Stuart periods: worldly deans holding plural livings, uninspired services and preaching, and more tourists and monuments, but less true religious devotion. The abbey was also enjoying a substantial income from its extensive urban and rural estates, some of which it had held since early medieval times, and it still played a predominant role in the government of the City of Westminster and of Westminster School, re-founded by Henry VIII and again by Elizabeth I. Thus regarded, the abbey seemed not so much a house of God, but rather an outwork of what radical critics called 'old corruption' – a world of patronage, pensions, sinecures, family connection and self-perpetuating oligarchy, where the great institutions of Church and state were agencies of private benefit rather than vehicles for promoting the public good. This negative impression was confirmed as the Dean and Chapter made money by allowing the proliferation of increasingly ornate monuments, some of which were undoubtedly merited by the stature and contribution of their subjects, but many were not. These defects were eventually remedied during the Victorian age of reform: pluralism and absenteeism declined, Westminster School and the City of Westminster were freed from the abbey's jurisdiction (although some links still remain), and it ceased to be a major landlord. Between 1864 and 1881, Arthur Penrhyn Stanley was a transformative dean, who made the abbey a place of broad, liberal and welcoming churchmanship, with better-sung services and memorable preaching, and with more grand public funerals and yet more (though better-deserved) monuments. As a result, the abbey again became increasingly central to the life of the nation as a whole, especially the imperial nation that the United Kingdom had progressively become during Queen Victoria's reign.

148

Yet during the nineteenth century, the monarchy itself played little part in the day-to-day life of the abbey: the great age of royal building and patronage was long since over (the Hawksmoor towers had been funded by parliament not by the sovereign), and George IV (r. 1820–30), William IV (r. 1830–37) and Queen Victoria (r. 1837–1901) rarely visited the place except for their coronations (and Victoria also for her golden jubilee service). The reign of Edward VII (r. 1901–10) may have witnessed the apogee of imperial consciousness and the first authentically imperial coronation, but the king–emperor felt no close affinity with the abbey (though he had been a pall-bearer at Gladstone's funeral in 1898, much to his mother's annoyance and disapproval); nor, initially, did George V (r. 1910–36), even as his coronation was grander and more imperial than his father's. But the First World War was as much a turning point for the abbey and the monarchy as for the British nation and empire: there were new annual services, such as that marking Anzac Day, which the monarch and the royal family habitually attended; the Unknown Warrior was buried in the presence of the sovereign in 1920, and his grave became a place of popular pilgrimage; and royal weddings returned to the abbey, where they had not been held since medieval times, and only rarely then. This new and close association between the monarchy and the abbey has been further consolidated since the second half of the twentieth century. Like all her predecessors since the Reformation, Queen Elizabeth II has been the abbey's Visitor, in that she exercises supreme authority over it; but she has also attended its services more frequently and assiduously than any previous monarch. She is thus its 'visitor' in both senses. It is, then, tempting to regard this close personal relationship between the abbey and the monarchy as having been the natural and permanent state of affairs since the time of Edward the Confessor, but it is in fact a recent, twentieth-century development.

120, 147

155

159

10, 162, 163

In seeking to convey the abbey's unique history, as both a house of God and a 'house of kings', and as a great church set in a broader context, this book focuses on ecclesiastical, political, architectural and ceremonial matters, as they have developed and

10   On the centenary of the Battle of the Somme, 2016, a vigil was held at the grave of the Unknown Warrior. Here lie the remains of an unidentified British soldier killed in battle during the First World War; buried on 11 November 1920 with due ceremony 'among the kings', the soldier represents the many hundreds of thousands of empire dead. His grave has become a place of pilgrimage for monarchs, world leaders, the armed forces and civilians alike.

interacted, and as they have been of different importance at different times. The impact of the Norman Conquest was profound, political controversies peaked during the Tudor and Stuart eras, and the crisis of faith during the late nineteenth century was also a major challenge. Architecture was more important before the Reformation than after (with the exception of the later construction of the towers on the west front), while the 'restoration' of the abbey fabric was more significant for much of the nineteenth century than it would be during the twentieth, when very different approaches to conservation were adopted. Ceremonial flowered during late Tudor times, during the early and late seventeenth century, and again during the twentieth century. There have also been high points in terms of music – the Elizabethan era, the late Stuarts and early Hanoverians, Elgar and Parry, Vaughan Williams and Walton – but there have been low points as well. The nation in which the abbey has long been embedded has itself changed significantly over time, in terms of its territorial jurisdiction, its political structures, its social hierarchies, its gender relations, its ethnic composition and the intensity and pervasiveness of its commitment to Christian religion. In more ways than one, it has been a very long, varied and unpredictable journey, linking the abbey where pilgrims worshipped at the shrine of Edward the Confessor with the abbey where visitors in their thousands pay their respects at the grave of the Unknown Warrior.

Nor do the paradoxes and unexpected outcomes end there. We know more than ever before about the abbey's history, but that merely reinforces the view that it is impossible to predict what the remainder of the twenty-first century will bring, or how its future will unfold. The abbey itself seems adamantine and immutable, with its towers and pillars and flying buttresses; yet it is the third building on the site, construction and demolition are as much a part of its history as religious, political and social change, and the recently completed Queen's Diamond Jubilee Galleries, located in the triforium, represent a wholly new phase in its existence, purpose and appeal. The abbey is very royal but also very popular, it is very sacred yet also very secular, it is very old but with a constant capacity for unexpected renewal. It is the setting for great ceremonials, focused on the monarchy and royal family, the like of which occur in no other church in Christendom (and which, thanks to the media, now attract billions of viewers from around the world), yet it is also a place for private devotion and contemplative prayer. Its history is simultaneously one of extraordinary continuity, and no less extraordinary discontinuities, which the fabric itself disguises yet embodies, conceals but proclaims. With the possible exception of the Tower of London, it is England's greatest building, and it has no rival in its claim to be England's greatest church. The result, as Kenneth Clark once observed, is that 'the weight of so much history, the resonance of so many moving ceremonies, must touch even the most prosaic mind'.[2] Such, indeed, is Westminster Abbey today, 750 years since the consecration of Henry III's new church. But it cannot be too often stressed that none of this could have been foreseen when a group of monks founded their small monastic community, to the west of the city of London, on Thorn Island, in what may have been, or perhaps was not, the year AD 604.

11 The central scenes of the Bayeux Tapestry provide a striking visual image of Edward the Confessor's church, the first in England to be built in the Romanesque style, with a large tower and an arcaded nave.

1

From Legend to History:

*c.*604–*c.*1100

HENRY SUMMERSON

1065. And King Edward came to Westminster at Christmas and had the minster consecrated which he had himself built to the glory of God and of St Peter and of all God's saints. The consecration of the church was on Holy Innocents' Day. And he died on the eve of the Epiphany, and was buried on the feast of the Epiphany [6 January 1066], in the same minster.

Anglo-Saxon Chronicle[1]

THE CHURCH NOW RECOGNIZED THROUGHOUT THE WORLD as Westminster Abbey is essentially the one that Henry III began to erect in 1245. It was not, however, the first church to occupy the site, for Henry's magnificent building replaced an earlier one, the great Romanesque basilica that King Edward the Confessor[2] began to construct in the 1050s, until he was able – as the Anglo-Saxon Chronicle recorded – to order that it should be consecrated at the end of 1065. And Edward's church itself replaced an even older one, dating back at least to the middle of the tenth century. Nevertheless, despite frequent change and development, Westminster Abbey has maintained a persistent underlying continuity, in terms of form and function, and also of association. At no time has this been truer than in the Middle Ages, when the abbey's prestige and prosperity alike owed much to its relationship with the Confessor, a king who, for his Norman and Plantagenet successors, personified continuity with the Anglo-Saxon past.

Early Times: Foundations and Forgeries

That past was an ancient one, so old, indeed, that by King Edward's time it had become thoroughly obscured by legend. Various stories, of varying degrees of plausibility, were told of the foundation of Westminster Abbey. By the fifteenth century it had been extended as far back as the second century AD, to the mythical King Lucius.[3] In the Confessor's own time it was attributed to the cooperation of King Æthelberht of Kent and Mellitus, a companion of St Augustine who became the first Bishop of London. In around AD 604, so the story went, Mellitus was called upon to consecrate the new church, but was anticipated by a mysterious night-time visitor who turned out to be St Peter, the Prince of the Apostles, to whom the future abbey was to be dedicated.[4]

12   Lundenwic, to the west of Roman Londinium, was one of the most important centres of commerce in southern England in the 7th and 8th centuries. A little way upstream, Thorney – an island separated from the riverbank by the two branches of the Tyburn – was the site of a minster (probably from the 7th century), whose location to the west of St Paul's Cathedral presumably accounts for the name 'Westminster'. The site benefited from the proximity of Lundenwic's industry and trade, with its network of roads and movements of people and goods, as well as from the protection of watercourses.

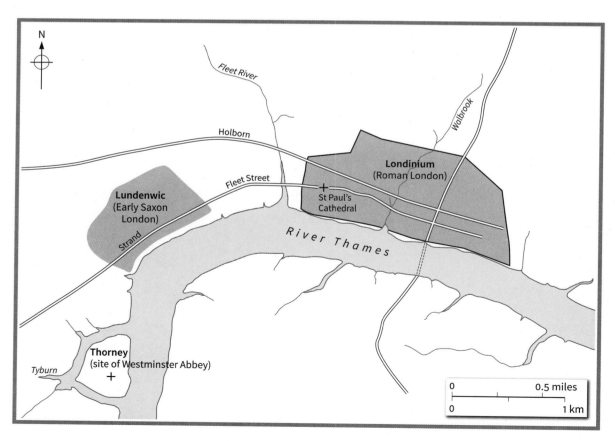

It is hardly possible to say what substrata of truth may underlie this story. The site of Westminster Abbey was known in the Anglo-Saxon period as Thorney (literally 'Thorn Island'), alongside the north bank of the Thames, a short distance up-river from the city of London. It is likely that it had been occupied from an early date, and conceivable that a church was established there in the seventh century, not least because it was at that time that London began to emerge as a major centre of commerce – 'an emporium for many peoples who come to it by land and sea', according to Bede[5] – though less within the old city walls than to the west of them, in a settlement recorded as 'Lundenwic' along what is now the Strand.[6]

In 604 a minster was founded at St Paul's, inside the city walls. An important church constructed on Thorney might well have come to be known as the 'west' minster, but it remains uncertain when or by whom a church was first built there. A supposedly late eighth-century charter refers to 'the awesome place (*loco terribili*) called Westminster', which could be interpreted as implying that Thorney had a rather desolate reputation.[7] Yet it is just as likely that the phrase was intended to suggest religious awe, appropriate to a place occupied by men devoted to the pursuit of holiness, for there was nothing exceptional about the site itself as the place for a minster.[8] Indeed, its position, on an island in the Thames, at a point at which a secondary stream (the Tyburn) ran into the river, had many close parallels among similar communities in southern England at this time – unsurprisingly, in light of the ease of communication, movement of people and goods, and protection that such a location enabled or provided.[9] The 'Palace of Westminster Sword', datable to the late eighth century, which was found in 1948 in Victoria Tower Gardens, at the southern end of the Houses of Parliament, and the large early ninth-century wooden hall, discovered in the early 1960s under the north side of Downing Street, less than half a mile north of the abbey, together provide clear evidence for activity in, and occupation of, the area by high-status people in the years around 800.[10]

13   An Anglo-Saxon sword, excavated at Westminster in 1948, offers evidence for the occupation of the Thorney area by people of wealth and importance in the late 8th century.

The charter mentioned above, said to have been given by King Offa of Mercia (r. 757–96), is a forgery, one of many concocted in the abbey that both illuminate and confuse – often at the same time – the early history of Westminster. Forgery today implies criminality, the creation of false writings (among other things) for the benefit of the person responsible. There were certainly medieval forgeries of this kind, but documents like those produced at Westminster should not necessarily be seen in a wholly sinister light. They proliferated throughout medieval Europe, but in England especially in the years on either side of 1100, at a time when written documents were just starting to be regarded as essential evidence for property rights; they set down in writing, often for the first time, the abbey's ownership of estates which it might genuinely have possessed for many years, even centuries, but of which it had previously had no record of a kind that the law courts, in particular, were willing to accept.[11] But forgeries were produced in earlier periods as well, as the community's needs required, their forms dictated by the particular challenges to which they were intended to be responses. Some were complete fabrications, but many more were 'improved' versions of genuine grants, in which the forger doctored, or even created, a text, less as a deliberate act of deception than as a kind of creative interpretation – for instance, by adding rights that were unknown, or at any rate unspecified, at the time when a gift was first made. To do this was no crime – so he could tell himself – but rather a praiseworthy attempt to fulfil the intentions of a long-dead benefactor, by ensuring that the abbey possessed all those lands and privileges that he would certainly have wished it to enjoy.

The problems that such attitudes have created for historians can be vividly demonstrated from another charter – indeed, the one with which the continuous history of Westminster Abbey arguably begins. In this, King Edgar (r. 959–75) ordered Dunstan, Archbishop of Canterbury, to restore to monastic ownership an estate ostensibly granted to Westminster by King Offa of Mercia with the encouragement of Archbishop Wulfred.[12] To all outward appearances it is a conventional Anglo-Saxon royal charter, the only problem being that it is explicitly dated to the year 951 – that is, eight years before either Edgar became king or Dunstan archbishop – while Offa died in 796, nine years before Wulfred succeeded to the see of Canterbury in 805! Underlying all these misdatings there probably lurks a genuine grant, but it can be seen that distinguishing truth from falsehood in texts like this is a task bristling with difficulties. Nor is it always much easier to interpret the few eleventh- and twelfth-century chronicles and saints' lives that also shed an occasional flickering light on the abbey's early history. Sulcard, a Westminster monk who compiled a history of his abbey in the late eleventh century, was clearly an honest man, but he no less clearly relied heavily on traditions of debatable reliability.[13] The questionable trustworthiness of these sources, and the

14   King Edgar's purported charter of 951, returning to Westminster lands originally granted by King Offa. Probably an 'improvement' on an authentic original, it shows the monks of Westminster almost from the outset resorting to forgery in order to reinforce their claims to lands and privileges.

gaps within and between them, mean that conjecture all too often has to do duty for certainty. But it is still possible to use them, with due caution, and with the occasional assistance of archaeology, to construct an account of Westminster Abbey's development in the early Middle Ages, until a clearer light begins to dawn in the reign of Edward the Confessor.

The first monastery on the site of what became Westminster Abbey was what is now conventionally described as a 'minster'.[14] Although the word shares its roots with 'monastery', it defines a settlement that later monks would have found hard to recognize as anything resembling their own, though many such institutions were established in north-western Europe in early medieval times. Set within an enclosure containing a church and other buildings, a minster was a community that could consist of monks – men vowed to poverty, chastity and obedience – or of secular priests, or of the two together, along with the servants needed for their support (there were also communities staffed by nuns, or by both nuns and monks). But although each minster had an abbot, responsible for the direction of its affairs and the maintenance of discipline, there was no uniformity of rule at this date, as there was with later monasteries, and those who lived in one were not secluded from the world, as monks were expected to be in later periods. Indeed, a minster was usually a mission centre for the conversion of the countryside around it, with the work being carried on by its clergy. Minsters were maintained from the produce of their own estates, given to them by their founders and other donors, who in return benefited from the prayers offered in them to God and the saints. They also provided religious services for places in their vicinity – usually on their own property – where Christianity had become established. The functions and requirements of a well-endowed minster were often such as to make it the focal point for its neighbourhood, both economically and socially, thanks to its constant demand for supplies of food, clothes and other necessaries, its need to dispose of the surplus produce from its lands, and, at a humbler level, the almsgiving that was another of its functions. The fact that it was intended to be permanent made it a potential force for stability in its neighbourhood, a consideration that doubtless appealed to the king or lord who contemplated establishing one. In the early twelfth century, the figure of Sæberht, King of the East Saxons (d. 616/17) and a nephew of Æthelberht of Kent (d. 616?), was brought into Westminster's foundation story, and there may, in fact, be elements of truth behind this.[15] Seventh-century London did indeed form part of the East Saxon kingdom, making it perfectly possible that Sæberht gave or confirmed the land on which the early minster was built.

The forged charter allegedly originating with Offa in the 780s may well have been based on an authentic document. If that is so, the Mercian king granted an estate at Aldenham, Hertfordshire, to the Westminster community, which demonstrates both that the minster's interests were by now extending out of London, and also that the most powerful English king of his time regarded it as worthy of his benefaction. That must remain hypothesis, less certain, indeed, than that, in the following century, the Vikings saw Westminster as an irresistible target for pillage, drawn by the minster's movable wealth, particularly in the form of church plate and vestments, and also by the human resources associated with it, the men and women who could be seized and sold into slavery. Minsters were hardy institutions, so much so as to make it unlikely that the 'west minster' succumbed completely to such attacks. But by the time King Alfred of Wessex recovered London from the Danes in 886, the minster was probably in a seriously run-down state, unable to protect itself effectively against its friends, let alone its enemies, with the result that many of its lands were quietly absorbed into the holdings of Alfred and his successors, as they extended their rule north over the former kingdom of Mercia. The continuous history of Westminster Abbey begins in the second half of the tenth century with what was effectively a new foundation.

★

The Origins of Westminster Abbey in the Tenth Century

Enough evidence survives to allow Westminster to be set securely among the houses founded in the mid-tenth century that had long and distinguished histories thereafter. The cause of religious reform, as the necessary response to what was seen as drift and decline (not always the result of Viking attacks, though they cannot have helped), originated on the continent, but was soon taken up in England, where the political, economic and cultural developments associated above all with the reigns of three kings – Alfred (r. 871–99), his son Edward the Elder (r. 899–924) and his grandson Æthelstan (r. 924–39) – created the conditions in which new aspirations might flourish. On both sides of the channel, reform meant, above all, monastic reform. In England, as many as thirty or forty religious houses were founded, re-founded or reformed in the tenth century, as part of what began as a series of separate initiatives but by c.970 had become an organized movement. When embraced whole-heartedly by King Edgar (r. 959–75), this movement developed in ways that extended far beyond the regulation of the observances practised within each community, important though that was to the reformers. Not only could reformed monasteries have the same sort of impact on their localities as minsters had had before them, but they could also become centres of royal power, or centres from which a bishop or an abbot exerted influence in a neighbourhood, or a lay patron of the abbey could do the same. Many powerful men, laymen as well as ecclesiastics, were caught up in the religious fervour generated by the re-foundation or reform of a religious house in their vicinity, displaying their support by giving land or money to a monastery or nunnery, or simply by joining one.

The details of how Westminster re-joined the monastic mainstream are once more obscured by forgeries. The abbey's tradition, as it was plausibly set down in one of them, was that Dunstan, Bishop of London and later Archbishop of Canterbury, gave King Edgar an armband worth 120 golden *solidi* for the church at Westminster, for the purpose of founding a monastery there, most likely in 959.[16] It was not intended to be a large house – the chronicler William of Malmesbury, writing in the early twelfth century but a well-informed source, records that at first it had only twelve monks, living according to the Benedictine rule[17] – but perhaps because the powerful and influential Dunstan acted as its first abbot, it soon appears to have attracted other grants of land.   15

Not everybody welcomed or approved of the donations made so lavishly to religious houses in the reign of Edgar, however, and after the king died in 975 there was a sharp move against the monasteries, many of which lost a good deal of their recently acquired property. Some of Westminster's early forgeries show how the abbey was seriously threatened by this so-called 'anti-monastic reaction', but also how the monks were active in protecting their abbey's property, and successful in recovering it when lost,

15 St Dunstan, first Abbot of Westminster, bows down before Christ, in a mid-10th-century drawing that may be by Dunstan himself.

16 The opening of Psalm 1 from the Bosworth Psalter, a magnificent late 10th-century manuscript, written and illuminated by a member of Westminster's monastic community.

whether in and around Westminster itself, where the abbey's core estate was recorded as extending as far east as the walls of London, or further afield – for instance, at Hendon, Hampstead and Sunbury-on-Thames in Middlesex.[18] They were ready to take on those who coveted their lands, and they busied themselves in preparing the documentation needed for the purpose. The clause added at the end of one of their charters (in a different-coloured ink), threatening with divine punishment anyone who might dare to take any part of the land 'from the church of St Peter which is situated in Westminster', shows them deploying religious sanctions alongside legal ones.

The monks of tenth-century Westminster were not concerned only with their material possessions. They would, indeed, have regarded the defence of their properties, given as they often were to God as well as to themselves, as part of their religious duty (it was in that spirit that they forged so many charters), but they also attended to the regular work of a monastic community, and did so, moreover, using the same skills. It has long been recognized that the charter setting out the defence of their rights at Sunbury-on-Thames was written by the same scribe who wrote and decorated a magnificent psalter, known as the Bosworth Psalter, which is among the most spectacular of late Anglo-Saxon books.[19] No doubt he was a member of the community of Westminster Abbey, though this superb example of his craftsmanship did not, in fact, stay there for long, for by the end of the tenth century it was certainly at Christ Church, Canterbury. Perhaps it was taken there by Dunstan himself, when he was moving between the two places; or it may have been given to Canterbury by one of the early abbots of Westminster, soon after Dunstan's death, as a mark of respect.

There is no sign of a person designated Abbot of Westminster in charters of the years before the death of Dunstan in 988, and it seems likely that the latter was from the outset regarded as founder and head of the abbey. From 960 onwards he also held the see of Canterbury, but surprisingly little is known of what he did there, and it may be that a base at Westminster proved more convenient for his work.[20] Following his death, however, the norms of monastic custom were soon reinstated, with Wulfsige, who is recorded as having been Dunstan's understudy at Westminster, emerging at once as abbot in his own right. It was as Abbot Wulfsige that shortly afterwards he attended an assembly at London convened under the next archbishop, and when he was made Bishop of Sherborne in 993 he was replaced promptly at Westminster by Ælfwig (993–c.1020), probably a monk from within the community.[21] Wulfsige concentrated thereafter on his responsibilities as a bishop, but retained close relations with his former house.

Ælfwig was a significant figure, both at Westminster, where he was probably chosen as abbot by the monks, in accordance with the Rule of St Benedict, and also at the court of Æthelred II (Unræd, the Unready, r. 978–1016), where, from 993 onwards,

17   Aethelred II (the Unready), is represented in armour and helmet on the obverse of this early 11th-century silver coin; the inscription reads ÆDELRED REX ANGL ('Æthelred king of the English'). The early 11th century saw the beginnings of a closer link between the crown and Westminster.

during the worst of the Viking wars of the late tenth and early eleventh centuries, he attended royal assemblies and attested royal diplomas. Among the latter was a charter of 998 confirming the re-foundation and endowment of Westminster itself.[22] Although it is inauthentic as it stands, it appears to be largely trustworthy in its details, and sheds valuable light on the recent fortunes of the abbey, referring to acquisitions of property which show that its endowment had continued to grow. Most of these were owing to Dunstan, who at considerable personal expense bought a number of estates in Middlesex on the monastery's behalf. The charter concludes with a statement that the text had been drawn up when the king visited the abbey on his way to the fleet – a reference, no doubt, to attempts to counter that year's attacks by the Danes on the southern coasts of England. It was common for kings to take advantage of monastic hospitality as they moved round their territories. There is no evidence for a royal palace at Westminster as yet, but Æthelred's visit may have helped to prepare the way for one.

Four years later, in 1002, when the Danes were at their base on the Isle of Wight, the king and his councillors decided (not for the first time) to give provisions and make a payment of tribute to the invading army. Abbot Ælfwig was among those who contributed funds, being reliably recorded as having made a payment to the king of 100 mancuses of pure gold (the equivalent of 3,000 silver pennies), and as receiving in return a grant of two hides of land 'at the berewick' (æt berewican), for the monastery of St Peter 'in the noble place' called Westminster.[23] The grant was conditional upon the community's offering 300 Masses and reciting as many Psalters for the king, in aid of efforts to ensure that at this critical time God would help the English in their cause. The property in question lay directly to the north of the abbey, and shows how land that controlled the approaches to London from the west and from the north-west was now safely in the abbey's possession – possibly a pointer to the king's expectations that, at need, its men might be called out to defend the city by protecting its own lands.

It was in London, with the Viking forces closing in upon him, that King Æthelred died in 1016. Many years later, his surviving son, Edward, might have remembered how, and why, his father had taken an interest in the 'noble place' called Westminster.

An abbot like Ælfwig moved among the great men of the kingdom, and some of these followed the king in making grants to Westminster, though only two of them can be identified by name – Ælfhelm Polga, a thegn of some standing in eastern England, who in his will, made *c*.990, left the monks an estate at Brickendon, Hertfordshire, and Leofwine, son of Wulfstan, who in 998 bequeathed lands at Kelvedon, Essex.[24] It was by such means that the monastery continued to add to its estates. Yet it may be a pointer to the insecurity of the times that only one of these grants took lasting effect, for although Kelvedon remained in the monks' possession until 1540, Brickendon had within barely half a century fallen into the hands of the canons of Waltham Holy Cross.[25] A clause in his will showing that Ælfhelm's loyalty to King Æthelred had been called into question may help to explain why nothing ultimately came of his bequest to Westminster.

The age was one of uncertainty, beginning early in Æthelred's reign and continuing after his death, when the throne was contested by the Danish king Cnut (r. 1016–35) and Æthelred's eldest son, Edmund Ironside (r. 1016). The latter's death in November 1016, which left Cnut as sole ruler, brought a degree of stability to English affairs, but only modest benefits to Westminster: a much later source claims that the new king made a gift of relics to the abbey,[26] but it is certain that Cnut was buried at Winchester, as many previous English kings had been. Nevertheless, it is possible that the early eleventh century saw the beginnings of a closer link between the crown and Westminster. It has been argued that Cnut had a residence there and, when his son and (after a further period of competition) successor Harold Harefoot (r. 1035–40) died at Oxford, it was to Westminster – presumably with the approval of Abbot Wulfnoth (*c*.1020–1049), Ælfwig's successor – that his body was brought for burial.[27] Harold's remains did not stay there long, since his half-brother and hated rival Harthacnut (r. 1040–42) soon had them dug up and thrown into a marsh. But a precedent had been set which the next king was to follow, with momentous consequences for Westminster.

Edward the Confessor and Westminster

King Edward the Confessor (r. 1042–66) needs no introduction in his own abbey.[28] His knowing eyes and gentle smile, lighting up his bearded face, are familiar to all from the opening scene in the Bayeux Tapestry, where he sits crowned and enthroned in a fine palace, engaged in intimate conversation with two of his courtiers.[29] It is the

18

18   Edward the Confessor re-endowed and greatly enlarged the existing Benedictine monastery at Westminster, building a stone church in honour of St Peter the Apostle. The opening scene of the Bayeux Tapestry (probably commissioned within about fifteen years of the Battle of Hastings in 1066) shows him enthroned in his palace, instructing Harold Godwinson to depart for Normandy, thus setting in motion events that came to a climax in 1066.

image of a king who has come to be renowned most of all for his wisdom and piety, who seemed latterly powerless to deal with the affairs of this world, whereupon he turned his mind to the project at Westminster that he had chosen to make his own. This perception of King Edward originated in the anonymous *Vita Ædwardis Regis qui apud Westmonasterium requiescit* ('Life of King Edward who rests at Westminster').[30] The Life was written for Edward's widow, Queen Edith, and was intended to honour and console her. An invaluable source for our knowledge and understanding of the Confessor, its historical value derives from its early date – very possibly begun while Edward was still alive, it could have been completed as early as 1067 – and from the fact that it emanated from the king's circle. It also represents an important early stage in the development of the cult of Edward as a royal saint, showing that this originated very soon after his death, among people who must have known him well.

After the Danish interlude of Cnut and his two sons, Edward's reign was seen from the outset as constituting a glorious revival of the English royal line, reinstated after an interval of twenty-five years. The new king, now aged about 40, had returned to England in 1041, having spent the reigns of the Danish kings in exile, mostly in Normandy. A contemporary source described him as 'the legitimate heir, a man notable for the eminence of his power, endowed with virtue of mind and counsel and also with quickness of intellect, and marked out by the sum of all desirable things'.[31] The writer was doubtless partisan, but great things were certainly looked for from Edward, as the very embodiment of a re-established English kingship, and it was in keeping with these expectations that he was crowned on Easter day (3 April) 1043. The place chosen for the ceremony was Winchester, not because coronations were customarily performed there – most of Edward's tenth-century predecessors had been crowned at Kingston upon Thames in Surrey – but probably because of the city's place at the heart of the old kingdom of Wessex, which was itself still the core of the English realm. The rites of coronation were similarly respectful of tradition: already well over a century old, they had originated in the reign of King Alfred.[32]

The service began as the king was led by two bishops into the church, where he prostrated himself before the altar, and was then formally 'elected' by the bishops and the people. At this point, the king took a threefold oath, setting out his fundamental responsibilities to his people:

> In the name of the Holy Trinity, I promise three things to the Christian people who are subject to me: first, that God's church and all Christian people in my dominions preserve true peace; the second is that I forbid robbery and all unrighteous things to all orders; the third, that I promise and command justice and mercy in all judgements, so that the kind and merciful God because of that may grant us all his eternal mercy, who lives and reigns.[33]

Prayers were said for the king, and for the good of all. The ritual of anointing followed, and the antiphon 'Zadok the priest and Nathan the prophet anointed Solomon king' was sung. After further prayers, the king was given the ring and the sword; then the archbishop performed the crowning, after which the king was given the sceptre and the rod (*virga*). A blessing, and further prayers, followed. By the 970s it had become customary for the officiating archbishop to deliver a short homily on kingship, and in 1043 Archbishop Eadsige appears to have followed this practice, since he is recorded as giving Edward 'good instruction before all the people'.[34] The order of service followed at Edward's crowning had deep roots, and set the new king on his path. It also provided the basis for the orders of service used for William the Conqueror and, with appropriate modifications, all his successors – though not, however, at Winchester.

Writing in the late 1060s, the author of the Life of King Edward contemplated the magnificent church that, by then, Edward had had built at Westminster, and looked back to imagine its origins:

> Outside the walls of London, upon the River Thames, stood a monastery dedicated to St Peter, but insignificant in buildings and numbers, for under the abbot only a small community of monks served Christ. Moreover, the endowments from the faithful were slender, and provided no more than their daily bread. The king, therefore, being devoted to God, gave his attention to that place, for it both lay hard by the famous and rich town and also was a delightful spot, surrounded with fertile lands and green fields and near the main channel of the river, which bore abundant merchandise of wares of every kind for sale from the whole world to the town on its banks. And, especially because of his love of the Prince of the Apostles, whom he worshipped with uncommon and special love, he decided to have his burial-place there.[35]

It is not, in fact, known for certain when, or why, Edward began to take a special interest in Westminster. By the late eleventh century the story was circulating that, after his accession, he planned to make a pilgrimage to Rome, to offer thanks at the shrine of St Peter for his peaceful succession, but was discouraged by his advisers, fearful for the stability of the realm in the absence of its recently installed king, who persuaded him that, instead, he should restore a shrine dedicated to St Peter in England.[36] In its original form the tale may contain an element of truth, though it was later amplified out of all credibility, and in any case there are other possibilities that could help to explain Edward's support for Westminster Abbey. He might have visited the monastery as a boy, with his father, Æthelred, and remembered it with affection; and if he liked its setting, and its convenient location, he might also have liked its separation from established political and ecclesiastical interests of the kind that had overseen his own installation in power – in which case, extending his patronage to Westminster could have been a gesture of independence. Or he may simply have resolved to support an abbey that King Æthelred before him had supported, as one that could serve the interests of the revived dynasty – in which case, he may have had Westminster in mind from the outset as the place of his burial.

Once the king had decided to concentrate his attention on a single house, the process of endowment would have been carried forward most conspicuously at royal assemblies. Such gatherings were convened perhaps four or five times a year, over the major festivals or whenever a special need or opportunity arose. On such occasions, the king would meet with his archbishops, bishops, abbots, earls and thegns, who came together from various parts of the kingdom. After a day or two, the business might draw to a close with a ceremonial session for announcing and approving the

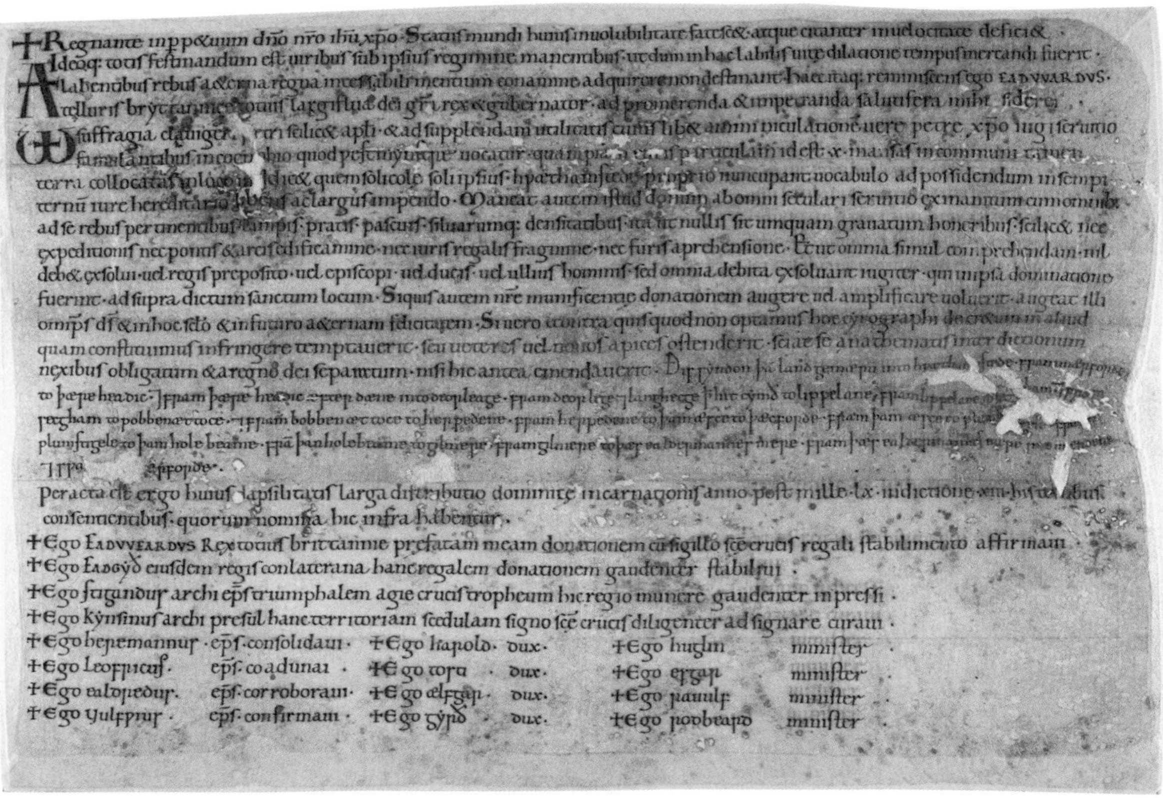

19   King Edward's charter of 1060, granting lands at Wheathampstead in Hertfordshire to Westminster Abbey.

king's grants of land to various parties. Of the many such documents that must have been drawn up on Westminster's behalf, one survives in the abbey archives, a fine example of a royal diploma, dated 1060 and written in Anglo-Caroline script of the mid-eleventh century, recording in the solemn formulation of its day King Edward's grant to the community at Westminster of a considerable estate – perhaps 1,000 acres – at Wheathampstead in Hertfordshire.[37]

Westminster was already a reasonably wealthy house, with estates worth around £80 per annum.[38] Nonetheless, without being extravagant, Edward was generous to the abbey, extending the distribution of its properties into the west of England and the Midlands by making grants of lands, either by gift or bequest, in Berkshire, Gloucestershire, Hampshire, Hertfordshire, Middlesex, Northamptonshire, Oxfordshire,

Staffordshire and Worcestershire, altogether worth about £270 per annum. He also confirmed a number of grants made by others. A few donations were frustrated after 1066, and precision is in any case difficult, but it would appear that out of the abbey's endowment as it was recorded in Domesday Book, compiled in 1086, over 60 per cent had been acquired by the time of Edward's death, the rest being added under William I.[39] In terms of its gross yearly income, Westminster was not yet close to the famously wealthy abbeys of Glastonbury (£840) and Ely (£768); but at the end of William's reign it was already in seventh place, with an estimated £583 per annum, comfortably ahead of Abingdon (£462) and the remaining thirty-eight religious houses, down to Swavesey (£2).[40] By the end of the eleventh century it was able, if only briefly, to support about eighty monks.[41]

King Edward and the Rebuilding of the Church at Westminster

Adding to its estates was not, of course, all that King Edward did for Westminster Abbey, for he transformed it architecturally as well. A few traces of the buildings and their contents that constituted the monastery re-founded by Dunstan have survived to the present day. A Roman sarcophagus of unknown origins was apparently re-used for an Anglo-Saxon interment in the years around 1000, having had a cross roughly carved on its lid (excavated on the abbey's North Green in 1869, it is now in The Queen's Diamond Jubilee Galleries).[42] Excavations carried out in 2011 in the cellarium, on the west side of the cloister, revealed the chalk rubble foundations of an earlier structure, along with some pieces of late Anglo-Saxon pottery, and a small bone object decorated in a recognizably Scandinavian style, all also datable to *c.*1000. In 2018 a broken part of the limestone cover of a child's grave, with panels of Anglo-Saxon interlace ornament, came to light during drainage works in the cloister garth.[43] But these are mere fragments: everything else has been swept away by the ambitions first of Edward the Confessor and then of Henry III.

In the contributions that both kings made to the abbey, their successive rebuildings of its church have inevitably bulked largest, but they also spent lavishly on its monastic buildings. In Edward's case, new and larger buildings would anyway have been required thanks to the growth in the number of monks that his own generosity made possible. Some impressive remains of the structures begun by him (they were completed after his death) can still be seen – notably parts of the dormitory and refectory, off the south and east sides of the cloister.[44] But the most striking of these survivals is the dormitory's undercroft, which now constitutes the Pyx Chamber and the rest of the vaulted passageway that extends southwards from it; some of the

20   An Anglo-Saxon door in the
vestibule of the chapter house,
dating from the mid-11th century, is
a rare survival from King Edward's
original monastery, and is perhaps
the oldest surviving door in Britain.

chamber's original brown-glazed tiles also survive, having been re-used to patch its
20   floor. No less remarkable is a nearby door, leading from the south-east corner of the
outer vestibule of the chapter house into a storeroom; this has been securely dated by
dendrochronology to the middle of the eleventh century, and thus has a good claim
to be the oldest surviving door in Britain.[45] But all these structures would have been
overshadowed by Edward's magnificent new church, executed in a style that had no
known precedent in England.

There is no record of when Edward embarked upon the building of a new
church – one intended to be on a scale fit for the dynasty that he represented, and
appropriate to the status it could expect to have as his own resting-place – but a date
around 1050 seems likely. The Life of King Edward represents the king and queen as
working in competition: the king at Westminster, setting out to build a magnificent

21 (FACING PAGE)   William the Conqueror's Domesday survey of England and parts of Wales,
completed in 1086, established that Westminster Abbey exercised direct lordship over sixty manors.
The number reflects the remarkably rapid expansion, both numerical and geographical, that had
taken place since the 1040s in the holdings of a monastery founded only a little more than a
century earlier. The extent of the abbey's estates increased somewhat during the Middle Ages, and
grew significantly in the early 16th century, thanks mainly to Henry VII's generous endowment of
his own chantry in the Lady Chapel at Westminster. All sixty estates recorded in 1086 are marked
on the map with black dots. Numbered locations (listed in the key) indicate valuable properties
– that is, those worth more than £40 in 1540. Centres of ecclesiastical and royal significance are
named.

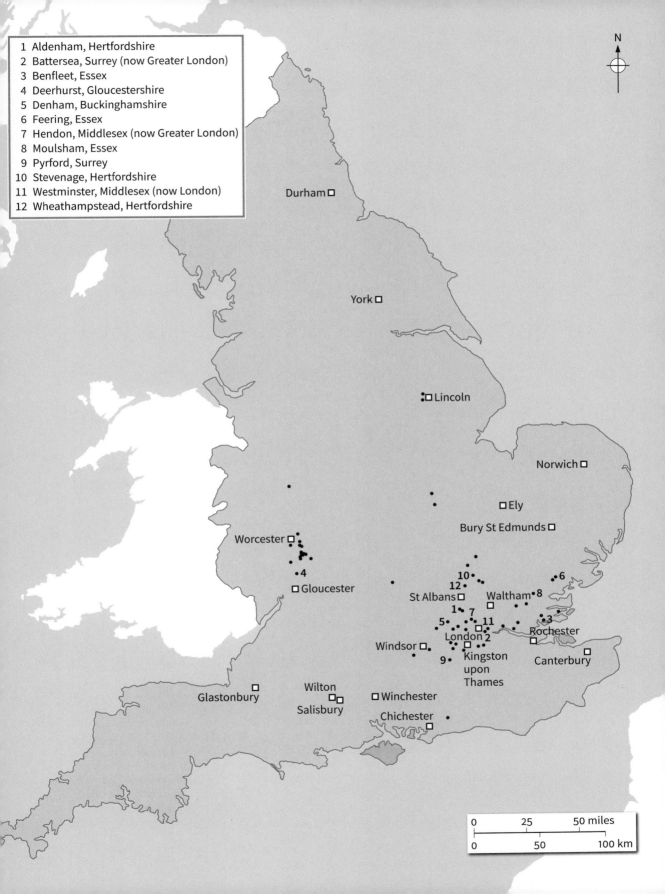

1 Aldenham, Hertfordshire
2 Battersea, Surrey (now Greater London)
3 Benfleet, Essex
4 Deerhurst, Gloucestershire
5 Denham, Buckinghamshire
6 Feering, Essex
7 Hendon, Middlesex (now Greater London)
8 Moulsham, Essex
9 Pyrford, Surrey
10 Stevenage, Hertfordshire
11 Westminster, Middlesex (now London)
12 Wheathampstead, Hertfordshire

N

Durham

York

Lincoln

Norwich

Ely

Bury St Edmunds

Worcester

Gloucester
4

10
12
St Albans
1 7
Waltham
8
6
5 11
3
London 2
Rochester
Windsor
9
Kingston
upon
Thames
Canterbury

Glastonbury

Wilton
Salisbury
Winchester

Chichester

0   25   50 miles

0   50   100 km

church in a new style; the queen at Wilton in Wiltshire, where she had been brought up, building a church in stone to replace an existing wooden structure; and each racing the other to bring their respective projects to completion. In the event, the queen's church was finished a few months before the king's, 'because it was more modestly planned'.[46]

The author of the Life, who may have known both places well, continues his description of Westminster with an appropriately detailed, if sometimes rather opaquely phrased, account of the building work there:

> Accordingly he [Edward] ordered that out of the tithes of all his revenues should be started the building of a noble edifice, worthy of the Prince of the Apostles; so that, after the transient journey of this life, God would look kindly upon him, both for the sake of his goodness and because of the gift of lands and ornaments with which he intended to ennoble the place. And so, at the king's command the building, nobly begun, was made ready, and there was no weighing of the cost, past or future, as long as it proved worthy of, and acceptable to, God and St Peter. The house of the principal altar, raised up with most lofty vaulting, is surrounded by dressed stone, evenly jointed. Moreover, the circumference of that temple is enclosed on both sides by a double arch of stones, with the structure of the work strongly consolidated from different directions. Next is the crossing of the church, which is to hold in its midst the choir of God's choristers, and, with its twin abutments from either side, support the high apex of the central tower. It rises simply at first with a low and sturdy vault, swells with many a stair spiralling up in artistic profusion, but then with a plain wall climbs to the wooden roof which is carefully covered with lead. And indeed, methodically arranged above and below, are chapels to be consecrated through their altars to the memory of apostles, martyrs, confessors, and virgins. Moreover, the whole complex of this enormous building is set at a sufficient distance from the east end of the old church to allow not only the brethren dwelling there to continue with their service to Christ but also some part of the nave, which is to lie in between, to advance a good way.[47]

William of Malmesbury, who produced his compendious *Gesta regum Anglorum* ('History of the English kings') and *Gesta pontificum Anglorum* ('History of the English bishops') in the 1120s, was better able to appreciate the significance of the changes taking place. He wrote of Edward that he was buried 'in the church which he himself had built, using for the first time in England the style which almost everyone now tries to rival at great expense', and that 'he gathered there a larger body of monks and built a church in a new style'.[48] What he was describing was England's first Romanesque church, planned, it seems impossible to doubt, under the influence of churches Edward

22   King Edward may well have modelled his new church at Westminster on the grandeur and scale of the abbey church of Jumièges in Normandy, with its soaring lantern tower attached to a three-storey nave, and twin towers at its west end.

had seen in his youth, when he was an exile in Normandy. The great abbey church of Jumièges, begun in 1040 on the Seine west of Rouen and still majestic in its ruined state, is likely to have been especially influential, not least because one of its abbots, Robert, became Bishop of London in 1044 and (briefly) Archbishop of Canterbury in 1051. With twin towers at its west end and a mighty lantern tower over its crossing, a three-storey nave flanked by groin-vaulted aisles, two transepts, and an extended choir terminating in an apse, Jumièges was conceived and executed on a scale with no known English parallel.[49] But such was the building that Edward nevertheless aspired to emulate, and such, on the evidence of the Bayeux Tapestry, was the church he built. A very grand sacral building, it is shown there with an apse and windows, a large tower with turret stairs, and an arcaded nave of conventional basilican type with aisles. There are no west towers, but a man puts up a weathercock at the east end, symbolizing either the consecration or the completion of the building, while the hand of God reaches down in blessing.[50]

It is not known who designed Edward's church, though it seems more than likely that a Norman architect was employed. (A grant of land at Shepperton in Middlesex — an estate actually belonging to the abbey — which Edward made to Teinfrith his 'churchwright', probably identifies one of the masons.)[51] But archaeology (which also shows that the building was of Reigate stone) and written records, despite inevitable gaps in both, make it possible to say a good deal about its form.[52] That there was a central tower with turrets is evident from Matthew Paris's chronicle description in 1245 of the demolition of the east end and crossing of the Confessor's church, which refers to its 'middle towers'.[53] The same chronicler, who though based at St Albans had certainly seen that church, in his Anglo-Norman French *Estoire de Seint Aedward le rei* ('Life of St Edward the king') describes its east end as 'rounded', confirming its apsidal shape.[54] The earlier Life of King Edward (quoted above) has been interpreted as describing a building with a sanctuary surrounded by high arches and walls of squared stones, and a nave of stone arcading of strong construction.[55] The terms used are not technical, but were intended rather to emphasize Edward's munificence as a patron — very appropriately, since, as the Life records, he devoted a tenth of all his revenues to paying for it.

23   An imaginative drawing by David Gentleman, looking from above the chancel through the crossing and down the aisled nave towards the west end, and showing King Edward and his architect directing the construction of the church, conveys an effective impression of the church's internal dimensions, of the scale of the operation as a whole, and particularly of the length of the building.[56] Naves of English Romanesque churches were often exceptionally long, suited above all to the staging of processions, and Westminster's was no exception; indeed, it was considerably longer than any of the Norman churches on which it was modelled.[57] But the nave is also shown as having been architecturally sophisticated, thanks primarily to the rhythm given to the structure by its sequence of six double bays. Each bay was made up of two arches, resting alternately on cylindrical columns and composite piers — rectangular pillars with a half-column on each side, the one facing into the nave continuing up to the base of the roof. Above the nave arcade, moreover, there was no blank expanse of wall, for Norman examples and archaeology together suggest that, instead, there was a series of 'triforia', that is, of arches opening into the spaces above the aisles, while over them was set a clerestory, a sequence of windows under the wooden ceiling.

It would be difficult, however, for a present-day artist to produce a similar reconstruction of the church as seen in the opposite direction, looking from the nave into the choir. Clear evidence is lacking, and to make matters more difficult, the east or main ritual ends of such churches, with their altars and shrines, were much more variable in form than the nave. The usual alternatives for a large stone church on the European

23   A drawing (1987) by David Gentleman imagines King Edward and his architect directing
the building of the church as it approached completion in the mid-11th century; the royal party
stands in the triforium looking through the crossing and down the aisled nave to the west end.

model were an apse with an ambulatory – as at Norwich cathedral, and the churches of
Bury St Edmunds abbey and St Bartholomew the Great at Smithfield in London – or
graduated stepped apses in an 'echelon', as at Canterbury cathedral. Limited excavation
suggests that Westminster had an apse enclosing the high altar, and a crossing in about

the same position as that of the thirteenth-century replacement, but it is not known, for lack of archaeological investigation, whether there was some form of walkway or ambulatory surrounding the high altar, though Jumièges is known to have had one.

The Dedication of King Edward's Church at Westminster

The abbey church was not King Edward's only building project at Westminster. It was usual at this time for royal palaces to be built close to cathedrals and great churches, and it was in accordance with this practice that, while the new church was in progress, the king had such a palace erected for himself a short distance to the north-west.[58] The central panels of the Bayeux Tapestry are a priceless visual source not only for the events surrounding the dedication of the new church but also for the setting in which they occurred. Although the Tapestry does not represent the whole of Edward's palace, which was probably an extensive complex of buildings – for instance, there is no representation of the spacious hall, for ceremonial and feasting, which was surely one of its principal features – it still shows that it contained a throne room (where Harold reports to the king after his expedition to Normandy), and that at least part of it was laid out on two floors, within a building with turrets and doors at each end. Edward's decision to build a palace at Westminster proved to be of critical importance for the abbey, creating a lasting association between the two, which in turn helps to explain why the abbey became a family burial church for English royalty.

Queen Edith's church at Wilton was probably dedicated in the summer of 1065, when the nave of Edward's church at Westminster was still unfinished.[59] It would appear that the old abbey church, which Edward's new one was in the process of replacing, still stood to the west of its successor, so that monastic worship could continue as usual, though with the old building steadily coming down as its successor was going up. In the autumn of that year, however, the king appears to have suffered a stroke, and thereafter his health steadily declined. Nevertheless, in the closing weeks of the year it was decided to press forward with the formal ceremony of dedication, since the church was now almost complete – a fragment of the Life of King Edward which survives only in an Elizabethan translation records that 'there remained nothynge unbuylded but the Entrye or porch'.[60] An assembly was convened in the royal palace at Westminster over the Christmas season. On Christmas eve the king's condition worsened, and although he was able to sit at table in a festal robe for the three days over Christmas itself, he retired thereafter to his bedchamber, and could not be present at the ceremony of dedication on Holy Innocents' day (28 December). The forger of charters ostensibly issued on this day appears to have had access to authentic documents, whose witness lists give a largely realistic idea of the attendance on this momentous occasion. The prescribed rites were said to have been conducted in the presence of the king and queen (the twelfth-century forger was presumably unaware that Edward had in fact been too ill to attend), the Archbishops of Canterbury and York, nine other bishops, seven abbots, three royal chaplains, Duke Harold (Queen Edith's brother), and eighteen earls, thegns, officials and clerks.[61] Nor, indeed, was that all, for every effort had been made to attract as large an attendance as possible. The Elizabethan fragment records that 'longe howses' had been prepared 'for such as were willinge to see the celebration of this feaste', thereby allowing the presence of 'noble men & commen people comen from all partes of the realme [...]'.[62] The dedication of Westminster Abbey was a great occasion, bringing in people of every social rank.

It would appear that in his last days King Edward made further grants of 'properties, ornaments, and possessions' to the abbey. Books, vestments, vessels and other precious things would have been handed over to the monks, and also lands, perhaps through the transfer of existing title-deeds from the king's archives into those of the abbey.[63] He died a few days after the dedication of the church, on the eve of the Epiphany (5 January 1066), in the royal bedchamber on the upper floor of the palace. The Bayeux Tapestry shows him addressing his attendants, while Queen Edith sits mournfully in the background. Then, following his death, we see his corpse being prepared for burial at ground level, and carried on a bier to the nearby church, where, 'washed by his country's tears', it was laid to rest before the altar of St Peter the Apostle.[64]

24

The cult of relics was central to medieval religion. The bodily remains of holy men and women, or physical objects associated with them, were venerated in the belief that these relics not only possessed miraculous powers by virtue of their origins, but also constituted points of contact with the saints in heaven, who could now intercede with God on behalf of those who implored their aid on earth. The burial of King Edward in Westminster Abbey meant that its church was thereafter more than a place of regular monastic worship: it also aspired to something of the character of a vast and magnificent reliquary, a container for relics, with the same wonder-working power. The author of the Life of King Edward, writing within a year or two of the king's death, closes with striking words of contemporary testimony:

> For at the tomb through him the blind receive their sight, the lame are made to walk, the sick are healed, the sorrowing are refreshed by the comfort of God, and for the faith of those who call upon Him, God, the King of kings, works the tokens of his goodness.[65]

The number of miracles recorded in the Life is in fact modest. And the image of the saintly ruler projected there, although not entirely false, is one that most of

24   The Bayeux Tapestry depicts the death of Edward the Confessor in January 1066, surrounded by his wife and attendants, in the first-floor bedchamber of his palace at Westminster; in the room below, the king's body is prepared for its burial, which would take place in the recently consecrated abbey church.

Edward's contemporaries would have found unsatisfactory, or at least incomplete. He had led an active life – his favourite occupation was hunting – and exercised a largely effective kingship, maintaining order and dominating England's British neighbours. For Anglo-Saxon Englishmen, however, such engagement with the world was not necessarily a bar to the attribution of sanctity (they were notably ready to perceive their kings as saints), and in Edward's case their willingness to regard him as having been a holy man was strengthened by the nostalgia for England's pre-Conquest past, focused upon his reign, which grew in the decades after 1066. In the pages of the Life, a more positive basis for the Confessor's sanctity is found in the lifelong chastity there ascribed to him. Whether or not this was a virtue grounded in fact, in secular terms it meant that Edward could have no direct heir. So it was that on his deathbed Edward had entrusted the realm to Harold, who as his own brother-in-law had long

HAROLDO: REGIS

HIC RE REX: AN SIDET: HAROLD GLORVM:

STIGANT ARCHIEPS

25 Edward's burial and the coronation of his successor, Harold, took place in Westminster Abbey on the same day, 6 January 1066; the Bayeux Tapestry shows Harold crowned and enthroned, holding the sceptre and orb, attended by the Archbishop of Canterbury, and with bystanders acclaiming their new ruler.

been the most powerful man in England after himself, and who was now consecrated king on the same day that Edward was buried, 6 January 1066.

    A scene at the very heart of the Bayeux Tapestry shows the newly crowned Harold 25 enthroned and holding the sceptre and orb, between two men on the left who stand for the secular order (one holds a sword), and Archbishop Stigand on the right, representing the ecclesiastical order, while five bystanders acclaim their new ruler. Better than anything else, this gives a sense of the occasion, and of the ceremonies accompanying it, in the first coronation to take place in Westminster Abbey. The new coinage struck in Harold's name bore an image of the crowned king on the obverse, and the word PAX displayed across the reverse, but in the knowing words of the Anglo-Saxon Chronicle, King Harold 'met little quiet in it as long as he ruled the realm'.[66] His kingship was soon contested, in the north by Harald Hardrada, King of

Norway, and then on the south coast by Duke William of Normandy, who claimed that in 1051 King Edward had promised him the succession. 1066 was famously a year of battles, and among its casualties was a thegn named Ingulf, recorded in Domesday Book as having given Westminster Abbey land at Paglesham, in Essex, 'when he went to battle in York[shire] with Harold'.[67] He may have been among those who died on the victorious English side at the Battle of Stamford Bridge on 25 September, or perhaps he was killed three weeks later at the Battle of Hastings on 14 October, fighting alongside his stricken king.

Westminster Abbey and the Norman Conquest

> 1066. Then on Christmas Day, Archbishop Aldred consecrated William king at Westminster. And he promised Aldred on Christ's book and swore moreover (before Aldred would place the crown on his head) that he would rule all this people as well as the best of the kings before him, if they would be loyal to him. All the same he laid taxes on people very severely [...] and always after that it grew much worse. May the end be good when God wills.
>
> Anglo-Saxon Chronicle[68]

The defeat and death of Harold left the way clear for Duke William to take the throne. Duly recognized as King of the English, on 25 December he was consecrated at Westminster by Aldred (or Ealdred), Archbishop of York, probably with an order of service modelled on that used at the coronation of Edward the Confessor.[69] Both the rite itself, and now the place chosen for it, underlined William's claim that he ruled as the Confessor's kinsman and designated successor (the two men were first cousins once removed, Edward's mother, Emma, having been William's great-aunt), while Harold had been an oath-breaker and usurper, who, according to Norman sources, had disregarded a solemn promise he had made – probably in 1064 – that when Edward died he would support William's claim to the throne. The new king's support for the abbey conveyed a similar message. Building works continued apace, on the monastic buildings as well as on the completion of the church, and William, like Edward, gave protection, lands and privileges to Westminster.[70] A writ drawn up in English, probably soon after his accession, notified officials in Staffordshire that land at Perton was to belong to St Peter's, Westminster, just as his kinsman King Edward had given it – illustrating not only how King William regarded Edward, but also how continuity of possession from 1066 to 1086 was subject to authorization by the king.[71] Maintaining a different sort of continuity, Abbot Eadwine (1049–c.1071) remained in office for a few years after 1066, though his successors were Norman.

Looking back from the 1120s, William of Malmesbury was well aware of the new king's wish to establish continuity with the Anglo-Saxon past: 'King William did no less, indeed much more, to exalt the place, lavishing on it revenues from estates, for it was here that he was crowned. So the custom has been established among his successors that, in memory of Edward's burial place, kings should receive their crowns there.'[72] It was William's coronation, so the chronicler emphasized, and not Harold's, that set the precedent, and under the new regime Westminster came fully into its own, its association with a major palace and its familiar roles as a royal mausoleum and coronation church being now established, if not yet wholly guaranteed. The coronation of Queen Matilda soon followed her husband's, on Whit Sunday 1068,[73] its significance for the abbey underlined by a diploma of King William in favour of St Martin-le-Grand, granted at Christmas 1067, but confirmed on the day when Matilda was consecrated queen 'in the basilica of St Peter of Westminster'.[74] Equally important in this context was the funeral of Queen Edith, widow of King Edward, in 1075. She died at Winchester shortly before Christmas, whereupon King William had her 'brought to Westminster with great honour', and 'laid her near King Edward her husband'.[75] His respect for Edward's widow was, of course, intended to impress, but is nonetheless striking.

Reconnecting to the Anglo-Saxon Royal Line

In the late eleventh century, Westminster continued to thrive as a royal palace for the Norman regime. It acted regularly as a place of assembly for the king and the leading men of the realm, sometimes with solemn crown-wearing over the Whitsun festival.[76] Both William II (Rufus; 1087) and Henry I (1100) were crowned there, and the former also built an enormous hall to the east of the abbey, today known simply as Westminster Hall, most of which still stands. All this owed much to the example set by William the Conqueror, and even more to Westminster's particular associations with King Edward. As time passed, however, it began to seem important to find a sounder foundation for the link back to Edward than one based on a contested designation and allegations of perjury, and also to foster a reconciliation of the Norman regime, forcibly imposed in 1066, with England's pre-Conquest past. To meet this need, stress was increasingly laid upon a story related in the Life of King Edward. In his last days, the king had awakened one night from a bad dream, and told those in attendance on him what he had seen.[77] Two monks he had known in Normandy had spoken to him of the wickedness of the leading men in the kingdom, warning him that, as a consequence of their wrongdoings, within a year and a day of his death the kingdom would have been delivered by God 'into the hands of the enemy'. The king assured

26 Assisted by its associations with King Edward, Westminster thrived as the seat of the Norman kings of England. The gigantic hall, which William II (Rufus) built there in the 1090s as part of his palace complex, had stone walls 2 metres thick; the lower parts of them still stand today.

them that he would tell the people, and that the people would repent. The monks responded that the people would not repent, which prompted the king to ask when remission of such ills might come. They replied obliquely: only when two parts of a severed tree, separated by some distance, would join together of their own accord and bear fruit again – in other words, that it could not and would not happen.

For the author of the Life, writing in the immediate aftermath of the Conquest, there seemed little prospect of an improvement in England's fortunes. And yet sooner rather than later, the severed tree of Edward's dream was to be mended and seen to grow again. The Confessor had died childless, and his nearest kin were the children of Edward Ætheling (Edward the Exile), son of King Edmund Ironside. The eldest of these was a daughter, Margaret, who in 1070 married Malcolm III, King of Scots. Thirty years later, on 11 November 1100, in yet another act of political theatre conducted in Edward's church at Westminster, Henry I, the youngest son of William the Conqueror, married Edith, also known as Matilda or Maud, daughter of King Malcolm and Queen Margaret. The service was conducted by Archbishop Anselm, 'with great ceremony', and was followed by Matilda's consecration as Henry's queen. The marriage between Henry and Matilda was seen at the time as marking nothing less than the attachment of the Norman royal dynasty, established by William I, to the old royal line of Anglo-Saxon England, stretching back to King Alfred and beyond. A contemporary annalist described Matilda's mother as 'the good queen, the kinswoman of King Edward, of the true royal family of England'.[78]

The outcome was not entirely as intended. Queen Matilda died at Westminster on 1 May 1118, and was buried there. For Henry I, the hope lay in their eldest son and heir, William Ætheling (a telling use of the standard Anglo-Saxon term for a king's son). Tragically, William was among those lost on the night of 25–6 November 1120, when the *White Ship*, in which he was crossing the channel from Normandy to England, struck a rock and sank off Barfleur.[79] In his *Gesta regum Anglorum*, written at about this time, William of Malmesbury, who was himself Anglo-Norman by birth, was despondent. When writing about Edward, he told the story of the king on his deathbed, and accepted without comment the wretched future for England implicit in the message concerning the shattered tree. But in recording the wreck of the *White Ship*, he spoke in terms suggesting he had hoped for a miracle that God's providence might after all bring to pass. And so it was with sorrow that he reported that God had had other plans. 'In him [William Ætheling] it was supposed King Edward's prophecy was to be fulfilled: the hope of England, it was thought, once cut down like a tree, was in the person of that young prince again to blossom and bear fruit, so that one might hope the evil times were coming to an end.'[80]

Fortunately, there would be further opportunities. Young William had an older sister, Matilda, successively German empress and Countess of Anjou. In his tract *Genealogia regum Anglorum* ('The genealogy of the kings of the English'), written in 1153–4, Abbot Ailred of Rievaulx addressed Henry of Anjou, Matilda's son from her second marriage, as 'truly heir to England'.[81] Some ten years later, in his *Vita Sancti Eduardi regis et confessoris* ('Life of St Edward, king and confessor'), after Henry of Anjou had become Henry II, Ailred looked to the new king, in a passage making extended reference to Edward's dream, as the one whose accession would represent the rejoining of the severed tree. 'Now certainly England has a king from English stock,' he exulted.[82] When the story came to be told yet again, in the mid-thirteenth-century Anglo-Norman Life of St Edward the king, a work in verse based on Ailred's earlier treatise, the king whom its author (the chronicler Matthew Paris) had in mind was none other than

27 By *c.*1100 Westminster Abbey and the adjacent palace were laid out at the southern end of
Thorney (re-created in this drawing by Terry Ball, 1980). Nearest the river (to the east), stands
William Rufus's great hall, completed in 1099, and other buildings of the palace complex. Inland
(to the west) stands the abbey church, built in the new Romanesque style: shown in cut-away,
one of its twin west towers, the nave (with triple elevation and aisle), and the central tower
(flanked by matching transepts) can all be seen. On the south side of the church, the cloister is
under construction: in the east range are the foundations of the chapter house with its apse, and
the partly built dormitory, extending beyond the cloister, with the reredorter (lavatories) set across
its end; the south range consists of the refectory, with the kitchen nearby; work has yet to begin
on the west range. All around are fields, mostly part of the abbey's home farm, an important
source of food for the monks.

Henry III ('li terz Henri'), at about the time of the birth of his first son, significantly
named Edward.[83] Henry III's devotion to St Edward reflected his own awareness of
the place he could claim in a line that reached back through St Margaret to the most
renowned of the royal dynasties of Anglo-Saxon England. He could imagine what
St Edward's church had meant for that king when it was built in the 1060s; and,

by replacing it with a larger church, for the grander shrine he planned for his holy predecessor, he was able in his own way to proclaim a new beginning.

In all periods, Westminster was a place of innovation, but also one of imitation, rivalry and recurrence. Other great churches were being built at this time. After a fire in 1087, St Paul's Cathedral was substantially rebuilt in particularly magnificent form, about 155 metres in length: Westminster, even at 98.2 metres long, was soon superseded in scale by the giant churches of London, Winchester, Canterbury and Bury St Edmunds, also important shrine churches.[84] The Conquest released an entirely new form of architectural ambition: some of these great churches explicitly modelled themselves on the dimensions of Old St Peter's in Rome. Yet regardless of competition – a constant in Westminster's history – in the late eleventh century it still stood among the largest of all European churches. The same grandeur was thought appropriate to the nearby palace. By 1100, when William Rufus's splendid great hall was already in use ('only half large enough' in the reported words of the king), Westminster possessed one of the most impressive royal building complexes in Christendom.[85]

27

2

A House of Kings:

1100–1307

PAUL BINSKI AND JAMES G. CLARK

WILLIAM THE CONQUEROR'S WESTMINSTER became a church like no other in medieval England. 'This place of ours . . . since ancient times rightly has been called the chief, the head of England, the kingdom's coronet', reflected the monk John Flete four centuries after the Norman Conquest, 'and has been known as such for ages past, from the very beginning.'[1] This was no windy boast. The abbey that had arisen at Westminster under Edward the Confessor took on a shape and a stature that set it apart from the many institutions that made up the Church in England before the Reformation. It consisted, not least, of a fine Romanesque great church, the first built in that style in England. The monastery had become the very embodiment of Norman glory. It held a commanding position not only beside a burgeoning capital city but also in the country beyond. The lands and properties of Westminster extended north to the Humber, south to the Sussex downs, up-river on the Thames as far as its source, and westward to the Severn Sea. Together they generated greater wealth than any other institution, abbey or cathedral. Neither the oldest nor the largest monastery in medieval England, nor the one that had the most extensive network of daughter houses, still Westminster was seen to be pre-eminent. It was to this abbey church that England's premier bishops and her two archbishops were called for their consecrations.[2] Westminster was the keeper of the kingdom.

Westminster secured this singular status in little more than a hundred years from the death of William I. To a very great extent this was the achievement of the sequence of Norman abbots who led the monastery from Conquest to Magna Carta, from Vitalis

28 (FACING PAGE)   On 17 May 1220 the 13-year old Henry III was crowned at Westminster; a portrait in Matthew Paris's *Historia Anglorum* (written 1250–55), shows him holding a representation of the abbey church (which he was to rebuild in the Gothic style), in recognition of the love he bore for his predecessor St Edward.

(1076–*c*.1085) to William du Hommet (1214–22). It was unusual that each of them should have been a Norman incomer; they also represented Normandy's quite different monastic customs, and the two longest-serving, Gilbert Crispin (*c*.1085–1117/18) and Gervase of Blois (1138–57), were, respectively, of ducal and royal rank.[3] It was fitting that all but one of them were buried together, lying head to foot in the south cloister, a reminder to the remaining generations of monks who passed them on their daily route from the dormitory that it was their century of leadership that had made their church *caput Anglie*.

One of their first achievements was to garner the interest of the new monarchy. The first authentic writs of William I, issued in the interest of Abbot Vitalis, show the king requiring rival claimants to respect the wide reach of Westminster property.[4] He intervened to ensure the restoration of lands seized by rivals in the wake of the Conquest, by which many of the greater Anglo-Saxon abbeys had been wasted.[5] The chain of confirmations of territory and legal and fiscal privileges did not break even as far as the reign of King John (r. 1199–1216). At the coronation of the Conqueror's second son, Henry I (r. 1100–35), if not before, Westminster was designated one of the festive venues where the monarch could wear the crown: in effect the ceremony of coronation was reserved for Westminster.[6] The privileges that Gilbert Crispin secured from Henry I were decisive in positioning the abbey ahead of other churches. There was also a covert side to the progress of the abbey after the Conquest. The century of Westminster's rise to power was a golden age of medieval forgery. Its abbots effectively created a series of royal charters granting properties, protections and privileges over and above those that were genuine.[7] Forgery was widespread in medieval monasteries, but Westminster's enterprise was rare, even staggering, in its coordination and longevity, continuing even after the canonization of Edward the Confessor in 1161. The mind behind them was almost certainly the Prior of Westminster Osbert of Clare (d. *c*.1158).

Yet, although the abbey possessed a truly great abbey church, Westminster was unusual in the relatively modest size of its community of monks.[8] The Norman abbots aimed at a convent of no more than about eighty to serve the church, whereas other Benedictine houses of national importance, such as Christ Church Canterbury, Bury St Edmunds, Gloucester, Glastonbury and St Albans, had as many as one hundred, while by the turn of the twelfth century the monastic chapters of the cathedral churches at Canterbury, Durham, Norwich and Worcester numbered as many as seventy. At the start of the reign of Henry III (r. 1216–72), the Westminster community was somewhat smaller, and the choir stalls provided for Henry's new church, dedicated in 1269, provided for no more than about sixty monks and guests, so further expansion was not envisaged.[9] In the late Middle Ages it did not rise above fifty. The social profile of the monastery was as distinct as its size. The home-grown abbots who led Westminster from the

29   The century of Westminster's rise to power was a golden age of medieval forgery, staggering
in its co-ordination and longevity; this forged charter (dated 5 August 1100) records Henry I
taking the abbey into his protection, acknowledging it as the coronation church, and confirming
its liberties and privileges.

early thirteenth century mostly came from one of the districts where the abbey held
property, and their families were modest: property-owning, perhaps, but not gentry or
nobility. After 1200, no abbot was appointed to Westminster from elsewhere until 1533.

A Royal Role Model: St Edward

A keystone of Westminster's faith was the abbey's patron saint, Peter the Apostle.
However, unlike Canterbury, Winchester, Ely, Bury and Durham, also great Benedictine
establishments, the abbey in 1100 lacked a major shrine. It was not to become a true
shrine church until Edward the Confessor's canonization in 1161. Saints were made
by two methods: by popular canonization or, more recently, by papal process.[10] In
England the first had been usual: St Edward was the first English saint to be canonized
by Rome; the second was Thomas Becket (1173). In the earliest years after his death,
Edward was not a saint but a king worthy of praise: his first biography, compiled for
the Godwin family by a monk of Saint-Bertin in the 1060s, celebrates his foundation
of Westminster and his decision to be buried there. It is dedicated to his queen, Edith,
a Godwin, who was buried with him in the abbey. A second part of the Life records
various miracles performed by Edward as a saint-to-be, and his tomb was duly opened

and inspected in 1102 for signs of sanctity.[11] What was lacking was evidence of a popular cult, the old means of canonizing English saints. Edward did not enjoy the same level of regional support as Cuthbert, Edmund or, eventually, Thomas at Canterbury. Instead, his early cult was largely dependent on its energetic promotion by specific individuals or groups, especially the abbey and the king. One fervent supporter was Prior Osbert of Clare, who in 1138, during the reign of King Stephen (r. 1135–54), composed a formal proposal to the papal legate, Alberic of Ostia, that Edward should be canonized.[12] Support from the royal circle was notably lukewarm. What is evident from Osbert's process is how promotion of Edward's cult was strategically connected to the issue of the abbey's rights and privileges. What concerned the abbey especially was the power over it of the Bishop of London; the aim, with the help of a new saint, was to get the abbey exempted from diocesan control and instead placed directly under the pope as, in Osbert's words, a 'special daughter of the Roman church'.[13] St Edward was an agent in the simultaneous promotion of the rites of the abbey and the sacrality of English kingship. There was always to be a political dimension to his cult.

Alexander III eventually promulgated the canonization of St Edward early in 1161, after Osbert of Clare's death, but probably as a result of the pope's inspection of Osbert's compilation of Edward's miracles. Whatever the pope's motives, the roles of Lawrence, Abbot of Westminster (c. 1158–1173), and Henry II (r. 1154–89) seem to have been decisive. Lawrence pressed the process through and then persuaded his kinsman, the eminent Cistercian monk Ailred of Rievaulx, to write an official Life of Edward based on all the earlier sources. Ailred's preamble duly mentions the support of Henry II.[14]

It was at this time that the essentials of the later medieval cult of St Edward were formed. St Edward never displaced St Peter as the presiding figure of the monastery's devotional life. But Edward was useful. He quickly became a sign of the authority and independence of the abbey, the performer of an accepted body of miracles and a mirror of kings. As Ailred's opening address to the notoriously ill-tempered Henry II says, 'the justice of such a great king deserves imitation'. Into his concise and elegant Latin Life, Ailred imported the finest traditions of classical Stoic ethics, which now informed standards of civil or courtly conduct originally intended for the monastic novitiate. As a model, Edward was in no sense 'chivalrous'. But he was instantly transformed into a courteous, gentle and prudent king, whose powers, particularly his visions, stemmed from his chastity with his queen, Edith. His virtues of temperance were those of monks and Anglo-Saxon virgin saints, resembling the claims made for the episcopal saints canonized in England particularly in the thirteenth century. Ailred's Life, together with its surviving Anglo-Norman reissue by Matthew Paris, is among the central monuments of the history of courtly conduct, of the 'civilizing process' aimed directly at royal patrons in an era when the reform of the conduct of clergy

30 Ailred's Life of Edward the Confessor represented the king as the embodiment of saintliness, whom all later monarchs should aspire to imitate; in a miniature from Matthew Paris's mid-13th-century reissue (in French) of the Life, the King of England (probably Henry I) kisses the uncorrupt body of Edward when his tomb is opened.

and the pastoral education of the laity became preoccupations of the Church.[15] Vital to this process was the political and ethical objective of toning down the English kings' thuggish tendencies to tyranny, wilfulness and violence. In contrast, as depicted by his later and most widely read hagiographers, Edward represented a balm of saintly niceness, the very embodiment of a Virgilian golden age of peace and tranquillity before the Conquest. Edward's harmonious nature and especially his peaceful relations with his baronage were therefore a sort of prescriptive mythology, a necessary nostalgic fiction, for the Plantagenets.

After the canonization there followed the symbolic moving or 'translation', the physical elevation, of the relics of the saint, for whom a new shrine was raised high above the pavement directly behind the abbey's high altar on 13 October 1163, a date for ever marked in royal feasting and possibly chosen because it was the eve of the anniversary of the Battle of Hastings, which had inaugurated the new dispensation. Henry II and Thomas Becket, still in harmony, presided at the event. Raised shrines were becoming a norm in twelfth-century churches, as at the French royal abbey of Saint-Denis and soon at Canterbury. The vacated grave of the saint in the apse was thereafter marked as an independent site of veneration.[16] In 1272 it was to be opened again to receive the body of Henry III until his tomb was built.

It has long been recognized that the outer form of a great church in the era of pilgrimage was, at least to an extent, a mirror of the cult and shrines within.[17] Had the abbey's practices of historical writing been as strong at this time as its skill in forging documents we might have been able to establish whether the 1163 translation had any material consequences for the now century-old and increasingly superseded building. It was not uncommon for the east ends of shrine churches to be extended with grand ambulatories and retrochoirs, as was to happen for the sake of St Thomas at Canterbury in the years after 1174. The rebuilding of the east end of Canterbury cathedral in the latest French Gothic mode was a spectacular challenge to all English shrine churches, and to Benedictine establishments especially. We know that Lawrence, the Abbot of Westminster who achieved Edward's canonization, was also a builder, because he restored Westminster's conventual buildings in 1158–73.[18] But whether his abbey church was amplified by an enlargement of its east end with walkways or chapels is hidden from view, and it remains possible that the Confessor's church already had an ambulatory.[19] There is no evidence for a pilgrimage cult at Westminster in these years to compare with Canterbury's, however, and the kings of England were all buried elsewhere in England or in France. The cult of St Edward was never a popular cult, though its hagiography and imagery insinuated the contrary. By the 1200s the abbey, so far as we know, was becoming outmoded as a building, and it was to take the energy of a true devotee of St Edward to remedy this.

Popes, Government and Saints

In 1170 the new cult of St Edward was overtaken, if not swept away, by one of the most dramatic episodes in English history. The martyrdom of Thomas Becket in December 1170 and the controversy that followed for a half century were the most cogent demonstration in the history of the English people of the necessity of inculcating virtue into kings.[20] St Thomas of Canterbury started as a spectacular wonder-worker, and remained the pre-eminent English saint and the principal focus of miracles and pilgrimage. He had far more churches and (no less importantly) holidays dedicated to him than did St Edward. St Edward was to remain a saint of the political elite that had created him: Thomas was a man of the people, and especially the people of London.

The great English Benedictine houses of Durham (St Cuthbert) and Bury (St Edmund) housed the most ancient and the most important regional saints. Neither Henry II nor his successors Richard (r. 1189–99) and John (buried, respectively, at the abbey of Fontevraud and Worcester cathedral priory) showed interest in Westminster. Benign neglect in these years could have been disastrous, had not international forces prevailed.

If two archbishops of Canterbury, Baldwin of Forde (1184–90) and Hubert Walter (1193–1205), had had their way (and if the protestations of the monks of Canterbury are to be believed), the primatial throne and the relics of St Thomas could have been moved from Canterbury cathedral and away from its troublesome and conservative monks, to a new church staffed by canons charged, like an electoral college, with the election of Archbishops of Canterbury, to be built either at Hackington in Kent or in London. By the end of the twelfth century, plans were afoot to erect a new collegiate church dedicated to Sts Stephen and Thomas on the opposite side of the Thames from Westminster, at Lambeth.[21] Had all this happened, London could have displaced Canterbury to become the head of the southern province of England, and Westminster would have been permanently sidelined. The profile of glorious Gothic buildings along the Thames, including St Paul's Cathedral, would have surpassed even Paris. But an exceptionally dynamic pope, Innocent III, took the side of the Canterbury monks and in 1199 squashed the scheme, of which Lambeth Palace is the only remnant.

Westminster's relationship to the pope was vital. In the twelfth century the abbots had pursued a special status for the abbey beyond the realm of England, with the authority of Western Christendom's leader. A battery of benefits followed: the right to appropriate the income from the parish churches in its possession; a general exemption from the jurisdiction of any bishop; and the grant to the abbot of the regalia (mitre, staff and ring) and the powers of a bishop.[22] Definitive freedom from the jurisdiction of the Bishop of London was not won until 1222, when the abbey gained the formal exemption from diocesan control that it had sought in the previous century; by then, Westminster's status as a church, subject only to the ultimate authority of the papacy, seemed well established.[23] The abbey enjoyed unrivalled independence from ecclesiastical authority and a presiding role in the affairs of Church and state. The idea of a special relationship with the papacy stayed with the Westminster monks for generations, and St Edward was its guarantor.

The relationship to the crown was no less important to Westminster as a whole. In the town of Westminster and the city of London, the passing of the last of the Norman abbots, William du Hommet (1222), represented the high-water mark of the abbey's profile. At this stage, the abbot and his brethren might still have travelled a mile to the north from their church as far as what is now Oxford Street without leaving their own domain. Eastward, within the city, they could claim valuable property, including riverside wharfs and some of the Londoners' largest parishes, such as St Alban Wood Street and St Magnus the Martyr.[24] London was rising politically and economically. Westminster to its south-west nevertheless had two advantages. The first was that by the early thirteenth century, the machinery of royal administration, including the exchequer and the common bench, was now sited in its palace. The royal residence, begun before the Conquest and expanded after it, had become an administrative machine. Westminster had totally superseded Winchester as the administrative capital, as Archbishop Hubert Walter, a great administrative reformer, may have reckoned when planning to move to nearby Lambeth. The second advantage was that, after the loss of Normandy in 1204, the kings of England spent less time in their French territories and more time at what was becoming the premier royal palace, Westminster. Of this idea of political centralization and unification, St Edward was to become an articulate and explicit symbol.

Westminster Abbey was at an apex in Church and public life when Henry III, its most celebrated patron, acceded to the throne in 1216 at the age of 9. Henry's sheer youth may have been one factor in his powerful personal identification with a venerable and virtuous father figure, St Edward – a tendency, too, of the other English king who acceded to the throne as a boy, Richard II. Henry also had the support of a particularly brilliant Archbishop of Canterbury, Stephen Langton, who had influenced the content of Magna Carta in 1215 and who had a politician's eye for orchestrated symbolism, especially anything that reinforced the unity of the community of the realm after John's reign. Henry's reign had begun with the occupation of London by Louis VIII of France; the young king was crowned first at Gloucester Abbey in late October 1216 under difficult circumstances. The year 1220 saw Henry's second coronation, this time at Westminster, the spectacular translation of St Thomas to his new shrine at Canterbury, at which Henry III assisted, the canonization of Hugh of Lincoln, the re-foundation of Salisbury cathedral, and, at Westminster, the foundation by Henry III of a new Lady Chapel at the axis of the abbey's east end.[25] In 1228 Henry gained his majority, and in 1236 he married Eleanor of Provence.

The renaissance of St Edward as a patron saint occurred in the years 1233–8 for a combination of political and personal reasons, probably under the guidance of one of Henry's advisers, the Westminster monk Richard le Gras. St Edward is first explicitly described as Henry's patron in a royal charter granting liberties to the abbey in 1235.[26] This new role immediately received its most enduring literary and artistic expression in a new, and this time illustrated, Anglo-Norman verse Life of St Edward, executed between 1236 and 1239 by the versatile St Albans historian–artist Matthew Paris (d. 1259), and dedicated to Henry and his new queen, a slightly later copy of which, graced with courtly illustrations in gentle pen and wash, survives.[27] Matthew's *Estoire de Seint Aedward le rei* ('Life of St Edward the king') was adapted from Ailred's Latin Life by amplifying it with racy and often violent historical narrative and political opinions particular to him – Matthew seems to have been adept at composing booklets of this sort for aristocratic women. The cases of Richard le Gras and Matthew Paris show that Benedictine monks retained a pastoral role at court before the friars took over as royal confessors.

28

31 A miniature from Matthew Paris's *Estoire de Seint Aedward le rei* (in a copy from *c.*1250–60) shows pilgrims coming to seek a cure at the tomb of St Edward in Westminster Abbey; behind the kneeling figures (one of whom has crawled into the tomb itself), stand a patient crowd waiting their turn, including a child, a man with a crutch and a blind man. The saintly king was fashionably mythologized in the 13th century as a wonder-worker, with the same powers as St Thomas of Canterbury.

La Estoire de Seint Aedward le rei elegantly encapsulates all the fashionable doctrines of the time about restrained courtly behaviour, good manners, styles of devotion and devotional objects such as the Eucharist. St Edward re-founded Westminster Abbey at the very centre of his land (*en mie . . . terre assise*, as the French puts it), and got on with his barons in what the verses call 'parliament' (an early instance of the word in the thirteenth century); his court was a very 'school' of courtesy. In the wake of Magna Carta, the outstanding innovation in royal government was the advent of a new form of representative assembly to replace the old, occasional Great Council of prominent nobles, in which the monarch might be accountable to the political nation at large. The first sequence of parliaments was summoned to Westminster from 1258, but the notion was clearly older. The regular transaction of parliamentary business confirmed Westminster Palace as the site for all forms of royal government.

The *Estoire* also shows long queues of pilgrims waiting for cures at St Edward's tomb, as if he, like St Thomas, were a wonder-worker. Pastorally, St Edward was a perfected model or pattern for kings to imitate, except in one regard: his quasi-monastic chastity, which had left him heirless. Still, the idea of a pattern materially affected the abbey, even if it could not entirely recommend itself to kings. While Edward had rebuilt the church for his love of St Peter, Henry did so for the love of St Edward;[28] just as Edward nominated the abbey as his burial place, so did Henry, in 1246. And just as Edward was a great builder, so Henry III also proved to be. Matthew's verses claimed that St Edward's new abbey 'Arises, grand and royal' (*Surt l'ovre grantz e reaus*),[29] a fair description of what Henry was to accomplish after 1245.

Henry III's New Abbey Church, 1245–1272

La Estoire de Seint Aedward le rei may even have been intended to nurture sympathy for the renewal of the shrine and the abbey church itself. By 1241 Henry had begun to refashion the shrine of St Edward; this may imply that he already had in mind the total rebuilding of St Edward's church on up-to-date Gothic lines that began in 1245.[30] The construction of any great church inevitably posed financial and logistical questions. Henry was almost alone among Western European patrons in himself funding the erection of a giant Gothic great church: at Westminster this necessitated a dedicated exchequer.[31] In all, by 1272, the works were to cost about £41,000, an extraordinary outlay on an English church of unprecedented lavishness if not absolute scale. The king's investment was critically important, since the abbey, like all the greater monasteries in England, was steadily being drained of its cash resources by the demands of domestic taxation and papal levies. In the course of the rebuilding, it was essential that the monastic routine be disrupted as little as possible; but although the new lofty east end, cloister, chapter house, transepts and choir rose with remarkable speed, given constant financial and political hindrances in the years 1245–69, some dislocation was inevitable. In 1245 the old east end, transepts and tower and a part of the nave were demolished, and the offices decanted into what remained of the old church. In the mid-1170s Canterbury had undergone the same upheaval for the sake of St Thomas, and its chronicler, Gervase, shows how it coped: the juncture of the functioning church and the building site was sealed by a huge wooden wall, while the conventual Masses and offices were performed in the nave at the altar of the Holy Cross.[32] After 1245 at Westminster about ten bays of the old nave still stood. We learn of a new great rood with two cherubim to either side of the cross, set up in 1251 in the nave over the temporary high altar, with the royal throne nearby.[33] Here, too, must have been placed the major shrines. Edward's and Edith's bones were immediately moved from the old east end in their twelfth-century containers. Queen Edith's tomb was certainly opened, because in October 1245 an orphrey found on her body (she was a noted embroiderer) was used to adorn a choir cope to be presented to the shrine of St Edward.[34] The abbey was already a small-scale Anglo-Saxon mausoleum. In all probability, Edward's shrine was moved behind the temporary high altar where it could continue to generate donations.

As rebuilt by Henry III because of his love of St Edward, the abbey church demonstrates the emulative and eclectic aspect of magnificent courtly patronage. Since the twelfth century, royal support at Westminster had been important. Such limitations as were imposed on the new scheme were physical rather than economic. The nave and west end of the old church were retained, as were the general positions of the choir, crossing and high altar, meaning that the new building could expand only very slightly eastwards before it encountered the axial Lady Chapel begun in 1220 and the palace, with the Thames lying beyond. The east walk of the cloister was therefore absorbed into the west aisle of the south transept, and space was left for a magnificent octagonal vaulted chapter house. So the decision to adopt a polygonally formed, compact and high-rise French-style *chevet*, or apse with radiating chapels, possessed a greater logic for this specific, cramped brief than an English-style, broad, spreading, ground plan as at Salisbury.[35]

Great buildings, like great saints, could be formal 'models'. It is impossible to ascertain whether there was any survival at Westminster of the idea that St Edward's church had itself been innovative in its day. Canterbury cathedral's internationalism of style, witnessed by Henry III in 1220 and again in 1236, when he was married there, will have been a powerful example for this century of saints. Gothic architecture had entered England in the course of the mid-twelfth century in a variety of forms. Some (in the north) were Cistercian (therefore Burgundian) in origin; others, like Canterbury, were derived from the new Gothic abbey and cathedral churches of Paris and north-eastern France. In 1246 King John's Cistercian foundation at Beaulieu was consecrated, but up to this point English kings did not build great churches: in both England and France, the truly large projects were diocesan. Henry's Capetian brother-in-law, Louis IX of France (r. 1226–70), was emerging as a significant builder in these years. In 1239 Louis had begun an extraordinary chapel in his main palace in Paris, to house the newly acquired Crown of Thorns.[36] This was the Sainte-Chapelle, dedicated in 1248 and rising fast enough to be consulted by Henry's chosen masons throughout the late 1240s. That the Sainte-Chapelle was at least one motivating factor in Henry's decision to rebuild the abbey church is suggested by the fact that he took it as one model for his work at Westminster.

What is also striking is that, while Canterbury cathedral priory had employed a French architect, William of Sens, to erect its new Gothic choir in 1174, Henry III appointed a master whose work discloses that his origin was English – even if (as seems likely from his name) Henry of Reyns had some professional association with Reims cathedral and had certainly studied it.[37] Had Henry employed an uncompromising French mason, Westminster would have risen in the 1240s in the new so-called Rayonnant style of the nave of Saint-Denis (started in 1231) and the transepts of Notre-Dame in Paris (designed in the 1240s). It might even have resembled the masterpiece of this style, Cologne cathedral, begun in 1248. But this did not happen. Instead, the new abbey retained the relatively thick walls of the Anglo-Norman tradition, but had inserted into them the huge 'bar'-tracery windows, including magnificent and structurally daring rose windows, that had been developed in the Paris area. This mixture very probably signalled a belief that English Gothic masons and their buildings were not inferior to the French, and had to be taken into account.

As a matter of record we have no clue as to what thinking dictated the form of the new abbey church, despite the extraordinary and entirely new level of documentation available from the prodigious English chancery and exchequer records. The brief must have been mixed. The abbey was presumably to match and surpass Canterbury and all other English cathedral and shrine churches, such as Salisbury, Ely and Lincoln, taking into account, especially, their eye-catching architectural forms and lavish use of native marbles, of which Purbeck, used extensively at Westminster, was the most famous. These rich and telling features might be matched in a smaller French scheme, such as the Sainte-Chapelle, which, like the abbey, has rich interior sculpture, but they were quite untypical of the rather severe interiors of the vast and lofty French cathedrals. Westminster has marble columns like those at Salisbury, a complex middle stage in its elevation (like those at Lincoln and Ely), fronting deep galleries of uncertain function. This middle stage, or tribune, is faced with ornamental carved diaper-work as if it were made of patterned gold. An important gauge of prestige was interior height: the vault of the new church reached 31 metres, matching that of the nave of St Paul's Cathedral and surpassing all other English churches, but falling well below the great heights attained by Chartres, Reims and Amiens – the last being at least 10 metres taller. For Henry, Westminster was to be the greatest of English shrine churches.

Rivalry with the French achievement still mattered because emulation and imitation were as important to building as they were to kingly conduct, of which patronage was an aspect. The various patterns taken from France have long been known. The abbey's polygonal *chevet* was arranged according to that of Reims cathedral, set out around 1211.[38] The huge portals of the north transept, facing Charing and the road to London, were based on those of Amiens, with vigorous crenellations, reminiscent of fortifications, added on the city side as a warning to the populace. The slim proportions of the interior were also modelled on High Gothic buildings such as Reims

32 (FACING PAGE)   The new abbey church, built in the Gothic style by Henry III between 1245 and 1272, retained from the old church the general positions of the nave, choir, crossing and high altar; proof that the master mason, Henry of Reyns, had studied contemporary building trends in France, notably at Reims, is amply provided by the aisle and clerestory windows. Although it was no match for Chartres, Reims or Amiens in loftiness, the height of Westminster's nave surpassed that of most other English churches.

33

and Amiens. The aisle and clerestory window tracery derives from Reims cathedral, while the triforium and transeptal rose windows were plainly modelled on patterns known in Amiens and Paris (Notre-Dame and the Sainte-Chapelle) by 1245; the same is true of the windows of the chapter house, which was the first building on the site to be completed and furnished, by about 1253. Henry of Reyns shows such detailed knowledge of the Sainte-Chapelle that he must have had a royally sponsored entrée to study it. But his studies, undertaken doubtless on more than one visit to France to catch up with the latest trends, included also the new Rayonnant nave at Saint-Denis, from which the abbey's chapter house trefoil arcading is derived. Because the influence of such buildings is often visible in projects undertaken by the royal works, it seems likely that drawings of them were stored systematically for reference by architects, joiners, painters and sculptors. There was no notion of intellectual or artistic property in the thirteenth century. What constrained artists, instead, was a sense that certain designs had royal lineage, a sort of aesthetic bloodline or family likeness, appropriate to some classes of patronage but not to others. Clearly Henry III for the most part acted under advice. He did not actually see the Sainte-Chapelle until 1254 and was reported (by the French) to have admired it so much that he wished to take it back to London in a cart.[39] But the choice of Reims as a model – like Westminster, a coronation church, but one passing out of fashion stylistically by the 1240s – indicates that the thinking of his artists was also symbolic and functional: authority counted as much as 'modernity'.

Abbey and Palace: Sacral Space

With the possible exception of Canterbury, Westminster Abbey is the only English great church where the sheer reach of power is consciously put on display. Power is usually mediated by personality: the personal character of the kings of England had always been a major political factor, and Henry's was complex. He was impatient, spendthrift, critical of eye (Matthew Paris nicknamed him 'the Lynx' after that sharp-eyed animal), fastidious and, to some, untrustworthy. He drove forward the new construction with vigour, and was prepared to implement any expedient, financial or human, to gain his end. His deadlines were often liturgical: in 1254 workmen were to be recalled to the site so that the church might be consecrated on the next feast of St Edward, 13 October – a key date in Henry's mental calendar.[40] Two years earlier he had wished in vain that the raising of the marble work might be hurried up.

Henry's ambitions affected both the abbey and those buildings that formed its context, since the abbey functioned in part as a royal chapel in close proximity to what had become the major royal palace. It is helpful to consider the porous boundaries

33 (FACING PAGE)   The chapter house was the first Gothic building on the site to be finished, in about 1253; the windows imitate French patterns, as at the Sainte-Chapelle in Paris, dedicated in 1248, and the arcading copies that of the nave of Saint-Denis, started in 1231.

between the palace and abbey, and so between the temporal and the religious, for just as sacrality entered politics, so politics were not separable from the sacred. Here, what counted was the extraordinary concentration of Westminster's great buildings.

A key building in this regard was the new chapter house, built in the years 1246–53 and in use by 1257.[41] Centralized chapter houses were rapidly becoming a mark of status: examples already existed at Worcester, Lincoln and Beverley; Westminster's was to be copied at Salisbury. As a building type, chapter houses were intended to house separate meetings of the monastic chapter, at which the business of the monastery was discussed and discipline administered. Westminster's differed because there is some evidence that Henry III wanted to use it for state purposes as well as for chapter meetings. Abbey buildings such as the refectory and infirmary chapel had long been used for royal meetings, which, for some unknown reason, were not held in the great hall of the palace, or in its second or 'lesser' hall, or in the king's chamber; meetings, with or without the king, occurred in the new chapter house in 1257 and 1265.[42] Later, between the 1350s and the 1390s, the chapter house was used for the assembly of the Commons. In 1259 Henry commissioned a second lectern for the chapter house, which might indicate the need for his own personal visibility and audibility at such occasions. The chapter house's permanent imagery consisted of sculpted images of the Virgin Mary, a Tree of Jesse and an Annunciation at its portal, and a splendid tiled pavement with a repeated motif of the royal arms, images of St Edward giving a ring to

34, 35

34, 35 and 36 (FACING PAGE AND LEFT)   One of the finest medieval pavements in England, the tiled floor of Henry III's chapter house features the royal arms, images of St Edward, and copies of Westminster's rose windows.

St John, and beautiful copies of the church's rose windows. In their design, the chapter 36 house's magnificent, spreading windows, based on recent Parisian models, provided a glamorous backdrop.[43] The pavement could as easily have been planned for a palace. Its display of the arms of England reminds us that, as the nave progressed, carved and coloured stone shields with the arms of St Edward, England and many of the senior nobility were placed in the aisle wall arcading around the choir as an assertion of that unity of the king and his peers promoted by the example of St Edward, and so sorely tested by Henry himself in the troubled years after 1258, when England descended into civil war and Simon de Montfort became de facto ruler.[44]

Just to the east of the abbey, towards the Thames, lay an older but extensive complex of palatial halls and chambers, whose decorations might have belonged in an ecclesiastical context. After the giant great hall raised by William Rufus, the best-known of these, a sizeable chamber running east–west and looking over the Thames, was later known as the Painted Chamber.[45] In the thirteenth century it was called the 'king's great chamber' and held at its far end the king's bed of state, reminding us that the body politic was always a public body. Much is known about this and the adjacent queen's chambers, partly because Henry III is the first really well-documented English royal patron, and also because, though the great chamber was destroyed in the palace fire of 1834, its wall-paintings had been copied in 1819. Many of the most important images dated from the last years of the reign of Henry. The four-posted and canopied

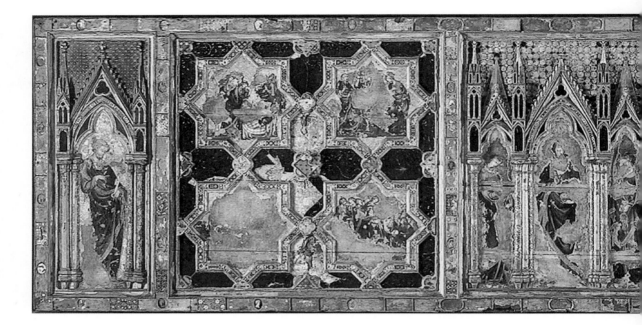

bed was surmounted at its head end by a large painted image of the coronation of
St Edward and a guardian of King Solomon's bed, with adjacent images in the window
embrasures of St Edward's virtues (including *Largesse*, or 'generosity', and *Debonereté*,
or 'calmness') and of St Edward giving a ring to St John the Evangelist. St John had
appeared to Edward as a poor pilgrim, begging for alms; Edward gave him a ring,
which was eventually returned to him as a token of his imminent death. The same
35 scene appeared on the pavement of the chapter house, and the transepts of the abbey
also display sculpted images of St Edward and St John beneath their great roses,
overlooking the coronation arena. Henry liked to transpose entire systems of imagery
in familiar patterns of association from one context to another. His message to his
court of unity, civility, virtue and peace was consistent.

In style and technical splendour, these pictures (as copied in 1819) were close to the
one surviving example of sacral painting from Henry's reign, the magnificent carved,
gilded and painted altarpiece provided for the abbey's own high altar between 1259
37, 7 and 1269.[46] The Westminster Retable shows the patron of the abbey, St Peter, to the
left, with Christ as Saviour, the Virgin Mary and St John at the centre, and tiny but
exquisite oil-based images of the Miracles of Christ. All the scenes are framed with
gilded, painted and bejewelled miniature Gothic architecture of Parisian type, even
inlaid with pretty decorative stained glass. The retable is the supreme instance of

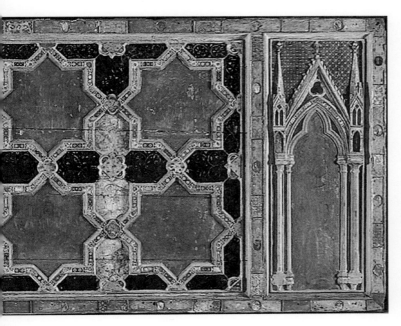

37   The Westminster Retable, an unsurpassed example of French influence on courtly art in England at this time, was created for the high altar of the abbey church between 1259 and 1269; the wall-paintings in the halls and chambers of Henry's adjacent palace (lost in the fire of 1834) would have matched those of the retable in style and splendour.

French influence on the figurative arts at court, and in England more widely, in these years. Clearly Henry had a scheme to 'Frenchify' the fittings of his new church, since he also asked a French goldsmith to guide the design of the chalice used at the high altar.[47] His palace murals were executed in the same style. They fundamentally altered the direction of English art.

How medieval patrons made aesthetic choices and perceived the values implicit in them is a complex problem that rewards investigation. At Westminster, whether as anointed sovereign, seated in estate in his chamber, or present at his abbey's high altar, Henry III showed that at some level he perceived in French or French-influenced art something not merely fashionable and pleasurable, but beautiful in the sense that it conveyed and made fully present his idea of the sacred. The function of the works of art alone cannot explain his choices, though it is true that Henry and his advisers probably looked to Reims cathedral as a model because of its role as a coronation church, and to the Sainte-Chapelle because it was the most beautiful stone reliquary in the known world. Henry's vision was not exclusively French in character, however. His patron cult was English, and Henry, like most great patrons, was not ideologically committed to a single style or taste. The richness and power of English art were not lost on him. He wanted the best and the most convincing, and in selecting the best from the best he was acting as great patrons have always done in the pursuit of excellence.

The ability to pick and choose, and to afford the best, is a sign not of ideology at work, but of the ultimate freedom of power.

Henry was a collector in more than one sense. His observance of the October feast of St Edward at Westminster was remarkably strict throughout his reign, but his devotion to the saints generally, including pilgrimage to other shrines, was very like that of most Plantagenet kings. Henry paid due respect to St Thomas of Canterbury. He never went to Jerusalem, Rome or Compostela, though he did know the major French shrines at Saint-Denis, Pontigny and Chartres, which he visited in the 1250s and early 1260s, and his normal itinerary often included shrine visits in England.[48] Instead, Rome, Jerusalem and other holy sites came to him via the culture of relic giving. He benefited particularly from the extraordinary movement of relics following the sack of Constantinople, a storehouse of religious remains, in 1204. Like most great churches, the abbey preserved, as well as its main relic of St Edward, numerous smaller relics. These included St Edward's regalia, used at the coronation. A methodical list of the relics remaining in the fifteenth century was made by the abbey monk John Flete, in the conventional order of a litany. Royal donors included King Sæberht (now firmly established in Westminster's historiography as the founder of the abbey) and Offa, Æthelstan, Edgar, Cnut, St Edward, William I, Henry III and his son Edward I (r. 1272–1307).[49] Of relics of Christ, Henry III gave some blood from the side-wound of Christ, a thorn from the Crown of Thorns and a stone with the footprint of Christ left at the Ascension. St Edward gave arm relics of St Bartholomew and St Thomas, and in addition Henry III gave various fragments of the heads of St Christopher and St Maurice. The thorn relic was probably that given to Henry by a Franciscan in 1235.

Of the relics of Christ, that of Holy Blood shed at the Crucifixion was the most important, earning a visitor an indulgence of more than nineteen years, according to Flete.[50] It was also the most fashionable and controversial of the relics. At first sight it was a more than impressive counterpart to Louis IX's acquisition of the Crown of Thorns and other relics of the Passion purchased by him from the Latin Emperor of Constantinople. It had been sent to Henry in 1247 as a gift from the Patriarch of Jerusalem and, according to Matthew Paris, ranked above the Crown of Thorns, as a physical relic of Christ, not a contact relic that had simply touched him.[51] It was also a political relic, designed to inspire English royal support for the crusade, and was deliberately paraded by Henry III in front of the English nobility summoned to Westminster for the feast of St Edward in October 1247, in a kind of sacral ambush.[52] On St Edward's day, Henry, humbly barefoot and dressed in a poor cloak, carried the Holy Blood in its crystal phial from St Paul's Cathedral through London to Westminster, and around the abbey and palace, including his own chambers. It was deposited somewhere in the abbey. Matthew's own illustration of the event in his

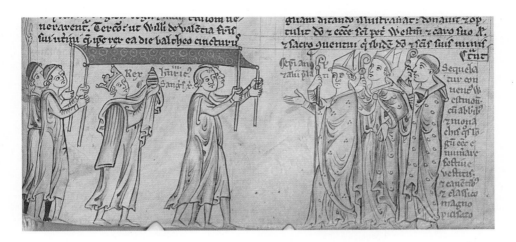

38   In his *Chronica majora* (mid-13th century), Matthew Paris depicts King Henry's devotion to the relic of the Holy Blood as he carries it to Westminster for the feast of St Edward in 1247.

Chronica majora, showing Henry captivated by the relic held up in his hands beneath a portable canopy, is rather like a late-medieval Corpus Christi procession.

The mix of reverence, ostentatious humility and grand public gesture seems typical of Henry's marked sense of occasion and place. That the relic served to consecrate the king's chambers indicates the connection of sacrality that held Westminster's great church and palace together as a single political and religious entity. Possibly its public role was to enhance the otherwise fairly narrowly based cult of St Edward; but at a deeper theological level such relics – others were at Hailes abbey and Ashridge priory, also Plantagenet foundations – proved problematical, because they contested the doctrine of the Resurrection: if Christ had resurrected, why had not his blood too?[53] In fact – and perhaps because of these difficulties – we know little or nothing of the subsequent history of the Holy Blood at Westminster, including how and where it was displayed in the abbey church.

Very few physical traces of Westminster's lesser relic cults survive, but the abbey possesses one remarkable piece of evidence in the form of the large wall-paintings of St Thomas the Apostle and St Christopher on the south wall of the south transept,   39 discovered in the 1930s and dating to the period of the decoration and furnishing of the new abbey church, perhaps even to the late 1260s.[54] The paintings are bold interpretations of the style of the abbey's new high-altarpiece, but the notable thing is the way they emphasize the saints' physical proximity to – indeed, contact with – Christ: Thomas putting his hand into Christ's side with the Saviour's help, and the Christ

39   Remarkably vivid wall-paintings on the south wall of the south transept, thought to date to the late 1260s, show St Thomas thrusting his hand into Christ's wound (*left*) and the Christ Child carried by St Christopher (*right*); the choice of subject matter reflects the presence of relics of St Thomas and St Christopher in the collection of the abbey church.

Child wrapping his arm around St Christopher's head, gestures that point to the relics of Thomas's arm and Christopher's cranium in the abbey's collection.[55] Whoever planned these images thought with some care, and it is notable that in 1244 Henry III had ordered that a ring should be made for the hand of St Thomas's arm reliquary, bearing a verse inscription from John 20:29: 'Blessed are those who have not seen and yet have come to believe.' High above the two paintings, just under the rose window, are the carved images of St John with his ring, and St Edward. Presumably other paintings relating to the relic collection were originally in the wall arcading here, near the south transept entrance from the palace. Once again the model at work might have been the upper chapel of the Sainte-Chapelle, where the glittering relic display was introduced by lively wall-paintings of the martyrs whose cults were celebrated in Paris and especially at court. The Westminster image of St Christopher is probably the earliest surviving English example in wall-painting of a theme that became common in parish churches, and Henry III had chosen the image for his palaces even earlier.

The Dedication of the New Church and the Translation of St Edward: 1269

In 1259 the east end and transepts of the abbey church were complete, and so more of the Confessor's nave was knocked down by royal order to make way for the continuation of the nave and the completion within it of the liturgical choir.[56] Much of the nave continued to stand throughout the fourteenth century. But the time for the dedication of the new church had clearly arrived. Potential deadlines of symbolic importance for the translation and dedication will have included 1263, the centenary of the first translation of St Edward, and 1269, the year that calendrically resembled 1163 (the dates falling on the same days of the week and Easter on Sunday 24 March) so possessing special significance.[57] This was the date at last earmarked by the king. For the dedication and translation to be celebrated satisfactorily, the abbey required a functioning high altar, choir and shrine. The high altar and its altarpiece appear to have been commissioned and finished within the decade 1259–69; the choir stalls had long been in manufacture. For Henry the situation was significantly complicated by the state of violent political conflict with his barons that ended in the years 1264–7 with the defeat of Simon de Montfort and the passage of the Statute of Marlborough. Henry had to establish clear priorities, the first of which was the completion of St Edward's new shrine, undertaken in 1241. The shrine's history illustrates the financial perils of civil war. A goldsmith's account for the period 1257–72 makes it clear that basic elements of the design, such as the arcading on its sides, were still unassembled by the late 1250s.[58] Worse, the silver-gilt figurines within this arcading remained uninstalled, and at least one of them boxed up, in June 1267, when they and the jewels on the shrine – technically called the 'feretory' or ornate metalwork coffin – were temporarily pawned by a cash-strapped Henry.[59] They were handed to the Archbishop-elect of York and then to Ottobuono, the papal legate; many went abroad. Henry undertook to

40

restore the pawned items to the abbot, prior and convent of the abbey by Michaelmas
1268, and was borrowing money from Boniface, Archbishop of Canterbury, in June
1268; redemption was still under way in the summer of 1269.[60] February 1269 – eight
months before the scheduled translation – seems to have marked the start of the final
assembly, since by then the goldsmith William of Gloucester was at work on the shrine
with five assistants.[61]

On 13 October 1269 and on schedule, the dedication of the new church was
effected by Hugh of Taghmon, Bishop of Meath, in the presence of the king and his
magnates, and the translation took place.[62] Exactly how this was done is not known,
but it can be inferred from the manufacture of an ornately painted and enamelled
wooden coffin for St Edward that the old reliquary containing the saint was first
positioned next to the coffin on the high altar; the reliquary was then opened and
examined and the remains of the saint were duly transferred to the coffin.[63] In 1163,
at the first translation, the body of St Edward had been exposed to view in a chest
carried in procession around the cloisters by Henry II and his principal nobles, before
being located in the precious reliquary in a raised place.[64] Presumably the same rite
occurred in 1269. The chronicler Thomas Wykes tells us that St Edward was raised from
a modest to a more eminent place in the presence of an immense gathering, his bones
being moved *de veteri scrinio . . . in sublime* ('from the old shrine . . . to on high') and
processed on the shoulders of Richard, Earl of Cornwall, the Lord Edward, Edmund
Crouchback, John de Warenne and Philip Basset.[65] Not everything went smoothly:
the occasion was marred by unseemly squabbling among the bishops about their
precedence, thirteen of whom did not follow the procession: this at least suggests that
the processional act was intended to be splendid and prolonged.[66] Finally, the coffin
was placed in the space in the top of the stone shrine base, a short distance behind
the high altar, and over it the metal feretory was lowered. A London chronicle states
that the reliquary was not yet finished at the time of the 1269 ceremony; Hugh of
Taghmon's post-translation indulgence of January 1270 mentions further donations to
the making (*reparacione*) of the feretory, and work was still continuing as late as August
1272.[67] In a sense, no shrine is ever complete and the inlaid stonework of the shrine
was not signed off (*factum* according to its inscription) until 1279. But when he died
in November 1272, Henry III will at least have honoured his commitment. He was
buried in the old grave of St Edward near the high altar because no tomb had yet
been built for him. In the spring of 1290 the king's remains were finally moved to his
new papal-style tomb 'suddenly and unexpectedly' by night, just as if he himself was

40 (FACING PAGE)   The Confessor's wooden coffin still lies in a cavity in the top part of the
Purbeck marble structure, planned in the 1260s, that dominates the shrine of St Edward; the
gilt wooden canopy that surmounts it is a 16th-century addition. Five kings and four queens lie
buried in the same chapel, Henry III among them; visible in the background, his marble tomb is
inset with slabs of purple and green antique porphyry and inlaid with gilded Cosmati mosaics,
coloured marble and glass.

a saint.[68] His heart, significantly, was removed and presented in the following year to the ancient Angevin burial church of Fontevraud. Old loyalties ran deep.

The Royal Mausoleum

Before 1245 the kings of England had no single recognized burial place in England or France, though the royal abbey at Fontevraud near Chinon in Anjou had seen the burials of Henry II and Richard I. Henry III's father, John, was buried at Worcester near St Wulfstan, and Henry himself will almost certainly have quickly marked out the site of his permanent tomb on the north side of the shrine platform next to St Edward at Westminster: in England, royal death was never wholly free of the aura of sanctity. Many of the Anglo-Saxon kings and queens of England were traditionally venerated as confessors or martyrs, and extraordinary numbers of the wider family of Henry III himself were credited with posthumous miracles.[69] Westminster was already a minor mausoleum of royalty, because with St Edward lay his queen Edith and also Matilda, the first wife of Henry I. The relics of King Sæberht were retained in the nave during the thirteenth century.[70]

So when, in 1246, Henry reversed an earlier decision to be buried at the Temple church in London in favour of Westminster, 'out of reverence for St Edward' as the charter effecting this stated, he was not only imitating St Edward but joining a minor clan of the royal dead.[71] The abbey was a monastic burial church too, but it was very quick to attract non-monastic burials: Henry's little disabled daughter Katherine (d. 1257) was buried near the high altar, even as work on the church's east end continued; and throughout this period other members of the Plantagenet dynasty were granted this favour, such as the children of Edward I and William de Valence. This familial aspect of burial distinguishes Westminster from Saint-Denis, the burial place of anointed French sovereigns, and draws it closer to a church such as Fontevraud, where Henry II and Richard I and their families were laid to rest, or the Cistercian Royaumont, founded by Louis IX and Blanche of Castile, where family members and not just sovereigns were buried in tombs of striking diversity.[72] Westminster's quite different character as a premier royal residence must have been a factor in the formation of a mausoleum in the abbey as a family burial place.

The important point is that the rather inclusive decisions taken in regard to court burial from the 1250s profoundly affected the abbey's long-term character as a national church. After the retreat from Normandy in 1204, Westminster was now at the political and symbolic centre of things, and from the family mausoleum could eventually grow the idea of a great national pantheon of the dead. At the abbey's heart, by the shrine

41 The exquisite gilt-bronze effigy of Eleanor of Castile, wife of Edward I, was cast by goldsmith William Torel in 1291; she holds the string of her cloak in one hand but the sceptre that was once in her other hand is now lost. The tomb slab and pillows beneath her head are covered with the emblems of Castile and León (castles and lions).

of St Edward, lay the most privileged burial positions. The tomb of Henry III himself is by far the most striking monumental work of art surviving from the abbey in these years. Designed and largely manufactured by Roman mosaicists, its design is based on papal tomb models, such as that of Hadrian V (d. 1276) at Viterbo.[73] It originated in the circle of the major Italian architect and sculptor Arnolfo di Cambio. The beautifully sensitive gilt-bronze effigy of Henry was made by an English artist, William Torel, and installed only in the 1290s, at the same time as the manufacture of the no less outstanding effigy on the tomb of Eleanor of Castile.[74] After Henry's death in 1272 41 the momentum of patronage had been lost, and the completion of Henry's projects by Edward I was becoming untidy. What is evident is that Henry's tomb was intended to signal its identity as a potential shrine by means of its altar-like base and niches. An indulgence was issued for it to pilgrims in 1287. Henry, however, did not commit many post-mortem miracles, and no campaign for his canonization was undertaken; in 1297, in contrast, Louis IX, the most Christian king in Europe, was canonized by Pope Boniface VIII. The age of royal canonization was drawing to a close.

Whether or not Henry's decision in 1246 to be buried with the Confessor was the first shot in a campaign to found a royal mausoleum at Westminster is not explicitly confirmed by the sources, though it cannot be ruled out. The planning of the building in that year created spaces for burials between the columns of the sanctuary and apse, as well as the radiating chapels – spaces that were promptly filled by members of Henry's own family from as early as 1257. Henry's unique quasi-papal monument was followed in quick succession by those of Eleanor of Castile (d. 1290), Aveline de Forz (d. 1274), the first wife of Edmund Crouchback, Earl of Lancaster and brother of the king, Crouchback himself (d. 1296) and Edward I (d. 1307), some around the shrine, some in the sanctuary, but all or most on the privileged north side, to which they were entitled as Henry's children or children-in-law.[75]

Whatever the plan, the outcome even by 1307 was the single most eclectic and important group of Gothic tombs ever designed in England, and, with the exception of Saint-Denis, possibly in Europe. What matters here is that the decision to use the leading royal master masons of the day to design tombs – the Crundales, Michael of Canterbury and later Henry Yevele – resulted in monuments of exceptional quality, enhanced by a careful distinction between tombs for sovereigns with gilt-bronze effigies, and those for unanointed Plantagenet family members with painted or alabaster tomb effigies. Eleanor of Castile's burial places at Lincoln (her entrails), Blackfriars in London (her heart) and Westminster (her body) remain the most important of any English queen to date, to say nothing of the twelve funeral wayside crosses erected in the 1290s at the stopping places of her cortège as it travelled from Harby in Nottinghamshire to Westminster, via Cheapside and Charing, a route chosen deliberately to pass through London, and reminiscent of Henry III's conscious orchestration of the city when he processed the Holy Blood. Aveline's tomb, with its paintwork and simple canopy in the cusped French style of the Sainte-Chapelle, was widely copied in tombs made for the knightly classes within a decade or two. Edmund Crouchback's tomb, with a fabulous array of French-style steep gables, miniature tabernacles, painting and glassware, restated the styles and techniques of Paris introduced by Henry III. Again, within a generation, canopied tombs in this spirited and colourful style became the monument of choice for dozens of aspirant patrons throughout southern and eastern England. Such tombs were readily imitable, unlike the solemn mosaic floors and tombs imported to Westminster from Rome: these were far more specialized.

42

★

42   The elaborate
canopied tomb of
Prince Edmund
Crouchback (d. 1296),
Earl of Lancaster, the
second son of Henry
III, shows a knowledge
of French Gothic
tombs and portals; the
tomb effigy depicts
the prince dressed
in mail armour, in
commemoration of his
death during the Siege
of Bordeaux.

Rome, Coronation and Empire

The cumulative effect of a sequence of clashes between the crown and the papacy
in the reigns of John, Henry and Edward I was a general suspicion of Rome and its
representatives, and a resistance to its involvement in English affairs. The medieval
Roman, or Cosmati, mosaics in Westminster Abbey accordingly pose questions of
an unusual order, because no other north-western European great church, royal or
otherwise, was ornamented with this specifically papal art form in the Middle Ages.[76]

This has never been satisfactorily explained. There are three major Cosmati works: the sanctuary pavement before the high altar, the raised shrine base still containing the relics of St Edward, and the tomb of Henry III. The sanctuary pavement is a

43   large version of at least two Cosmati pavements in Rome, those in the naves of the basilicas of San Crisogono and Santa Francesca Romana.[77] It bore an ingenious Latin inscription (surviving only in fragments), which yielded by its method of addition the dates of the pavement, 1268, and of Henry III's death, 1272, and the length of his reign, fifty-six years.

> In the one thousandth year of Christ, twice hundredth, twelfth, with the sixtieth minus four, the third King Henry, Rome, Odoric and the Abbot joined together these porphyry stones.
>
> If the reader carefully considers everything set down here, he will discover the end of the Cosmos; if you add hedges thrice, dogs and horses and men, stags and ravens, eagles, enormous sea monsters and the world, each thing following triples the years of the one going before;
>
> Here the spherical globe shows the archetypal macrocosm.

The conventional narrative suggests that Henry and the then abbot, Richard of Ware (d. 1283), between them took the initiative to procure the pavement from Rome. Abbot Richard was not the humble monk of the Benedictine ideal. He was eager to use Westminster's status to win a role for himself in high politics, although the favour and influence he gained ebbed as much as it flowed during his long abbacy.[78] He provided the abbey with a new manual to guide its worship – a 'customary' – which was modelled on that of the cathedral monastery at Canterbury.[79] He also had international connections. Because the abbey was exempt from diocesan control, the newly elected abbots had to go to the pope to be confirmed, and that entailed going to Italy in person. Another key element in the acquisition of the pavement was the vigorous support lent to Henry III by the papacy during the disastrous civil war of the early 1260s. Popes such as Alexander IV had already supported English royal ambitions, including the claim to the throne of Sicily. The English had a strong presence at the papal curia, and the pope, the Frenchman Clement IV (1265–8), was important to this. In 1263 Clement had acted, as papal legate to England, in support of Henry against the baronial rebels, and it was he who in 1265 not only defended Henry staunchly but excommunicated his opponents.[80]

Once again Westminster's absolute openness to the latest and best in European fashion can be seen to have been a product of a unique and in many ways exceptionally difficult political situation, as well as of papal privilege. The pavement, the first of the abbey's Cosmati works to be begun and completed, may be seen as part of a post-civil

43   The Cosmati mosaic pavement in the sanctuary of Westminster Abbey is an example of a
specifically papal art form, found in no other church in north-western Europe; Abbot Richard
of Ware almost certainly brought back the material and craftsmen to create it when he visited
Rome for Henry III in 1266, and Edward I later commissioned the same artisans to work on his
father's tomb.

war papal *rappel à l'ordre*, started by Roman authority and aided by the offering of favourable rates for (or even the donation of) the stone inlays and craftsmen to work them; Richard of Ware fetched the materials and craftsmen from Rome himself, at some personal cost. This visit was almost certainly the one conducted by the abbot to Rome on the king's business in November 1266; Henry issued his safe-conduct from Kenilworth at exactly the time that the papal legate Ottobuono was disseminating the terms of the Dictum of Kenilworth at Coventry. Richard of Ware's journey to Rome falls very satisfactorily into line with the first references to the pavement work and shrine area in the accounts for 1266–67, enrolled around September 1267,[81] and the pavement was set down in time for the consecration in 1269.[82] When Abbot Richard returned to Rome in 1276, in connection, no doubt, with the commissioning of Henry III's own tomb, he already had established contacts. The tomb was under way in 1279–80, and may have been made by Peter the Roman citizen, the artisan whose name was placed at the very centre of the inlaid inscription formerly on the nearby shrine of St Edward (now lost but known from a fifteenth-century copy), which dates its completion in 1279:

> In the thousandth year of the Lord with the seventieth and twice hundredth, with another tenth nearly complete, this work was finished which Peter the Roman citizen fashioned. O man, if you wish to know the cause, it was King Henry the friend of the present saint.

Much commentary has been devoted to the numerical aspects of the inscriptions on the mosaics, that on the sanctuary pavement especially, which uses an arithmetical riddle about the ages of things and animals to explain the duration of the cosmos as 3^9 (19,683 years). There is an incessant play on the number three in the inscription.[83] This was clearly a compliment to the third King Henry: Henry, the 'friend' of St Edward, as he is called in the inscription on the shrine, is absorbed numerically into an altogether larger cosmic order. The Roman mosaics were intended to be harder-hitting than has hitherto been imagined.

In particular, they would have made a fine setting for the coronation of Edward I on his return to England from crusade in 1274, the inscriptions on the sanctuary pavement – the very place of anointing and coronation – demonstrating the stable relation between cosmic and political order after the upheavals of the 1260s. Coronations were uncommon events; yet the abbey, as designed, catered for them physically with its ample crossing space and galleries. Only two coronations had occurred in the thirteenth century (those of Henry III in 1220 and Edward I in 1274), and four were to happen in the fourteenth (those of Edward II in 1308, Edward III in 1327, Richard II in 1377 and Henry IV in 1399). Inevitably, the coronation 'order', as it was known, had to be written down as a formalized liturgy. The firmest record of English medieval coronations begins with the 'fourth recension' (or edition), which set down the ritual for the coronation probably used for Edward II (r. 1307–27) in 1308 and certainly used in 1377 for Richard II (r. 1377–99), and recorded in a handful of manuscripts, of which two are at Westminster: the Litlyngton Missal of 1383–4, and the *Liber regalis*, probably made in the following decade.[84] It was not uncommon for the coronation rite to be written out in other sorts of manuscript, and indeed the Litlyngton Missal, a very rare survival of an English Benedictine missal, may owe its preservation entirely to the presence within it of the coronation order.

44, 52, 55, 56

Earlier rites, such as those for Henry III and Edward I, must have been ancestral to the fourth recension. Some points of continuity from the earlier versions are clear. For instance, near the start of the ceremony of anointing and coronation (the anointing was, and remains, the sacred part), a form of election took place. The prince, positioned on a raised platform or scaffold in the centre of the church called the 'pulpitum', to ensure absolute visibility, was presented to the public gathered in the abbey. At this moment the prince was acclaimed. The French coronation order used at Reims refers to a similar platform in the midst of the church, and its points of similarity to Westminster's ritual may have directed Henry III to consider Reims cathedral as a model for Westminster in 1245. There were differences. Unlike Reims, the new abbey church retained spacious tribune-level galleries, possibly used by those gathered in the church for the acclamation, and its Cosmati pavement and inscriptions would have connected the cosmic order as a whole to the initiation and legitimization of royal power, of which the anointing and coronation rite was guarantor.[85] And the cult of the English royal patron saint, of course, lent to the English rite specific content and patterns of association. The use in the ritual of St Edward's own regalia, deposited at the abbey as one of its most important privileges, indicated the gradual assimilation of St Edward, until then a personal role model, into impersonal rituals of state. These regalia were solemnly returned to the abbey at the end of the ritual. They easily surpassed the royal relics of Wales and Scotland, which were essentially trophies of subject territories.

The coronation order was structurally quite simple, since it was analogous with other consecratory rites, such as the inauguration of a bishop. The day before the coronation the prince was to display himself to the public by riding to Westminster from London, that route also traced by the major relics; a night vigil in the palace then followed, when the prince contemplated the virtues of Solomon. On the morning of the coronation, the prince processed under a canopy to the abbey with St Edward's regalia and then mounted the pulpitum for his election and the acclamation *Vivat Rex!* In due order there followed the oath, the anointing during the singing of the

44 A miniature of a coronation ceremony, from the Litlyngton Missal, 1383–4, one of only a few manuscripts that set out the conduct (or 'order') of the ritual; parts of the coronation order of Westminster dated back to the time of Charlemagne, crowned Holy Roman Emperor in 800. The abbey, with its galleries and a large crossing, was well suited to coronations.

anthem 'Unxerunt Salamonem', and the investiture and coronation, after which the king was presented again at the pulpitum accompanied by the *Te Deum*. A Mass and the return of the regalia followed.

At its heart the coronation ritual was ancient, and elements in the orders of Westminster and its French counterpart, Reims, dated from the Carolingian era. In 800

Charlemagne himself had been anointed on the porphyry roundel in the centre of the pavement of the nave of Old St Peter's in Rome. The Cosmati mosaics at Westminster, which also used porphyry, were provided by popes and legates, but significantly extended by a king, Edward I, working with Abbot Richard. Edward's patronage has always suffered by comparison with his father's. Unlike Henry III, Edward had travelled in the Mediterranean while on crusade in the 1270s: his actual experience of European art and culture was wider. Yet his expenditure on the abbey as a whole was negligible, easily overshadowed by his building of the castles in Wales and by his works on Westminster Palace nearby, where he rebuilt St Stephen's Chapel in the palace from 1292, and repainted its various chambers. Edward anticipated the pattern of late-medieval English monarchs, such as Edward III at Windsor, who spent far more on domestic than on great church building.

What Edward's policies did point to was a new imperial drive, of which his patronage was a sign. Between 1204 and 1259, when Henry relinquished his rights in Normandy and Anjou, the old Plantagenet empire in France had fallen apart. Having annexed the Welsh territories in the years 1274–84, Edward, with characteristic ruthlessness, removed major Welsh relics and transferred them to the high altar and St Edward's shrine at Westminster, the centre of the land; in 1284 his eldest surviving son, Alfonso, gave the crown of Llewellyn to the high altar, where it was joined the following year by a glittering reliquary containing a relic of the True Cross, the 'Cross Neith', taken from Aberconwy and processed through London by Edward in a fashion reminiscent of Henry III's parading of the Holy Blood nearly forty years earlier.[86] The design of Caernarvon castle, established at this time, echoed the polygonal towers and Byzantine-style banded masonry of the Theodosian walls of Constantinople.[87]

Scotland's relics of state were to follow, also drawn by the magnetic power of St Edward's shrine at the heart of the realm. In 1296 Edward removed chests with jewels and documents from the Scottish royal treasury in Edinburgh to the King's Wardrobe at Westminster. From Scone abbey he took the stone that the kings of Scotland were accustomed to use as a seat at their coronations, and presented it to the shrine of St Edward in June 1297. Edward, a great politician, understood that in order to subjugate a people it is necessary to erase their history and so their sense of tradition and identity. The relics of Welsh and Scottish kingship and history added nothing practical to the royal power of Westminster since formally these domains were little more than subject territories. What mattered was the pull of Westminster, the symbolic concentration of relics with the saint who now symbolized the heart of the English nation, St Edward.

Edward I's sense of gesture and place, of the significance of moving stones to Westminster, whether from Rome or from Scotland, was powerful. It was for this

45   The Stone of Scone (or Stone of Destiny), used as the seat of the kings of Scotland at their coronations, was one of the treasures that Edward I removed from Scotland in 1296; to secure and display the stone, he commissioned a chair reliquary, which stood beside the shrine of St Edward. Although the stone was returned to Scotland in 1996, it will be restored to its place beneath the chair for the next coronation ceremony.

45   reason that he immediately commissioned a gilt-bronze chair, in effect a chair reliquary, to house the Stone of Scone beside the shrine of St Edward, the chair echoing the shape of the 'relic' in the same way that the arm reliquaries of St Thomas and St Bartholomew echoed what was within. Unfortunately, Edward's military expenditure produced such a financial crisis that all royal works were halted in 1297 bar those on the palace at Westminster and the castles in Wales – a fair indication of Edward's priorities. So instead of the bronze throne, a wooden copy of it was made, set upon a step next to the shrine, and finished by about March 1300.[88] This, the surviving coronation chair, was not initially planned to be used in the coronation ritual. The name of Scotland was never added to the royal style by Edward I, and the regalia that mattered in the actual coronation rite were the regalia of St Edward.[89] The chair

was a piece of fixed state furniture, on a par with the chapter-house lectern and the great bed in the palace. Like the palace bed, with its Solomonic guardians, it made reference, through the carved lions once on its arms, to the biblical image of King Solomon on his throne, a universal type of wise kingship anticipated on the Great Seal of England formulated specially for Henry III in 1259. Though executed and decorated by the favourite royal painter, Walter of Durham, the chair was probably designed by the leading master mason at court, Michael of Canterbury. Its openwork structure and panelled surfaces, devised to secure and display the stone, anticipated the Perpendicular style developed at court and in London in subsequent decades. The chair is without question the single most important surviving example of medieval royal furniture of this period.

For as long as it took for Eleanor's tomb to be completed, Edward's interest in the role of the church as a physical memorial and a place of commemoration was as intense as his father's. Yet Edward's attention to the abbey faded almost as quickly as it was aroused. Between 1291 and his own death in 1307, he showed no conspicuous interest in Westminster; nor did he develop a patronal relationship with another church. Unlike his father, he was seldom at Westminster for St Edward's October feast. The support of monarchy had been vital to Westminster's cultural development for two centuries; its gradual but obvious withdrawal ushered in a new, less cheerful phase in the fortunes of the abbey, and its monks especially. Down-river at St Paul's Cathedral, a magnificent new Gothic choir was rising to house the shrine of St Erkenwald. It was to outstrip Westminster physically, if not in artistic importance. The new and lavishly equipped churches of the mendicant orders in London, the Franciscans and Dominicans, were competing for the patronage of royalty, dead and alive. A golden age was passing.

The Impact of Westminster's Great Age of Patronage

By 1307 the accomplishments had, nevertheless, been great. It is a simple enough matter to list the various national 'firsts' notched up by Westminster between the Conquest and the death of Edward I, the English Justinian: the first English Romanesque great church and cloister; the first response to the court art of Paris under St Louis in the thirteenth century; the production of the earliest surviving English oil painting (the Westminster Retable); the possession of the earliest surviving image of St Christopher in English wall-painting; the manufacture of the only English royal throne to survive from the High Middle Ages; the first building to display heraldry as a significant part of its interior decoration (in its choir aisles); the first and only major Cosmati mosaics in north-western Europe. The very fact that the abbey still possesses its shrine with the saint within, its high altarpiece, its throne and most of its tombs is itself exceptional among northern European churches. And that Westminster was a place of innovation, as well as of the recurrence of familiar but symbolically important patterns, we have established in our narrative. The abbey, though still incomplete in 1269, with its Romanesque nave still standing, set an ambitious yardstick for future royal dynasties.

For specialists in the history of English Gothic art and architecture the abbey remains a happy hunting-ground of ideas dispersed throughout the nation's building history. Without the abbey, it is still likely that St Paul's Cathedral would have adopted a mighty French-style rose window to light its great new choir, begun in 1258 and following the latest fashions of Paris. From 1291 again, French influence, wholeheartedly from the Rayonnant style, determined the main elevation of the giant new nave begun at York minster. That Westminster had re-ignited English emulation of French Gothic cannot, however, be doubted. By the 1260s the canons of Salisbury had rapidly taken up the most impressive aspects of Henry III's dazzling chapter house for their own. Sometimes, as with the 'war of the roses' between Westminster and St Paul's Cathedral, architecture could express an older and deeper ecclesiastical rivalry. Other connections were more specific, more related to curial circumstances. The north transept of Hereford cathedral, built for Bishop Peter d'Aigueblanche (d. 1268), a Savoyard courtier favourite of Queen Eleanor of Provence, is manifestly informed by aspects of the abbey's French-style window designs, as well as by its use of marble and diaper ornament. The nave of Lichfield cathedral, built under Bishop Roger of Meyland (1257–95), a cousin of Henry III and protégé of Henry's brother Richard, Earl of Cornwall, was designed in the 1260s, again using motifs derived from Westminster and the Sainte-Chapelle.

At both the greater and the lesser scale, Westminster had opened a kind of cultural floodgate. Its court painters and illuminators helped to determine the appearance of English figurative art throughout the thirteenth and fourteenth centuries in its various phases of French and Italian influences. Courts were always international, and when English designs began to spread throughout the court networks of southern and western France, Iberia and the German-speaking lands from around 1325 – whether at Prague or Avignon, Pamplona or Santes Creus – a genealogy for those motifs can often be traced back to Westminster and London in the second half of the thirteenth century: here, in part, lay the origins of the so-called English Decorated style that represented England's one great moment of artistic influence abroad before the early modern period, thanks to international power.[90] Westminster, too, indicates the force of the accidents of patronage that political events provoke. Without the legatine presence in England supporting Henry III during the civil war of the 1260s, the Cosmati mosaics very probably would not have arrived or been adopted by the court. The role of a court was to assimilate and adapt as much as actually to create; Westminster had become as much a reservoir of ideas as a wellspring. And clearly, as always with such powerfully political media, not all patrons could avail themselves of these great effects. Courts created possibilities and disseminated them: but the very power of court patronage also imposed limitations on how and whether those possibilities could be adopted elsewhere. Not everything that the English kings did was loved, and the kings themselves were not always lovable. Such adjudications belong to the specialized history of patronage and the general moral thrust of history. Westminster's unique and in some ways providential position as an important national church owed much to its association with the seat of royal ritual, power and residence, and to the fact that it was blessed by a measure of kingly patronage of its art and architecture.

It is worth recalling that, by contrast, in its heyday the monastery itself had no particular tradition of artistic or literary activity. The only home-grown propaganda produced in these centuries was the very slight account of the foundation by the late eleventh-century monk Sulcard.[91] It is true that Henry III's activities spurred on the process of historical inquiry. Henry's presentation of the Holy Blood relic in 1247 very probably stirred the community into making a new annal of the abbey's recent past, the *Flores historiarum* or 'Flowers of history', kept up at Westminster by the 1260s. Although the *Flores* was derived from a chronicle already compiled at St Albans abbey by the monk–historian Matthew Paris, who had authored the Life of St Edward for Henry III, for a short period the abbey became a hub for the collection and circulation of the news of royal affairs. A Westminster narrative of current events was transmitted to a network of monasteries in south-east England; possibly it was also passed back to the king, both Edward I and Edward II.[92] But the abbey was not, at this time, a major centre of literary or scholarly endeavour, and did not measure up to its French near equivalent, the abbey of Saint-Denis, as a home of official royal history writing.[93]

Indeed, at the beginning of the fourteenth century, the abbey had reached a kind of nadir in its fortunes. In a literal sense, the proximity of the royal palace had damaged

46 (FOLLOWING PAGES)   In *c.*1300 the profile of Westminster had already changed dramatically through the investment of its royal patrons. The outline of the Norman abbey church had been embellished by the addition of a Lady Chapel, projecting east from the presbytery, and a unique, octagonal chapter house for the monastery. A magnificent belfry, the tallest structure in the vicinity, now stood sentinel on the border of the Sanctuary. But south of the church, the old monastery buildings, ravaged by fire, were barely habitable. The western edge of the precinct had changed little since the 12th century, though the almonry and its meadow were now fringed by the houses and shops of the rapidly developing Tothill Street. As a whole, the abbey complex seemed to be overshadowed by the enlarged and enriched royal palace to the north-east. The tall, slender, two-storey chapel of St Stephen had just been begun – a new adornment to the great hall of the palace, erected by William Rufus.

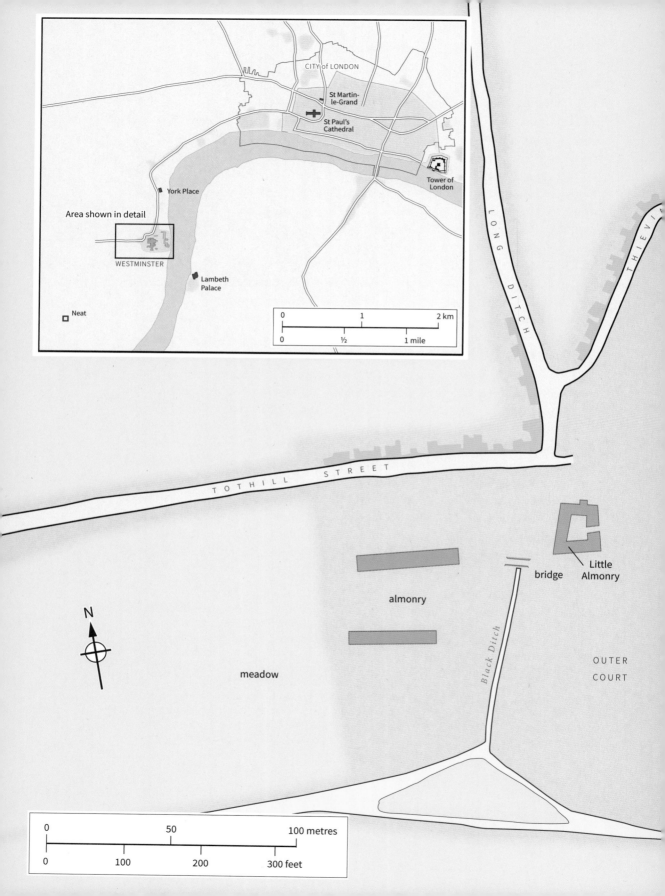

CITY of LONDON

St Martin-
le-Grand

St Paul's
Cathedral

Tower of
London

York Place

Area shown in detail

WESTMINSTER

Lambeth
Palace

Neat

| 0 | | 1 | | 2 km |

| 0 | ½ | 1 mile |

LONG DITCH

THIEVI

TOTHILL STREET

bridge

Little
Almonry

almonry

Black Ditch

OUTER
COURT

meadow

N

| 0 | | 50 | | 100 metres |

| 0 | 100 | 200 | 300 feet |

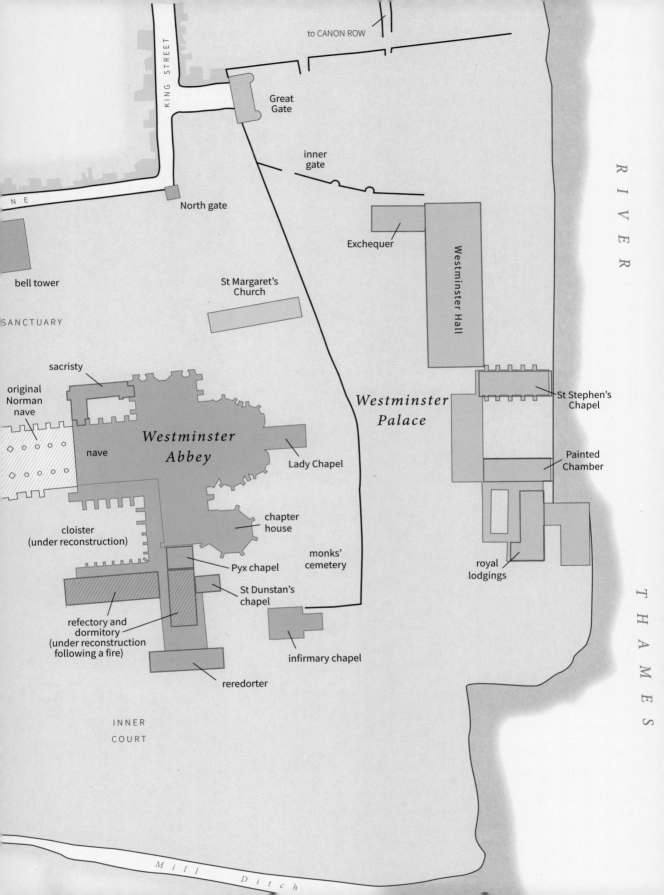

to CANON ROW

KING STREET

RIVER

Great
Gate

inner
gate

North gate

NE

Exchequer

Westminster Hall

bell tower

St Margaret's
Church

SANCTUARY

St Stephen's
Chapel

sacristy

original
Norman
nave

*Westminster
Abbey*

nave

*Westminster
Palace*

Lady Chapel

Painted
Chamber

cloister
(under reconstruction)

chapter
house

Pyx chapel

monks'
cemetery

royal
lodgings

St Dunstan's
chapel

refectory and
dormitory
(under reconstruction
following a fire)

infirmary chapel

reredorter

INNER

COURT

THAMES

M i l l   D i t c h

it. A fire there in 1263 had reached across to the buildings of the monastery. A more severe blaze in 1298 was said to have reduced the monastery to cinders; only the chapter house was spared.[94] The town of Westminster and the city of London beyond posed new threats. The rising urban and suburban populations, their housing and their commercial activities, could not be contained by the original terms of the abbey's endowment. By concession and compromise, its provisions were steadily eroded. A watershed was marked by the surrender of territory for the formation of St Martin's parish, which effectively ended Westminster's reach north and west of the city.[95] The territorial advance of town over abbey continued to the very end of its history in 1540, accelerated at the end by Henry VIII's scheme for Whitehall Palace (1509) and his coercive exchange of the abbey's remaining town estate for country properties.

In contrast, what strikes us about Westminster's royal art patronage before 1307 is its sheer visual range, its almost imperial reach, which made the abbey quite exceptional among the great churches of medieval England, and unusual even in the wider context of Western Europe. Westminster is a place of recurrence but also of paradox, and for a much more local reason. When, by the thirteenth century, Westminster emerged as, in effect, the court and administrative capital of England, the home both of kings and of administrative power, this idea of a political centre, of 'Westminster' as the shorthand for all matters political, found its symbolic form in a person: St Edward the Confessor. St Edward constituted the first great English myth of the happy antiquity of the nation's political institutions, and of their fundamental virtue. He provided an idea of what might be restored to an ailing polity. Regardless of his actual nature as a king, Edward as a saint became more than a charismatic role model for kings: he became a sign, a symbolic form, assimilated into the traditions of power of the nation expressed in the idea of a capital city. The ultimately classical idea of a golden age, revived in early modern England, had begun with Edward: one of the earliest rehearsals of the concept of political nostalgia is found in Herbert of Bosham's account of the translation of St Edward in the presence of Thomas Becket and Henry II.[96] Just as the dying Edward's vision of the severed tree whose growing together was understood as representing the union of the English and Norman elements in the twelfth-century kingdom, so, for Herbert, St Edward himself symbolized the happy if brief unity that had been lost at the Norman Conquest.

It might be thought that the history of a great institution cannot be told by means of its buildings and artworks. Yet at the level of grand narrative it was well said – by Winston Churchill – that we shape our buildings, and afterwards our buildings shape us.[97] Churchill was thinking of the present form of the House of Commons with opposed rows of benches, structurally favouring a two-party system of representation – government and opposition. The model was the arrangement of cathedrals and collegiate chapels, in which choirs ranged in opposing stalls, sang the services of the Church antiphonally, though in harmony. Those who built the new Houses of Parliament in 1834 will have recalled the seating arrangement in St Stephen's Chapel in the palace, used as the House of Commons from 1549 until the great palace fire of 1834, and planned by Edward I. British oppositional politics had been enshrined by the confronted arrangement of stalls proper to a chapel. Had the House of Commons continued to meet in the abbey's circular chapter house (as it did in the fourteenth century until the monastery complained about the damage done by the MPs to its tiled floor) a different style of politics might have emerged.[98] The physical heritage of Westminster as established by Henry III and Edward I was more than a built encyclopaedia of form: its shapes and myths moulded our institutional life for centuries to come.

3

Plantagenet Tragedies to Tudor Triumphs:
1307–1534

JAMES G. CLARK AND PAUL BINSKI

THE BURIAL OF KING EDWARD I (r. 1272–1307) was perhaps the most muted royal event that Westminster witnessed in the Middle Ages. The king was almost four months dead when his body finally arrived at the abbey. There had been acute apprehension that news of the great king's sudden passing while on campaign would galvanize the Scots for a ferocious attack; the government was so concerned to give an impression of continuity that writs continued to be issued in Edward's name for more than a month. His body was not brought south until October and then it lay in state at the royal abbey of Waltham (Essex) before it was brought to London. There was no public ceremony at Westminster. Although Edward was buried in the shadow of the Confessor's shrine and his father's burnished effigy, every expense seems to have been spared. The temporary timber figure that topped the coffin on its final journey was left to stand in favour of any grander sculpture. The only memorial inscription on the tomb was not added for another 250 years, at the behest of John Feckenham (1556–60), the very last of Westminster's abbots: 'the hammer of the Scots' would have had a very hollow ring at the time of Edward's death, when it was obvious, even as far south as Westminster, that his tireless warring had served only to heal the divided nation on the northern border. Soon it was Edward's eldest son, Edward II (r. 1307–27), who would suffer their hammer-blow, at Bannockburn. In 1307 there was little lustre left on the Plantagenet monarchy. Its authority was challenged abroad, and at home its resources of money and political support were running very low; without the commanding presence of the old king they called 'Longshanks', there was an impending crisis of leadership as well.[1]

47 (FACING PAGE)   The interior of Henry VII's Lady Chapel is distinguished for its pendant fan-vaulted ceiling; the architectural scheme was devised by the English master Robert Janyns the younger, and the decoration was intended to honour the apostles, the Church Fathers, saints and the English crown – not least Henry himself.

Fall from Grace

It was inevitable for a church that had pledged itself to princely authority that at the start of the fourteenth century Westminster's fortunes should falter with those of the crown. The monastery's sixty-year collaboration in the personal and political schemes of the Plantagenets had carried a heavy cost. Now its effects were rudely exposed. Royal patronage had set the abbey above its peers, but when Abbot Walter of Wenlock (1283–1307) died at the Westminster manor of Pyrford (Surrey) on Christmas day 1307, its credibility as chief among the churches of England was steadily ebbing away.[2] The abbey was in debt for many thousands of pounds; the total can only be estimated, but it was easily more than the annual income of any other church in England. Walter himself was perhaps guilty only of trying to spend his way out of a crisis he had inherited. The enduring legacy of Abbot Richard of Croxley (1246–58) had been his debts; although his successor, Abbot Richard of Ware (1258–83), is remembered for his royal service and the installation of the Roman pavement, he was the prisoner of creditors who were still baying at his heels as he lay dying.[3]

While the weight of debt grew, the abbey's relationship with the royal family fell into a headlong decline. Edward I had not shown himself at Westminster after the completion of the tomb for his queen, Eleanor of Castile (d. 1290). In retrospect, there is a valedictory note to his dispatch of Abbot Walter to bury the heart of Henry III (r. 1216–72) at another royal church (Fontevraud) in 1291.[4] Edward last requested prayers from his abbey in 1297; for protection in battle for another ten years he looked elsewhere.[5] Now that the crown held it at arm's length, the abbey became an object of suspicion. In September 1303 the abbey fell lower in the crown's estimation than it had ever done, and would ever do before the Reformation. When the vast sum of £100,000 was missed from the royal treasury, the king's justices looked at once to the monastery, arresting the abbot and all forty-eight monks and casting them into the gaol of the Tower of London.[6]

At the time of Walter's death, the monastery itself was on the point of dissolution. Dissent and division had been deepening ever since Abbot Richard of Croxley had been publicly vilified for his part in tax grabs by the crown and the papacy in the 1250s.[7] Westminster's self-image of sacred independence had been undermined by the venal politicking of its leadership. Croxley's successors had healed nothing. Abbot Walter, who travelled the country with a baggage train as long as the royal household's, looked on his monastery like a pirate, plundering its assets for a private glory that was more imagined than real.[8] The monastery rebelled against his authority, causing a legal battle between them that lasted three years and led all the way to the papal court. While the abbey still retained some material assets to be exploited, the power-hungry courtiers were tempted into this battlefield. The rider who brought word of Walter's death to the king carried coinage to bribe those who would decide the abbey's fate.[9] At a moment when the age-old argument over the primacy of princes and the papacy was again intense across Europe, Westminster Abbey was becoming an object lesson for clergy in the danger – indeed, the assured destruction – that would come of any affinity between state and Church.

Neither a new abbot nor a new monarch eased Westminster's malaise. The abbey's debts persisted as the creditors continued to hold their ground, just as their forbears had done against Richard of Ware. It was not without irony that a church that had so long benefited from the authority of Rome should now find itself in ransom to a resurgent papacy. Abbot Richard Kedington (1308–15) just borrowed more, and hid himself out of town, taking his medicine.[10] His successor, William Kirtlington (1315–33), was more circumspect but no less desperate. Just after his election he mortgaged all of the abbey's manors across three counties.[11]

There was no thaw in the relationship with the monarchy. By custom, Edward II was crowned in the church, but it was a poor show and set the tone for the reign; the material condition of the abbey could not have been clearer when, at the trumpets' blast, a wall collapsed, killing one of the watching knights.[12] Edward aimed to break free from the strictures of tradition in his kingship, and it appears that Westminster was among the ties he wanted to cut. He turned instead to the older royal abbeys of provincial England, such as Bury St Edmunds and St Albans (from where he embarked for his first Scottish campaign), and to the newer order of friars, the Carmelites, acting as founder for several of their convents.[13]

Meanwhile, the conflict inside the monastery intensified. The election of Kedington was disputed by an influential faction that purchased the support of opposing parties at court – the queen, Isabella of France (1295–1358), and the king's favourite, Piers Gaveston (d. 1312) – to advance their cause.[14] The abbey was left without a confirmed leader for almost two years, while 'the dissolute monks consume the goods of the house', as the king himself described it in an angry letter.[15] For the second time in twenty years a truce was brokered only by the personal intervention of the pope. The conduct of Westminster's monks was becoming a matter of public notoriety. The revelation of scandalous living at St James's Hospital, a royal foundation in the parish of St Margaret under their jurisdiction, was regarded as a reflection of the state of the monastery itself. The king's treasurer stepped in to restore order at the hospital, and the abbey suffered the humiliation of being deprived of its historic charge. The future abbot Simon Bircheston (1344–9) was twice arraigned for committing grievous bodily harm, first on the king's mason and then on a member of the royal family itself, William de Bohun (c.1312–1360), the grandson of Edward I.[16]

Spurned and shamed, in his later years Edward II threatened to strip Westminster of its remaining material assets. He placed the burden of his final military campaigns disproportionately on the abbey, calling on Abbot Kirtlington to procure transport and provide oak timbers for every conceivable weapon, from siege engines to the shafts of lances.[17] At the last, he also appears to have contemplated relieving the church of some of its most prized regalia. When the Scots made their first serious petition for the return of the Stone of Scone in 1324, the king seemed ready to comply, despite the fact that it was bolted to the floor beneath Edward the Confessor's chair. This was one of the few inclinations that the young king Edward III (r. 1327–77) shared with his father: less than a year into his reign, he also thought to remove it.[18] Abbot Thomas Henley (1333–44) objected, but perhaps only in remembrance of times past.

In 1328 the abbey was a remnant of a style of kingship long out of living memory, and its qualities as a church were no longer quite so singular. The nearby London skyline was now filling up with spires and towers. Rising above them all was the new cathedral church of St Paul's, completed in the first years of Edward III's reign, offering a fresh template for the Gothic to the city and to the world. Westminster, whose unfinished state was compounded by the effects of the fire of 1298 and would remain shrouded in timber scaffold for another fifty years, was now, undeniably, in its shadow.

Monastic Renaissance

In adversity, Westminster's abbots returned to the first principles of a medieval monastery: endowment, governance and the maintenance of good religion. Edward the Confessor had given the abbey estates which, together, cut a path across England, from the home counties, through the Thames valley, to the Malvern hills. Their two centuries of unbroken crown patronage had garnered them a cluster of choice manors and churches to the north and east of London, from Middlesex to Hertfordshire and Essex. There were also prosperous pockets of property reaching northwards to the foothills of the Pennines. Now, the proper exploitation of these estates was paramount. The main manorial complexes at Islip (Oxfordshire) and Sutton (Gloucestershire) were comprehensively rebuilt.[19] The income of outlying churches was appropriated – that is to say, redirected from their respective parishes to meet the needs of the distant abbey.[20] In their straitened state, the abbots did not always stay within the bounds of customary lordship. Remembered by his brethren as 'a man of perfect religion, devout, simple, just', Abbot Henley was reported to have trespassed on the estate of a neighbouring Essex landlord to steal away 'many valuables'.[21] Both Kirtlington and Henley proved better men for a fight than their predecessors. Between them, they finally

21

relieved the abbey of its 75-year-old obligations to the papal court and reasserted its claim over historic rights, including, for a time, the jurisdiction of the hospital of St James.[22]

These men embodied a new Westminster, largely released from its turn-of-the-century trials, which would recover much of its former presence and influence in the years after the Black Death (1348–50). It was powered by its great patrimony which reached out across the countryside, not only the money, food and raw materials it yielded, but also its harvest in men. Kirtlington, Henley, Colchester, Islip: the leaders that did most to mould the abbey from the late Middle Ages to the coming of the Tudors were raised in these Westminster heartlands, from the valley of the Colne to the source of the Thames, all of them far from the metropolis itself.

Inside the monastery, the authority of the abbot, and good (or, at least, better) order of the community of monks was restored, arguably for the first time since the election of Walter of Wenlock in 1283. The abbey monks, and those of the outlying cells at Hurley (Berkshire) and Malvern (Worcestershire), were subject to the regular scrutiny of visitation. The meagre, and now more strictly regulated, life of the house at Hurley was held over the Westminster men as a warning: persistent indiscipline could be punished with a sentence of banishment there. Abbot Henley made himself a champion of claustral discipline, not only for his own house but for the Benedictine order as a whole. Chosen as the first president of the Benedictines' new general chapter in 1338 – the first time Westminster had been involved in the affairs of the order for fifty years – he took responsibility for introducing the reforms of Pope Benedict XII (1334–42).[23] The master copy of the papal reform code was lodged at the abbey, so that disciplinary cases – of individual monks or whole monasteries – might be adjudicated and corrected from Westminster.

The principal aim of the papal reforms was to ensure that the worldly business of managing an institution did not displace the primary purpose of the monastic life, to provide a perpetual cycle of prayer. Abbot Henley reinforced this with a measure of his own, a new edition of the 'customary' of the monastery – that is to say, the manual that described the religious duties of the monks and how they were to be conducted. First compiled under Richard of Ware in 1266, the customary suggests that Westminster's pattern of worship was firmly imprinted with the Cluniac traditions of its first Norman abbots.[24] The custom of Cluny, the Burgundian abbey that had reformed Benedictine monasticism at the turn of the millennium, had been to heighten the spiritual power of the monks' worship by extending its scale and scope, adding to the sequences of psalms and readings laid down in the Rule of St Benedict. By the beginning of the fourteenth century, the Benedictines in England had generally stopped such elaborate observances. But at Westminster a trace survived, nurtured, perhaps, by Marian rituals

that were avant garde and by the unique responsibilities the abbey had acquired for
the commemoration of kings and queens.

In Abbot Henley's edition of the customary it was revived. The monks were committed
to observe no fewer than ten feasts as 'principals' – that is to say, requiring the highest
form of ceremony performed by the whole convent and not only on the feast day
itself but also on its vigil and for the week following.[25] The customary also required
brethren otherwise occupied outside the choir of the abbey to maintain the routine of
the monks' offices.[26] This challenged the prevailing trend in monasteries for the daily
schedule of offices to be consigned to a token number of 'cloister monks' unsuited to
any other duty. The customary attached great importance to the commemoration of
the community's dead, the monks and the abbot.[27] Here, also, Westminster appeared
to resist the tide of change. It was a common complaint of later medieval reformers
that the monastic tradition of the Office of the Dead had been abandoned and that
the anniversaries of their predecessors had been ignored. Perhaps it was a further effect
of the abbey's early relationship with the crown that its pattern of monastic religion
had been reorientated towards ad hominem commemoration. This reached back to a
much earlier tradition of a monastic church, the basilical monastery of late antiquity,
where the worship of the monks served the spiritual needs of a defined network, an
extended family.

The customary is also notable for the central importance it attached to the cult of
St Benedict of Nursia (c.480–c.547), founding father of the monastic order. The monks
were required to observe both the traditional feasts of the saint, his death and the
translation of his relics. By the fourteenth century the translation feast was disappearing
from the calendars of English monasteries and even his main anniversary (11 July)
was no longer marked as one of the principal feasts.[28] At Westminster, the observance
was to be led by no fewer than five monks vested as priests, a level of ceremony
second only to the feasts of the Blessed Virgin Mary.[29] At the altar of St Benedict a
lamp was to be kept alight 'day and night', one of only a handful of locations in the
abbey church distinguished in this way.[30] The customary also called for the cult to
be shared with the abbey's lay patrons. The form of words to be used in grants of
spiritual confraternity invoked the abbey's patron saint, St Peter, its founder, Edward
the Confessor, and then St Benedict, 'the institutor of our order'.[31]

At the same time that the customs of worship were refined, the abbots added
another distinction. They introduced the latest modes of musical performance. The
traditional plainsong of the monks' chants was supplemented with polyphony – that
is to say, music set for multiple voice-parts. An inventory of the Lady Chapel of c.1304
recorded the presence of two organs, as well as books of 'pricksong', meaning antiphons
set to polyphonic music.[32] The original purpose of the organ was only to rehearse
the chant, but the presence of pricksong books points to the preparation, now, of a

48   Benedictine monks, with their choirboys, gathered at a lectern in the presence
of a royal patron, illustrated in a miniature from John Lydgate's Lives of St Edmund
and Fremund, 1434–9(?). Westminster's 14th-century abbots introduced the latest
modes of musical performance, with music for multiple voice-parts, pioneered
in France; by the end of the century, boys were brought in to sing alongside
professional singers employed by the monastery.

group of singers. The performance of the liturgy in multiple voice-parts was a great
novelty, pioneered in France, where it was known as the *ars nova*, in the years before
1300. Its appearance at Westminster may be its very first occurrence in an English
church. Perhaps it marked a positive effect of Abbot Walter's courtly preferences. It is
very likely that polyphony was first heard in England in the secular entertainments
enjoyed by the Plantagenet household, especially after the arrival of Edward II's queen,
French Isabella.[33]

By the end of the fourteenth century the musical repertoire of the Lady Chapel
must have grown, because the monastery began to employ professional singers; soon
after that, boys from the grammar school based in the abbey almonry were brought in
to sing the treble part.[34] In the fifteenth century the taste for polyphonic sacred music   48

spread, and even the larger, wealthier parish churches invested in pricksong books. The greater monasteries were aware of the new trend and the opportunity it offered to attract the attention of the laity. The Westminster monks used their purchasing power to secure professional singing-men from churches in the city of London.[35] Perhaps it was these singers who performed the memorable vocal music at Henry V's coronation in 1413.[36] A century on, and the abbey was reaching the cutting edge of English music. The first singing-master of the Lady Chapel whose name is recorded was William Cornysh (d. *c.*1502), whose son, also William (d. 1523), was a composer of sacred music and a dramatist and orchestrator of Henry VIII's famous pageant of the Field of Cloth of Gold (1514).[37]

The Return of the King

Just as the abbey returned to its monastic roots, its relationship with the royal family revived. Edward III was the opposite of his father in many respects, unemotional, instinctively tactical, and not given to outward displays of the fervent religious belief he probably sincerely held. The change was signalled at the coronation itself in 1327, conducted with deliberate haste after he was proclaimed king. This time there were no mishaps, and it was remarked how well the 16-year-old Edward spoke the words of his oath, and how stably the crown rested on his head, helped by the padding that someone, perhaps one of the monks, had thought to add to the inside.[38] His interest in Westminster grew slowly over the course of his long reign. By the time he died in 1377, it seems likely that he recognized again the abbey's importance not only for the institution of the monarchy but also for the Plantagenet family. Yet it was more than a decade after his accession before there was the hint of a rapprochement. In 1339 he requested the relocation of the burial of his younger brother, John of Eltham (1316–36), to the chapel of St Edmund, where he might lie 'among the royals'. Like his grandfather, Edward I, his awareness of what the abbey church might offer him seemed to sharpen in personal grief. When two of his children died, William of Hatfield (d. 1337) and Blanche (d. 1342), he looked at once to Westminster for their burial. [39]

By now Edward had begun his campaign to recover the crown of France. His ambitions for a role on the mainland European stage surely also quickened his interest in the old royal abbey. Westminster was tailor-made for the displays of sacral kingship that were essential if Edward was to command the attention, and perhaps the subjection, of Europe's princes, secular and ecclesiastical. Marking a decade of offensive land and naval warfare, which had proved him invincible, Edward came to Westminster in 1351 with a relic of continental significance, the head of St Benedict, encased in silver.[40]

After another ten years, when the utter defeat of France had been capped with the capture and ransom of their king, Jean II, Edward laid his claim to a saint even more central to the identity of the European church, presenting Westminster with the priest's robes said to have belonged to St Peter himself.[41]

In his later years, the tenor of Edward's relationship with the abbey changed from the political to the personal. The loss of his second son, Lionel, in 1368, and of his wife, Philippa of Hainault, the following year, affected him as deeply as the loss of Queen Eleanor had affected his grandfather. The family mausoleum at the abbey was a source of solace to him, more so as his own powers failed and what is now known to have been dementia took hold of him. The elderly Edward was the first monarch since Henry III regularly to witness Mass at Westminster.[42]

His last intervention at the abbey was to plan a dual tomb for himself and his lost queen. The project must have been the last to occupy his mind before his powers finally faded: he appears to have been discussing the crafting of copper angels with their maker, John Orchard, in his last year – 1376 – though it was almost a decade after his death before the work was finished.[43] Cut from alabaster, Philippa's effigy was sculpted by the Brabantine artist Jean de Liège (c.1330–81).[44] Edward's tomb was topped with a gilt-bronze effigy, a product of the same craft workshop responsible for the effigy of his eldest son, Edward, the Black Prince (1330–76), at Canterbury.[45] This expression of family ties was strengthened by the choice of gilt bronze, which replicated the tombs of Edward's royal forbears, and the claim in the tomb epitaph that the king was 'a Maccabee in wars', which echoed the martial reputation of his grandfather.

49

The return of the king to the abbey reflected a transformation of royal government over the half-century of his reign. The greater stability of his regime allowed the institutional development of government departments to resume. The mobilization for war on many fronts over many years caused it to accelerate. Westminster Palace was now the undisputed centre-point of the Plantagenet monarchy. The logistics of war also changed the nature of parliament, from an occasional, volatile arena in which the limits of royal authority might be tested, to a recurrent forum for the review of the crown's 'policy', and in particular its financial administration.

As the political nation gravitated towards Westminster in ever greater numbers and for ever longer periods, its business encroached on the abbey. The church and the communal chambers of the monastery, such as the chapter house and the refectory, were too convenient not to be commandeered for the King's Council and, during sessions, which now continued for three or four months, for various functions of parliament. The Lords convened in the chapter house. Petitions were heard there, and those arraigned for a felony were brought there for trial. The business of government,

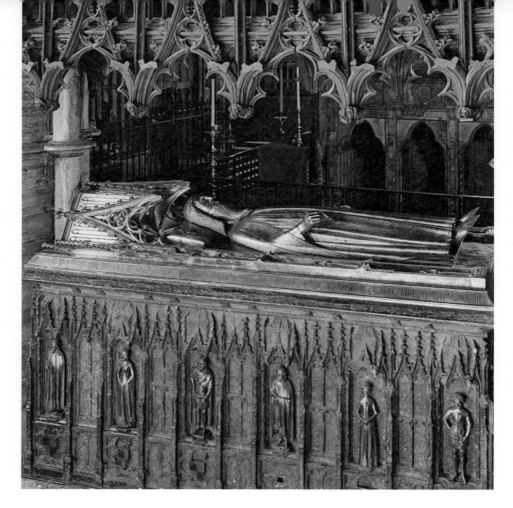

49   The tomb of Edward III, before 1395, with its gilt-bronze effigy, replicates the tombs of the king's forbears and marks the revival of the monarchy's affinity with the abbey after a period of relative detachment during the first half of the 14th century.

much of it pretty rough, cut across the regulated climate of the cloister. During Edward II's reign the nobility had doubted that parliamentary process could resolve their divisions and had arrived at sessions *a force e armes*, literally arrayed for war.[46] Edward III's martial achievements assured only a temporary suspension of these hostilities. As he lay dying, the Lords were again sharpening their swords against the abbey's stonework as his third son, John of Gaunt, Duke of Lancaster (1340–99), was rumoured to be raising an army to seize the throne.

The new world of Westminster government also presented the abbey with a more insidious threat to its pre-eminent position: to meet the spiritual needs of his expanding government, Edward III had turned the palace chapel of St Stephen into a royal church

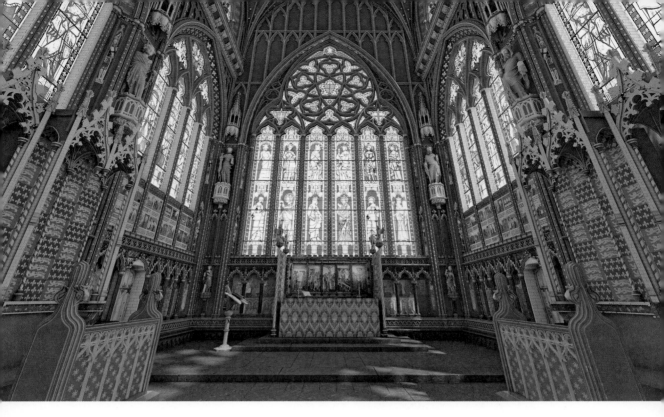

50 By the middle of the 14th century, Edward III had completed St Stephen's Chapel in Westminster Palace to meet the needs of his expanding government; it was largely destroyed in the fire of 1834, but this modern digital reconstruction shows the splendour of the new building, which posed an unwelcome challenge to the pre-eminence and privileged status of the abbey.

of a quite different scale and constitution. In 1348, he re-founded it as a college of 50 twenty-five secular priests, supplemented by a permanent choir of singing-men and boy choristers. The total was equivalent to three-quarters of the abbey's comparatively small cohort of monks. The chapel itself was enlarged and a bell-tower added, and the king assigned a substantial portfolio of properties to assure its income. Of even greater value, he set up a protective cordon of exemptions from tax and other dues and extended the chain of papal indulgences open to those who gave it their patronage.[47]

This was the first challenge to the exalted, exempt status that the monastery had enjoyed since its final detachment from the jurisdiction of the Bishop of London more than a century before.[48] Inevitably perhaps, the two churches were drawn into a dispute. In 1375 Abbot Nicholas Litlyngton (1362–86) asserted his authority over the parish of St Margaret, in which the palace and its chapel stood, and therefore his right to the income from the tithes and oblations and the probate of wills currently collected by the chapel clergy.[49] The king intervened and the dispute was carried to the papal court, which after seven years of indecision finally favoured the abbey's position and enforced a settlement that imposed much more limited rights on St Stephen's. The monks may have won this contest, but, in the competition for favour, the clergy of the chapel retained the upper hand. Even without all of its exemptions, its wealth continued to grow, above all from the patronage of courtiers and officers of government concentrated on Westminster. At the Reformation, St Stephen's annual income was £1,082 – not very far short of half the income of abbey.

Public Service

The pride of the monks may have been dented by the advent of the new St Stephen's, but the chapel did not seriously challenge their position at the centre-point of public affairs. In fact, the development of the government domain and the renewed affinity with the royal family acted to raise the abbey to a new level of influence in the second half of the fourteenth century. These same forces may also have insulated it from any lasting effects of the Black Death, despite the decimation of the monastic community, and from the troubled administration of Abbot Simon Bircheston (1344–9) that preceded it. He had brought the abbey close to a reprise of the condemnation provoked at the accession of Edward II. Despite their sorrow for their lost brethren, the monks seem to have remembered his own death, from plague at Hendon, as something of a blessing.[50]

51   Bircheston's successor, Abbot Simon Langham (1349–62), capitalized on the king's new patronage of the church, securing his personal favour and a place at his court and in his counsels. His assistance in the peace negotiations with France orchestrated by the papacy in 1357 won him special acclaim and, according to his contemporary the monk John Reading, 'from here he made a name for himself, and fat benefices'.[51] Within three years (1360), Langham had been appointed royal treasurer, the prized role that Abbot Richard of Ware had aspired to for longer than he held it a century before.[52] After two continuous years in an office that was notorious for its sudden ejections, Langham was rewarded with the Bishopric of Ely (1362), requiring him to resign the abbacy. Four years later he was appointed Archbishop of Canterbury and called upon to serve concurrently as royal chancellor. It was a remarkable trajectory, which might have set him at the apex of the Edwardian regime to the end of the king's life. But as John Reading had observed, Langham's hunger was greater, and he reached out for papal promotion as a cardinal, which he attained in 1368. For Edward, whose aim was to set his authority above that of the princes of Europe, he had reached too far. Langham could not serve two masters. The king forced him to resign as archbishop, and the former abbot spent the rest of his life in exile.[53]

Langham's fall does not appear to have affected the abbey's influence on the counsels of the king. His successor, Nicholas Litlyngton (1362–86), seems to have been known to the king from earlier, unspecified services rendered. A Tudor rumour told that he was the king's son, or his half-brother; the latter suggestion may have some substance to it. Edward kept a close watch on the election after Langham's resignation, and his call to the convent to choose one who was 'faithful and useful to us and our realm' may have been a knowing glance towards Litlyngton, their eventual choice.[54] Where Langham had applied himself to the administration of government, Litlyngton acted the courtier. He served Edward Despenser (1336–75), household knight of the king's eldest son, the Black Prince, and patron of the chronicler of chivalry Jean Froissart (1337?– c.1404) when he was campaigning in France in 1372. This might account for Litlyngton's personal collection of helms and body-armour, inventoried at the time of his death.[55]

The public service and court life of Westminster's abbots left an indelible mark on their monastery. The household and income of the abbot had been separated from the convent for more than a century, but now he inhabited an entirely different world. Litlyngton looked to re-create at the abbey the grand apartments of the palaces he frequented, and to which, perhaps, he believed himself to have been born. His mason, John Palterton, created a suite of chambers for him on the cloister's west side, among them what is now known as the Jerusalem Chamber.[56] Fit for a king, it was to Jerusalem that Henry IV (r. 1399–1413) was taken when he was unexpectedly seized by his final illness. In practice, from the time of Langham to the end of the monastery's history, the reign of the abbot was lived out on a circuit of his manor houses in the suburbs and the country provinces. Islip was their home when conditions of climate or health called for them to be out of town; Neat, just over a mile from the abbey precinct, in the region of Pimlico, allowed them to keep a watch on their church while affirming to their own monks, as much as to outsiders, that theirs was a separate sphere.[57]

53

46

51 Simon Langham, successively Abbot of Westminster, Bishop of Ely and Archbishop of Canterbury, was raised to the cardinalate in 1368 – the only monk of Westminster to gain such international recognition. His alabaster altar tomb, by Henry Yevele and Stephen Lote (1389–95, viewed here from above), shows his recumbent figure, with hands at prayer, dressed in Mass vestments with crozier and pall.

52 The armorial
bearing of Abbot
Nicholas Litlyngton,
from the Litlyngton
Missal, 1383–4.

The grand separation of the abbots transformed them from brethren of the monastery into patrons. The paeans of praise sounded for Langham at his death were akin to the commemoration of a royal or noble benefactor. Nor were they misplaced. After almost fifty years when building works at the abbey had been at a standstill, Langham's personal investment saw the cloister and nave completed. Like many a lay funder, he fussed over the detail of the construction work, trying to derail the use of marble in the nave piers. Litlyngton's contributions to the abbey buildings were more self-interested, concentrating on his own lodging and a chantry chapel for his own commemoration and that of his family; a companion chantry was raised at Malvern. Yet he also provided a dinner service for the use of the entire monastery – complete with forty-eight trenchers and matching pairs of salt cellars – for use on those pittance-days when meat was permitted at table.[58] Late medieval Westminster witnessed two parallel expressions

52 of regality, that of a secular and an ecclesiastical prince.

The public prominence of these abbot–prelates won Westminster a place in the leadership of the Church for the first time since the twelfth century. Before Langham's death, the abbey's prior, Richard Merston was drawn into curial business on the cardinal's behalf.[59] When, in 1378, the College of Cardinals sought news of the heresy of John Wyclif, rumoured to be spreading in England, it seemed natural for them to make first contact with Westminster, which they designated the 'first of all the churches in England'.[60] Litlyngton's successor, William Colchester (1386–1420), was chosen as

53 (FACING PAGE)   The Jerusalem Chamber is the principal room of Cheyneygates, the lodging of the medieval abbots of Westminster; it was commissioned by Abbot Nicholas Litlyngton in 1369 as part of a suite of rooms for himself.

president of the Benedictine general and provincial chapters recurrently for most of his thirty or so years in the abbacy.[61] At the very end of his life he represented the English clergy at the ecumenical Council of Constance (Baden-Württemberg), convened to resolve the forty-year-old schism in the papacy. In the last weeks of Colchester's life, Henry V looked to him to join a council to discuss the reform of the monasteries.[62]

The entry of the late fourteenth-century abbots into the affairs of state and Church opened the monastery to cultural influences that, while not entirely new, had not penetrated very far in previous generations. Langham was one of only a handful of Westminster men to have experience of university, and his reign was marked by a more concerted embrace of academic study. In this respect, the abbey remained far behind its peers. It was one of the only premier Benedictine monasteries that did not establish its own *studium* or house of studies at either Oxford or Cambridge.[63] The education of a representative number of monks to university level was a requirement placed on the Benedictines under the papal reforms for which Westminster itself had been made responsible. Yet over the course of the centuries between the Black Death and the break with Rome (1534) its own traffic in student monks was notably sparse, and was often initiated only when a rebuke was received from the president of the order's general chapter.[64]

But Langham's background and, especially, his exposure to the principled debates over papal authority and the privileges of the friars, in which the royal government intervened in the 1350s and 1360s, seems to have engendered a new intellectual engagement in the cloister. The future abbot William Colchester was professed in Langham's last year at Westminster, and soon progressed to a period of study at Oxford.[65] Another monk, Richard Cirencester, a generation older, was his exact contemporary at university.[66] Cirencester returned from the university with a habit of researching and writing books, which had not been seen at Westminster for almost a century. The fruit of his labour was a compendium of Westminster's Anglo-Saxon records which he called the *Speculum historiale* ('The historical mirror'). He may also have been responsible for beginning the abbey's annal of Richard II's reign – the first and only original chronicle ever written at Westminster.[67]

Perhaps it was his awareness of a nascent climate of learning that persuaded Langham to leave his entire library to the abbey at his death in 1376. His collection of bibles, bible commentaries, theological manuals of the staple authors of the university syllabus, and compendia and commentaries on canon law represented the raw materials for a college of university masters. The books filled eight barrels when they were packed for shipping back to the abbey, and they were valued at £1,186.[68] For a generation at least, Langham's general legacy, if not the individual books themselves, appears to have inspired several Westminster monks to step into the world of academic argument

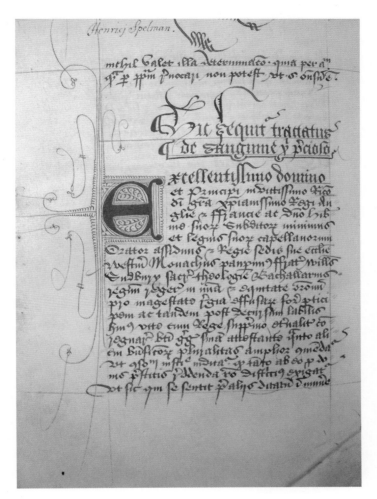

54 William Sudbury's defence of the Holy Blood relic was written in the 1380s or 1390s and dedicated to Richard II; a detail from the opening page of his *Tractatus de sanguine Christi precioso* is reproduced here. Sudbury was a monk at Westminster and member of the king's inner circle at the height of Richard's interest in the abbey church and its religious traditions.

and public controversy. William Sudbury, who made his profession shortly before Langham's death, studied at Oxford for at least a dozen years. On his return he prepared a study aid for fellow students before applying his training in disputation to a defence of the abbey's relic of the Holy Blood.[69] Unnamed monks who surely followed William to Oxford made a valuable collection of scholarly tracts on the papal schism and its resolution, perhaps at the request of Abbot Colchester in preparation for his appearance at the Council of Constance. Another of Sudbury's peers, Thomas Merk, followed a different path at, and beyond, Oxford. At university he appears to have built a reputation as a master of Latin rhetoric and he may have even taught the subject to student monks from other monasteries. Perhaps it was his unusual literary

54

tastes that propelled him towards the court of Richard II, where he joined the young king's inner circle of clergy. A courtier monk not unlike his abbots, he was rewarded (1397) with the Bishopric of Carlisle.[70]

By contrast with Langham, Abbot Litlyngton carried into the abbey a trace of the aesthetic interest in books cultivated in the Edwardian and Ricardian courts. Again acting as a lay patron of the abbey in all but title, he commissioned a deluxe missal of the size and style that might be found in the private chapel of a royal or noble household.[71] It was written out by a professional copyist, Thomas Preston, who lived at Westminster and wore the abbot's livery for the two years it took to complete. Preston's contribution, which accounted for little more than 10 per cent of the total cost, was eclipsed by the sequence of illuminations added by artists recruited from a London workshop responsible for some of the finest book art known from this period. The initial capital letters of each section were filled with figures representing its subject, the seasonal festivals and saints' feasts celebrated in the calendar, and, for the order of the Mass itself, the story of Christ's Passion. The materials, style and mode of production of Litlyngton's missal belonged to the world of high-society books not to the traditions of the monastery scriptorium. But Litlyngton was enough of a monk, and a monk of Westminster in particular, to make the book an expression of the abbey's identity and devotional values. Neatly, it captured some of the dominant features of the fourteenth-century community: the reassertion of its claim to be a coronation church and the distinctive character and colour of its monastic observance, its commitment to post-mortem ritual and polyphonic music. After the order for the Mass, the missal reproduced the order for the coronation of the monarch, with miniatures showing the crowning of a king and a queen, and the conduct of a royal funeral. There followed the monastic Office of the Dead, with a miniature showing a catafalque flanked by burning tapers and hooded mourners, while in the wide margin of the book, there was a scene of monks in mourning robes singing from a lectern. It might be said it was a visual summary of the recovery that had been achieved since the death of Edward I.

55

Plantagenet Finale

It was a changed abbey to which the 9-year-old Richard II (r. 1377–99) was brought for his coronation on 16 July 1377. The church and convent buildings were more complete than they had been for as much as 200 years. The young prince's grandfather and great-grandfather (Edward III and Edward II) could not have failed to see a contrast between the damaged and undeveloped site of the self-styled national church

55   This folio from the Litlyngton Missal, 1383–4, includes a miniature showing hooded monks and, in the margin, singing-men in mourning robes performing the Office of the Dead.

and the many others they encountered across their kingdom. Now the position was reversed. In 1377 many of England's premier monasteries stood incomplete, their own redevelopment arrested by the economic effects of the Black Death. Langham's and Litlyngton's investment had recovered Westminster's visual ascendancy, just as they had advanced the abbey into state and Church affairs. Richard's reign would be framed by the highest measures attendant on this new-found status: in 1378 the Roman cardinals declared Westminster's abbot to be 'the father and first lord of our order'.[72] At his penultimate parliament of 1397, when the presiding seat in the chamber of prelates had fallen vacant, Abbot Colchester staked his claim; only one of those present objected.[73]

If the monastery had anticipated with the new king a resumption of the relationship on the terms they had known before, almost immediately they discovered that the mood and manner of the royal party was quite changed. At the coronation, Richard's advisers rode roughshod over the established customs, as they saw it to exalt the sacred dignity of the crown. The king's oath was sworn at the high altar before the archbishop, not in the face of his subjects gathered in the nave. At the end of the ceremony he left the abbey still clothed in the precious regalia. One of the slippers, said to have come from Alfred the Great and so already 500 years old, fell from the boy-king's foot. The monks were outraged and held on to their sense of offence for years, scolding Richard in person when he came of age.[74]

In fact, from his first encounters Richard did regard the ancient treasures of the abbey with a reverent awe. There was generally little continuity in his two decades as king, but he returned to these sacred spaces at regular intervals. On the feast of the king–confessor (13 October) the monks would not be surprised to find him 'and his chapel' (his chaplains) seated with them in the choir.[75] He sought the spiritual charge of the relics in adversity, as when an army of rebellious peasants poured into the city in June 1381. The protective embrace of the Confessor was turned from private succour into the public symbol of his kingship in the 1390s: after the death of his queen, Anne of Bohemia, in 1394, he impaled the arms of St Edward with his own in an unprecedented form of heraldic marriage.[76] When he was able to play the prince of power he represented himself as the proud custodian of the abbey's treasures. Receiving Leo VI, King of Armenia, in November 1389, who had come as a peace envoy to mediate in the Anglo-French conflict, Richard insisted that the visitor should see the coronation regalia, and at dusk stole into the abbey to take him through the treasures by candlelight.[77] His powerful affinity for the place was apparent in the first public ceremonies of his reign in which he had any personal agency – his marriage to Anne, followed by her coronation, in January 1382. It was the first royal wedding at Westminster for 150 years. The town and the city came out en masse for the procession of the wedding party, celebrating the imperial alliance with a couplet that represented Anne as 'manna from heaven'.[78]

As in any very intense attachment, Richard's relationship with the abbey was volatile, his behaviour beseeching and bullying in equal measure. Raised by the courtiers who had stage-managed his coronation to regard Westminster not as the coadjutor of kingship but rather as its servant, he asserted his authority over the church and its community in all their dealings. With self-conscious insensitivity to the traditions of the place and the preferences of the monks, he appropriated the east end of the church for the burial of his clique of courtier favourites. The memorial brass for John Waltham, Bishop of Salisbury (d. 1395), was intruded directly into the mosaic flooring of the shrine. The

56 Richard II's marriage to Anne of Bohemia on 20 January 1382 was followed two days later by her coronation; an illuminated manuscript in the abbey library, the *Liber regalis*, is said to have been written for use at Anne's coronation, and depicts a king and queen enthroned together.

monk chronicling these years noted that even when he stole into the choir to watch their observances, Richard was wearing his crown. After the resurgence the abbey had known under Abbots Langham and Litlyngton in the last years of his grandfather, Richard's instinct was to check its institutional power. In the bitter jurisdictional battle of the abbot and monks with the dean and canons of St Stephen's, the king was inclined to take the side of the royal chapel. When in 1383 the monks broke a previous bond not to pursue the matter in the papal court, Richard did not hesitate to seize the temporalities – that is to say, to take the income of the abbey's estates into his own hands. Three years later, he challenged their election of Litlyngton's successor, William Colchester, with a view to interposing his own candidate, John Lakenheath.[79] It was the first interference in the governance of the abbey since 1307, and where Edward II's motivation then had been to hold the monastery to account for its misrule, it seems Richard's impulse was to establish a principle that Westminster was subject to the crown. As the chronicler recalled, the king called on the community to accept John as their abbot 'out of respect for himself'.[80]

Yet Richard's preference for Lakenheath in itself reflected ties to individual members of the community of monks that ran counter to his treatment of the abbey as an institution. Lakenheath was responsible in the monastery for the financial management of the ongoing 'new work' on the church, and it is likely that Richard saw him as an adviser for his own investment in the building. The king was also drawn to the scholars of the abbey. He asked William Sudbury to satisfy his fascination with the coronation regalia by writing an account of their historical origins.[81] Thomas Merk he took into his household as his chaplain. Once the matter of his election was settled, William Colchester also became a confidant of the king. Near the end of Richard's reign, it appears that Westminster provided him with a personal priesthood: Colchester and Merk went with him on his final, fateful campaign to Ireland in 1399; and Merk stood by him until the very moment he surrendered the crown.[82]

While his handling of the institution and its individual members ebbed and flowed, Richard's interest in its physical fabric was a constant. From the moment he began to assert his personal rule in 1385, he continually sought out, purchased or commissioned new decorations for the shrine of the Confessor. He gave a portable altar, depicting the story of the saint in enamel in a silver frame; a gold ring set with a 'costly and valuable ruby'; several 'Mass sets' of vestments, for the celebrant and his assistants, embroidered with the figures of the royal saints Edward and Edmund and the Blessed Virgin Mary; for the funeral of his favourite counsellor, John Waltham, a cope covered with the Tree of Jesse; and an altar frontal carrying fleurs-de-lys, together with banners bearing the arms of Edward and the Holy Roman Empire.[83]

After the settlement of the dispute over St Stephen's, Richard invested heavily in the abbey's principal building project, the 'new work' to complete the church. He assigned to it the income of two monasteries, at Folkestone and Stoke-by-Clare, sequestrated because of the Anglo-French war. He also made cash payments of his own, more than £200 in the years 1394–6 alone. By the end of that decade, and his reign, Richard had contributed £1,685 for the completion of the 'new work'; if the sum he put down for the completion of his own tomb (£950) and the likely value of the plate, jewels and vestments is added, it may be estimated that in total he channelled more than £10,000 into Westminster.[84] This was no more than half the figure Langham had invested, but it was sufficient to engage the services of Henry Yevele, one of the most influential practitioners of the Perpendicular style. The work continued until the flow of royal funding was stemmed at Richard's deposition in 1399; Yevele died the following year. Much of the nave's triforium, clerestory and vaulting were unfinished.[85]

The death of Queen Anne in 1394 caused Richard to concentrate his attention on a commemorative scheme for them both. Contracts for builders and craftsmen were made ready within the year.[86] One was for the marble tomb-chest, designed by Henry Yevele and Stephen Lote and represented by a drawing copyrighted by the seal of the royal treasurer, which must have resembled the finished tomb of Edward III by the same team. The other was for the gilt-bronze effigies and associated metalwork, to be made by the London coppersmiths Nicholas Broker and Godfrey Prest. To them was shown some sort of official drawn likeness of the king, which they were to follow, and exact instructions were issued for a double tomb, showing Richard and Anne as sovereigns holding hands with an orb between them, and for the associated fixtures, images and heraldry. All this was to cost around £900, the work to be done in two houses in Wood Street, London, over the next four years.[87]

49

The model for the tomb was probably the destroyed double tomb made for Charles V (d. 1380) and his queen, Jeanne de Bourbon (d. 1378), at Saint-Denis near Paris, but the choice of gilt bronze and not French white marble for Richard's tomb created scope for its treatment with fabulous and minutely engraved fluffy detailing and chasing, with Richard's various emblems such as broom-pods, tree-stocks, sunbursts and crowned As and Rs. The epitaph likened Richard not to a warrior Maccabee but to Homer, true in speech and prudent in mind. Like the Wilton Diptych – an exquisite painted altarpiece that depicts the youthful king in the company of Christ and the patron saints of England, apparently offering up his island kingdom to the Blessed Virgin Mary[88] – the tomb is a fastidious condensation of an entire world-view: magnificence in small things. Yet the thinking could be that of a Renaissance prince–patron as much as of a Gothic king. Richard manifestly also thought on the grander scale, as shown in his rebuilding and spectacular re-roofing of the great hall in Westminster Palace in 1396–1401 under Henry Yevele and the carpenter Hugh Herland. This was now the most breathtaking royal secular interior in Europe, but its inclusion of a new sculpted gallery of the kings of England since St Edward proved that Richard kept an eye on the similar displays in the main royal palace in Paris, just as he probably gleaned information about the tombs at Saint-Denis.[89]

The French kings, notably Charles V's father, Jean II (d. 1364), had also been the subjects of small painted portraits of themselves shown in profile, but nothing known

57   The portrait of Richard II (late 1390s), which hangs on a pillar outside
St George's Chapel in Westminster Abbey, is the earliest known contemporary painted
portrait of an English sovereign.

in France can explain Richard II's large frontal portrait, over 2 metres in height, which   57
hangs in the abbey's nave. This is, properly speaking, a revolutionary image in the sense
that it is the first near full-length, frontal, painted portrait of a known individual in
European art. It shows Richard crowned, collared and enthroned with orb and sceptre,
dressed in a blue tunic sparkling with gilt crowned Rs, and addressing the spectator
with a steady gaze. Of this the word 'iconic' seems, for once, appropriate. It was painted
in oil on gesso on oak, a technique already used on the abbey's thirteenth-century
high-altarpiece, and its ground was of gilt gesso diapering resembling the textured   37
stonework of the main elevation of Henry III's church. This indicates that it was
intended for display, either in the choir of the church or in the nave, of which Richard
considered himself the founder. It may have been the painted image of a king in the
choir of the abbey paid for in 1395, in which case its most likely point of display was
in the royal *cawagium* or seating enclosure to the south of the high altar. It may also
not have been the only version of an image that could as easily have been intended
for the palace.

To describe the portrait as autocratic is not wholly misleading. As well as likening
him to Homer, Richard's epitaph says that he laid low whoever violated the regalia – in
other words, all things pertaining to the dignity of a king. Anti-Ricardian propaganda
during the 'tyranny' at the end of Richard's reign includes a chilling description of
Richard seated in state in silence, surrounded by his courtiers, fixing them with his
gaze and forcing them to genuflect: not necessarily fact, but like much propaganda
revealing of what some people considered true and vivid, symbolically real. The picture
was certainly painted late in Richard's reign. But psychologizing about medieval kings
carries risks. Richard's image is also quite deliberately one of absolute formality, an
accumulation of signs and attributes, betraying nothing of his inner life but pointing
to his public sovereignty. What we can say more confidently is that at this point
Westminster Abbey and the court produced something truly new in the history of
Western art, an autonomous picture of a patron, whose steady look, no matter how
inscrutable, greets ours indomitably.

A Communal Church

Richard II, like his forbear Henry III, had taken possession of the abbey church for
himself and his family. Yet beyond its role as royal mausoleum, by the end of the
fourteenth century Westminster was a place of public worship. This reflected the fact
that the monks and their special patrons were no longer the exclusive possessors of,
and worshippers in, the space. The community of religious men was itself increasingly

diverse. In general, the greater independence of late-medieval monks, and in particular
the public careers of several Westminster men, saw a number of monks enjoying a
private life (and a pension, sometimes paid by the crown), in the precinct but not
inside the enclosure of the monastery. There were always several lay brothers, men
who had committed to live in the community of the monastery under the authority
of the abbot but would not make the solemn profession of monastic vows.[90] In
the fifteenth century, if not before, there was also a recluse, a former monk who
contrary to the general drift of the times, wanted to be more, not less withdrawn from
the world.[91]

The community of men professed to live under these different vows was surrounded
by a population of secular clergy, which was expanding steadily. The pairing of the
Convocation (the governing assembly) of the Church in England with parliament
from 1295 brought the kingdom's prelates to Westminster on an almost triennial cycle.
The re-creation of St Stephen's Chapel as a collegiate church introduced a further
twenty-five secular priests into the environs of the abbey. Although hardly on the same
scale, the increasing autonomy of the monks' own parish church of St Margaret, on the
northern boundary of the precinct, led to the arrival of other secular priests – among
them, from 1482, a stipendiary preacher.[92] By the fourteenth century the monastery
itself was reliant on a cohort of clerks for the prosecution of its legal causes at home
and at the papal court. There is some irony in the fact that in the church often
identified as an abbey for the nation the clergy most visible at Westminster would
not have been monks. This conspicuously mixed economy of clerical men moulded
the memorial schemes devised by the abbey's last medieval patrons. In their plans for
funeral services and posthumous commemorations, Henry V and Henry VII sought
to mobilize all orders and ranks that the foundation maintained.[93]

The vowed and clerical communities, in their turn, shared Westminster with an
expanding lay population. The monastery's own staff grew to a level that outnumbered
the monks by as many as three to one. The succession of royal building schemes brought
skilled and unskilled labour into the precinct for long enough for some to become
residents. The volume of government business likewise kept officers of the crown at
Westminster for much of their working lives; it was sheer practicality for them to
look to make their home in the precinct of the abbey.[94] It was this that persuaded
Geoffrey Chaucer to haunt the precinct as he climbed from collector of customs in
the port of London to clerk of the king's works. This trend was most pronounced
towards the end of the monastery's history, perhaps especially after Henry VIII's chief
minister, Thomas Wolsey, took possession of nearby York Place (1514), and many of
those disposed to work with him and those determined to work against him, followed
him into the lee of the abbey.

It was their presence that roused the abbey church into serving as a place of sanctuary – that is, secure protection for those outside the law, which, in principle, could not be challenged. The origins of Westminster's claim to sanctuary and its documentary authority (if such there had ever been) were long since lost in time. But as a growing number laid claim to it from the beginning of the fourteenth century, the monastic community was receptive and when their church's status was challenged the monks sprang to its defence.[95] When, in 1378, a veteran of the war in France, Robert Hawley, was dragged out of sanctuary as the gospel was read during High Mass, the monks represented it as nothing less than an assault on their spiritual authority as a church subject only to Rome. The outrage was repeated a decade later when the king's chief justice, Sir Robert Tresilian, a target for the appellant lords in their attempted coup for control of the king and his council, was taken from Westminster's sanctuary and summarily executed.[96]

The people of the precinct and its environs reached for the spiritual aid of the abbey not only *in extremis* but as a focus of their devotional life as important as any parish. The sacrists' accounts record steadily rising returns from the nave altars from 1350 to the end of the fifteenth century. In 1355–6 the stonemason John Palterton made a cash donation of 1 mark (13*s*. 4*d*.) to the 'new work' of the abbey buildings, in which he was already engaged as a craftsman, and pledged himself to make a pilgrimage.[97] The pioneer printer William Caxton (*c*.1422–92), whose premises stood between the precinct and King Street, is rarely visible in the abbey records but after his death he

58

58   The printing pioneer William Caxton established a shop on the edge of the abbey precinct in a property he rented from the monks. This advertisement (*c*.1477), the earliest surviving in English publishing history, publicizes Caxton's affordable edition of the Sarum Ordinal, a guide to the liturgy most commonly used in England's churches; it includes directions to his premises 'at the reed pale' (that is, 'at the sign of the Red Pale').

was recorded in the sacrist's roll as the donor of a paper Mass book of the Use of Salisbury, deposited in the Confessor's chapel.[98]

The increasing independence enjoyed by the monks meant that they too endowed the church with expressions of their own private devotion. A full measure of their impact is impossible, given the later adaptations of the interior, but it is likely that before the Reformation the decoration and furnishing of the main body of the church reflected the tastes of successive generations of monks. From the fourteenth century onwards, individual monks made substantial investments in particular altars, adding to the quality of their furnishings.[99] Some of those charged with the custody of the chapels acted independently to renew and elaborate the decorations and the vestments available for observances there. Even at the centre of the monastic community, in the chapter house, the cycle of wall-paintings depicting the Merciful Judge and the Apocalypse were the result of the patronage of an individual monk, John Northampton.[100]

The Hollow Crown

When Richard II returned from Ireland to north Wales in August 1399 to meet an invasion force led by Henry Bolingbroke, Duke of Lancaster, he was carrying with him sacred oil for a second coronation at Westminster; far away in a London workshop the component pieces of his tomb at the abbey were more or less ready to be assembled. But Bolingbroke's force was too great, and support for Richard, personally, and for his plans, too faint: he surrendered, his schemes for his kingdom and his tomb interrupted.[101]

Westminster's history with Richard was a reproach for his Lancastrian usurper, Henry IV (r. 1399–1413). Henry needed to harness the abbey's authority, and did so hastily, staging a coronation, with the same tactical calculation that had won him the throne, on the very feast day of the king–confessor, 13 October 1399. His triumph over Richard was very deliberately demonstrated in the ritual of the ceremony. Henry retrieved from the Tower of London the legendary oil of St Thomas Becket, stored in a phial in the shape of an eagle, the subject of a celebrated prophecy that one day it would anoint the King of England to recover the Holy Land for Christendom. Richard had rediscovered the phial and had taken it as a talisman on his fateful journey to Ireland.[102]

Westminster was necessary for Henry to lay claim to the institution of monarchy, but he did not want its spiritual traditions for himself or his dynasty. Henry's instinctive choice for a family church was Canterbury cathedral, where his grandfather, Edward III, and his father, John of Gaunt, had been generous patrons, and with which his half-brothers, the Beauforts, were already allied. It is possible that he was also inclined to acknowledge the part the Archbishop of Canterbury had played in supporting his seizure of the crown. If Abbot Colchester and his monks were in any doubt that the royal affinity of the Ricardian age had been shattered, that was soon confirmed when Henry took the side of the Beauchamp family in their bitter dispute with Westminster over property rights. It appeared the new Lancastrian monarchy would be neither the abbey's patron nor its protector. For a man who believed himself to be stalked by fate, there was a hint of nemesis in the fact that Henry's final illness overcame him when he was passing through Westminster en route for Canterbury, and death came before he could get back on the road.[103]

His son, Henry V (r. 1413–22), recognized the need to be reconciled with the tradition of Westminster if the legitimacy of the Lancastrian dynasty was not to be doubted. After his own coronation, the first public spectacle of his reign was the reburial of the remains of his deposed cousin, Richard II. The ceremonial and the outlay of expense were as great for the deposed king as they were for any who died in office. The bier bearing the coffin from its temporary tomb at King's Langley (Hertfordshire) was surrounded by 120 burning torches; 1,000 marks were distributed in alms for the poor along the way. In a real-life act in keeping with the character of Prince Hal as celebrated by Shakespeare, Henry recalled from Canterbury the royal banners, which had been used for his father's funeral, so they could greet Richard's coffin as it entered the abbey.[104]

In the months that followed, Henry planned a permanent realignment with his Plantagenet forbears. It was a measure of the priority he attached to the task in the first eighteen months of his reign that in his will, dated 24 July 1415, just three weeks before he led his army to France for the first time, he was able to give a very detailed description of the memorial he planned. His tomb was to be contained within a chantry chapel, whose altar was to be dedicated to the Annunciation of the Virgin Mary. It was at least as ambitious in its architectural fabric and decoration and as rich in its imagery as Richard's own aborted scheme. The altar was to be flanked by statues representing the Virgin, the Trinity, the English royal saints Edward the Confessor and Edmund the Martyr, St Denis (the patron saint of the French crown) and St George. Henry's own antelope badge and the swan badge of the Bohuns, his maternal family, were to decorate the chapel's vaulted ceiling; on its outer walls at the front a frieze would feature Henry's coronation. The English saints established a direct connection to his cousin Richard, to whom he owed his throne. The presence of St Denis underlined that the design of the chantry was, in fact, an adjunct of Henry's preparation for war with France, which, even in 1415, he intended to be nothing short of a war of conquest.[105]

When Henry came to revise his plan seven years later, it is possible his relationship with the monastery had deepened. He had turned to Westminster, and perhaps its

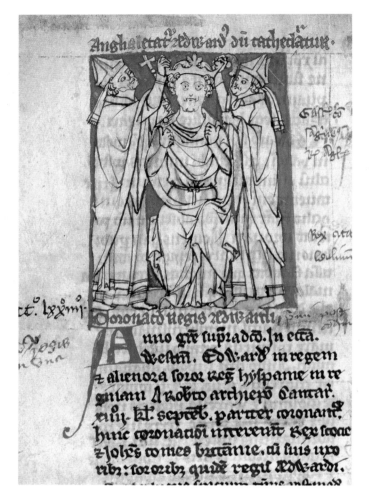

59 This depiction of the coronation of Edward I comes from the 13th-century annal of English history *Flores historiarum* ('Flowers of history'), a copy of which was bequeathed to the monastery by Henry V. The miniature was certainly painted by a Westminster artist: it affirms the conviction that the abbey was central to the making of any legitimate English monarch.

abbots, to convene a council to consider the reform of the Benedictines in May 1421, one of his last acts before leaving England for the final time. Henry's revised will, made just before his military embarkation, added details of the form and style of observances to be followed in his chapel. He showed an awareness of the monastery's own particular form of literary heritage in his bequest of a psalter and a copy of

59 the *Flores historiarum* ('Flowers of history', the abbey's annal). Yet he also broke with monastic practice, requiring the presence of secular mourners. From the day of his burial for a year, thirty poor men were daily to recite the psalms of the Virgin Mary. The Requiem Mass to be performed on the anniversary of his death was to be attended by twenty-four poor men, each bearing a torch, and at the end of the Mass there was

to be a distribution of alms to the poor to a value of £20. The revised will also called for a funeral fit for his royal dignity but eschewing 'damnable excesses'. The hearse was to be illuminated by fifteen candles, graduated in size.[106] Not described in the will, a solid oak effigy was carved to crown the hearse – a feature that was later repeated for the funeral of Henry's consort, Catherine of Valois in 1437.[107]

60

Henry's two wills give the impression that, in a rapid reversal of his father's policy, he had taken possession of Westminster as his church. Yet the chantry at the abbey competed with another, grander scheme, which, remarkably, was also initiated in the opening months of his reign. Soon after his accession, Henry conceived a plan to create a wholly new sacred landscape, close to his capital city, but up-river from Westminster at Sheen. His aim was to raise three new monasteries of the reformed orders, the Bridgettines, Carthusians and Celestines.[108] Their collective capacity for intercession would make them a chantry for the house of Lancaster on an unprecedented scale. The prospect of the third monastery soon faded but the first two were founded successfully, and although it was on a much larger scale than at Westminster, the work proceeded much faster. The Bridgettine abbey, known as Syon, and the Charterhouse on the opposite bank at Sheen were in operation within three years of the king's death in 1422. If the king's new land of Zion was emerging as the spiritual centre for the dynasty, it may be that Henry's thoughts for Westminster were taking a more personal direction. When his intimate friend and most trusted counsellor, Richard Courtenay (c.1381–1415), died from dysentery during the Siege of Harfleur, the king directed that his friend's body should be buried at Westminster, in the space he had planned for his own tomb.[109] No record of Courtenay's burial survives but it was not (at least not explicitly) displaced by his revised scheme and it

60   An effigy of Henry V was displayed on his coffin during the solemn funeral procession from Dover to London after his death at Vincennes in 1422; although the king's funeral effigy does not survive, it would have been carved from oak, as was that of his consort, Catherine of Valois (shown here), fifteen years later.

61   Henry V's tomb (probably completed 1431) lies beneath an arch in the chantry chapel in the abbey, built in accordance with the directions in his will; the tomb effigy of black oak, which rests on a monument of Purbeck marble, would originally have been decorated with silver-gilt ornaments and regalia.

may be that Henry was settling on the idea of Westminster serving as the memorial for an exclusive, if extended, family group.[110]

Henry's immediate family showed some commitment to realizing the Lancastrian monument at the abbey. His uncle, Henry Beaufort, Cardinal and Bishop of Winchester (1375?–1447), though ousted from the regency government that wielded power for the infant Henry VI (r. 1422–61, 1470–71), still guided the building work, which proceeded, albeit at a snail's pace. The chantry was finally finished in 1437, fifteen years after the death of the king.[111] Already the dynastic ties to the chantry were weakening. When Henry's queen, Catherine of Valois died in 1437, she was interred in the Lady Chapel. She had remarried, controversially, but her burial place may have been as much a practical as a political decision, since the finishing touches to the chantry were not yet complete.[112] Lacking the attention of a living patron, Henry's own memorial soon fell into neglect. Perhaps as early as the middle years of the century, his effigy had been stripped of some its silver-gilt ornaments and the painted funeral figures of Henry and

61

his queen had been discarded.[113] They later joined other threadbare funeral effigies to form the 'ragged regiment', an amusing talking-point for visitors to the abbey in the eighteenth and nineteenth centuries.[114]

Henry's and Catherine's son, Henry VI, had succeeded his father in September 1422, when he was just 9 months old, and inevitably his outlook as he grew up was moulded by the older generation that governed in his name. Their vision remained that of the boy-king's late, lamented father, the victor of Agincourt, crowned Regent of France, who held a dual monarchy that would make England the dominant power on the European mainland. It became abundantly clear at the child's coronation, conducted in his 8th year, that Westminster would now lose its primacy to the royal churches of France. The ceremony was timed to allow the royal party then to cross the channel for a second coronation at Rouen, the capital of conquered Normandy. As the boy was balanced precariously on a platform so that he might play some part in the ritual of which he was the focus, the customs so solicitously curated by the monastery were changed. Henry was anointed with one oil only, in the French style.[115]

The boy-king assumed his personal rule just as his father's chantry was finished. As they unfolded, his own plans for religious patronage carried the mark of Henry V's conception of the crown's role in the Church. This Henry also saw his role as that of a champion of the reform of the clergy and a renewal of their Church. He too aimed to raise new foundations in his own name, and embarked on a dual establishment at Eton College and King's College, Cambridge, which would dominate what remained of his active life. Westminster had been kept at the margins of his Francophone formative years; now, in the pursuit of his personal chantries, it was permanently eclipsed.

The early years of the war between the houses of Lancaster and York (1455–71), commonly remembered as the Wars of the Roses, were matched by disorder within the Westminster community. William Colchester's death in 1420 ushered in more than half a century of instability. Between then and 1474 no abbot died in office. Richard Harweden (1420–40) resigned, perhaps under some pressure, exhausted as much by the factional climate of the house as his advanced age. Edmund Kirton (1440–1462/3) was forced out of office after his scandalous conduct as 'a fornicator, dilapidator, adulterer, simoniac' was reported to Pope Eugenius IV. George Norwych (1463–9) was likewise removed after his misrule was made known to Edward IV (r. 1461–70, 1471–83). His successor, Thomas Millyng (1469–74), possessed the capacity to be a competent abbot but not the disposition, preferring court life, where he found a role as tutor to the king's eldest son, Edward. He went on to act as administrator in the household of the teenage prince and finally won release from Westminster when the king appointed him Bishop of Hereford.[116]

By the time Edward IV resumed his reign in 1471, after six months in exile, there can have been scarcely any monk of Westminster who could recall the collaboration of the monarch in the cult of their church. Perhaps the first Yorkist king shared the unease of the Lancastrian usurper Henry IV at the abbey's place in the royal tradition, which seems to have haunted Henry. Edward was an attentive patron of churches, but Westminster was only once, tangentially, drawn into his schemes. He attempted to restore the Benedictine priory at Deerhurst (Gloucestershire), which had been an outpost of the French royal abbey of Saint-Denis. Since a large part of the manor of Deerhurst had been granted to Westminster Abbey by the crown, it was natural for Edward to draw the monks into the re-foundation. One of the monks, William Buckland, was chosen as Deerhurst's prior. Like so many of his brethren, it seems Buckland was reluctant to take responsibility so far from the metropolis; Edward soon removed him and the plan was abandoned.[117] Generally, Edward held the abbey at arm's length, under suspicion. He staged his public wearing of the crown at St Paul's Cathedral. He criticized the continuing operation of the abbey's sanctuary. When he died, suddenly, in April 1483, there was no question but that he would be buried elsewhere – in the event, at Windsor.

While it could not claim any affinity with the king, for the first time in its history the monastic community in these years formed a close relationship with the queen. Perhaps Elizabeth Woodville first looked to the abbey as a place of protection, but over time it became her preferred recourse during the king's long periods of absence. She bore her eldest son in the sanctuary on 2 November 1470, while Edward was away, again fighting to recover the throne. The monastery was her surrogate family. The sub-prior baptized the baby; Abbot Millyng stood as his godfather. When her husband died a dozen years later and his brother Richard reached for the throne, her first thought was to return to the embrace of this second family. She fled to the abbey.[118]

Richard of York, who succeeded in taking the throne from his nephew, was crowned as Richard III (r. 1483–5) at Westminster with unprecedented display. It was said that as many as 6,000 knights were in his train. For the first time, the abbot, John Eastney (1474–98), came to the west door to meet the new monarch, bearing the ancient regalia, which he then surrendered. Eastney's predecessor was godfather to the rightful king, Edward V, whom Richard had surely had killed;[119] Edward's mother, the dowager queen, was the monastery's long-term guest. Abbot Eastney's welcome for King Richard was realpolitik at its most stark. Richard's presence at the abbey was purely tactical, however, and his well-established interests as a patron lay elsewhere, especially in the Church's northern province, at Barnard Castle, Middleham and the province's capital, York.[120]

Even though, in this period, it saw in its precinct only those members of the royal family who were on the margins of power, like the long-lived, loyal Elizabeth Woodville, Westminster was now remoulded in the image of this political nation. When Abbot Eastney commissioned deluxe manuscripts, he employed a professional scribe, William Ebesham, who also worked for court patrons.[121] William Caxton's printing enterprise, established in 1476 at a property on the edge of the precinct, rented from the monastery, clothed the abbey in the literary style of the Yorkist court, classical in theme and vernacular in language. Meanwhile, the church, and in particular its crowd of subsidiary altars, reflected the devotional fashions of an exclusive, cosmopolitan elite. Elizabeth Woodville invested in a chapel dedicated to St Erasmus, whose cult was increasingly in vogue in the second half of the fifteenth century.[122] Elizabeth also gave a relic of St Mary Magdalene in a silver casket, together with a velvet purse containing unnamed relics. It may well have been from the court circle of Lancaster or York that the abbey took possession of a silver-cased relic of the leg of St George.[123] It was surely to respond to the modish interests of this same circle that the monks set up an altar dedicated to the Holy Name of Jesus. Later, Abbot John Islip (1500–32) made the altar the focus for his own chantry chapel.[124]

The imprint of court culture weakened Westminster's standing as a communal church. By the middle years of the fifteenth century it was increasingly separated from the religious life of the town and the expanding metropolis. The monks very rarely ministered outside the abbey. There were university-trained theologians but they did not preach to the people. Westminster did not set up an open-air preaching cross as there was at St Paul's. In fact, in a capital city to which graduate preachers gravitated in growing numbers, there is no record of a Westminster man ever stepping into a public pulpit in this period. A weekly sermon at the abbey was assured only when it was made a requirement of Henry VII's grand commemorative scheme.[125] The sacrist routinely paid 2d. for the principal feasts of the church to be announced in the town of Westminster and in the city (at Temple Bar), but these occasions were not taken as an opportunity to expound to the people.[126] When, in *The Canterbury Tales*, Geoffrey Chaucer recalled the 'cleere' and 'eek loude […] chapel belle' and the 'murie orgon' (merry organ; ll. 170–71; 2851), probably he had in mind the sounds that reached his doorstep at Westminster, which he shared with residents of the town and the city. The worship of the abbey was heard but not seen.[127] The separation of the abbey from secular religion was reinforced by the vigour of the two churches in the lee of the abbey, the palace chapel of St Stephen and the parish church of St Margaret. The parish church capitalized on the monastery's detachment, developing devotional attractions that directly rivalled the abbey. A Guild of the Assumption of the Virgin Mary was established in 1431.

Polyphonic music was introduced. From 1482 a benefactor funded a university graduate
to lecture on the Bible.[128]

Westminster was moving away from the religious life of the neighbourhood at a
moment when many of the greater monasteries in England were as closely engaged
with it as they ever had been – as preachers, confessors, even as parish priests. It was
one symptom of a greater transformation of the abbey, apparent by the turn of the
fifteenth century, that while the community's obligations to the endowed chantries may
not have displaced the core monastic routine, its manner of life was less and less like
that of a monk. Whether the monks were chapel wardens, celebrant priests or lowly
torch-bearers, much of their routine activity now saw them dispersed through the
church and its surrounding offices, acting in capacities – administrative, priestly – which
were not drawn directly from the monastic rule to which they had been professed.
This routine was still communal in many ways, but the community that shared these
duties did not share the rule for monks. They were secular priests, or clerks not even
in holy orders, lay brothers, or illiterate poor men who had come there to live 'of the
foundation'. The change in their life might be described as a turn from 'regular' (that
is, following a rule) to secular clergy, but since each of the forms of clerical office
was to be found in the abbey church it would be more accurate to see their new
status as a hybrid.

The Tudor Mausoleum

At the coming of Henry Tudor to the crown as Henry VII (r. 1485–1509), the monks
of Westminster knew of a royal presence in their religious life only as the legacy of
their earlier history. They may have feared being edged even further to the margins
when, on entering his capital for the first time as king, just five days after victory at
Bosworth Field, Henry celebrated a service of thanksgiving at the cathedral church
of St Paul's. But for his coronation, conducted just two months later (30 October),
without hesitation Henry honoured the abbey's customary role. The 'device', or plan,
drafted for the staging of the ceremony was copied from the one used for Richard
III which had been drawn up from the pages of the *Liber regalis* itself. Indeed, Henry
seemed disposed to allow the abbey the final say on the ancient rites, since the device
carries a note explaining that not every detail need be written out 'because this be
sufficiently recorded at Westminster'.[129] The public spectacle of the coronation was
at least as great as Richard III's. There was such a crowd that one of the scaffolds
on which the people were standing gave way, although 'none [was] slayne, blessid be
God'.[130] In the opening months of his reign, Henry returned three times to the abbey

for further ceremonial acts. Only ten weeks after he was crowned, he came to the high altar to marry his queen, Elizabeth of York (d. 1503); theirs was the first royal wedding at Westminster for almost a century (18 January 1486). Again at the abbey, in the spring of the same year, Henry embarked on a first royal progress through his kingdom. Finally, after Henry had seen off two challengers for his crown, Elizabeth was herself crowned at Westminster in November 1487.

These orchestrated displays were designed to engender a new unity in the realm, but they were followed almost immediately by the first of a series of challenges to the Tudor claim on the crown. It was the reality of Henry's dynastic insecurity that returned him to Westminster and the capacity of its religious culture. Like his Lancastrian forbear Henry V – whose profile was clearly focused for the new king by his mother, Margaret Beaufort, herself the granddaughter of Queen Catherine of Valois – Henry was first conscious of the need to resolve the status of an earlier, anointed monarch who had been deposed, in this case Henry VI. There was already a popular cult of St Henry.[131] Now the king dispatched a formal petition to Pope Innocent VIII (1490) for his canonization, and began to plan for the reburial of his remains (which had already been transferred from Chertsey to Windsor) in a grand tomb. Rome sanctioned the translation of the remains of the would-be saint, ruling also that if it was so privileged as to receive them Westminster Abbey should contribute £500 to the costs. But official recognition of Henry VI's sanctity was slow in coming. Further petitions were made to Innocent's successors, continuing as far as 1504.[132] The proposal for a tomb also drifted, as a variety of possible sites were considered.

Finally, towards the end of 1497, the king resolved on Westminster. Abbot Eastney had made clear his enthusiasm for the project, but the decisive influence was that of the king's mother, who was deeply attached to the Lady Chapel tomb of Queen Catherine, mother of the saint-in-waiting. Lady Margaret had already endowed two chantries of her own at the abbey, in the chapel of Our Lady of Pew (1494) and in St Edward's Chapel (1496). She surely cemented Henry's choice of the abbey when, in 1499, she transferred her nascent scheme for a further chantry and a chain of university lectureships from Windsor. Like Elizabeth Woodville, in her long old age Margaret adopted the abbey as a second home. After burying her son, whom she outlived by two months, and seeing her grandson Henry VIII securely into his place she withdrew to Cheyneygates to prepare for her own end. For a time, her own tomb in the Lady Chapel was a focus for devotion, perhaps encouraged by the monks, who acknowledged her part in the recovery of royal patronage.[133]

Having committed to Westminster, Henry now aimed for more than a memorial to his Lancastrian forbear. There was to be an entirely new Lady Chapel, which, as well as accommodating the last Lancastrian king, would be built to contain the tombs of Henry himself, his queen, Elizabeth, and his mother. The architectural scheme was the most ambitious conceived by any of the Tudors. In its execution it was judged by the generation that saw it completed to be the finest church building in England. The court historian John Leland, who knew most of the kingdom's churches at first hand, called it *miraculum orbis universali*, the wonder of the entire world.[134] It was distinguished, above all, for its tall proportions, for the parallel pendant points of its fan-vaulted ceiling, and for the sculpture at its altar, in the apsidal chapels, and on the royal tombs. The main structure may be attributed to the English master Robert Janyns the younger (d. 1506). The designers of the interior sculpture are unknown, but the king's tomb was a masterpiece of the Italian Pietro Torrigiano (1478–1528). His involvement began only in 1511 at the invitation of Henry's son, Henry VIII, who then intended Torrigiano to design a tomb for himself and Queen Katherine.[135] By contrast with the family themes of Henry V's chantry, here the decorative scheme represented subjects of universal devotion, the apostles, the Fathers of the Church, and saints, male and female, familiar from English calendars, conjuring an impression of the whole company of heaven. As a deliberate counterpoint, the gates, the stalls and the window glazing conveyed secular imagery, Henry's own arms and those connected to the history of the English crown, with whom he claimed association. The decorative centrepiece was to be an image of the king himself, 'wrought [. . .] with plate of fine gold', shown as knight–prince, 'with a swerd and spurres, a coote of armour of our armes of England and of Fraunce enameled', clutching the coronet he had claimed at Bosworth field.[136]

The programme of commemoration Henry proposed for his chapel was on the same scale as the building. He conceived a collegiate structure in which the votive acts would be the collective responsibility of several tiers of clergy and laymen, priests, lay clerks, choristers, monastic lay brothers and poor almsmen. The almshouses for the last group were to be a new creation, on the edge of the abbey precinct.[137] The chapel men would observe daily commemorations, and his own and his family's anniversaries were to be marked with vigil, procession and Requiem Mass. They were to be provided with specially commissioned vestments, among them six copes of Italian cloth of gold designed by Antonio Corsi of Florence, and a complete set of priests' vestments in black silk for funerary observance; each robe was to be blazoned with the Tudor rose and portcullis symbol. Simply the best ceremonial costumes seen in Tudor England, later Henry VIII borrowed them for his 1520 summit with the French king at the Field of Cloth of Gold.[138] Perhaps the most remarkable provision of all was that the votive acts of the chapel men were to be syndicated across the English Church. A chain of twenty-one churches spread wide across the country – including cathedrals, abbeys, friary churches, charterhouses, the royal chapel at Windsor and the universities of Oxford and Cambridge – were to be bound to the Westminster scheme under a

62　On 24 January 1503, at the instigation of Henry VII, the foundation stone was laid for a
new Lady Chapel in an ambitious, late Perpendicular style, to replace the older, simpler structure.
Contemporaries considered it the finest church building in England.

formal indenture, issued to them under the royal seal. They had two obligations: to
stand as guarantors of the perpetual commemoration of the royal anniversaries and to
mirror them with their own clergy. The cooperation of affiliated churches in fulfilling
the requirements of a lay patron was not unprecedented, but the Tudor indentures
mapped out a new national union of monks, friars and secular priests, a new form of
ecclesia Anglicana (English Church) for the new dynasty, with Westminster at its head.[139]　63, 64

The cost of the scheme as it progressed from a proposal in 1498, the inception of
the building work in October 1502 and the completion of the main structure, perhaps
by 1509, was close to £14,000; by the time the interior and adjunct facilities, such as
the almshouses, were finished, perhaps half as much again had been required, raising
the total to £20,000. Remarkably, cash sums were deposited at the abbey at intervals
during the construction. A payment of £5,000 was made weeks before the king's
death in 1509 'for the perfitte finisshing [...] of the said werkes'; another £5,000 was

128 WESTMINSTER ABBEY

63 and 64   Illuminated initials from the Quadripartite Indenture of 1504 depicting Henry VII and Abbot John Islip, respectively, with the monks of Westminster. The king placed the abbey at the head of a chain of twenty-one churches across England, each bound by a formal indenture that committed them to the commemoration in perpetuity of the anniversaries set down by their royal patron.

released by his executors.[140] The king also assigned new endowments to the chapel, among them the old royal foundation of St Martin-le-Grand, though, since the abbey was obliged to maintain its services, the financial benefit was limited.[141] By contrast with Richard II and Henry V, Henry VII saw at least the outline of his scheme realized. The first formal commemoration enacted in the new chapel was in 1504 for the first anniversary of the death of Henry's queen, Elizabeth of York. Perhaps the king himself was present; certainly he came in his remaining years.[142]

Even before the building of the Tudor Lady Chapel, commitment to royal commemoration placed heavy demands on the monastery. The administrative burdens were at least as great as the cost. From the death of Henry V to the dissolution, the annual account of the sacrist opened with details of his purchase of the thousands of pounds' weight of wax to supply the royal chapels. The devolved structure of the abbey's income sources aided cash flow, though within fifteen years of the raising of

65   By *c.*1500 Westminster Abbey was a monument to 150 years of Plantagenet patronage. The outline of the old Norman church was now scarcely visible, being covered almost completely by arched windows and angular buttresses in the Gothic style. Since the beginning of the 14th century the nave had been extended, doubling its length from the crossing to the west door, though the great west towers were as yet unbuilt. The domestic buildings of the monastery had been much improved. After years under construction, the cloister was at last complete, and there were now well-appointed private suites for the abbot and the prior. The working buildings had expanded hugely to the south-west of the church, and the precinct was now subdivided into different quarters, each serving a distinct purpose. To the south-west of the west door was a garden for the abbot; due south of the cloister there was perhaps an orchard and to the east of this a kitchen garden. Meanwhile, the large open quarter to the north of the nave was the main concourse for the outside world to approach the abbey church and to gain access to its social services in the almonry. Outside the north gate, the royal palace of Westminster had also grown in scale and scope. The chapel of St Stephen was now flanked by a quadrangle for the college of its canons, and to the south of the royal family's private apartments rose the great Jewel Tower of Edward III.

Henry V's chantry fresh endowments were needed. By the fifteenth century many of England's monasteries that had accepted the chantry obligations of royal and noble patrons conflated them into a single general act of commemoration to spare time and resources. Sometimes they simply let them lapse. At Westminster the separate administration of each foundation was maintained. The rolls show that the lavish lights and vestments of the royal chapels continued to be made ready, perhaps even in the last year of the independent abbey, 1539–40.[143]

The changed culture of the monastery and its position at the head of the Tudors' chain of churches appeared to be leading Westminster into a new public role by the accession of Henry VIII (r. 1509–47). It was prefigured in the ceremonial performance of Henry's coronation. The route all the way from Westminster Hall to the pulpit in the abbey was laid with blue ray-cloth. Where his father's masters of ceremonies had been six senior bishops, Henry's 'device' gave the abbot a leading role, 'for his informacion in such thynges as concerneth the solempnitee of his coronacion', made him the very embodiment of the ritual lore contained in the *Liber regalis*. The abbot was also called upon to perform the most intimate action of the ceremony, 'to dry all the places of his body wher he was annoynted'.[144] The bond with the Tudor crown took on a yet more personal character when the grandson of Jasper Tudor, the king's great-uncle, was professed as monk. In his time, Thomas Gardiner was given a responsibility that was his birthright – to officiate in the chantry founded by his kinsman Henry VII. He also pored over the abbey's history books to pen his own apologia for the Tudor seizure of the throne.[145]

The king and his first minister, Thomas Wolsey, were seeking to establish a new dispensation between the crown and the ancient monastic estate. From the time that his dominance was assured, Wolsey appears to have been building a network of prominent abbots who might be persuaded to exchange their traditional independence for a role in the shaping of a new English Church. Westminster's abbot, John Islip (1500–32), was among the first to find a place in this clique. His status as collaborator was publicly signalled in November 1515 in the extraordinary ceremony of the reception of Wolsey's cardinal's hat, the hat itself being processed into the abbey church in a stately ritual previously reserved for a coronation.[146]

Wolsey aimed not only for authority over the traditional Church but also for the advance of reform. His design was made clear to Islip in 1518, when he made Westminster his permanent residence and the base of all his operations, a move that marked a watershed; in retrospect it was perhaps the end of the independent abbey. Wolsey was diverted from any root-and-branch reform, but only because he raised his sights to a greater prize, a programme of reform for the Benedictine order as a whole.[147] Islip was advanced further in Wolsey's service, modelling for monastic England the cardinal's vision of a royal monasticism. In 1522 he was given the responsibility of swearing in the new abbot of St Augustine's Abbey, Canterbury; in 1525 he presided over the election of the Abbot of Glastonbury.[148] It might not be too much to suggest that Islip was moulded into a Tudor prelate on the Wolseyan model. There was more

66   Thomas Wolsey was invested with his cardinal's hat in Westminster Abbey in 1515, at a ceremony that, for solemnity and splendour, rivalled a royal coronation. When in London, Wolsey would ride daily in procession to Westminster Hall, his four footmen bearing silver poleaxes, and a peer or a gentleman usher carrying the hat; it is visible at the centre of this illustration of 1578 from a copy of George Cavendish's Life of Wolsey.

than a hint of the cardinal's Renaissance ambition in Islip's completion of the nave and west front of the abbey church, no less than 200 years after it was first contemplated. Like so many of Wolsey's projects, they were stamped with Tudor badges. It was surely only Islip's age that prevented his promotion to a bishopric, the due reward for several of Wolsey's abbot allies. His funeral procession commanded the presence of a cross-section of the clerical nation, the city and the court, as if acknowledging his position at the head of a new order.[149]

There are signs that the mood of the monastery was turning towards reform. The sudden appearance of professed men choosing names in religion that stood for Christian virtues – Charity, Faith, Grace, Hope and Virtue – or recalled the Fathers of the early Church – Chrysostom, Gregory, Jerome – reflected the self-conscious piety that Wolsey aimed to promote.[150] A sermon exclusively addressed to them by Bishop

67 A contemporary drawing, attributed to Gerard Horenbout, shows the funeral of Abbot John Islip in 1532, with the abbot's hearse standing before the high altar of Westminster Abbey. Islip was one of a handful of abbots to find a place of influence in the Tudor regime; his death marked the end of the abbey's long tradition of independence and self-governance, which had endured for 400 years.

John Longland of Lincoln carried the reformist message that the strictly observant monk was 'especially chosen for the household of Christ'.[151] The mood may have passed through the Westminster family – it might explain the Malvern monks' appeal to Thomas Cromwell in 1536 for the reform of their own 'monkery'.[152] Yet it was axiomatic that a place in Wolsey's Church would be at the expense of Westminster's self-governance. When he arrived at York Place, the cardinal had demanded sight of the foundation charters and insisted that his agents 'nottid suche thyngis as be off most importance as the fundation off the place, the sanctuarie and the exemption there'.[153] By the time he was dead, a dozen years later, he had appropriated much of the abbey's Westminster property.[154] When Islip died in 1532 it was inevitable that his successor would be a crown appointee, the first since the Normans had made the abbey their own four centuries before. Henry VIII's control of the appointment at Westminster anticipated his assumption of the headship of the Church across his kingdom as a whole, articulated in the Act of Supremacy of 1534. The authority of the Roman papacy in England was extinguished. The medieval history of the abbey was at an end.

4

The Great Transition:
1530–1603

DIARMAID MACCULLOCH

I N THE 1520S, A DECADE BEFORE ROYAL Dissolution of the Monasteries, the abbey was one link in a spiritual and temporal chain of power on the Westminster skyline. To the south was the Archbishop of Canterbury's headquarters at Lambeth, a barge journey across the Thames. To the east was the royal palace of Westminster. The purely residential heart of the palace had been wrecked by fire in 1512, and, for the time being, Henry VIII (r. 1509–47) was forced to live elsewhere. Nevertheless, the undamaged part of the complex remained home to the ecclesiastical foundation of St Stephen's College. Its prominent, free-standing bell-tower, beside Westminster Hall, signalled a not always easy relationship between the two adjacent royal churches; more deferential to the abbey church was the lesser tower of Westminster's newly rebuilt parish church of St Margaret. Abbey and palace together formed a miniature walled and gated city; parliament customarily divided its meetings between the two institutions. Beyond their walls to the west straggled the houses, shops and inns of the 'vill' of Westminster. North of the royal palace walls, England's second primate, the Archbishop of York, boasted a home equivalent to Lambeth Palace: York Place. From the 1520s, York Place was being rebuilt by the cheerfully ostentatious current archbishop, Cardinal Thomas Wolsey; the Caen stone façade of its great dining-hall was already gaining this new work the name 'Whitehall'.[1] Whitehall was sited between the Thames and the road (appropriately called King Street) leading from the vill towards London and into the wider manor of Westminster, with its second parish church of

68 (FACING PAGE)   In the late Tudor age, Protestant worship made redundant the many side-chapels, such as St Edmund's Chapel. These became shelters for an array of funerary monuments as diverse in style as the occupations of the men and women they commemorate. In 1561 the abbey verger began charging fees to view the tombs, and the tour of the monuments was soon illuminated by William Camden's guidebook of 1600 (page 174).

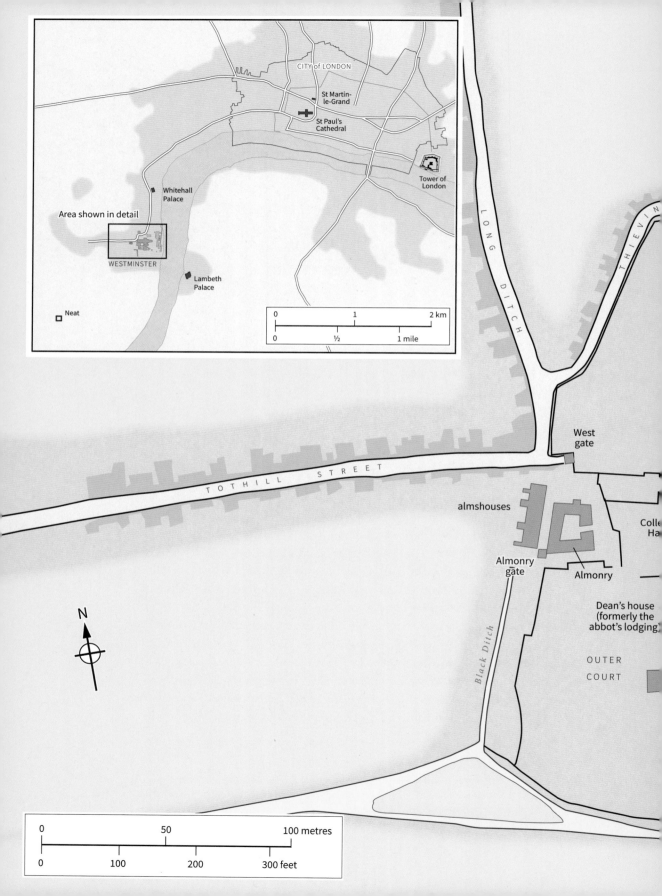

Inset map

CITY of LONDON

St Martin-le-Grand

St Paul's Cathedral

Tower of London

Whitehall Palace

Area shown in detail

WESTMINSTER

Lambeth Palace

Neat

| 0 | | 1 | | 2 km |

| 0 | ½ | | 1 mile | |

Main map

LONG DITCH

THIEVIN

West gate

almshouses

Colle Ha

Almonry gate

Almonry

Dean's house (formerly the abbot's lodging,

OUTER COURT

TOTHILL STREET

Black Ditch

N

| 0 | | 50 | | 100 metres |

| 0 | 100 | 200 | 300 feet | |

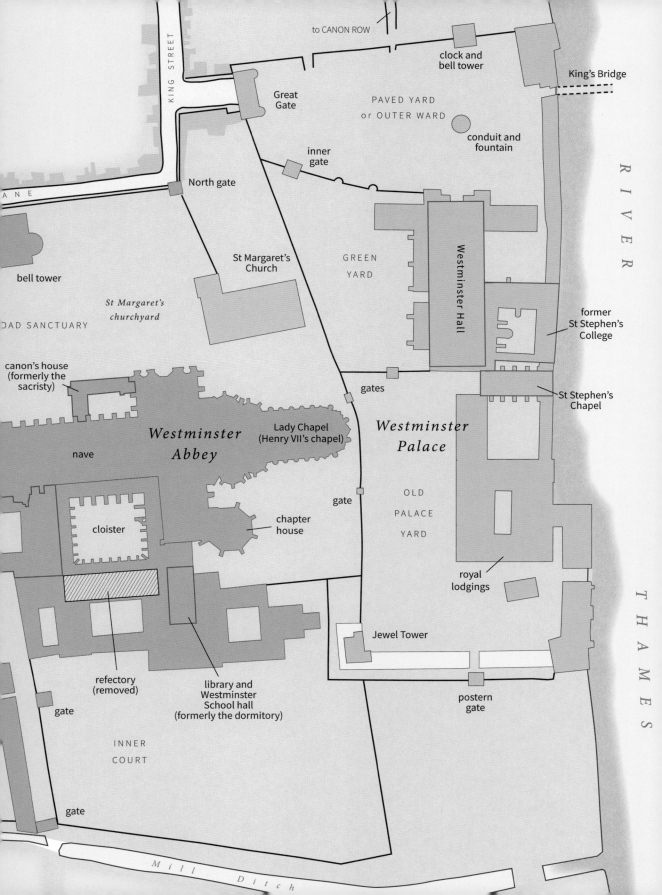

to CANON ROW

clock and
bell tower

King's Bridge

Great
Gate

PAVED YARD
or OUTER WARD

conduit and
fountain

inner
gate

KING STREET

North gate

St Margaret's
Church

GREEN
YARD

Westminster Hall

former
St Stephen's
College

bell tower

St Margaret's
churchyard

AD SANCTUARY

ANE

canon's house
(formerly the
sacristy)

St Stephen's
Chapel

gates

Westminster
Abbey

Lady Chapel
(Henry VII's chapel)

Westminster
Palace

nave

gate

OLD
PALACE
YARD

cloister

chapter
house

royal
lodgings

refectory
(removed)

library and
Westminster
School hall
(formerly the dormitory)

Jewel Tower

gate

postern
gate

INNER
COURT

gate

Mill Ditch

RIVER

THAMES

St Martin-in-the-Fields. Overall, there were perhaps three thousand inhabitants under the abbot's jurisdiction, and the abbey owned the majority of Westminster properties.[2]

By the end of the sixteenth century, the same view across the river testified to a great adjustment between royal and ecclesiastical power. The dean and canons of St Stephen's were long dispersed, and York Place was now formally the royal palace of Whitehall, after the brusque eviction of the Archbishops of York in 1529. Whitehall proved an ideal solution to the inadequacies of the old royal palace. Under Henry VIII's enthusiastic direction, it became a vastly expanded royal complex, so large that it spanned King Street, which was now far more obviously a royal processional way, a means of impressing the hordes of visitors to parliament and palace. Much of the abbey's former land now made up part of the royal estate, but still at the centre of all this stood a collegiate ecclesiastical corporation, proudly beyond the control of Lambeth Palace across the river, and still informally, if inaccurately, known to many as 'Westminster Abbey'. The formidable bulk of its great church crouched without tower or spire to grace it; for the time being, there was no appetite to finish its prolonged scheme of rebuilding, given the Protestant mood of the Reformed Church of England.

A Cardinal and his Servant

The first signs of change appeared with the fall of Cardinal Wolsey in 1529–30. He was felled by his inability to solve a problem that, indeed, seemed to lack a solution: the ending of the king's marriage to Katherine of Aragon. King Henry's aspiring bride-to-be, Anne Boleyn, developed an implacable hatred for Wolsey because of his failure, and was a further driving force behind his misfortune. Accordingly, Henry allowed him to be indicted on a charge of praemunire in October 1529. This crime,

69 (PREVIOUS PAGE)   The abbey and its environs, c.1600. The main footprint of the abbey and its precincts was little changed by the Dissolution of the Monasteries in 1540: the new cathedral and collegiate institution simply adapted existing buildings to new uses. One major demolition was the monks' refectory on the south side of the cloister, but the dormitory on the east side survived, divided into the church's library and Westminster School hall. The buildings of St Stephen's College and Chapel also remained after the dissolution, but now put to use by parliament and government. To the north of St Margaret's Church, beyond the immediate environs of the abbey, Henry VIII's transformation of York Place into the Palace of Whitehall involved much demolition of private property along King Street, to allow for the extension of the palace. Whitehall's role as the centre of royal and later Interregnum government cemented the continuing ceremonial importance of the nearby abbey.

aiding and abetting a foreign jurisdiction in the realm, was particularly unjust, since it was the king who had insisted on furthering Wolsey's ambitions to become papal legate in the realm. Yet King Henry was never inclined to see all sides in any question, and the praemunire indictment had an incidental benefit for him: through acknowledging guilt, Wolsey, at least in theory, lost title to all estates in his many ecclesiastical offices, the archdiocese of York being only chief among them.

While, in practice, negotiation followed over the package of confiscation, the immediate fruit King Henry plucked from Wolsey's tree was York Place, now to replace the old Westminster Palace as premier royal palace near the capital. It was the capstone in a project to create a wide zone of royal palaces around London, from Hampton Court to Greenwich. Immediately, a great many transactions with local landowners built up a coherent local estate for the king around Westminster, and chief among landowners was the abbey. It would have been foolish, but also disloyal, to refuse sales or exchanges, and there was no question of Abbot Islip's doing so; he had begun the process already, thanks to Wolsey's ambitions for expanding York Place, and the terms were not desperately unfair. As these complex transfers went ahead, increasingly prominent among royal officials carrying out the work was one who knew Wolsey's palace very well, his former senior servant Thomas Cromwell.

Cromwell was a familiar face at the abbey from at least 1524, when he entered Wolsey's service with a brief to administer the cardinal's 'legacy project'. This intricate business centred on a monstrously expensive tomb, and a pair of memorial colleges: a 178 feeder-school at Ipswich to prepare pupils for higher education at a college at Oxford. Imitation is the sincerest form of flattery; these projects mimicked Henry VI's foundations of Eton and King's College, Cambridge, but of course also sought to outdo them. The cardinal may also have been inspired by Pope Leo X's project in 1521 to finance an equally lavish tomb for Henry VIII. Leo had intended that gift as a token of his gratitude to the king for writing against Martin Luther: events rendered the proposal richly comic in retrospect, and it came to nothing.[3] It is still not absolutely clear where Wolsey planned his tomb to end up – in Westminster, Ipswich or Oxford – and perhaps he himself left the matter open, waiting to see what the most splendid setting might be. Yet the Italian craftsmen busied themselves in workshops at Westminster, 176 and certainly the intention was to surpass the new Italian-made tomb for the king's father in the abbey. The twin Cardinal Colleges would stand as both chantries for Wolsey's soul and places of education, for education was always of great importance to the former Oxford don, and one of his solaces amid the crushing burden of his royal duties. Cromwell managed all that went forward, most importantly the prima-donna sculptors and gilders working on the tomb, but also the dissolution of superfluous monasteries to finance the colleges.[4]

As a result, Cromwell became more familiar with the world of English monasticism than any other Tudor layman of his generation. His relationship with Westminster Abbey grew ever closer as his career in royal service spectacularly expanded. Two circumstances encouraged this. The first was a characteristic piece of heroic selfishness on the part of the king in seizing the almost finished elements of Wolsey's tomb for his own use, so Cromwell continued useful in managing what was now Henry's legacy project (though it too came to nothing). Second was the abbey's intimate link to English parliamentary business. Since 1485 parliamentary sessions had begun with a service in the abbey church, and, once ordinary business began, the House of Commons normally met in Westminster Abbey's refectory. This was a room of appropriate size for a large assembly, and because of the structure of the Benedictine day, it was reliably available for most of the morning, while the monks were in church at their devotions. We must think of Commons sessions before the 1540s dominated by the lingering smell of monastic cooking.[5]

Cromwell's preoccupation with parliament was even greater than his involvement with monasteries; his enthusiasm for managing parliamentary business, using parliamentary sessions to solve the king's present problems, was probably his principal recommendation for royal favour. He himself sat in Commons sessions from 1523 until 1536, when his expanding power took him to the Lords. In a typical example of Cromwell's acquiring apparently trivial or even menial offices with a particular usefulness, in 1535 the Westminster monks granted him the position of their gatekeeper, a duty separate from the far more honourable stewardship they had already given him. We need not think of Master Secretary grimly brooding, Holbein-portrait-like, from the abbey gatehouse lodge: the point of being gatekeeper was that it gave him or his nominated underlings free access to the abbey precincts while the House of Commons sat in the refectory, together with the right to exclude on the spur of the moment anyone who might be a political nuisance.[6] By 1535 a new abbot was proving admirably compliant with his plans, to their mutual advantage.

The Coming of Abbot Benson

Abbot Islip's death in 1532 opened the way for a royal nominee at a crucial moment in Henry VIII's plans to restructure his spousal portfolio. What contemporaries called, with nervous tact, his 'Great Matter' was widening into a plan of startling boldness; since the pope seemed incapable of granting Henry the annulment of his Aragon marriage, it was worth trying to deny papal jurisdiction in England on such matters, claiming that the monarch enjoyed 'imperial' jurisdiction. That would enable the king to demand adjudication on his own case within the realm, without deferring to any superior under God. Among a fleet of canon lawyers and theologians drafted in to formulate justifications for this revolutionary programme was the recently elected Abbot of Burton upon Trent, a former monk of Peterborough abbey, whose surname in the world was Benson and as a monk (echoing his family's Lincolnshire home) Boston.

Among William Benson's great friends was a current royal ambassador called Thomas Cranmer, who likewise was doing good service on the king's case; he may have known Benson since boyhood, but certainly since Cambridge days.[7] They formed an effective duo in scheming for the Boleyn marriage. Cranmer appeared in the House of Lords in 1533, after a startling promotion from relative obscurity in the University of Cambridge to become Archbishop of Canterbury. But Benson anticipated Cranmer: summoned to that session, he was the first abbot in Burton abbey's history to sit in parliament. Evidently he was a safe man to swell the vote for the regime's plans to break with Rome, which duly became law that spring through an 'Act in Restraint of Appeals': the act declared England to be an 'empire', and therefore immune from appeals to the pope, such as that Queen Katherine had already made to save her marriage. It passed just in time for parliament's prorogation on 7 April; during the following week, Benson moved smoothly over administrative hurdles to become Abbot of Westminster.[8] He was actually the first abbot to be chosen from outside the community since 1214, but in present circumstances he showed every sign of being a sound choice for the abbey, given its role at the heart of very controversial current royal proceedings. On 1 June he and Cranmer shared top billing for the clerical roles at Anne Boleyn's coronation in the abbey – the only separate coronation to be held for any wife in what became a sequence of six for King Henry. Cranmer crowned her and Benson was principal celebrant at High Mass.[9]

The new Abbot of Westminster was part of what, in the mid-1530s, became an establishment group of religious Reformists negotiating the ambiguities of Henry's new Church, with definite purposes of their own. It is too early to call them 'Protestants', a word only really understood in England as we now use it during Queen Mary's reign (and not initially in a good way). A term that made more sense in King Henry's days was 'evangelical', characterizing those seeking to remould the Church from its medieval state according to the gospels (evangelia): the models were provided for England by Luther's 'evangelical' Reformation in Saxony and by others in south Germany and Switzerland. In England, the chief movers, within constraints ordained by King Henry's never predictable whims, were Cranmer, Cromwell and the new Queen Anne, leading a not altogether stable coalition of courtiers and senior churchmen (Benson included), and interacting with a variety of discontents in the wider population, both Lollard and newly Reformist.

70   Hugh Latimer (1487–1555), Bishop of Worcester from 1535 to 1539, is portrayed in Foxe's *Acts and Monuments* (1563) preaching in the Privy Garden pulpit at Whitehall Palace. The king and courtiers in the galleries had the advantage of shelter – a useful privilege, as many sermons were preached in winter or early spring.

Various vivid glimpses of Benson's evangelical circle appear through the eyes of his friends, and one or two enemies. Chief among the former was the great evangelical preacher Hugh Latimer, who would have got to know him at Cambridge. The abbot prevailed on Latimer to play his part in the preaching rota created by the abbey's agreements with Henry VIII's father for regular sermons; in 1535 Latimer wrote to Cromwell, excusing himself from meeting on business, because 'thys day my Lord of Westmynster hath putt unto me to prech there w'th hym'.[10] After ex-Bishop Latimer was deprived of any home or living for opposing the conservative turn in Henry VIII's religious policy in 1539, Benson remained a good friend to him. He gave Latimer the use of one of his houses, in Long Ditch in Westminster, and the preacher featured prominently in his will of 1549. Benson made him one of his executors, left him generous and very personal bequests, and furthermore set up elaborate arrangements to secure Latimer's life occupation of the Long Ditch house. This was the base for Latimer's celebrated preaching ministry under Edward VI (r. 1547–53), much of it conducted a short walk from home in a special open-air pulpit built in the Privy Garden of Whitehall Palace.[11]

Equally significant are warm references to Benson in the elegant Latin of an evangelical French poet under Anne Boleyn's patronage, Nicolas Bourbon, who found France too hot to hold him in 1535 and went into enjoyable exile at the English court, until Anne's downfall forced him to move on once more. His English stay prompted him to reissue his collected Latin poetry and letters (entitled *Nugae*, 'Trifles') in 1538; much of the new content was addressed to the emerging English evangelical establishment, with whom he became acquainted during his stay in England. Among a mass of complimentary letters and verse for Latimer, Cranmer, Cromwell and the king's evangelical physician, Dr William Butts, Benson's prominence is striking. He was involved alongside Bourbon himself in educating various teenage sons of courtiers to the high level that the king's enthusiasm for humanist learning made fashionable, teaching not just Latin but also Greek. Benson was, after all, a Cambridge DD.

A further and cheerful theme in Bourbon's compliments to Abbot Benson was their mutual love of wine. As he teasingly begged his English patron, translating a couplet from Greek to Latin, 'Most excellent prelate, you make me a gift of a mighty wine-bowl, beautifully wrought [in] silver; give me vintage wines at the same time!' (*Ingentem pateram, argentum tornatile, dono / Optime das praesul; da mihi vina simul*). In the course of a long and elegant letter to Benson, the main subject of which was the pleasures of Greek and Latin philology, he reminded the abbot of the time when Dr Butts was treating one of Bourbon's servants. Butts forbade his patient wine, and the servant sickened further. The doctor's son Edmund advised him to take refuge in Benson's rural retreat, the Neat, in what is now Pimlico. There, teased Bourbon, the abbot's well-stocked cellar did a better job than Butts had managed.[12]

Abbot Benson, whose health was latterly not robust, was himself a great believer in the restorative properties of alcohol. In one of his letters to Thomas Cromwell in 1535, he let him know that in his current illness, he had presumed on their friendship: 'I was so bolde to sende for some of your ale, wiche (I ryghte hertely thanke youe), dide me greate pleasure, prayenge youe I may eftsoynes [another time] upon my nede, doo the same.'[13] Benson's penchant for good wine led him into a prolonged stand-off in the late 1530s with the then deputy of Calais, Arthur Plantagenet, Viscount Lisle (not, in any case, a religious soulmate), about a large consignment of wine from Calais. The abbot seems to have been in the right about demanding it in settlement of a legal dispute, and he would not take prevarication for an answer, to the extreme annoyance of the Lisle household: 'I would he had a tun of wine, and the cask, in his belly' was a repeated bitter joke of Lisle's servant John Husee.[14] It is hardly speculation to suppose that a good deal of Benson's fine cellar was expended on the appreciative palates of government officials, peers and MPs, particularly during the frequent meetings of the Commons held within the precinct.

Benson thus displayed a winning combination of scholarship, evangelical religion, conviviality and ease at the royal court, putting him in an ideal position to defend his monastery's interests as the tide of dissolution gathered strength between 1536 and 1539. In fact, in the 1510s and 1520s, a number of leading abbots had shown sympathy with Wolsey's programme of Church reform; Cromwell was the inheritor of their interest, which, after all, reflected his own work under the cardinal in converting monastic assets to the creation of two great colleges. Now, in the late 1530s, amid the general Dissolution of the Monasteries, nunneries and friaries, a real prospect emerged that many of the most venerable English monasteries, principally Benedictine houses, would transition into colleges of secular priests such as Wolsey had planned for his foundations at Ipswich and Oxford. This appears to have become official policy in summer and early autumn 1538, when a remarkable number of senior figures in Church and commonwealth, Cromwell among them, made proposals for such schemes.[15]

Plans for Survival

In winter 1539–40, a policy document produced in Cromwell's office, which he personally pondered over and emended, gave a no-nonsense description of the monastic dissolutions so far, but went on to say that 'som other house[s], for respect of the places they stand in, his Grace woll not dissolve'.[16] Although the programme of converting monastic to secular foundations was much cut down because of Henry VIII's urgent need of finance for a huge campaign to build coastal defences, it was not abandoned altogether. It took concrete form in plans also reviving Wolsey's proposals for new dioceses and cathedrals, using greater monasteries. Plans for turning other great abbeys into colleges of priests pure and simple were drastically curtailed, but they did go ahead in two instances, and those new colleges both survived for another decade or so before final dissolution in changed religious circumstances. One – surely significantly – was William Benson's former abbey of Burton upon Trent (the other, Thornton in Lincolnshire, cries out for further explanation).

71   Among the new cathedrals was Benson's present abbey of Westminster. In adding Westminster to the tally, the strongest card he could play was the presence of royal tombs – probably also a major reason for putting Gloucester and Peterborough on the list, respectively the resting places of Edward II and Henry's first wife, Katherine of Aragon (in his eyes, widow of his elder brother Arthur). In the end, after much argument and horse-trading, Westminster was joined by five other leading monasteries as brand-new cathedrals, together with eight cathedrals lately monastic but now transformed into collegiate bodies. Collectively, these were (and nearly all still are) Henry VIII's 'New

71 In the illuminated initial from Henry VIII's charter establishing the abbey church as a cathedral, 5 August 1542, Dean William Benson (d. 1549) kneels to receive the charter from the king.

Foundation' cathedrals; they remain the one lasting unaltered achievement of Henry VIII's confused and shapeless effort at Reformation.[17]

As this programme took concrete shape, Benson was simultaneously caught up in one of the worst political crises of the realm. It developed out of Cromwell's ambitious programme to solve both the king's latest lack of a wife and various other dynastic problems. By the end of 1539, Henry was scheduled to marry the last lady available and willing on the European marriage market, in fact rather scraping the bottom of the barrel: Anna, from the hardly even middle-ranking power of Jülich-Cleves-Berg. Cromwell calculated that these nuptials would stop the king turning his eyes again to some lady from the English nobility, a constant worry for the minister who had pulled off the coup of marrying his son Gregory to the king's sister-in-law Elizabeth Seymour. The princely family of Cleves were also pleasantly ambiguous amid the developing Reformations in mainland Europe, and definitely a counterweight within the Holy Roman Empire to the imperial Habsburg family.

Simultaneously there was the need to find a suitable partner for Henry's elder daughter, Mary, who happened to get on very well with Thomas Cromwell, but would probably be a princess too far for the dumpy widower himself. Consequently,

Cromwell laid the groundwork for a marriage for Mary into another German princely family: the prospective groom was Philip, Duke of Bavaria. Like the Cleves line, the Bavarian Wittelsbachs represented an alternative power base to the Habsburgs within the empire. Remarkably, the duke journeyed to London in person, though with little fanfare. Mary seemed happy enough with this marital prospect, and consented to meet him face to face on Boxing day 1539, in the garden of the Abbot of Westminster, an arrangement that would involve no more than a discreet stroll from Whitehall Palace. On this occasion she even allowed Duke Philip to kiss her, against all protocol.[18] All seemed well that Christmastide, but then Cromwell's plans for Mary's future were overwhelmed by a totally unexpected catastrophe to his cherished royal marriage alliance with Cleves.

At Rochester on new year's day 1540, King Henry had his first glimpse of his new bride, Anna. Over the next few months, only a handful knew just how visceral was his revulsion against poor Anne of Cleves, but there is one hint that Benson knew more than most – his sudden aversion to staying on at a remodelled Westminster after the dissolution, expressed in a note to Cromwell, which he may have written in the week after formally surrendering his monastery on 16 January 1540. He made his excuse ill health, begging Cromwell to devise a way 'that I may be delyvered from the cure and to me the unportable [unbearable] borden in governance of this house, in suche sorte as the Kynges Maiestyes indignation be advoyded'. Evidently his retirement on a pension would upset government plans already well advanced, but, regardless, he sounded adamant beyond conventional pleas: 'my feblenes is such by reason of dyverse most grevouse dyseases, that I know well (tarying here) I shall not only have a very short paynfull bodlye lyeff, but also put my soule in dawnger. Alas, my Lord, what shall it profett eny creature, that I put eyther of them in pearell?'[19]

If it was not the sense of impending political crisis that affected Benson, it might have been the structural consequence of Westminster's new arrangements. A bishop for a new diocese required a house, and inevitably the best in the abbey complex: that would be the current abbot's lodging. The new dean would be installed in a different house, elsewhere: the prior's lodging (where Ashburnham House now stands, on Little Dean's Yard). If the dean was Benson, that would mean an infuriatingly inconvenient move across the cloister, accompanied by continuing administrative burdens in a new post, at a time when his health was no doubt perfectly genuinely fragile. Moreover, it may already have been clear, when the abbot-quondam wrote, that the bishop-designate was the Dean of the Chapel Royal, Richard Sampson, whose conservatism would not be congenial to either Benson or Cromwell.

In fact, matters took a different turn, and Benson's concern for his soul subsided. Amid bewilderingly rapid moves and counter-moves that spring, as traditionalists and evangelicals battled it out for the king's favour, Cromwell's party seized what seemed a decisive advantage towards the end of May 1540. Late that month, on the very day that Sampson was publicly named as Bishop of Westminster, he was suddenly arrested and sent to the Tower of London, along with another prominent conservative, also designated for a bishopric, Dr Nicholas Wilson.[20] The successor-bishop eventually chosen was Thomas Thirlby, a career diplomat but also very close to Benson: back in 1536, in writing to the abbot, Nicolas Bourbon had singled out Thirlby as being 'the greatest admirer of your virtues'. The new Bishop of Westminster would not have far to travel to his new home, since one of his already numerous preferments was a canonry of St Stephen's; his house in Canon Row was no more than a few minutes' walk from the abbey. He duly surrendered that office on becoming bishop in the autumn.[21] Benson swallowed his pride for the sake of his friend, and his bags were trundled across the precinct from the former abbot's lodging to a new home.

The continuing prosperity of the likes of Benson and Thirlby is a witness to the peculiarity of the political crisis in winter to summer 1540. It culminated in the execution of Thomas Cromwell and three close evangelical protégés of his, but otherwise harmed Cromwell's associates not a whit. King Henry kept his options open, and in fact soon regretted the loss of 'the most faithful servant he ever had'.[22] Westminster played its part in resolving the Anne of Cleves problem, via notably brisk proceedings to annul the marriage while Cromwell was still languishing in the Tower of London. The chapter house was the setting for a joint meeting of the Convocations of Canterbury and York on 9 July: on the same day, in the abbey refectory, Cranmer's decree of annulment was witnessed by Benson, three of his brethren and Thirlby, who in these proceedings was described for the first time as bishop-designate.[23] This prominence of the abbey was perhaps inevitable, since the annulment was only one aspect of the current crisis needing to be tackled, particularly alongside the attainder of Cromwell: Convocation and parliament had to work together at close quarters. Benson's and Thirlby's prominence in oiling the wheels of proceedings safeguarded their future positions. A contrasting fate befell one former Westminster monk, whose face did not fit in King Henry's present dispensation: Thomas Epsam was executed on 4 July after three years in prison on treason charges. At his death, he was said by the chronicler Edward Hall, who witnessed the execution, to be the last monk seen in his habit in all England.[24]

Once what passed for normality in Henrician politics was restored, the details of the new cathedral's future were created piece by piece, although it took a year or two to finalize everything and formally restore an independent administration. In place of the monks was a college, headed by a dean with a chapter of twelve canons, leaders of a community of around 150 people, young and old, including the boys in the school.[25] In personnel, there was remarkable continuity with the previous monastic community. The abbot, prior and five other senior monks became members of the chapter; they would no doubt have been joined by Richard Gorton, an Oxford DD, and a monk of Burton before following Benson to Westminster, for he was much favoured by Cranmer and Latimer and was therefore another card-carrying evangelical, but he died before formalities were completed.[26] Among the fourteen junior cathedral clergy were five former monks, and five other monks received university studentships that were part of the new foundation. Most lay officials and servants of the community were kept on; so too were boys already in the grammar school and their master.

Of the six newcomers among the canons, four were unmistakable protégés of Thomas Cromwell.[27] The common factor was that they all had other concerns elsewhere, and would fit in responsibilities in the Westminster chapter as proved possible. This became a recurring pattern in the chapter into the Victorian age; what their position in the new cathedral gave such frequent absentees was a highly convenient base at the centre of politics when necessary, and that consideration was a useful centripetal force binding them to the foundation. Most far-flung was Simon Haynes, Dean of Exeter cathedral from 1537, who was fighting a lonely battle to impose evangelical reformation in the West Country in the face of resistance from his bishop and Old Foundation chapter; the company at Westminster would be a good deal more congenial. The most prominent canon not aligned with Cromwell was John Redman, who likewise soon had a major preoccupation elsewhere, as first master of King Henry's allied new foundation, Trinity College, Cambridge. Redman, a distinguished scholar of Erasmian sympathies, did his best to create a very personal middle way between traditional and evangelical views on salvation and the Eucharist, and his position was still evolving at his death at Westminster in 1551. It would be too early in the Church of England's history to see this attempt at nuance and avoidance of dogma as something called 'Anglicanism', but few enough tried anything so sophisticated at the time, and theologically aware contemporaries followed Redman's efforts with much interest.[28]

The new diocese, formally created by royal letters patent on 17 December 1540, consisted of most of the county of Middlesex, detached from the diocese of London (which was still substantial enough, comprising the City of London, Fulham and the counties of Essex and Hertfordshire). Making the abbey a cathedral involved the vill of Westminster formally becoming a city, and from 1545 it returned two MPs to Parliament; this survived the subsequent seesawing of the abbey's status.[29] The incumbent London diocesan registrar, Robert Johnson, remained Westminster's registrar, and naturally cloned his record-keeping from what he did in London; it is appropriate that when the dioceses were reunited in 1550, Westminster's diocesan register was bound up with those of the contemporary Bishops of London.[30] More important than Westminster's designated geographical territory was that its mother church was the king's cathedral. That was underlined when the new bishop, Thirlby, also replaced Richard Sampson as Dean of the Chapel Royal. Thirlby actually spent most of his episcopate both of Westminster and then of Norwich abroad on diplomacy, but in such service, the prestige of his royal and episcopal dignity would be very useful.

Westminster was therefore treated like nowhere else. A mark of King Henry's personal interest in the new institution was that he spent his own money on new accommodation for the school that continued the monastic school, for which his provisions specified two masters and forty boys: the building work he paid for has recently been revealed by dendrochronology at 19 Dean's Yard.[31] To recognize him as founder, rather than his daughter Elizabeth, to whom the school has generally given the credit, is only fair.[32] This character of the abbey as royal cathedral was useful background mood-music in its later survival: as late as the 1570s, there was a suggestion of merging the abbey, St George's Chapel, Windsor, and the queen's peripatetic Chapel Royal under the Dean of Westminster, who would become a single 'Bishop of the Court' and royal almoner, complete with a place in the House of Lords.[33]

Thanks to its special status, Westminster's endowment was exceptionally generous among Henry's new foundations, and its complexity may account for the length of time taken to set it up – well into summer 1542. Only re-founded Canterbury and Durham exceeded Westminster's income, but they had been cathedrals before; among the brand-new cathedrals, Westminster stood out bizarrely.[34] Some 83.5 per cent of its new endowment had belonged to the abbey, and other former abbey lands went to fund the bishop. To the cathedral's existing ancient core estates were added lands from other great monasteries, chiefly Pershore and Evesham, building on Westminster's existing strengths in Gloucestershire and Worcestershire, and other lands were granted in Nottinghamshire, Lincolnshire and Yorkshire. Moreover, unlike the other ancient royal chapel of St George's, Windsor, the majority of this endowment was not 'spiritual' (tithes or income from rectories), but good solid land for renting out, including much property for lease in the City of London – as gilt-edged an asset then as now. The largest single sector was rent from manors, bringing in a handsome £1,500 per annum.

Throughout the late Tudor period, Westminster like all ecclesiastical landlords found itself constantly besieged by powerful outsiders wanting to benefit from its generous holdings, but it escaped further permanent alienations of estates, with one exception. Henry VIII's original vision in his New Foundations was to provide studentships and readerships linked to his cathedrals; Westminster was by far the most substantial contributor, with no fewer than ten academic posts to fund, besides twenty students. Evidently most cathedrals found this arrangement a nuisance, and, like others, Westminster was relieved of the obligation in 1545–6, in exchange for returning to the crown property

72 A drawing in Abbot Islip's obituary roll shows that, in 1532, the abbey church had a small central lantern tower with a stumpy cupola, visible at the top of the initial letter.

worth £567 per annum. The beneficiaries were the king's even newer foundations, Christ Church, Oxford, and Trinity College, Cambridge, and the academic posts soon become the most honourable in the realm, gaining the title of 'regius professorships'. Predictably, the Dean and Chapter groused about the income they were losing, and they also lost Westminster's formal institutional link to the universities, which, thanks to Henry VII and his mother Lady Margaret Beaufort, pre-dated the dissolution. Yet the long-term result was a permanent escape from a considerable burden.[35]

Cheeringly fortified with royal bounty, the cathedral could begin adapting for new purposes. Liturgical change would be most obvious – probably not to us, if we had visited, for traditional Latin rites continued with all the old splendour, but to contemporaries, much would stand out as different. Naturally the monastic dress of the community was changed to that of secular priests, but in a startling novelty, as in all the monastic churches now become colleges, the laymen and boys of the choir,

73 By the mid-16th century, a decision had been taken to remove the cupola completely, as this sketch of the east end of the church proves.

singing Latin polyphony, moved from the Lady Chapel to occupy what had been the monastic choir, where the monks had sung their plainsong. One might think that it was in connection with this shift and consequent adjustments that the new Dean and Chapter commissioned a survey of the eastern parts of the church in December 1543, but since the report was to be made to the Privy Council, fabric concerns are likely to have been more serious. Something must account for the fact that the abbey lost its low central lantern tower with a stumpy cupola just around this time. It is shown on what remains of Abbot Islip's obituary roll in 1532, but it is not present in Anton van den Wyngaerde's drawing made in the mid-1540s, and a mid-sixteenth-century drawing shows a most uncomfortable and obviously temporary arrangement of roofs where the tower cupola had been. The cupola does not look much of an architectural loss.[36]

72

73

    Much remains to be discovered about such changes, but drastic adjustments were made to the abbey's domestic buildings, to create separate residences for the new chapter and lesser clergy out of buildings designed on a monumental scale for a different communal life. In practice, the creation of personal spaces had started well before the dissolution, with comfortable separate houses for abbot and prior, and the huge monastic dorter had already been divided up into little cells for individual monks; but now all twelve canons must have their own houses, even before the ending of clerical celibacy – one ingenious conversion was from the now redundant infirmary chapel of St Catherine.[37] Nor were the canons to eat in common, so the monastic refectory, as vast in scale as the old dorter, was superfluous. On 5 November 1544 the Dean and Chapter abruptly decided to demolish the refectory, 'for the awoiding of ferther inconveniences' unspecified, but perhaps including its habitual use by the House of Commons.[38]

Certainly this destruction was not done in consultation with officials of Westminster Palace, since the next month, when the king summoned parliament to Westminster, there was official disarray; parliament's meeting was eventually postponed to the following November, and, although Windsor and Reading had been suggested as venues, it returned to Westminster. But where? Possibly the Dean and Chapter made available the vacant dorter (now cleared of its cell partitions) for the 1545 session of the Commons and that which followed in 1547, but parliament's eventual solution was to move out of the abbey altogether. Their chance came after the death of Henry VIII, when the government set up for his young son, Edward VI, gleefully forwarded an increasingly more pronounced Protestant Reformation for the English Church. St Stephen's College in Westminster Palace was desperately vulnerable to closure in what became a general attack on chantries, and, since its ecclesiastical neighbour was now also a collegiate church, St Stephen's did not have the advantage enjoyed by the other great royal college of St George's, Windsor, of lacking any local competition. By the end of 1548 it was gone, and the Commons moved permanently into the chapel building, whose footprint still forms St Stephen's Hall in the Houses of Parliament.[39]

The carcass of the surviving Westminster dorter found a continuing use: by the beginning of the seventeenth century it was divided between a large schoolroom, Henry VIII's original provision for the school having proved inadequate, and a library for the use of the Dean and Chapter.[40] The chapter house also survived, despite being entirely the wrong scale for a collegiate body. It had always served a wider function than simply the abbey's needs, and soon it was preserved as a principal store for government records. When Westminster was re-founded as a college under Queen Elizabeth (r. 1558–1603), that use became permanent; it is interesting that the building was not used for a major public debate on religion in 1559, perhaps because it was already too cluttered, and the event went forward in the choir. The shelving for the records grew

74 The abbey's library is now housed in what was formerly part of the dorter (dormitory), where the monks slept; it has been a repository since the 16th century for the abbey's valuable collection of printed books and manuscripts. A spiral stair leads from the library up to the muniment room, where the archive is now kept.

more and more elaborate; this providentially preserved a wonderful building that might otherwise have perished. In the long term it also accidentally saved a great mass of one of Europe's richest archives that might have met fiery oblivion in 1834 if it had been stored in the neighbouring palace complex.[41]

Mid-century Instability

The disappearance of St Stephen's College was only one component in the thoroughgoing Reformation of the English Church, spearheaded by the ministers of Edward VI, with the warm approval of a young monarch who quickly proved to have a will as strong as his formidable father. The council of evangelical politicians who took over on the old king's death, headed by Henry's brother-in-law Edward Seymour, in effect represented the revenge of Thomas Cromwell's partisans on the conservative politicians who had engineered his downfall. Their religious programme relentlessly moved England way past the Lutheran Reformations of northern Europe, to the iconoclastic changes in southern Germany, Geneva and Switzerland – what would soon be called 'Reformed Protestantism', in contrast to Lutheranism. In the opening months of the regime, the concern was to avoid too much alarm to the conservative majority of the political nation, so the coronation of the 9-year-old king at Westminster was a traditional affair.[42] A little abbreviated in consideration of Edward's 'tendre age', it still lasted seven hours, including the banquet in Westminster Hall: the abbreviations did give an excuse for omitting some 'old observvaunces' which the records do not further specify. Nevertheless, at its core was a pontifical Latin High Mass, celebrated by Archbishop Cranmer. (A fiery Protestant speech credited to him on this occasion is a piece of late seventeenth-century fake news, though it has deceived very many modern historians, including, for a time, myself.)[43]

This policy of conciliatory gestures towards conservatives was not to last long, once the new regime of the young king began to consolidate. The leadership of Westminster cathedral was well disposed to making their highly visible church a beacon of change, particularly important for spreading the government's message when members of parliament came up for their sessions, or for showing off the evangelical revolution to visiting foreign ambassadors. In late August 1547 the regime launched a kingdom-wide royal visitation, designed to destroy much traditional religious practice, including church furniture and ornaments that embodied it. In an extension of Thomas Cromwell's order of 1538 to remove images 'abused with pilgrimages or offerings', the visitation injunctions condemning 'feigned miracles, pilgrimage, idolatry and superstition' said that even images in stained-glass windows should be removed if they had been the object of devotion.[44] Such devotion was in reality highly unlikely, and the order went well beyond what connoisseurs of iconoclasm in mainland Europe would have considered necessary, but it provided an excuse for wholesale destruction of stained glass at Westminster, right at the beginning of the visitation.[45] New priorities were clear: a new theological library, required by the visitors in all cathedrals, was financed in 1549 by selling off ecclesiastical plate and metalwork, by then considered as relics of a popish past.[46]

Liturgical change was a high priority in this religious revolution. It is possible that at the coronation the choir performed an anthem in English, 'The king shall rejoice' by Christopher Okeland, though the work does not survive and not much is known of the composer – a pity, since this is the first known musical composition definitely associated with an English coronation.[47] Then, in autumn, at an event almost as high-profile as the coronation – the opening of parliament – the Lords and Commons were

treated in the customary Mass to a demonstration
of choral liturgy in English: the cathedral choir sang
vernacular settings of the main customarily choral
components, the Gloria, Creed, Sanctus and Agnus
Dei. Matters moved on again for another royal
event, Westminster's continuing statutory obit to
commemorate Henry VII. Before this, at Easter, a
vernacular rite for communicants to receive bread
and wine had been published for insertion into the
celebration of Mass, and this 'Order of Communion'
was used in the obit Mass; once more, the main
choral elements of the service were in English.[48]
In effect, Westminster was turned into a miniature
version of the Reformed city-states of mainland
Europe. The royal injunctions for Westminster
diocese in September 1547 specified that Sunday
service was to end in the four parish churches of the
city by nine o'clock, for priests and laity to resort
to the sermon in Westminster cathedral, unless the
churches themselves had a sermon. All Westminster
clergy were also to attend every divinity lecture in
St Stephen's College.[49]

By the time of Dean Benson's death in September 1549, the government had imposed a fully
vernacular Book of Common Prayer throughout
England, despite major rebellion in the West

75 This portrait of Richard Cox (c.1500–81), Dean
of Westminster from 1549 to 1553, comes from his
later years as Bishop of Ely – a very typical image
for a bishop in the Elizabethan Church. A militant
evangelical in Edward VI's time, Cox found himself
outflanked and harassed by younger Puritans in his
years at Ely.

Country against its introduction. Benson, whose ill health meant that in his last years
he was more frequently in his country homes than at Westminster, was generous in
his will, not merely to Latimer but to the distinguished Reformers in English exile
Martin Bucer and Paul Fagius, and his executors were a roll-call of Cranmer's friends
and employees.[50] Inevitably, he was succeeded by a like-minded evangelical, and the
royal choice was the man who in 1540 succeeded Bishop Thirlby in his canonry of
St Stephen's, Richard Cox. King Henry had chosen Cox as principal tutor to young   75
Prince Edward, but he was also an obvious member of the court clique of evangelicals
who already dominated the new dispensation at Westminster.[51] Cox now had much
else on his mind, as Dean of Christ Church, Oxford, and university chancellor, and he
was not going to obstruct new plans for Westminster, which emerged the following
year as part of a general consolidation of evangelicals on the Bishops' Bench in the

House of Lords; among other considerations, this would ease the passage of further reforming legislation in the Lords by changing the balance of votes.

By 1551 the government had seen to the removal of seven traditionalist bishops from their dioceses, and in 1550 Thirlby was also moved out of Westminster. His religious views had not marched in step with those of his old friend Benson, and if he had been more present between his various diplomatic missions he might have caused trouble. He was therefore shuffled off to the diocese of Norwich, and his see of Westminster simply reunited with London, now under the leadership of Cranmer's energetic lieutenant Nicholas Ridley, promoted to London from the much less significant Bishopric of Rochester, as well as from a canonry of Westminster cathedral.[52] Now the diocese of London had two fully functioning cathedrals: a situation paralleled in the Tudor realms only in the city of Dublin, though a further amalgamation of dioceses soon produced a similar pairing at Worcester and Gloucester. It was a puzzle as to what even one cathedral per diocese was doing in the increasingly stripped-down Edwardian Church; two seemed like carelessness. An act of parliament in 1552 recognized the re-foundation of Westminster as a subordinate cathedral for London; it made clear that the chapter of Westminster had no share in the (admittedly nominal) role of electing the Bishop of London; nor did it play any part in business transacted by the Dean and Chapter of St Paul's.[53]

Curiously, amid the confusion, Westminster cathedral went on administering the probate of wills in its privileged jurisdictions of Westminster and St Martin-le-Grand (a misleadingly grandiose name for a small liberty in the City of London). This is all the more odd because Abbot Benson had lost these rights in 1533 to a royal commission, but they were restored to the new Westminster dispensation in 1540, and the cathedral made sure that it would not lose them again, along with the notorious rights of sanctuary in the privileged enclaves, which had survived all attempts under Thomas Cromwell to undermine them.[54] It continued in its showcase role for religious change: Edward's second Book of Common Prayer, of 1552, meant a radical simplification of ceremony, which needed less liturgical equipment. On 20 May 1553 royal commissioners took away all remaining cathedral plate, apart from two communion cups, a silver wine-flagon (essential now that all those present at Communion received both bread and wine) and various cushions and hangings.[55]

Edward VI's fatal illness that spring did not suggest any let-up in religious change. His chosen successor was his enthusiastically Protestant cousin and contemporary Jane Grey – a decision of the dying king himself, in an effort to preserve his religious revolution; but an immediate coup d'état in July by Henry VIII's daughter the Lady Mary exploited her father's enduring charisma to galvanize legitimist support across the kingdom. A profound shock to the nation's leading politicians, it brought an abrupt end to the Edwardian religious experiment. Mary (r. 1553–8), in her devout Catholicism, was a symbol of traditionalist resistance to Protestant advance, confirmed by her clashes over religion with her royal half-brother. Once Mary replaced Queen Jane, Edward's corpse was hostage to the latest turn in England's religion. He died on 6 July and did not find his resting place till 8 August: this unprecedented delay was thanks to Queen Mary's wrestling with her conscience as to whether her half-brother could be rescued from the damnation awaiting a heretic.

In the end, pragmatic advice from representatives of the Emperor Charles V persuaded Mary that Edward could not be denied burial according to the rites of the Book of Common Prayer he had enthusiastically authorized. She consoled herself by not attending the funeral, instead staging three days of Requiems for Edward in the Tower of London, which included a guest appearance as celebrant from her lord chancellor-designate, Bishop Stephen Gardiner, not long since released from a cell in the Tower after close Edwardian imprisonment. The night before the funeral, Cranmer transferred Edward's body from Whitehall across to the abbey, with none of the Catholic ceremony that had escorted Henry VIII to the grave. In the church gathered the ghost of Edward's court to say farewell to the king in the context of the 1552 Communion service, conducted by the archbishop. No foreign ambassadors felt able to put in an appearance. Richard Cox was released from prison to attend, as both dean and Edward's former tutor. The preacher chosen by the queen for the occasion was, like Stephen Gardiner, newly released from detention: Bishop George Day, now restored to his old see of Chichester (and a former canon of St Stephen's). He undermined the spirit of the occasion by a sermon which an observer bitterly said 'prepared the way for papistry just like an advance raiding party'.[56] Once Edward's other half-sister, Elizabeth, was safely on the throne, she planned a splendid tomb for him in the abbey, but it was never built, and his present modest but seemly commemorative floor-slab in the Henry VII chapel is a gesture of gratitude from his personal charitable foundation, Christ's Hospital, made only in 1966.

Dean Cox was the first married man to head the church of Westminster in its history, and that alone would have been enough to end his career under Mary, even if he had not been an active supporter of the Jane Grey regime. His release from imprisonment continued long enough for him to preside over a routine chapter meeting on 26 August.[57] August was a rather surreal month, generally, in the kingdom, with the queen not yet fully showing her hand in repressing Protestantism; yet she could not tolerate Cox in place at Westminster for her meticulously traditional coronation on 1 October. In September he was removed (and was later allowed to escape to mainland Europe without much fuss). His replacement was a very different Oxford don, Hugh Weston, already marked out as a pillar of the new regime, and given a prominent

76
77

78

77 (ABOVE) In place of a monument,
Edward VI has a modest floor-slab in the
Lady Chapel; the first acknowledgement of his
grave, it was installed some four centuries after
his death.

76 (LEFT)   The design for the elaborate
canopied monument, planned by Elizabeth I
for Edward VI, who had died in 1553, is
attributed to Cornelius Cure (c. 1573?) but was
never realized.

part in heresy trials for senior Protestant clergy like Archbishop Cranmer, who were
not let off as lightly as Cox.[58] Inevitably, accompanying Weston's arrival was a purge
of unreliable elements among the cathedral staff. A simple rule of thumb right across
the kingdom deprived (that is, removed from office) all married clergy, a process
carried out in March 1554. Cox had already gone, but among those now dismissed
was the former senior monk Humphrey Perkins, who is likely to have been one of
those steering the abbey on Reformist paths before the dissolution; he had taken the
distinctive and unusual surname in religion of 'Charity', rather than the place name
that was the general Benedictine custom. Along with him departed eight others among
the twelve canons, together with two minor canons.[59]

   Weston's duty was to preside over a new and opposite phase of the abbey's demonstration of official religion to the nation, restoring old splendour. That involved massive
financial outlay, since Catholic worship is a good deal more expensive than Protestant.
In came new vestments, plate and liturgical books, and restored statues, including the
great rood and its attendant figures of the Virgin Mary and St John the Evangelist above

78 Dean Hugh Weston (d. 1558; far right) is one of the leading Catholic clerics depicted with wolves' heads, who drink blood spurting from Christ the Lamb hanging in the centre, in this satirical print from the Protestant exile presses in Emden, Germany, *c.*1555; Protestant sheep – Cranmer, Ridley and others – lie at their feet.

the principal screen: altogether a loving attention to detail, right down to the purchase of box and yew branches for the Palm Sunday procession of 1554, and flowers for the choirboys who sang the solemn *Gloria Laus* that morning.[60] All this cost more than £300 in one year, the equivalent of the annual income of a particularly prosperous gentleman, and it was achieved partly by cutting back on annual expenditure on such charitable obligations of the cathedral as almsgiving to the poor and road-mending.[61] In addition, the queen was generous in giving vestments, as well as jewels to beautify the proposed new shrine of St Edward and its altar.[62]

The kingdom was now deeply divided on religious lines, the divisions accentuated by xenophobia; Mary's insistence on marrying her Habsburg cousin, Philip II of Spain, alarmed politicians and generally stirred fears of England being absorbed into the already vast agglomeration of Habsburg territories. At Westminster, the new dispensation provoked some violent protests, since most of King Philip's courtiers and friars brought from Spain were lodged around the court and abbey; one Spanish priest, Alfonso de Salinas, who had served the queen's mother, was actually appointed a canon. Among various confrontations was a full-scale fight in the cathedral cloister between some servants of Dean Weston and a group of festively inclined Spaniards, who had imported some female companions into the precinct. Spanish pistols were fired and a resident Spanish friar sounded an alarm on one of the cathedral bells; disturbances spilled on to Westminster's streets before being curbed by the authorities – a deep embarrassment to fragile official relationships around the court.[63] The clash reflected tensions made worse in Westminster by an even more serious incident at Easter 1555. The perpetrator was William Flower, a former monk of Ely, who stabbed John Cheltenham, a cathedral minor canon and former Dominican friar, while he was distributing Easter Communion in St Margaret's. Flower received exemplary punishment, even though he was said to be mentally disturbed: on the urging of the prominent Spanish Dominican Bartolomé Carranza, then lodging in the precinct, he was tried for heresy and burned in St Margaret's churchyard, after his offending hand had been chopped off.[64]

A Revived Monastery

Now came a new departure, reversing the great change of 1540 in order to restore a Benedictine monastic community. The initiative came from the diocese of London's other cathedral, St Paul's, whose newly appointed dean was John Howman (in religion, Feckenham), a former senior monk of Evesham. He used his newly acquired wealth as dean to gather other Benedictines in resuming their former monastic life; in early March 1555, they appeared before the queen, dressed in their monastic habits. Queen

Mary was no doubt genuinely moved, though it is likely that the ground was well prepared for her show of happy tears at this ostentatious public challenge to her father's policy. She appointed a team of senior politicians, one of whom (Sir William Petre) had been much involved in King Henry's Dissolution process, to decide on a suitable home for the fledgling community.[65] Where could be better than the superfluous cathedral at Westminster?

There needed to be compensation for the resentful Dean and Chapter, none of whom – rather remarkably – had ever been a monk (ironically, Mary had already deprived all former religious in the chapter). It took till September 1556 to work out a final solution. The evangelical John Bradford, burned at the stake in June 1555, told friends during his imprisonment that Dean Weston had been assigned to visit him and persuade him out of his heresy; Weston excused a significant hiatus in their encounters because he had been holding out against 'certain monks, which would have come again into Westminster' – that was in April, only a week or two after their appearance before the queen.[66] Weston was eventually consoled with the deanery of another royal collegiate church, St George's, Windsor, though he had less than a year to enjoy it before being deprived on charges of fornication (which, it ought to be said, he denied). Feckenham became abbot at Westminster.

This new Westminster Abbey would once more stand as a flagship, this time for a revived English religious life, for which the queen was providing a variety of exemplars, besides the Westminster Benedictines: Dominican and Observant Franciscan friars, and aristocratic Bridgettine nuns in their old house at Syon.[67] Among these various projects, Westminster was particularly advanced by Mary's new Archbishop of Canterbury, the papal legate Reginald Pole; he saw this as the first in a series of Benedictine foundations. Thanks to the papal bull of June 1555, *Praeclara*, recognizing all the new cathedrals created by Henry VIII, Westminster had to be a new foundation, not a restoration of the ancient abbey; indeed, of the sixteen brothers in the initial community, only two had been monks of Westminster. That would not have worried Pole. His vision of a renewed Catholic Church was formed in his two decades of exile in Italy, and his enthusiasm was for a reformed variety of Benedictine observance: although it was a creation of early fifteenth-century austerity in an abbey of Padua, it programmatically took its name from the wellspring of Benedictine monasticism, Monte Cassino, as the 'Cassinese Congregation'. This chimes interestingly with the reformist mood in the last decades of the old Westminster Abbey, and it is significant that Feckenham was a veteran of another among that old elite of reforming abbeys, Evesham. The continuity was not institutional, but of the spirit: the Benson of the 1530s might well have approved.

There are interesting glimpses of this new ethos at the Marian abbey in the admittedly dim reminiscences of the very last monk to survive from it – indeed, the last monk of all English monasticism alive in Protestant England: Robert (in religion, Sigebert) Buckley. He was a very old man when, at the end of the century, one of the most distinguished in a new wave of post-Reformation Benedictines in exile, Fr Augustine Baker, eagerly sought him out for reminiscences of Marian Westminster. Baker was rather disappointed by the banality of the replies. Buckley's significant memories were about the menu at meals, which was solidly based in the normal Tudor diet of meat: Baker tartly commented 'it seemed a fare somewhat heavy for digestion to them that rise at midnight'. Moreover, Buckley recalled that in the refectory the monks had 'satt face to face on both sides the table, being fowre to every messe as they do in the Innes of Court' – each 'mess' of four sharing their servings. Baker's summary of his various enquiries on the long-lost community was that Feckenham 'had not insisted much upon monastick regularities, . . . but contented himself to have sett up there a disciplin much like to that which he saw observed in cathedral churches, as for the Divine Office; and for other things, he brought them to the laws and customs of colledges and Inns of Court'. After all, Feckenham's founding community were all in late middle age, and a majority of them had spent much time in the former Oxbridge monastic colleges.[68]

This way of life ironically reflected Wolsey's and Cromwell's proposals for reshaping England's greater monasteries. The same lay receiver who had served the Dean and Chapter since 1545, John Moulton, went on doing good service to the new corporation, just as he would to its successor church under Elizabeth. Abbot Feckenham was not averse to the splendour of his medieval monastic predecessors, but it was probably out of concern for the dignity of his house that he retrieved the former abbot's lodging from its long lease to the Protestant peer Thomas, Lord Wentworth (agreed after the see of Westminster was dissolved in 1550, making the bishop's house redundant). He sealed the deal by granting Wentworth the east London manor of Canonbury. His act of rescue remains one of the permanent legacies of the new abbey to the present foundation.[69]

In its brief existence, the new abbey underlined its place in royal ceremony with the restoration of its shrine of Edward the Confessor, two funerals and a coronation. The restored shrine was completed in spring 1557, though Queen Mary's gift of jewels in 1555 suggests that this was a project inherited from Dean Weston. King Edward's body had to be restored to its old location from the discreet reburial afforded most saintly corpses affected by Henry VIII's destruction of pilgrimage sites. Much remained of the old structure, both its medieval base and probably the present wooden canopy, which may be a product of reconstruction under Abbot Islip; although most of its Marian magnificence was censored away, no doubt, in Elizabeth's time, it remains a rare example of a saint's shrine substantially standing in Protestant England. Few shrines

79   The tomb of Anne of Cleves (1515–57), shown in a watercolour by John
Chessel Buckler, 1829, is attributed to Theodore Haveus of Cleves, 1606. Queen
Mary insisted on full Catholic rites for the funeral of her father's fourth wife; the
restrained stone and marble tomb, which may have been intended as the base of
a larger monument, stands in a place of honour in the sanctuary.

were restored in Marian England; this one was a nudge to the rest of the kingdom to
embrace this major aspect of traditional religion.[70]

The first royal funeral, on 4 August 1557, was a curious link to those charged months
of 1540 that brought Cromwell's downfall as well as the abbey's transformation, for the
deceased was Anne of Cleves, Henry VIII's last surviving wife, the only one of six to
be buried at Westminster. For nearly two decades, she had lived in England on estates
gratefully granted her by her unwilling husband, enjoying not being married to King
Henry or anyone else. The Protestant Reformation was congenial to her, but she was
friendly with her near-stepdaughter Mary; her tomb is, appropriately, reticent.[71] The
second funeral, on 14 December 1558, was effectively a death announcement for the
abbey as well, for it was Queen Mary's own. With her half-sister, Elizabeth, marked
indelibly as a Protestant despite her tepid outward conformity to the Marian Church,
everyone knew that England's developing experiment in Counter-Reformation was at
an end. The only thing that could have saved it was an heir of Mary's body to succeed

79

her and King Philip. Dean Weston had been one of those working hard on prayer for
a successful outcome to Mary's supposed pregnancy in 1554 and 1555, recruiting the
boys of the school to help him 'morning and evening' in the second of his specially
composed prayers in elegant Latin; both were put into print.[72]

It was Mary's tragedy that nothing followed her hopes except terminal illness. The late
queen's will remembered her burial church with characteristic generosity, leaving £200
or the equivalent in church treasures.[73] As if in confirmation of Catholic England's end,
ten days later the monks held a Requiem for her late cousin, father-in-law and lifelong
supporter, the former Holy Roman Emperor Charles V, who had died in retirement
some three months earlier.[74] Inevitably they would already have been preparing for
the transition to national celebration, the required mood for the coronation of Mary's
half-sister, Elizabeth, in the abbey on 15 January 1559. This was always going to be an
uncomfortable affair; so many eyes were scanning it for possible meanings that the
considerable number of reports disagree on details of what happened.[75]

The new queen was constrained by the existing law, so no vernacular liturgy
was currently legal, apart from the English litany of Henry VIII and the traditional
intercessions in English called 'the bidding of the bedes'. For her crowning, she needed
one of the bishops in current post, and the only one willing was Owen Oglethorpe
of Carlisle, though he had already clashed with her about her private modification of
the Catholic liturgy in her Chapel Royal. She spared Catholic and indeed Protestant
blushes by receiving Communion 'in both kinds' (bread and wine) within a curtained
enclosure. The Latin Mass framing the ceremony was celebrated by her newly appointed
Dean of the Chapel Royal and former chaplain, George Carew, like herself a closet
Protestant, or, in the sneering contemporary phrase, a 'Nicodemite'. Elizabeth was to
surround herself and seek to fill the most prominent clerical posts of her Protestant
Church with such Nicodemites. Catholics later circulated the story that she offered
Abbot Feckenham the vacant see of Canterbury around this time. In view of the
forensically Protestant character of the settlement she and her advisers imposed on the
Church in 1559, this is unlikely, but it does resonate both with the curious reminiscences
in Feckenham's abbey of reformist monasticism in the 1530s, and with the fact that
virtually no one, Protestant or Catholic, had a bad word to say for this thoughtful,
generous and scholarly man. He defended the Church of Rome through all triumphs
and adversities up to his death in prison in 1584.[76]

Elizabeth gave ample proof of her real intentions at the customary Mass for the
opening of parliament, only ten days after the coronation. In a famous incident, she
waved away the procession of monks bearing candles to receive her with the words
'Away with these torches, for we see very well.' Even more pointedly, the preacher
was the deposed Dean Cox, soon to be Bishop of Ely, who did not mince his words

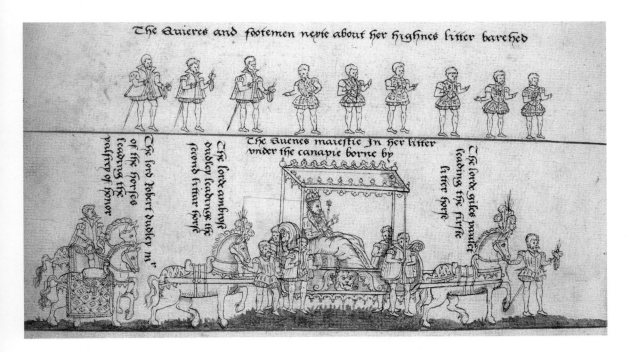

80   On the day before her coronation in January 1559, Queen Elizabeth travelled in triumphal procession from her ceremonial apartments at the Tower through the City of London to Westminster (an occasion recorded in pen and ink drawings in this manuscript from the College of Arms). Later that year, she dissolved the monastery, and in 1560, by royal charter, established the abbey in its present form as a collegiate church.

about his reluctant hosts at the abbey or the deaths of Protestant martyrs under Queen Mary. His hour-and-a-half-long diatribe must have made up considerably for his earlier ejection and years of exile abroad.[77] Soon after, while parliament was in recess for Easter, the abbey played its part in a vital stage in the official move to Protestantism: a theological debate between leading Catholic and Protestant clergy was staged in the choir before a large and influential audience. It gave an excuse for arresting the two Catholic bishops who spoke, now accused of sedition simply for what they naturally argued in the debate. Their imprisonment conveniently prevented them henceforth from voting in the House of Lords; by this means, Elizabeth's parliamentary settlement of religion just squeezed through in the Upper House.[78] Inevitably, the abbey's dissolution followed, achieved not by surrender but parliamentary statute.[79] Most of the ejected monks remained staunch in their Catholicism, though at least one (more likely two) did become a minor canon in the new Westminster foundation that followed.[80]

A Collegiate Future

This might have been an anxious moment for the church of Westminster's future, but in fact was not. By her charter of 1560, Queen Elizabeth re-founded a collegiate church retaining endowments, jurisdictions and all (with a convenient vagueness in some aspects, such as the continuing role of sanctuary). It was a royal peculiar, and so remains: separate from the Archbishop of Canterbury's jurisdiction, having no bishop, and under the monarch's direct control. This had not merely local significance. Elizabeth was as conservative a Protestant as one could be while still being a Protestant: her religious formation had been as a teenager, amid the splendid choral and ceremonial tradition of her father's court in its last years, and under the pious influence of her kindly evangelical stepmother, Katherine Parr. She had never been in total sympathy with her half-brother's rapid moves towards Reformed Protestantism. Although a symbol of Reformation through her very birth to Anne Boleyn, she did not have much room for manoeuvre in her re-established Church of England; yet in her own Chapel Royal and allied dynastic enclaves, she could give full rein to her love of church music and fend off the austerity of Edwardians like Bishop Cox.

A restored choral foundation at Westminster would fit this agenda, and all the signs are that restoration was agreed early on. A sure indication was the amount of trouble devoted to repairing what was now to be called 'the Dean's House' – that is, the abbot's lodging, over whose recovery Abbot Feckenham took such trouble. (Lord Wentworth was in no position to try to retrieve it, being currently in disgrace for having been lord deputy of Calais when the town was lost to the French.)[81] Feckenham was characteristically helpful to his supplanters in making the transition. Elizabeth's choice to replace him was not the former dean, Richard Cox. For all his forthright defence of Cranmer's second Prayer Book against more radical spirits among the exiles in Mary's reign, on his return Cox was pugnacious in two causes that both annoyed Queen Elizabeth: defending clerical marriage, and protesting against the crucifix and candles she displayed in her private chapel. Instead she chose William Bill, a senior Cambridge academic for whom she had already shown her esteem by appointing him royal almoner, among other promotions. Bill was yet another 'Nicodemite' Protestant, who had sat out Mary's reign as a parish priest in Bedfordshire. He achieved one lasting result, in drafting statutes for his new church and its school, which are still the basis of its constitution, but he died on 15 July 1561 after little more than a year in office, and the queen must think again. She chose Gabriel Goodman, a man of the same stamp, rector of a parish in Rutland in Queen Mary's last year.[82] Significantly, both Bill and Goodman were unmarried, unlike Cox; the queen felt uncomfortable with married clergy.

81   William Cecil, Lord Burghley (1520–98) – shown here in an anonymous
portrait (after 1587), wearing the robes of a knight of the Garter and
holding the staff of office of the lord treasurer – dominated Westminster in
Elizabeth's reign even more than he dominated English government; he was
a benevolent supporter of the new collegiate foundation.

Goodman's appointment was as crucial for the future of Westminster as William
Benson's in 1533, but needs to be read alongside another career at the centre of
Elizabeth's regime, which was now central to both abbey and city. William Cecil,   81
a Cambridge-educated civil servant under Edward VI, was her lifelong friend and
for four decades principal minister, from 1571 1st Lord Burghley.[83] He had lived in
Westminster since King Edward's reign, moving into one of the houses previously

occupied by the canons of St Stephen's, like a number of influential Edwardian politicians, including his first major patrons, the Seymour family. Although Cecil later moved to a much grander mansion on the Strand, his interest in Westminster endured, and it was based on the peculiar government (or lack of it) of the new city, dependent on the continuing power of the Dean and Chapter, who did not allow the setting up of any corporation to resemble the formidable body that ran the City of London. The only major opportunity of office Westminster offered a layman was the high stewardship, a recent creation evolved from the abbey stewardship last held by Thomas Cromwell. In theory this was an appointment of the Dean and Chapter, but in practice it was given to a courtier chosen by the crown.

Cecil, now principal secretary to the queen, became high steward in 1561, and was succeeded on his death in 1598 by his son Robert, a statesman of equal national significance. William's connection to the abbey was signalled in 1560, when Dean Bill made him one of the supervisors of his will. Cecil influence thereafter became all-pervasive, including the choice of the city's two MPs, who in any case would customarily be prominent government men living in Westminster. Cecil was deeply interested in the good government of his little fiefdom, whose social problems were mushrooming as its population swelled; it was very necessary to minimize trouble in this home of monarch and parliament. He did not strive officiously to back the townsmen's vigorous efforts to gain proper self-government in a royal charter, as so many aspirant Elizabethan urban communities were doing. The most that he and the Dean and Chapter allowed to pass into law from legislation proposed in the Commons in 1585 was a Court of Burgesses for administering justice – really little more than a glorified manorial court, with no mayor or corporation.[84] His emotional investment in the church was considerable. His own death and the deaths of Mildred, Lady Burghley, and their beloved daughter Anne, Countess of Oxford, all produced exceptionally grand funerals in the abbey, and the joint monument to the two ladies is the second tallest in the church (the tomb of Queen Elizabeth's cousin Lord Hunsdon just tops it).[85]

In Mary's reign, Cecil had been the arch-Nicodemite Protestant in the realm after Princess Elizabeth, sheltering a clandestine Protestant press on his Midland estates but outwardly conforming to official Catholicism and taking a modest part in government.[86] Goodman had been schoolmaster in his household and remained his chaplain; their shared memories of some very tricky times were the basis for Cecil's lifelong support for Goodman, which had the most benevolent consequences for his church. Goodman proved a good deal more conservative in his Protestantism than his patron, though Cecil did move in the same direction in his last years.[87] The dean's Welsh background (he came from Ruthin) inspired him with enthusiasm for promoting the ultimately successful Elizabethan project for publishing a Bible in Welsh, but his religious outlook

82   The lower part of the magnificent monument to the formidably learned Mildred Cecil, Lady
Burghley (1526–89), and her daughter Anne, Countess of Oxford (1556–88), two of the many noble
women memorialized during the Elizabethan period, is located in the St Nicholas Chapel. The
effigies, attributed to Cornelius Cure, are set in an elaborate structure some 24 feet high, inscribed
with a lengthy text by Lord Burghley recording the family's grief.

D. O. M.

GABRIEL GOODMAN SACRÆ THEOLOGIÆ
DOCTOR, DECANVS HVIVS ECCLESIÆ
QVINTVS, CVI CVM SVMMA LAVDE XL AÑOS
PRÆFVISSET, ET RVTHINIÆ IN COMITATV
DENBIGHÆNSI VBI NATVS HOSPITALE FVN-
DASSET, SCHOLAQ INSTITVISSET, VITÆ SANC
TIMONIA DEO BONISQ CHARVS IN COELESTÈ
PATRIAM PIE EMIGRAVIT XVII IVNII ANNO
SALVTIS. M D C I. ÆT: SVÆ LXXIII.

was more like that of the monarch; they were lonely, almost Lutheran, figures in a Protestant Church now looking to Zürich and Geneva for its inspiration. They valued ceremony and seemly liturgical furnishing far more than did most leading figures in the Elizabethan settlement.[88] Goodman was considered the sort of Protestant who might persuade or charm more thoughtful Roman Catholics into conformity with the new settlement: Abbot Feckenham was one of those entrusted to him; another was the East Anglian Catholic magnate Sir Thomas Cornwallis. Equally, those of Puritan inclination might find him too much to stomach – and that meant most of Elizabeth's enthusiastic Protestant subjects.

It is a mark of just how unusual Goodman was among leading clergy of the Elizabethan settlement that the abbey kept a large store of vestments, rich cloth canopies and altar frontals passed on from Abbot Feckenham. Many survived into the seventeenth century, when the choir still displayed a splendid set of tapestries given by the thirteenth-century abbot Richard of Barking, with narratives of the lives of Christ and Edward the Confessor. Consequently, although Goodman had powerful friends in both Cecil and that further Nicodemite Protestant Matthew

83   Gabriel Goodman, Dean of Westminster from 1561 to 1601, is buried in St Benedict's Chapel – appropriately for such an important player in the abbey's story. A Welshman, his merchant father had adopted an English surname; the dean was generous to his native Ruthin as well as to the abbey.

Parker (Elizabeth's first Archbishop of Canterbury), none of a number of proposals to promote him to a bishopric came to anything. He simply would not have been acceptable in the average diocese, and those few like-minded senior clergy who did become bishops, such as Richard Cheney at Gloucester or Edmund Freke at Norwich, had unenviable experiences.[89] So Goodman was stuck at Westminster for what turned out to be an extremely long incumbency as dean, right up to 1601. Quite apart from the duration, his constant residence made him very different from either Richard Cox or William Bill, much of whose attention was elsewhere (Bill was at his death also master of Trinity College, Cambridge, and provost of Eton). Moreover, among the job lot of Protestant canons Goodman inherited or saw appointed during his years in office, most of the ambitious or energetic were conveniently distracted from taking much interest in the abbey by other ecclesiastical preoccupations. The most potentially troublesome was the fiery Puritan Percival Wiburn, who managed to outlive Goodman in his canonry and regularly attended chapter meetings, but whose strenuous godliness was mostly devoted to Reformation elsewhere, in the Channel Islands, Northamptonshire and Rochester.[90] Other high flyers would rarely be seen gathered in chapter at Westminster, unless there were matters of estate management to settle. Furthermore, Goodman was extremely restrictive in whom he allowed to preach in the abbey; Puritans were not welcome.

That left a conveniently open field for those in actual long-term residence, from the dean downwards, who were, in their different ways, really interested in their church, indeed probably loved it. Goodman's long tenure left them undisturbed by any of the new generation of English Protestant senior clergy who might have changed things considerably. There were some extraordinary stories of longevity and continuity. We have already encountered Humphrey Perkins, who was at Westminster from his days as a monk, to restoration under Elizabeth and up to his death in 1577, a veteran of the early English Reformation; and John Moulton's record in administration from the days of Abbot Benson till 1563 is hardly less remarkable. The especial continuity on the musical side represents one of the great legacies of Goodman's Westminster to the Anglican future. The most impressive example is Christopher Bricket or Birkhed, who started as a chorister in the monastic Lady Chapel choir and was then a scholar on the post-1540 foundation, before re-joining the choir in 1549 and singing on till he died aged 77 in 1596; he was buried in the cloister, where his monument made a point of recording that he died on Ascension day.[91] There is more than chronological continuity in the career of William Mundy, head chorister in 1543. He blossomed into a composer of talent, both in the Latin that would have been legal in the liturgy at the beginning of his career and in the English of the Elizabethan Reformation. Alexander Peryn was one of a number who transferred from the distinguished musical   84

84   One of the great
legacies of Dean Goodman's
tenure was the management
of the abbey's music by
experienced musicians such
as Alexander Peryn; Peryn's
name, and four staves of
chant, are handwritten on
the last page of a printed
edition of the Sarum
Processional (1545), a
liturgical book from which
the choir would have
sung during processions in
the short-lived cathedral
foundation or the briefly
restored abbey.

foundation of St Stephen's on its closure in 1548; although under Mary he was expelled
from Westminster office, probably for having married, he promptly returned in 1559,
overseeing the transfer of the organ in the Henry VII chapel to the choir, and managing
the abbey's music till his death in 1569.[92]

From Abbot Feckenham's choir of laymen and boys, ten continued to serve the
new collegiate foundation, and, in what seems a gracious gesture towards the new
institution that was about to supplant his monastery, Feckenham appointed another
singing–man as late as March 1559.[93] Another new arrival, just as the college was
being set up, was John Taylor, master of the choristers, who was poached by Salisbury
cathedral in 1569 and replaced by Robert White, the first senior music official to have
a university degree in music. White was married to the daughter of the Ely cathedral
musician Christopher Tye, who like him composed in both English and Latin. Some
of White's Latin compositions may have been written for Mary's Church; since it is
unlikely that even Queen Elizabeth's Chapel Royal choir got away with singing in

Latin, it could not have happened in Elizabethan Westminster. White did achieve a coup for his church in arranging for the transfer to the abbey of the organ his grandfather had given to the London church of St Andrew, Holborn, its loss much upsetting some of the parishioners there.[94] This was at a time when, in many parts of the realm, pipe organs were being dismantled in parish churches, and singing was increasingly confined to metrical psalms in the developing Reformed tradition. Westminster's tradition was radically diverging from the new norm in nearly all the thousands of English places of worship.

A 'Westminster Movement'?

Goodman, therefore, fostered a ceremonial and ritually splendid version of Reformation Protestantism at Westminster, whose nearest rival in Elizabethan England was the queen's own Chapel Royal. His successor in 1601 was one of his former canons, Lancelot Andrewes, who in changed times, was the standard-bearer of the same outlook on a broader national canvas. Their collegiate church behaved more like a cathedral than most English cathedrals at the time. Not only that: it encouraged the parish church of St Margaret in its shadow to behave in a most untypical way, even in comparison with St Martin-in-the-Fields down the road. St Margaret's enjoyed its own rich choral tradition before the Reformation (the prolific composer Nicholas Ludford, long on the staff of St Stephen's Chapel, was an active parishioner up to his death in 1557), and this continued in Goodman's time, with abbey singers enriching its worship at festivals; the church even bought one of the abbey's organs second-hand in the 1590s.[95]

All this is so *sui generis* – as distinctive as the High Churchmanship of the Oxford Movement three centuries on – that it might be called the 'Westminster Movement'. In the period before 1600, this coinage would make more sense than using anachronistic labels like 'Arminian' or 'Laudian', which draw their meanings from the early seventeenth century. Westminster set patterns for a future aspect of the Church of England that was an unexpected, even paradoxical, direction for a Church set on an unmistakably Reformed Protestant path under Edward VI and even, perforce, Queen Elizabeth herself. One senses the queen behind Goodman, nerving him to think the liturgically unthinkable, while never considering it wise to let him loose on the wider Church of England as one of its bishops. It was not only Goodman who found a successor in office to carry the torch of ceremonialism. William Cecil had once been a major player in the Edwardian Reformation that destroyed so much of beauty in the abbey. His son Robert became an enthusiastic supporter of ceremonialist worship and of the clergy who valued it, and the private chapel that Robert built at Hatfield House at

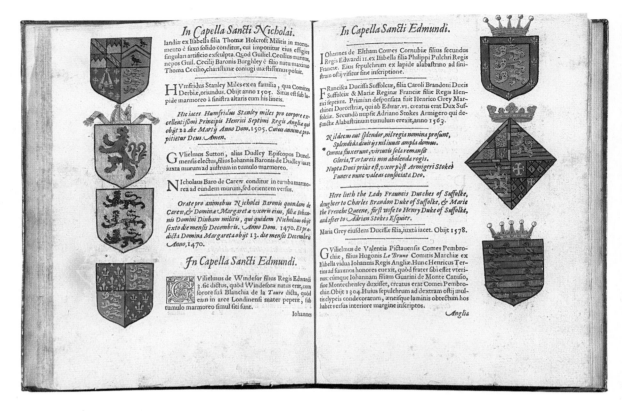

85   An opening from William Camden's pioneering guidebook to the abbey's monuments, *Reges, reginae, nobiles* […] *Westmonasterij sepulti* (1600), showing the monuments to be found in the chapels of St Nicholas and St Edmund.

the beginning of James I's reign boasted a startlingly novel assemblage of pictures and stained glass, to emphasize that God should be worshipped in the beauty of holiness. It was the message already sedulously cultivated in the abbey.[96]

Equally significant was the school that Elizabeth nominally re-founded, and in which she took a particular personal interest; she visited the abbey only for state openings of parliament, but she frequently enjoyed watching plays put on by the Westminster boys.[97] Westminster School was one of the big three, alongside Eton and Winchester Colleges, and like them boasted direct links through scholarships to Oxbridge – in this case, Henry VIII's foundations of Trinity, Cambridge, and Christ Church, Oxford. It is worth noting just how many of the senior clergy of the Church of England over the next two or three centuries were Westminster schoolboys, educated in the devotional and liturgical atmosphere that Dean Goodman first fostered; by the seventeenth century, they far outnumbered the products of Eton and Winchester as leaders in the Church.[98] One of the earliest examples was a boy who actually grew up in Westminster in the parish of St Margaret, and who received much patronage from the Cecils: Richard Neile, who returned as Dean of Westminster from 1605. He was later Archbishop of York, and in his turn patron of another archbishop who shaped the complex identity of 'Anglicanism', William Laud.

A long-term agent in creating the 'Westminster Movement' was a younger protégé of William Cecil, the great historian William Camden, who was on the school staff from 1575 for twenty-two years, latterly as head master; he was also librarian for the Dean and Chapter. Camden had a deep sense of a national past and deplored the Reformation destruction of beauty. Predictably, he loathed Puritans – for instance, sneering in his *Remains*, a discursive analysis of English culture, at Puritans' 'singular and precise conceit' in giving newly invented, pious names to their children. His views may have inspired the memorable stereotypes of Puritans in the plays of one of his most distinguished students in the school, Ben Jonson.[99] But in another major respect, Camden was in the right place at the right time. In 1600 he published a marvellously comprehensive guidebook to the funerary monuments of the abbey,   85 from earliest Catholic times right up to the present day, nearly eighty pages long; the very last entry in his tour was an inscription in the cloister for the precentor who had died three years before.[100]

Camden's book witnessed that the abbey's royal tombs were only the prime exhibits amid an astonishing array of monuments old and new, all the more appreciated in the late Tudor age because so many others had recently disappeared in the general wreck of the monasteries. The many side-chapels, which Protestant worship made redundant, now proved hugely useful in sheltering tombs and inscriptions of all sizes (and, in fact, their old saints' dedications were a handy way of locating them for visitors, as Camden's guidebook demonstrated). The abbey verger was put in charge of the tombs in 1561, and there was a regular fee for tours, or a simple penny admission to the premises for browsing, a move that marked an early start to the great debate on admission charges for churches.[101] One peculiar speciality of the Elizabethan foundation was the erection of monuments to noble ladies, of whom the Cecils were only one example; it has been plausibly argued that in the first place this arose because the dissolution had disrupted various arrangements for burial with pre-deceased husbands in other monastic or friary churches.[102] The whole array at Westminster was coming to be seen as a record of national history; it was a significant moment when, in the era of the Marian abbey, an exchequer official put up a new monument in the south transept for Geoffrey Chaucer, duly celebrated by Camden.[103] The addition of Edmund Spenser's   86 grave nearby, in 1599, made the area the nucleus of Poets' Corner.

86   In 1556 a simple epitaph brass for the poet Geoffrey Chaucer near St Benedict's Chapel was replaced by a new marble altar tomb with canopy, in which his remains were reburied more than 150 years after his death; the tomb is in the eastern aisle of the south transept, now known as 'Poets' Corner', and began the association of this part of the church with poets and dramatists.

Attempted theft might be considered a sincere form of flattery. In May 1602 Dean Andrewes and the chapter collectively wrote to their patron and protector Robert Cecil complaining that one of the choirmen of Queen Elizabeth's Chapel Royal wanted to be granted a place in Westminster, which would of course really become a sinecure while he did service for the queen's music; influential courtiers had written to them backing up his impudent attempt. It would only encourage Westminster choirmen, they said, to desert to the Chapel Royal, while keeping a nominal place back in the abbey. They reminded Cecil that his father had always seen off such attempts, mindful that the 'Queere' of Westminster should be kept up to strength, for all the reasons by now familiar: it was, more than any other church, 'in the eye of all comers to this great place of the land', near to the law courts and parliament, and visited for 'the beautiful monuments of her Majesty's progenitors'. Such visitors must not be disappointed in the music.[104]

One can understand the Dean and Chapter's annoyance, but the situation was actually a back-handed, if striking, compliment to the vision and achievement of Dean Goodman in creating a new standard-bearer of choral and ceremonial excellence. Almost as remarkable was the fact that one of the signatories to this ringing defence of all that the college of Westminster stood for was that grizzled old Puritan among the canons, Percival Wiburn. The Tudor age saw Westminster Abbey triumphantly overcome the greatest threat in its history, in good heart to bid its own ceremonial greeting to a new dynasty. Of three great royal monastic foundations from the last years of Anglo-Saxon England, Wilton, Waltham and Westminster, two vanished in the Dissolution of the Monasteries. This fate could easily have overtaken Westminster. Its survival is extraordinary, as is the influence the new foundation exercised over the long-term formation of Anglicanism.

5

Monarchy, Protestantism and Revolution:
1603–1714

JULIA F. MERRITT

T HE DEATH OF QUEEN ELIZABETH IN 1603 marked the end of an era that had ultimately brought stability to the English Church and state. It also marked the end of the Tudor dynasty, which had so dramatically shaped the character of the late medieval abbey, its dissolution and the subsequent creation of the collegiate church of Westminster. Thousands of people gathered to see the old queen's funeral procession to the abbey on 28 April 1603, when there was 'such a generall sighing, gro[a]ning and weeping as the like hath not been seene or knowne in the memory of man'. The coffin, covered in purple velvet, was borne on a chariot drawn by four richly caparisoned horses, while a painted effigy of the queen, crowned, and in her parliament robes, lay on top of the coffin. The funeral was a lavish affair, though not attended by the new king, James VI of Scotland, first of a Stuart line of English monarchs, who arranged tactfully to arrive in London after the ceremony was over.[1]

The Tudors had come to the throne in the wake of the Wars of the Roses, but the first Stuart King of England succeeded without bloodshed as an unequivocally Protestant monarch, thus ensuring religious continuity. However, the following century was to see royal authority challenged as never before, leading to the execution of one king and the ousting of another, along with the abolition and Restoration of the monarchy. Every Stuart monarch faced the challenge of asserting the legitimacy of their rule and demonstrating their authority over Church and state, and in this struggle Westminster Abbey had a vital part to play. The abbey would itself endure a century of religious turbulence that included the temporary abolition of cathedrals and

87 (FACING PAGE)   The remains of Mary Queen of Scots were interred in 1612 in a spectacular tomb by William and Cornelius Cure in the south aisle of Henry VII's chapel; by locating her tomb opposite that of Elizabeth I in the north aisle, the Stuart king, James I, pointedly asserted his mother's equality with the last Tudor monarch.

the established Church, and it would serve, perhaps incongruously, as the ceremonial centre of a parliamentarian, and then a republican, regime. This was nevertheless the century in which the abbey could legitimately claim to be the undisputed church of the nation as never before.

A New Dynasty – and a New Role?

England's new monarch in 1603 was already ruler over an independent Scotland as James VI. At the news of Elizabeth's death he now travelled down from Edinburgh to take his place as James I of England (r. 1603–25). James's succession to the throne had been far from assured, as the old queen had always refused to name an heir, but secret correspondence with members of Elizabeth's council as well as leading English Catholics, such as the Earl of Northampton, helped to smooth his way.[2] It soon became clear that James had an especial interest in the abbey, and felt that, as the ceremonial heart of the English monarchy, it had an important and distinctive part to play in manifesting the dynastic legitimacy of the Stuarts, and the sanctity of the monarch. His accession marked the beginning of a new and more systematic use of the abbey by the executive power for ceremonial and political purposes – a trend that would persist in different ways for the rest of the century.

James's sense of the importance of Westminster Abbey as a vehicle for establishing the Stuarts' dynastic legitimacy was perhaps most strikingly illustrated in his decision to rebury his mother, the Catholic Mary Queen of Scots, there. This was no mere act of filial piety on James's part, but reflected his determination to establish the dynastic credentials of the new Stuart monarchy, and to do so in the most important royal space in his English kingdom. Initially, a 1603 proclamation asserting James's rightful claim to the throne had emphasized only his Tudor descent, describing him as 'lineally and lawfully descended' from Margaret Tudor, daughter of Henry VII, the founder of the Tudor dynasty. No mention was made of Mary, but James remedied this omission within a month of his coronation, by having a pall decorated with the royal arms placed ceremoniously upon the grave of the executed queen in Peterborough cathedral, accompanied by a sermon delivered by the dean. This was soon followed by a far bolder plan to emphasize the link between the Tudor and Stuart dynasties; in early 1605, news circulated of the commission to erect tombs for both Elizabeth and Mary in Westminster Abbey.[3]

The scheme involved moving Elizabeth's body from its location in Henry VII's grave, so that the two queens faced each other in splendid monuments located in opposite aisles of Henry VII's chapel. Mary's body was not only re-interred in the abbey, it was

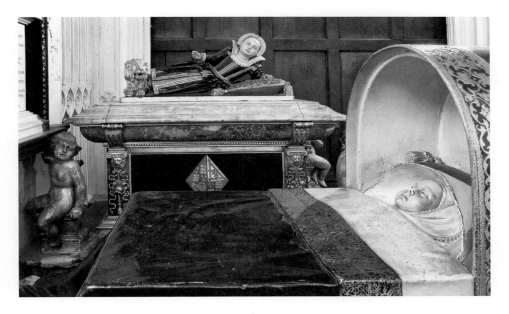

88   The tombs of the Princesses Sophia (d. 1606, aged 3 days) and Mary (d. 1607, aged 2 years), beloved daughters of James I and Anne of Denmark, in the north aisle of Henry VII's chapel; the portrayal of the baby Sophia lying in her cot was an innovation in tomb design that was imitated throughout Stuart England.

also strategically placed next to an earlier monument to Margaret Douglas, Countess of Lennox, mother of Lord Darnley, the king's father.[4] Here, situated prominently within the English 'house of kings', was an extraordinary assertion of the Stuart dynasty, and of the right of dynastic succession regardless of the religion of the monarch. The Scottish queen who had been executed for plotting the assassination of Elizabeth and the reintroduction of Catholicism into England was now memorialized – almost apotheosized – in the abbey in a position of equality with the last reigning member of the Tudor dynasty. Her monument bore verses that celebrated her and her lineage, and condemned those involved in the 'violent murder' of an anointed queen. This was also a message that complemented the more positive treatment of Mary in the *Annales* penned by William Camden, the celebrated antiquary, herald and former librarian to the Dean and Chapter, and head master of Westminster School.[5]

In fact, a Stuart presence in the abbey had already been secured well before the reburial of Mary Queen of Scots, owing to the deaths in quick succession of the infant daughters of James and Anne of Denmark: the Princesses Sophia (June 1606) and Mary (September 1607). Both had tombs erected for them by their grief-stricken parents.   88

It is also in James's reign that we first have clear evidence of the public display of royal effigies, including those of Elizabeth I and, later, Prince Henry and King James himself. Equally important, though, was the refurbishment of images commemorating earlier English monarchs. In preparation for the visit in 1606 of Christian IV of Denmark (James's brother-in-law), the effigies of Henry VII, Elizabeth of York, Edward III, Philippa of Hainault, Henry V and Catherine of Valois were 'repayred, robed and furnished at the King's Majestie his charge', at a cost of £70, and they were rehoused in a specially constructed 'presse of wainscott'.[6] King Christian was taken specifically to view the monuments in Henry VII's chapel, which included those under construction, and he reportedly took a special interest in Edward the Confessor's shrine.[7] It has not hitherto been noticed that Christian may well have been inspired by this occasion when launching his later campaign to refurbish and beautify Roskilde cathedral, a burial place of Danish kings, and in particular the separate chapel, which was under construction between 1614 and 1641 and would ultimately accommodate Christian's own monument.[8]

Perhaps one of the most celebrated funerals to take place at the abbey during the reign of James was that of the heir to throne, the 18-year-old Prince Henry. He was the golden young man whose demise in 1612 not only overshadowed the wedding of his sister to the Elector Palatine but also came hard on the heels of the interment of his grandmother Mary of Queen of Scots (the arrival of James's impending Protestant son-in-law only days after Mary's reburial may have been more than just a happy coincidence if there was a desire to reassure James's Protestant subjects).[9] Henry's unexpected death from typhoid fever in November unsettled the dynastic security that the Stuarts had seemed to provide, and prompted an outpouring of publications lamenting his promise and the loss that he represented to the nation. Despite this, no funeral monument to the prince was erected in the abbey: perhaps the magnificence of the funeral and the display of an elaborate hearse of the sort normally reserved for reigning monarchs was deemed to have already fulfilled memorial requirements (and may also have exhausted the funds required for a suitably lavish monument).[10]

The Stuart dynastic occupation of the abbey was fittingly encapsulated in James's own funeral in 1625. His death brought to an end a period that had seen the establishment of a new Protestant dynasty, the union of the crowns of England and Scotland and a religious settlement for both disgruntled Catholics and Protestants, and his funeral celebrated these achievements in distinctive ways. Not only did the abbey memorialize the dynasty, but it now played host to new European styles in funeral pageantry. The king's handsome effigy, with its spectacular hearse (strongly influenced by Italian Renaissance models) attracted the widespread admiration of contemporaries. The lying-in-state itself – it has been suggested – reflected the desire of James's son Charles

89

not to fall behind his continental counterparts in funeral pageantry.[11] The funeral sermon by the dean, Bishop John Williams, praised the king as a modern incarnation of Solomon, the Old Testament king renowned for his wisdom, and also drew attention to the classical figures representing Religion, Justice, War and Peace on the hearse.[12] This hearse was not only fit for a king but was also significant as a Protestantized version of Catholic funerary architecture. The result was, arguably, a distinctively Stuart mix of continental fashion with a hint of apparent Catholicism that would alarm the more rigidly Protestant observer. But if the dramatic use of candles at the corners of the bed of state where the king's effigy lay might suggest Catholic ideas of intercession for the dead, the service itself was unequivocally Protestant, and Charles (who was in the process of seeking funds for war with Spain) banned Catholic nobles from attending the funeral and stipulated that they were not entitled to receive the mourning 'blacks'.[13] The lavish funeral procession, from Denmark House to the abbey, included up to nine thousand mourners, and it is particularly striking that after the service the king's body was taken to the vault of Henry VII, thus placing him not among his immediate family, but with the founder of the Tudor dynasty and architect of one of the most important parts of the abbey.[14]

The Mausoleum in Westminster Abbey at the Funeral Obsequies of K. JAMES I.

89 The elaborate hearse designed by Inigo Jones for the funeral of James VI and I in 1625 (reproduced in Francis Sandford's *Genealogical history*, 1677) was the centrepiece of a grand procession from Denmark House to Westminster Abbey, where the obsequies, including a two-hour funeral address by Dean Williams, were performed.

James's revival of the abbey in the first decades of the seventeenth century was not limited to the needs of Stuart dynastic legitimation. It also encompassed the abbey's enhanced importance as a site of revived religious ceremonialism and as an emblem and encapsulation of the liturgical splendours of the national Church. Under a series of high-profile and activist deans – such as the clerk of the royal closet Richard Neile, (1605–10) and the urbane courtier John Williams (1620–44) – the abbey was repaired and its worship, music and furnishings restored and revitalized. Dean Neile, for example, proudly documented the considerable amounts

90

spent on improving the decaying fabric and furnishings of the abbey during his tenure – including more than £100 on new communion plate and hangings made of cloth of gold and blue velvet for the Communion table.[15] In addition, he installed a new organ in Henry VII's chapel and boosted funding for the choir, including a fund to support an anthem to be sung every day at Morning Prayer.[16] The musical interests of Dean Williams are likewise well documented, and he oversaw a significant programme of music copying.[17] Williams is also credited with spending over £4,500 of his own money on restoring the still dilapidated abbey. This programme of repair and beautification included the addition of 'elegant statues', one of which commemorated Abbot Islip (1500–32), another powerful clerical statesman with whom Williams may well have identified himself.[18] Despite the need for constant repairs, contemporaries such as William Camden and John Weever still extolled the abbey's splendour and celebrated its medieval past, while King James explicitly praised the singing of the choir before Convocation in 1606.[19]

The abbey was increasingly used to impress foreign visitors and ambassadors, not just as the burial place of kings and venue for royal coronations, but also as the most distinguished exemplar of the religious services celebrated by the Church of England. In 1624, for example, King James asked Dean Williams to entertain the French ambassadors and their entourage at the abbey during the negotiations for the marriage of the future Charles I and the Catholic Henrietta Maria. Before a feast held in the Jerusalem Chamber, Williams conducted his guests to dinner through an elaborately adorned abbey so that they 'might cast their Eyes upon the stateliness of the Church', while the organ 'was touch'd by the best Finger of that Age, Mr Orlando Gibbons'. The dean then presented his guests with French translations of the English Book of Common Prayer while the music continued, asking that 'their Lordships at Leisure might Read in that Book, in what Form of Holiness our Prince Worshipp'd God, wherein he durst say nothing savour'd of any Corruption of Doctrine, much less of Heresie, which he hoped would be so reported to the Lady Princess Henrietta'. The 'Lord Embassadors and their Great Train took up all the Stalls', while the choir 'in their Rich Copes' and the choristers 'sung three several anthems with most exquisite Voices'. Although the French king's secretary, La Ville-aux-Clercs, kept his hat on and pointedly left his prayer book in the stall, another member of the entourage, a scholarly lay *abbé*, asked to read over his copy more carefully and then to see the liturgy performed in the abbey, since the English liturgy had a reputation 'for Profaneness'. Williams therefore arranged for him to witness secretly the Christmas day service, hidden behind a lattice and curtains, with the dean's secretary helping him to follow the responses. There the *abbé* watched the dean sing the service, preach and distribute Communion to 'great multitudes', and reportedly admitted afterwards that he had been

90   The urbane Dean Williams (1620–44), a generous benefactor to the abbey, was a favoured courtier of James I and the first cleric since Archbishop Nicholas Heath in 1558 to hold the high office of lord keeper of the Great Seal; in this portrait (*c.*1625, attributed to Cornelius Janssen or Gilbert Jackson), he is shown with his left hand resting on the seal-bag.

misled by 'lying Varlets', who had maintained that the English Eucharistic service was 'a prodigious Monster of Profaneness', whereas he had witnessed the sacrament being given and received with all 'Decency'.[20] Williams, who strongly supported the French marriage, is credited with having later added an intricately carved wooden mantel to the fireplace in the Jerusalem Chamber to commemorate this visit.[21]

91   The title-page of the first edition of the King James Bible (or Authorized Version), 1611. Two of the six 'companies' (committees of scholars) working on this pivotal new translation met in the abbey's Jerusalem Chamber (the other four were based – two each – at the universities of Oxford and Cambridge). Lancelot Andrewes, Dean of Westminster from 1601 to 1605, was the head of the First Company of Westminster translators.

The abbey's special relationship to the Church of England was also demonstrated by the number of times it played host to leading events in the Church's history in these decades. Perhaps most famously, two of the six 'companies' working on what would become the 1611 King James translation of the Bible met in the Jerusalem Chamber at Westminster, where Dean Lancelot Andrewes (1601–5) served as the head of the First Company of Westminster translators.[22] More generally, meetings of the Southern Convocation (separate assemblies of the clergy that met when parliament was in session) were held in the abbey.[23] The abbey thereby played host not only to the debating and passing of the Laudian canons in 1640, but to a famous speech to the Lower House later in the same year, in which the very same canons were denounced by Thomas Warmstry.[24] Similar critical sentiments would have been heard in the spring of 1641, when (under the chairmanship of Dean Williams) the abbey was selected as the venue for a series of important meetings of Churchmen to consider the further reformation of the English Church in the wake of the attacks on Laudian innovations. It was therefore only appropriate that from 1643 onwards, when a national synod assembled to debate and agree far-reaching reforms of the doctrine and government of the national Church, the famous Westminster Assembly met in the Jerusalem Chamber.[25]

Beyond its specifically religious and political uses, the abbey also attracted increasing numbers of visitors in the early seventeenth century. From the 1590s onwards, members of the gentry and aristocracy increasingly came up from the country to stay in the capital, often when the law courts were in session or to attend the royal court or parliament, and Westminster society assiduously catered for these new visitors with leisure facilities, gardens, eating and drinking establishments, and new building developments such as Covent Garden, with its fashionable piazza.[26] The abbey was clearly a popular attraction among these gentry visitors, as revealed in the diaries of Sir Richard Paulet (attending parliament in 1614) and the godly Lady Margaret Hoby, who chose to attend its sermons.[27] One sermon delivered in the abbey in the 1620s attacked the fopperies and indolence of fashionable society, and presumably was intended to be heard by at least some of those who moved in these circles. Among those ridiculed were time-wasters, 'these brave Gallants and noble Sparkes', who 'half the night gamed and revelled, and as much of the day slept out'. Similarly, the preacher characterized fashionable women as spending the morning dressing, trimming and painting, while the afternoon was squandered 'in idle visits, and seeking after the fashions'.[28] The fantastic fashions sported by ladies attending the abbey so outraged Dean Robert Tounson (1617–20) that he banned yellow ruffs from the abbey church in 1620, but, this 'being yll taken and the King moved in yt', the dean backed down, explaining rather lamely that he did not specifically mean yellow ruffs as such, but only 'other manlike and unseemly apparell'.[29]

The usual weekly congregations at the abbey may have been limited to abbey clergy and officials, high-ranking visitors and the notables of St Margaret's parish, but scattered evidence suggests the attendance at evening service by non-elites. As a public building, the abbey was also a reluctant host to other activities. The cases heard before local justices of the peace document criminals loitering in the church with stolen goods and fights breaking out in the aisles.[30] In one case heard in the local court, a mariner claimed that he arranged with a friend to view the monuments in the abbey – a reminder that this activity was not limited to the prosperous visitors who describe it in their letters and diaries. Viewing the monuments became one of the indispensable features of any visit to the abbey and thus a potentially lucrative fashion. The Earl of Huntingdon paid 2s. to see the 'toomes' in 1606, while a copy of Camden's guide to the monuments could be purchased at the abbey for 10d. Small wonder, then, that a

85

patent for the post of official keeper of the monuments – which included the profits from 'showing' the monuments – was sold for £250 in 1615.[31]

The royal tombs were not merely of historical interest, though. Newer monuments increasingly incorporated important innovations of Renaissance architectural and monumental style, which invited imitation. This influence can be traced through the spread of new iconography, while specific references to abbey monuments can be found in some surviving contracts for new tombs. The arch-like canopies of the tombs of Queen Elizabeth and Mary Queen of Scots inspired other monuments, while the depiction of the infant Princess Sophia (d. 1606) in her cradle soon prompted cradles and cots to be incorporated in a range of tombs from Kent to Lincolnshire. It was not only royal monuments whose features gained wider circulation among potential patrons and craftsmen alike. A distinctive seated effigy (*c.*1602–3) of Elizabeth Russell, daughter of Lord John Russell, was similarly copied, the stance being favoured particularly in tombs for women. Fashions in the style of monuments for legal men, a group with increasingly social aspirations in early modern England, also fanned out from the abbey. These could be more conservative, but the elegant tomb provided in 1635 for the judge Sir Thomas Richardson by the court sculptor Hubert Le Sueur in the French Mannerist style was widely imitated.[32] In other cases, the abbey showcased important classical styles of commemoration, as in the monument for the young Francis Holles, son of the Earl of Clare. Although he died abroad defending the Protestant cause in 1622, his monument depicts him in Roman armour with a shield, in imitation of a Medici monument in Florence.[33] Even for the dead, the abbey was the fashionable place to be seen.

The fashionableness of the abbey also reflected the fact that its immediate vicinity was a hub of cultural and intellectual activity – as well as gentry society – in the early Stuart period. Westminster School itself enjoyed an enviable reputation as a nursery of talent and scholarship. The area also boasted the most notable libraries in the capital, including the royal library, the abbey library and, most famously, the library of Sir Robert Cotton. The last was one of the richest collections of private manuscripts ever amassed. Cotton's library served as a meeting place for the Society of Antiquaries until 1614, while in 1622 he purchased a house near the Court of Requests and the House of Commons, where his collection was frequently consulted by scholars and was also employed by MPs in important parliamentary debates over the nature of Church and state in the pre-civil war period. Meanwhile, the pulpits of the neighbouring Westminster parish churches attracted famous preachers whose sermons often touched on the contentious politics of the period. The centrality of the abbey and its environs to the country's political and cultural life was destined to increase still further over the course of the century, as we shall see.[34]

92 (ABOVE LEFT)   The monument to Elizabeth Russell (d. 1601) shows the pensive figure of a young woman, her right foot resting on a skull, the symbol of mortality; mounted on a decorated pedestal in marble and alabaster, it was the first memorial in England to depict a seated figure on a free-standing monument, and the pose was widely imitated.

93 (ABOVE RIGHT)   The monument by Nicholas Stone to Francis Holles, son of the Earl of Clare, who died in battle in 1622 while still only in his teens. One of the earliest memorials in England to depict a seated figure in the round, the young soldier is portrayed as a Roman warrior, a type that became increasingly common in the second half of the century.

The first half of the seventeenth century was distinctive for the high calibre and political importance of the deans who served at the abbey. King James not only attached importance to the abbey, making his appointments carefully, but also used the position of dean as a promotion route for clergy: all the early Stuart deans went on to hold major episcopal posts.[35] Dean Williams was also the first cleric in more than sixty years to hold the legal position of lord keeper of the Great Seal.[36] These were men who moved easily at court, and were not simply hangers-on there but men of talent, looking for preferment. The financial rewards of the deanery were very limited but, nonetheless, its proximity to the court prompted one contemporary to liken it to 'the Office of the King of Persia's Garden at Babylon, which was stored with his most delicious Fruits . . . [and] He that was trusted with that Garden, was the Lord of the Palace'.[37] Certainly John Williams went to extraordinary lengths to remain dean, in spite of further preferments and later attempts by King Charles (r. 1625–49) to remove him.

Religious Politics under the Early Stuarts

We have already noted the abbey's increasing prominence as exemplar of the ceremonial splendours of the English Church. But those splendours were to become an increasing source of controversy in this period. After the Elizabethan settlement, more advanced forms of Protestantism struggled to secure the 'further reformation' of a Protestant national Church that still retained elements of its medieval Catholic past in its liturgy and government. While English cathedrals had experienced determined efforts to transform them into institutions that would serve the demands of Protestant evangelism, they were nevertheless potential repositories of more conservative styles of religion. The continuation of older ceremonial practices within cathedrals, including the use of rich vestments, elaborate polyphonic music, the use of wafers (rather than bread) at Communion and the retention of images in stained glass, were seen by some as clouding the understanding of Protestant doctrine or as promoting outright idolatry. This reflected the fact that in cathedrals there had been much more continuity with pre-Reformation forms of worship, in contrast to parish churches, with their white-washed walls, congregational psalm-singing and pared-back services.

Westminster Abbey, in particular, remained a very public example of cathedral-style worship. By the seventeenth century, however, its practices did not simply represent a thread of continuity with the pre-Reformation period. Instead, a more positive attitude towards ceremonies and aspects of the medieval church was becoming dominant, and could build upon the inertia of the Elizabethan decades that had allowed the shell of the medieval abbey to remain. Andrewes, Neile and Williams all helped to promote these more elaborate forms of worship, which meant that the abbey served as an important and influential centre of ceremonialism.[38] However, the more public adoption of such practices within the Church of England intensified existing fears of Catholic influence at the highest levels of society, including among privy councillors and at the royal court. In 1612 Lewis Bayly, chaplain to the late Prince Henry, delivered a notorious sermon at St Martin-in-the-Fields – a short distance from the abbey – in which he condemned Catholic privy councillors, who 'tell theyre wives what passes [in council], and they carie yt to theyre Jesuities and confessors'.[39] These concerns were epitomized in a dispute in 1614, when the Commons refused to celebrate Communion in the abbey and moved instead to St Margaret's Church. Their objection was to the abbey's use of wafers – a Catholic practice now present only in cathedrals and not in parish churches. Given that the compulsory attendance at Communion was intended to flush out any potential Catholics among MPs, the conservative practices of the abbey were held to be an inadequate test of Protestantism.[40] Suspicions that abbey ceremonialism might pave the way to Roman Catholicism were fuelled by the apparent deathbed conversion to Rome of the prebendary Theodore Price in 1631.[41]

Fears of the 'popish' nature of High-Church ceremonial rose to a fever pitch with the policies pursued by William Laud as Archbishop of Canterbury (1633–45) during the Personal Rule of Charles I. The abbey's high-profile ceremonialism might have provided some inspiration for the emerging Laudian movement.[42] Another key feature of Laudianism was its determination to defend and restore the power, wealth and secular jurisdiction of the Church, which had been eroded since the Reformation. And here, too, there was much for Laudians to admire in the remarkable authority and influence that the abbey had continued to wield over the locality, where it owned most of the land and exercised substantial jurisdictional power and patronage.[43]   94

94   This topographical view of Westminster (c. 1643–50), after Wenceslas Hollar, shows figures promenading in Tothill Fields, with the abbey, Westminster Hall and St Paul's Cathedral in the background; the abbey was the principal landowner in its locality, which gave it very considerable secular power and patronage.

Deans of Westminster served as local JPs, and they (or rather their deputies) presided over the local court, the Westminster Court of Burgesses. Deans also wielded influence in the town's parliamentary elections, Williams, notably, intervening in the 1621 parliamentary election.[44] All attempts by the townspeople to gain true corporate status for the City of Westminster (analogous with that held by the City of London) were blocked by the abbey. These included, in particular, a concerted attempt in 1607 that seems to have received the royal assent (it is perhaps noteworthy that the only surviving draft of this sixty-five-folio charter is among the abbey's own records).[45] While the decade that Laud was in power witnessed a determined attempt by cathedrals across England to reclaim some of their authority and jurisdiction from city corporations, Westminster Abbey was in the fortunate position of there being no powers that it needed to regain. Indeed, in 1633 Dean Williams actually mooted a compromise in the form of a restricted incorporation for Westminster's inhabitants 'under the shadowe of the Church'.[46]

Despite the fact that the abbey might seem to encapsulate so many aspects of the Laudian vision for Church and state, it actually had a very ambiguous relationship with the Laudian movement. Laud had played no obvious role while he was a prebendary there (1621–8). The abbey's prebendaries had in the past encompassed moderate Calvinists as well exuberant ceremonialists and conservatives, and Williams himself combined a taste for ceremony with more orthodox Reformed doctrinal opinions.[47] In fact, the long-running political feud between Williams and Archbishop Laud meant that in the 1630s the abbey was actually a focus for potential opposition to the new ecclesiastical policies, with Dean Williams writing and publishing an anonymous tract against Laud's altar policy. Charles I had previously disagreed with Williams over government policy and it was Laud, not the dean, who was asked to officiate at the new king's coronation in 1625. Williams was pursued by Laud's clients. His tract against altars was in its turn attacked by Peter Heylyn (one of the most notorious apologists for the Laudian movement), who had been deliberately placed in the Westminster chapter and was busy orchestrating a whole range of charges against the dean with the other prebendaries.[48] The prosecution of Williams in 1637 and his imprisonment in the Tower of London brought the abbey firmly under crown supervision. A royal commission undertook the management of the institution in the late 1630s, the king claiming the power to appoint all abbey officers and to dispose of all the abbey's fines and leases 'according to our royal will and pleasure'.[49] Thereafter, the abbey operated with Laud's supporters largely in the ascendant, but it was not the focus of new royal initiatives. By contrast, with the support of a royally sanctioned funding campaign, St Paul's Cathedral benefited from a new, classically inspired west front designed by Inigo Jones.[50] Unlike his father, Charles does not seem to have had a distinctive place for the abbey in his political and cultural vision. The abbey was ultimately, then, the precursor rather than the focus of Laudian innovations.

On one occasion, however, the abbey briefly became the ceremonial focus of Charles's crumbling Personal Rule. The king's confrontation with the Scottish Covenanters had seen the abolition of episcopacy in his northern kingdom and the extraordinary flight of the bishops, including John Spottiswood, the Archbishop of St Andrews and Primate of Scotland. Spottiswood died in London in November 1639, and the king clearly resolved that his funeral in the abbey should be a magnificent celebration of beleaguered Scottish episcopacy. The corpse was attended by 'at least 800 torches' and 'the whole Nobility of England and Scotland (then present at Court) with all the Kings servants and many Gentlemen came out of their Coaches, and conveied the body to the West-dore' of the abbey.[51] The message of state support for government by bishops was clear, but in fact this proved to be the death knell of Scottish episcopacy, and of the Personal Rule itself. The political crisis caused by the failure of Charles I's Scottish policy forced the calling of two parliaments in 1640. The abbey attracted hostile attention when Convocation continued to meet there, after

PETRUS HEYLYN, S.T.P.
Ecclesiæ Collegiatæ Sancti Petri Westmonasteriensis Canonicus, Martyri & superstiti CAROLIS Patri ac Filio, Magnæ Britanniæ etc. Monarchis, dum viveret, à Sacris.

95 Peter Heylyn (1599–1662), right-hand man of Archbishop William Laud, was made a member of the Westminster chapter in order to engineer charges against Dean Williams in the 1630s; at the Restoration, he returned to the chapter as sub-dean, and it was he who presented Charles II with the sceptre at the coronation in 1661.

the dissolution of the so-called Short Parliament, in order to pass a set of new Laudian canons. Ultimately, though, the rioting crowds in May directed their attention to Laud's   96 residence at Lambeth Palace rather than the abbey itself. The meeting of the Long Parliament from November 1640 was accompanied by fears of a Catholic conspiracy at the heart of Church and state, and a crescendo of attacks upon episcopacy and 'popish' ceremonies within the Church.[52] The situation in the capital was particularly tense in November and December 1641, when trained bands were called out to clear apprentices from the vicinity of parliament, and, in late December, troops were needed in Westminster to disperse anti-episcopal mobs. The abbey itself came under attack

The rising of Prentises and Sea-men on South-wark side to assault the Arch-bishops of Canterburys House at Lambeth,

96   A hostile mob threatened Archbishop William Laud's residence at Lambeth Palace in 1640 (depicted here in an engraving from John Vicars, *A sight of ye trans-actions of these latter yeares*, 1646); there were similar scenes outside the abbey the following year, as a crowd, bent on destruction, tried to enter the building.

as a band of apprentices reportedly attempted to enter the building 'to pull downe the organs and altar', but were thrown back by Dean Williams, his servants and 'some other gentlemen that came to them'.[53]

The transformed political situation had initially given Westminster's dean the opportunity to play the decisive political role that he had always craved. Williams had been released from the Tower at the order of the Lords in November 1640 and did his best to broker a settlement with the king's critics, proposing, among other things, a bill that would ban clergymen from exercising the power of a JP, while astutely securing an exemption for the Dean of Westminster.[54] But Williams found himself in the Tower again after drawing up the 'Bishops' Remonstrance' (against the forced exclusion of bishops from the House of Lords) on 30 December 1641. The departure of Charles I from London in 1642, however, marked a turning point in the capital, and not long afterwards most members of the chapter fled, while Williams, again at liberty and now Archbishop of York, managed to follow the king into Yorkshire.

The capital remained in the hands of parliament during the civil war. Nevertheless, some members of the abbey staff remained. In April 1643 one of the singing-men was convicted of setting up a royal proclamation in St Peter's Street, prohibiting the collection of parliament's weekly assessments to support the war effort; the following year all abbey employees were required by parliament to swear to the Solemn League and Covenant in the abbey.[55] By this point, parliament was firmly in charge of the abbey, having taken effective control from the absent Dean and Chapter by January 1644, when it entrusted management to a parliamentary committee.[56] Both Commons and Lords routinely issued detailed instructions, to authorize burials, arrange pews, direct the ringing of bells, and require abbey officials to act promptly to prevent people walking and talking there and children playing during divine service.[57] Parliament's control was formalized still further when the Committee for Westminster College was established by ordinance in November 1645, consisting of eleven members of the Lords and twenty-two of the Commons. It was to prove a very active body, whose powers and membership were regularly enhanced thereafter.[58] By contrast, parliament did not assume similar control over St Paul's Cathedral, which ultimately found its way into the hands of the City of London.

Parliament's power over the abbey is usually associated with scenes of sacrilegious destruction. There are the reported desecrations by soldiers in the summer of 1643, the breaking open of doors to seize and remove the royal regalia, and Sir Robert Harley's notorious 'cleansing' of the abbey of superstitious objects in 1644. Much damage undoubtedly occurred, but these vivid snapshots can easily give a distorted view of the abbey's fate in the 1640s and 1650s. Images and painted glass were removed in profusion in the 1640s, it is true, especially in the chapel of Henry VII, where the altar was destroyed and some two thousand feet of stained glass removed. But this was not an iconoclastic fury: the activity took place over the course of two years, and was a cool and clinical dismantling of decoration. Moreover, this work was carried out by craftsmen and abbey officials, many of whom had served during the Laudian period. They included Adam Browne, the abbey surveyor since 1639, who would remain in post until his death in 1655.[59]

In fact, this 'reform' of the abbey's interior was not simply prompted by iconoclastic zeal, but was intended to prepare it for regular use by the parliamentarian regime. Windows were reglazed, and new galleries built.[60] The Puritan John Vicars noted with approval 'the most rare and strange alteration of the face of things in the Cathedrall Church of Westminster'.[61] It is also significant that parliament gathered in the abbey when its military victories were formally celebrated. This was where the House of Lords kept every one of the monthly fast days (and other thanksgiving days) until April 1648, and at least forty-one of these abbey fast sermons were printed. Not only did peers and judges have separate pews kept for them, but the wives of peers clearly attended these events in the abbey as well, having seats reserved for them in what was referred to as 'the Honourable Pew'.[62]

So it was that parliament gradually oversaw the conversion of the abbey from a centre of elaborate ceremonial religion into one of the nation's most famous preaching places. Dedicating one of the morning sermons in 1648 to the committee established to administer the abbey, the preacher Thomas Hill exclaimed 'O how many people doe blesse God for the sweet change they finde in their Morning Exercises; now they have rather the meanes of a heart and life Religion amongst them[!].' He expressed his satisfaction that the abbey offered 'Not Pompous Altars only to humour the Eyes, and talking Musick to please their Eares'. Instead, he asserted that 'many will tell you to the Praise of God' that they had found 'saving' edification in 'these Morning Exercises'.[63]

Particularly important in this regard was the rota of daily sermons established in the abbey in the 1640s, to which Hill's sermon referred. While traditional accounts emphasize the importance of the monthly fast sermons delivered to the House of Commons in the neighbouring church of St Margaret's, they neglect the more constant and immediate opportunities for political direction that these daily abbey 'lectures' afforded.[64] The team of ministers appointed by parliament contained some of the most politically important Presbyterian clergymen of the period, including Charles Herle, Thomas Hill, Herbert Palmer, Edmund Staunton, Jeremiah Whitaker and Stephen Marshall. They preached every single morning at 7.30 a.m. (or sometimes earlier) 'to Builders of Church and State', as one contemporary put it. Here was a means by which preachers could respond to daily events. MPs could be advised or exhorted with an eye to the day's forthcoming business, just minutes before they crossed the short distance from the abbey and entered the chamber, where prayers would usually be led by the same minister who had just preached to them.[65]

97   The events of the 1640s and 1650s saw the abbey turned into what was effectively a state church. In the past, St Paul's Cathedral and Paul's Cross had partly served as national religio-political venues. Paul's Cross, however, had been removed in the 1630s and its former pulpit was not rebuilt, while the cathedral suffered serious neglect, culminating with the collapse of the south transept vault in 1654, and was repeatedly occupied by quartered soldiers and horses.[66] With preaching at St Paul's subsequently confined to a chapel, it was now the abbey that served as the religious heart of government. Given its importance to the state, it was only appropriate that the abbey should also have played host to the Westminster Assembly during the nine years in which that body met to oversee the reformation of the English Church (and its prolocutor, William Twisse, was given an abbey burial in 1646). The abbey was complemented as a focus for state religious activities by its daughter church of St Margaret Westminster, which famously hosted the fast sermons delivered to MPs, and was decorated with the state's arms in the 1650s at the state's own expense.[67] St Margaret's had, in the past, enjoyed intimate links with the abbey, which exercised sole right of visitation over the parish

Cinitatis Westmonasteriensis pars.

ament House   the Hall   the Abby

97   The skyline of Westminster, as depicted by Wenceslaus Hollar in 1647, shows the meeting
place of the House of Commons (the 'Parliament House'), Westminster Hall and the abbey.
During the 1640s and 1650s, the Commons became increasingly involved in the government of
the abbey and often commandeered it for ceremonial purposes. To the right of the abbey, the
tower of St Margaret Westminster, the location of many fiery sermons to parliament, can be seen
next to the much larger detached bell-tower of the former St Stephen's Chapel.

and had played a vital role in shaping the notably conservative approach to religious
worship that characterized the parish.[68] Now St Margaret's followed the abbey in
becoming the chosen venue for the very different style of evangelical Protestantism
that was promoted by the Long Parliament.

Regicides and Interregnum

The trial and subsequent execution of Charles I at Whitehall in January 1649 was one
of the most dramatic events in the history of England, and of Westminster itself. It was
accompanied by the abolition of the House of Lords and the purging of parliament, and
the establishment of a new republican government. But the abolition of the monarchy

did not lead to the eclipse of the 'house of kings'. On the contrary, the abbey now had an important part to play in the establishment and legitimation of the new regime. From the outset, it was bound closely to the new political establishment. Authority over the abbey was devolved from an earlier parliamentary committee and was more formally established in September 1649 in a new body with the misleadingly bland title of 'Governors of the School and Almshouses'. This humdrum name disguises what was actually a very powerful organization, which controlled the abbey's lands and revenues and its religious patronage. Ironically, this product of revolutionary government actually strengthened the traditional secular powers that the abbey exercised in the locality, appointing local officials and frustrating local inhabitants' renewed bid for incorporation.[69] It also commanded a substantial annual income.[70] The importance of the governors as a body is reflected in the list of prominent names appointed to serve on it.[71] Most striking of all is the fact that it included no fewer than fifteen men who had signed Charles I's death warrant. The erstwhile 'house of kings' was now a 'house of regicides'. Among these regicidal governors, perhaps most emblematic of the change of regime is the name of John Bradshaw, who had served as lord president of the High Court of Justice set up to try Charles I. Bradshaw dwelt in the increasingly well-appointed Dean's House throughout the 1650s and enjoyed surroundings of some luxury.[72] He also regularly attended services in the abbey, his name appearing in a partial seating plan that survives from the 1650s, along with those of other members of the governors such as Colonel Fielder, Edmund Ludlow and Sir John Trevor.[73] Bradshaw's dominant presence, and his active role as a member of the governors, were a very public reflection of how the most prominent and publicly recognizable regicides had taken over the abbey.

The strong bonds that tied the abbey and its governors to the new republican regime were made still more explicit in the new seal that was created for the governors. This was designed in 1649 by Thomas Simon, who had made the new Great Seal of the Commonwealth. The governors' seal features the great porch of the abbey on one side and an image of parliament in session on the other.[74] There could hardly be a more explicit statement of the sense of the co-identity of the two institutions. It must have seemed only appropriate when, in 1656, the Council of State proposed that parliament's records should be kept in the chapter house of the abbey. In the past, the abbey had preserved the royal regalia; now it was envisaged as the custodian of the goods of parliament.[75] It was in keeping with this institutional link that one of the houses in the abbey complex was now directed to be preserved for the serjeant-at-arms.[76]

When it came to religious matters, the political triumph of the Independents in this period ensured that there would be no national Church imposing compulsory attendance at its services. The monthly parliamentary fast sermons that had been such

98   The seal of the Governors of the School and Almshouses (the governing body of the erstwhile abbey) was designed in 1649 by Thomas Simon, who also designed the Great Seal of the Commonwealth; it shows the porch of the north transept on one side (*left*) and parliament, now the supreme authority, in session on the other (*right*), thus presenting the abbey as a 'house of parliament' rather than a 'house of kings'.

a distinctive feature of the 1640s were also discontinued in the 1650s. But the abbey continued to play a significant religious role. Its preachers acted as a barometer of the regime's religious complexion, with a regular roster of prominent Independents in the pulpit, including John Rowe (who preached to parliament on various occasions, and delivered the funeral sermon for Bradshaw), Philip Nye and Joseph Caryl. They were, nevertheless, supplemented by the eirenically minded Presbyterian Thomas Manton.[77] The victory of the Independents ensured the defeat of the various Presbyterian attempts in the 1640s to remodel the Church's institutions. Among the casualties of this power shift appear to have been proposals that the abbey should be constituted as a separate parish.[78] Instead, and in a perfect reflection of the changing balance of political power, it became host to one of most famous separatist congregations in the country, which

gathered there under William Strong, and subsequently John Rowe. This congregation reportedly included many 'Parliament men, and persons of quality residing in
Westminster'.[79] It had first assembled in the 1640s, when a number of petitioners
had requested to use Henry VII's chapel for a lecture on Sunday afternoons, asking
that the organization of the lecture should be allocated to 'Mr Peters, Mr Legate and
Mr Henry Walker, able godly orthodox and wel-affected ministers of gods word; or to
Mr Scobell Clerke of the parliament'.[80] While the abbey provided a meeting place for
this Independent congregation presided over by Strong and Rowe, it seems nevertheless
to have sustained a more orthodox local congregation as well, with pews accommodating
various governors and abbey officials.[81]

The abbey's chief importance in the 1650s, however, lay less in its purely religious
functions than in its role as a focus for state pageantry. For example, it was the venue
chosen for the formal commemoration and thanksgiving by parliament on 3 September
1652 for the victories that its forces had achieved at Dunbar and Worcester in the
previous two years.[82] The abbey also hosted the processions and sermons preceding the
openings of the various parliaments of the 1650s.[83] It is true that, under the Protectorate,
Cromwell generally observed these days of public thanksgiving with his council and
senior army officers at Hampton Court or Whitehall Palace, with sermons and a feast,
rather than attending a public event.[84] But there were other major state occasions in
which the abbey figured prominently.

It is important to realise that parliament's deployment of the abbey was directed
by more than its usefulness as a substantial building in close proximity to Whitehall
Palace and Westminster Palace. The continued use of the abbey was also crucially
bound up with issues of legitimation. As we have seen, under the early Stuarts, funerals
and monuments had been used as devices to legitimize royal dynastic claims, and we
find a similar process during the 1640 and 1650s. This made the abbey – as it was
still often termed – one of the most important buildings of the non-monarchical
governments of the civil war and Interregnum period. What has gone unrecognized,
though, is the abbey's vital role in establishing a sense of physical continuity with past
royal government and in providing opportunities for propaganda and display.[85] Even
when the abbey itself was not used, it provided the trappings of legitimacy, as in the
case of the coronation chair, which was moved to Westminster Hall for the second
installation of Oliver Cromwell as lord protector in June 1657.[86]

From early on in the civil war, the abbey had been chosen as the venue for
elaborate state funerals: that of the leading parliamentary leader John Pym took place
in 1643. The parliamentarian regime carefully honoured its most faithful servant as
a hero whom it had a right to bury and memorialize where kings lay. The Venetian
ambassador cannot have been alone in suggesting that parliament's decision to erect 'a

99   The regicide Richard Deane (d. 1653), shown in this portrait by
Robert Walker painted around the time of the general's death, was killed in
the war against the Dutch; his burial in Henry VII's chapel, accompanied
by great pomp and spectacle, exemplifies the honour accorded prominent
figures who died in the service of the Interregnum regimes.

sumptuous monument' to Pym 'in the chapel of the kings at Westminster' showed 'what
their ends are to the reflecting eye'.[87] Other burials associated with the parliamentary
regime followed, and by the 1650s the abbey was notable for the lavish state funerals
and burials provided there for major military figures, especially those dying in battle
for the Commonwealth. A striking example was the funeral of the regicide General
Richard Deane (who died in 1653 in the Anglo-Dutch War). His body was brought   99
from Greenwich, 'in a very rich and stately manner', the state's arms were carried before
the hearse, and the general was buried, a contemporary pamphlet noted, in 'the burial
place of all the kings and queens of England', while 'guns were fired throughout the
ceremony and the streets were lined by all the cavalry and infantry' then quartered in
the city.[88] Similarly, Admiral Robert Blake's magnificent state funeral ended with his
burial in the chapel of Henry VII.[89]

   After the regicide, the abbey was the burial place of choice for the Republic's
servants. Especially significant in starting this trend was the treatment of the Republic's
first martyr, its ambassador to the Netherlands, Isaac Dorislaus. He was assassinated by
royalist refugees in May 1649 in revenge for his involvement in the trial of Charles
I. After lying in state at Worcester House, 'hung with black baize and escutcheons',

Dorislaus's body was conducted 'in stately pomp' to Henry VII's chapel in the abbey by the lord chief justices, the general officers of the army, the Commons and the Council of State, 'in regard that he had beene a publick Agent for the State' (as one newsletter observed); he was interred in the chapel at the state's expense.[90] The spectacle clearly inspired Thomas May's friends to arrange a similar state funeral and abbey burial for the Republic's first historian.[91] Other state servants buried in the abbey with a fair degree of pomp and circumstance included John Bradshaw, whose burial in 1659 was reported by an observer to have been marked with 'very noble and great atendence with much of haroldy [heraldry]'.[92]

Grand state funerals were not merely magnificent theatrical events, however. They also generated memorials and monuments that enshrined the parliamentarian and republican presence in the abbey. The abbey became a virtual mausoleum of the parliamentarian and republican cause. Parliament ordered that the funeral hearse of the parliamentary war hero the Earl of Essex (d. 1646) should remain in the chancel indefinitely for those paying their last respects. The catafalque (based on a design by Inigo Jones) was, however, mutilated soon afterwards, and the effigy was ordered to be reclothed and placed in a glass case near to the Stuart Earl of Lennox in Henry VII's chapel, where it remained for the next fifteen years. Essex's effigy was tellingly clad not in a peer's robes but in the buff coat that he had worn at the Battle of Edge Hill.[93] In effect, the revolutionary government turned Westminster Abbey into a parliamentarian shrine. The new monuments were now added to the familiar tourist route through the abbey. The satirical royalist newsletter *The Man in the Moone* had imagined in 1649 how the current 'shower of the Monuments' would now guide tourists around, identifying the tombs and monuments of the traitors Dorislaus, Pym, William Strode and Essex. This sardonic prediction was soon fulfilled: a foreign visitor shortly afterwards described how Dorislaus and Essex were pointed out to him in precisely this way.[94] The parade of Commonwealth heroes in Henry VII's chapel would be augmented in the 1650s by Henry Ireton, Deane, Blake, and also Colonel Mackworth, who had famously refused to surrender Shrewsbury to the young Charles II in 1651.[95] In a sense, then, every stage of the struggle against the Stuart monarchs and the triumph of the Commonwealth was represented among the exhibits in the abbey.

The most famous Commonwealth leader to be buried in the abbey was Oliver Cromwell himself. His funeral invited parallels with those of Stuart monarchs, embracing monarchical ritual more unambiguously than had any ceremony during Cromwell's own life. Most notable was the use of a crowned effigy, both for the lying-in-state and also for the lavish funeral procession, and ultimately for display in a splendid catafalque – 'a most Magnificent Structure built in the same Form as one before had been (on the like occasion) for King *James*, but much more Stately' (as one commentator observed). Another visitor observed that the effigy was placed in the abbey 'in a triumphant, ritch and artificall monument in Henry the Seventh Chappell . . . where it lies in a magnificent manner and shall remaine for a certain tyme to be seene'.[96] It is also tempting to see the burials of his mother and favourite daughter in Henry VII's chapel as Cromwell's attempt to use the abbey to make the same claims to dynastic legitimacy as James I had done. But it must be noted that these were still private funerals, and were carried out, it was observed, 'without Funeral pomp'.[97] More generally, the exclusive focus upon Cromwell and monarchical emblems has led historians to miss the wider context of the 1640s and 1650s – the series of grand state funerals in the abbey occurring at roughly the rate of one a year from 1643 onwards. The extraordinary scale and some of the monarchical features of Cromwell's funeral were, of course, unique, but arguably it should be seen as the culmination and apogee of established Commonwealth display, and of the broader appropriation of the abbey by the governments of the Interregnum. The prominence of the state's arms and the pronounced military features of funerals at the abbey in the 1650s also demonstrate that these were not simply feeble echoes of royal ritual, but in fact enshrined specific features of the Interregnum regimes.

Making the abbey the state's mausoleum and placing these fallen leaders in locations such as Henry VII's chapel were particularly crucial as a legitimizing symbol and as a form of state propaganda for regimes that struggled to maintain order and their own authority. The sustained use of the abbey as the sepulchre of the state's military heroes was a novel development in England, but it is striking that there was a similar contemporary development in the Netherlands, in the shape of the Nieuwe Kerk in Amsterdam, rebuilt after a fire of 1645. Although it was the city rather than the state that was behind the construction, the church was the work of a new Dutch republican establishment (Holland and Amsterdam were very much the heartlands of Dutch republicanism), and within it were erected monuments to military heroes such as the vice-admiral Jan van Galen, at precisely the same time as the English monuments appeared in Westminster Abbey (and to commemorate heroism in the very same Anglo-Dutch conflict).[98] Ironically, just like the abbey, the Nieuwe Kerk would subsequently become tied to the monarchy as the venue for Dutch royal investitures.

The abbey's prestigious position in the 1640s and 1650s as the ceremonial heart of the Interregnum regimes and effectively the state church was itself part of a broader process whereby the area of central Westminster came to have a more exclusively 'national' meaning in this period. A decisive factor here was that the executive was a more constant presence in the area than hitherto: parliament was in continuous session until 1653, and the late Protectorate ignored the royal custom of going on progress. It was also in the 1640s that St Margaret Westminster truly began to serve

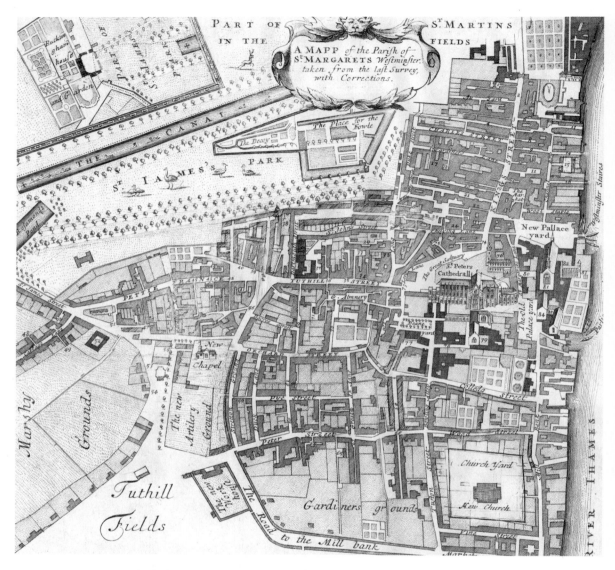

100   In the 17th century, the area around the abbey was mixed in character. The bustling
thoroughfares of Westminster were lined with inns, taverns and shops, which served those
attending the law courts, government offices, parliament (which met with increasing frequency
in this period) and the royal court. Crowded alleys housed poorer residents, often unskilled
migrants from the countryside, who lived in dilapidated tenements. However, a new demand for
aristocratic houses in the capital prompted building on the open fields located to the north and
west of the abbey. After the Restoration, some of these were built on fields to the north of
St James Park (visible in the upper left-hand corner of this map, printed in John Strype's *Survey of
the cities of London and Westminster*, 1720).

as the church of the House of Commons, though it had enjoyed episodic use earlier. Additionally, these years saw the state intervene more decisively in the locality than ever before, not only systematically taking it upon itself to house its officials within the immediate proximity of parliament, but also seizing many of the most important noble town houses in the Westminster area and converting them to the state's use. It also intervened in local parliamentary elections and the choice of preachers by local parishes, while security concerns placed the whole area of central Westminster literally under the eyes of the state in the shape of the troops garrisoned at Whitehall and St James's palaces throughout the 1650s.[99] Just as the town of Westminster now acted as the host of national government in a more intensive and constant fashion, so Westminster Abbey played a more continuous national role, in contrast to its more intermittent deployment under the early Stuart monarchs.

It would be misleading, though, to suggest that the abbey complex and its surroundings simply reflected Cromwellian sympathies in these years, for all the prominence of the regicides. Nowhere was this less true than in Westminster School, presided over by the notorious royalist sympathizer Richard Busby. Robert South later famously recorded that Busby had ensured that Charles I 'was publickly Pray'd for in this School, but an Hour, or two (at most) before his Sacred Head was struck off', and the schoolmaster doubtless instilled royalist sentiments into his charges thereafter, albeit with the discretion that underlay his remarkable self-preservation.[100] The swiftness with which the school resumed its teaching (minus some of its staff) after the end of the civil war – and despite Busby's known antipathy to the subsequent regimes – also underlines its importance to the nation's elite. Busby is a telling reminder that there were significant numbers of ex-royalist divines and gentry who lingered in Westminster during the

101   The royalist sympathizer and head master of Westminster School, Richard Busby, with one of his pupils, in a portrait by John Riley. Busby maintained his royalist allegiance, while working successfully with the regicides and others who ran the abbey in place of the Dean and Chapter.

1650s, generally treated with tolerance but occasionally subject to temporary expulsion when there were security scares.[101] The cloisters and Dean's Yard housed a population remarkable for the heterogeneity of its politics, from republicans to die-hard royalist absolutists, such as Sir Robert Filmer.[102] In the churchyard of St Margaret's, next door to the abbey, dwelt Godfrey Goodman, the Catholic-leaning former Bishop of Gloucester and nephew of the Elizabethan dean. He enthusiastically observed (in a rather optimistic dedicatory epistle to Oliver Cromwell) the parish's restoration of their font and the revival of perambulation in the early 1650s.[103] St Margaret's itself was served by two remarkable clergymen in the late 1650s, in the shape of their lecturer, Thomas Warmstry, and their minister, John Vyner – both dedicated royalists. This extraordinary situation came to the authorities' attention only in 1657, when a preacher failed to turn up to deliver the scheduled sermon at an abbey service being attended by MPs, and Warmstry stepped in to take his place. Subsequent complaints by the Commons led to the expulsion of the two notorious royalists, to be replaced by two Independent preachers, one of whom was already based in the abbey. Just as the abbey had promoted conservative religion at St Margaret's in the past, so now it promoted radical religious views in its daughter parish.[104]

The exequies of Oliver Cromwell in the abbey marked the beginning of the gradual unravelling of the Interregnum regimes. The unseating of his son Richard as lord protector in the spring of 1659, the restoration of the Rump Parliament and its subsequent dissolution and reinstatement by different factions of the army fully revealed a terminal crisis in government legitimacy. This culminated in the final march on London by General Monck, which prepared the way for the Restoration of the monarchy. Charles II (r. 1660–85) landed at Dover on 25 May 1660, and triumphantly entered London four days later. For all the initial enthusiasm that greeted his return, there was an obvious need to re-establish the symbolic trappings of the monarchy, to reinstate its legitimacy and to ensure its longer-term survival, and here the abbey would, as ever, have a central part to play. Efforts to 'reclaim' the abbey at this time would be crucial to the re-establishment of the monarchy and the Church of England. What happened at the abbey also formed part of broader efforts to renegotiate and reinterpret the nation's immediate past.

Restoration and Revolution

It was to be a year before Charles II's formal coronation in the abbey, but the reoccupation and rebranding of the abbey by the Stuarts was under way well before that. Henry VII's chapel was reclaimed for specifically royal funerals and interments within only a few months of Charles's return, as several members of the royal family died in quick succession. These included Charles's younger brother Henry, Duke of Gloucester, and his sister Princess Mary (mother of the future William III), while his aunt Elizabeth of Bohemia died less than a year after the coronation.[105] The use of Henry VII's chapel for this series of royal funerals will undoubtedly have drawn attention to the jarring presence there of the iconic figures associated with the regimes of the 1640s and 1650s. What followed was one of the most notorious actions of the Restoration: the removal from the abbey of the bodies of those associated with the Interregnum regimes. While Cromwell's and Ireton's bodies were hanged and then publicly displayed, the rest – including Dorislaus, Deane, Blake, Bradshaw, Pym, Twisse and others – were buried in a pit in St Margaret's churchyard.[106] The ejections were not merely an act of revenge; they were also a very public purging of a building that had been systematically taken over by the republican regimes. This symbolic sanitizing of the abbey was all the more significant as Charles's government was otherwise notably restrained in its treatment of adherents of the Interregnum regimes, most notably in the passing of the Acts of Oblivion, which provided a general amnesty.

It was precisely the very public role the abbey had performed in the regimes of the 1640s and 1650s that made it so important that it should play a national role at the Restoration. This applied not just to the monarchy, but also to the restoration of the Church of England, with its traditional system of government by bishops. The potential of the abbey as a prominent stage for the restored episcopalian Church may have been seized upon at an early stage, when Robert Skinner, the pre-war Bishop of Oxford, reportedly ordained no fewer than 103 ministers at a ceremony at the abbey immediately after Charles II returned from exile.[107] But the abbey played an even more important role as the site chosen for a remarkable series of episcopal consecrations. The restoration of a national Church governed by bishops required the creation of a large number of them as a matter of urgency. Westminster Abbey was certainly not the traditional venue for episcopal consecrations, which had typically taken place in the chapels of episcopal palaces.[108] Yet, beginning with a notable ceremony on 28 October 1660, when five bishops were consecrated on one occasion, no fewer than sixteen were consecrated, all at the abbey, within the space of ten weeks. All these consecrations took place in Henry VII's chapel, until recently a mausoleum of republican heroes. The choice of the chapel for episcopal consecrations doubtless reflected a strong desire to link the revival of episcopal government with the Restoration of the monarchy in the public eye and mind. The abbey was also the venue for the consecration of four Scottish bishops in December 1661 (by contrast, a comparable institution of three Scottish bishops in 1610 had taken place at the residence of the Bishop of London).[109] The royal associations and High Churchmanship that the

102   The coronation procession of Charles II, 23 April 1661, depicted by the Dutch painter
Dirck Stoop in 1662; the magnificent coronation ceremony followed traditional forms and
powerfully expressed the significance of the Restoration of the monarchy.

abbey had encapsulated clearly seem to explain its use for these occasions, and – appropriately – it was one of the first venues to restore its organs, exciting much public
interest.[110]

The organs were just one element of the gradual restoration of the abbey building itself. The re-acquisition of the necessaries for Church of England services was
soon in train, and the Dean and Chapter issued an order seeking to track down in
the immediate locality 'any money goods or utensills' which had been 'deteyned or
imbeazeled' from the abbey in the 1640s and 1650s. Preparations were also soon in
order for the coronation, hampered by some confusion over the correct procedures

for the ceremony, and the fact that the ancient regalia had been broken up over the years since the previous coronation.[111]

106

The coronation itself was vested with much symbolism. The original date was moved

102

from February to 23 April, presumably because of its significance as St George's day, commemorating the patron saint of England. The ceremony, not surprisingly, was modelled on the last pre-civil war coronation – that of Charles's father – though it also included the traditional procession the day before, which had been omitted in 1626 owing to plague and concerns over cost.[112] The coronation was also the first to be described in print: the official account emphasized the scale and lavish ceremonial involved, the abbey itself paying for sumptuous vestments. Pepys found the spectacle of the copes of cloth of gold and the members of the nobility 'all in their Parliament

103   Triple portrait (after 1660) by Sir Peter Lely of the Restoration divines John Fell, Dean of
Christ Church, Oxford (*left*), John Dolben, Dean of Westminster (*centre*), and Richard Allestree,
canon of Christ Church (*right*). Allestree points to a copy of the Book of Common Prayer held
on his knee, in recognition of the three men's adherence to the prayer book at Oxford in the
1650s, when its use was forbidden.

robes . . . a most magnificent sight', and he described how the king took part in all
the ceremonies of the coronation, 'which to my great grief I and most in the Abbey
could not see'.[113]

The restored deanery was placed in the secure hands of two clergymen with strong
loyalist backgrounds: John Earle (1660–62), who died in post, and John Dolben (1662–83),
who ultimately became Archbishop of York. At the time of their appointments, these
men lacked the profile of those who had occupied the Jacobean deanery. But they
both had impeccable royalist credentials, and in Earle's case a close personal link to
the king: Earle was a former tutor to Charles II and had followed him into exile. John
Dolben had also won his royalist spurs. He fought for Charles I at Marston Moor

and was later wounded, while his attendance at proscribed prayer book services in
Oxford in the 1650s (along with John Fell and Richard Allestree) was celebrated at
the Restoration in a triple portrait, in which Allestree points meaningfully to an open
copy of the Book of Common Prayer. At the Restoration, Dolben was sufficiently
trusted to be commissioned by the king to visit the condemned regicides and exhort
them (though unsuccessfully) to repent. He seems to have owed his position as dean
to the patronage of his father-in-law, the Bishop of London, Gilbert Sheldon. But
Dolben also had notable local credentials for the office. He had been admitted as
a king's scholar to Westminster School by his great-uncle, Dean Williams, and was
curate of the adjacent St Margaret's at the time of his appointment.[114] Links to the
royalist experience of civil war and exile characterized other members of the abbey
community as well in these years. If Earle represented continuity with the king's
period of exile, then the redoubtable Richard Busby at Westminster School provided
a notable example of loyalty to the Church of England that had endured throughout
the inhospitable climate of the Interregnum. Busby would remain an active member
of the Westminster chapter virtually until his death in 1695.[115]

   The complex process of disentangling the collegiate church's legal and financial
affairs and improving its furnishings and fabric gradually built up momentum, especially
under Dolben's lengthy tenure. On the very day of his installation, Dolben persuaded
the chapter to enhance the financial provision for the repair and upkeep of the abbey.
Pepys described visiting him in his lodgings in 1668, and finding him living 'like a
great prelate'.[116] Like his great-uncle, Dolben was able to retain the deanery, despite
being subsequently raised to a bishopric (in his case, the see of Rochester), and he
would subsequently play an active role in defending the Church on a national level
in the House of Lords.[117]

   If the abbey had sometimes eclipsed St Paul's Cathedral as the nation's pre-eminent
church under James I and during the various civil war and Interregnum regimes, this
was a situation that inevitably intensified under Charles II, with the destruction of
St Paul's, along with no fewer than eighty-eight city churches, in the Great Fire of
1666. The abbey stood out as the capital's unchallenged principal church during the
subsequent decades when the cathedral was being rebuilt. It is debatable, however,
how far it was equipped to capitalize on this, or to replace St Paul's as a major centre
of preaching. The physical limitations of the abbey building – its narrowness and lack
of extensive seating – had drawn complaints when it was called upon to play a more
prominent role in the 1640s. By contrast, the adjacent church of St Margaret's held a
great advantage, having been remodelled and expanded in the late fifteenth century,
providing a space more conducive to preaching (perhaps reflecting here the influence
of the friars' churches).[118] The abbey, nevertheless, had no competitors for the moment

in its role as the religious heart of the Restoration regime, and it would continue to play a significant part in the series of convulsions that now shook royal government later in the century.

Although the Restoration of Charles II re-established the Church of England, religion remained a highly politicized issue, and fear of Catholicism, which had been so prominent in the first half of the seventeenth century, re-emerged, especially in relation to the royal court. The king's marriage with the Catholic Catherine of Braganza was childless, and it became increasingly clear that the succession would pass to the king's brother, James, Duke of York, whose Catholicism became public knowledge. This situation prompted not only the Popish Plot of the 1670s, but also attempts to exclude James from the succession, something that Dean Dolben strongly opposed, as did many of the clergy for whom the link between the divinely appointed monarch and the Church remained paramount.[119]

The position of the monarch as Supreme Governor of the Church of England, which was represented and symbolized in the coronation service, was therefore likely to prove problematic when James came to the throne in 1685. Attempts to promote a Protestant alternative, in the shape of the illegitimate son of Charles II, the Duke of Monmouth, were firmly blocked by Charles himself, and Monmouth's Rebellion, which took place in the first year of James's reign, was crushed and the duke executed. A sermon preached in the abbey condemning the rebellion was one of the few abbey sermons to be published in the decades after the Restoration. But this did not necessarily reflect the views of everyone in the abbey: it is notable that Dolben's successor as dean, Thomas Sprat (1683–1713), who had written an official account of the Rye House Plot of 1683 for Charles II, refused to a write a similar piece after the Monmouth Rebellion.[120]

If the coronation of Charles II had been a key expression of the Restoration of the monarchy in England, the principle upheld at the coronation of his brother, James II (r. 1685–8), was more specifically the lawful succession of the monarch regardless of religion. This was, in a sense, an application of the message laid down implicitly by James's grandfather when he had re-interred his mother, Mary Queen of Scots. The abbey was naturally the venue where this principle was reasserted. Sprat was a vigorous supporter of royal authority in all its forms, and he initially supported James and took part in his coronation.

As we would expect, the more precarious the position of the new monarch, the more crucial it was to convey an impression of continuity in the coronation service. The coronation of James II took place on 23 April 1685 – the choice of St George's day undoubtedly a deliberate echo of that of Charles II. The king was crowned by Archbishop Sancroft, but the king's Catholicism meant that the ceremony omitted the

104   The coronation of James II at Westminster Abbey in 1685, from Francis Sandford's illustrated account of the ceremony. *The history of the coronation of the most high, . . . most excellent monarch, James II* (1687) was the first publication to reveal the regalia employed for the crowning of a new monarch, and to depict not only the coronation itself, taking place in the sanctuary before the high altar, but also the general scene in the abbey.

Communion service, something that the archbishop seems to have accepted after much hesitation. Instead, James and his wife, Mary of Modena, had apparently been anointed and crowned the day before in a Catholic rite conducted at Whitehall Palace.[121] It was perhaps partly to compensate for this that the music at the coronation was even more elaborate than it had been at the coronation of Charles II, and that it formed a more prominent part of the service. Our knowledge of the coronation ceremony at the abbey derives from a beautifully illustrated account commissioned by James II from the Lancaster Herald, Francis Sandford, which pointedly includes full details of the earlier coronation of Charles II. Sandford's 'History' of the new king's coronation lists the names of all those in the procession from Westminster Hall to the abbey, and includes engravings of both the coronation procession and of the ceremony itself. The   104 illustrations of the volume are unusual in showing not only the moment of crowning but also the interior of the abbey, with galleries of spectators, instrumentalists, and

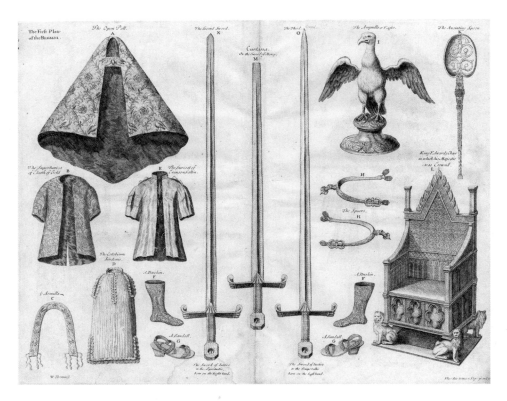

105   Engraving of the vestments and regalia used at the coronation of James II in 1685, from Francis Sandford's *The history of the coronation of the most high, . . . most excellent monarch, James II* (1687), including the coronation chair, with the Stone of Scone beneath, the anointing spoon and ampulla, and three ceremonial swords.

the choirs of both the abbey and the Chapel Royal conducted by John Blow. Indeed, Sandford's work was the first publication to illustrate fully for the public the interior of the abbey, revealed in all its glory and depicting the sacred ceremonies that took place within its walls. If Pepys had earlier been frustrated by his inability to glimpse the ceremonial of Charles II's coronation, Sandford's work now offered the best possible view of the proceedings for loyal subjects (albeit, only those who could afford to buy this expensive work). Even the principal objects employed in the coronation service, from the ancient chair to vestments and other items of the regalia, were the subjects of exquisite engravings. The king ordered that the figures depicted should be actual portraits of 'such Persons in the Proceeding'. The text emphasized the nobility's support for James, but also noted that he had graciously granted a dispensation 'without great prejudice' to those who had felt unable to attend. By the time Sandford's coronation

105, 106

106   The coronation anointing spoon and ampulla (the vessel that holds the consecrated chrism or oil), are part of the abbey's regalia. The spoon (thought to date from the 12th century) was used at the coronation of James I in 1603 and at all later coronations. It was sold off in 1649, but fortunately a member of Charles I's household purchased it (for 16s.) and returned it after the Restoration; it was used at Charles II's coronation in 1661, as was the eagle-shaped ampulla, which was made for that occasion.

volume was published in 1687, though, events had already overtaken this exercise in royal public relations, as the goodwill that the king had initially enjoyed had begun to decay as a more authoritarian style accompanied James's promotion of Catholicism.[122]

Support for the king divided the realm and also its clergy. At the abbey, Dean Sprat continued to serve James II loyally at first. Historians have characterized Sprat in terms of his 'political malleability', but the main constant in his career was complete loyalty to the restored monarchy. Indeed, he ensured that the Declaration of Indulgence (which suspended penal laws enforcing conformity to the Church of England) was read out in Westminster Abbey. It was one of only a few churches in the capital where this was done, as even those Anglicans who were most loyal to James had baulked at this

apparent betrayal of the established Church. An eyewitness in the abbey reported that
when it was read 'there was so great a murmur and noise in the church that nobody
could hear' the words, while Sprat himself 'could hardly hold the proclamation in
his hands for trembling'.[123] In this obedience to the regime, the abbey was swim-
ming against the tide. When, in autumn 1688, James's son-in-law William, Prince of
Orange, landed his Dutch army on the Devon coast, having pledged to defend 'the
Protestant religion and . . . the laws and liberties of those kingdoms', he met with
little opposition. The incongruity of the Glorious Revolution, in which James was
decreed to have abdicated by his flight and his daughter Mary was deemed to be his
successor (passing over his young son, James Francis Edward, whose legitimacy was
conveniently questioned), was something that called more than ever for the reassuring
balm of abbey ceremonial to emphasize dynastic continuity and legitimacy. But things
would not be quite so straightforward.

The reign of William and Mary (1689–94) is well known for the changes it brought
to the political landscape of England and the shifting balance of power between
parliament and the monarchy. It was perhaps only appropriate that the period also
witnessed a significant change in the relationship between the abbey and the monarchy.
The succession of William and Mary could have been expected to have created
problems for the abbey, given the personal links that the dean and several of the
prebendaries had enjoyed with James II. Certainly, many clergy (not least Archbishop
Sancroft himself) found it difficult to reconcile their consciences with the new political
settlement. Sprat, however, who had been a pugnacious defender of monarchy in the
past, ultimately found it possible to shift his support to William and Mary. In fact, the
changing relationship between monarch and abbey had less to do with the previous
loyalties of the dean or mixed loyalties of the prebendaries, and more to do with the
attitudes of the new monarchs themselves.

107   The coronation service itself reflected the changed political circumstances while
also preserving some of the older traditions. William and Mary were proclaimed joint
monarchs on 13 February 1689, and their coronation at the abbey took place relatively
swiftly on 11 April – a reflection of the urgent need to establish the legitimacy of the
regime with all the appropriate ceremony. The coronation sought to emphasize continuity
with that of Charles II: his effigy was on display in the abbey to observe proceedings, while John Ogilby's official account of Charles's coronation was republished.[124]
Nevertheless, while legitimacy demanded some continuity with previous ceremonies,
there was also a clear need to distinguish events from the very recent past. As Mary
herself later noted, the Communion service was reintroduced specifically to provide
a contrast with her father's coronation.[125] The Protestant nature of the ceremony was
also emphasized in other ways, with the novel presentation of a Bible to the royal

KROONING VAN WILLEM DE III. EN MARIA, TOT KONING EN KONINGIN VAN ENGELAND, ENZ. IN WESTMUNSTERS ABDY DEN ¼ APRIL 1689.

107   The joint English and Dutch interest in the coronation of William and Mary in 1689 was catered for by the Dutch artist and propagandist of the king, Romeyn de Hooghe; these scenes include the coronation procession itself and medals being thrown to spectators, while the engraving also shows how, elsewhere in the capital, the event was celebrated with fireworks.

couple, to remind them of their role as godly magistrates, after the models of David, Solomon and Josiah.[126] The new political realities were also reflected in the formal presence of the House of Commons at the coronation for the first time.[127] William and Mary were not crowned at the high altar; instead they were led to their 'Regal Chairs' (Mary's had been made especially for the occasion), so that, as a contemporary account pointedly explains, 'they might be more Conspicuous to the Members of the House of Commons' when they were crowned.[128] Significantly, the new rulers swore to govern according to the statutes agreed upon in parliament, while they also took the oath to maintain the Protestant religion. The prominent position given to the parliamentarians who assisted the new monarchs to the throne also suggested the new constitutional arrangements, though these were skirted around in the sermon that accompanied the service.[129]

   An engraving of the coronation procession outside the abbey can be seen to epitomize a clear and orderly devolution of power, but the circumstances of the ceremony were anything but conventional. The capital was occupied by Dutch troops for a year following William and Mary's arrival, and for the coronation itself the Commons asked General Schomberg (William's second in command during the invasion) to provide foot soldiers to guard the passage to and from the abbey.[130] The military presence was not, then, simply an echo of the martial pageantry that had marked grand public events at the abbey in the 1650s; this was a matter of armed security. The fact that the soldiers were Dutch also reminds us that William was a foreign ruler, who could be expected to have a rather different sense not just of kingship, but also of the function of the abbey. If the changed understandings of the meaning of kingship that were evident in the coronation service would inevitably have some long-term implications for the 'house of kings', the new sovereigns also seem to have had an instinctive distaste for the abbey and its ceremonial style of English Protestantism. Despite being a Stuart on his mother's side, William had been brought up within the Dutch Reformed Church, with its Presbyterian form of Church government. While it is true that he had taken Communion with Mary at the coronation and thereafter regularly attended the services of the Church of England, he had only contempt for some of the rituals of sacred kingship (he dismissed touching to cure the king's evil as 'a silly superstition' and suggested supplicants should go to the exiled James II instead).[131] William also initially struggled to grasp that his sympathy for Dissenters would antagonize his Anglican supporters.[132] Given that he remained a practising member of the Dutch Reformed Church whenever he visited the Netherlands, it is not surprising to find that William seems to have had very little interest in the abbey or, indeed, its potential for promoting royal authority. The queen seems to have shared her husband's indifference. She had complained that at the coronation there was 'so much pomp and vanity in all the ceremony that it left little time for devotion', and directed her efforts towards making services in the Chapel Royal more frequent and public, rather than making use of the abbey.[133]

Mary's death in 1694, however, provided the customary opportunity for the monarchy to reclaim the ceremonial prestige that the abbey afforded. Ironically, the demands of royal ceremonial meant that Mary – who privately desired a simple service – received the most lavish and expensive royal funeral of the century, which has been estimated to have cost approximately £50,000. The funeral service was more than two months in the planning, and included music specially composed by Henry Purcell, an elaborate funeral procession and a catafalque designed by Sir Christopher Wren, the architect of the newly emerging St Paul's. In a nod to the new political situation, the coffin of the monarch was for the first time accompanied by both Houses of Parliament. After the sermon, the body was lowered into the tomb, though an effigy of the dead queen remained on display above the ground (as had been the case for her uncle,

108

Charles II).[134] Historians have debated the decision to turn Mary's funeral into a grand, state occasion, and it seems likely that the reasons were political, helping to boost and legitimize the position of her co-ruler, William. It has also been suggested that William himself was influenced by the tradition of great public funerals in Delft of the Dutch stadholders. The Dean and Chapter influenced the timing of the funeral, and petitioned the Privy Council for a daytime, and hence public, funeral. However, their request was practically motivated, as they feared the risk of fire at a night-time service, 'to the manifest danger of our fabrick'. Whatever the case, the occasion was treated as a public holiday; contemporaries noted that shops were shut throughout the city.[135]

Mary's extravagant funeral did not herald an immediate revival in the abbey's public political role, however. The burning down of Whitehall Palace in 1698 had long-term implications in removing the monarch from physical proximity to the abbey, and also simply exacerbated William's retreat from it and his general unwillingness to participate in pageants, displays and courtly ritual (he was even absent from Mary's funeral).[136] When the king died in 1702, there was no repeat of the lavish ceremonial of his wife's funeral. He was

108   Henry Purcell's manuscript of his setting of the Second Funeral Sentence for Queen Mary, 'In the midst of life we are in death', composed for her elaborate and costly funeral at Westminster Abbey in 1695.

buried in the abbey privately by the Privy Council, which partly reflected his own desire but also the sober wartime mood. However, even this 'private' funeral was not as obscure as has sometimes been suggested: it included a chariot and 130 coaches in procession, and followed a precedent for private nocturnal royal funerals that had been set by Charles II (in whose vault William's body was interred).[137]

Beyond its role in coronations and royal funerals, the religious complexion of the abbey in the post-Restoration period reflected the changing policies of the crown and fortunes of the Church of England. While the deans tacked their way prudently through the tumultuous religious politics, different prebendaries encapsulated different responses and churchmanships. Simon Patrick, a prebendary from 1671, was a charismatic preacher and pastorally minded minister, applauded for remaining in his parish of Covent Garden during the plague of 1665, and a noted anti-Catholic polemicist during James's reign (despite having begun the reign as one of James's royal chaplains). His experience of the 1680s led him to seek some form of accommodation with Protestant dissent. By contrast, the convictions of the prebendary Robert South headed in the opposite direction. South had attended the clandestine prayer book services conducted by Dolben and his colleagues in Oxford in the 1650s, and was a prebendary from 1663. While Patrick ultimately repented of his early opposition to Dissenters, South's views hardened.

The two prebendaries responded to the Glorious Revolution in starkly different ways. Patrick was one of a group of more accommodating London clergy consulted by William at the start of his reign, who hoped to entice moderate Protestant Dissenters back into the Church, with the new king's backing. Significantly, when a meeting of the Ecclesiastical Commission was held in the Jerusalem Chamber to discuss reforms to the Book of Common Prayer, Dean Sprat soon slipped away, while Patrick remained and even suggested the creation of a new holiday commemorating both the Gunpowder Plot anniversary and William's landing in England. Patrick was swiftly promoted to become Bishop of Chichester, though he continued to preach occasionally at the abbey.[138] By contrast, South was clearly placed in a quandary by the events of 1688. Having served as chaplain to James as Duke of York, South delayed declaring for either James or William as long as he could. He took the new Oaths of Allegiance on the last day possible to avoid suspension, and left money in his will for twenty ejected 'nonjurors'. His hostility towards Dissenters made him a natural opponent of William's policies, but unlike Patrick he remained an important and active presence in the Westminster chapter until his death in 1716 (and even in his 80s was chosen by the chapter to serve as Archdeacon of Westminster).[139] South's attitudes were echoed by another pupil of Busby, Francis Atterbury, who would eventually succeed Sprat as dean in 1713. From the 1690s onwards, Atterbury was an outspoken defender of the right of Convocation to meet at the same time as parliament, in opposition to William III's determination to dispense with the assembly as a potential focus of criticism of his ecclesiastical policies.[140] As William was forced to yield, and Convocation assembled amid acrimonious exchanges over its independence (not least between the Upper and Lower Houses themselves), the abbey was very much in the eye of the storm as the venue for meetings of Convocation throughout this period (the bishops meeting in the Jerusalem Chamber, and the Lower House in Henry VII's chapel).[141]

At the succession of Queen Anne (r. 1702–14), the abbey greeted a monarch more sympathetic towards its ceremonial religious style, and her accession to the throne was welcomed enthusiastically by the Tories. The coronation was less contentious than had been those of her predecessors, and the queen reassured her subjects that her heart was entirely English. For the English musical establishment, the occasion presented an opportunity to revive music at the Chapel Royal and at court, and the music performed at the coronation was publicly disseminated afterwards. As with previous coronations, the event was the subject of extensive coverage in print, including the sermon by Archbishop Sharp, celebrating the new queen as a 'nursing mother' to her subjects (a reference to Isaiah 49:23).[142] While enhancing the ceremonial aspects of the service (and happily restoring St George's day as the coronation date), Anne's coronation nevertheless retained some of the innovations of William and Mary's service: the queen received the Bible, was attended by parliament, and also (tellingly) took not only the coronation oath but also the Test, thereby confirming her rejection of Roman Catholicism.[143]

The queen's poor health and numerous pregnancies meant that at her coronation she was carried in a 'low open Chair all the way' along the route of the procession to the abbey. More generally, Anne's health meant that she was less of a public figure manipulating royal ceremonial for political purposes, albeit she restored the ceremony of touching to cure the king's evil.[144] She was personally devout and unflaggingly loyal to the Church of England, its doctrines and ceremonies, and believed implicitly in the mutually supportive role of Church and state. More pertinently, the reign saw extensive church-building in the capital, bolstered by the Fifty New Churches Act of 1710. For the abbey, her reign was a period of consolidation, with Dean Sprat, at the suggestion of Archbishop Sancroft, introducing Holy Communion every Sunday after Morning Prayer. A far larger undertaking, though, was the major restoration of Westminster Abbey. The Dean and Chapter had been forced to petition parliament in 1697 for its assistance in paying the £40,000 that they had been told would be required to repair the 'very defective' structure of the church.[145] The parliamentary grant that eventually followed was said to be 'for the honour of God, the spiritual welfare of Her Majesty's subjects, the interests of the established Church and the glory of Her Majesty's reign'.[146] To this project Queen Anne donated, in 1706, an altarpiece designed by Christopher Wren for James II at Whitehall Palace.[147] This vast building programme at the abbey – lasting for almost fifty years – was the most expensive and prominent restoration project of its day, overseen by Christopher Wren and, later, Nicholas Hawksmoor. The grants by parliament of huge sums specifically for the work indicate that the abbey was still regarded as a major public building of national significance. Nevertheless, it would now be rivalled by the splendid new cathedral of St Paul's, and it is notable that the series of thanksgiving services held for military victories during Anne's reign all took place at St Paul's rather than the abbey.[148]

109

It is, perhaps, significant that the initial parliamentary grant was actually appended to a statute 'for compleating the building and adorning' of St Paul's.[149]

The Abbey and the Stuart Century

At the end of the Stuart century, the abbey found itself in a profoundly transformed capital city. London was now the most populous city in Europe, overtaking Paris,[150] and a great international trading power, while new post-Fire building meant that much of the capital presented a very different face to the world from its old medieval aspect. In addition, the ancient abbey found itself on the fringes of a new and fashionable West End, whose growth prompted the subdivision of parishes and the creation of new local churches designed for Protestant worship. The nexus of power on the abbey's doorstep had also changed. At the start of the seventeenth century, a politically powerful and confident monarchy was still based at Whitehall Palace, virtually adjacent to the abbey, where the key rituals of monarchical authority were enacted and the memory of a series of royal dynasties was preserved. By the end of the period, the role of the monarch had been redefined and Whitehall Palace ravaged by fire; new and less powerful sovereigns retreated to leafy royal palaces further west, leaving the abbey to present a key – if somewhat isolated – symbol of the symbiosis between Church and state.

The Stuart century was one in which the nature of monarchy, the claims of dynasty and the role of religious difference were in a constant process of review, revolution and retrenchment. Far from being sidelined by these political convulsions, the abbey was an active participant at the centre of events, reflecting changing realities but also providing the ceremonial continuities that could serve to legitimize them. In the process, it served as the effective national church, and as the crucial ceremonial arm of a bewildering range of governments – monarchies, parliaments, Republic, Protectorate – who could all recognize its importance, however different may have been the precise messages that they wished it to convey.

109 (FACING PAGE)   As part of an essential and far-reaching restoration project at Westminster Abbey, funded by parliamentary grant, in 1706 Queen Anne donated an elaborate, two-tiered altarpiece, originally designed by Christopher Wren for James II at Whitehall Palace. It was removed to the abbey and installed there – as shown in this print by Frederick Mackenzie from Rudolph Ackerman's *History of the Abbey Church of St. Peter's Westminster* (1812) – but was later dismantled.

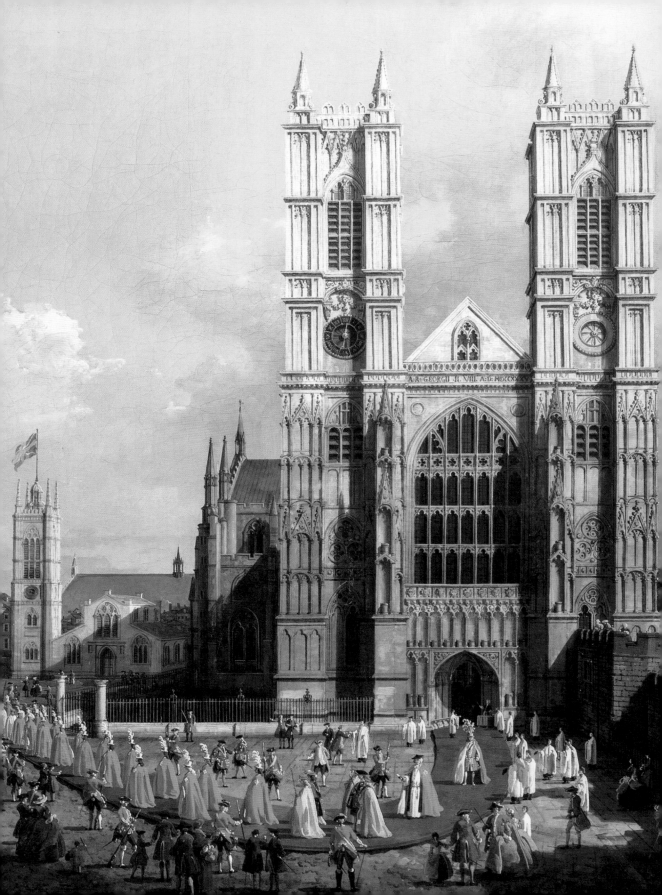

6

Old Corruption and New Horizons:
1714–1837

WILLIAM WHYTE

Painted in 1749, canaletto's great canvas *Westminster Abbey with a Procession of the Knights of the Bath* still hangs in the abbey's Deanery, as it has done since the end of the eighteenth century. It may not, in truth, be 'a particularly sensitive rendering of Gothic architecture or a very lively portrayal of the worthy knights'. It may not have made Canaletto's career – and, indeed, he would return to Venice for lack of work shortly afterwards.[1] But it does show the institution as it wished to be seen, and as it still wishes to be seen. Here is pomp and circumstance. Here are Church and state, monarchy and pageantry, religion and ritual. Applauded by a polite and decorous crowd, and processing beneath the Union flag flying from St Margaret's Church, the ancient roof of Westminster Hall just visible behind, the knights, and the canons, choir and dean of the abbey seem to symbolize something unchanging and essentially English. And yet, this scene also shows a place in transition, one experiencing significant change. The Order of the Bath was an innovation, created only in 1725. The west front of the abbey – with its two imposing towers and monumental window – was brand new. The tower of St Margaret's was similarly recent in design, and the clear streets and public spaces that surrounded the site were equally novel. Further change was coming, too, not least because the whole picture was conceived from a vantage point – the top of the Sanctuary gate – that would shortly be demolished.

The abbey in this era was a meeting place for court, parliament and wider public life, an ancient building strongly associated with long-standing traditions. It was also a very modern place: a tourist attraction and art gallery *avant la lettre*; a charged and sometimes contested space, where even the monuments might have a political purpose.

110 (FACING PAGE)   Encapsulating the combination of elite and bourgeois culture that transformed Westminster in the 18th century, Canaletto's *Westminster Abbey with a Procession of the Knights of the Bath*, 1749, depicts the knights leaving the abbey by the main door, dominated by Nicholas Hawksmoor's newly completed west towers.

111   A view of the nave in 1723 in an engraving from John Dart's two-volume guide to the abbey and its monuments, *Westmonasterium, or The history and antiquities of the Abbey Church of St. Peters Westminster*. At this period there were no pews, and elegant visitors promenaded in the open space; the plain choir screen with wooden obelisks was replaced in the 19th century by one designed by Edward Blore.

It was highly fashionable and very well connected. Indeed – and this is surely something Canaletto captures – it was remarkably well integrated within the society around it. The Dean and Chapter alike owed their places to their connections. The minor canons, the singing-men, the everyday administrators and the tradesmen all had other jobs and were parts of other networks, too. The Victorians, and many subsequent historians, would look on all this as an abuse. For one well-placed historian, this whole period could be written off simply as 'the bad times'.[2] With its non-resident clergy, its vast revenues, its tiny congregations, Westminster Abbey would come to seem synonymous with old corruption. With all the petty squabbles, all the talk of crumbling masonry, and all the sums of money exacted from the dead or grieving – be they funeral fees charged by the chapter or the 'Tomb Money' pocketed by minor canons and the choir for showing tourists round the place – it can look a little like Gormenghast. Reality was certainly very different from the high ideals regularly articulated by its deans.[3] But the abbey of the long eighteenth century was typical of its times, and reflected – even led to – wider movements in contemporary religion, society and the arts. It also, perhaps, represented an element of continuity with the old, medieval Westminster – a dispensation that would be radically modified in the years after 1837.[4]

Pluralism and Politics

Eight deans and more than eighty prebendaries oversaw the abbey in this era.[5] At any one time, twelve prebendaries, who were canons of the college, served under the dean as the chapter. Some spent most of their life there; others passed through so quickly that they can barely have seen the place. Almost all, however, were important men, and even the most unimpressive was inevitably well connected. These were crown appointments and it required patrons at the very highest level of society to obtain this sort of post. Robert Hay Drummond, for instance, served as a canon for six years, before moving on to still greater preferment as Bishop of St Asaph and then Archbishop of York. 'A man of parts, and of the world', in Horace Walpole's words, he was the son and son-in-law of aristocrats, a courtier, and a friend of front-rank politicians.[6] It was said that he first gained the patronage of Queen Caroline, wife of George II (r. 1727–60) owing to his 'singular presence of mind when the ostrich plumes on his costume caught fire during a [Westminster] school production of *Julius Caesar*'.[7] Not untypical of the less stratospheric, rather longer-lasting canons was William Bell: a learned scholar, astute operator and popular preacher, who dedicated his first book to that great fount of ecclesiastical patronage, the 1st Duke of Newcastle, he owed his stall at Westminster to his role as domestic chaplain to Princess Amelia, the aunt of

George III. Small wonder that among his most notable contributions to public debate was a sermon defending the necessity of a well-funded order of clergy. He died, at his prebendal house in Little Dean's Yard, in 1816, having served the abbey since 1765.[8]

All the deans and canons were pluralists. The deans were almost invariably Bishops of Rochester and, generally, rectors of Islip in Oxfordshire too. The abbey had a range of livings, to which it presented its prebendaries and their friends: St Margaret's and St John's in Westminster, St Bride's in Fleet Street and Christ Church in Newgate Street, as well as a clutch of proprietary chapels and other churches in more rural spots. Service in the Chapel Royal was often a qualification for appointment to Westminster Abbey and continued thereafter for most canons. Almost all prebendaries also had other jobs in other parishes, cathedrals, or colleges. Writing from his parish in Surrey in April 1768, the sub-dean John Thomas, who combined his parochial cure and his Westminster prebend with the rectory of St Bride's and the role of sub-almoner of York, regretted that he had been unable to prepare properly for his annual period of service as a royal chaplain because of his duties as a magistrate.[9] Yet other canons had still more challenging responsibilities. In the early 1830s, for instance, the twelve prebendaries included the Bishops of Gloucester, Lichfield and Coventry, Hereford, and Bristol, as well as the Dean of Ripon.

Pluralism did not necessarily betoken neglect. Notwithstanding their other responsibilities, chapter minutes show that the canons of the 1830s who also held bishoprics were diligent in discharging their duties as governors of the abbey, as had been many of their predecessors. Nor was pluralism understood as a problem. It was seen, rather, as the natural reward for good service, real talent or genuine piety. Indeed, contemporaries expressed themselves surprised and even alarmed when pluralists sought to disencumber themselves of their roles.[10] On learning in 1764 that the dean, Zachary Pearce, was intent on resigning either his bishopric or the deanery, a former prebendary who had gone on to become both Bishop of Bristol and, at the same time, Dean of St Paul's, repeatedly wrote to remonstrate that 'It would really be hurting the church to separate two preferments each of which adds so much to the value of the other.'[11]

Nonetheless, these multiple responsibilities did mean that Westminster was only ever a part — and sometimes rather a small part — of the prebendaries' lives. It was assumed that even the most devoted would spend much of their time elsewhere.[12] Others, as the disgruntled reformer John Jebb put it, would stay away 'except during the height of the London season'.[13] Several omitted to meet even the minimum requirement of residing and attending daily service for least a month a year.[14] In 1797, for example, nine of the twelve prebendaries were fined for non-attendance in the preceding year: Joseph Hoare and William Cleaver failed to make all thirty of the thirty days allotted to them. As Hoare was the principal of Jesus College, Oxford, and Cleaver combined

133

By an account of Mulcts for failure of attending Divine Service in the year ending with November last

		£	s	d
Sir Rich.ᵈ Cope is to pay	for 9 days in March	6	0	0
D.ʳ Hoare	for 30 days in September	20	0	0
D.ʳ Bell	for 1 day in April	0	13	4
D.ʳ Wake	for 3 days in May	2	0	0
D.ʳ Wetherell	for 11 days in July	7	6	8
Bp. of Chester	for 15 days in Oct.ʳ & 15 in November	20	0	0
D.ʳ Smith	for 8 days in December	5	6	8
D.ʳ Cole	for 1 day in June	0	13	4
M.ʳ Moss	for 1 day in January	0	13	4
		62	13	4
Whereof				
To the several Prebendaries attending		55	6	8
And there remains for the Poor		7	6	8

The course of Residence observed since the first day of December last and to be continued for one year is as follows

1796 December D.ʳ Finch

112   This entry in the abbey's Chapter Act book, 23 February 1797, records the fines ('mulcts') levied against nine of the abbey's prebendaries for absence from services in the year to November 1796; as it attests, dereliction of duty was common.

his headship of Brasenose College in the same university with his role as Bishop of Chester, presumably they had better – or, at any rate, other – things to do.[15]

In the absence of consistent prebendal presence, much depended on the person of the dean. Here, too, pluralism was potentially problematic. After all, in 1802, it was the dean, Samuel Horsley, who led the way in absenting himself from services, neglecting to turn up no fewer than forty-two times in his two months of required residence.[16] Several deans spent much of the year at their episcopal palace in Bromley. Others occupied themselves in the parsonage at Islip. Attendance at court and parliament often proved onerous, too, while the advanced age of some deans – whether at the time of their appointment or after years of service – could cause difficulties.[17] Samuel Bradford, who initially combined his roles at Westminster and at Rochester with the mastership of Corpus Christi College, Cambridge, was described as 'indeed super-annuated when he became Dean'. At the coronation of George II and Queen Caroline in 1727 he was not only unable to walk unaided, but 'At the Sacrament had like to have pour'd the Wine in the Cup into the King's Bosom.'[18] Moreover,

113   The brilliant but combative Francis Atterbury became Dean of Westminster in 1713, just before the death of Queen Anne and the accession of George I (which he deeply deplored); his support for the Jacobite cause led to his arrest and conviction for treason, and his enforced exile. This portrait, after Godfrey Kneller, was painted in the year of his preferment to the deanship.

even the most robust and assertive deans always had to contend with their chapter and the strong views of the strong men that comprised it. In the end, however, John Dart was not wrong to suggest in 1723 that 'The Dean may now be said to enjoy all the Honour, Power and Prerogatives the former Abbats did.'[19] When a dean truly exerted himself, things did change, no matter who he was. Old and infirm he might be, yet even Bradford 'would never hear of the least abatement of the highest of the pretensions, his predecessor had set up'.[20]

113   The predecessor who had bequeathed to Bradford such an exalted view and whom Dart envisaged as a latter-day abbot was Francis Atterbury (1713–22). He was an intriguing, troubling figure. A brilliant product of Westminster School and Christ Church, Oxford, Atterbury was a friend of poets and a patron of the arts. A powerful speaker and 'as Judicious, Instructive, Convincing, Persuasive, and Delightful a *Preacher*, as ever *England* bred', he was also a gifted writer and a corrosively ingenious polemicist, whose work, as one historian observed, 'set the tone' for the great debates about Church and state that racked parliament, the court and the Church's ruling body – Convocation – in the first few decades of the eighteenth century. His learning, his wit and his 'lively piercing eyes' made him an attractive figure. But his pugnacity, his ruthlessness, his

ambition and his incivility made him an intolerable – even a dangerous – person to cross. He was, as Daniel Defoe put it, 'insufferably haughty, superrogant [overweeningly arrogant] and enterprising, restless and indefatigable in pursuing his designs'.[21] This combination of ability and ambition was to prove almost fatal.

Atterbury bullied his way to preferment and remained unceasingly belligerent thereafter. As Dean of Carlisle from 1704, his furious rows with the cathedral chapter grew to such an intensity that, in the words of his biographer, 'it was thought wise to obtain a royal licence excusing him from further attendance'. His time as Dean of Christ Church (1711–13) proved no less traumatic. Nonetheless, his importance within Convocation and his fierce support for the ruling Tory ministry meant that he believed himself entitled to still greater honours. With much reluctance – 'I never knew the Queen do anything with so much reluctancy', recalled one observer – Anne grudgingly agreed to make him Bishop of Rochester and Dean of Westminster. As Atterbury arrived at the abbey to take up his duties, a 'terrible storm' broke out in the skies overhead.[22] Never was a pathetic fallacy more prescient.

'Frank Scammony', as his Whig critics dubbed him, was far from unsympathetic to the place. Indeed, as an old boy of the school, he was emotionally invested in Westminster, and at the death of Joseph Addison in 1719 was to call the scholars into the north aisle of Henry VII's chapel to attend the funeral, clad in white surplices and holding tapers in their hands. As this suggests, Atterbury was attracted to the rituals and robes as well as the associations of the abbey. He was already, as a founder of the St Cecilia Society, publicly committed to the revival of choral music. Just as important, perhaps, was the fact that Westminster had been the scene of so many of his triumphs – not least as an orator and operator in Convocation, which met within the abbey. Atterbury intended to be buried there, commissioning a tomb at the west end of the nave, 'as far from Kings and Kaisars, as the space will admit of'. As a leading figure in the establishment of the Commission for Building Fifty New Churches, he was also well placed to funnel money intended for new buildings into an old abbey. Although he played little role in the commission itself, the act of parliament that he helped to inspire ensured that Westminster continued to receive substantial sums every year for its restoration.[23] The architectural improvements enacted across this period would be attributed to other people, but owed something to Atterbury's manoeuvrings.

Yet for all this, as one historian puts it, 'in many ways the Abbey brought out the worst' in Atterbury, whose irascibility was compounded by the painful bouts of gout he increasingly endured. He found the Deanery dark and disagreeable, and far preferred spending time at his palace in Bromley. Worse still, his attempts to run Westminster by diktat provoked a predictable response from the prebendaries: exactly the same response, in fact, as he had encountered at Carlisle and Christ Church. 'To *live peaceably with all*

Men', he had once preached – and in a sermon on the 'Duty of living peaceably' – 'is a Thing absolutely impossible.' Thus, although apparently capable of comprehending that fellow deans, like his friend Jonathan Swift, should use subtlety and discretion, Atterbury, in his time at Westminster, revealed that he himself knew no other mode than aggression, assertion and imposition on others.

After some initial skirmishes, battle began in 1715 over the appointment of a new high steward for Westminster. A year later, the chapter split over the vacant Westminster archdeaconry and then the living of Islip. Two years after that, civil war broke out as Atterbury attempted to force through his proposals for a new dormitory at Westminster School. The argument was ostensibly one about planning, as prebendaries disagreed with Atterbury and with each other over the impact of the building on their garden. But it was also – perhaps chiefly – about authority, the senior members of the chapter setting themselves against the presumptions of their uppity dean. Remarkably – unprecedentedly – the case eventually found its way not only to law but to the House of Lords. Atterbury won. The dormitory was built. Worse, however, was to come.[24]

As a convinced High Churchman and a passionate High Tory, Atterbury struggled with the Hanoverian succession of 1714. Before Queen Anne's death, there had been talk of his elevation to the see of Canterbury. The accession of George I (r. 1714–27) brought all such hopes to an end, while the prorogation of Convocation in 1717 was designed to frustrate attempts by Atterbury and his allies to institutionalize Tory opposition within the Church.[25] In 1715 he was even excluded from the Commission for Building Fifty New Churches by a Whig government bent on revenge. It was, then, scarcely surprising that although he remained superficially loyal to the crown Atterbury flirted with treason: composing anonymous anti-governmental pamphlets in 1715; raising funds for the Jacobites in 1716; and even writing to James III, the Old Pretender, in 1717. Nothing came of these indiscretions, but age, disappointment and ill health turned this flirtation into a more serious relationship in the early 1720s. Atterbury began to act as James's English agent, acquiring money, establishing a network and plotting a coup. There was even a suggestion that the Jacobites would use the Westminster funeral of the Duke of Marlborough as the occasion for their rising. As it was, this would be Atterbury's last service in the abbey. On 24 August 1722 – just over a fortnight after the ducal interment – he was arrested. He was imprisoned in the Tower of London, tried in the House of Lords, found guilty and exiled for life. Atterbury died in France in 1732, a disappointed and undeniably tragic figure, having lived for a decade as a 'man with whom it was a felony even to hold a conversation'.[26]

★

After Atterbury

Westminster was kind to its disgraced dean during his imprisonment in the Tower. Servants brought him fresh water from the abbey's supply twice daily, and the chapter met frequently to ensure that he received a fair share of the moneys that were accruing in his absence. But on his conviction, the government rushed to replace him, ensuring, with the appointment of Samuel Bradford (1723–31), that they had installed a loyal, Low Church Whig instead of a resentful, treacherous Jacobite Tory.[27] Bradford was not the only person to benefit from Atterbury's fall. The enterprising Edward Willes, who had deciphered the letters that provided crucial evidence of the Atterbury plot, was rewarded with a Westminster prebend a year after the trial, in 1724.[28]

The new dean was a perfect symbol of the new dispensation, and, indeed, Bradford may be seen as exemplary of the Hanoverian Church as a whole: a figure firmly committed to unity and concord, a Protestant state and an Erastian Church.[29] He had been among the leaders of the opposition to Atterbury within the chapter, and made his disapproval of Jacobite pretensions apparent in a series of public statements, not least in one of the annual sermons preached before the House of Lords in Westminster Abbey to commemorate the death of Charles I. While Atterbury used such occasions to extol the Christ-like nature of the martyred king and to prophesy further national disaster until the power of the Church to extirpate sectaries was fully restored, Bradford focused firmly on the blessings accrued from the Hanoverian succession and a Church so 'firmly established' that it could tolerate 'those who dissent from it, to worship God according to their own apprehension'.[30]

Bradford, in short, could almost have been born to serve as a sharp contrast to his predecessor. Educated at Cambridge, rather than Oxford, far from sharing Atterbury's desire to rise from 'the irksomenesses of a college life' into the grander world of clerical preferment, he had left the university without a degree, having experienced 'scruples of conscience' that made him unwilling to subscribe to the Thirty-Nine Articles.[31] Instead of espousing an unimpeachable orthodoxy, he had associated with freethinkers and, most notoriously, with the heretical William Whiston, whose writings – under the influence of Atterbury – became a *cause célèbre* in the Convocation of 1711. As master of Corpus Christi College, Cambridge, Bradford had battled with Tories and been defeated in his campaign to become vice-chancellor by a group opposed to him as a famous 'whig and a decided friend of the house of Hanover'.[32]

Some of his early decisions as dean suggested that Bradford's policies as well as his past would distinguish him from his predecessor. He stopped any payments to Atterbury and regulated bell-ringing so that the abbey commemorated only suitably loyalist causes. He relied more heavily on others, and was particularly dependent on his son-in-law

John Denne, a former fellow of Corpus Christi College, Cambridge, and author of *The blessing of a Protestant King and royal family to the nation* (1727), whom he made Archdeacon of Rochester. Most of the dean's actions, however, revealed continuity. Just like Atterbury, his elevation was marked by the acquisition of a new canopy and cushion for his stall. Just like Atterbury, he had a high ideal of the power of the Church to regulate behaviour in general, and of his own right to oversee the abbey in particular. Although aged and often unwell, he was drawn into elaborate liturgical events like the glittering coronation of George II and the first installation, in 1725, of knights of the Order of the Bath. More tangibly still, he continued to oversee the restoration of the building and the campaign for further parliamentary grants to effect it. With Bradford's appointment, the regime – and the regime to which the dean was loyal – had certainly changed. The role of the abbey and its head had certainly not.[33]

The same would prove true of Bradford's successor, Joseph Wilcocks, who served as Dean of Westminster and Bishop of Rochester from 1731 until his death in 1756. A fervent Hanoverian Whig, he was a chaplain to George I and a tutor to George II's daughters, and had been elevated to a Westminster prebendary and the see of Gloucester in 1721 as a reward for his conspicuous loyalty. As Bishop of Gloucester, he had repaired the episcopal palace, and delivered a series of strikingly obsequious sermons on the blessings of a Protestant monarchy – most notably, perhaps, one preached at Westminster Abbey to the House of Lords, celebrating the failure of Atterbury's 'secret and clandestine Plot'. Under him, there could be no fears of a recrudescence of treachery within Westminster and, indeed, the chapter responded to the Jacobite rising of 1745 by donating £300 to help combat the rebellion.[34] Wilcocks, it is true, was more eirenic than his predecessors: he agreed to confirm with the chapter all his appointments to posts within the abbey; it was also settled that nominations to livings would be doled out strictly according to seniority. But he was no less committed to the place. When offered the Archbishopric of York, he quoted another Bishop of Rochester, the saintly John Fisher, 'Though this my wife be poor, I must not think of changing her for one more opulent.' He worked to enforce residence requirements on the canons and engaged in an almost perpetual effort to petition parliament for further resources. Under Wilcocks, the restoration of the building was completed and the two west towers built, a fact commemorated in a relief on his memorial at Westminster. In a conscious imitation of Atterbury, indeed, he was granted permission to create a family vault and was buried at the west end of the abbey.[35]

Zachary Pearce, who presided – despite growing disability and deepening disengagement – as dean from 1756 to 1768, followed in this tradition of assertive Whig loyalty, combined with a respect for precedent and a strong desire for an untroubled abbey. In many respects, he personified such attitudes. A scholar at Westminster and then at Trinity College, Cambridge, he was quickly picked up by a rising figure, the lawyer and future lord chancellor Thomas Parker, ennobled as Lord Macclesfield in 1716. With Macclesfield as his patron, Pearce experienced a steady ascent within the ranks of the Church. He was also employed to publish anonymous defences of the government's treatment of Atterbury. Even Macclesfield's own impeachment in 1725 did not ultimately disturb Pearce's progress, for he had established connections with other important sources of support: the Duke of Newcastle; his old schoolfriend William Pulteney, the future of Earl of Bath; and Queen Caroline, who insistently pushed for his preferment. Lord Bath's letters reveal just how hard he exerted himself on Pearce's behalf, a campaign that eventually resulted in the deanship of Winchester and the see of Bangor, and then promotion as Dean of Westminster and Bishop of Rochester. Small wonder that critics would dub Pearce 'a Court-Clergyman, a Hunter of Preferments; a man who is for obtaining a Mitre, by Methods which ought in Justice to exclude him from a Curacy'.[36]

In fairness, this was somewhat unjust. Whatever Pearce's motivations as a younger man, by the time he arrived at Westminster his ambition had rather played itself out. Having inherited a fortune from his father, who set an encouraging example by retiring at the age of 40, he similarly hoped, as he put it, 'to retire to a private life'. This inclination, combined with growing age and infirmity, and a congenital incapacity to make decisions swiftly, which left him 'purring and puzzling' over matters that others might dispatch in minutes, ensured that his years at Westminster were filled with repeated attempts to resign. With no precedent for a bishop to do any such thing, Pearce's efforts at retirement relied on his ability to mobilize exactly the same sorts of patronage that his progress up the ranks had deployed. Meetings with the king and conversations with the Archbishop of Canterbury, lobbying by prominent politicians and hints from third parties, when the time was right, to intercede with the current ministry: Pearce deployed all his arts, and in 1768 was finally able to leave Westminster, though he remained at Rochester for another six years, recording his half-triumph in a *nunc dimittis* which began, 'From all Decanal cares at last set free, / (O could that Freedom still more perfect be)'.[37]

During the campaign to facilitate his protégé's retirement, Lord Bath referred to the deanship as 'the troublesome part of your preferment', and it is evident that Westminster did take up a lot of Pearce's time and effort. Under Pearce, the everyday work of the place went on, of course; the estate was developed yet further; the coronation of George III (r. 1760–1820) and funerals and memorials of numerous figures great and small were undertaken. The bicentenary of Queen Elizabeth's charter was celebrated in 1760, the dean preaching a sermon that characteristically eulogized monarchy, learning and Protestantism alike. Pearce had to contend with disputatious canons, not

114   During his long deanship (1768–93), Dean John Thomas (depicted here wearing the robes of the Dean of the Most Honourable Order of the Bath) made many charitable donations out of his personal wealth; his determination to care for and enhance the abbey and its buildings is reflected in the inclusion of the first few bays of the ambulatory as the backdrop to this portrait attributed to Joshua Reynolds, c.1780.

least Thomas Wilson – that 'dirty disappointed hunter of a mitre', as Horace Walpole described him – who quarrelled unceasingly with his fellow prebendaries, and whose negligence necessitated a rebuke from the dean.[38] Above all, Pearce's correspondence shows that his work involved endless permutations of patronage, as he responded

114 to requests and made supplications of his own. Prebendaries sought places for their relatives and hangers-on, and noblemen hoped to impose their clients. Perhaps his greatest achievement in this respect was ensuring that his successor was his own candidate, the sub-dean, John Thomas, who would serve as dean from 1768 to 1793 and became Bishop of Rochester on Pearce's death in 1774.[39]

Admired not least for 'the urbanity of his manners, the suavity of his disposition', Thomas was yet another in the lengthening line of establishment figures to inhabit the Deanery. He was, as his contemporary Edward Gibbon might have described him, 'a respectable prelate, alike qualified for this world and the next'. Thomas would also follow his predecessors' more unhappy example by becoming progressively less capable, to the extent that, in his last few months, he was replaced by a proxy. But from the moment of his appointment, he showed a real determination to improve the abbey, combating laxities in the liturgy, the failure of prebendaries to preach when required, and pursuing changes to the

115   Under Dean Thomas's tenure, the abbey's 13th-century choir stalls (shown in this painting of the choir by a Dutch artist, *c.*1700) were demolished in 1775 and replaced with new fittings designed by Henry Keene.

fabric. The Jerusalem Chamber was restored, the Deanery radically refitted, Dean's Yard laid out and the choir stalls replaced. Such zeal was not always welcomed. Like   115 Pearce, Thomas found the deanship 'a troublesome post', and, like Pearce, he found Thomas Wilson an incorrigible absentee. He struggled to establish consensus over the reordering of the choir, as well as encountering opposition over his rights and his ability to appoint his clients. Nonetheless, it was under Thomas that Westminster came to host successive choral festivals. Moreover, as a wealthy and generous man, he was an important benefactor to the abbey, and his work on the Deanery, in particular, helped to make it a suitable home for a Georgian gentleman – an 'extravagant folly', in his own words, for which he paid the lion's share, allowing a whole year's salary to be eaten up in these refurbishments.[40]

At first sight, Thomas's successor similarly seems like business as usual, and, in some respects, he was; as a godson of Zachary Pearce, it might even be argued that he was, by adoption, one of the Westminster family. Samuel Horsley (1793–1802) had – like all his eighteenth-century predecessors – risen through patronage and pluralism. He was renowned as a fierce loyalist and earned his preferment, so it was said, with a highly emotional defence of the British constitution in Westminster Abbey at the annual House of Lords service commemorating the death of Charles I. Yet, if John Thomas had been an improver, Horsley was a keen reformer – albeit one with a decidedly conservative cast of mind. If Thomas was suave, Horsley was brusque. Possessed of a 'perpetually sharp manner', as his biographer puts it, 'it is easier to believe that he was respected than . . . beloved'. Almost from the moment he arrived, he was determined to shake up the sleepy institution. New bibles and new music books were bought; the garden was re-gravelled and the library rearranged, with unbound texts sent for binding 'under the direction of the Dean'. Two bell-ringers were sacked 'for neglect of duty', and the abbey's baker was given new instructions for the composition of his bread.[41]

True enough, Horsley's wider responsibilities – not least his active role within the House of Lords – frequently distracted him from the quotidian business of the abbey. Nevertheless, his willingness to take on vested interests did effect a particularly important reform in the choir, ensuring greater continuity of personnel from one service to another. His efforts to entrench reforms in Westminster's rental roll also paid – literal – dividends, with receipts rising significantly throughout his time and afterwards. The abbey's annual income of £5,139 in 1793 had become, by 1803, one of £8,123; five years later, it would reach £11,428.[42] This was not entirely due to Horsley's work, to be sure; but a less active dean might not have seized the opportunities so firmly or successfully.

More important even than these changes was the consequence of Horsley's departure, for he was to be the last dean who also served as Bishop of Rochester. William Vincent, who succeeded him (1802–15), was a very different figure: a Westminster schoolboy, under master, second master, head master, and then prebendary; except for a few years in Cambridge, he had barely left the precincts of the abbey since the age of 7. 'For exercise', it was recalled, 'he made no allowance; and generally had no more than could be gained in walking to and from the school.' This was no prince of the Church. In fact, Vincent had been appointed to his stall in 1801 as a sort of pension. Worn out by teaching, he was intended to be able to retire on the proceeds of his prebend. He owed his elevation as dean to his educational rather more than his political or ecclesiastical commitment. Although he was a royal chaplain and sub-almoner to the king, and although he repeatedly – and, on occasion, famously – preached sermons

116   An entry in the Chapter Act book, 20 June 1807, refers to the 'decay and ruinous appearance' of the fine Gothic chapel of Henry VII, details expenditure on the fabric met by the Dean and Chapter in recent years, and petitions parliament for restoration funds.

defending the constitutional status quo, it seems that it was a pamphlet defending the public schools that led to his preferment. As dean – against some opposition from members of his chapter and much obstruction by members of parliament – he oversaw the restoration of Henry VII's chapel and a series of repairs that followed a serious fire in the roof of the abbey in 1803.[43] He also served as a notably engaged rector of Islip. But, in many respects, his main importance was what he stood for: an abbey still governed by pluralists, perhaps; yet now with a dean who no longer also served as a bishop and sat in the House of Lords.

116

John Ireland (1816–42), belongs as much in the next chapter as in this, but he was, essentially, a figure from the eighteenth century and a natural successor to Horsley and

Vincent, both of whom had been his friends. Like all the Georgian deans, he had been vocal in his defence of Church and king; he had also acquired an important patron in the shape of Lord Liverpool. He grew rich on preferments, leaving substantial sums to Westminster School, his own home town of Ashburton in Devon, and the University of Oxford, which still appoints a Dean Ireland professor. For the son of a butcher, this was no small achievement. Like his immediate predecessors, too, Ireland continued the process of incremental change. Under him, pressure on the minor canons and members of the choir to fulfil their contracts was intensified; the occupants of abbey livings were increasingly encouraged – and sometimes compelled – to reside in their parishes and undertake a conscientious parochial cure. Parsonages were built and the value of stipends augmented. The prebendaries also experienced some change. It was agreed that they should no longer rent out their houses, and that accommodation would be allocated on the basis of need rather than simple seniority. Ireland, however, found that such change was seen by outsiders as neither fast nor fundamental enough. The Ecclesiastical Commission, established in 1835, was to force though more radical reforms.[44] Ireland, like the abbey, discovered that the old ways – old connections and old loyalties – which had sustained the place throughout this period, had lost their former purchase.

Loyalty and Royalty

The unalloyed loyalism of successive deans – at least after Atterbury – reflected the general temper of the eighteenth-century Church of England. It was also a consequence of the patterns of patronage that shaped Church and state.[45] But there was a more particular reason why it mattered that Westminster Abbey should be governed by safe and safely dependable men. The dean was a figure at court, not least through his annual sermons preached in the Chapel Royal on Good Friday. He was also an active participant in politics, and, when Bishop of Rochester, a member of the House of Lords as well. Not the least of the reasons that the government punished Atterbury so severely on his fall was the fact that he used his role as head of the Court of Burgesses in Westminster to sway elections in the Jacobite interest. Under more reliable deans, the ministry could rest easy, knowing that the full force of the abbey's influence would be used on its behalf. In 1727 and 1734, the chapter exercised such tight control that loyalist Whigs were elected unopposed to the two Westminster City seats. In 1741 the high bailiff of Westminster, John Lever, received £1,500 from the secret service fund to oversee a fiercely contested poll, while the high constable, Arthur Rawlinson, hired a gang of heavies led by 'a profest Boxer' to bully the electors into line. Eight years later, in 1749, the dean himself was drawn into the fray, applying pressure to vote appropriately on such apparently insignificant figures as 'Mr Cornwall who shows ye Tombs at West' Abbey.'[46]

The abbey itself also played an important part in the political life of the nation. Some of the site was appropriated to state functions; the chapter house – described in 1755 as 'The Kings Record Room' – was used to store official papers, and the Pyx Chamber beside it housed the country's standard weights and measures.[47] More publicly, the abbey was the site of important national events, not least parliamentary sermons. Each year, to commemorate the accession of the reigning monarch, the execution of Charles I, the restoration of Charles II and the 'Deliverance from the Gunpowder Plot', members of the House of Commons would process to St Margaret's and members of the House of Lords to the abbey, where peers assembled in the choir – laymen sitting in the south stalls and bishops in the north stalls.[48] The fast on 30 January, the anniversary of Charles I's death, was seen as especially significant, though, to be sure, it was not always a well-attended event: 'emotive as this occasion was' for some, 'it rarely tempted them to endure the ritual tedium of an official sermon'. But the rite had an important symbolic role, as it brought Church and state together. The sermons were publicly printed, and sometimes very widely distributed.[49] And it was, after all, a sermon on precisely this occasion that propelled Samuel Horsley's preferment.

Loyalty to Church, to state and – for that matter – to party thus dictated much about Westminster life. It even influenced the chimes of St Margaret's Church, which, from 1748, rang out 'God save the king'.[50] This amalgam of loyalties can likewise be seen in an important innovation of the eighteenth century, albeit one disguised as a revival of medieval practice. The Order of the Bath was inaugurated in 1725. It served a twofold purpose: intended, in Horace Walpole's words, 'to supply a fund of favours in lieu of places', it was also meant to cement the legitimacy of the Hanoverian regime.[51] The decision to make Westminster Abbey the order's home and the chapel of Henry VII the location for the knights' installation was thus highly significant. Choosing the   117 abbey over Windsor or Winchester or some other place ensured that 'the pageantry would be accessible to large metropolitan crowds'. Choosing the chapel helped to make it 'not just a shrine, but a living monument to the new dynasty'. Installations were infrequent – they took place in 1725, 1732, 1744 and 1749, and almost a decade apart thereafter – but they were undeniably splendid affairs, not much less elaborate than coronations. The processions to and from the abbey – with the knights and the dean in red robes and the prebendaries in their white mantles – were certainly sights worth seeing, while the chapel, even in later installations such as that of 1788, 'was superbly decorated' with crimson velvet. The standards, hung in the chapel, were a constant reminder of the order's existence.[52] Here were loyalty, royalty and pageantry, indeed.

118   James Watts's wooden model, 1818, for the royal vault beneath Henry VII's chapel, intended by George II as a Hanoverian mausoleum. The space is divided into separate chambers to accommodate sarcophagi and urns of family members; the far end was reserved for the marble sarcophagus and urns containing the remains of George II and Queen Caroline and their deceased infants.

The installation of knights of the Order of the Bath was not the only way in which the Hanoverian regime sought to use Westminster. Although, in 1725, Henry VII's chapel was described as 'entirely out of use', it was already beginning to be turned into a royal mausoleum. Here it was that George II had interred his infant son George William in 1718, and here, too, he would himself be buried in 1760, just as, more importantly, it was here that he commissioned a vault for his much loved wife, Queen Caroline, in 118 1737, and here that he buried his estranged son, Frederick, Prince of Wales, in 1751. The external signs of this royal crypt were not, it must be said, all that prepossessing. Histories and guidebooks would complain that the only monument to the king and

117 (FACING PAGE)   The choice of the abbey as the home of the Order of the Bath meant that the people of London were able to witness the splendid pageantry of the installations of the knights, which in turn promoted the popularity of the Hanoverian regime; this engraving of the 1812 ceremony (published by Rudolph Ackermann) shows Henry VII's chapel festooned with standards, the knights in their plumed helmets seated in the pews, and the royal box at the east end.

his family was a plate of perforated brass set into the floor of the chapel.[53] Nor was the trend perpetuated by George II's successors, who chose Windsor rather than Westminster for their last resting place. The interminable fights between the abbey authorities, the Office of Works, and the lord chamberlain's department over control of the space would also cause significant problems long after George II's death.[54] But he left behind what has been described as 'the largest and most sophisticated vault yet created in the Abbey', and the scale of these funerals was equally unprecedented – a choir made up of 100 singers attended Queen Caroline's and one of 155 George II's. This revival of the abbey's role as what Addison called 'the repository of our English kings' both confirmed and heightened its significance to the dynasty.[55]

Above all, of course, Westminster was the site of successive coronations. To be sure, these events were neither the sacral, solemn Stuart coronations of the past, nor the elaborately choreographed confections that would be offered by the Windsors in the future. The early Hanoverians – like their continental counterparts – rejected notions of mystical kingship in favour of more enlightened attitudes.[56] Later kings broadly followed this tradition, even if they differed in the enthusiasm with which they embraced the ritual. The lavish coronation of George IV (r. 1820–30) was underwritten by a parliamentary grant of more than £240,000.[57] The grudgingly conceded celebration for William IV (r. 1830–37) was so meagre that it was referred to as his 'half-Crownation'.[58] But neither of these events was in any respect a mystical moment. Even George IV's *Gesamtkunstwerk*, in which almost all attendees wore pseudo-Tudor dress designed especially for the occasion, was more like 'a gigantic fancy-dress pageant' than a consecration.[59]

An absence of sacramentalism, however, did not denote a lack of significance. There can be no denying the importance of these events to the kings or to the abbey. For the sovereigns, the coronation was the public confirmation of their legitimacy; for the abbey, it was a proof of the institution's role not just as the resting place of kings but also as the site where mere mortals were made into monarchs. George I's coronation in 1714 may have been hastily assembled, modelled essentially on that of Queen Anne, and explained inexpertly by his ministers, 'who could not speak German, to the King, who could not speak English, in Latin, which they must [all] have spoken very imperfectly'. But it was attended by thousands, and some sense of its grand scale may be gauged from the remarkable range of textiles it called for: 20 yards of 'silk stuff', 21 yards of carpeting, 22 yards of gold brocade, an 'Anointing Pall' 11 yards long.[60] The ceremony for George II (1727) was exceptionally impressive: 'a return to royal display on a scale that had probably not been seen since 1685'. Reputedly, jewels worth £10,000 were sewn into Queen Caroline's dress, making it so heavy that she struggled to kneel for the sacrament. Handel's four coronation anthems, including 'Zadok the priest', were composed – on the king's request – for the occasion, and were performed by the largest group of professional singers and musicians ever assembled in England up to

119

119   The opening bars of George Frideric Handel's original manuscript score for 'Zadok the priest', one of four anthems commissioned from the composer by George II for his imposing coronation ceremony in 1727.

that time; the occasion would be remembered as 'the first grand Musical Performance in the Abbey'.[61] George III's coronation in 1761 was, in its turn, so gargantuan that the opening alone was staggeringly lengthy. Starting from Westminster Hall at 11 a.m., the procession was of such a scale that it was not until 1.30 p.m. that the king and queen actually entered the abbey. The whole service took six hours to complete.[62] Significantly, even though William IV believed that the lavish affair of his brother George IV in 1821 had been inappropriate, and that the dinners and balls associated with the coronation were now 'at variance with the genius of the age we live in', he nonetheless fully accepted that he could not dispense with the service at Westminster.[63]

    For the inhabitants of the abbey, a coronation meant hard work, not infrequent arguments, and substantial modifications to the site. The work was various: the choir needed to master new music and cope with the addition of extra, sometimes unfamiliar, choristers; the abbey staff were required to locate and prepare the great robes that were used only on these occasions, as well as acquire bibles and prayer books, furniture and

120

120   George IV's opulent – and extravagantly costly – coronation took place in the abbey on
19 July 1821; the king commissioned a new crown and a train 27 feet long for his robe,
and selected costumes inspired by Tudor styles for all the participants. A banquet for 300 at
Westminster Hall followed the five-hour ceremony in the abbey.

fittings, carpets and cloths, new gowns for the vergers, a new coat for the beadle, and
new surplices for the singers; glaziers, smiths, carpenters, clerks, mat-makers, organ-
builders and others were all taken on for the occasion. The arguments were had with
an equally remarkable range of people – not only craftsmen and tradesmen, but, above
all, with the officials of the court, for at a coronation, just as at a royal funeral, the
abbey became a sort of no-man's-land, with the Dean and Chapter facing off against
the earl marshal, the lord chamberlain, the Office of Works, even the Archbishop of
Canterbury, all of whom had interests in and authority over aspects of the service. The
modifications to the building were all-encompassing, transforming the place into an

auditorium, with what was called 'the Theatre' at its heart. At a cost of many thousands of pounds, scaffolding for seats and viewing platforms was erected inside the abbey and all around it. The organ was dismantled, the altar removed, the choir stalls altered, and even the trees in St Margaret's churchyard were cut down.[64] Never did the abbey look less like itself; yet never, in the minds of many, did it seem more like itself.

Arthur Penrhyn Stanley (dean 1864–81) was almost right when he observed in his history of the abbey that 'The Coronations are but as the outward wave of English history', breaking on Westminster and on the wider nation 'without leaving any permanent mark.'[65] There were, after all, some lasting effects: the new organ of 1730, installed to replace the one removed for George II's coronation; the new choir stalls of 1775, 'contrived to make room for more splendid arrangements, as for the coronation of the British sovereigns'; and the potentially serious subsidence caused by the scaffolding set up for George IV's.[66] The memory of these great events also lingered on, perpetuated by the regal symbols, the royal tombs and the coronation chair in Edward the Confessor's chapel. Guides and guidebooks similarly emphasized this link – as they had done as far back as the seventeenth century.

Not least, the link between abbey and monarchy was reinforced by the extraordinarily popular waxwork collection, which moved from Henry VII's chapel to Abbot Islip's chapel in 1767, and ended up in Henry V's chapel nineteen years later. An eclectic mix of funerary effigies and specially commissioned images, the figures that made up this

45
85

121

121   In this caricature by Richard Newton (1792), visitors from the countryside gawp at waxworks of George III and Queen Charlotte, under the aegis of an official guide; Westminster's motley collection of effigies and wax figures may have been derided by art connoisseurs, but they associated the abbey with the monarchy in the public mind, and entrance fees provided a valuable source of revenue.

'ragged regiment' experienced what has been described as 'the heyday of their career' in the eighteenth century.[67] Particularly significant in this respect were the expensive models of William III and Mary II, which cost as much as £187 in 1725, and the figure of Elizabeth I – 'whose face is pinched into most expressive and venerable old-maid*ism*' – bought to celebrate the bicentenary of 1760. These may have appalled the artistic elite, who bemoaned such 'rubbish', but they served as important reminders of temporary events as well as an ongoing tradition, confirming the abbey's place as a royal peculiar and as peculiarly royal.[68]

Form and Function

The links with court and parliament, the networks of patronage that sustained and were sustained by the abbey, had still more material consequences. State support for restoration work was justified – and by Sir Robert Walpole, no less – on the grounds that it was a national disgrace for Westminster to remain visibly decaying. 'Should we let the Church where the Bodies of our greatest Princes are deposited, and which lately received the Remains of a Princess [Queen Caroline] whose memory must ever be dear to Britain, to be the only Church in the whole Kingdom not properly provided for', he argued in the House of Commons, 'we should justly expose ourselves to the Censure of the rest of Europe, and of every Stranger who visits us.'[69] And it was not rhetorical support alone that helped the abbey's case. Petitions to parliament for financial support were backed by George II and championed by the Westminster MP William Clayton, Lord Sundon: a Whig loyalist, a cabinet minister and a man whose wife was one of Queen Caroline's closest friends.[70] Like many others, the abbey helped him politically and he helped the abbey financially as it sought to rebuild itself.

Thus, although the abbey remained conspicuously unrevolutionary throughout this period, it experienced an alteration of its form, and a subtle, but no less important, transformation in its function. From outside, for much of the eighteenth century, Westminster Abbey would have resembled less a church than a building site. Its interior, too, was profoundly changed, not least through the accumulation of an ever larger collection of monuments. Always a tourist attraction, the abbey became a place to see and be seen – 'a site of promenade', a 'gallery' where artists exhibited their talents and men of taste displayed their connoisseurship.[71] It became a testing ground for attitudes to art and architecture and also, increasingly, a state-sponsored pantheon for national heroes. One of eighteenth-century London's unacknowledged 'spaces of modernity', the abbey evolved a hybrid identity.[72] It was very old, it was very proper – indeed, it was intimately linked to the monarchy and the very highest echelons of society – but it was also, not least because of these associations, fashionable, popular and polite.

Visitors at the beginning of the eighteenth century struggled with the same obstacles identified by Henry Keepe in his guide of 1682. Not only was the abbey 'incumbred with private buildings by which she seems in some places altogether hid and obscured'; it had also suffered neglect and decay. 'On the North part', he wrote, in words that would be quoted for decades to come, 'you rather behold the *Skeleton* of a Church than any great comeliness in her appearance, being so shrivelled and parcht by the continual blasts of the Northern Winds, to which she stands exposed, as also the continual smoaks of Sea-Coal . . . which have added more furrows to her declining years, that little of her former beauty now remains.'[73] Attempts at repair were almost equally damaging. In 1713, Sir Christopher Wren's survey of the abbey deplored the plaster patching of the great north window, the cropping of pinnacles, the covering of staircases with 'very improper roofs of timber and lead which can never agree with any other part of the design'. He observed that the west window was 'too feeble', the roof inadequate and the west towers incomplete; the crossing lacked a 'Steeple', and the north side of the abbey was, in a paraphrase of Keepe, so 'incumbered with private tenements', he could not determine what needed to done there.[74] All this would change, in what has been described as 'the most prominent and costly restoration of its day'.[75]

Wren's restoration began in 1697, when parliament made its first grant for the purpose. By the time he produced his survey of 1713, he had already spent almost £50,000 and was able to report repairs to about a third of the south side, the east window and the buttresses in the cloister, as well as some of the roofs.[76] But this was, he made clear, only a start; it was the £4,000 a year produced by the Atterbury-inspired Fifty New Churches Act (1711) that enabled Wren's assistant, William Dickinson, to restore the north transept, with 'the Time-eaten Sculpture and Masonry pared away, the *Gothick* Order justly preserved, the whole adorned with a magnificent Window', as John Dart noted in 1723.[77] Wren's successor, Nicholas Hawksmoor, continued the process, moving to the west front, replacing the great west window and undertaking other major projects.[78] His work was completed, in turn, by the new surveyor, John James. After the expending of another £60,000, the parliamentary grant ceased in 1745.[79] It had been a far from unproblematic process, during which the chapter was forced to petition the Commons again and again for support. It had also left the chapel of Henry VII almost untouched, and in the early nineteenth century the abbey threw itself on parliament's mercy once again, successfully persuading MPs to grant ever increasing sums of money to effect James Wyatt's restoration at a cost of something like £50,000.[80]

These restorations were remarkable in two respects. In the first place, they showed a consistent and somewhat surprising sympathy for what less complimentary critics, such as John Evelyn, regarded as the 'Heavy, Dark, Melancholy and *Monkish Piles*' of the medieval past.[81] Dickinson's plan for the north transept, for instance, though criticized by antiquaries and effaced by the Victorians, nonetheless retained the scale and something of the style of the original building.[82] Henry Keene, who served as surveyor of both the abbey and its wider estates between 1752 and 1776, was even more enthusiastic in seeking to evoke medieval themes. Although Keene was not, in Howard Colvin's words, 'a serious student of Gothic architecture', he was a committed advocate for medieval modes and a sensitive exponent of contemporary Gothic forms.[83] His successor, James Wyatt, would be roundly criticized for his work in other great churches. He even came to be known as 'Wyatt the Destroyer'. But, acting with the master mason Thomas Gayfere, he would prove unusually sympathetic in his treatment of the Tudor details of Henry VII's chapel.[84]

The second and still more striking aspect of these restorations was the fact that they went far beyond repair, and envisaged the final completion of the building. In his letter of 1713, Wren had projected a central tower 'in the *Gothick* form'. He had also observed that the west front should be finished, and the two towers completed.[85] Under Hawksmoor, these projects went forward. Just as he did for Beverley Minster, Hawksmoor produced designs for a central tower, and for what he called the 'sad Ruinous and unfinish'd' west façade.[86] With the enthusiastic encouragement of the dean, Joseph Wilcocks, and the somewhat more reluctant support of parliament, the twin west towers would finally be built. They were an artful composite of classical and Gothic details, combined to create a medieval silhouette – not unlike the towers of Wren's and Hawksmoor's city churches.[87] They were thus a wonderful symbol of the way that the abbey was modernized through using ancient forms.

This balancing act was carried on within the abbey too. The creation of the Order of the Bath necessitated the destruction of the stone screens and the re-creation of the Tudor stalls in Henry VII's chapel – a programme carried out with such stylistic sensitivity in the 1730s and again in the 1770s that its history has only recently been fully uncovered.[88] The gift of a new organ in the aftermath of George II's coronation likewise led to the erection of a new screen, built to plans by Nicholas Hawksmoor. He offered two alternatives: a piece of Doric, swiftly rejected; and the 'Gothic Design' that was approved in 1728.[89]

Nor was this the end of the changes, as Henry Keene's enthusiasm for the medieval past did not prevent him from replacing the choir stalls in 1775. The alteration could have been more dramatic still, as the dean, John Thomas, initially hoped to remove the stalls altogether, with the intention of pushing the choir further eastward to supplant the chapel of Edward the Confessor. This would have been a modish move, and it was one he had admired in James Essex's recent reordering of Ely cathedral.[90] It was

122   In a painting of the abbey (*c.*1734–40), the Italian artist Pietro Fabris depicted a central tower, as proposed by Nicholas Hawksmoor, and lofty spires surmounting the towers at the west end; the central tower was never built, but Hawksmoor's design for the west towers (without spires) was realized. The painting also gives a good impression of the crowded precinct of the abbey, showing the houses and shops that stood against the north wall of the building at this time.

also a suggestion supported by two leading architects in addition to Keene – Essex himself and James Wyatt – and similar programmes would soon be carried out in other cathedrals across England, as they sought to open up their interiors and improve the views along the nave.[91] After much debate and several votes in chapter, however, the choir remained effectively in place, though it was rebuilt in what guides would describe as a 'light and elegant Gothic' of Keene's own devising.[92] That it continued to be acceptable to make changes in Gothic guise is similarly apparent in the decision, taken in 1820, to dismantle Wren's baroque altarpiece, which had been so expensively installed a century before. Despite its authorship, it was now seen as 'decidedly inappropriate in its character to the style of the structure in which it stands'.[93] The logic of Wren's argument, in other words, now dictated his own work's destruction.

109

   All these changes took place within an altered urban environment. The price of parliamentary support for restoration was the removal of those buildings that stood

123   The medieval
gatehouse to the abbey
precinct, used as a prison
after the dissolution of the
monastery, was demolished
in 1776 as part of a
campaign of improvements
to the area. The monument
to former pupils of
Westminster School who
died in the Crimean War
and Indian Mutiny now
stands on this spot, outside
the west door.

against the north wall of the abbey: a development that took decades, speeded up in
the 1770s, and was finally completed at the beginning of the nineteenth century. At
the same time, the precincts were opened up by the demolition of the dilapidated
123   gatehouse gaol and almshouses, which improved access and the view from the west.[94]
This was partly a matter of fashion: at Salisbury, after all, similar improvements led
to the destruction of numerous buildings surrounding the cathedral. It also reflected
parliamentarians' desire to raise the tone of their own immediate environment. But,
above all, this was the outcome of a trend that was remaking Westminster as a whole.
124   The opening of Westminster Bridge in 1750 transformed the prospects of the area,
and the city would go on to pioneer a series of other urban improvements, not least
paving and lighting the streets.[95] Although the Dean and Chapter initially opposed
much of this work, the abbey would come to be a key player in the process, as it
knocked down houses to create Dean's Yard, widened streets, speculated in property
development, and developed the previously barren, debatable and somewhat dubious
94   Tothill Fields.[96]

These wider Westminster improvements have been portrayed as quintessentially
modern. The paving is seen as evidence of 'a desire to create the appropriate urban
geography for a commercial and civilized nation.'[97] The bridge is depicted as an equally
important intervention: a 'space of polite entertainment' within a modernizing city.[98] If
this was so for the streets and the bridges, then it was also – perhaps still more – the
case for Westminster Abbey. As the building and its surroundings were improved, so it

124 The desire to improve the urban environment of parliament and the abbey led to the construction of a new river crossing, opened in 1750; Samuel Scott's painting *The Building of Westminster Bridge*, *c.*1742, shows, on the north bank of the Thames, Westminster Hall and the abbey, with Hawksmoor's new west towers.

became a yet greater draw to casual visitors, not least those entering through the newly commodious west entrance.[99] The restoration of the abbey can even be compared to the rebuilding of the fashionable Vauxhall Gardens – that popular pleasure ground on the south bank of the Thames, in which the management 'took an already existing and somewhat decayed public resort and turned it into a more elegant attraction'.[100] Indeed, the abbey was longer-lasting and more popular than Vauxhall, becoming 'the most public indoor space in eighteenth-century Britain'.[101]

The Tourist Attraction

What did people come to see? There was the abbey itself, of course; and its many antiquarian associations too. There were the waxworks and other objects of rather varied value: 'black coffins, rusty armour, tattered standards', in Oliver Goldsmith's words.[102] Connoisseurs like the sculptor Joseph Nollekens complained that the serious-minded could not pursue their interests 'without being bothered with Queen Catherine's bones, the Spanish Ambassador's coffin, the Lady who died by pricking her finger, and that

128

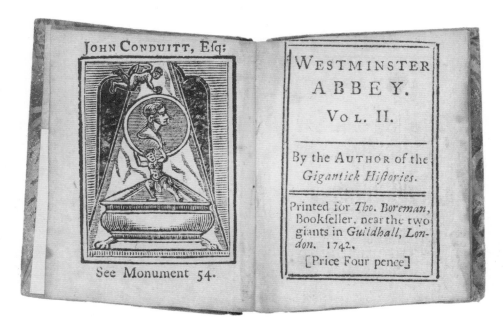

JOHN CONDUITT, Efq;

See Monument 54.

WESTMINSTER
ABBEY.
VOL. II.

By the AUTHOR of the
Gigantick Hiftories.

Printed for *Tho. Boreman,*
Bookfeller, near the two
giants in *Guildhall, London.* 1742.

[Price Four pence]

125   As footfall through the abbey increased, large numbers of guidebooks to the building, the tombs of national figures and other curiosities were produced for visitors; this early guide to Westminster Abbey by Thomas Boreman (1742), the second of three volumes, has a frontispiece depicting the monument of the politician and scientist John Conduitt (1688–1737).

nasty cap of General Monk's'.[103] To judge by the ever increasing number of guidebooks produced in this period, which generally devoted most of their pages and the majority of their illustrations to the subject, it was the tombs and funerary sculpture that most attracted visitors.[104] The French traveller Pierre-Jean Grosley expressed amazement to find the abbey 'incessantly filled with crowds' admiring the monuments. 'I have seen',

125   he went on, 'herb-women holding a little book which gives an account of them; I have seen milk-women getting them explained, and testifying, not a stupid admiration, but a lively and most significant surprize.' He had even witnessed 'the vulgar weep' at the sight of the 'beautiful and expressive' statue of Shakespeare by William Kent and Peter

126   Scheemakers, put up in Poets' Corner in 1741.[105] The smarter guides tried to train readers to value these works for their aesthetic more than their associational qualities, to appraise them 'with the eye of a man of taste', and to judge as worth noting only those pieces 'which are calculated to charm by their inherent perfections'.[106] In that way the abbey became both museum and art gallery in this period.

As a museum, the abbey offered a variety of attractions. It was in the eighteenth century that the notion of 'Poets' Corner' became firmly established, and Westminster

126   The marble monument to William Shakespeare, designed by William Kent and sculpted by Peter Scheemakers, was erected in the south transept of the abbey – Poets' Corner – in January 1741. The life-sized figure of the playwright leans on a pile of books and points to a scroll on which lines from *The Tempest* are inscribed; the heads of Henry V, Richard III and Elizabeth I adorn the pedestal.

began to be seen as a 'national literary pantheon'.[107] Visitors could also find a history of recent political and military heroes. It had long been the resting place for many of the great and the good, a tradition that gained renewed importance in the seventeenth century and was celebrated by Francis Atterbury's friend the poet Alexander Pope, who hoped to make Westminster into 'a great national Pantheon'.[108] Not until the turn of the nineteenth century would St Paul's offer any sort of competition. A memorial in the abbey could confirm a person's importance or buy back their reputation.[109]

From the 1750s, parliament began to sponsor this process, and the colonial legislatures followed suit, the province of Massachusetts, for example, voting money in 1758 to commission a magnificent effigy by Peter Scheemakers of General Lord Howe, hero of the wars against the French. The East India Company also came to commemorate its heroes, again employing Scheemakers to create an extraordinary orientalist fantasy in memory of Admiral Charles Watson – a statue framed by chained and kneeling subcontinental inhabitants and flanked by Gothic columns turned into golden palm

127 Louis-François Roubiliac's monument to Lieutenant General William Hargrave (d. 1751), erected in the south aisle of the nave in 1757. Roubiliac's dramatic funerary sculptures drew crowds to the abbey: in this most astonishing example, the naked figure of Hargrave is seen emerging from his sarcophagus beneath a tumbling pyramid; in the clouds above, an angel sounds the last trump, while, to the right, the figure of Time grapples with Death.

trees.[110] Still more striking were Louis-François Roubiliac's 'spectacular, highly illusionistic, military allegories in the Abbey', which had 'the effect of transforming the nave into a theatre of militaristic spectacle . . . a public forum for the promotion of nationalistic sentiments'.[111] Certainly, by the 1760s, Grosley could observe that 'Westminster-abbey receives every day new monuments of the successes of England in the last war.'[112] Following the death in 1778 of Pitt the elder, a similarly patriotic monument, costing no less than £6,000, was erected – as the inscription still pointedly asserts – 'by the King and Parliament as a testimony to the virtues and ability of William Pitt, Earl of Chatham; during whose administration in the reigns of George the Second and George the Third Divine providence exalted Great Britain to a height of prosperity and glory unknown to any former age.'

128 *Death and the Antiquaries*, 1816, by Thomas Rowlandson, satirizes the public's insatiable
interest in the abbey's unique collection of monuments and relics. The figure of Death climbs off
his plinth to wreak vengeance on a group of 'burglarious' antiquaries, who disinterred the body
of Edward I for closer inspection and were widely believed (though falsely) to have stolen one of
the king's fingers.

Not all of the monuments were safely patriotic, of course; nor was patriotism always
safely on the side of the state. There were important opposition statements too. Indeed,
the statue of Shakespeare that Grosley admired was sponsored by 'patriot' opponents
of Sir Robert Walpole; the memorials to Isaac Newton and Walpole's great rival in
politics, the 1st Earl Stanhope, placed on Hawksmoor's choir screen, have been seen as
'a kind of appropriation of the nave by opposition sympathizers'; and Pope's epitaph
to the politician James Craggs included an attack on government corruption.[113] There
were hints of Jacobitism, too. Atterbury composed his own epitaph, but it was so
scurrilous and offensive to the government that his tomb remained unmarked until
1877, while the Buckingham memorial in Henry VII's chapel possessed an inscription
composed by Atterbury and intended to present the family as an alternative to the
Hanoverian dynasty.[114] Small wonder that the loyalist chapter resolved in 1727 to
vet inscriptions in advance, a decision that clamped down on dissent.[115] Yet even less
obviously controversial works could carry a kick. The first parliamentary memorial – to
the naval captain James Cornewall (d. 1744) – was, it seems, intended to be as much an
indictment of his colleagues as a commemoration of his own life. The next great state
monument, to General James Wolfe, was the product of an unseemly tussle between

129   In this portrait of
Louis-François Roubiliac by
Adrien Carpentiers, 1762,
the French sculptor is shown
working on a model for a
figure of William Shakespeare,
commissioned by David
Garrick, one of a string of
fashionable patrons.

king and parliament. George II had originally offered to pay for it, but his prime
minister, William Pitt the elder, made political capital by insisting that the House of
Commons should undertake this duty.[116] In such ways, like any good museum, the
abbey and its monuments had the potential to tell many, sometimes competing, stories
about the recent past.

It would be hard to argue that all the monuments were great works of art. But they
were all assessed in these terms, the *London Chronicle* lamenting in 1757 that 'one was
more likely to visit the Abbey for the pleasure of looking at the art of sculpture, rather
than moral edification'.[117] And there could be no doubt that the creators of some
memorials were among the leading artists of the age, nor that 'The best advertisement
for a sculptor was undoubtedly a major monument in Westminster Abbey.'[118] 'I find
in Westminster Abbey', observed Oliver Goldsmith's citizen of the world, 'several new
monuments erected to the memory of several great men. The names of the men I
129   absolutely forget, but I well remember that Roubiliac was the statuary who carved
them . . . "Alas! alas!" cried I, "such monuments as these confer honour not on the
great men, but on little Roubiliac."'[119] Moreover, the impact of such exposure was
felt far beyond the abbey itself. Public commissions were often the outcome of widely

publicized competitions, and even more private projects were frequently exhibited in public. Monuments in Westminster were copied and – sometimes – improved in other locations. The most famous were re-created as mass-produced miniatures. They were also subject to wide criticism – wider, in many respects than any other art, because they were so much more public. The abbey was a gallery in every sense: a place to admire beauty and also 'a shop window for the sculptors'.[120]

The effect of this monumental mania on the abbey was extraordinary, every bit as transformative as any building programme. Original fabric was effaced or demolished to make room. Almost all available wall space was deployed, and as the competition between artists increased, so their designs became larger and more eye-catching.[121] To their credit, the chapter agreed in 1740 that no further memorials could be set up in Henry VII's chapel;[122] they also, six years later, observed that the abbey itself was now 'almost full' of monuments.[123] But the demand just kept growing – as did the number of monuments and the volume of people wishing to visit. In that way, the abbey was confirmed not just as a place of worship, nor merely as a site of royal significance, much less as an anachronistic backwater or untouched relic of an ancient past, but as an integral part of London – indeed, national – life: a thoroughly modern mausoleum, in other words. It was 'New coated and improved', as one guidebook put it in 1783.[124] It was filled with 'funerary art' superior to that of any other church in England – and perhaps Europe, as another purred twenty years later.[125] Westminster Abbey had become 'alike Venerable from its Age, its Architecture, and the Uses to which it has been appropriated', as a third opined in 1818.[126]

The Quick and the Dead

It was not a disinterested love of art or an ostentatious patriotism that led the Dean and Chapter to fill their abbey with memorials: it was money, for death paid in Westminster. And it paid a lot. Death was thus a way of life for the abbey and its inhabitants. This contributed, doubtless, to the 'Melancholy' mood that its 'Solemnity' inspired in Joseph Addison in 1711, a sensibility that would be echoed by other authors for decades to come.[127] More tangibly, too, the abbey's dependence on the funerary trade, and on the tourism it inspired, created an entire ecology. Individuals prospered, whole families – successive generations – lived off the profits of memorialization. Nor was this the only way that the abbey interacted with wider society. As landowner and landlord, school governor, and prison and poorhouse manager, it was a powerful presence in the lives of thousands. More than the great events it staged and the rich associations it possessed, these everyday connections drew the abbey into the world around it.

As critics were quick to point out, burial or the erection of a memorial in Westminster owed little to merit.[128] Most of those commemorated were neither obviously great nor self-evidently good, and the majority were not even interred in the abbey, but were simply commemorated there. Some hoped to attain distinction through a form of osmosis, with Goldsmith observing that many who had been 'hated and shunned by the great while alive, have come here, fully resolved to keep them company now they are dead'.[129] Others had some connection with the grander people memorialized, even if it could not be publicly admitted. In death, the three illegitimate daughters of the Duke of Northumberland all secured admittance near their father's more magnificent tomb, for instance.[130] Yet others did not aspire to distinction, but did imagine that a memorial in the abbey would grant a sort of immortality. Writing to Alexander Pope in 1731, the dramatist Aaron Hill explained that he wanted to erect a monument to his wife 'in so frequented a place as *Westminster-Abbey*' because it would return her 'to a kind of second life, among the living'.[131] Most of those commemorated were locals, who had lived less than five minutes from the abbey, and used it rather in the way that other people might have used their local parish church.[132]

What united all but the chosen very few – whose costs were borne by the crown, or parliament, or a local legislature, or the East India Company – was the ability to pay for a place in the abbey. In the 1720s a substantial, well-situated monument might set you back 20 guineas.[133] By 1801 the smallest relief in an already congested side-chapel cost a grieving father 50 guineas.[134] Three decades later, in 1831, the site for the memorial to Sir Stamford Raffles was priced at a cool 200 guineas.[135] Funerals could be just as expensive. Conducted in the evening, or even at night, torchlit, crowded and chaotic, they were a major public spectacle – and sometimes a public danger too. The fight that broke out at the Earl of Bath's funeral in 1764 'inflicted permanent damage' on the tomb of Edward I; the turmoil at the Duchess of Northumberland's interment a decade later led to the collapse of the screen of St Edmund's Chapel.[136] Funerals attracted all manner of mourners, from the boys who clambered over ancient tombs to get a better view, to the two women once 'intimately connected' to the Duke of Cumberland, but 'at present sincere Penitents', who hoped to join his funeral procession in 1765.[137]

Any profits accrued from this trade were shared between the Dean and Chapter, who charged additional amounts for their services and a bewildering array of expenses for others involved. The 'Fees for the Burial of an Earl' noted in around 1730 came to more than £100, and included sums for the surveyor, the registrar, the bell-ringers and beadle, a dozen 'Almes-men', and even mourning materials for the dean's four servants.

In total, something like seventy individuals stood to benefit from such a bereavement. Private funerals, like those of the three Percy sisters in the 1790s, benefited fewer people but still netted several hundred pounds apiece. Dividing the spoils left over from a large public funeral could also be lucrative: the linen sheet, purple pall, cushions and canopies at George II's funeral brought in more than £70. The funeral of such public figures as William Pitt the younger could prove almost as advantageous – his yielded just over £50.[138]

Nor did the opportunities to cash in end there. The abbey charged visitors to view the east end, and until 1826 distributed this 'Tomb Money' among the choir and the minor canons.[139] Many thought this disgraceful – and the canons themselves objected to it – but there was no denying its value, especially when augmented by the strategic purchase of new and alluring waxworks to drive up trade. Moreover, the money charged – 3d. in the 1760s, as much as 2s. by the early nineteenth century – was widely shared, for neither the canons nor the choir wanted to spend time guiding visitors round the tombs themselves and thus employed others to do the job.[140] 'As for that there threepence', Oliver Goldsmith's fictional Chinese visitor records one of their agents explaining, 'I farm it from one, – who rents it from another, – who hires it from a third, – who leases it from the guardians of the temple, and we all must live.'[141]

Memorial-making had an impact outside the abbey, inspiring an industry of sculptors and masons in the streets around it. Here, in the 1710s and 1720s, could be found such front-rank figures as Pierre-Denis Plumier, Edward Stanton and Peter Scheemakers. Here, too, the entrepreneurial Henry Cheere made his fortune, coming to employ as many as forty men in his workshop, first in St Margaret's Lane, abutting the abbey, and then in Old Palace Yard. By the 1750s his work in Westminster had placed him at the head of 'the most successful sculpture business in London'. He was a tenant of the abbey, renting properties around it from 1726. He was employed by the abbey, working as a 'carver' from 1743. He was an agent of the abbey, serving as churchwarden and as an important election manager for the parish of St Margaret's, where his enthusiasm was such that he once illegally persuaded a Dutchman to vote in the government's – and hence the Dean and Chapter's – interest. Cheere's connections were personal as well as professional, for he had been a schoolboy at Westminster, trained nearby with the sculptor Robert Hartshorne, and then entered a partnership with Henry Scheemakers, whose workshop was also in St Margaret's Lane. His entrée to work on the abbey was probably due to his friendship with the Tufnell family, who produced successive master masons of Westminster.[142] Although exceptional in his wealth, his success and the baronetcy that these brought him, Cheere is thus a sort of exemplar, providing an excellent illustration of the ways in which the abbey reached out into the everyday lives of locals.

130 and 131   Tickets for admission to the coronations of George III (*left*) and George IV (*right*). Money-making enterprises proliferated at all levels in the abbey's hierarchy, and the musicians did a roaring trade in coronation tickets.

130, 131

Another example of this theme can be found in the experience of the musicians and members of the choir, for they too helped to widen the network of associations that stretched out from the abbey. Like their superiors, they supplemented their income by selling tickets for coronations and installations of knights of the Bath. George III's elaborate service in 1761 brought in a profit of no less than £6,272.[143] Like their superiors, the musicians were also pluralists. John Robinson, for instance, served as organist at the abbey and also at St Lawrence Jewry and St Magnus the Martyr. His successor, Benjamin Cooke, was equally busy as organist of St Martin-in-the-Fields. Samuel Arnold was offered the post in 1793, and turned it down because he was unwilling to resign his many other commitments; the Dean and Chapter responded by enabling him to appoint at least three deputies.[144] Almost all of the choir members sang in the Chapel Royal, and it was customary for them to leave the abbey for St James's during Sunday services to undertake their other duties.[145]

The minor canons proved similarly enterprising. Anselm Bayley, for instance, combined his role at Westminster with a canonry at St Paul's, the sub-deanery of the Chapel Royal and the vicarage of Tottenham. He even found time to invent and patent 'an elastic girdle for the prevention and relief of ruptures, fractures, and swellings'.[146] The disputatious John Pridden, who was noted for the 'sublimity' of his burial services and who served as a sort of shop steward for the choir and minor canons at the turn of the nineteenth century, spent years bemoaning his lot: the humiliation of collecting Tomb Money, the problems of organizing coronation tickets, the inadequate accommodation, the 'scanty income'. Yet he also received remuneration as canon of St Paul's, priest of the Chapel Royal, vicar of Caddington, and honorary secretary of the Sea-Bathing Infirmary at Margate. He spent most of his time in his parish and let his minor canon's house back to the abbey for the sum of £5 a year.[147] It was hardly an ideal situation for Pridden – or the abbey, for that matter – but it did confirm the fact that Westminster was never cut off from the rest of the world.

The abbey was a family business for many. In the choir, the mason's yard, the garden, and among the chapter clerks, son succeeded father, and widows took on the work of their dead husbands.[148] It cannot have hurt Benjamin Deane Wyatt's cause as surveyor that his father had preceded him and his uncle was the dean.[149] Abbey servants were abbey tenants.[150] But like some ancient rhizomatic organism, the abbey also cropped up all across the city and the country in the most surprising places. The Dean and Chapter were important players in the project for a new Westminster fish market, for instance, intending, at a stroke, to increase their income by £20 a year, satisfy the demands of the locals for cheap seafood and contribute to a parliamentary campaign to promote the British fishing trade.[151] They numbered among their tenants those imprisoned for debt and forced to beg for money at the gateway of the abbey, and those they nominated for a place in the local almshouses, as well as such luminaries as the Duke of Chandos, the Earls of Bath, Chesterfield, Jersey, Upper Ossory and Winchelsea, Viscounts Beauchamp and Bulkeley, the Bishop of Salisbury and Jeremy Bentham.[152] Their interests comprehended tenements in Westminster, bridges in Oxfordshire, fields in Worcestershire, farms in Essex and the preservation of game in Berkshire.[153] Westminster Abbey may have become a place synonymous with – even, to a degree, dependent on – death. It was nonetheless teeming with all sorts of life.

The Bad Times?

Many images and events might sum up the abbey in this period. Canaletto's painting of the procession of the knights of the Bath is one, of course. So too is Francis Atterbury's most lasting legacy: the dormitory he imposed on Westminster School. As built between 1722 and 1729, this was a shrine to taste. Intended to replace the crumbling monastic granary that had served as a dormitory since 1540, the new building was designed

110

132

132   Charles Walter Radclyffe's lithograph *Westminster School: Interior of the Dormitory*, 1845, shows the spartan conditions in which the scholars lived in Victorian times. The boys were frequently likened to juvenile delinquents for their riotous behaviour and for vandalizing the abbey's monuments and furnishings.

by the increasingly fashionable amateur architect Lord Burlington in the very latest style.[154] A cool, chaste, but ruinously expensive exercise in Palladian classicism, it was a monument to its creators as much as a home for schoolboys.[155] Seen from College Garden, its arcades and blind windows – reconstructed and filled with glass after the Second World War – provided a stately yet modish backdrop for the abbey's inhabitants as they enjoyed their grounds. Indeed, as an aspect of estate improvement, it was all of a piece with the near contemporaneous resolution to pay the Beadle an extra £10 'for keeping the Abby and Cloisters clear of Boys & Beggars'.[156] It even attracted royal patronage: George I donated £1,000 to the building fund and the Prince of Wales chipped in another £500.[157] In years to come, it would host royalty and nobility alike, all of whom flocked to attend the annual school play held within. More than a century after its opening, in December 1834, in fact, money would be set aside to erect an awning for William IV to process into the dormitory for just that purpose.[158]

The dormitory is indeed a marvellous microcosm of Westminster life in the long eighteenth century. It links the abbey to the school and to the wider world in the streets beyond. It illuminates the tiny community of the canons – for, of course, Atterbury's plan provoked furious rows among the members of the chapter.[159] It similarly speaks of the ways in which Westminster was rebuilt in this period. The abbey that emerged from the eighteenth century was almost unrecognizable: not only had the west towers been completed and the choir reordered, but restoration and urban improvement meant that both the fabric of the building and its setting were changed for good.[160] The Westminster dormitory affair, likewise, illuminates other themes, not least the connection between the abbey, the parliament and the court. The king's support for the project has been seen as an attempt to conciliate the many aristocratic old boys produced by the school.[161] More remarkably, it has been argued that the serious financial problems caused by this project were the result not of mismanagement but of treason, as the Jacobite Dean Atterbury siphoned off funds and sent them to France, making the dormitory less a white elephant than a red herring.[162]

The school itself might serve as another image of eighteenth-century Westminster. Certainly, it would be wrong to ignore the frequent references to the scholars of Westminster fighting in the cloisters, clambering over the monuments, annoying visitors and locals alike. In the 1740s four carved their names on the coronation chair; two decades afterwards, another delinquent stole the jawbone of Richard II, an object returned by the boy's family 140 years later.[163] They were undoubtedly one of the sights of the place: guides complained of 'young men of *family* and high blood skipping from tomb to tomb', and Horace Walpole was scared off from a visit by a group of schoolboys he found 'as formidable . . . as the ship carpenters at Portsmouth'.[164] The fact that the Dean and Chapter instructed the butler 'always to take care to supply

133 (FOLLOWING PAGES) Westminster in 1819 (shown in this detail from a revised edition by William Faden of Richard Horwood's *Plan of the Cities of London and Westminster*, with the boundary of St Margaret's parish marked in yellow) was already recognizably modern. Parliament Square (to the north of the abbey) was taking shape, the Sanctuary had been cleared of its gatehouse and debtors' prison (to the west), (Great) Dean's Yard had been laid out, and the houses abutting the north and east end of the church had at last been removed. But an older dispensation persisted. The ramshackle Westminster Palace beside the river still stood. The chapter house still held the 'Records', with the official weights and measures of the kingdom in the adjacent Pyx Chamber. And the area around the abbey retained some insalubrious buildings – not least the enormous workhouse to the south-west, beneath the Great Almonry, which accommodated over 400 inmates. Beyond that was a congeries of narrow streets and yards, many of which would be demolished in the urban improvements of the subsequent decades.

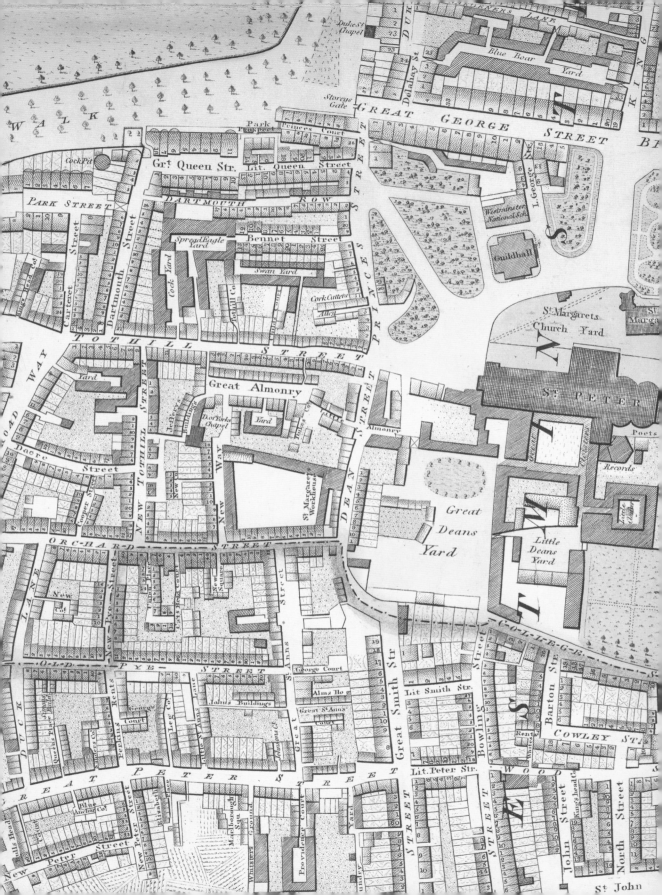

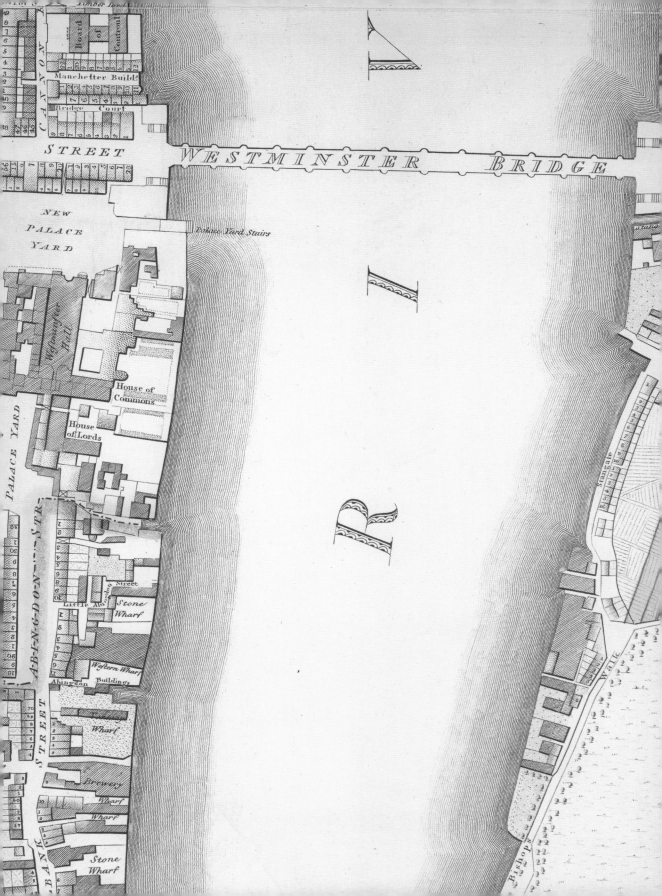

WESTMINSTER BRIDGE

CANNON STREET

Board of Control

Manchester Build:

Bridge Court

STREET

NEW
PALACE
YARD

Palace Yard Stairs

PALACE YARD

Westminster Hall

House of
Commons

House
of Lords

A-B-I-N-G-D-O-N STR:

Little Abingdon Street

Stone
Wharf

Western Wharf

Abingdon Buildings

Wharf

STREET

Brewery

Wharf

Wharf

BANK

Stone
Wharf

R I V E R

Stangate

WALK

Bishops

the Scholars with as much beer as they shall desire', presumably did little to improve matters.[165]

But it is another, more specific occasion that most effectively exemplifies the abbey in this age. The Handel Commemoration of 1784 was just one of the musical events staged under Dean Thomas, but it was undoubtedly the most spectacular of the decade – if not the century – and the concerts would be both remembered and repeated for years afterwards. It was a deeply aristocratic occasion: overseen by the earls of Exeter and Sandwich, viscounts Fitzwilliam and Dudley and Ward, and by a clutch of other peers, baronets and knights. It was also a royal occasion – ordered and attended by the king – and, as such, it could hardly fail to be a political event as well. The scale of the spectacle ensured that it was, above all, a popular occasion, one that expressly linked the abbey to another fashionable place of entertainment, the Pantheon on Oxford Street. Sacred music was performed at the former; more 'miscellaneous' music at the latter. Thousands flocked to Westminster, paying half a guinea apiece to attend the rehearsals alone. The west end of the abbey was transformed by the surveyor James Wyatt into a huge sacred theatre, with stacked seats, packed galleries, and a royal box; the choir alone numbered hundreds.[166]

'Here', in the words of the historian John Brewer, 'was the polite nation as it wished to imagine itself: respectful, silent, serious, harmonious and united – no discord was heard.'[167] It was, in this way, an apotheosis of all that the abbey had become and all that it wished to be. A well-connected, well-financed, much frequented place of resort, Westminster served many purposes in this period. It was not always so respectful, and such respectability may not have satisfied the generations that followed, who came to see the eighteenth-century abbey as corrupt and neglectful. Yet it evidently reflected and satisfied the changing demands of its age.

134 (FACING PAGE) Edward Edwards, *An Interior View of Westminster Abbey on the Commemoration of Handel, Taken from the Manager's Box*, c.1790. The Handel Commemoration of 1784, which became a legend in its own time, marked the twenty-fifth anniversary of Handel's death; one of the five concerts that made up the celebration was a performance of *Messiah* by more than 500 musicians given before an audience of some 4,500 people.

7

Towards a Broad Church Valhalla:
1837–1901

J. MORDAUNT CROOK

During the night of 16 october 1834, the ancient Westminster Palace was destroyed by fire. Two years after the passing of the Great Reform Bill, the home of the unreformed parliament had itself been consigned to history. 'The whole calamity', recorded *The Examiner*, 'reads like an allegory'. From the roof of Henry VII's chapel two figures gazed out over the inferno: John Ireland – dean since 1816 – and Francis Palgrave, newly appointed keeper of records in the chapter house. Burning sparks fell about them, thick as snowflakes. The painter and diarist Benjamin Robert Haydon was ecstatic: 'Good God . . . it was sublime.'[1] Surely, Palgrave suggested, at least Domesday Book might be moved to safety? Ireland is said to have replied: 'I must first ask Lord Melbourne.'

Dean Ireland (1816–42) was an old-world pluralist, notable only for his endowment of biblical and classical studies at Oxford. He clearly held deferential views on the relationship of Church and state. Of humble origins, he had risen through the ranks, thanks to the patronage of Lord Liverpool. Like his immediate successors – Dean Turton (1842–5), Dean Wilberforce (1845), Dean Buckland (1845–56) and Dean Trench (1856–64) – Ireland depended seriously on the skills of the sub-dean, Lord John Thynne, the third son of the 2nd Marquess of Bath, who was a canon of Westminster for exactly half a century (1831–81). Thomas Turton lasted only two and a half years en route to the Bishopric of Ely; 'Soapy Sam' Wilberforce, occupied the Deanery for less than a year on his way to the Bishopric of Oxford. As for William Buckland, he was a learned geologist, whose eccentricity verged on madness. He crowded the Deanery with 'eagles, serpents and monkeys', and seems to have been peculiarly proud

135

136

135 (facing page) A detail from a lithograph by Thomas Picken showing the calamitous fire that consumed the medieval Westminster Palace on the night of 16 October 1834. The abbey escaped untouched but both Houses of Parliament were destroyed, leaving Westminster Hall and the Jewel Tower as the most visible survivals.

136　Lord John Thynne, appointed a canon of Westminster in 1831, was sub-dean from 1835 until his death in 1881, responsible for the everyday running of the abbey. His lifelong mission to recast the abbey as a national mausoleum was to prevail in spite of ever present financial constraints.

of the new system of sewers he installed in school and abbey, cleansing, in the process, cesspits blocked with the ordure of centuries. His sermon of 1849, giving thanks for the abatement of cholera, took as its text: 'Wash and be clean'. Finally, Richard Chenevix Trench, a future Archbishop of Dublin, was a learned lexicographer; he was also a noted hypochondriac. Neither factor particularly assisted the day-to-day running of the abbey. Nevertheless, it was during the tenures of Buckland and Trench that the abbey finally awoke from its later Georgian slumbers.[2]

The Ecclesiastical Commission and the Abbey

In 1835, as part of a concerted programme of reform, the Whig government established a new Ecclesiastical Commission. Its remit was wide. It proposed little less than a wholesale restructuring of the economy of the Church of England. A year later, in 1836, the commission was made permanent by law. That would have long-term implications for Westminster Abbey, especially in matters of finance. Inevitably there was opposition. But the new Conservative prime minister, Sir Robert Peel, was prepared to face it down. 'Is the Church', he wrote to the politician and historian J.W. Croker, 'to be a provision for men of birth, or for men of learning? or is its main object the worship of God according to the doctrines of the Reformed faith?'[3] The answer to that question had already been implied in the text of Peel's Tamworth Manifesto (1834). First in the line of fire were the inhabitants of Barsetshire – not least the Dean and Chapter of Westminster. For all his energy in matters of liturgical planning, Lord John Thynne was known for his conservative views when it came to government interference in questions of income and expenditure. In this he found himself at odds with the momentum of political pressure. The days of 'old corruption' – to use the language of the philosophical radicals – were numbered.

The scope of the new commission, led by Bishop Blomfield and Archbishop Howley, ranged widely across the gamut of Church finance.[4] As regards Westminster, one result of its activity – removing pluralists in favour of what Peel called 'the working clergy' – was the reduction in 1840 of the number of canonries and prebendaries from twelve to six. Furthermore, in 1843 and 1853, by Orders in Council, the income of the dean was fixed at £2,000, and the incomes of the canons at £1,000 per annum each. Nor was that the end of it. In 1865 the commission began negotiating with the Dean and Chapter for the commutation of the abbey's rental and investment income. In 1868 the Ecclesiastical Commissioners' Act cleared the way for the transfer of episcopal and capitular estates to the management of the Ecclesiastical Commission itself. By 1869 a totally new system was in place. The commissioners took over the bulk of the abbey's property in return for a payment of some £20,000 per annum. A single payment of similar size was assigned for immediate repairs.

Henceforward, the chapter became less and less involved in matters of estate management. The dean himself emerged as a stipendiary cleric rather than an ecclesiastical landlord. And other – more secular – factors were working in the same direction, divesting the Dean and Chapter of extraneous responsibilities. Thirty years after the reorganization of 1869, even the deanship's ancient involvement with the government of Westminster was abolished. Already vestigial, this responsibility became entirely symbolic with the passing of the London Government Act of 1899. By then – thanks to this purposeful process of redistribution – the Dean and Chapter had been pruned of nearly all their peripheral powers and perquisites. As Bishop Blomfield told the House of Lords as early as 1840, the whole manoeuvre ultimately represented 'a sacrifice from one part of the Church to another – from the less useful to the more efficient'.[5]

Meanwhile another set of commissioners were progressing with another tranche of institutional reforms. This time Westminster School was the target. When Samuel

Wilberforce was appointed dean in 1845 he recognized at once that the school was 'in a dreadful state'.[6] The following year, Peel himself decided that reform was indeed necessary. Peel seems to have alerted Prince Albert and the queen. They in turn alerted Palmerston. And in June 1854 the prime minister found time – despite the Crimean War – to present his thoughts on the subject.

> To make Westminster [School] what it ought to be and is capable of being, it ought to be removed into the country . . . [perhaps] some place in the neighbourhood of Henley-on-Thames . . . [Then] the 12 acres which are now occupied by the school and buildings . . . might . . . be converted into the site of a great and striking improvement of the town in connection with Westminster Abbey, the Houses of Parliament, the parks and Palace; and that district which is now a reproach to London might be rendered one of its distinguishing ornaments.[7]

Those themes would recur, and recur again, throughout the rest of the century.

In 1846 and 1865 two great head masters – H.G. Liddell and C.B. Scott – were appointed in succession. But again major changes were shelved. There were too many competing interests. It was not until 1861 that serious reforms were set in motion. In 1862 and 1863 the Public Schools Enquiry Commission took evidence on the state of Westminster School. Its report in 1868 was highly critical. The school was found wanting: in numbers, in standards, in governance, in accommodation. In effect, the Dean and Chapter stood accused of contributory negligence. That was a little harsh. Westminster, in fact, was suffering from the competition of newer public-school foundations and grammar-school revivals. But the resulting Public Schools Act took justifiable action: it separated school and abbey, guaranteeing the school's independence in terms of governance and finance, and at the same time making possible a programme of future expansion. Therein lay considerable potential for territorial dispute. The school's gain was the abbey's loss. Thanks to some nimble parliamentary footwork by two former pupils of the school, the site of the old prior's lodgings and monks' refectory in Little Dean's Yard was lost to the abbey forever. By the terms of the 1868 Act, Ashburnham House – built on that site – was designated to be passed to the school, but not until the demise of its occupant, Lord John Thynne. That did not take place until 1881. As the years went on, the head master, the formidable Dr Scott, became increasingly impatient. One day, thinking that Thynne was away from home, he procured a ladder and climbed the garden wall to catch a glimpse of the promised land. From an upper window came the icy voice of the octogenarian sub-dean: 'Not yet dead, Dr. Scott.'[8]

From the abbey's point of view there were advantages and disadvantages in this process of overall contraction. The twin acts of 1868 – the Ecclesiastical Commissioners' Act and the Public Schools Act – drastically reduced the abbey's *imperium*. The London

Government Act of 1899 confirmed the process, depriving the Dean and Chapter of their powers of oversight of the City of Westminster. On the credit side, Dean and Chapter could now concentrate on their core liturgical functions. On the debit side, they had been deprived of the revenue necessary to make those functions possible. In 1869 the abbey had lost the potential capital gains that might have accrued from urban redevelopment. But while its income was now constrained, the future cost of fabric maintenance remained variable. Just how were these unpredictable costs to be met? On 1 March 1870, in his capacity as sub-dean, Thynne felt obliged to issue a solemn warning to the chapter: the gap between guaranteed income and variable costs now seemed to him not only alarming but ultimately unsustainable. His pessimism proved correct. Despite some tinkering with the figures – the Westminster Abbey Restoration Act of 1886 and the Westminster Abbey Act of 1888 alleviated the situation by allowing the chapter to borrow from the commissioners – the second half of the nineteenth century revealed only too clearly the tension between the level of income and the rate of expenditure. One man who felt that tension with particular force was George Gilbert (later Sir Gilbert) Scott.

From Collegial Retreat to Public Forum

The process of opening up the abbey began in 1827. That was the year in which one of the canons, J.H. Monk – regius professor of Greek at Cambridge, and Bishop of Gloucester and Bristol – seems to have engineered Edward Blore's appointment as surveyor.[9] Monk had already been responsible for the partial opening up of Peterborough cathedral. Westminster gave him a bigger canvas still, and the death of Dean Ireland in 1842 eventually supplied an opportunity. Thynne had surely been preparing for just such an event. Within months, Blore's plans were ready. These involved the removal of Henry Keene's choir stalls of 1775; the partial restructuring of Blore's own screen of

139

137, 138

137 (FOLLOWING PAGE)   The choir as it looked in 1811, facing east, with the transepts to either side and the sanctuary beyond, is shown in this aquatint by John Bluck after a watercolour by Frederick Mackenzie (1812). Blore's plan to open up the crossing involved the removal of the 18th-century choir stalls and the screens that divided choir from transepts; the black and white marble paving, the gift of Dr Richard Busby in 1677, was taken up and then relaid after the floor was lowered.

138 (PAGE 277)   The redesigned choir and transepts of the abbey, which offered vastly more seating for worshippers, were dedicated at Easter 1848. They are shown here in a chromolithograph by Leighton Bros. published in the same year.

139   Edward Blore, shown
here in a portrait in chalks
by George Koberwein,
1868, was best known for
his work on Buckingham
Palace. He was appointed
surveyor of Westminster
Abbey in 1827; his radical
scheme to open up the
choir and transepts, backed
by Lord John Thynne
but publicly opposed by
a number of influential
figures, was finally
completed in 1848.

1829 and 1831 to allow for the division of the organ;[10] the 'throwing down' of Keene's
wooden parclose screens of 1776 separating choir and transepts; and, most drastic of
all, lowering the floor of the choir – three steps down – to create an uninterrupted
north–south vista.

Here was a dramatic reversal of cathedral custom. One newly elected canon,
Christopher Wordsworth, objected vehemently. In a pseudonymous pamphlet – *A Letter
. . . on the Intended Alterations in the Interior of Westminster Abbey* (1844), by 'A Clergyman
of the Church of England' – he proposed an alternative plan, just as drastic as Blore's.
His idea was quite simple: bring the nave into liturgical use, with a 'people's altar' in
front of the screen, instead of opening up the choir. *The Ecclesiologist* vainly protested
against both schemes; its critical language waxed 'hyperbolical'.[11] But then Tractarians
invariably deplored any tampering with screens (A.W. Pugin famously christened
the process 'Ambonoclasm'). And Wordsworth did receive some mainstream support.
'Throw open the nave to the people,' demanded *The Guardian*. 'Let the congregations
henceforth be counted in thousands instead of tens.'[12] Still, Thynne, working with

Dean Buckland, had his way. In 1845 the chapter formally agreed to Blore's proposals. Keene's screens and stalls were dismantled. Hundreds of tons of earth were removed from the ancient choir and deposited in the churchyard of St Margaret's.

By 1847 the new choir was almost ready, in time for the consecration of four colonial bishops. Wordsworth was unrepentant. 'A crowded sculpture gallery of . . . glaring white marble [now] bursts upon the view from the two transepts on both sides of the choir,' he complained. 'Some of these statues are of colossal size, some are clothed in fantastic modern costume, some have no clothing at all . . . [As it stands] we see huge marble mausoleums . . . a pantheon of pagan deities . . . gigantic figures of Judges seated on rock-like pedestals, Naval and Military Commandos . . . breathing war and carnage in a temple of peace.'[13] He protested in vain. At Easter 1848 the dramatic new space – bold in conception, tripartite in disposition – was opened in full, with a fighting sermon by Dean Buckland. Choir and transepts together could now accommodate 1,600 people, more than could be fitted into the whole of the nave. Thynne was understandably delighted. 'You have [created]', he told Blore, 'the greatest work which has been executed in the Abbey for generations.'[14]

After Blore's retirement in 1849 his successor, George Gilbert Scott, added three final touches to the new system. In 1853 he replaced Blore's spindly wooden pulpit in the choir with a sizeable marble pulpit of his own. In 1854 he inserted a pair of low, wrought-iron screens, rationalizing the threefold space of choir and transepts. And in 1862 he added a substantial nave pulpit of magnesia limestone and grey alabaster.[15] The transformation of the abbey's layout was now complete. The way was open for the development of choral liturgy before a much larger congregation; and the regular procession of surpliced choirs would add new dignity to Evensong.

When Thynne secured the appointment of Scott as abbey surveyor, his arrival had been welcomed by High Church critics. They hoped for more Tractarian planning, with a fresh emphasis on sacramental ritual. They complained that the abbey was no longer 'a House of Prayer'; it had become 'a show-place', filled with wax dolls and naked effigies. They were unimpressed by the opening up of the abbey for larger congregations: such changes merely turned 'a Cathedral' into 'a large area for preaching'. Would that Blore had been replaced 'much sooner'.[16] In years to come these same Tractarian critics must have regretted their optimism. Scott proved himself – as he later admitted – an architect not of the High Church but of 'the multitude'.[17]

From 1852 onwards Thynne supported manfully not only Scott's immediate programme of restoration but his increasingly ambitious plans to turn the abbey into a 'National Mausoleum' or 'Valhalla'. That 'idea', as the dean, Arthur Penrhyn Stanley (1864–81), later confirmed, 'first arose' with Thynne; and ever afterwards it was 'never far from his mind'.[18] For fifty years the day-to-day governance of the place was Thynne's

140

140   George Gilbert Scott
was the abbey's surveyor
from 1849 to 1878; an
architect of the people,
he was often at odds with
the High Churchmen
of his day. His work at
Westminster included the
restoration of the chapter
house, the installation
of a new high altar and
ambitious designs for the
north front.

responsibility. At the same time he had somehow to deal with the financial constraints
created by the prevailing climate of Whig improvement. As Dean Stanley put it, it was
Thynne who had to 'set a falling house in order'. Stanley himself would prove to be
perennially unbusinesslike. When in 1868 he was faced with the effective separation
of Westminster Abbey and Westminster School – by the Public Schools Act of that
year – he seems to have accepted the recommendations of the commission readily
enough. Perhaps too readily.

★

Programmes of Restoration

As guardians of the abbey fabric, the chapter and its architect inherited a twofold responsibility: an immediate programme of restoration, plus an ongoing search for some sort of solution to the problem of overcrowding. They took both responsibilities very seriously.

Westminster Hall had survived the great fire of 1834, but St Stephen's Chapel – home to the House of Commons since the Reformation – had been reduced to a skeleton. The Painted Chamber – seat first of the Commons, then of the Lords – was now no more than a shell. But the heart of Westminster – the abbey itself, focus of Church and state – remained unscathed. The palace would have to be rebuilt, and its setting could at last be replanned. A new set of symbols would emerge: Big Ben and Victoria Tower; Sir Charles Barry's river frontage; A.W. Pugin's glittering House of Lords. In this process – prolonged, expensive, beset by controversy – the abbey would have a key part to play. The Dean and Chapter found themselves drawn into a sequence of schemes stretching over more than a century. The aim of these plans – at least twenty in all – now seems, with the benefit of hindsight, curiously inflated. At the time, however, they generated enormous public interest. Over the years they came to involve a mighty memorial extension to the abbey: in effect a mausoleum of British greatness. Hesitant at first, touched in the end by more than a hint of megalomania, one after another each of these projects came to nothing. 'What a chance', Barry is said to have remarked on the night of the fire: 'What a chance for an architect!'[19] There would be no shortage of designs. Potentially, there was even no shortage of cash. But where was the political will?

Scott's programme began, in effect, with his reports of 1854.[20] He was well aware of their significance, and he insisted on their preservation in a government archive. Here was the basis of everything that came afterwards. His comments on the exterior of the abbey were devastating. Much of the original Reigate stone had long ago decayed. Wren had replaced it with stone from Oxfordshire. This in turn had decayed – partly because of the use of iron cramps – and would soon itself have to be replaced. In 1854 Scott was faced with a building largely denuded of its Gothic ornaments: 'so altered and impoverished . . . as to destroy the greater part of its beauty . . . every costly feature pared down so as to leave the Abbey a mere block model of the original design.' The magnificent façade of the north transept, he noted, had suffered 'most cruelly':

> every vestige of sculpture [has been] removed . . . the gabled canopies . . . entirely done away with, and the whole reduced to a mere Caput Mortuum . . . [In effect] with the exception of the Cloisters . . . there remains scarcely a fragment of the original work in the whole [exterior of the] Abbey . . . The whole [building has

been] debased and deprived of its ornamental features. [Moreover Wren's work is now itself] in a state of advanced and rapidly progressing decay.

There was only one reassuring piece of news, apart from Thomas Gayfere's restoration of Henry VII's chapel: the 'design [of the west towers] is not bad in general outline, though their details bear little resemblance to the style with which they were intended to harmonise. They [at least] are very substantial and, being executed in Portland Stone, are but little decayed.'

As to the interior of the abbey, Scott had to admit that 'we probably owe to [Wren] the preservation of the vaulting'. Otherwise it was all 'in a most dangerous condition'. Moreover, he shared his contemporaries' horror at the range of monuments that had come to fill the place. 'Surely no church was ever so cruelly outraged by incongruous obstructions!' he exclaimed. 'Being the Great National Mausoleum it has become so crowded with monuments, and these display such utter disregard for the building, and are often . . . in such barbarous taste, that it is really marvellous how any building can bear up against them as this does.' His solution was their complete removal: he proposed that some be sent to the lobby of the House of Commons, others to some 'new depository', and yet others to the triforium. That last suggestion – like his dream of a leaded timber *flèche* above the crossing – was certainly optimistic.[21] The triforium would remain a lumber room of fragments – 'an architectural charnel house' – for years to come; no public access would be achieved until 2018. Still, Scott's principal conclusion was at the time definitive. 'There is no more room in the Abbey', he stated firmly; and 'if public ridicule' is to be avoided, some new arrangement 'seems to have become absolutely necessary'.[22] Thynne was persuaded. Dean Stanley was persuaded. The chapter was persuaded.

Crucially, the chancellor of the exchequer was also persuaded. The chapter house, at the very least, was a government responsibility. For years it had been used as a makeshift public record office. There could be no denying that, here at least, parliament should supply the funds. In fact, it was Gladstone's conclusion in 1854 that the abbey's restoration as a whole could be accomplished only by 'joint action between the State, the Chapter, and the Public'.[23] That tripartite solution was never, in fact, achieved. As a result, Scott's programme of action was intermittent and underfunded. It involved, principally, four overlapping campaigns: the chapter house, the sanctuary, the north transept and – tantalizingly – the *campo santo* (literally a 'holy field' – that is, a burial ground).

Rescuing the chapter house was Scott's first priority. When he began his investigations, in 1849, he found the crypt piled high with dust and rubbish: Stygian darkness, he remembered: 'blacker than Rembrandt';[24] 'I had more the look of a master chimney-

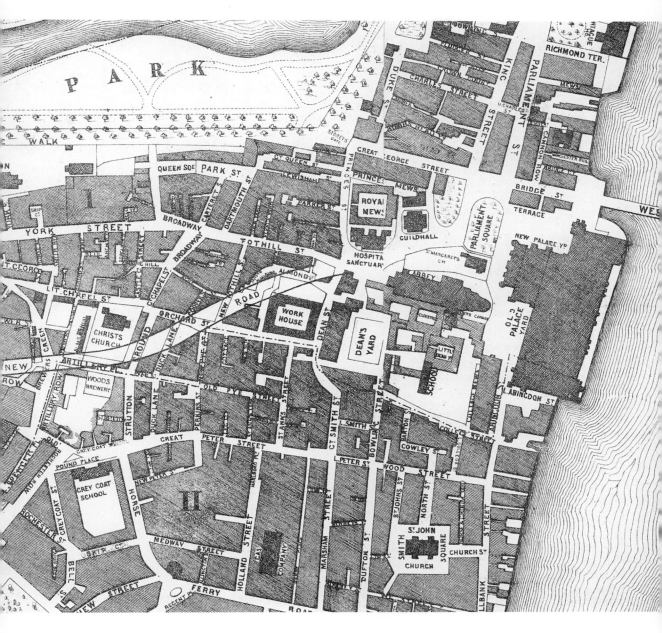

141   This detail from Thomas Cooke's *Map of the City and Liberty of Westminster* (1847) shows
Westminster in the mid-century as a place in transition. After the fire of 1834, the new Palace
of Westminster was under construction – a process that would take many decades. The sinuous
white shape to the west is a planned new road, opened as Victoria Street in 1852, a development
that would necessitate the demolition of many old buildings, including the huge workhouse
in the former almonry of the abbey. To the north of the Sanctuary is the newly constructed
Westminster Hospital, which would remain on this site for a century. In the abbey precinct itself,
Dean's Yard was finally complete and George Gilbert Scott's restoration was under way; not yet
begun was Scott's re-creation of the chapter house, almost lost here amid a collection of other
buildings to the south-east of the abbey.

sweep than an architect.' Still, it was a challenge that he willingly undertook. In fact it became a veritable 'labour of love'.[25] It proved also to be a long, protracted process.

On 18 March 1854 direct negotiations began between the abbey and the chancellor of the exchequer. What Scott had in mind was a twin-track programme: first save the chapter house; then create an adjacent cloister, or *campo santo*, for future burials of 'men of eminence'.[26] In one sense, the time at last was ripe: work was already progressing on a new public record office in Chancery Lane. In another sense it was wildly inopportune: nine days after that initial meeting, the Crimean War broke out. Still, Scott went ahead and exhibited a prize-winning perspective at the Paris Exhibition of 1855, showing the chapter house in reconstructed form. Four years later nothing had yet been done. The *Illustrated London News* published an engraving showing the abbey's disconsolate surveyor inspecting the mutilated interior: 'seldom do we see a noble work of art reduced to such a wreck!'[27] And five years after that, in 'the degraded Chapter House' itself, Stanley chaired a meeting organized by the Society of Antiquaries, consisting of 'men of eminence in art and literature without distinction of party'. This time Gladstone, by now prime minister, welcomed the petitioners, and agreed to fund the project. But in 1866 he was still reassuring Stanley that – though his opinion was unchanged – the time, politically, was still unripe.[28] Government caution about cost proved to be justified. Scott's first estimate in 1866, for the chapter house alone, was £25,000. By 1869 the figure was £30,000. By 1872, when the public were at last admitted, it was clear that the bill would be still higher, and that Scott himself would lose money on the project.[29] Between 1874 and Scott's death in 1878, the abbey was constantly seeking further support to guarantee completion.[30]

Since the Middle Ages, stained glass has seldom been the abbey's greatest asset. During the Victorian period the process of reglazing was made more complicated by changing taste and changing techniques. When, in 1840, the Dean and Chapter determined to renew the rose window and lancets of the south transept of the church, they decided to give 'native artists . . . an opportunity of proving that they are capable of providing work in no respect inferior to the boasted works of the continental glass makers [of Munich]'. Blore advertised for tenders, and selected the firm of Ward and Nixon. At the same time, Thomas Willement, already well established, was made responsible for repairing the work of James Thornhill and William Price in the west window of the nave.[31] Neither operation proved wholly satisfactory: Ward and Nixon were noted for their blazing colours and uncertain firing. By 1860 Blore's choice of glass – once considered an improvement – was now seen as 'very objectionable' in view of recent 'improvements in glass-making'.[32] In 1854 Scott had suggested the commissioning of new glass for the south transept 'in strict harmony with the building'.[33] That proved easier said than done. In 1859 he went to a rising firm, Clayton and Bell, to prepare six windows for the north transept.[34] The same firm were chosen for a south transept window in 1869. In 1882 they also won the belated contract for windows in the chapter house. Scott remained loyal to Clayton and Bell's literal style.

But there were already hints of an alternative taste. In 1861 Scott chose William Wailes to design a window in memory of the railway engineers George and Robert Stephenson. He approved of its engineering images: 'representations of the great works and great facts of our day'; otherwise, as he pointed out to Trench, contemporary art would become 'very dead'.[35] In 1868 he tried another firm, Heaton, Butler and Bayne, for a memorial window to Isambard Kingdom Brunel. This time the cartoonist was Henry Holiday. That was as close as Westminster came to the stained glass of Morris and Co. When, in 1873, it was suggested by Thynne that William Morris's firm might at least be consulted over the high altar, Scott became very defensive. 'Messrs. Morris and Faulkner are very talented artists, rather of the Pre-Raphaelite School,' he explained. 'Tastes differ', he went on, 'respecting their works, though they are pretty generally admitted to be men of superior talent.' 'They are', he added with a final touch of faint praise, 'men of education and even I believe of some literary position.'[36]

142   The memorial window to Isambard Kingdom Brunel, designed by Richard Norman Shaw and manufactured by Heaton, Butler and Bayne, was originally installed on the north side of the nave in 1868, but was later moved to the south side; the figures were drawn by the Pre-Raphaelite artist Henry Holiday and the window depicts biblical scenes of the building of Solomon's Temple and Christ's teaching there.

142

Westminster Abbey missed its chance. By 1902 taste had veered dramatically towards a later style of glass: paler, sweeter, more luminescent. Burlison and Grylls were called in to replace the windows of 1847 in the south transept. So the abbey boasts no vintage glass from James Powell's renowned Whitefriars workshop; no windows from cartoons by Burne-Jones; and nothing at all from William Burges, though he had once been Blore's assistant in Dean's Yard and had actually written the most learned sections of Scott's *Gleanings from Westminster Abbey* (1863). Burges had even produced a speculative design for the restoration of Edward the Confessor's shrine. That was in 1852.[37] But by then he was operating firmly within the orbit of Beresford Hope and his High Church allies. Scott belonged to a rather different milieu. He was cut off by the imperatives of patronage from the achievements of High Church aesthetics. In his own words he was architect not to the High Church but to the multitude. There was no room for Pre-Raphaelitism in Stanley's Broad Church Valhalla.

143

Scott was never happy with talk of 'restoration'. 'I would almost wish', he explained in 1861, 'the word restoration expunged from our architectural vocabulary.' He preferred the term 'reparation', which meant tactful repair. And to this end he developed a technique known as 'induration'. This involved the application to existing masonry – by means of a syringe – of a weak solution of white 'shell-lac' dissolved in spirits of wine (a form of methylated spirit).[38] The process seems to have had the required adhesive effect. But it produced a dismal brown overlay, masking the original silvery masonry. Scott told Stanley that its use had been *'the saving of the Abbey'*.[39] Well, perhaps. At least, it satisfied his criterion of repair: not archaeology but simply renovation for use. 'Individual genius or invention', he believed, 'should be banished.'[40] When it came to the chapter house, however, he found so much had vanished – destroyed, as he put it, by 'some barbarian' – that individual genius and invention were, indeed, necessary.

Years later Scott confessed that several major sections of his exterior work on the chapter house were, in fact, conjectural: the parapet, the pinnacles, the gables on top of each buttress, and of course the dominant pointed roof.[41] Inside, there were further innovations, and it was these that especially irritated critics – in particular, the trumeau above the inner doorway: he crammed the tracery of the inner portal with sculptured imagery of Christ in Majesty. The carving on this occasion, by James Redfern, is admittedly accomplished. But it should not be there: the tracery of the upper portal would have been open, as at Wells and Southwell. John Carter had spotted that in 1799.[42] On the other hand, most of Scott's carved work is admirably discreet. The rich ornament of the central column of the chapter house, for example, is in fact of the thirteenth century, most carefully restored by Scott. However, the massive iron hooks inserted above the band of carving on this column almost certainly supported eight radiating tie-bars, as originally at Salisbury. It was the architect William Lethaby

143 William Burges's visionary proposal for the reconstruction of the shrine of Edward the Confessor, 1852. Dean Stanley and George Gilbert Scott's conception of the abbey as a 'Broad Church Valhalla' had no place for Burges's idiosyncratic Gothic Revival style, which they associated with High Church aesthetics and values.

who spotted that in 1925.[43] Still, only a pedant would now call for their reinstatement. The present roof structure – by R.M. Ordish, who worked with Joseph Paxton at the Crystal Palace and with Scott at St Pancras – is both ingenious and substantial. The idea of an iron frame seems to have come initially from the Office of Works. Scott at first preferred a flatter, timber structure. Fortunately, he changed his mind. The new roof managed, as he put it, 'to relieve the central pillar of the weight of the vaulting'.[44] And it did so – as Lethaby explained – by hanging the masonry vault from the iron-shod roof framework above, using eight wrought-iron hangers, each running downwards from its own cast-iron rafter, to join a massive iron plate hidden beneath a layer of concrete above the great central pillar below.

144

144   George Gilbert Scott's creative restoration of the chapter house (first envisaged in 1849 and still not completed when Scott died in 1878) deployed cutting-edge engineering techniques to reveal the building's graceful original architecture. Seemingly weightless, the vault is hung from an ingenious framework of iron, hidden from view.

Here architecture and engineering – Scott and Ordish working together – combined to produce a triumph of creative restoration. 'There has been no re-chiselling or meddling with the old carvings', noted James Thorne (somewhat optimistically); no 'touching-up' of the old painting.[45] Perhaps, or perhaps not. But even the influential High Church journal *The Ecclesiologist* seems to have been satisfied: 'every atom of . . . stone in the old structure has been used again in the new'.[46] Scott inherited no more than the shell of a building: vaulting hidden, tracery ripped out, windows blocked, tiles broken, sculpture smashed, interior subdivided and filled with galleries. He left it a luminous octagon, nobly presented, archaeologically plausible.[47] G.E. Street, never one to over-praise a rival, admitted that Scott's restoration of the chapter house was indeed 'a good work, well done'.[48] Generations later, Sir Nikolaus Pevsner was more generous. There may be errors of scholarship, he noted; but 'if we have an idea today of [this building's] noble original beauty, Scott's work has given it to us'.[49]

Scott's reordering of the sanctuary achieved rather less critical acclaim. Liturgically and architecturally, the sanctuary lay at the heart of the abbey. It had been altered in the seventeenth, eighteenth and early nineteenth centuries. It was an obvious target for treatment. The reredos of 1823–4 – designed by B.D. Wyatt and executed in plaster by Francis Bernasconi – seemed to High Victorian eyes too late in style and almost frivolous in execution. Scott's replacement of 1866–73 – high altar, reredos and screen; sculpture by H.H. Armstead; mosaic by Clayton and Salviati – was designed as a glittering backdrop to the precious Cosmati pavement.[50] 'Alabaster from our Midland quarries, . . . marble from our Cornish rocks, mosaic colours from the isles of Venice, . . . porphyry from the shores of the Nile or the Bosphorus, . . . jewels from the far off coasts of Asia and America . . . '.[51] There was no doubting the sumptuous construction of the reredos, paid for from the abbey's fabric fund. It was the theological implications of the design that aroused concern. Low Churchmen attacked the four sculptured statues – Moses and David, Peter and Paul – as idolatrous. One protest received by Dean Stanley began: 'Thou miserable idolator'.[52] But High Churchmen were equally aggrieved. In 1849 Tractarians had welcomed Scott's appointment. They had reckoned without his instinct for compromise, and they were unprepared for the effects of Stanley's Broad Church attitudes. They were soon disillusioned. By 1865 Scott had been revealed as an ecclesiological *politique* and Stanley as a theological liberal.

In December of that year, *The Ecclesiologist* carried a preview, written perhaps by Beresford Hope – highest of High Church Tories – regarding Scott's proposal for the reredos. It was damning. It began by explaining that the theme of the central mosaic was an adaptation of Leonardo's *Cenacolo* – that is, the celebrated *Last Supper* at Milan. There was a recent precedent for its use, at Durham Cathedral. But whereas the short-lived sculptured reredos at Durham (1849) seemed to High Church eyes

145

merely 'ridiculous', the proposal for Westminster was a serious matter. It supplied an insight into what Beresford Hope dismissed as 'the Protestant mind'. In the first place, 'what is eminently suited to a refectory does not necessarily suit a church . . . [still less] a cathedral'. 'No Catholic Churchman' (note the Tractarian language) should be 'content with styling the great Christian mystery [as merely] the Lord's Supper'; for that is 'a low, insufficient, English view of the Eucharist.' Equally important, the medium itself – mosaic imitating fresco – was intrinsically false. J.C. Clayton had not 'thought in mosaic'; his cartoon 'would make a good oil painting' and a better fresco, if executed at life size. Ideally, mosaic 'requires gigantic proportions'. By comparison with Leonardo's work, this was 'a mere toy'; like 'the Fates on the Parthenon done in *bisque*, and on a Parian mantelpiece'.[53]

Most important of all, the circumstantial figuration of Leonardo's masterpiece – in truth, the Discovery of Judas – had been fatally misapplied. There is a serious distinction, noted the reviewer, 'between the Cenacolo as a work of art and the Eucharistic symbols'. In fact, a mere Last Supper 'cannot, except proleptically, fulfil the idea of the Eucharist'. What was needed was at least some element of abstract imagery: 'something ideal, suggestive . . . mysterious'. Some visual implication, perhaps, of the subject's sacrificial significance: 'Psilo-Protestantism has no objection to the Crucifixion – much to the Crucifix.'[54] After all, even the plainest cross tells more and means more than the most elaborate piece of historical representation. As it stood, Scott's reredos – Dean Stanley's reredos – was held to be 'not . . . in keeping with the highest religious feelings'. By showing Christ standing – in a gesture of consecration, not seated as in Leonardo's version – Scott had tried to emphasize the Eucharistic character of the Last Supper. But, to be consistent, the apostles would have had to be shown kneeling. By High Church standards, Stanley's Broad Church theology had been found wanting. The 'heretic' dean can hardly have been surprised.

The chapter house and the sanctuary occupied Scott's best years. He did not start research on the north transept portals until 1871.[55] Work began only in 1875. By then his health was failing fast: he had suffered a serious stroke in 1870. But the restoration of Solomon's Porch had long been his most 'intense ambition'.[56] 'May I be spared', he noted in 1872, 'to see [this project] perfected.'[57] That was not to be. In March 1878 the audit chapter urged their dying architect to reorder his priorities: to deal with the superstructure of the north transept before tackling the portals; and to grapple with the south clerestory before turning to its counterpart on the northern side. All these sections of the abbey were in a state of impending ruin. Part of the south clerestory had actually fallen through the triforium.[58] But Scott had set his heart on re-creating what he regarded as the royal entrance to England's 'National Mausoleum'. In a letter of 1875 he waxed eloquent on this theme: 'It will immortalize the Dean and Chapter

145 (FACING PAGE)   George Gilbert Scott's reordering of the sanctuary, 1866–73, introduced a new high altar, reredos and screen, intended to complement the Cosmati pavement (foreground). The statues, sculpted by H.H. Armstead, and mosaic depictions of saints by Clayton and Salviati incensed High and Low Church critics alike.

146   The uppermost tier of the tympanum of the abbey's north door, 1885, represents Christ enthroned in glory as ruler of the world, surrounded by angels; the porch was completed, after Scott's death in 1878, under his son John Oldrid Scott. Although Scott had intensively researched the most renowned medieval models for his theme, the architectural masons who carried out the work produced rather lifeless and undistinguished sculpture.

who undertake it! . . . Let me earnestly (on my knees if necessary) intercede for this work!'[59] Three years later he was dead.

Scott's approach to the north transept reveals much about his strengths and weaknesses as an archaeologist–architect. His model for the detailing of these portals was, confessedly, the south-east porch at Lincoln. This he rightly admired as 'a contemporary and exquisite work'.[60] But the overall disposition of Scott's porches derives rather more from Amiens. With what results? The architectural detail now seems a little mechanical: 'endless monotony' was one near-contemporary criticism.[61] But let that pass. Less easy to accept is the figured sculpture of the central tympanum over the north door. Here it has been suggested that Scott's model may have been the Puerto del Sarmental at Burgos in Spain, though preliminary drawings also suggest the inspiration of Lincoln, Reims and Amiens. Mid-Victorian architectural sculpture is seldom strikingly individual. And the work of the contracting masons – Poole and Piercey, and Farmer and Brindley – was hardly fluent. Lincoln, Burgos, Amiens, Reims: Scott did not suffer

146

from lack of scholarship. Rather he was a victim of his own learning. The inspiration of thirteenth-century models sucked the life out of his own powers of creation.

Worse was to come under Scott's successor, J.L. Pearson. In 1884–92 it fell to Pearson to attempt the restoration of the upper parts of the north transept portals. His choice of stone – Chilmark limestone from Wiltshire – had been inherited from his predecessor. But since Scott's time acidic pollution had already much increased. A very hard, carboniferous sandstone might have been wiser.[62] But it was his treatment of the great rose window that aroused the strongest criticism. Misguidedly following a seventeenth-century engraving by Wenceslaus Hollar, he replaced the eighteenth-century window with a piece of conjectural restoration. It was widely denounced as a failure. Even the radiating lights of the tracery were reduced, thus cutting off the feet of the stained-glass apostles by James Thornhill and Joshua Price. 'An incredible piece of bungling,' noted *The Builder*.[63] 'All false,' agreed Lethaby, particularly the foiled circles in the upper spandrels – 'blank, blind and foolish'.[64]

It was this reaction to Pearson's work that finally swung Victorian attitudes away from 'restoration' towards 'repair'. That it took so long was not for want of trying: William Morris, among others, had been agitating for change for some time. But Pearson's pursuit of a mechanical ideal – he was rumoured to employ several left-handed masons to guarantee authenticity of finish[65] – proved to be a methodological cul-de-sac. Not unfairly, he has been labelled the last of the restorers.[66]

'Throw open the nave to the people'

As a ceremony, Queen Victoria's coronation in 1838 was not without fault. When two pages of the service book were turned over together by mistake, the young queen had to instruct her clergy to begin that section of the proceedings all over again. And when the aged Lord Rolle – nicknamed 'Rigmarolle' by the Foxites – tumbled down the steps in front of Her Majesty, the occasion threatened to descend into farce. But the event went off well enough, with all its traditional drama. And the future Dean Stanley was there to record it.

147

> At half-past 5 we started; London all awake; the streets crowded . . . This was [my] first view of the Abbey . . . [From high up among] the vaultings [at the West end, it was all] most glorious . . . At 9 the guns announced that the Queen had left the Palace; an electric shock ran visibly through the whole Abbey . . . At 10 ½ another gun announced that she was at the Abbey door . . . and in they came: first the great dukes, struggling with their enormous trains; then bishops etc. [including Stanley's

147   The coronation of Queen Victoria in Westminster Abbey on 28 June 1838, depicted by George Hayter, 1839; the queen is seated on the coronation chair, wears the imperial state crown and holds the sceptre with the cross in her right hand and the sceptre with the dove in her left.

father, the newly consecrated Bishop of Norwich]; and then the Queen with her vast crimson train . . . The orchestra broke out into the most tremendous crash of music I ever heard. 'I was glad when they said unto me, Let us go into the house of the Lord'. Everyone literally gasped for breath . . . the rails of the gallery visibly trembled in one's hands . . . The very moment the crown touched her head the guns went off – the trumpets began, and the shouts . . . [Then] at 3½ . . . she went out . . . with her crown, her orb, and her sceptre. I walked home . . . the crowd in the streets . . . was stupendous. It was all more like a dream than a reality.[67]

All his life, Stanley would love nothing better than a state occasion. Standing in for the aged Dean Ireland that day was the indispensable Lord John Thynne. In all he did, he had gravitas; he had presence. When Ireland appointed him, the dean is said to have remarked: 'Now I can go to bed.'

It was certainly Thynne, making up for the unpredictable Dean Buckland, who energized the slow process of opening up the whole of the abbey to a wider public. The population of Westminster was increasing fast. Not all areas neighbouring the abbey were salubrious: the slums around Tothill Street survived until the 1840s. But from the mid-century visitors to London multiplied as the railway network developed, and Westminster gradually developed a new constituency with an appetite for full-scale sermons. There was a newly curious audience now, and a bigger congregation to satisfy. From 1826 onwards – partly under parliamentary pressure – nave and transepts were at last opened to the casual public, free of charge. From 1841 onwards admission to the entire abbey was free, apart from the payment of 3d. for the north transept and 3d. for the royal chapels. Visitors were now welcomed and instructed: lithographed plans were displayed on prominent boards, though sightseers were reminded that 'all Sticks, Whips, Umbrellas and Parasols [are] required to be left at the Door'.[68]

Years afterwards, in 1876, F. W. Farrar, author of *Eric, or Little by Little* – then a newly appointed canon – was scheduled to deliver a Sunday evening sermon on the nature of eternity. Disraeli was anxious to be there, but incognito. Stanley arranged to smuggle him in via the north transept. The congregation were tightly packed. Prime minister and dean wormed their way inside and clambered up onto the plinth of the monument to the Three Captains. From that vantage point, they could see – if not entirely hear – the celebrated preacher. After five minutes they slipped away. 'I would not have missed the sight for anything,' remarked Disraeli: 'the darkness, the lights, the marvellous windows, the courtesy, the respect, the devotion – and 50 years ago there might have been just 50 persons.'[69] Thynne's programme of half a century before had, indeed, been vindicated in full.

During the 1850s and 1860s it was Thynne who turned to advantage the crowds of visitors who came to London in the years following the exhibitions of 1851 and 1862. Notices for foreigners were posted in French and German. From 1856 gas lighting was installed; hundreds of chairs were borrowed from the Crystal Palace; the words of psalms and hymns were printed on large posters mounted on calico, framed and hung from the columns of the nave. From 1858 onwards, regular Sunday evening services were held, filling nave and transepts to overflowing. From the new choir pulpit (1853), Francis Jeune of Oxford even delivered an entire sermon in French. In 1856 one attendant explained that he had himself guided over 100,000 visitors around the royal tombs.[70] Sunday evening congregations regularly topped 2,000, many of those attending being the working people of Westminster. By the 1860s there were three services per day on weekdays and four services every Sunday.

Such changes proved crucial to the future of the abbey. The guns of radicals in parliament had effectively been spiked. For some years reformers had been calling for Westminster to be 'compulsorily thrown open to the public as a Valhalla for the State'.[71] Thanks largely to the activity of Dean Trench and Thynne, the abbey was now in practice a public space. However, its role as a focus of national identity had yet to be developed. That would come under Dean Stanley. And it would involve a fundamentally different concept of Anglicanism. Westminster was about to become Broad Church.

Dean Stanley and the Broad Church

148

Arthur Penrhyn Stanley was born to the purple: son of a bishop and nephew of a baron, he married the daughter of an earl, who also happened to be maid of honour to the queen. But it was his precocious academic career – Dr Arnold's pupil at Rugby School, Benjamin Jowett's colleague at Balliol College – that established him as the rising star of liberal Churchmen. For many years, in Oxford, Canterbury and Westminster, he was the leading spokesman of Broad Church Anglicans. The term 'Broad Church' seems to have been coined in the early 1840s not by Stanley himself but by the poet Arthur Clough. However, it was Stanley, writing in the *Edinburgh Review* of 1850, who made that label a shibboleth of the new Anglicanism: 'not High, or Low', as he put it, 'but *Broad*'.[72]

Broad Church thinking is perhaps best understood as an attempt to solve what historians call the Victorian Crisis of Faith. In effect there were two crises: one relating to Darwinian evolution, the other to German biblical criticism. The first of these posed no problem for Stanley: scientific discovery simply revealed more of the glory of divine creation. 'Good science', he wrote, 'is good theology.'[73] The second crisis – extricating religious truth from the allegories of holy scripture – proved rather more difficult. It involved the separation of necessary and unnecessary myths. Broad Church ideas were involved in both debates. They set out to supply some sort of bridge between science and religion, between evolving ethics and identifiable scriptural authority. Hence, Stanley's own personal faith. In articles, books and sermons, and in innumerable statements as a public intellectual, he propounded a rational form of Christianity: demystified, demythologized, a religion fit for an age of change.

It was Baron von Bunsen, Prussian ambassador to London from 1842 to 1854, who seems to have introduced Stanley to the Prince Consort. In 1847 Albert made him a prince's chaplain.[74] When the future King Edward VII became a temporary undergraduate at Oxford in 1859–60, Prince Albert – whose background was firmly Lutheran – specifically chose Stanley as the Prince of Wales's mentor. When, in 1862, a visit to the Holy Land was planned for the heir to the throne, Stanley was the obvious choice as guide and guardian. In effect, he was now a courtier. And his marriage a year later to Lady Augusta Bruce consolidated his position. Lady Augusta's brother, Lord Elgin, was already governor to the Prince of Wales's household. Here, surely, was an alliance made in court. Within hours of his engagement, Stanley was invited by Prime Minister Palmerston to become Dean of Westminster.

Queen Victoria always thought of herself as 'Protestant to [her] very *heart's core*'.[75] The Scottish Kirk was really her spiritual home. And Stanley's liberal vision of Church inclusion – which he shared with charismatic Scots preachers like John Tulloch and Norman Macleod – was warmly supported by Victoria herself. After all, she was both Supreme Governor of the Church of England and a loyal member of the Established Presbyterian Church of Scotland. Throughout her life, the queen remained Broadly inclined. She preferred her clerics to be 'Moderate, sensible, and clever men; neither Ritualist nor Evangelical.'[76] Men rather like Dean Stanley.

Stanley was a Protestant Whig. He believed in progress; in civil and religious liberty; in the evolution of Christian thinking within a context of cohesive liberalism. Above all he supported the union of Church and crown. He believed in religious diversity, sheltered by the framework of an established Church, guaranteed by the crown in parliament. 'A free development of religious thought', he came to see, was the only pathway appropriate to an 'age of flux and transition' like the mid-nineteenth century. 'No one creed or confession', he explained, 'has exhausted the whole of Christian truth'; 'each form of theology is but an approximation to the truth'.[77] The Church of England, as he put it in 1850, 'was meant to include, and always [has] included, opposite and contradictory opinions'.[78] After all, the prayer book had been a statement of faith, composed by Protestants; but the Thirty-Nine Articles was a statement of law, formulated by parliament. Ambivalence, if not doubt, was thus built into the very fabric of Anglicanism.

From Thomas Arnold, Stanley inherited the conviction that 'rites and ceremonies' were but 'things indifferent', because the essentials of religion are rooted not in vestments or dogma – not even in the sacramental system – but in the values of Christian morality.[79] And those values, as Arnold had explained, were subject to the operation of reason buttressed by scripture: what he described as 'the moral reason acting under God'. In other words, they were the product of an informed conscience independent of priestly mediation, operating without the validation of what Stanley learned to call 'the monstrous . . . unchristian, unanglican . . . tendency of the Apostolical Succession'.[80] Stanley never matched the doctor's vehemence of speech, but his views were indeed the views of Arnold of Rugby. Predictably, the 'heretic' dean preferred the Sermon on the Mount to the Athanasian Creed. Over the years, Stanley became increasingly convinced that some form of rationalized Christianity – with its freedoms guaranteed

148   Arthur Penrhyn Stanley,
the great Victorian Dean
of Westminster (1864–81),
seen here in a portrait of
1877 attributed to Heinrich
von Angeli, believed that
the abbey should be
the home 'of the whole
Anglo-Saxon race'; he was
untiring in his efforts – often
controversial – to promote an
inclusive form of Anglicanism
and a close alliance between
Church and state in every
aspect of Westminster's life.

by the judiciary of a secular state – would triumph in the end. 'As Christianity is the salt of the world,' he wrote, 'so . . . Protestantism is the salt of Christendom.'[81]

Such opinions were not entirely welcome when Stanley arrived at the Deanery in 1864. They smacked too much of Balliol College Common Room. One of the canons, the redoubtable Christopher Wordsworth, went so far as to issue a formal protest.[82] Stanley's easy charm was brought into play: he politely invited his opponent to dinner. The chapter was initially suspicious of their new dean's 'Oxford friends': men like Benjamin Jowett, Frederick Temple, Mark Pattison and Goldwin Smith. Several of these had been contributors to a highly controversial volume of liberal articles entitled *Essays and Reviews* (1860). Their names, Stanley remembered in later years, were 'odious in the eyes of the theological world'. And when the dean invited one of them – the future Archbishop Temple – to preach at Westminster, the chapter broke into open rebellion. Stanley coolly addressed his canons as follows: 'you may sign [your] protest, but there is one thing that you can never do, and that is to make me quarrel with any of you'. The protest, as he recalled in old age, was simply 'signed and [then] buried in the Chapter archives'.[83]

Thereafter, Stanley cast his net widely. The variety of invitees was striking: Broad Church Jowett as well as High Church H.P. Liddon; Christian Socialist F.D. Maurice as well as the liberal Temple. Some – like Maurice, Liddon and Jowett – at first declined, then eventually agreed. Even the philologist and Sanskrit scholar Friedrich Max Müller of Oxford was in the end persuaded, though he discreetly spoke in the chapter house. Then there were the Presbyterians of the Scottish Kirk, John Tulloch and John Caird. Stanley thought Caird's address of 1874 'the best I ever heard within Westminster Abbey'.[84] Charles Kingsley, a very Broad Church canon – a Christian Socialist and author of *The Water-Babies* (1862) – most certainly agreed. But among those who long resisted Stanley's invitation were E.B. Pusey, Liddon and John Keble: Keble out of reticence; Pusey and Liddon on dogmatic grounds. Liddon did eventually speak, in 1876; and four years before that Keble had actually been given his own memorial in the abbey. But Pusey remained aloof. When Stanley suggested he might preach on the Christian values that Broad and High Church ultimately shared, the invitation was brusquely rejected. 'I do not know', announced Pusey, 'what the common Christianity of myself and Professor Jowett is. I do not know what single truth we hold in common, except that somehow Jesus came from God, which the Mohammedans believe too.'[85] 'This tide of rationalism', Pusey explained – like J.W. Colenso's unpicking the veracity of the Pentateuch – was 'frightfully unsettling to the faith of the lower classes.'[86] Liddon agreed: 'you must draw the line somewhere'.[87]

That High Church line was drawn tightly along the boundary of doctrinal authority. '*Mere* moral goodness', Liddon argued, 'is not a sufficient basis for . . . a common faith . . . fixed doctrines are necessary.'[88] Such a position was far removed from Stanley's vision of an evolving Christian community. High Church spoke the language of revealed faith: corporate, hierarchical, theocratic. Broad Church spoke for the verities beyond Church dogma: in Stanley's words, for 'the religion . . . behind the religion'.[89] What he was groping towards – in his abbey sermons and in his theological writings – was a morality independent of sacramental mediation, free from 'the magical offices of a sacerdotal caste'.[90] That disposed of one priestly trump card, the Catholic Eucharist. 'We must', he wrote towards the end of his life, 'incorporate in ourselves – that is, in our moral natures – the substance, the moral substance of the teaching and character of Jesus Christ. That is the only true transubstantiation.'[91]

Now, that particular line of argument – emphasizing the non-magical miracle of Christ's goodness – bypassed much of the traditional dogmatic system upon which High Church authority was based. 'Whole continents of useless controversies', Stanley told theology students at St Andrew's (Tulloch's university): 'baptismal regeneration, predestination, justification by faith'; 'whole systems of false doctrine . . . whole fabrics of barbarous phraseology, have [now] received their death blow . . . Theology has . . .

changed, [and] Religion has survived those changes.'[92] Only by means of an evolving language of theology could Christianity be reconciled with 'the progress of civilisation'. That, he explained right at the end of his life, would not come quickly: 'The Sacraments – the Clergy – the Pope – the Creeds – will take a long time in dying.'[93]

Not surprisingly, his attitude to Rome itself varied between tolerance and exasperation. 'Stanley', wrote the Jesuit poet Gerard Manley Hopkins, 'is a man who means well . . . he emphatically means well.'[94] All his life he showed some sympathy towards Catholics, rather less towards Catholicism. 'Catholics', young Stanley had explained to his sister Mary in 1835, were, after all, 'Christians . . . fellow-workers with all good Protestants against their common enemies, the world, the flesh, and the devil.'[95] But he had no time for the papacy's accumulated mythology. When in 1852 he heard the *Dies irae* chanted in the Sistine Chapel, he was initially much taken; but then reacted strongly against the 'superstition and falsehoods of 1,500 years'.[96] When Mary went over to Rome in 1856, Stanley's powers of sympathy were tested to breaking point – as were those of his friends. 'Is she mad, bad, or silly?' enquired Florence Nightingale.[97]

Stanley's ecumenical instincts – as expressed in the daily functioning of Westminster Abbey – were therefore mostly limited to the Protestant world – in effect, to the British Empire. Matins and Evensong, of course, continued. But there was a new emphasis on the abbey's communicative and coordinating role. Between the 1870s and the 1890s the abbey could boast a team of outstanding preachers: first Stanley, Farrar and Kingsley; then B. F. Westcott, Charles Gore and Basil Wilberforce. Each of these was capable of attracting packed congregations. Stanley himself was particularly anxious to bring in the working people of Westminster. During long summer evenings, he especially enjoyed 'taking large parties of working men through the Abbey and providing them with tea in the Jerusalem Chamber'. Children were particularly welcome on the feast of the Holy Innocents, when the service was followed by charades in the Deanery.[98] And, on a wider – indeed, imperial – scale he made it a definite policy to continue and elaborate the installation of colonial bishops within the precincts of the abbey. He had little to say about Islam, except to imply that it needed a good dose of reformation. As for the Greek Orthodox Church, though he admired its instinct for inclusion, he thought it 'in some respects more stagnant, more retrograde even than the Church of Rome'. His ideal was very different. What he admired most was the primitive simplicity of the catacombs.[99] During his time no vestments were worn at the abbey: simply a black Geneva gown or else a plain surplice. Daily Communion had to wait until after the death of Queen Victoria. Stanley's liberalism was essentially the liberalism of a progressive nonconformist mind. And he stretched the elasticity of that mentality to surprising degrees. There was more than a touch of Puritanism in all this. His religion was not a matter of aesthetics.

Dean Stanley had no ear for music. Notoriously so. After hearing her sing at a concert, his congratulations to the soprano Jenny Lind were oddly ambiguous: he compared her performance to the thunder of distant drums. In essentials, his ministry was a ministry of the word. Still, his appointment to the deanship in 1864 suited fairly well the pre-Tractarian practices of early Victorian Westminster. Trollope's description of daily service at the abbey in his novel *The Warden* (1855) seems to have come uncomfortably close to the truth:

> The minor canon . . . hurried in, somewhat late, in a surplice not in the neatest order, and was followed by a dozen choristers, who were also not as trim as they might have been: they all jostled into their places with a quick, hurried step, and the service was soon commenced. Soon commenced, and soon over.[100]

A few years before that, in 1847, Sir John Sutton – a pioneer of organ studies – had made no bones about the inadequacy of many contemporary cathedral services:

> the modern Cathedral organist scarcely ever accompanies six verses on the same stops, or even on the same row of keys, and keeps up a perpetual thundering with the pedals throughout the Psalms, [while] perhaps the choir he is accompanying consists of ten little boys, and six or at most eight men, three or four of whom are either disabled by old age, or by a long continued habit of drunkenness . . . Where will it end?[101]

Well, as far as Westminster Abbey was concerned, this sort of thing had certainly ended by the late 1850s. But it was a slow process. The appointment of James Turle in 1831, as both organist and master of choristers, signalled at last the possibility of better discipline and higher standards. He favoured full 'rolling' chords, which reverberated through the abbey with telling effect. Turle held office for fifty-one years (1831–82). He was noted for his composition of psalm chants and hymn tunes; less noted, perhaps, for attendance at rehearsals. In 1848 a separate school was begun for choristers. But real change proved sluggish. It was not until the future Sir Frederick Bridge – 'Westminster Bridge' as he was known – was promoted to organist (he had been deputy to James Turle since 1875) that the turning point in the revival of choral music at Westminster became clear. Bridge found the daily service in a condition of 'artistic poverty' – a condition that Stanley seems to have had little inclination to rectify. Admittedly, it was Stanley who authorized – and partly subsidized – a memorable performance of J. S. Bach's *St Matthew Passion* in 1871. But the choir itself remained underpaid, poorly housed and under-rehearsed until Bridge took it in hand. It was thanks to Bridge that a proper choir school was at last established. During his time, the organ was rebuilt by Pearson as a tribute to Henry Purcell (organist at the abbey from 1679). And it

149

149   The abbey choirboys, *c.*1908–9, with Frederick Bridge (*left*), the precentor Howard
Daniell-Bainbridge (*centre*) and the head master of the choir school William Dams (*right*). Bridge's
appointment as organist in 1882 marked a sea change at the abbey choir school: under his aegis,
living and working conditions for choristers and lay vicars (professional adult male singers)
improved, and so too did the standard of musicianship. Bridge presided over the music at many
landmark events and services during his nearly forty years at the abbey.

was under his regime that what he called 'the venal system' of choral pluralities – the
engaging of individual choristers and minor canons employed at the same time in
various royal chapels – was at last abolished.

   The extraordinary events of the queen's golden jubilee in 1887 had significant musical
consequences. A national and international event – attended by the crowned heads of
Europe and Hawaii, by princes from India and from Japan – it symbolized the way in
which the abbey had become an imperial redoubt. It was Bridge's role to celebrate
the occasion with an anthem of his own composition and to prepare a performance
of a *Te Deum* composed some years before by Prince Albert. Not long after Bridge's
appointment, Stanley had arranged to introduce him to Robert Browning: 'Poetry and
Music should know each other.' Some years later, for Browning's funeral in 1889, it fell
to Bridge to set to music Elizabeth Barrett Browning's poem 'He giveth his beloved

sleep'. And in 1892, for Tennyson's funeral – a major state occasion, marking the death not just of a great poet but of a figure some believed to have been the greatest of all poets laureate – it was Bridge's privilege, at no more than a few days' notice, to set to music the poet's immortal farewell: 'Crossing the Bar'.[102]

Burials and Memorials

Stanley's tolerance was certainly taxed by his battles with High Churchmen in Convocation. Between 1717 and 1852 the Convocations of Canterbury and York had been in abeyance. Their revival – first Canterbury, then York – reopened a contentious forum for ecclesiastical politics. Since, in his time, meetings were regularly held in the abbey's Jerusalem Chamber, Stanley was doubly involved. In 1870, for example, to mark the opening meeting of the committee appointed by Convocation to revise the Authorized Version of the New Testament of 1611, Stanley invited all its members to a service of Eucharist in the abbey. A new altar table, designed by Scott in jet-black marble, had been set up in Henry VII's chapel over the grave of England's first Protestant monarch, Edward VI.[103] Participants included an American scholar, Dr George Vance Smith. Now, Smith was a Unitarian who denied the Nicene Creed. The invitation to take part – Stanley was generally on good terms with Unitarians – was denounced as one of 'insult and defiance to the whole of Catholic Christendom'. As a precaution against protesters, the 'heretic' dean 'stationed behind the altar rails two stalwart policemen in plain clothes'. Similarly, in 1872, during one of the periodical debates about the Athanasian Creed, Stanley found himself denounced once again. G. A. Denison stormed out of the Jerusalem Chamber in protest. A petition – only narrowly defeated – attempted to remove Stanley from the list of Oxford select preachers. A combination of 'defiant pluck' and 'rhetorical skill' – to say nothing of royal favour and personal charm – kept most of his critics at bay. After a typical outburst by Denison, Stanley was seen to guide his opponent amiably towards lunch. But over the years, disputes with the 'bigots' of Convocation, as he called them, must have drained away a good deal of his creative energy. In 1867, when a Pan-Anglican Synod was summoned to Lambeth – partly as a vehicle for the condemnation of J. W. Colenso, Bishop of Natal, to whom Stanley was sympathetic – he felt obliged to exclude it altogether from formal use of the abbey.[104]

As dean, Stanley became notorious for accepting the burial in the abbey of non-Anglicans and even crypto-agnostics. His rights in this matter were indisputable: they stemmed from a royal grant of 1560. The dean, it was agreed by a royal commission of 1890, was head of the abbey, there being, of course, no bishop.[105] Stanley felt strongly that his abbey must be 'a sanctuary not of any private sect, but of the English people'.[106] During his time, there was only one notable exception: George Eliot – despite expressing a wish to be buried in the abbey – had to wait until 1980 to be commemorated in Poets' Corner. Her relationship with a married man produced implacable opposition, which overcame even Stanley's desire to honour her. Otherwise the dean was open to all. Lord Palmerston, Charles Dickens, William Herschel, George Grote, Sir Charles Lyell, David Livingstone, the American philanthropist George Peabody, Connop Thirlwall, Sir Rowland Hill: believers, unbelievers, half-believers – he buried them all. Gladstone was the last statesman to be buried in the abbey and commemorated by a standing statue. The solemnity of his state funeral in 1898 – which resounded to the strains of Beethoven and Schubert as well as Purcell – was long remembered. Thereafter a plaque, or a bust, or simply an inscribed stone would have to suffice. But during his own lifetime, Stanley had done more than enough to establish the principle that great-

150 ness – however defined – should, wherever possible, be commemorated in the abbey.

Thousands filed past Dickens's grave. Tens of thousands filled the streets for Livingstone's funeral. No wonder the queen once referred to her favourite cleric as that 'body-snatcher Arthur Stanley'.[107] Almost his last act was to dictate from his deathbed a letter to the *St James's Gazette* calling for a monument of reconciliation to the regicides exhumed at the Restoration.[108] And when it came to the choice of pall-bearers at his own funeral, the list was as comprehensive as his vision of a national Church: the Duke of Westminster, a territorial magnate; Bishop Temple of Exeter, a future Arnoldian Archbishop of Canterbury; William Spottiswoode, president of the Royal Society; Matthew Arnold and Benjamin Jowett, leaders of Oxford liberalism; Bishop Westcott of Cambridge, a less obviously Broad Church sympathizer; John Stoughton, representing nonconformity; Robert Story representing the Scottish Kirk; and W. H. Smith (Tory) and W. E. Foster (Liberal), representing both sides in the House of Commons. Only one figure was symbolically missing: a representative of the Church of Rome.

Stanley's sense of inclusion had been infectious. When it came to the burial of Charles Darwin, scarcely an objection was heard. Broad Church Canon Farrar was there to give the address. By the 1890s the process had become almost formulaic. The story of Tennyson's funeral is instructive. Even as an adolescent, one relative remarked, he revered the abbey: 'it suited the pensive habit of his soul'. When he attended the wedding of Stanley's niece in 1878, he was seen looking round the abbey 'as if he felt the Immortals were his compeers'. He was there for Dickens's service; he was there again, in spirit, for Browning. And he long anticipated his own obsequies. When that day came, in 1892, the nave was lined by men of the Balaclava Light Brigade; among the pall-bearers were one duke, two marquesses, two earls and a baron. It was 'a lovely day', noted Henry James; 'the Abbey looked beautiful'. But somehow it was all too

150   Arthur Penrhyn Stanley, Dean of Westminster (1864–81), is buried in Henry VII's chapel beneath this fine alabaster tomb effigy by Joseph Edgar Boehm, completed in 1884.

official: 'too many masters of Balliol, too many Deans and Alfred Austins'. Burne-Jones found it all 'so flat and flattening . . . there should have been street music . . . and bells muffled all over London, and rumbling drums . . . I wish I hadn't gone.'[109]

If Stanley and his successors succeeded in transforming much of the abbey's form and function, they were less successful in providing extra space for additional memorials. Indeed, successive schemes produced no more than a catalogue of counterfactual dreams. Scott's first plan of 1854 had involved a 'wide and lofty cloister', approached from the west walk of the Great Cloister and running alongside College Garden, all hidden on its southern flank by the existing row of eighteenth-century houses in Abingdon Street.[110] This was the plan – 'a national mausoleum for men of eminence' – first suggested by Thynne in 1852, endorsed by Gladstone in 1854, and submitted to the Westminster Improvement Commissioners in 1855 and 1857.[111] Scott's second scheme, of 1863, was more ambitious: 'a sort of campo santo'; a 'double cloister' flanking two sides of College Garden. This was the scheme much favoured by Prince Albert as well as by Dean Stanley; submitted to the Thames Embankment Commission in 1863,[112] and again in 1873.[113] In 1873–8 a number of the more egregious classical monuments – memorials to General Wolfe, Captain James Cornewall and the politician

151

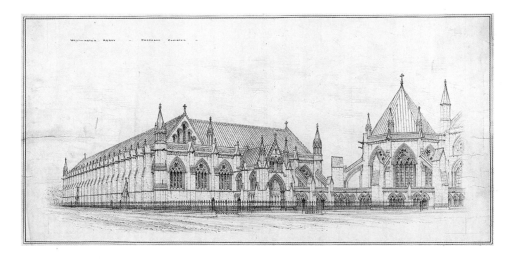

151   George Gilbert Scott's ambitious scheme for a 'National Campo Santo' for future burials of 'men of eminence', was a double cloister of magnificent proportions adjacent to the chapter house; this view, dating from *c.*1873, was reproduced in *American Architect and Building News* (29 February 1884).

James Craggs, for instance, as well as Admiral Richard Tyrrell's cloud-capped marble fantasy – were arbitrarily pruned.[114] But that secured only temporary relief. The increasing acceptance of cremation in the 1870s and 1880s in no way reduced the public appetite for memorials. 'We have already more than rivalled Santa Croce in Florence,' mused Stanley. 'Let us hope in future days to excel even the Campo Santo at Pisa.'[115] Interestingly, this *campo santo* idea was also supported by Beresford Hope. In good hands, he thought, a new sepulchral building – replete, perhaps, with Gothic domes – might even launch 'an era in monumental sculpture'.[116] Dean Bradley (1881–1902), however, had reservations. Opening up the south-east corner of the abbey site would have created a space of magnificent proportions between the future Parliament Square and Millbank. But it would ultimately also have involved the purchase and demolition of all the houses between Abingdon Street and Great College Street. The cost of that would have been at least £500,000.

Meanwhile, Parliament Square was still waiting to be born. Space had been prepared by statute as long ago as 1806. Schemes for 'Westminster Improvements' were already being hatched in 1832. In 1840, in 1853 and again in 1855, Charles Barry produced plans for developing the area between the abbey and the new Houses of Parliament.[117] St Margaret's Church was to go. A grand entrance to the House of Commons – the Albert Tower – was to balance the newly built Victoria Tower and act as a focus for

152   The ancient Egyptian obelisk known as 'Cleopatra's Needle'
arrived in Britain early in 1878, and it was suggested that it be
installed outside the abbey on the empty site north of Henry VII's
chapel; a wooden replica was temporarily erected there by way of a
trial, but fears were expressed that the obelisk itself might threaten the
safety of the new District Line, which ran underneath, so the plan was
abandoned and the site became Parliament Square.

parliamentary offices on the site of Sir John Soane's Law Courts (not demolished
until 1883). Barry's master plan for a new Westminster – 'New Palace Yard, or Parliament Square, or whatever it is to be called' – was exhibited at Westminster Hall in
1857, and then submitted to Palmerston in 1864.[118] But neither in conception nor
in detail did it achieve consensus. Scott, for example, always opposed the demolition
of St Margaret's.[119] As late as 1878 there was talk of giving the whole site north of
Henry VII's chapel a new focus with the installation of Cleopatra's Needle.[120] But   152

E.M. Barry's more sensible proposal of 1868 eventually gained majority support and was carried through as Parliament Square. Here, at last, was an urban reservation for departed statesmen, raised on plinths and cast in bronze. First Canning and Peel, then Palmerston, Derby and Disraeli.

But that idea approached only half the problem. The notion of a full-scale replanning of Westminster – mooted by Charles Barry so long before – returned in the shape of a comprehensive scheme drawn up in 1878 by H. Heathcote Statham.[121] Now, Statham was an influential editor of *The Builder*. His ideas carried weight. From Embankment Gardens to Lambeth Bridge; from Abingdon Street (rejigged as Abingdon Place) to St John, Smith Square (ensconced in a layout to rival Eaton Square); with an opera house on the site of the future New Scotland Yard, as well as a towering *flèche* for the abbey itself: Statham staked out the potential for an aggrandized Westminster as a focus for the conjunction of Church and state. He even resuscitated Charles Barry's dream of a quadrilateral *campo santo* in Embankment Gardens, approached this time by a 'Campo Santo Road' no less.

Nothing came of it. But the cause of monumental extension – an abbey fit for the memorials of another thousand years – still had its champions. Dean Stanley himself never wavered: his 'dreams [it was said, were] haunted by the genius of the place'. To walk through the abbey with the dean was like walking through antiquity with Plutarch.[122] For Stanley the abbey embodied, uniquely, that necessary nexus of state and Church; 'Union and reconciliation'; 'Medieval and . . . Protestant', within a single building. A union, moreover, fortified by countless memorials, past, present and future. 'It is not only Rheims Cathedral and St Denys . . . in one', he wrote, 'but . . . also what the Pantheon was intended to be in France, what the Valhalla is to Germany, what Santa Croce is to Italy.'[123] Westminster Abbey, he believed, was destined to be 'the peculiar home of the entire Anglo-Saxon race on both sides of the Atlantic'. It was 'the Fortress of the Church of England . . . [and] whilst Westminster Abbey stands, the Church of England stands'.[124]

Even before Dean Stanley had himself been interred in Henry VII's chapel, however, a new player had entered the field. George John Shaw-Lefevre, Baron Eversley, was a radical politician with energy to burn. As Gladstone's commissioner of works in 1880–84 and 1892–4, he made metropolitan planning his speciality. He even moved the Wellington arch at Hyde Park Corner to facilitate traffic flow. And he campaigned – volubly, obsessively – for a national mausoleum at Westminster.[125] First Dean Stanley, then Dean Bradley, found him an eager, if wayward, ally.[126]

In 1882 and 1884, in two fighting articles in the journal *Nineteenth Century*, Shaw-Lefevre set out his stall. As he saw it, the rebuilding of Whitehall and Westminster – again that elusive symbiosis of Church and state – would not only 'ennoble and beautify this historic part of London'; it would create a group of buildings 'worthy of . . . the *mesomphalos* [the very heart] of the British Empire'.[127] The author of these dreams was no architect, but his proposals stimulated a number who were. Henry Travis suggested a *chevet* of chapels, disguising the 'debased' structure of St Margaret's and linked to the abbey by a subterranean 'catacomb' cloister.[128] James Fergusson – an architectural theorist of subtlety and power – proposed a massive 'new south transept', running between chapter house and Jewel Tower, with access to the abbey via a passageway at Poets' Corner.[129] The architect George Somers Clarke Jr – speaking out for Old England – called down a plague on all their houses: 'Being Englishmen we do not want Campo Santos, Pantheons and such outlandish things.'[130]

One architect who was certainly not afraid to dream outlandish dreams was John Pollard Seddon, diocesan architect for London. In 1888, in conjunction with a young City and Guilds instructor named Laurence Harvey, he began work on what would eventually become the most outlandish scheme of all. His first draft was simply designated a 'mausoleum in connexion with Westminster Abbey'. This was presumably designed to catch the eye of those who were at that point pressing for a golden jubilee monument to Queen Victoria. He resubmitted the idea to the parliamentary commission on Westminster Abbey in 1890.[131] And then, this time with Edward Beckitt Lamb (son of a more famous architectural father), he produced in 1904 a final, over-aggrandized version of the same scheme, now entitled 'Imperial Monumental Halls and Tower'.[132]

One of those promoting a state of mind sympathetic to such visionary schemes was, of course, the indefatigable Shaw-Lefevre.[133] In 1888 he specifically canvassed Dean Bradley in an attempt to turn the abbey's plan for a national memorial chapel into a permanent celebration of Queen Victoria's golden jubilee: he proposed a Victoria Chapel, no less, featuring a statue of the queen, surrounded perhaps by great figures of the age (some of them transferred from the north transept). A committee met in the Jerusalem Chamber: the Archbishop of Canterbury, the Duke of Westminster, W.H. Smith, Lord Wantage . . . .[134] They discovered, not surprisingly, that the queen had already given her approval to an 'Imperial Institute' in South Kensington.[135] Westminster Abbey had to be content with staging a golden jubilee service on 21 June 1887. The aged queen–empress graced the occasion, appropriately seated in the coronation chair.

Shaw-Lefevre was not yet defeated. He made a parallel approach to parliament in the form of a 'Monumental Chapel Bill'. Another committee was enrolled, packed this time with millionaires: Lord Brassey, George Cubbit, H.H. Gibbs, B.W. Currie . . . .[136] Meanwhile, the architect James Knowles – an old ally of Stanley – made play with a proposal of his own: 'a great National Pantheon' within the abbey's cloister garth, 'surrounded . . . by the most majestic memories in the world'. Here would be space

for 'the bodies of more heroes than England is likely to produce in the next 1,000 years'.[137] Then, just as Shaw-Lefevre's campaign was showing signs of progress, the London County Council pulled the financial plug: prospective revenues from the Coal Fund would no longer be available.[138] Bradley began to take fright at Shaw-Lefevre's scheme: 'needlessly ambitious'; 'needlessly destructive'.[139] Dean and Chapter turned instead to the Treasury for 'pecuniary aid'. Their case was strong. Since the commutation of the abbey's estates in 1869, agricultural depression had seriously reduced available income. The number of visitors had increased dramatically since the 1840s; 'from the United Kingdom . . . the Colonial Empire, as well as the United States'. There were 'no funds' available for future repairs, and no room at all for future memorials.[140] The Treasury fell back on a well-worn governmental device: a royal commission was set up in 1890 to explore 'the want of space for monuments in Westminster Abbey'.[141]

David Plunkett, MP, commissioner of works, was appointed chairman. The other members were Alfred Waterhouse, president of the Royal Institute of British Architects; Sir Alfred Layard, archaeologist; Sir Frederic Leighton, artist; a well-known journalist, L. J. Jennings, MP; and, of course, Dean Bradley himself. Four architects submitted five sets of plans. Pearson was the established competitor. He produced three schemes: a cloister north of the abbey; a chapel south-east of the chapter house;[142] and another chapel on the ancient refectory site to the south of the Great Cloister. The last of these seemed likely to carry the day until it was discovered – rather belatedly – that the land had already been transferred, along with Ashburnham House, to Westminster School in 1868.[143] The other competitors were outsiders. E. J. Tarver suggested girdling the chapter house with 'a wreath of chapels', approached by a 'low passage or ambulatory under the flying buttresses, supplying enough space for at least 400 years'.[144] J. P. Seddon and Laurence Harvey resubmitted their scheme of 1888 for a cluster of chapels south-east of the chapter house.[145] But none of these gained majority support. The votes regarding the site – south of the Great Cloister or south-east of the chapter house – were equally split. Bradley's own hesitation effectively guaranteed deadlock.[146]

By now another factor had entered the equation: the growth of the conservation lobby. First the Society of Antiquaries, then the Society for the Preservation of Ancient Buildings, led by William Morris, campaigned fiercely against interference – any interference – with the historic fabric of the abbey. It was Morris who led the charge: 'beastly monuments to fools and knaves'; 'ghastly pieces of perversion'. And the proposals for additional chapels seemed equally damnable. All the schemes considered in 1890–91, he explained, had missed the point entirely. Westminster Abbey was simply 'the noblest

153 (FACING PAGE)   In the late 19th century, the abbey's ancient fabric was increasingly assailed by teeming streets and polluted air, its environs staked out for grandiose development by architects and visionaries. This detail from a hand-coloured engraving by William Wyllie and Henry Brewer, *A Bird's-Eye View of London as seen from a Balloon*, 1884, shows, to the right of the chapter house, a huddle of houses and shops still clinging on in the shadow of Charles Barry's Victoria Tower, which was for many years the tallest secular construction in the world.

building ever raised by Englishmen'. No addition linked in any way to the ancient fabric should therefore be permitted. If there had to be a memorial chapel, the obvious site would be in Abingdon Street. As it was, the exterior had been 'hatched and cobbled . . . with restorations, and restorations of restorations, till it has been half destroyed as a work of art'. As for the interior, there was now little hope at all. It had been 'cluttered up with a huge mass of the ugliest and vilest undertakers' masonry that anywhere can be seen', leaving it in 'a state of sordid dirt which is disgraceful to both the Government and the Chapter'.[147]

153   And yet something, as Stanley used to say, had to be done. The contrast between the new Houses of Parliament on one side of Old Palace Yard and the huddle of houses immediately opposite was painful: 'pawnbrokers one side, palaces on the other'. And the prospect of rivalry presented by the proposed new Roman Catholic cathedral nearby must surely have given Anglicans pause for thought.[148] In 1893 Henry Yates Thompson − a benefactor with his eye on a baronetcy − stepped in. He offered to resolve the impasse with a gift of £40,000.[149] What he suggested, however, was rather vague: a chapel in Old Palace Yard dedicated 'to the Empire or the Anglo-Saxon race'.[150] The idea was quietly shelved, only to be resurrected after the First World War.[151]

Envoi

Looking back over his time at the abbey, Dean Stanley can have been only partly satisfied. He felt that the tempo of Churchmanship outside Westminster had for some time been shifting Higher. As ritualists moved to the right and evangelicals to the left, he sensed that the middle ground of Broad Church thinking was under threat. The abbey itself remained largely immune, at least until the end of the century. Elsewhere, that was not so. 'A cloud of superstition', Stanley noted in 1878, 'has settled down over a large part of the ecclesiastical world'.[152] The growth of ritualism certainly made him uneasy, but his basic attitude was one of tolerance. His heart was never really in the Public Worship Act of 1874. Had he lived longer, he might have accepted with good grace the compromise arrangements of the royal commissions on ecclesiastical courts and ecclesiastical discipline in 1883 and 1906. But then Stanley always had an eye for the wider horizon. His central aims − to make the abbey an emblem of national identity, a focus of reasonable belief, a symbol of inclusive Anglicanism on an imperial scale − had all, by the end of his career, largely succeeded; even if Valhalla, in the end, had to be indefinitely postponed.

Stanley's successor – and biographer – Dean Bradley perpetuated his approach, his Broad Church theology, and even his habit of showing working men round the abbey. He also inherited Stanley's financial and architectural problems and his willingness to turn to government for help and support. His long tenure – from 1881 to 1902 – ensured that Westminster remained both a liberal and a public place. But the role of the abbey was about to change once more. By the close of Queen Victoria's reign the abbey's inclusive ethos had begun to take on new resonance: not just national and imperial but consciously, inescapably global.

8

Imperial Zenith to Worldwide Communion:
1901–2002

DAVID CANNADINE

At the end of Queen Victoria's reign, Westminster Abbey was much more alive as a place of worship than it had been at the beginning. Yet in other ways, the picture was less optimistic, one indication of which was that many of the abbey's 'organic links with the nation' had been 'irreparably severed' during that period.[1] The Dean and Chapter had surrendered their estates, they had ceased to govern Westminster School and they had been deprived of their powers of oversight of the City of Westminster. At the same time, the construction of the Roman Catholic Westminster Cathedral (1895–1903) and the Methodist Central Hall (1905–11) on the abbey's very doorstep, challenged its claim to be the pre-eminent national church of the pre-eminent national faith. Moreover, the schemes to consolidate its position as the 'National Valhalla, or Temple of Fame', had come to nothing, and in his poem 'Recessional', written for the diamond jubilee in 1897, Kipling had drawn attention to the transience of earthly power and the ephemerality of worldly dominion.[2] It was a prescient poetic prediction, for one hundred years later the British Empire effectively came to an end with the handover of Hong Kong to the Chinese government. During the same century, attendance at the Church of England's services declined dramatically: until the 1950s, Britain remained a nominally Christian country, characterized by 'a deep if atavistic and largely unpractised Protestantism', but thereafter it evolved into a multi-faith nation that was also among the most secular in the Western world.[3] For a church that, by the 1890s, had increasingly sought to identify with the empire as well

154 (FACING PAGE)   The empty oak coffin, prepared for the Unknown Warrior, rested in the abbey before being taken to Boulogne to receive the body, which was then carried on HMS *Verdun* to Dover and travelled on by train to Victoria Station, where it arrived on the evening of 10 November 1920. On the following day the Warrior was transported on a gun carriage, first to the Cenotaph and then to the abbey for burial.

as with God, these destabilizing developments threatened to undermine its role in the life of the nation and the global English-speaking communion beyond.

Yet across an ever more godless century, which simultaneously witnessed the decline and fall of the British Empire, successive deans and their chapters defied these trends, embracing and creating futures their predecessors could not have imagined or foreseen; and instead of diminishing in importance, the abbey's national significance and global reach actually grew.[4] As a place of worship, as the pantheon of the great and the good, and as the church most closely connected to the monarchy, it became more central to the life of the nation than ever before, while also consolidating its position as the focal point of the post-imperial, English-speaking world, as a tourist attraction drawing millions of visitors from around the globe and as one of Christendom's greatest churches. But this was not a simple story or a linear trajectory. From the death of Queen Victoria in 1901 until the outbreak of the First World War, imperial consciousness was at its zenith, and in the abbey these sentiments were ceremonially articulated with remarkable power and resonance. But from 1918 until the end of the Second World War, there was a turning away from such hubris and swagger, in favour of a less histrionic ceremonial mode, as the abbey increasingly aligned itself with the sorrows and joys of ordinary people. From the late 1940s until the 1970s, it became the place where the transition from the British Empire to the multiracial Commonwealth was most significantly marked and recognized. Since then, it has gradually embraced a wider ecumenicalism, even as it has continued to be the setting for great ceremonials centring on the royal family, and for those many special services that have been put on more frequently than in the past.

Abbey and Empire

In August 1902 Canon James E.C. Welldon, previously Bishop of Calcutta, preached a sermon in the abbey not long after the coronation of Edward VII. 'The Abbey Church of Westminster', he insisted, was the 'Holy of Holies of the British race', which 'belongs not to England only, but to the Empire.' Indeed, for the duration of his canonry, from 1902 to 1906, Welldon sought to accentuate and intensify the 'imperial character' of the abbey as the 'heart and soul' of the 'English-speaking world'. For him, it was a palimpsest upon which had been inscribed 'the lives and the deeds by which England became Great Britain, and Great Britain became the British Empire, and the British Empire became, as it still remains, and . . . shall never cease to be, the greatest secular institution in the world.'[5] In terms of geography and history, the abbey was unique in the length and the intimacy of its association with the British parliament and also in its close connection with the sovereign, by virtue of its status as a royal peculiar. But by Welldon's time, the British monarchy was more than ever before an imperial monarchy, and between 1902 and 1953, four coronations took place in the abbey, each particular to its time, but together forming a unique sequence of sacred-cum-secular ceremonies, of local, national and imperial significance, for which there was no precise historical precedent, and the like of which will surely never happen again.[6]

These were developments all the more surprising because Queen Victoria's relations with the abbey had not been close and, although like all sovereigns she was its Visitor, she had only occasionally visited it, apart from her coronation and the golden jubilee service of 1887. And the abbey played no part in her obsequies, which took place in January 1901: there was no public lying-in-state, her funeral service was held at St George's Chapel, Windsor, and she was buried at Frogmore.[7] But her successor, Edward VII (r. 1901–10), would be a very different sort of monarch: less engaged politically, but far less reclusive than his mother had been after the death of Prince Albert, and eager to establish a new and changed royal style, in which ceremonial and splendour would be of great importance, and in which Westminster Abbey would play a significant part. To his mother's outrage, he had acted as a pall-bearer at Gladstone's funeral in 1898, and, as king, Edward determined that his coronation would be the most magnificent ceremonial display of modern times, surpassing similar events in the other great imperial cities of Berlin, Vienna and Moscow. The preparations were elaborate and meticulous, overseen by Lord Esher, the Duke of Norfolk and Sir Schomberg MacDonnell, and, since scarcely anyone could remember the last time a British monarch had been crowned, they were also lengthy and detailed. Edward's coronation was scheduled for June 1902, but, only a few days before, he was taken ill, and the ceremony had to be postponed while he recovered from an operation.[8]

Edward survived the surgery, and the delayed coronation took place six weeks later than planned. By a combination of design and default, context and circumstance, it was the most imperial event that had ever taken place in the abbey. The Treaty of Vereeniging, ending the Second Boer War, had been signed at the end of May, creating a much extended British South Africa. Edward Elgar composed his 'Coronation Ode', with expansive words by A.C. Benson: 'wider still and wider shall thy bounds be set; God who made thee mighty make thee mightier yet'. Sir Charles Hubert Hastings Parry produced a new setting of the processional anthem 'I was glad', which was the very quintessence of Edwardian pomp and circumstance, and has been sung at every coronation since.[9] King Edward was the first British monarch to come to his crowning as Emperor of India and as ruler of British dominions beyond the seas, while Queen Alexandra would wear a dress made of golden Indian gauze, and a new crown set with the Koh-i-noor diamond, which had been given to Queen Victoria after the

British conquest of Punjab in 1849. The postponement of the coronation also meant that many of the visiting monarchs and foreign dignitaries had gone home, and only the colonial delegations remained. So, when it eventually took place, in the presence of a congregation of 8,000 people, and featuring 'native soldiers' and ruling princes from many parts of the empire, Edward's coronation was even more of an imperial occasion than had originally been intended, and commentators such as John Bodley eulogized the ceremony as 'the consecration of the imperial idea'.[10]

155

But this was not the only way in which the coronation of Edward VII differed from that of Queen Victoria. Under Sir Frederick Bridge, who was the abbey's organist and choirmaster from 1882 to 1918, musical standards were greatly improved, the organ was rebuilt, the choir was remodelled and lit with electricity, the choristers were provided with scarlet cassocks at the instruction of Edward VII himself, and the establishment of a choir school meant that they were expertly drilled and trained.[11] Moreover, the appointment of Jocelyn Perkins as minor canon and sacrist in 1899, who cared deeply about ecclesiastical ceremonial, meant that by the time of Edward's coronation the abbey services were no longer drab and plain, as they had been for much of the nineteenth century, when elaborate rituals were deemed to smack of popery, but had become more colourful and stately, as well as better sung. Thanks to Perkins, the clergy were provided with colourful copes, the altars were vested with vivid frontals, and banners were borne in procession. This helped to make possible 'the attainment of a lofty standard of worship and ceremonial at the solemn sacring of Edward VII', which Perkins believed 'was felt on all sides to be imperative'. 'From end to end', he later recalled, 'did the [abbey] altar blaze with a display of alms dishes, flagons, chalices . . . Upon the amateur ritualist of the nineteenth century, with his tailor-made vases, his feeble floral decorations, the scene bestowed a sorely needed lesson.'[12] But, in addition, the unexpected postponement on account of the king's illness allowed more time for the choir to be rehearsed and for the processions to be organized and practised, with the result that the coronation of 1902 was not only more imperial, but also better performed than Queen Victoria's had been. It was rightly seen as 'an immemorial tradition celebrated under unprecedented circumstances', as 'the archaic traditions of the Middle Ages were enlarged in their scope . . . to include the modern splendour of a mighty empire'.[13]

The idea that the abbey coronation was not only a solemn sacrament for the monarch and his consort, but also a collective religious experience for the whole nation and empire struck a completely new note, even though the majority of the king–emperor's subjects did not profess the Christian religion. The press acclaimed the coronation as a superb and unprecedented spectacle, there were pictures in many newspapers and magazines of a sort that had not been available in 1838, and the procession to and

155 This painting, by Edwin Austin Abbey (*c.* 1902–7), of the coronation of Edward VII on 9 August 1902 shows the king, seated in the coronation chair, clothed in robes of state, and the Archbishop of Canterbury, with arms lifted, preparing to place the imperial crown on his head; princes and peers raise their coronets and lead the shout 'God save the king!' 'It was a sight indeed . . . I never saw so many jewels in my life,' remarked the artist.

from Buckingham Palace was the first of its kind to be filmed.[14] To be sure, there were mishaps and criticisms. The service was curtailed on account of the king's weakened condition, he was not strong enough to wear the traditional St Edward's crown, and settled for the lighter imperial state crown instead. Archbishop Temple was even more frail than the monarch: he was so blind that he had trouble reading the words of the service, put the crown on the king's head back to front and had to be helped from his knees after paying homage. These were minor glitches compared to the mishaps that marred Victoria's coronation, but the Bishop of London made a serious point when he regretted that the crowning had become 'too much a great show', and 'too little a great sacrament'. For the remainder of the twentieth century, the competing claims on the abbey, as a great Christian church, devoted to the worship of God, and as a secular shrine, playing an integral part in the life of the nation, empire and Commonwealth, would remain unresolved for some, but successfully reconciled for others.[15]

Soon after Edward VII was crowned, the octogenarian Dean Bradley finally resigned, and was succeeded by Joseph Armitage Robinson, who was not much more than half Bradley's age. He was a fine New Testament scholar and an impressive preacher, who had been appointed Norrisian professor of divinity at Cambridge in 1893. He had become a canon of Westminster and rector of St Margaret's six years later, and played a major part in the planning of Edward's coronation on behalf of the abbey. Armitage Robinson continued to be a prolific author while dean, producing a stream of theological and historical works, but his relations with the chapter were often tense and vexed, as his colleagues, especially Hensley Henson, considered that he exercised his extensive powers without adequate consultation.[16] Among his first tasks was to attend to the unveiling in 1903 of a statue of Gladstone, in the north transept, by Sir Thomas Brock. In the same year, Lord Salisbury died, and in 1909 he was commemorated in an altar tomb of black marble and bronze, with a recumbent effigy by Sir William Goscombe John, in the nave near the west door (though Salisbury's body had been buried at his ancestral home at Hatfield in Hertfordshire). These two memorials, which were undertaken at the behest of parliament, and which the abbey had no choice but to accept, were a further indication that the Victorian age was over. Between them, Gladstone and Salisbury had held the prime ministership almost continuously from 1880 to 1903: they were the last two great titans of nineteenth-century politics, and during their time in power the British Empire expanded spectacularly in Asia, the Pacific Islands and, especially, Africa.

156

The Gladstone statue and the Salisbury effigy were the last of their kind, as the unrelenting pressure on abbey space compelled the Dean and Chapter to consider different and less ostentatious forms of memorialization.[17] On the death of the author and critic John Ruskin in 1900, the dean had offered an abbey burial, but the

156   The marble statue of William Ewart Gladstone by Sir Thomas Brock, 1903, was the last standing statue to be erected inside the abbey; owing to lack of space, it was decided that future memorials should take the form of tablets, memorial stones or windows. An exception was made for Lord Salisbury, a recumbent bronze effigy of whom was set upon an altar tomb in the nave in 1909.

157   A profusion of floral tributes for the celebrated actor Sir Henry Irving piled up along the north side of the nave after his death in 1905; his body was cremated and the ashes buried in Poets' Corner – the first such burial in the abbey – where, marked with a small memorial stone in the floor, they lie next to the grave of the 18th-century Shakespearean actor David Garrick, and in front of Shakespeare's memorial statue.

family had declined, and instead Ruskin was given a memorial service, and a bronze plaque commemorating him was unveiled in Poets' Corner two years later. When Sir Henry Campbell-Bannerman died in 1908 – the first British prime minister to expire in office since Palmerston – he was also given a memorial service in the abbey, and four years later he was commemorated with a larger than life-sized bust in the north nave aisle. In the same year, a memorial window to John Bunyan was erected by public subscription in the west aisle of the north transept. But the most portentous memorialization of these years was of the actor Sir Henry Irving, who died in 1905.   157 He was accorded an abbey funeral, and his ashes were buried in Poets' Corner, next to the grave of David Garrick. This was an appropriate location, but the interment represented a major change in abbey policy, for Irving was the first person whose

158 In 1904 John Pollard Seddon and Edward Beckitt Lamb submitted an outlandish plan for what they called 'Imperial Monumental Halls and Tower', shown here in a perspective view from the north-east by John Gaye; the scheme's most startling features were a huge free-standing tower more than 200 feet taller than that of Big Ben, and a soaring crossing tower added to the abbey.

cremated remains were buried in the abbey. However, it took some time before this new policy, which was formally agreed by the Dean and Chapter in March 1908, was widely accepted.[18] On the death of the botanist Sir Joseph Hooker in December 1911, the dean offered burial for him in the abbey near the grave of his friend Charles Darwin, but only on condition that he first be cremated. His widow declined the offer, and Hooker was interred elsewhere.

At the same time, schemes for a great imperial mausoleum that would be close to or linked to the abbey, continued to appear, stimulated by the growth in imperial sentiment resulting from the coronation, and the belated but successful ending of the Boer War. Indeed, it may have been in anticipation of the realization of such a project that the Dean and Chapter turned away from corporeal interment in the abbey during these Edwardian years, in the hope that additional space might soon become available elsewhere. In 1904 the architects John Pollard Seddon and Edward Beckitt Lamb produced the most grandiose design yet, for what were termed 'Imperial Monumental Halls and [a] Tower', which would display 'monuments of high art to eminent men and women . . . of an Empire upon which the sun never sets'. The tower would be 550 feet high, dwarfing both the abbey and the Houses of Parliament, and in compensation, the abbey would be given a new and gigantic tower at the central crossing. Once again, the proposal came to nothing, and *The Builder* dismissed it as exhibiting 'a little too much megalomania', while two historians later denounced it as 'the most preposterous folly in London's history'.[19] But the problem of memorializing and accommodating the heroes of empire would not go away. As Welldon would later observe: 'the future of the Abbey, as the burying-ground of men and women famous in their generation throughout the country and the Empire, is a question which it is necessary to face, and, as I hold, to face at once'.[20]

Edward VII died in May 1910, and whereas Queen Victoria's obsequies had not involved Westminster in any way, those of her successor innovatively did. He was the first British monarch to lie in state nearby in Westminster Hall, allowing an extraordinary display of popular homage to a sovereign; if Archbishop Randall Davidson had had his way, the king would have been buried in the abbey itself, in recognition of the close rapport he had built up with the public during his short reign, and this would have revived the practice of royal interments that had ceased after the burial there of George II in 1760. But the new monarch, George V (r. 1910–36), insisted that his father be interred at Windsor. Even so, Davidson's idea recognized the growing feeling that the abbey was the place that brought together the monarchy, the nation and the empire.[21] Moreover, George V was an even more imperially minded sovereign than his father, and his coronation, which took place on 22 June 1911, was aptly described as a 'festival of Empire'. In 1902 standard-bearers had carried the banners of England, Ireland, Wales, Scotland and the United Kingdom; nine years later the flags of the home nations were joined by those of the four great dominions of Canada, Australia, New Zealand and South Africa, carried in procession by former governors general, along with one for the Indian empire, borne by a previous viceroy, Lord Curzon, of whom it was said that he 'processed as if the whole proceedings were in his honour: the aisle was just wide enough for him'.[22]

Curzon believed passionately in Britain's imperial mission, and he regarded George V's coronation as an emphatic reaffirmation of that purpose as the whole of the British Empire was impressively represented in the abbey on that June day. 'It is safe to say',

159   This interior view by John Frederick Bacon of the abbey, prepared for George V's coronation on 22 June 1911, shows the complex infrastructure of temporary galleries and boxes erected for all coronations to accommodate the congregation: the coronation chair faces the altar in a specially constructed raised area known as 'the Theatre'.

noted one observer, 'that never before have the grey walls of the Abbey held so varied and noble an assemblage, nor witnessed a ceremony so pregnant with the romance of the Empire.' It was the first time that the premiers of the 'self-governing Dominions of the British Crown and delegates from every other part of the Empire, and some of the princes and Feudatories of India' were brought together.[23] Indeed, according to the *Edinburgh Review*, the coronation afforded 'remarkable and most satisfactory evidence of . . . almost complete unanimity of national sentiment existing throughout the vast and scattered Dominions of the British Empire', as the king–emperor George V embodied a monarchy that 'united all, for it was the sole political institution that belonged to all'. All this meant that imperialism was 'much more to the front in the Abbey than it has been at the coronation of previous sovereigns, a fact that cannot but gratify the four hundred millions of people who acknowledge King George V's

160 (FACING PAGE)   To the delight of crowds on Fleet Street, George V and Queen Mary travelled in an open landau through London on the day after their coronation (23 June 1911). The following December they were crowned Emperor and Empress of India in Delhi, where the official ceremonies lasted for ten days.

rule'.[24] Soon after, King George and Queen Mary would be crowned a second time, as Emperor and Empress of India, at the greatest durbar ever held under the British Raj. This was the high noon of empire, and in the imperial capital it was Westminster Abbey that was the focus of such sentiments and ceremonials.[25]

Of course, St Paul's Cathedral claimed that it was 'the parish church of the Empire' and 'the central sanctuary, in some sense, of the English race', and these assertions had been strengthened by the decision to hold Queen Victoria's diamond jubilee thanksgiving service at the cathedral, rather than in the abbey. These claims were further consolidated in 1906, when a chapel was dedicated at St Paul's to the Order of St Michael and St George, membership of which was given to those who represented Britain overseas – either as ambassadors or as proconsuls – and an installation ceremony was devised for the most senior knights.[26] Yet since 1725 the abbey had been associated with the higher-ranking Order of the Bath, which by the nineteenth century was awarded to senior figures in the home civil service and in the British army and Royal Navy. The Dean of Westminster was its *ex officio* prelate, and the chapel of the order was Henry VII's chapel, where knights had been installed until 1812, after which the practice fell into desuetude. But soon after his accession, George V determined that the installation rituals should be revived, and forty-six senior knights paid for the creation of new stalls in the chapel. The first such ceremony took place in the abbey on 22 July 1913 in the presence of the sovereign, and installations have been regularly performed since then. And from 1916 the Anzac Day service, commemorating the part played by Australian and New Zealand troops in the Gallipoli landings, would be held annually in the abbey, as would Empire Day services from 1919, both of them regularly attended by George V and Queen Mary.[27]

While the abbey, in its imperial guise, was in the public eye as never before, its finances were far from robust. The single most reliable source of income remained the £20,000 from the Ecclesiastical Commissioners, a much smaller annual sum than the abbey would have enjoyed had it held on to its lands in London, which were significantly increasing in value. In 1909 the Dean and Chapter decided to levy a charge of 6*d.* on visitors to the royal chapels, but it yielded little in terms of revenue. It was becoming increasingly difficult to make ends meet, and the demands and depredations of the First World War only made matters worse. In July 1915 the coronation chair and stone were moved to the crypt of the chapter house; the windows in the apse were taken out, and the reredos of the high altar was stowed away. Early in 1916 sandbags were ordered for the protection of the monuments, and later that year the effigies in Henry VII's chapel were boarded over. In September 1917 the choir school was struck by a bomb, but the damage was slight and no one was injured.[28] By the end of the war, abbey finances were distinctly precarious: in 1920 the Dean and Chapter were

161

161   The tomb of Elizabeth I and the abbey's other monuments were protected by sandbags in 1916; in the event, the abbey itself came through the First World War unscathed, though the choir school was slightly damaged by a bomb.

in debt to the Ecclesiastical Commissioners, and parts of the fabric urgently needed attention. In a letter to *The Times*, dated 20 June 1920, Dean Ryle announced the abbey's first ever public appeal. Knowing that so many people had made such great sacrifices during the war, Ryle made his request 'with a sore heart, hating having to do so'. The ask was for £225,000, but only £170,000 was eventually raised.[29]

Unknown Warrior, Royal Weddings

Dean Herbert Ryle had been installed as the successor to Armitage Robinson shortly before George V's coronation, having previously been president of Queens' College, Cambridge, Bishop of Exeter and subsequently Bishop of Winchester.[30] But although he arrived at the height of the abbey's imperial phase, and had been a prime mover

in the revival of the installation rituals for the Order of the Bath, he made his lasting
mark by establishing a very different ceremonial idiom. Times had changed. The British
Empire had emerged victorious from the First World War, and reached its greatest
territorial extent when the new League of Nations mandates in the Middle East and
Africa were assigned to it. Yet almost a million men from the empire had been killed
in the fighting, and the spiralling cost of the conflict meant that the United Kingdom
had become increasingly dependent on the financial support of the United States.
Although the British government had declared war in 1914 on behalf of the whole
empire, by 1918 the dominions were eager to assert their own autonomy, and there
would also be serious unrest in Ireland, Egypt and India. The Fourth Reform Act (1918)
introduced mass democracy to Britain for the first time; but there were fears that it
might portend a continental-style revolution. The three great-power monarchies of
Russia, Austria-Hungary and Germany had been vanquished, republics now became
the norm across most of Europe and communism represented a new and hostile
threat to the established order. In such a changed climate, where imperial swagger and
sentiment had been replaced by widespread feelings of bereavement and bewilderment,
the pomp and circumstance that had characterized the abbey coronations of 1902 and
1911 no longer seemed right or resonant.

Ryle sensed this change in the public mood, he sought to align the abbey with
these very different feelings and sentiments, and recognized that it must offer comfort
and consolation to the bereaved and the wounded. The measured, conciliatory tone
of his appeal letter to *The Times* made this plain. 'Can any sacred building', he began,
quoting an American friend, 'in the British Empire compare with Westminster Abbey?
Is it not the most unique and priceless treasure of the English-speaking race?' Yet this
by then familiar formulation was no invitation to return to Edwardian braggadocio or
bombast. For while Ryle allowed that 'the Abbey is the heart-shrine of the world-wide
Empire', this meant that it was 'intertwined with the most sacred feelings and deepest
affections of brothers and sisters scattered over the whole world'. And he described
these 'brothers and sisters' not as prelates or princes, prime ministers or proconsuls, but
as 'working men, clerks, soldiers, factory hands, schoolboys and schoolgirls', the sorts
of ordinary people who made up the majority of the 'thousands who are swarming
through the Abbey'. And his final image was maternal and nurturing, rather than assertive
or boastful: the abbey, he urged, was 'the Mother Church of the Commonwealth'.[31]
This was the sort of emollient language, meant to bind up the nation's wounds and to
bring people together, that Stanley Baldwin would mobilize so powerfully for much
of the 1920s and 1930s.[32] But Ryle got there first, and in so doing he changed the
abbey's ceremonial style from the grandiose and hubristic towards the domestic and
intimate, thereby greatly widening its public appeal.

Yet it was not immediately clear that that was how things would work out, for there were alternative futures that the Dean and Chapter might have embraced in 1918. Even before the armistice, the architect William Woodward had proposed a Gothic 'Memorial Chapel and Valhalla', situated between the abbey and the Palace of Westminster, which would seat between three and four thousand people, and be large enough to house all the imperial heroes for a century and beyond. In January 1919, well before Ryle wrote his appeal letter, Major C.J.C. Pawley had produced a plan, drawn up for him by the architect Harold Oakley, for an even more grandiose 'Memorial Shrine' on the same site, overshadowing the abbey and the chapter house, and including seventy-eight regimental chapels. It would cost £800,000 and would, Pawley asserted optimistically, be paid for 'by the women of the Empire'. Once again, the scheme got nowhere: it was denounced by antiquarians as 'criminal lunacy', while the architectural writer Lawrence Weaver dismissed it as 'a castle in the air'. Yet as late as 1927, and at the behest of the Church Assembly, the Cathedrals Advisory Commission sought designs for a memorial chapel integrally attached to what was now described as the 'Valhalla of the British People'; but, as the shift in terminology from 'British Empire' to 'British People' suggests, the public were by then finding consolation elsewhere – and 'elsewhere' increasingly meant the abbey itself.[33]

One of Ryle's most significant and lasting innovations was to increase the number of special services.[34] Some followed previous precedents, as the abbey honoured the great and the good of the nation and empire: funerals for two first sea lords (Lord Fisher and the Marquess of Milford Haven, formerly Prince Louis of Battenberg), for Field Marshal the Earl of Ypres (formerly Sir John French), for Lord Curzon (Viceroy of India and foreign secretary), for Andrew Bonar Law (briefly prime minister in 1923) and for the composer Sir Charles Villiers Stanford, and memorial services for two proconsuls (Lord Cromer and Lord Milner) and the painter John Singer Sargent.[35] But Ryle was also determined to make the abbey a place where the lives and activities of ordinary people might be recognized and commemorated. During the First World War, special services were held to mark the jubilee of the involvement of women in the work of the Society for the Propagation of the Gospel, for the students, staff and professors of the University of London, for Welsh prisoners of war, and for solicitors and articled clerks who had fallen during the conflict. Thereafter, such services were held for members of the Royal Irish Constabulary who had been killed during the post-war 'troubles', for the crew of the airship R38 which had broken up and crashed into the Humber estuary in 1921, for the Mothers' Union and its founder, Elizabeth Mary Sumner, and for the golden jubilee of the Girls' Friendly Society in 1925. Here was a broad range of activities being recognized and celebrated – military and civil, Christian and secular, academe and the law – and women were prominently included.

Through services of this kind, Ryle's abbey reached out to ordinary people as never before, and in furtherance of this ambition, he also promoted a novel scheme that would make it a unique place of popular pilgrimage.

At the end of the First World War, a series of annual observances were gradually developed, centred on the Cenotaph in London, and replicated in cities, towns and villages across Britain and the empire. They involved the two minutes' silence in honour of the war dead on 11 November, the anniversary of Armistice Day and, eventually, the wearing of Flanders poppies in support of the work of the British Legion. The unveiling of a permanent Cenotaph by George V was scheduled for 11 November 1920, and while it was being planned, Ryle made the suggestion, originally put to him by the Revd David Railton, an Anglican army chaplain who had served on the western front, that one of the soldiers who lay in unmarked graves should be returned to Britain and interred in Westminster Abbey 'to represent all those who fell'.[36] His proposal was accepted and the body of an unidentified British serviceman was brought back from France. The coffin of the Unknown Warrior was conveyed on a gun carriage down Whitehall to the Cenotaph for the inauguration ceremony, and then to the abbey for burial, with the king as chief mourner, and senior military commanders among the pall-bearers. The abbey was filled with bereaved wives and mothers and one hundred nurses who had been blinded or wounded during their wartime duties; men who had won the Victoria Cross provided the guard of honour. After a short service, the Unknown Warrior was buried near the west door, in a grave filled with earth from the main battlefields of the war. In the days that followed, a million people passed through the abbey: a 'ceaseless stream' of those 'whom the Unknown and his friends had died to save'. As The Times noted, 'The authorities frankly admit that the extent to which the public imagination has been stirred exceeded all their expectations.'[37]

'In all its history,' Ryle would later write, 'the Abbey can have witnessed no such moving spectacle' – a nation brought together in grief, remembrance and homage. Although the royal family, the cabinet and senior military leaders attended the service, the majority of those in the congregation were 'widows and mothers of those who had fallen, especially in the humbler ranks', just as the Unknown himself was regarded as 'an emblem of "the plain man", of the masses of the people' – an appropriately classless hero for a nation that had just embraced democracy. In the words of The Times: he 'might be the child of any one of a million mothers. Therefore, all could mourn him better because he was unknown.'[38] As Ryle had intended, this meant that the abbey could serve a new and popular purpose as a place of solace, comfort and reflection for millions of ordinary people from Britain and the empire. In 1921, a black marble stone was placed over the grave, noting, in an inscription written by Ryle, that 'a warrior unknown by name or rank' had been 'brought from France to

BENEATH THIS STONE RESTS THE BODY
OF A BRITISH WARRIOR
UNKNOWN BY NAME OR RANK
BROUGHT FROM FRANCE TO LIE AMONG
THE MOST ILLUSTRIOUS OF THE LAND
AND BURIED HERE ON ARMISTICE DAY
11 NOV: 1920, IN THE PRESENCE OF
HIS MAJESTY KING GEORGE V
HIS MINISTERS OF STATE
THE CHIEFS OF HIS FORCES
AND A VAST CONCOURSE OF THE NATION

THUS ARE COMMEMORATED THE MANY
MULTITUDES WHO DURING THE GREAT
WAR OF 1914–1918 GAVE THE MOST THAT
MAN CAN GIVE LIFE ITSELF
FOR GOD
FOR KING AND COUNTRY
FOR LOVED ONES HOME AND EMPIRE
FOR THE SACRED CAUSE OF JUSTICE AND
THE FREEDOM OF THE WORLD

THEY BURIED HIM AMONG THE KINGS BECAUSE HE
HAD DONE GOOD TOWARD GOD AND TOWARD
HIS HOUSE

162   The Unknown Warrior, an unidentified representative of all those from Britain and the empire who died in the First World War, was buried in the centre of the nave just inside the west door of the abbey on Armistice Day 1920; a temporary stone with a brief inscription was laid over the grave, to be replaced, the following year, with a permanent gravestone inscribed with words by Dean Ryle.

lie among the most illustrious of the land'. Appropriately, yet uniquely, it is the only memorial on the abbey floor over which no one is allowed to walk, and laying flowers on the grave would soon become essential for any head of state visiting London. In 1928 the Empire Field of Remembrance was established in St Margaret's churchyard, where for a few days on either side of 11 November, crosses were planted in honour of fallen servicemen – temporary acts of homage to named comrades complementing the permanent memorial to the Unknown inside the abbey itself.[39]

As Ryle had intended, these were public ceremonies intended to assuage private grief – a very different purpose for abbey memorialization from the proposed Imperial Valhallas, as grandiosity and ornamentation had been superseded by understatement and a stripped-down style. It was also easier for the general public to relate to the observances and customs that built up around the grave of the Unknown Warrior than to the pomp and circumstance of coronations, which by definition were rites of passage exclusively confined to monarchs, and designed to exalt them high above ordinary mortals. Thanks to the burial of the Unknown Warrior, Westminster Abbey did more than any other church to help the British people and the British Empire come to terms with the devastating losses of war, and it was from just this time that it became a major visitor attraction, and its opening hours were extended.[40] During the inter-war years, the abbey also became the focus of very different ceremonials, evoking very different feelings and responses, but which were once again intended for the general public. In the aftermath of the First World War, as thrones fell, revolutionaries triumphed, republics were established and the United Kingdom became a mass democracy, courtiers feared that 'the position of the monarchy [was] not so stable now . . . as it [had been] at the beginning of the war'.[41] Accordingly, they looked for new ways to relate the British crown more closely to the British people, and in this repurposing of the monarchy, Ryle's abbey would play a major part, consolidating its connections with the throne and the nation.

In the post-war years of Ryle's deanship, royal weddings, previously held in the privacy of the Chapel Royal in St James's Palace, or St George's Chapel, Windsor, were transferred to Westminster Abbey, and transformed into grand metropolitan pageants. The first sign and portent of this major change came in 1919, when Princess Patricia, the daughter of Queen Victoria's third son, Prince Arthur of Connaught, married Commander Alexander Ramsay, in the first royal wedding to take place in the abbey since that of Richard II and Anne of Bohemia in 1382. Three years later, George V's only daughter, Princess Mary, wedded Viscount Lascelles, an equally remarkable occurrence, since 'no daughter of a reigning king was ever . . . married in Westminster Abbey before'. In 1923 the Duke of York married Lady Elizabeth Bowes-Lyon at Westminster, in another unprecedented event: 'not for five hundred and thirty years . . . had a prince of the royal house been wed in the Abbey'.[42] From one perspective, these ceremonially enhanced royal weddings were a natural development from the jubilees and coronations that had taken place between 1887 and 1911, involving elaborate processions through the streets of London, increasingly confident organization, and

163   Hundreds of thousands of people filed past the Unknown Warrior after his interment in 1920; most of the congregation at the burial itself and those who afterwards paid their respects at the nameless soldier's grave were ordinary people, united in their grief and their desire to honour the dead.

large and cheering crowds, especially in front of Buckingham Palace itself. And the abbey was the obvious setting for these public royal rites of passage, since it was 'not a private chapel but the sacred possession of the entire British race'.[43] But whereas coronations and jubilees were examples of extraordinary people doing extraordinary things, royal weddings, by contrast, were examples of extraordinary people doing ordinary things – albeit in the splendour of an abbey setting – to which ordinary people could easily and imaginatively relate.

    From the outset, it was clear that these new-style royal weddings were simultaneously special in their grandeur but commonplace in their meaning. As the Duke of York explained at the time of the marriage of his sister, 'it is now no longer Mary's wedding, but (this from the papers) it is the "Abbey Wedding" or the "Royal Wedding", or the "National Wedding", or even the "People's Wedding"'.[44] As with the burial of the Unknown Warrior, the congregations in the abbey came from more diverse backgrounds, the routes to and from the abbey were deliberately extended to draw in more people as spectators, the newspaper coverage was sentimental, unrelenting and global, and the processions and the abbey services were broadcast live on the recently established BBC, which rendered all listeners active participants in these 'audible pageants'. Never had Walter Bagehot's oft quoted observation been more valid: 'a princely marriage is the brilliant edition of a universal fact, and as such it rivets mankind'.[45] The inter-war abbey had thus become a place that offered men and women consolation through the grave of the Unknown Warrior, and hope through royal weddings which were also regarded as 'democratic marriages'. More than ever, it had become the people's church, offering tidings of comfort and also of joy. And with that sure touch for which she would soon become famous, Lady Elizabeth Bowes-Lyon recognized this new and important connection when, on her arrival in the abbey to marry the Duke of York, she placed her bouquet of white roses on the Unknown Warrior's grave, in homage to her own brother who had been killed in the war; subsequent royal brides have often done the same, though usually after the service.[46]

Ryle died in office in August 1925, but for the remainder of the inter-war years his vision of the abbey as a church for the people remained strong. His successor was William Foxley Norris, who had previously been Dean of York and was a talented artist and an expert on ecclesiastical treasures (he thought the abbey overcrowded with monuments).[47] Among the first services during his tenure was the funeral of Queen Alexandra, who received the most elaborate obsequies for a queen consort since the death of Queen Caroline in 1737, including a one-night lying-in-state, before being buried at Windsor. But this did not represent a general change of policy in royal funeral arrangements: since the nave of St George's Chapel, Windsor, was undergoing restoration at the time, it was necessary to find an alternative church big enough to accommodate all the mourners, and the abbey was the obvious place. The commemorations of the great and the good went on as before: funerals for Field Marshal Earl Haig, Archbishop Lord Davidson, admiral of the fleet Lord Wester Wemyss, the physicist Lord Rutherford, Thomas Hardy and Rudyard Kipling (the two latter both also commemorated in Poets' Corner); memorial services for Lord Asquith, Lord Birkenhead, Lord Grey of Fallodon and Arthur Henderson; memorial tablets for Asquith, Milner and Curzon; and a lying-in-state for admiral of the fleet Earl Jellicoe.[48] Foxley Norris also continued to extend the bounds of special services, as they were held for the diamond jubilee of the Canadian Confederation, and for the Boy Scouts, the Mothers' Union (again), the Lambeth Conference, the Church Lads' Brigade and the centenary of the temperance movement.

By the early 1930s, the political climate had changed again, with the Great Crash of 1929 and the ensuing Great Depression, soaring unemployment, the creation of a national government, and the advent to power of Roosevelt in the United States and Hitler in Germany. Against this generally sombre backdrop, it was hoped that two more royal weddings might once more lift the national spirits. In 1934 the Duke of Kent married Princess Marina of Greece, by which time (in the words of one newspaper) 'one thing is practically certain . . . the royal wedding will be solemnized in Westminster Abbey and there will be a drive in full state from Buckingham Palace to the Abbey and back';[49] the service itself was also broadcast. Similar arrangements were made for the marriage, in the following year, of Prince Henry of Gloucester to Lady Alice Montagu-Douglas-Scott. Only at the last minute was the wedding moved to the private chapel in Buckingham Palace, after the sudden death of the bride's father. But this was an aberration, for by then the 'tradition' that the children of the sovereign would be married in the abbey was well established.[50] This, in turn, was one of the many reasons why George V and Queen Mary visited Westminster Abbey more frequently than any of their predecessors. They also regularly attended the yearly special services marking Anzac Day, Armistice Day, and Empire Day; a service of thanksgiving for the king's recovery from illness was held there in 1929, and in 1932 the king distributed the Maundy money at the abbey – the first monarch to do so since 1685.[51] But George V's silver jubilee was celebrated in 1935 with a service at St Paul's Cathedral, following the precedent of 1897 rather than that of 1887; and although, on his death, the king lay in state in Westminster Hall, as had his father before him, there was in his case, too, no suggestion of an abbey funeral.

The coronation of the new monarch, Edward VIII (r. 1936), was scheduled for 12 May 1937, but on his abdication, the date was retained for the crowning of George VI and Queen Elizabeth. The planning was more meticulous than ever, and was dominated by two figures: the Archbishop of Canterbury, Cosmo Lang, and the earl marshal, the Duke of Norfolk. Lang was a determined and assertive Churchman, both men combined a flair for showmanship with great attention to detail, and the earl marshal soon acquired a reputation for punctuality and theatrical flair rivalling that of Lord Esher. The music was the most elaborate that had yet accompanied a modern coronation, and such traditional works as 'Zadok the priest' and 'I was glad' were interspersed with newly commissioned compositions by Arnold Bax, Arthur Bliss, Granville Bantock and Walford Davis, as well as a *Festival Te Deum* by Ralph Vaughan Williams, and a march in Elgarian idiom by William Walton, revealingly entitled *Crown Imperial*.[52] The 1937 coronation was the first to be broadcast live on the wireless, albeit without any commentary, and not only in the United Kingdom but on the BBC's Empire Service as well. It was also the first such service to be filmed: the forty-man camera crew inside the abbey were required to wear evening dress; and the archbishop and earl marshal were empowered to edit 'anything that may be considered unsuitable for the public at large to see' (in fact, they edited very little). Although afflicted by an embarrassing and debilitating stammer, the king spoke his sonorous words clearly and firmly. The result was the best-performed coronation yet: as the young Princess Elizabeth noted, 'I thought it all *very very* wonderful, and I expect the Abbey did, too.'[53]

This was another great pageant, in which the abbey, the monarchy, the nation and the empire were linked together in an act of worship and homage that combined sacred communion and secular celebration – and more so than ever, thanks to the BBC. But while it was undeniably another imperial occasion, the coronation of 1937 lacked the swagger and boastfulness of 1902 or 1911. Although his wife in many ways made up for it, George VI did not exude the charisma of his elder brother. The passing of the Statute of Westminster in 1931 had established legislative equality between the mother country and the settler dominions, and had effectively portioned the indivisible imperial crown between them; and nationalist opposition in India to the British Raj meant there would be no durbar for George VI and his queen, as there had been for his parents.[54] But leading colonial administrators, the premiers of the dominions, rulers of the Indian princely states and African potentates all attended, the banners of the dominions and India were again borne in the abbey, and there were more imperial troops on parade, from more parts of the empire, than ever before. This was still an imperial family, presided over by a benevolent sovereign, which was held together more by sentiment than by power, and by a shared loyalty to the throne. Such was the changed nature of the 'crown imperial', which Walton's march ignored rather than recognized. Yet the king had no doubt that his coronation had been an imperial gathering. As he put it in his broadcast later that day, 'I felt this morning that the whole Empire was in very truth gathered within the walls of Westminster Abbey.'[55]

Foxley Norris died in October 1937. His successor, Paul de Labilliere, was the first dean to have undertaken missionary work overseas, and he had previously served as Suffragan Bishop of Knaresborough and Archdeacon of Leeds.[56] His tenure (1938–46) would be taken up with preparation for war, the conflict itself and its immediate aftermath. Many of the muniments were moved out of London, the coronation chair went to Gloucester cathedral, and the Stone of Scone was buried. For much of 1940 and 1941, the abbey was subject to repeated enemy action, which damaged the west window, blew in the east window of Henry VII's chapel, destroyed most of the Deanery and several houses in the precincts, brought down the roof of the lantern tower and smashed the choir beneath. 'The Abbey, which is England, must suffer with

164   Dean Paul de Labilliere in the cloister viewing bomb damage caused in an air raid on the night of 10–11 May 1941; the debris came from the Deanery, which was largely destroyed.

England,' noted the dean.[57] But there were no fatalities, and, although the choristers were evacuated to Christ's Hospital School in Horsham, the work of the Dean and Chapter went on uninterrupted – indeed, intensified, as special services proliferated. Many were for familiar purposes: the burial of Neville Chamberlain's ashes; the funerals of Lord Willingdon, Sir Joseph Thomson, Admiral Sir Dudley Pound and Archbishop Cosmo Lang; and memorial services for Lord Tweedsmuir, George Lansbury, Lord Lothian, Lord Baden Powell, the Duke of Connaught, the Duke of Kent, Lord Lugard and Lloyd George. But many services were special to the war: for the Red Cross, the Home Guard, Empire Youth and the Civil Defence; for the restoration of independence to Ethiopia, for the suffering people of Greece and Yugoslavia; and thanksgiving for VE Day and VJ Day. And in September 1944 a service was held to commemorate the Battle of Britain which has taken place annually ever since.[58]

165, 166

At the end of the war in Europe, 60,000 sandbags were removed from the abbey, the treasures and muniments were returned, the temporary roof at the crossing was

165   Heroes of the Royal Air Force march away after the second Battle of Britain remembrance service to be held at the abbey, on 16 September 1945. During the Second World War many special services were added to the usual round of daily worship and the funeral and memorial services for national figures; the commemoration of the Battle of Britain continues to be held annually.

replaced by a permanent structure, and the Deanery and shattered houses in the Little Cloister were rebuilt and restored.[59] De Labilliere died in April 1946, and was succeeded as dean by Alan Don (1946–59). He had been chaplain to Archbishop Cosmo Lang, George V and the speaker of the House of Commons, and in 1941 he had been appointed rector of St Margaret's Westminster and a canon of the abbey. More than any of his recent predecessors, he knew his way around the cloisters and the corridors of power.[60] Among the earliest services during his deanship was the marriage of Princess Elizabeth to the Duke of Edinburgh on 20 November 1947, continuing the recently established tradition of abbey royal weddings into the next generation. From one perspective, the ceremony offered what Churchill called 'a splash of colour' amid the gloom and drabness of post-war austerity, and it was broadcast by the BBC on the wireless (George VI vetoed television cameras) to 200 million people around

166 (FACING PAGE)   To commemorate those who died in the battle fought over the skies of Britain between July and October 1940, Dean Paul de Labilliere dedicated the easternmost chapel in the abbey, which had been damaged by bombing in 1940, to the RAF; the refurbished chapel, with a memorial window by Hugh Easton, was unveiled by George VI in 1947.

the world; from another, it was more portentous than the earlier abbey weddings, because Princess Elizabeth was heiress presumptive to the throne, and her husband was descended from the Greek, German and Scandinavian royal houses.[61] The result was a unique gathering of European royalty (both regnant and exiled) for an abbey event that was not a coronation. Yet Princess Elizabeth had needed ration coupons to buy the material for her wedding dress, and in his sermon the Archbishop of York claimed that the ceremony was 'in all essentials exactly the same as it would have been for any cottager who might be married this afternoon in some small country church'.[62]

Empire to Commonwealth

Three months before this royal wedding, by turns grand yet ordinary, George VI had ceased to be Emperor of India, as the British Raj was ended in August 1947 by the last viceroy, Lord Mountbatten, himself a cousin of the sovereign. India and Pakistan joined the Commonwealth, but soon became republics, and their independence spelt the beginning of the end of the British Empire, of the British monarchy as an imperial monarchy and of Westminster Abbey as an imperial church. One immediate result was that schemes for a new Valhalla to accommodate and commemorate the heroes of an empire that had seemed so permanent in the 1900s finally fizzled out. During the Second World War, both Sir Edwin Lutyens and Edward Maufe had produced plans for a narthex to be added to the west front, which might have served such a purpose, but by that time the moment had gone, never to return.[63] It was, then, fitting that the two pre-eminent architects of empire were given their obsequies in the abbey: a funeral service for Lutyens in 1944, and the interment of Sir Herbert Baker's ashes two years later. To be sure, a portrait plaque of Cecil Rhodes would be unveiled in 1953, the centenary of his birth, in the Henry VII chapel, close by those of his fellow imperialists Lords Milner, Curzon and Cromer,[64] but as Dean Edward Carpenter would later note: 'these memorials of the Empire-builders are in rather an inconspicuous position. They excite a certain nostalgia, but the names convey little or nothing to many who read them there.' As he went on to observe, 'a different spirit has come over the nation as a whole, as Great Britain has shed much of the more recently acquired territories of what is now called almost exclusively the Commonwealth . . . The sentiment of the Empire only haunts the place as a ghost.'[65]

Yet, in the years following 1947, it was not immediately obvious that this was irreversibly the direction in which the empire, or the abbey, was going. The United Kingdom might not be in the same league as the two super powers, the United States and communist Russia, but it was still the third military force in the world. In

November 1948 a memorial to President Franklin Roosevelt was unveiled jointly by Clement Attlee and Winston Churchill, near the grave of the Unknown Warrior.[66] This was the first time a head of state of a foreign country had been commemorated in the abbey, and the memorial also celebrated the wartime Anglo-American alliance.[67] In June 1950 Lord Wavell was given a ceremonial funeral: having served as commander-in-chief in the Middle East and in India, and then as viceroy, he was the first of the great military leaders of the Second World War to die. His coffin was borne by water from the Tower of London (of which he was constable) to Westminster, and his obsequies were attended by virtually the entire British political and military establishment, along with mourners from the Middle East and South Asia. 'Nobody's burial arrangements', wrote the diarist Henry Channon, with characteristic but well-intended hyperbole, 'have been so elaborate and magnificent, but then who else has been a war hero, who captured the imagination of the whole world.'[68] And in January 1951 an intercession service was held at the abbey for Commonwealth prime ministers who were meeting in London, which was attended by George VI and Queen Elizabeth, and the premiers of New Zealand, Australia, Canada, Ceylon, Pakistan and Southern Rhodesia.[69]

Within little more than a year, the king was dead. On her 21st birthday in 1947, his elder daughter, Princess Elizabeth, pledged her 'lifelong service' to the 'imperial family to which we all belong', and her coronation, in June 1953, was both an imperial and a media event, which put the abbey on show as never before.[70] On the day, more people in Britain watched on television than listened on the wireless, which meant that Queen Elizabeth II (r. 1952–) was the first monarch to be crowned, as the rubric required, 'in the sight of all her people', in what was generally seen as 'an act of national communion'.[71] And as Richard Dimbleby's reverential commentary made plain, Elizabeth's coronation was widely regarded as the latest in a sequence of imperial enthronings extending back to that of Edward VII. Once again, there were newly commissioned compositions, from Bax, Bliss and Vaughan Williams.[72] The Queen's dress was embroidered with the floral emblems of the Commonwealth countries, many indigenous rulers from the African colonies attended, and contingents of Commonwealth and colonial troops marched in procession. On the very morning of the coronation, the news broke in London that a British-led expedition had been the first to conquer Everest, the highest mountain on the globe. 'Britain on top of the world', ran the jubilant headlines. The Archbishop of Canterbury declared that Britain was closer to the Kingdom of Heaven than ever before, and in her broadcast later that day the Queen caught the euphoric mood: 'I am sure', she insisted, 'that this, my coronation, is not a symbol of a power and a splendour that are gone, but a declaration of our hopes in the future.'[73]

168

167

167   Elizabeth II's coronation took place at Westminster Abbey on 2 June 1953; her dress, by Norman Hartnell, featured the floral emblems of the countries of the United Kingdom and of the other states of the Commonwealth, including the Canadian maple leaf, Australian wattle, New Zealand silver fern, South African protea, Indian lotus flower, the lotus flower of Ceylon, and Pakistan's wheat, cotton and jute.

Never before had a single church service attracted so much national engagement and global interest; yet this was not the only way in which Elizabeth II's coronation was seen. Far from being 'an act of national communion', some sceptics thought it little more than a blatant piece of ruling-class propaganda.[74] Unlike her three predecessors, the new monarch was neither ruler of 'the British dominions beyond the seas', nor Empress of India, but merely 'Head of the Commonwealth'. In the abbey she was crowned Queen of the United Kingdom, the premiers of Canada, Australia, New Zealand and South Africa attended as guests and onlookers rather than as active participants (though Elizabeth was separately sovereign of their dominions), and this time no imperial banners were carried in procession. Ireland and Burma had by then broken free from the empire and Commonwealth, India had become a republic and Pakistan was heading in the same direction. This sense that all was not quite as it seemed was also voiced by an American journalist, who suggested that what he called 'this show' was 'put on by the British for a psychological boost to their somewhat shaky empire'. And Walton's second coronation march, *Orb and Sceptre*, was but a pale

168   The newly crowned Elizabeth II holds the coronation regalia. More than 20 million Britons watched the coronation ceremony on television, almost double the number that tuned in on the wireless, and the event was the focus of worldwide attention within and beyond the Commonwealth.

imitation of *Crown Imperial*, lacking the stately grandeur and *nobilmente* confidence of its predecessor.[75] Five years after this last and only quasi-imperial coronation, Empire Day was superseded by Commonwealth Day, and by then the end was in sight for what remained of Britain's colonial realms. By the close of the 1950s, Sudan, the Gold Coast, Malaya, British Somaliland, Cyprus and Nigeria had gained their independence, and by the end of the 1960s virtually all that was left of the empire were the colonies of Southern Rhodesia and Hong Kong.[76]

Yet even as the British Empire declined and fell, its gradual evolution into the Commonwealth offered new opportunities for the abbey, which were avidly seized by Eric Abbott, who succeeded Alan Don as dean in 1959, having previously been dean of King's College, London, and warden of Keble College, Oxford. He would

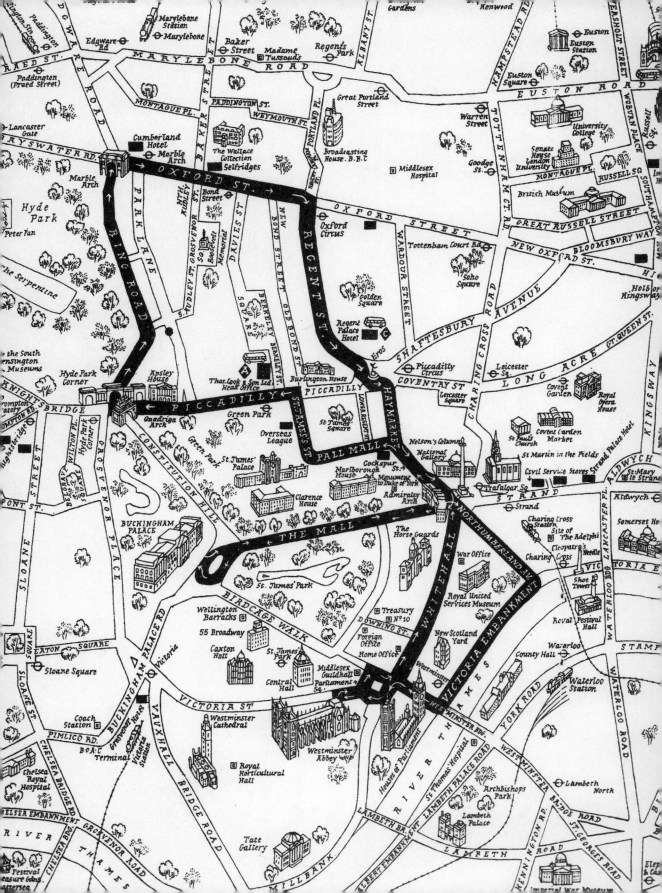

lead the abbey through a period of marked change during his term of office, which lasted until 1974, presiding over the 900th anniversary celebrations in 1966, and also creating a new, post-imperial identity for the abbey as 'the central shrine of the British Commonwealth'.[77] Even before his appointment, there had been significant straws in the wind. Beginning during the Second World War, it had become the practice to consecrate in the abbey bishops who would be serving in the empire and Commonwealth, in places such as Tasmania, Lagos, Bermuda, Northern Rhodesia, Gibraltar and Sydney. Special memorial services were arranged for such Commonwealth statesmen as John Curtin (Australia), R.B. Bennett and William Lyon Mackenzie King (both Canada) and Field Marshal Smuts (South Africa). In February 1948 a service of intercession was held for the peoples of India and Pakistan, which was in part a memorial service for the recently assassinated Mahatma Gandhi, in part a plea for the ending of the 'bloodshed and confusion' taking place in the aftermath of partition, and in part a call for peace as 'the only sure road to freedom and prosperity'. And the Anzac Day service also remained an annual fixture.[78] But the great innovation during Abbott's time, and the most significant since the changes wrought by Dean Ryle, was the institution of a sequence of services in the abbey to coincide with the independence celebrations that took place when former British colonies gained their freedom.

Between 1960 and 1983 twenty-one such services were held, beginning with Nigeria. Since most of the African colonies had been places of significant missionary activity, and there was a powerful continuing Anglican presence, this was an appropriate form of recognition, in a way that services to mark the independence of India and Pakistan and Ceylon, where the Anglican Church had been more marginal, would not have been. The idea originated at the Colonial Office and with the dean, and the service that was developed for Nigeria became a template for those that followed.[79] Those attending included a member of the royal family, representatives of the British government, the high commissioner of the new nation and his entourage, people belonging to the Christian bodies who had been at work in the former colony, men and women from other Commonwealth countries, and many recently arrived immigrants to Britain. The flag of the new country, 'the sign of its nationhood and the promise of its unity', was borne in procession in the abbey and placed on the high altar. The British national anthem was sung, along with such rousing hymns as 'Now thank we all our God' or 'Hills of the north, rejoice'. During the prayers, God's blessing was sought for the

169 (FACING PAGE)   On the day of her coronation, 2 June 1953, Queen Elizabeth II rode in procession from Buckingham Palace to Westminster Abbey and back again along an extended route, shown here in an illustration taken from a newspaper of the day. The map shows the abbey's close proximity to royal residences (Buckingham Palace, St James's Palace, Clarence House and Marlborough House), to the headquarters of political power and government (the Palace of Westminster, 10 Downing Street, the Home Office, the Foreign Office and the Treasury), to the armed forces (Horse Guards, the War Office and the Admiralty), and to centres of other religious denominations (Westminster (Roman Catholic) Cathedral and the (Methodist) Central Hall). This unique location continues to make Westminster Abbey the pre-eminent focus for royal ceremonial and public events at the heart of the capital.

new country: 'that it may be an instrument for good in His hands who is Lord of all nations'; 'that it may be strengthened against those forces that would divide or weaken it from without or from within'; and 'that it may never lack the men and women of wisdom, honour and righteousness to guide its destinies'. The high commissioner read the lesson, the sermon was usually preached by a former colonial bishop, and these services ended with the singing of the new country's national anthem (in the English version).

Within this rapidly established formula, there were some divergences and variations. At the service for Ugandan independence in 1962, the sermon was preached by the Revd J.V. Taylor, the Africa secretary of the Church Missionary Society, who warned that nationhood might open the way to bribery and corruption. At the service for Malawi (formerly Nyasaland; 1964), the procession divided at the grave of David Livingstone and did not walk over it, in recognition of his close association with the country. At the service for Zambia (formerly Northern Rhodesia; 1964), the hymn 'The Lord's my shepherd' was sung to the tune 'Crimond', at the explicit request of the prime minister, Dr Kenneth Kaunda. And when Southern Rhodesia finally became independent as Zimbabwe (1980), the prime minister, Robert Mugabe, requested that there should be no such service, but it took place anyway.[80] Sierra Leone had become independent before such observances became fully established, but a special service was put on to mark the tenth anniversary of its independence in April 1971; and, in the case of Jamaica, there was both an independence service and, in August 1987, a twenty-fifth anniversary commemoration. As Canon Adam Fox would later observe, 'no place but the Abbey is thought suitable for services such as these'.[81] Two additional services formed part of this British Empire-to-Commonwealth sequence, commemorating the lives of the West Indian cricketers Sir Frank Worrell in 1967 and Lord (Learie) Constantine in 1971. Worrell's was also the first memorial service accorded to a sporting figure, and West Indian workers for London Transport were given special permission to change shifts to attend it. Constantine had earlier read the lesson at the independence service for Trinidad and Tobago (1962), having been the country's first high commissioner in London.[82]

As the abbey marked the independence of former colonies, it also became the place for commemorating the Britons who had governed and administered them, but now celebrating these men as servants of humanity rather than as masters of empire. (What would Cromer, Milner, Curzon and Rhodes have thought of *that*?) In 1958, just over ten years after Indian independence, the Queen unveiled a plaque in the abbey's west cloister to commemorate the work of the Indian Civil Service. A former viceroy, Lord Halifax, gave the address, elaborating on the plaque's inscription: 'they served India well'. Two years later, the Duke of Edinburgh unveiled a plaque in the north cloister,

170

170 (ABOVE LEFT)   As one by one Britain's former colonies gained their independence, celebrations took place in the abbey, and the colonial bodies that had administered the empire were commemorated. The work of the Indian Civil Service, whose role was handed on to the newly independent states in 1947, is marked by a plaque unveiled by the Queen in 1958.

171 (ABOVE RIGHT)   Dean Eric Abbott and Queen Elizabeth stand before a memorial stone, unveiled in September 1965, to the former prime minister and statesman Sir Winston Churchill, who had died in January that year. His body is buried at Bladon, Oxfordshire, near his ancestral home, Blenheim Palace.

to remember 'The men and women of our race who laboured to serve the people of the Sudan', which had become independent in 1956. And in 1966 the Queen unveiled a third plaque nearby, honouring 'All those who served the Crown in the Colonial Territories'. Once again, the inscription drove home the same message: 'Whosoever will be chief among you, let him be your servant.'[83] A year before, at the Battle of Britain service held in September 1965, a memorial stone was unveiled near the grave of the

171   Unknown Warrior, honouring Sir Winston Churchill. It was, the architect Stephen
       Dykes Bower later noted, 'in striking contrast to the massive statue of William Pitt,
       towering above the west door'. But, he went on, 'grandiloquence in sepulchral art
       is no longer in favour'. That was true, but there was also a deeper explanation. The
       younger Pitt's father, the Earl of Chatham, commemorated even more grandiloquently
       in the abbey's north transept, had been, according to Churchill, 'the first great figure
       of British imperialism'; whereas Churchill himself, to his disappointment and regret,
       was the last.[84]

       Against this changed international background, there were some recognizable con-
       tinuities, in particular the weddings of members of the royal family, beginning with
       the Queen's sister, Princess Margaret, in 1960, which was the first to be broadcast live
       on television, adorned by another reverential commentary from Richard Dimbleby.
       This was followed by the marriages of Princess Alexandra (1963) and Princess Anne
       (1973), which conformed to what was by this time a well-established tradition, though
       their popular resonance may have been less than that of the royal weddings of the
       1920s and 1930s.[85] However, the most significant royal service in the abbey during
       this period was yet a further indication that the personnel of empire, like the empire
       itself, were passing away. In August 1979 Lord Mountbatten was assassinated by the
       IRA while holidaying in Ireland. He had been supreme commander in South-East
       Asia, the last viceroy of India, first sea lord and chief of the defence staff, and he was
       closely related to both the Queen and the Duke of Edinburgh. He held a very high
       opinion of his own abilities and achievements, and had planned to the last detail an
172   appropriately grandiose funeral for himself at Westminster Abbey. His obsequies were
       even more splendid than those accorded to his predecessor as viceroy, Lord Wavell,
       in that the entire British royal family attended, along with many of their continental
       cousins. If, Mountbatten had instructed, the prime minister felt inclined to give an
       address, he would like it to concentrate on 'his personal leadership in helping to set a
       line on which the British Empire changed itself into a Commonwealth of sovereign
       states'. But Margaret Thatcher, who never had much time for the Commonwealth,
       declined the invitation and therefore the instruction.[86]

       One person who continued to believe in the Commonwealth ideal was its head,
       namely the Queen herself, and this was scarcely surprising in the light of the commitment
       she had made in 1947. In 1963 and 1964, Commonwealth Day services were held for
       the first time in the abbey, following the renaming of Empire Day (the Empire Youth
       Service, into which the Empire Day observances had morphed in the late 1930s, had
       been discontinued after 1956). As special services, they were held according to the
       rites of the Church of England, but in 1965 there were calls from Commonwealth
       leaders who embraced other religions for a 'multi-faith' occasion instead. The Dean

172 The Prince of Wales reads the lesson at the funeral of his great-uncle Earl Mountbatten of Burma, assassinated in an explosion on board his fishing boat in August 1979; after the carefully planned obsequies at Westminster, Earl Mountbatten was buried at Romsey abbey.

and Chapter were unwilling to comply, there was criticism in the Church Assembly of such an 'inter-faith' gathering, and the service was transferred to the secular setting of the City of London Guildhall. But the Queen soon became dissatisfied with this arrangement, and asked Eric Abbott to permit the service to return to the abbey which, as a royal peculiar, was outside any sort of ecclesiastical jurisdiction.[87] The dean complied, but it was thought prudent to describe the event as an 'observance' rather than a 'multi-faith service', and on that basis the Commonwealth has been celebrated in the abbey in March every year since 1972, almost invariably in the presence of the Queen (and the occasion was renamed the Commonwealth Service in 2002). It was, Canon Trevor Beeson noted at the observance held four years later, 'impressive, indeed moving. The gathering together of so many people from so many different races, cultures and religions to affirm their belief in God and their solidarity within the Commonwealth can only be a good thing, and must contribute something to the furthering of the unity of the human race.'[88]

Yet for much of the time between the end of the Second World War and the funeral of Lord Mountbatten, the Dean and Chapter were preoccupied, more than their predecessors had been, with a variety of pressing practical issues. One was the increased number of visitors, averaging between 1.5 and 2 million a year by the 1970s, which meant the abbey was among the top tourist attractions in Britain. But overcrowding was, as a result, a regular occurrence, especially in the area of the royal tombs, and the noise and the hubbub were inappropriate in a consecrated house of God, the main purpose of which was supposed to be silent devotion and reflection.[89] As Canon Beeson noted, 'although Westminster Abbey was built primarily as a place of worship and prayer' it had become 'exceedingly difficult to experience between 10.00 am and 5.00 pm the kind of peace and tranquillity that most people need if they are to engage in private prayer'. A brief act of worship, lasting a mere two minutes, in which all tourists were invited to join, was conducted every hour from the nave pulpit, as 'a valuable way of reminding the visitors what the Abbey is for and also of involving them in its chief activity'. But obtaining the attention of 'the multitudes' was not easy – partly because many were eager to move on to Buckingham Palace, partly because many did 'not understand English and have no idea what we are talking about', and partly because 'the growth of secularization is making the idea of prayer seem alien to the British and some Europeans'.[90] This was a perceptive point. Until the Second World War, and perhaps on into the 1950s, the United Kingdom had, at least outwardly, conformed to Christian teaching and ethics; but from the 1960s onwards that was decreasingly the case.[91]

Whether they espoused other faiths or none, tourists generated revenue, as a result of the admission fees to the royal tombs and their spending at the bookshop, and these were essential contributions to the abbey's increasingly hard-pressed balance sheet. In coronation year, the Dean and Chapter had launched their second appeal, for £1 million, to fund the cleaning of the interior fabric, sculptures and statues. It was led off by Winston Churchill (though he donated only £1 to it), and was better organized and more successful than Ryle's earlier, reluctant ask. The target was considerably exceeded, and the burnished monuments and glowing interior, with the nave newly lit by sixteen Waterford glass chandeliers presented by the Guinness family in 1965, looked magnificent.[92] But by the 1970s, the abbey finances were becoming decidedly precarious, as soaring oil prices lead to rampant inflation across the Western world. In 1975 it ran a deficit of £42,000 on the general income and expenditure account, although that was an improvement on the previous year's loss, which had been £61,000. The annual running costs totalled £520,000, of which £325,000 went on salaries, wages and pensions, £100,000 on the provision of music, and £60,000 on the upkeep of houses within the abbey precincts. On the other side of the ledger, more than £300,000 in income came from visitors and spending at the abbey bookshop; although these revenue streams fluctuated unpredictably, year on year, they were a stark reminder that tourists, however noisy and irreverent, were vital to the abbey's financial sustainability. Here was the latest example of that 'tension between the sacred and the secular', or between 'cash and credibility', that have been recurrent themes across the abbey's long history, especially during the twentieth century.[93]

Towards Ecumenicalism

In 1974 Edward Carpenter had succeeded Eric Abbott as Dean of Westminster. He had been appointed to a residentiary canonry by Clement Attlee in 1951, and from that time on spent the whole of his Church life in the abbey until his retirement in 1985. Having already served as treasurer and archdeacon, he knew the abbey better than any other twentieth-century dean, and during the course of the thirty-four years he spent there, he became the very embodiment of its institutional memory and Christian mission.[94] Yet Carpenter's selection was unusual. He was appointed on the recommendation of the prime minister, Harold Wilson, and was the first holder of the office in modern times who had been educated neither at public school nor at Oxford or Cambridge universities. He wrote scholarly biographies, including those of two Archbishops of Canterbury (Thomas Tenison and Geoffrey Fisher), and also books on ethics and clerical life; in 1966, to mark the 900th anniversary of the abbey's dedication, he edited *A House of Kings*, which was its official history. Carpenter combined devotion to the abbey, its services and its traditions, with strong commitment to a variety of good causes: pacifism, the education of girls, animal welfare, the reform of clergy pay and the ecumenical movement. He was a man of great integrity and moral courage, prepared, if he saw fit, to defy prime ministerial edicts, even refusing to read a bidding prayer at the memorial service for Sir Arthur ('Bomber') Harris. But in turning the abbey away from what had still seemed to many to be Anglican exclusiveness and towards the embracing of other faiths, whether Christian or otherwise, 'he transformed a national shrine into a place of warmth and welcome'.[95]

In so doing, Carpenter did much to strengthen the 'ecumenical spirit' that had been proclaimed in the abbey in 1941, when a service of Christian witness was held, in which ministers of all denominations took part, and which continued annually during the war years. Moreover, Carpenter had been an enthusiastic supporter of the 'One People Oration', an annual lecture first delivered in 1966 as part of the abbey's 900th anniversary celebrations, the motto for which was 'Think not only of all Christian people, but of all mankind'; and as dean he welcomed many people of other faiths.[96] In 1976 he invited Basil Hume to the abbey following his inauguration as Roman Catholic Archbishop of Westminster; in 1978 he greeted the patriarch of the ancient

Coptic Church; in 1981 Bishop Desmond Tutu, 'perhaps the key figure in the struggle against apartheid', preached in the abbey; and in 1982 he (vainly) invited the pope to attend a service during his visit to Britain. As a result, the abbey was increasingly regarded not so much as a bastion of establishment Protestantism but rather as 'a national church whose doors must be open to everyone, and where a narrow ecclesiasticism should never erect fences to protect sectional interests – be they never so holy'. Another of Carpenter's 'special concerns' was 'the cultivation of links between the Abbey and the Commonwealth – inspired again by his vision of a multi-racial world community living in peace'. To that end, he initiated the practice, carried on ever since, of inviting the high commissioners of Commonwealth countries to attend evensong in the abbey on or near their country's national day, and to bring with them their staff and colleagues.[97]

Yet, at the same time, Westminster Abbey's role as the state church, which provided the unrivalled setting for national events, continued – albeit less completely than Carpenter would have wished. During his predecessor's deanship, in 1967, Earl Attlee's funeral had taken place, and his ashes had subsequently been interred; memorial tablets to Ramsay MacDonald and Lloyd George had been installed in 1968 and 1970; and there had also been a special service to mark the silver wedding of Queen Elizabeth and Prince Philip in 1972. While Carpenter was dean, there were memorial services for the Earl of Avon (Anthony Eden) in 1977, and for R.A. Butler in 1982, as well as the unveiling of memorial stones for Dame Sybil Thorndike and Noël Coward (who had been refused a memorial service in 1973).[98] During the last year of Carpenter's deanship, there were two events that well reflected his ecumenical and pacifist views: in May 1985 a service was held to mark the fortieth anniversary of the end of the Second World War, to which Church leaders from Germany, Poland, the Netherlands, Russia, the United States and Japan were invited; and six months later a memorial tablet was unveiled to the leading British poets of the First World War.[99] But there was also one great personal disappointment during his term of office – namely, the decision in 1981 to hold the wedding of the Prince of Wales and Lady Diana Spencer in St Paul's Cathedral, rather than in the abbey. 'The Dean', Canon Beeson noted, 'is deeply shocked by this decision, . . . he believed the Abbey itself has been in some way slighted. For the Royal Family to turn away from this Royal Peculiar, with which it has such an intimate relationship because of coronations and other special events, seems like some form of rejection.'[100]

Carpenter was succeeded as dean early in 1986 by Michael Mayne, the son of a clergyman, who had previously been head of religious programmes at the BBC and vicar of Great St Mary's in Cambridge. Among his first tasks was to conduct the abbey wedding of the Duke of York and Sarah Ferguson. 'We are', noted Canon Beeson with evident relief, 'back to normal with the venue for royal weddings': the marriage of the Prince of Wales had turned out to be 'a one-off departure from tradition'. An estimated 300 million people worldwide watched the wedding on television, and, in the spirit of ecumenicalism, both Cardinal Basil Hume and the Moderator of the General Assembly of the Church of Scotland were present. Yet, as Beeson also noted, harking back to the idiom of the inter-war years, 'the service itself was as simple as that of many a country church wedding'.[101] It would also be the last occasion on which a member of the royal house married in the abbey for the remainder of the century, as the subsequent collapse of the marriages of the Prince of Wales, Princess Anne and the Duke of York meant that the wedding of the Queen's youngest son, Prince Edward, in June 1999, took place, not in the abbey, as might otherwise have been expected, but in St George's Chapel, Windsor, instead. There would not be another such royal wedding in the abbey until April 2011, when Prince William married Catherine Middleton, making this the longest gap since the sequence of such public weddings began soon after the First World War.[102] And the decision of Prince Harry to marry Meghan Markle at Windsor in the spring of 2018 suggested that the next such abbey wedding, most likely to be that of the elder son of the Duke and Duchess of Cambridge (as Prince William and Catherine became on their marriage), must be some years off.

Mayne was a less avowedly ecumenical (and controversial) dean than his predecessor, and his term of office witnessed several high-profile memorial services, including those for three former prime ministers, the Earl of Stockton (Harold Macmillan; 1987), Lord Wilson of Rievaulx (Harold Wilson; 1995), and Lord Home of the Hirsel (Alec Douglas-Home; 1996).[103] More theatrical (Mayne himself had a lifelong interest in acting and the stage) were the services for Sir Frederick Ashton (attended by both the Queen Mother and Princess Margaret; 1988), for Lord Olivier (whose ashes were later interred in Poets' Corner; 1989) and for Bobby Moore, the captain of England's world-cup winning team of 1966 (1993).[104] Mayne also widened the range of those who were accorded such recognition in the abbey, sanctioning services for figures as varied as Sir Stanley Rous, Dame Anna Neagle, Dame Margot Fonteyn, Sir Geraint Evans, Sir Kenneth Macmillan, Les Dawson and Brian Johnston; he significantly increased the number of poets and writers commemorated in Poets' Corner, including Edward Lear, Anthony Trollope, Alexander Pope, A.E. Housman and Sir John Betjeman; and a memorial to Richard Dimbleby, the first broadcaster to be so honoured, was unveiled in 1990, twenty-five years after his death. There was also a special service in 1994 to celebrate the return of South Africa to the Commonwealth in the aftermath of the fall of apartheid.[105] Mayne was strongly committed to promoting inter-faith dialogue, to raising money for AIDS charities, and to working to support refugees and promote

173   The deanship of Michael Mayne witnessed the installation on the west front of the abbey of ten statues of 20th-century Christian martyrs. The figures include the civil rights leader Dr Martin Luther King Jr, the German theologian Dietrich Bonhoeffer, the Chinese pastor Wang Zhiming, and Manche Masemola, a young woman from the Transvaal murdered by her parents for her faith.

and defend human rights. During his time as dean, ten statues were placed in the empty niches on the abbey's west front, commemorating twentieth-century Christian martyrs – Anglican, Catholic, Orthodox, Lutheran and Baptist. And shortly before his retirement Mayne brought to fruition a project close to his heart, the creation of a monument outside the west front of the abbey to all innocent victims of oppression, violence and war, which was unveiled by the Queen.[106]

Mayne's deanship was not without its troubles. The appointment of Simon Preston, who had been organist and master of the choristers at Christ Church, Oxford, to the equivalent post at the abbey in 1981 was hailed as portending a significant improvement in the abbey's choral and musical life. But Preston was never happy in the post, he was often away and he resigned in 1987, soon after Mayne had taken office, 'to give more time to his professional career as a performer'.[107] His successor, Martin Neary, would have an even less tranquil time. The abbey's finances were also a continuing problem. A third appeal, headed by Prince Philip, had been launched in 1976, and eventually raised £36 million for the cleaning and restoration of the external fabric, a massive task that would be completed by the mid-1990s. For much of the 1980s, the abbey's annual balance sheet showed a surplus, but this was largely because of the ever increasing 'flood' of tourists, estimated at 2.5 million by 1980, and 3.5 million by 1986.[108] Yet, as Canon Beeson lamented, this meant that 'we are absolutely at the mercy of the number of visitors coming to London', the crowds of tourists were often noisy and ill-disciplined, and 'we are seriously under-capitalized'.[109] There were calls for the abbey to follow the examples of Salisbury and Lincoln cathedrals and to charge all visitors, not just those who wanted to see the royal tombs, in the hope that this might stabilize revenue and reduce the number of visitors. But although the Dean and Chapter discussed these matters on several occasions, they remained unresolved throughout Mayne's time.[110]

Like his predecessor, Mayne also suffered one major disappointment during his deanship; but it was of more lasting significance for the abbey than the rebuff Carpenter had felt regarding the Prince of Wales's wedding, for it was the removal of the historic Stone of Scone from the base of the coronation chair, and its return to Scotland.[111]   174 The chair had been custom-built to house the stone at the behest of Edward I, but for some Scottish nationalists this was an unacceptable symbol of their nation's continued and enforced subservience to the English-dominated Union. The stone had already been stolen from the abbey, on Christmas morning 1950, but had been recovered in the following year and returned to the abbey in February 1952. Forty years later, Scottish nationalism had become a far greater political force, which the prime minister, John Major, feared might result in the collapse of the Conservative vote north of the border. Urged on by Michael Forsyth, the secretary of state for Scotland, he peremptorily announced in 1996 that the Stone of Scone would be returned to Scotland (though it would be brought back to the abbey for coronations). The abbey authorities had not been consulted, but their opposition was to no avail, and on 14 November, the last month of Mayne's tenure of office, the stone was removed, while the Dean and Chapter, clad in black gowns, looked on in silent disapproval at what they regarded as a deplorable act of political opportunism and cultural vandalism.[112]

Mayne was succeeded as dean by Wesley Carr, who had previously been Dean of Bristol, and was a classicist, theologian and psychologist by training. He had been in post only a few months when, in late August 1997, Diana, Princess of Wales, was killed in a car crash in Paris. According to palace protocol, she had forfeited her royal status on divorcing the Prince of Wales. But she was the mother of a future king, she was eulogized by the prime minister, Tony Blair, as 'the people's princess', and it soon

174   700 years after it was taken by Edward I from Scone and housed in the base of his coronation chair, the Stone of Destiny was returned to Scotland; on St Andrew's day (30 November) 1996, Prince Andrew, representing the Queen, handed over the royal warrant for the stone's safe-keeping to the commissioners of the regalia in the Great Hall of Edinburgh Castle.

became clear that the public mood, which combined widespread grief with hostility to the allegedly 'uncaring' royal family, would not be appeased until she was given a ceremonial funeral in the abbey. As Carr later recalled, 'At one point it felt to me that I might even be the last Royal Dean of Westminster, and that the next one would inherit a republic.'[113] The hastily improvised obsequies were modelled on those already drawn up for the Queen Mother, and they took place on 6 September, watched by a global audience estimated at 2 billion people. The service was a unique amalgam of ceremony, celebrity and royal discomfiture. Elton John sang 'Candle in the Wind'; representatives of the many charities with which the princess had been associated were among the congregation; from the pulpit, the princess's brother Lord Spencer rebuked the royal family and the press, and the applause of the thousands gathered outside was taken up in the abbey itself. Not since the burial of the Unknown Warrior had there been such a powerful but unexpected response to an abbey event.[114]

Since the Second World War, grand, public abbey funerals had become increasingly rare events, while memorial services had become correspondingly more frequent.[115]

175   Elton John singing 'Candle in the Wind' in the nave of Westminster Abbey at the funeral of Diana, Princess of Wales, on 6 September 1997, which followed an unprecedented display of public mourning in the week after her death.

This continued to be the case during Carr's deanship, with such services for prime ministers and politicians (Sir Edward Heath, Lord Callaghan, Viscount Tonypandy, Lord Hailsham and Lord Jenkins of Hillhead), for figures from the arts world (Ted Hughes, Lord Menuhin, Dame Ninette de Valois and Dame Alicia Markova), for entertainers and journalists (Sir Harry Secombe, Dame Thora Hird, Alistair Cooke and Ronnie Barker), for two very senior clergy (Archbishop Lord Runcie and Bishop Trevor Huddleston), and for two more cricketers (Denis Compton and Lord (Colin)

Cowdrey). In terms of gender and occupation, this consolidated the wider range of people and professions commemorated in this way, which had been begun in Edward Carpenter's day. Memorial tablets had long since superseded statues as the prime form of permanent commemoration in the abbey, and although they were installed more sparingly in Carr's time than they had been when Mayne was dean, those honoured included Sir Frank Whittle, Dame Peggy Ashcroft and, belatedly, Lord Baldwin.[116] There were also many special services, including those to mark the fiftieth anniversary of the National Health Service and the end of the Korean War, the sixtieth anniversary of the Battle of El Alamein and the end of the Second World War, the centenary of Australian confederation, and the 125th anniversary of the Mothers' Union.

At the same time, the trend towards ecumenicalism, so powerfully expressed in the ten statues to Christian martyrs and the monument to the innocent victims of oppression, violence and war, continued. For the special service in November 1997 to mark the golden wedding anniversary of the Queen and Prince Philip, the Queen requested the presence of inter-faith representatives, prompting invitations to the chief rabbi and the director of the Muslim College. In 2000, and following the precedent set by Edward Carpenter, Wesley Carr invited the new Roman Catholic Archbishop of Westminster, Cardinal Cormac Murphy O'Connor, to attend evensong in the abbey. At the memorial service for Archbishop Lord Runcie, the Bishop of London, Richard Chartres, noted in his address that there had been 'a change of style within the Anglican primacy as we moved out of an era of Empire into one of Commonwealth and far beyond'.[117] The Commonwealth Day observance remained an important event in the calendar of both the abbey and the Queen, and was a celebration of diverse peoples and faiths. In March 2001 Sir Roy Strong, who had recently been installed as high bailiff of the abbey, noted the presence of an 'avuncular rabbi', 'a minister of the Church of Scotland' and 'Monsignor George Stack'. He also witnessed 'a group of Zulus singing and dancing their way around the Abbey. They really used the space and, at the very end, returned to burst out of the West Door to give the public something to think about.'[118] The evolution from empire to Commonwealth, and from Anglicanism to ecumenicalism, were closely interconnected, and the abbey was the place where these developments converged.

Dean Carr came to Westminster with a reputation for getting things done, but also for ruffling feathers along the way, and at Bristol he had been involved in the dismissal of the cathedral organist and the resignation of the cathedral school's headmaster. His years as dean, which lasted until 2006, merited the same description, yet he was also genuinely admired by the staff and supported by many members of the chapter. As his *Times* obituarist observed, he was, like all his twentieth-century predecessors, 'effectively chief executive of the Anglican church's most historic shrine'; and it fell to him 'to balance the competing interests of tourism, sanctity and tradition, while keeping enough money coming in to maintain the royal tombs, fan vaults, paintings, statues and a staff of 150'. Moreover, Mayne had left Carr with some serious and unresolved problems, which he was determined to resolve. As one observer commented, 'Show Wesley a nettle and he will grasp it.'[119] The first of these were the vexed and interconnected matters of the abbey's uncertain finances, along with the 'bedlam' resulting from too many tourists. St Paul's had addressed similar problems by imposing charges on all visitors in 1991, and from Easter 1998 Carr followed suit at the abbey. His aim was twofold: to place the finances on a more secure footing and to reduce the number of visitors, and thus the overcrowding and the noise. Revealingly, this policy was entitled 'Recovering the Calm'. Although initially controversial, it did succeed, in considerable measure, in realizing both of these aims.[120]

More controversial was Carr's decision in 1998, supported by the chapter, to dismiss Martin Neary, the organist and master of the choristers, along with his wife, Penny, who was the abbey's concert secretary, after allegations of financial irregularities,. Neary, who had succeeded Simon Preston, appealed to the Queen as the abbey's Visitor, and she put the matter in the hands of Lord Jauncey of Tullichettle, a retired law lord. Neary's supporters included the MPs Frank Field, John Gummer and Sir Edward Heath, and he hired the prime minister's wife, Cherie Booth, QC, to represent him. The result was a media circus, which brought the abbey much adverse publicity as an ecclesiastical drama unfolded that might even have surprised the inhabitants of Trollope's Barchester, and Carr was criticized for being authoritarian and high-handed. After a twelve-day hearing, Jauncey ruled in the abbey's favour, that the two dismissals were, indeed, justified, though the Nearys were cleared of any dishonest practice, and he gave the Dean and Chapter 'gamma minus' for their insensitive handling of the affair.[121] In response, an inquiry was set up into the organization of all the royal peculiars – not just the abbey, but also St George's Chapel, Windsor, and the Chapels Royal at St James's Palace, the Tower of London and Hampton Court – chaired by Professor Averil Cameron of Oxford University. It recommended that their independent status and close links with the crown should be maintained, but that they should be more transparent in their governance, and that they should be overseen by a standing commission, which would superintend the production of annual accounts by each church, receive an annual report and 'exercise a mediating role in the settlement of disputes'. One immediate result was a thoroughgoing review of the abbey's structure of governance, which had been based on and developed from the royal charter of 1560, and this would eventually result in the granting of its first statutes in 2012.[122]

★

Endings and Beginnings

As the twentieth century closed, and the twenty-first opened, two abbey events were further signifiers of the dissolution of the British Empire, which had seemed so potent and so permanent only one hundred years before. In 1998, in the aftermath of the transfer to China of sovereignty over Hong Kong, a service was held, in the presence of the Queen, to mark the formal termination of the Colonial Service (and thus of the British Empire). The address was given by Sir Richard Luce, the last district officer in Kenya, and at that time governor of Gibraltar, who was subsequently lord chamberlain to the Queen and high steward of the abbey.[123] At the end of March 2002 the Queen Mother died, and her funeral, planned since the mid-1970s and known as 'Operation Tay Bridge', was the grandest accorded to any British queen consort.[124] Like Queen Mary, she lay in state in Westminster Hall; but like Queen Alexandra, she was given a funeral service in the abbey, before a private interment at St George's Chapel, Windsor. The entire royal family attended, as did the reigning sovereigns of Spain, Belgium, the Netherlands, Denmark, Norway and Sweden, along with the prime ministers of New Zealand, Australia and Canada. Her imperial crown, placed on the coffin, contained the Koh-i-noor diamond (which gave rise to demands that it should be returned to South Asia, though there was no agreement as to which country should receive it), and her obsequies were the last in the Western world for a former empress (her only rival, the Habsburg Empress Zita, having died in 1989).[125] Exactly a century after King Edward's innovative imperial coronation in the abbey, which took place when the young Lady Elizabeth Bowes-Lyon was already alive, this did, indeed, seem to be the final imperial requiem.

181

Yet the Queen Mother's funeral also set a precedent, for, like her, Queen Elizabeth II will be accorded a lying-in-state in Westminster Hall and obsequies in the abbey, just as Archbishop Davidson had (vainly) urged for Edward VII. With the passing of the sovereign who in 1947 pledged her life to the service of the now dispersed 'imperial family to which we all belong', the last vestiges of the British Empire will surely be gone, and the ensuing coronation of Charles III will be the first post-imperial crowning of modern times. Just as Edward VII's grandiose ceremonial of 1902 provided the template for the three monarchs who came after him, so the less assertive and more ecumenical enthronement of Charles III may establish a new, updated precedent for his twenty-first century successors.[126] But while this seems a likely outcome, one of the conclusions to be drawn from the abbey's history is how unpredictable and unexpected its many possible futures have so often been. At the end of the nineteenth century, few would have foreseen that the next hundred years would witness, among other things, the performance of spectacular imperial coronations, to be followed by the decline and fall of empire; a significantly enhanced connection between the abbey and the British monarchy; the end of grand statues and a reduction in the number of funerals, and their replacement by the cult of the Unknown Warrior, memorial tablets and memorial services; the advent of film, wireless, television and the digital age, which created a global audience for the abbey; and the shift from a Broad Church Anglicanism to a multi-faith ecumenicalism. This, in turn, suggests that during the twenty-first century, the abbey will continue to evolve and develop in ways that cannot yet be predicted. In its constantly changing future, as in its long and variegated past, only time will tell.

Conclusion

DIARMAID MACCULLOCH

D URING THE BBC'S EXCELLENT SERIAL DRAMATIZATION of Hilary Mantel's *Wolf Hall*, it was amusing to spot that, despite the production's pride in period authenticity for costumes and locations, the standard background set for Thomas Cromwell's garden in early Tudor London was embellished by the emblematic twin west towers of Westminster Abbey. Perhaps this reference to Westminster would have been just about geographically possible if the putative scene was Cromwell's official residence at the Rolls in Chancery Lane, off Fleet Street, rather than his main London home at Austin Friars, yet there's no point in making excuses for the set designer: Cromwell would have had to wait two centuries to see those abbey towers. No viewer today would recognize the sorry stumps that were their predecessors in the days of Henry VIII.

At one level, this is a proof of the First Law of TV Period Drama, that if there are going to be anachronisms they will be in the portrayal of anything to do with the Church. But it is also a tribute to the charisma of the abbey that visual shorthand for Period London is precisely that unmistakable image of the west towers. So much of Westminster's imaginative power, it has to be said, is precisely the work of creative imagination. One might without inaccuracy or unkindness call it fiction, but that is often the way with religious narrative, which sets out its own sort of truth. A great deal in the eleven-centuries-long story traced through this volume has turned out to be purposeful fiction: right from very early days, with the startling revelation of the extent to which in the late tenth century the Benedictine monks of Westminster – only relatively recently installed where the abbey still flourishes – forged documents to defend their landed property from outside depredations. Their continued expertise

176 (FACING PAGE)   The gilt-bronze tomb effigies of Henry VII and Elizabeth of York, 1518, were executed in the Renaissance style by the Italian sculptor Pietro Torrigiano. The intricate bronze grille enclosing the monument is by Thomas Ducheman (whose name probably indicates that he was a German craftsman); it bears a Latin inscription, the end of which translates as: 'No earlier ages gave thee as great a king, O England; ages to come will scarcely give thee his equal.'

in forgery now makes the early archive of Westminster Abbey a playground for the highest levels of scholarly skill in palaeography and diplomatic.

Ancient people were as capable as we are of recognizing fabrication; but much of what we would confidently label forgery would in many societies rather be classed as necessary creative fiction. We live with a deluge of recorded information always threatening to overwhelm us; during the Enlightenment of the seventeenth and eighteenth centuries, people learned to refine the skills they needed to separate fake from real news, and that discernment forms the basis of whatever right judgement our present-day society possesses. Tenth-century monks lived in an age with the opposite problem: an archival shortage, which often, therefore, demanded the provision of a record for a truth that had no record. The abbey was early involved in this creativity, which also embraced an urge to will into existence new realities. That enterprise started extraordinarily early, when in Edward the Confessor's great remodelling of the existing monastery, his buildings precociously turned into stone something that had previously existed only on parchment: the four-alleyed square of a cloister at the heart of a harmoniously designed monastery, famously depicted as the ideal monastic layout in the ninth-century Plan of St Gallen.

That particular realization in the 1050s was part of something even more significant. In that decade, King Edward, Queen Edith and the future King Harold created three great religious foundations, Westminster, Wilton and Waltham Holy Cross, which helped to refocus (some might say skew) the Anglo-Saxon kingdom of England towards the regions in the extreme south of the island. These were the historic territories of Wessex at its greatest, before Scandinavian warlords shifted the focus of England northwards again, culminating in Cnut's North Sea empire. An England with a heartland north of the Humber would have been a much more geographically logical entity, and would have had a very different history, looking to the North Sea and the Baltic rather than south across the channel. Instead, by the thirteenth century, with heroic inaccuracy, Westminster could be described as 'in the middle of the land'.[1] President Barack Obama expressed its centrality more accurately in terms of history than geography; when Dean Hall gave him a personal tour of the abbey on his state visit in 2011 and asked him why he thought it had so many American visitors, the president observed that 'here you have the history of the United Kingdom and the Commonwealth, and of the whole English-speaking world'.

There are a good many early paths not taken: Westminster's story bristles with 'what ifs' in different possible configurations of Anglo-Norman politics. Faversham, a little market town in Kent, is now not greatly celebrated beyond its pleasant bounds, but for a brief time in the early twelfth century it looked as if it might be catapulted to fame with a new royal foundation, a richly endowed Cluniac priory that was to be a

177 Almost all heads of state who make a state visit to Britain pay their respects at the grave of the Unknown Warrior; here the American president Barack Obama, assisted by two members of the US armed forces and watched by the First Lady and the dean, the Very Reverend Dr John Hall, lays a wreath on the grave during his visit to the abbey on 24 May 2011.

royal mausoleum for the dynasty of King Stephen and his queen, Matilda. Yet with the defeat of Stephen's effort to establish his family line on the throne, Faversham subsided into the second rank of monasticism, an obscure (and now Benedictine) abbey on the London road to Canterbury. At the end of the century there was a potential danger from even more serious competition, this time in Surrey: namely, Archbishop Hubert Walter's scheme to move his primatial church from Canterbury to a new cathedral at Lambeth, across the river from Westminster and in full sight of the abbey, to which he planned to bring the relics of Archbishop Thomas Becket to confront the shrine of King Edward across the water. We have the forceful intervention of Pope Innocent III to thank for curbing that ambition. Such a relocation would have altered completely the dynamic of English government, creating a nexus of royal and ecclesiastical power far more concentrated than that between Paris and the royal mausoleum–abbey of

Saint-Denis. Could this alternative future have survived a truly revolutionary Reformation, or some Pullmanesque English parallel to the French Revolution?

Church and Dynasty

The abbey has thus been locked, ever since the time of Edward the Confessor, in an intricate and fruitful relationship with the house of worldly power to the east of its altars. Its own legends have entwined with that of English monarchy: one of the longest-lived of the world's political institutions, only marginally younger than the abbey itself. The conversation between them encouraged further creative fiction, as Plantagenet monarchs constructed an Edward the Confessor distinctly more characterful than the man in his lifetime, and turned him for a while into England's patron saint: a philosopher–king to act as potential example or reproach for monarchs who ignored the need for thoughtfulness and humility in government. It should be pointed out that role models change, and that even the fictional Edward was not exactly a *Guardian*-reading liberal. Ailred's Life of Edward depicted him dissolving in laughter during Mass after learning through Christ's revelation that God had drowned the King of Denmark during his preparations to invade; the Confessor could also sit back at table and enjoy the spectacle as God choked to death the deceitful nobleman Godwin. But, after all, a pious monarch would hardly venture to criticize the didactic techniques of the Deity.[2] As national patron saint, Edward was nevertheless always at a disadvantage in the popular imagination compared with the Churchman who was the property of the city down the road: that Cockney boy Thomas Becket. Becket's memory was kept fragrant down to the Tudor age by the firm belief of the yeoman in the street that the archbishop had been an opponent of royal taxation, and still was. None of Westminster's sacred cults allowed for anything so unruly.[3]

Once Westminster had become part of a monarchy that looked south rather than north, its building history and devotional cults reflected a constant tension in deciding how the southern part of this Atlantic archipelago related to the much greater territories of France. Was England to be partner, client or overlord of those fascinating, infuriating lands across the water? The question was opened by the monumentality of King Edward's abbey church, the first great example of Norman Romanesque building in England, before ever William the Norman stumbled ashore at Pevensey. So much of the later building on Edward's footprint furnishes the purest examples of French style that one can see this side of the channel, and there is irony in that, when according to the modern patriotic cliché, Westminster Abbey often stands as the epitome of ceremonial 'Englishness'.

While two royal dynasties, Plantagenets and Capetians, were in contention for the future of England and France, their strife continued to be reflected at Westminster. Plantagenet Henry III attempted to make the relic of Christ's Holy Blood the centre of a popular cult, to outshine the various holy bits and pieces gracing Capetian King Louis IX's Sainte-Chapelle in Paris. It never really worked: within the kingdom, Becket at Canterbury effortlessly outshone Edward at Westminster. It was perhaps a strategic mistake to go for a blood relic, because they always remained controversial until the time that Henry VIII swept all such things away.[4] Rather more successful in defining England's relationship at least to the Capetians' northern partner in hostility was the theft of Scotland's Stone of Scone by Henry's son, Edward I. This outrage was not remedied until the end of the twentieth century, when the stone finally exited the abbey and Edward's throne with the blessing of the Westminster government, after a previous brief unofficial Scottish holiday in the 1950s.

    38

    45

    174

There was a more international dimension to medieval Westminster's place in the Anglo-Norman polity than simple dynasticism. Literally at the heart of King Henry's splendid new work was a treasure with a different significance and a surprising co-sponsor, the pope: the great Cosmati pavement, which still astonishes with its richness and by its very survival – the most significant and historic floor in England. This was a symbol of Christendom's unity across medieval Europe's divisions, at a time when the papacy was making its authority felt with a new insistence throughout the Western Latin Church (witness its part in the routing of Lambeth cathedral). The Plantagenet monarchy continued to enlist international saints in its dynastic self-assertion: Edward III's acquisition of a major relic of Benedict of Nursia was a reflection of a new phase of rivalry with the Capetians in the Hundred Years War, since substantial portions of this father of the Benedictine way rested in an abbey beside the Loire. The local cult of Benedict was one good motive for Westminster to take on its own role in the Benedictine life of late medieval England, as premier house in the kingdom, just as, in other parts of Europe in the sixteenth century, other great Benedictine houses came to lead or lend their names to 'congregations' in their regions – Cassinese or Camaldolese, for instance.

    43

The modishness of late medieval Westminster's devotion is notable. It was a pioneer in the movement to enrich liturgical music in ways beyond that appropriate to monastic worship, by employing lay singers for services supplementing those sung by the monks in choir. The initiative at Westminster came as early as the fourteenth century; other great churches throughout the land followed suit, in a proliferating tradition particularly associated with Lady Chapels. In the case of the abbey, this took place latterly in the most spectacular Lady Chapel of them all, also the most elaborate chantry chapel and foundation in the kingdom of England: Henry VII's relentlessly lavish effort to smooth

    48

    47, 62

176   his path into the presence of the God who had so astonishingly promoted him to
the throne of England. There the king lies, turned monumental by Torrigiano, one
of the greatest sculptors of a new departure in art and architecture that moved away
from the inspiration of the abbey's Gothic into Europe's Renaissance. The splendour
inspired one of the greatest men of the early Tudor age, Cardinal Thomas Wolsey, to
jealous emulation: a still greater tomb, perhaps the finest in English history, if it had
ever been completed.

Survival amid Revolutions

This partnership with the monarchy stood the abbey in good stead in the Reformation
era and beyond, as we are inclined to take for granted without realizing how astonishing
its preservation was. An abbey survived here at least in name and in community life,
when all monasteries disappeared. A strong royal connection did not save Waltham abbey,
even though it was the last monastery to be closed for good, nor did royal foundation
save the nuns of Wilton. Hardly any significant fragments of those two houses remain,
though visitors to Waltham often mistake the grand Norman church there for part
of the monastery – it is more the equivalent of St Margaret's at Westminster. Beyond
it spreads an empty lawn, while at Wilton stands one of the stateliest mansions of the
Protestant nobility. With a little tweaking of history, one could see the same happening
at Westminster: the royal College of St Stephen in Westminster Palace might have
sneaked past the dissolution of chantries to fulfil the dynasty's ceremonial needs a good
deal more cheaply than the re-founded abbey. After all, its counterpart at Windsor
Castle, St George's, managed to survive. Then could follow a feeding frenzy among
Henry VIII's courtiers over Westminster lands: King Henry's brothers-in-law Edward
and Thomas Seymour did very well out of long leases of abbey property in the history
that actually happened, and they would have needed little persuasion to tear down
a redundant monastery and replace it with some fine new mansion, saving Edward
Seymour the bother of building his Somerset House on the Strand. If so, the odds
are that the Victorians would in turn have knocked down a Tudor white elephant for
government offices or a grandiose road system.

Enough of such depressing counter-factuals. One or two other great monasteries
pulled off something like Westminster's trick around 1540 to become cathedrals, notably
two churches also dedicated to the Apostle Peter, Gloucester and Peterborough abbeys.
The dedication of all three is a rather curious coincidence, accounted for by their
antiquity, for Anglo-Saxon England had been very fond of invoking the powerful sanctity
of the 'Prince of the Apostles'. Henry VIII, a man immune from irony, is unlikely to

have wished to honour the putative first Bishop of Rome, but he did appreciate the custodianship of a significant royal tomb, which in the case of Peterborough was that of his much wronged first wife, Queen Katherine of Aragon. The new cathedrals were the one lasting legacy of the Henrician Reformation apart from the break with Rome itself. The corpse of Henry's father in its magnificent setting must have been the clincher that saved Westminster, but the royal generosity to Westminster and its school is so marked and exceptional that special credit needs to be awarded to the discreet diplomacy and well-stocked cellar of Abbot Benson.   71

Even before the Dissolution, visitors were already making their way to Westminster who must be called not pilgrims but tourists. The church was one of the must-see sights of the English capital. One of the earliest tourist visits is rather a surprise; it comes in the travel diary of a two-month tour in 1537, compiled by a teenage traveller from Protestant Zürich, Rudolph Gwalther, given a celebrity welcome to England by court evangelicals since he was the adopted son of the internationally respected chief pastor of Zürich Heinrich Bullinger. The young man was delighted with Henry VII's chapel, 'surpassing the skill of Daedalus in its building', and he carefully copied out the inscriptions framed by the gilt and marble of the royal tomb; his reward for such earnest morning diligence was quality time after lunch with the leopard and the lions in the Tower of London.

Young Rudolph also greatly admired Syon Abbey up the Thames, but, for all Syon's royal connections, that was a great church not destined to remain on the tourist trail.[5] Otherwise, he was, in 1537, treading a future standard circuit, followed in similar fashion, with lions and tombs, by Osip Nepeya Grigor'ev, ambassador from Ivan the Terrible twenty years later.[6] Naturally the abbey and its friends exploited this theme for all it was worth: when the Elizabethan statutes were finalized only a year or two later, the church was said to represent a mausoleum both royal and noble for the whole realm (*quasi publicum quoddam sepulchrum asylumque regum et nobilium Anglorum*). By the end of the century, that cliché could be casually inserted by Thomas Middleton in one of his satires, *The Ant and the Nightingale*, as the epitome of a fine show of riches: 'the Pillars in Powles, or the Tombes at Westminster'.[7]

Curiously, the one tomb that Westminster does not boast is that of its great transformer Henry VIII. In what some might see as poetic justice for his cannibalizing of Wolsey's tomb, the hugely extended project to build a fitting royal resting place – more than half a century's labour – came to nothing, despite all the busy activity in Westminster workshops. The king decided in the end to be buried at Windsor, and though the monumental components of his tomb followed his corpse there in due course, somehow they never got assembled. Most were sold off or melted down by the republican regime in the 1650s. There are magnificent bronze candlesticks in Ghent, and – most happy

178   This beautiful angel is one of four commissioned by Cardinal Wolsey from the Florentine sculptor Benedetto da Rovezzano, active in England *c.*1519–40, for the elaborate and costly tomb he planned for himself; after Wolsey's downfall, Henry VIII seized the completed pieces and the materials, intending to use them for his own monument at Windsor, but this was never finished. The angels were sold off during the Commonwealth and were long used to ornament the gateposts of Harrowden Hall (Northamptonshire).

178   and surprising of rediscoveries – four lovely bronze angels that for a long time did service as gatepost ornaments at a Midlands country house.[8] The greatest fragment of all is now Nelson's black marble sarcophagus in that other London church, St Paul's. All these were once sitting in a chamber at Westminster. One last reminiscence of Henry VIII's body has its own chilling Westminster resonance. Just over a year after the death of the former dean Hugh Weston (so briefly and anticlimactically Dean of Windsor and custodian of the royal corpse), the popular Protestant historical publication *Coopers Chronicle* reported that the disgruntled Weston nearly made a sensational revelation to revenge his public disgrace and dismissal: 'It was the common opinion, if he had not so sodenly ended his lyfe, that in displeasure of the [Marian] Byshops and Clergie, he woulde have opened and revealed their purpose to take up kynge Henries bodye at Windsore and burne it.'[9]

Moving on from that macabre possibility (fire does rather obstinately remain in the memory from the reign of Mary Tudor), we arrive at the plans of the most enigmatic of Tudors, so adept at keeping her counsel: Queen Elizabeth. The Elizabethan religious settlement has long been read in terms of compromise between Catholics and Protestants. That narrative suited Church historians of Anglo-Catholic sympathies from the nineteenth century onwards, but ignored the fact that 1559 saw a reimposition of Edward VI's Church entailing abolition of the Latin liturgy, papal jurisdiction, monasteries, chantries and compulsory clerical celibacy: hardly much joy for Roman Catholics there. What compromises there were in the settlement were really between different sorts of Protestant. For all that her life and history were guarantors of the Protestant Reformation in England, the queen represented a conservative extreme in a spectrum of Protestantism, with her love of music and ceremony and her disapproval of clerical marriage (actually, her personal history made her uneasy generally with the marriage of anyone close to her). This was a monarch who unsuccessfully tried to preserve the rood figures above chancel screens, together with the rood lofts that bore them; and who issued an angry proclamation forbidding her subjects to desecrate the monuments of the dead, likewise without much success. She was also marked by her outward conformity to Mary's Catholic restoration between 1553 and 1558: the Protestant Church of England had a Supreme Governor who would fully deserve John Calvin's contemptuous label of 'Nicodemite', emulating the timorous Nicodemus, who would approach his Saviour only secretly by night.

The collegiate church of Westminster represented Elizabeth's personal preferences as closely as was possible in the conditions of Elizabethan England. It used the martyred Archbishop Cranmer's prayer book with a ceremonial and formal dignity not envisaged at the time of its publication in 1552. It was presided over in succession by three unmarried clergy, William Bill, Gabriel Goodman and Lancelot Andrewes, their married predecessor Richard Cox, who might have resumed the deanship, being removed 75 elsewhere. Moreover, Bill and Goodman were also Nicodemites, like so many of the queen's close associates – principally William Cecil and Nicholas Bacon, and her first 81 choices as archbishops of Canterbury and York, Matthew Parker and William May respectively. If there were hot Protestants in the English Reformation, there were also tepid Protestants, though no less Protestant for being tepid. Perhaps a less freighted adjective would be 'thoughtful' or 'nuanced'. Dean Goodman might be seen as their 83 patron saint. Like his sovereign, he knew the unglamorous heroism of making choices about concealing opinions and making compromises in dangerous times, rather than the luxury of proclaiming convictions in unsullied purity, like martyrs and exiles. No other Protestant Church in Europe had such a beginning as the Elizabethan settlement. Its queen showed sympathy for traditionalist English Catholics, whose religious convictions she deplored, but who kept similarly quiet in her own Church and did not indulge in religious histrionics.

All this is of great importance for the future of the Church of England, because other English Protestants had made a different choice in the face of the moral dilemmas presented by Mary's Catholicism: they resisted, and more than two hundred died a terrible death as a result. Other strenuous souls, like Richard Cox, had marked out a choice as well when they suffered exile abroad till better times came; their Protestantism was worn on their sleeve, and reinforced by their international experiences, and they were celebrated in that hugely influential textbook of anti-Catholicism, John Foxe's 'Book of Martyrs'. Elizabeth found to her disappointment that only one of Mary's bishops would carry on serving in her Church, so she was forced to turn to exiled clergy, to the extent that seventeen of them ended up occupying her twenty-five bishoprics; but she kept such evangelical stalwarts at bay from her Chapel Royal, and from Westminster Abbey. The consequences for the future of, first, the Church of England and, then, worldwide Anglicanism have been profound. Anglicanism still experiences the struggle between these two styles of sixteenth-century Reformation, though many of its battlegrounds may now wear a different aspect. Westminster and Elizabeth's Chapel Royal fostered what is often called – slightly misleadingly – the 'cathedral ethos' within Anglicanism: dedication to a regular round of beautifully performed ceremony and sacred music, and to thoughtful consideration of how to justify such things in a Church of the Reformation. Cathedrals, encouraged by royal example, annexed the Tudor prose of Thomas Cranmer's prayer book for this ancient (and very unProtestant) liturgical duty, and they still do. What is more Anglican than sung Evensong, even if Archbishop Cranmer himself would have deplored such choral excess?

In the Jacobean age, the abbey's function as royal mausoleum was cemented when King James VI and I moved his mother's remains there from Peterborough cathedral (that other victim of the Reformation, Katherine of Aragon, had to stay put). James clearly felt a strong affinity with the church of Westminster, and, rather remarkably, the Stone of Scone played a positive part in this, as metaphor of a potential new age. Its ancient theft was a symbol of the long-standing feud between the English and the Scots, formally at war for two centuries from the time of Edward I; but, after the Reformation radically changed the atmosphere between them, the stone's presence at Westminster took on a more pacific meaning, with the prospect of two Protestant kingdoms ruled by a single Protestant Stuart (Stewart) monarch, fighting Antichrist for godly causes. No-one was more excited than the poetically inclined Scottish religious reformer and scholar Andrew Melville. With his gritty Presbyterianism, Melville was in many ways a profound nuisance to his sovereign, but the expectation of King James succeeding to the English throne inspired Melville, in the 1590s, to hymn 'the noble stone which on the banks of the beautiful Thames now demands a Scoto-Britannic

87

king, and a kingdom owed to the seed of the Scots'.[10] Thus the abbey beckoned King James to his new prospective land, and over the next century, the personal union of crowns fought its way to a Protestant constitutional Union of kingdoms that still creakily survives the loss of its world empire.

The events of the 1650s at Westminster are another hugely significant testimony to a charisma that had survived and was even renewed by the great caesura of the Protestant Reformation. Now the abbey as royal mausoleum was transformed into national mausoleum. Far from being pulled down as the monument to popish idolatry that it undoubtedly was, it was honoured by the English Republic with the grave of John Pym and a good many others, to form the beginning of a new republican state [99] narrative. The abbey was to be an English anticipation of Paris's Panthéon, a stately symbol to reassure the English political nation that revolution could exist alongside respect for a decorous continuity with a suitably purged version of the past. That story has, till now, been left obscure, because history took another turn. If Roundheads could feel the fascination of the abbey church, it was hardly surprising that the effect continued at the Restoration of Charles II and of an episcopal Church of England; this meant that the returning Dean and Chapter of Westminster could celebrate their good fortune with expenditure on rich new copes and other appropriate liturgical [179] paraphernalia. Indeed, the speedy reassembly of the English cathedral corporations alongside Westminster Abbey, complete with estates worth £½ million and a vigorous programme of physical restoration, was one of the wonders of Charles II's return to his throne. It was a testimony of how desperate the nobility and gentry of England were to forget the alarming adventures of the Interregnum that they meekly surrendered their perfectly legal gains of Church lands back to the returning bishops and refurbished cathedrals.

The building of an entire new cathedral for London after the Great Fire of 1666 was also an eloquent symbol of an extraordinary posthumous triumph for the cathedral ethos and for Archbishop Laud's ceremonialist vision. His victory was not complete in the Church of England, and never has been: at the end of the century, for instance, the joyously inquisitive but Puritanically inclined Celia Fiennes on her tour of cathedrals could find the copes of the Durham cathedral clergy an exotic sight in England, and not a pleasant one.[11] The misfortune of St Paul's Cathedral's being wrecked in the Fire and then demolished for rebuilding was, for the time being, the abbey's gain; it stepped into the ceremonial vacuum to take on the great national ceremonies of the late Stuart age and the decades that followed. On the back of that new prominence came fifty years of major building and restoration, which at last gave us those unmistakable twin west towers, vision of an architect of genius whose waywardness could appreciate and [frontispiece] encompass Gothic as much as his own, often intimidatingly inventive, classicism. It is equally symptomatic of this loving appreciation of the past that in 1758 St Margaret's acquired – in a piece of antiquarian philanthropy – some of England's most precious pre-Reformation glass, Christ crucified, with Henry VIII and Katherine of Aragon in attendance. With pleasing symmetry, this glass, now to be admired as St Margaret's east window, may originally have been placed in the royal abbey of Waltham, but it came to Westminster via the former royal country house of New Hall at Boreham in Essex.[12]

The late seventeenth century also saw the beginning of an era of music forever associated with Westminster in the memory of the whole musical world. At one end of solemnity is Purcell's funeral music for Queen Mary, but at the other, one of the greatest products of the Protestant musical tradition, Handel's coronation anthem 'Zadok the priest'. 'Zadok' is a joint Lutheran–Anglican triumphal shout of Hanoverian victory, as recognizable as the towers that went up in the same generation. Even those who commission television advertisements recognize its power. Yet one cannot ignore Westminster's stagnation of the late eighteenth century into the nineteenth, when congregations were tiny and it would have been difficult to predict the abbey's present-day popularity. The compensation of those years was that, without any effort on its own part, global historical circumstances were preparing the abbey for a new place in national life.

Church and Empire

The church of Westminster had been founded and fostered by island monarchs, then drawn into the brief splendour of Henry II's empire, embracing English, Irish and French territories. Three subsequent centuries of struggle sought – ultimately unsuccessfully – to re-create that moment in the sun. England's thoroughgoing defeat by the French monarchy in the Hundred Years War left an island kingdom that started to look in different directions. In partnership with the kingdom of Scotland, it began creating a new empire across far wider seas: a Protestant enterprise that required the new name of 'British Empire'. As this conglomerate recovered from the blow of losing its thirteen colonies on the American seaboard in 1783, it was undertaking a second expansion of the British Empire, but this had an awkward characteristic in comparison with other contemporary European constructs of empire: its unsought but inescapable religious pluralism. Protestant the British imperial power might be, but this was no longer a single form of Protestantism: it comprised two established Churches of different character and polity, side by side, in England and Scotland,

179 (FACING PAGE) After the depredations of the Interregnum, costly new vestments were made to mark the restoration of both the monarchy and the Church. The purple velvet cope (*left*), worn at Charles II's funeral in 1685, is decorated with pomegranates, trefoils and stars in gold and silver thread. Dean Alan Don wore one of the crimson copes originally made for Charles II's coronation in 1661 (*right*) at the coronation of Her Majesty Queen Elizabeth II in 1953.

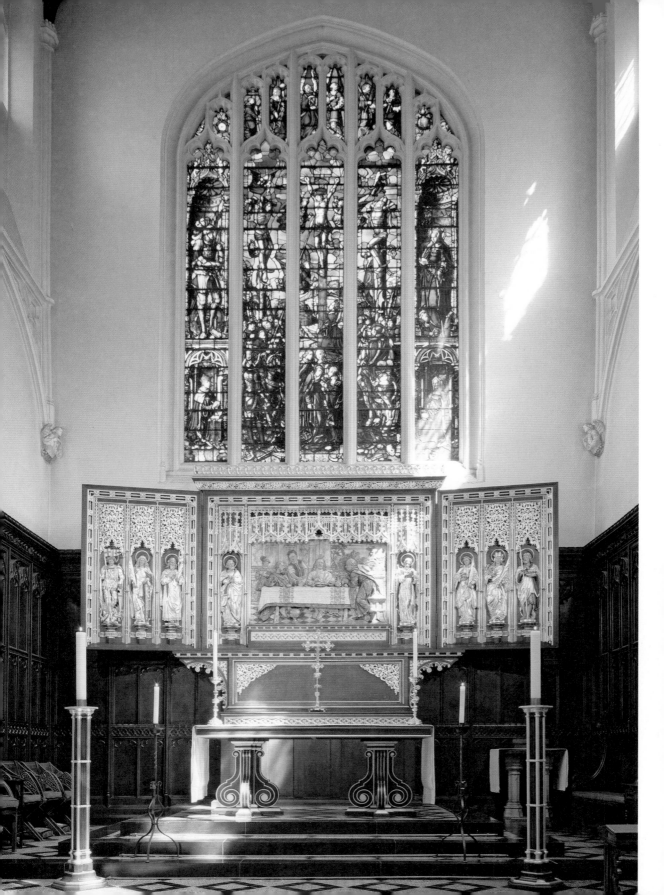

plus a good deal of healthily cussed Protestant Dissent. To survive, the empire would have also to make accommodations with the old enemy, Roman Catholicism, which still overwhelmingly outnumbered the official episcopal Church in Ireland and enjoyed virtually established status in the important newly acquired North American territory of Quebec. Even more perplexingly, there would have to be an understanding with great religions of the East, which were beyond any realistic possibility of subjugation, even if they had not fascinated many of those pushing forward the frontiers of British rule.

In the nineteenth century struggle to express the paradoxical and diverse character of British rule in forms of public ceremony and observance, Westminster had a unique advantage among the great churches of the Church of England. It was not a cathedral with a bishop. In fact, outside the private world of the royal family, there was nothing else like it in English public life; singularity can be the mother of flexibility. Cometh the Victorian age, cometh the man. Dean Stanley was a judicious Broad Churchman, at a time when the rival Big Church at the top of Ludgate Hill was going in a distinctly High Church Anglican direction; even though Queen Victoria took little personal interest in the abbey, her own undemonstrative Protestantism was a parallel to his own. Stanley's ability to lower theological and practical barriers around his church shocked the more ideologically pure, just as Elizabethan copes and anthems had shocked Puritans in the days of Dean Goodman. Following the generous precedents created by Dean Stanley, there was an honoured grave within the church for Charles Darwin: a name that is still reviled among a distressingly large number of Christians. 148

The Abbey in a Democratic Age

The Victorian era also saw the abbey (like other great corporations of the established Church) lose its temporal estates to the Ecclesiastical Commissioners, and its temporal power in government to local democratic institutions. The financial compensation provided – £20,000 per annum – now seems laughably small (and inflation has merely increased the hollowness of the laughter), but other compensations of history are worth considering. It is astonishing that as late as 1899 the abbey authorities were still formally in charge of the administration of the City of Westminster. In the early twenty-first century, that would have given them final responsibility for the public housing in the Borough of Kensington and Chelsea, which in 2017 endured the awful disaster of the Grenfell Tower fire. Secular power brings with it some dark responsibilities. Contrariwise, as the abbey's centuries-old secular responsibilities eroded into democracy, its ceremonial public profile grew ever greater. One new feature of that ceremony over the last century has been a less inhibited adoption of a

180 (FACING PAGE)   The east window of St Margaret's Church contains precious pre-Reformation glass, originally installed elsewhere and brought to Westminster only in 1758. The centre three lights depict the Crucifixion, and the outer two show Henry VIII (*bottom left*) and Katherine of Aragon (*bottom right*) kneeling beneath their respective patron saints

Catholic approach to liturgy in the worship of the abbey generally. This is a mark of the cooling of sectarian Protestant passions in the British establishment, a benevolent public expression of twentieth-century ecumenical openness.

Reconciliation is a cold and abstract word for a warm idea: good old Anglo-Norman terms such as sorrow, forgiveness, ruefulness, new friendship, express it better. One of the best aspects of modern Westminster is the way it has drawn on such thoughts in reconsidering its history. Benedictine monasticism is no longer simply a memory of a lost past at the abbey. Until the mid-twentieth century, collegiate Westminster's regard for the monastic past was essentially antiquarian. Even the historically minded Dean Armitage Robinson thought the original Dissolution timely, because it preserved buildings that might have disappeared in later monastic reform.[13] An aged Tudor survivor, Sigebert Buckley, originally a monk of Westminster, who died at the age of 93 in 1610, formed a lineal connection between the revived Westminster monastery of Mary's time and the community of Benedictines that now flourishes at Ampleforth abbey in Yorkshire. It was a graceful gesture to ask one of the community, the historian Dom Hugh Aveling, to write the medieval chapter for the abbey's previous official history, *A House of Kings* (1966). Ten years after that publication came a properly liturgical celebration of more generous times: the then Abbot of Ampleforth, Dom Basil Hume, was installed as Archbishop of Westminster in his cathedral, and later that day brought the Ampleforth community to sing Vespers in the abbey. Many representatives joined the congregation from other Benedictine communities; it has been suggested that this was the largest gathering of monks in the whole history of the abbey.[14]

175, 181 In later years, in different but nevertheless complementary ways, the funerals of Diana, Princess of Wales, and of Queen Elizabeth, the Queen Mother, formed a wholly appropriate end point for the abbey's twentieth-century history, which effectively began with the coronation of King Edward VII in 1902. Once again, these were royal ceremonials that held the attention of the nation, the English-speaking world and a global audience beyond. Yet such undoubted continuities in the abbey's public and ceremonial role also conceal many significant changes, reflecting unexpected developments in national culture. At the beginning of the century, Canon Welldon, in his sermon in the abbey to imperial troops soon after King Edward's coronation, was one of many who believed that the British Empire would be permanent. But by the end of the century, this vast territorial sprawl had been transformed into the very different Commonwealth.

During the same period, the United Kingdom evolved from being a Christian nation, in its public life and moral code, into a society both multi-faith and more secular. Simultaneously, the successive inventions of wireless, television and social media have brought the abbey and its services into the lives and homes of millions of people

181   The coffin of Queen Elizabeth, the Queen Mother, is placed on the catafalque at the foot of the chancel steps at the beginning of her funeral on 9 April 2002. Her death prompted reflection on a century of British history: within her long lifetime – she was born in 1900 – profound changes had occurred in every realm of national life, political, social and religious.

around the world, in ways undreamed of at the beginning of the twentieth century. This mid-twentieth century child is just too young to remember his experience in 1953, settled down with mother and father at the house of one of their friends lucky enough to own a television, to watch the young Queen move through ancient ceremonies in rather foggy black and white. The connection between the abbey and the monarchy has become much closer than it was a century ago: whereas Queen Victoria rarely set foot in the church, and King Edward VII only for his coronation, their successors and their families have become regular visitors, for annual services, special services, and royal weddings and funerals.

   Visiting monarchs are only a few among the countless thousands who arrive at Westminster Abbey throughout the year, in an age of mass tourism that would have been unthinkable in Dean Stanley's day. The grave of the Unknown Warrior has made

182   The choir and clergy process through the nave at the beginning of one of the many special services that take place in the abbey – this one in 2016. The congregation sings a hymn as the procession makes its way to the choir and the high altar.

the church a place of remembrance for all who mourn, not simply for the ruling elite whose tombs have accumulated there over the centuries; it is a place for individual silent thought, even amid the crowds flowing in through the west doors. Throughout the Western world, we now unite in silence to remember the dead, since silence is the universal property of religion, and also of human seriousness, beyond creeds or doctrines. All this, combined with the increasingly successful efforts to make the abbey a place of welcome for all people, meant that by the end of the twentieth century, it had become more central to national life than a hundred years before.

In the present century, the church that takes its place in national life does so in partnership with diverse democracy amid many religions and none. In this, the function of Anglicanism as umpire, so deftly anticipated by Dean Stanley, is finely expressed in the abbey's presentation of great national ceremony. Much of it is to do with those universals of human experience beyond particular creed or doctrine: marriage and burial. As the story of Westminster Abbey has been told in this book, various themes have recurred through nearly eleven centuries, ebbing and flowing in prominence. You have read of devotion, beauty, power, charisma, and, to a rather surprising extent, fiction. From the very early days of the monastic foundation, the monks of Westminster had proved adept at 'making things up', for often good purposes and with the good outcome of creating reality from invention. Their church was built as an icon in stone of a vision larger than the frontiers of the kingdom. One can hardly call that internationalism, as the concept of a nation sits uncomfortably in the medieval world or even the world of the sixteenth-century Reformation. By contrast, we now have too much nationalism, a product of the confused break-up of empires over a century and a half. Keeping our eyes open to the world beyond our borders is an urgent necessity at a time when this modern nation is in danger of turning inwards in self-absorption. Westminster can play its part in that too.

The abbey's modern history exemplifies the adage that the more things change, the more they stay the same. To a greater extent than is true of any other religious building, the abbey embodies continuity since before the Norman Conquest until the present day. Its unique location, close to the palaces of Westminster and Whitehall, and its unusual status as a royal peculiar mean that it has always been close to government and crown. The claims of the sacred and the secular, the spiritual and the terrestrial, have always competed, and have been reconciled with varying degrees of conviction and success. Yet, as throughout its history, the abbey is first and foremost a house of God, devoted to prayer and worship, and in that lies its fundamental purpose and   182 abiding continuity. Accordingly, when Canon Adam Fox predicted, towards the end of his contribution to *A House of Kings*, that it was 'fairly certain that in the next sixty years changes everywhere will continue to be rapid', he was half right, but also half wrong. Like many venerable British institutions, the abbey has both changed and yet endured, and there seems every good reason to suppose that the same will be true during that greater part of the twenty-first century that still lies ahead.

Appendix 1

Monarchs

PRE-CONQUEST KINGS

Only during the tenth century did a united English realm come into existence. Æthelstan (r. 924–39), the grandson of Alfred the Great (d. 899), was the first acknowledged king of all England, a position consolidated by his nephew, King Edgar.

Edgar (Pacificus) *Anglo-Saxon*	959–75
Edward (the Martyr)	
Anglo-Saxon	975–8
Æthelred II (the Unready)	
Anglo-Saxon	978–1013 (exiled)
Swein (Forkbeard) *Danish*	1013–14
Æthelred II	1014–16
Edmund II (Ironside)	
Anglo-Saxon	1016
Cnut *Danish*	1016–35
Harthacnut *Danish* ⎫	
Harold I (Harefoot) *Danish* ⎭	jointly 1035–7
Harold I	1037–40
Harthacnut	1040–42
Edward the Confessor	
Anglo-Saxon	1042–66
Harold II (Godwinson)	
Anglo-Saxon	1066

HOUSE OF NORMANDY

William I (the Conqueror)	1066–87
William II (Rufus)	1087–1100
Henry I	1100–35
Stephen	1135–54

HOUSE OF PLANTAGENET

Henry II	1154–89
Richard I	1189–99
John	1199–1216
Henry III	1216–72
Edward I	1272–1307
Edward II	1307–27
Edward III	1327–77
Richard II	1377–99
Henry IV *House of Lancaster*	1399–1413
Henry V *House of Lancaster*	1413–22
Henry VI *House of Lancaster*	1422–61
	(imprisoned 1465–70)
Edward IV *House of York*	1461–70
Henry VI	1470–71
Edward IV	1471–83
Edward V *House of York*	1483
Richard III *House of York*	1483–5

HOUSE OF TUDOR

Henry VII	1485–1509
Henry VIII	1509–47
Edward VI	1547–53
Mary I	1553–8
Elizabeth I	1558–1603

HOUSE OF STUART

James I (VI of Scotland)	1603–25
Charles I	1625–49

COMMONWEALTH

After the execution of Charles I, republican government was established under the Commonwealth (1653–9).

Oliver Cromwell
(lord protector)   1653–8
Richard Cromwell
(lord protector)   1658–9

HOUSE OF STUART

The monarchy and the House of Stuart were restored in 1660.

Charles II   1660–85
James II (VII of Scotland)   1685–8
William III and Mary II (d. 1694)   1689–94
William III   1689–1702
Anne   1702–14

HOUSE OF HANOVER

George I   1714–27
George II   1727–60
George III   1760–1820
George IV   1820–30
William IV   1830–37
Victoria   1837–1901

HOUSE OF SAXE-COBURG AND GOTHA

Edward VII   1901–10

HOUSE OF WINDSOR

George V   1910–36
Edward VIII   1936
George VI   1936–52
Elizabeth II   1952–

Appendix 2

Abbots and Deans of Westminster

This list is based on *VCH: County of London*, I, 1909; E.H. Pearce 1916; D.M. Smith, 1972–2008; *ODNB*; and on notes and indexes in WAL. For an account of the Dissolution of the Monasteries see chapter 4 in this volume, pp. 135–77; for terminology see the Glossary, pp. 387–95.

ABBOTS

As a monastic community of the Benedictine order, Westminster Abbey was ruled from its foundation by an abbot.

Dunstan	959?–988
Wulfsige	988–93
Ælfwig	993–c. 1020
Wulfnoth	c. 1020–1049
Eadwine	1049–c. 1071
Geoffrey	c. 1072–1075
Vitalis	1076–c. 1085
Gilbert Crispin	c. 1085–1117/18
Herbert	c. 1121–36
Gervase of Blois	1138–57
Lawrence	c. 1158–1173
Walter	1175–90
William Postard	1191–1200
Ralph of Arundel	1200–14
William du Hommet (Humez)	1214–22
Richard of Barking	1222–46
Richard of Croxley (Crokesley)	1246–58
Philip de Levesham	1258
Richard of Ware	1258–83
Walter of Wenlock	1283–1307
Richard Kedington	1308–15
William Kirtlington	1315–33
Thomas Henley	1333–44
Simon Bircheston	1344–9
Simon Langham	1349–62
Nicholas Litlyngton	1362–86
William Colchester	1386–1420
Richard Harweden	1420–40
Edmund Kirton	1440–1462/3
George Norwych	1463–9
Thomas Millyng	1469–74
John Eastney	1474–98
George Fascet	1498–1500
John Islip	1500–32
William Benson (name in religion William Boston)	1533–40

DEANS

After the Dissolution of the Monasteries, the former abbey church became a cathedral, led by a dean.

William Benson	1540–49
Richard Cox	1549–53
Hugh Weston	1553–6

ABBOTS

During the reign of the Roman Catholic queen Mary I (r. 1553–8), the monastic community was restored under an abbot.

John Feckenham	1556–60

DEANS

After the accession of Elizabeth I (r. 1558–1603), Westminster
Abbey was re-founded as a collegiate church, under the direction
of a dean.

William Bill	1560–61
Gabriel Goodman	1561–1601
Lancelot Andrewes	1601–5
Richard Neile	1605–10
George Mountain (Montaigne)	1610–17
Robert Tounson	1617–20
John Williams	1620–44
Richard Steward	1645–51
(never installed)	

During the Interregnum, the Dean and Chapter were abolished,
and were reinstated only at the Restoration in 1660.

John Earle	1660–62
John Dolben	1662–83
Thomas Sprat	1683–1713
Francis Atterbury	1713–22
Samuel Bradford	1723–31

Joseph Wilcocks	1731–56
Zachary Pearce	1756–68
John Thomas	1768–93
Samuel Horsley	1793–1802
William Vincent	1802–15
John Ireland	1816–42
Thomas Turton	1842–5
Samuel Wilberforce	1845
William Buckland	1845–56
Richard Chenevix Trench	1856–64
Arthur Penrhyn Stanley	1864–81
George Granville Bradley	1881–1902
Joseph Armitage Robinson	1902–11
Herbert Ryle	1911–25
William Foxley Norris	1925–37
Paul de Labilliere	1938–46
Alan Don	1946–59
Eric Abbott	1959–74
Edward Carpenter	1974–85
Michael Mayne	1986–96
Wesley Carr	1997–2006
John Hall	2006–19

Glossary

For architectural terms as they relate to Westminster Abbey, see Plans 1 and 2, on pp. viii–xi.

abbey A religious establishment, home to a community of Christian monks, canons or nuns of a particular religious order, conducting its affairs under the direction of an abbot or abbess; also, the buildings of such an establishment.

abbot The superior officer or head of an abbey.

aisle A relatively narrow flanking section of a church, running alongside the nave and choir, and sometimes the transepts. At Westminster there are north and south aisles to the nave and choir, aisles on both sides of the north transept, and an aisle on the east side of the south transept, where Poets' Corner is situated.

almoner The official responsible for the charitable work of an income-generating institution, such as a monastery. The office of royal almoner, a member of the monarch's household, dates from the early 12th century, and the office of the abbey almoner from at least the 13th.

almonry The department responsible for the administration of an institution's charitable work, generally housed in a purpose-built range, including offices, accommodation for the almoner and his staff, and space where care might be provided to the poor and alms dispensed. In monasteries, as at Westminster, the almonry was often located near the gatehouse so as to minimize disturbance to the monastic community.

altarpiece A painting or sculpture set up behind and above an altar.

ambulatory An aisle running round the east end of a large church behind the high altar, linking the north and south aisles of the chancel; on the inner side of the ambulatory is the sanctuary, and on the outer side chapels might open off it. At Westminster, the ambulatory gives access to the chapels of Sts Benedict, Edmund (the Martyr), Nicholas, Paul and John the Baptist, the Islip Chapel, the chapels of Our Lady of Pew and St John the Evangelist, the Lady Chapel (Henry VII's chapel), and also the Chapel of Edward the Confessor behind the high altar.

apse (Fr. *chevet*) The rounded or polygonal end of an arm of a church, especially the east end behind the high altar; it may be surrounded by radial chapels, a layout often found in medieval French churches.

arcade A row of arches in the same plane, supported by columns or piers; the arcades of the nave and choir consist of a series of such arches, separating the main body of the church from the aisles, and supporting the clerestory above.

archbishop In episcopal Churches, the chief bishop and highest dignitary of a province or archdiocese, responsible for superintending its bishops, each of whom, in turn, is responsible for a diocese. From the 6th century there have been two archbishops in England, exercising authority respectively over the Provinces of Canterbury and York.

archdeacon Originally the chief attendant on a bishop, who came to occupy a role superior to the priests and next in importance to the bishop within a diocese; there were usually several archdeacons in each diocese, responsible for the oversight of the clergy and the administration of church courts within their archdeaconries.

bar-tracery   *See* TRACERY.

basilica   *See* ROMANESQUE.

bay   In church architecture, the space between two architectural elements – usually an opening between two columns or piers in an arcade; the structure created by the piers and the arches that spring from them continues into the vault, so that the bay forms a lateral subdivision of the body of the building. The nave of Westminster Abbey has ten bays.

benefice   An ecclesiastical LIVING.

berewick   An outlying estate, dependent upon and answering to the residence of a lord.

bishop   In episcopal Churches, a senior priest consecrated for the spiritual direction of a diocese, including the superintendence of its priests and deacons; a bishop ranks below and is answerable to the archbishop.

Book of Common Prayer   The official service book of the Church of England; it includes the orders of service for daily and Sunday worship, for the sacraments of baptism, confirmation and marriage, and for funerals. It was first published in 1549, in the reign of Edward VI, under the supervision of Thomas Cranmer, Archbishop of Canterbury, and radically revised in 1552; the 1552 version remained the basis for further revisions until 1662.

Broad Churchmanship   A form of Churchmanship that interprets the Church of England's doctrines and liturgical rituals in a liberal spirit, favouring an inclusive and tolerant attitude.

buttress   A pier-like structure, usually of stone or brick, built against a wall to strengthen or support it. A flying buttress is an external arched structure connecting the upper part of a wall to a free-standing pier, usually to counter the outward thrust caused by a stone vault.

calendar   [kalendar]   In the ecclesiastical sense, a table showing the liturgical seasons and main festivals of the Church's year (such as Advent, Christmas and Easter), and other days on which the events of Christ's life are celebrated and the saints commemorated; the dates of some festivals, such as Easter, Pentecost and the Ascension, vary, and so are called 'movable feasts'.

canon   A cleric living with others within the precinct of a cathedral (unless it is also a monastery) or in a collegiate church. After the successive dissolutions of Westminster's two monastic foundations, the collegiate church of Westminster Abbey has been run by the canons, under the jurisdiction of the dean. See also PREBENDARY.

celebrant   The priest who presides at the EUCHARIST.

chancel   The eastern area of a church, used by those conducting services; it contains the sanctuary and the high altar, and often (though not at Westminster Abbey) includes the choir. It may be separated from the nave by a screen, railing or steps.

chantry   An endowment to finance the celebration, by one or more dedicated priests, of Masses for the souls of the founder and his or her dependants; an altar or chapel erected for this purpose.

chapel   Within a large church, a separate area or compartment of the building, usually dedicated to a saint, and having its own altar for prayer and worship. A chapel may also be part of, or attached to, a secular building, such as a palace, college or hospital.

Chapel Royal   The body of clergy and musicians whose duty it is to serve the spiritual needs of the monarch and the royal household.

chapter   As a term of ecclesiastical governance: (i) The daily assembly of a community of monks or nuns, the principal tool of its internal governance, presided over by the abbot or abbess; it is named for the chapter from the rule (for instance, that of St Benedict) that was read aloud at the opening of each meeting. (ii) More generally, the body of clergy attached to a cathedral or collegiate church, who assist the dean in maintaining the establishment and its spiritual life. In the case of Westminster Abbey, which is not under the jurisdiction of a bishop (being a ROYAL PECULIAR), the chapter consists of the college of canons, presided over by the dean, who together are responsible for the life of the church and its associated activities.

chapter house   A separate building or room in a monastery, cathedral or collegiate church in which the chapter meets. In a monastery (and at Westminster Abbey) the chapter house was usually attached to the cloister.

charter A written document, authenticated – and so given legal force – by the grantor's seal, most often used to convey land or privileges.

chevet (Fr.) *See* APSE.

choir [quire] In church architecture, the part of the church to the east of the nave (sometimes within the chancel), set aside for the singers; the choir stalls run longitudinally down either side of the choir so that two bodies of singers face each other across a central space. At Westminster Abbey, this part of the church is properly called the 'quire'.

clerestory The uppermost tier of the nave, choir and transepts of a church; its windows light the central parts of the building.

cloister In a monastery or a collegiate church, a covered walk, usually with arcades opening into a central square or rectangular open court or 'garth'; the cloister provided a route between different buildings, such as the chapter house, the refectory and the church, and was also used for study. It is commonly, as at Westminster Abbey, built on the south side of the church in the angle of the nave aisle and the south transept. In a figurative sense, 'the cloister' refers to the monastic life.

collegiate church A church run by a community or corporation ('college') of resident clergy, who, with the dean, constitute the chapter that governs the foundation.

Communion [Holy Communion] *See* EUCHARIST.

Convocation The law-making body of the Church, comprising the higher clergy (e.g. bishops) and representatives of the lower clergy, which usually meets in parallel with parliament. There are Convocations for the provinces of Canterbury and York, but, over time, the Convocation of Canterbury has become the more important and is often referred to simply as 'Convocation'.

cope A full-length vestment, consisting of a semicircular piece of cloth (usually embroidered or otherwise decorated), worn as a cloak by a cleric, in processions and on other occasions.

Covenanter The name given to those who signed the National Covenant of 1638, which bound them to maintain the 'true' (that is, Calvinist and anti-episcopal) religion in Scotland, and to oppose those who tried to change it.

crenellation A pattern of usually square notches, cut in the top of a parapet; originally of practical use, to allow arrows or shot to be fired against assailants, crenellation afterwards became part of architectural decoration on churches and other buildings.

crossing In a cruciform (cross-shaped) church, the rectangular area at the intersection of the nave and chancel (running west–east) with the transepts (running north–south); Westminster Abbey now has a low tower over the crossing (*see also* LANTERN TOWER).

crypt In a church, a vaulted chamber built partly or wholly underground, usually under the chancel. It might have a nave and aisles, and chapels with their own altars for worship; crypts were often used for burials. At Westminster Abbey there are burial vaults beneath the Lady Chapel, but the only true crypt is under the chapter house.

cupola A dome forming the roof of a building or part of a building; more specifically, any small domed form, visible above the level of a roof.

customary A book that describes the forms of worship of a particular monastery, cathedral or collegiate church.

deacon In episcopal Churches, an order of clergy ranking below bishops and priests.

dean The superior of the body of clergy attached to a cathedral or collegiate church, and president of the CHAPTER. At Westminster Abbey, which is not under the jurisdiction of a bishop, the dean is the ORDINARY responsible directly to the monarch for the well-being and good order of the foundation.

diaper-work A decorative pattern on a flat surface, consisting of the repetition of a simple geometrical form, usually a diamond, sometimes embellished with a central motif, such as a dot, leaf or rosette; diaper-work may be carved, painted or executed in bricks of lighter and darker shades. Diaper-work is found in Westminster Abbey on the interior walls of Henry III's 13th-century church.

diocese The area under the jurisdiction and pastoral care of a bishop.

Dissenter   The name given to those who refuse to follow the rules of the established Church or to attend its services systematically, instead conducting their own forms of worship and services.

Dissolution of the Monasteries   The suppression, between 1536 and 1540, of monasteries, priories and other religious communities in England and Wales, by means of a series of administrative and legal measures, starting with the Act of Suppression in 1536. Henry VIII, as Supreme Governor of the Church of England (thanks to the Act of Supremacy, 1534), dissolved more than 800 religious foundations and appropriated their lands, revenues and other assets. Westminster Abbey was dissolved as a monastery on 16 January 1540 and again (after Mary I's restoration of the monastic community) under legislation passed on 8 May 1559.

dorter   The dormitory in a monastery or convent.

east end   The easternmost part of the main body of the church, housing the chancel, sanctuary and high altar, and chapels behind the altar.

elevation   A vertical face of a building or part of a building, internal or external – for example, the nave arcade (internal) or the west front (external); the term is often used synonymously with FAÇADE.

episcopacy   The system of Church governance by bishops as the successors of Christ's apostles.

episcopal   Relating to a bishop or to the governance of the Church by bishops.

Erastianism   The doctrine that, in Church affairs, the ecclesiastical power is subordinate to the state.

Eucharist   The sacrament of the Lord's Supper or Holy Communion, and (by extension) the consecrated bread and wine (standing for the body and blood of Jesus Christ) consumed at this service.

evangelical   During the Reformation, the name given to Protestants who sought to reform the Church by bringing it as close as possible to its origins as described in the gospels. From the 18th century, the term (usually with a capital initial) came to mean a form of Protestantism that believes the essence of the gospel to be the doctrine of salvation through faith

in the atoning death of Christ, rather than through good works or receiving of the sacraments.

façade   The external face or front of a building, as it is seen from the street or other vantage point, especially the principal (west) front.

fan vault   In the PERPENDICULAR style, a vault having pendant trumpet or cone shapes covered with blind panel tracery. One of the most spectacular examples of fan vaulting is to be found in the Lady Chapel (Henry VII's chapel) in Westminster Abbey.

feast day   A day on which, annually, the Church celebrates an event – such as the Nativity (Christmas) or Resurrection (Easter) of Jesus Christ – or a person, each saint being commemorated on a particular date in the Church's calendar (his or her saint's day).

flèche (Fr.: 'arrow', 'spire')   A small spire, set upon a roof, often that of the crossing in a Gothic church.

friar (from Latin *frater*: 'brother')   A member of one of the mendicant religious orders founded in the 13th century under the patronage of the papacy to support the church's ministry in lay society, through preaching, receiving confession and assisting the work of parish priests; friars were distinguished from monks because they were supported by charity rather than the income from property, and were not confined to their church and cloister but moved from place to place. The main orders of friars are the Franciscans, Dominicans, Augustinians and Carmelites. Cf. MONK.

frontal   A covering for the front of an altar, usually a cloth, but sometimes made of metal, stone or other material.

gable   On a building with a pitched roof, the vertical section of wall that closes the end of the roof; also, a gable-shaped top – for example, to a buttress.

gallery [tribune]   In church architecture, an area constructed over the aisles of the nave, which might contain altars, or provide additional space for worshippers; structurally, a pair of galleries could act as buttresses for the nave. More loosely, a gallery may be any accessible area of a large church above ground level – for example, the TRIFORIUM.

Gothic   A style of architecture, originating in France in the 12th century and prevalent in Western Europe until the 16th century, characterized by pointed arches, pointed ribbed vault-ing, external buttresses, and large windows filled with stained glass, all combining to create a sense of soaring verticality. In England, the period of Gothic architecture is subdivided into Early English (or 'First Pointed'; *c.*1175–*c.*1275), Decorated (or 'Second Pointed'; *c.*1275–*c.*1375) and Perpendicular (or 'Third Pointed'; *c.*1375–*c.*1640).

groin vault   A vault of four segments, formed of two round-headed arch shapes set at right angles.

high altar   The main altar of a large church, usually in the sanctuary at the east end.

High Churchmanship   A form of churchmanship in the Church of England, identified from the 17th century onwards (and – with different nuances – in other Churches of the Reformation), that emphasizes the importance of liturgical ritual, priestly authority and the centrality of the sacraments, and asserts historical continuity with the pre-Reformation Western Church.

High Gothic   A style of French Gothic architecture current from *c.*1195, characterized by flying buttresses (allowing higher building and more windows) and the enlargement of the transepts and choir; typical of High Gothic are the northern French cathedrals built *c.*1195–*c.*1230, notably those at Chartres, Bourges, Reims and Amiens.

High [Solemn] Mass   A Mass celebrated with full ceremonial, in which most parts of the liturgy are sung and the priest (celebrant) is assisted by other clergy.

high steward of Westminster   An office created in 1545, after the dissolution of the abbey, to oversee the abbey's liberty of Westminster; the steward's role was expanded with the formation of the Court of Burgesses in 1585, over which he or his deputy presided to protect the abbey's interests. Although nominally appointed by the Dean and Chapter, in practice the high steward was a high-status crown appointee. Today the high steward acts as principal adviser to the Dean and Chapter and takes part in the ceremonial of certain services.

Independent   A member of a self-governing congregation, independent of any external Church authority; the term 'Independent church' was later displaced in England by 'Congregational church'.

indulgence   In the Western medieval Church, the full or partial remission of punishments for sin, imposed after death and undergone in purgatory; remission could be obtained through good works – prayer, pilgrimage and charity – but, under the complex penitential system of the Church, by the 12th century the principal means of obtaining release from purgatory (for the dead, and for the living who wished to escape its future pains) was through indulgences, which were in the sole gift of the pope and higher clerics, and mainly secured by monetary payments. By the late 15th century, the system of indulgences had become increasingly controversial; Martin Luther's protest against it sparked the REFORMATION.

infirmary   In a monastery complex, the building set aside for the care of the sick and the elderly. At Westminster, the infirmary complex stood around the site of what is now the Little Cloister and had its own chapel (now ruined), dedicated to St Catherine.

Lady Chapel   A chapel dedicated to the Blessed Virgin Mary ('Our Lady'), usually the biggest chapel in a cathedral or other large church and located to the east of (and behind) the high altar. The present Lady Chapel of Westminster Abbey was financed by Henry VII, begun in 1503 and dedicated in 1516 after his death; it is also known as the Henry VII chapel and serves as the chapel of the Order of the Bath.

lancet   A tall narrow Gothic window with a pointed arch at the top, or a single light of this shape as part of a larger window.

lantern tower   A tower, usually rectangular but sometimes octagonal, over the crossing of a church, with openings to light or ventilate the building.

Laudian movement   The policies and ideas associated with William Laud, Archbishop of Canterbury (1633–45); they included enhancing the 'beauty of holiness' in church decoration and worship, and placing the Communion table at the east end of the church. In Church governance, they aimed to boost the authority of the clergy and Church courts.

litany   A form of penitential prayer, led by a member of the clergy, in which the people respond at the end of each clause; the Book of Common Prayer contains a form of litany for regular use at Morning Prayer.

liturgy   A prescribed form for the conduct of services for public worship.

living [benefice]   In the Church, a position as a rector, vicar or other official, which brings with it property or an income or both, and in return requires the incumbent to conduct services and exercise care for the spiritual welfare of the parishioners.

Lollard   A member of a heretical religious movement current in England from the late 14th century to the Reformation; the Lollards followed the teachings of John Wyclif, looked to scripture as the basis of religion and sought the reform of the Roman Catholic Church.

Low Churchmanship   A form of Churchmanship in the Church of England that accords little importance to liturgical ritual, the authority of the clergy and the sacraments. The term 'Low Churchman', first used in the 18th century, is often used synonymously with 'evangelical'.

Mass   The liturgical service of the EUCHARIST, especially, after the Reformation, as interpreted and celebrated in the Roman Catholic Church.

mendicant orders   *See* FRIAR.

minor canon   A priest in the service of a cathedral or collegiate church, but not a member of the chapter.

minster   An early medieval enclosed community consisting of monks or secular priests or both, directed by an abbot; within its local area, it acted as a centre for conversion and for the maintenance of religious life. A minster had a church and other buildings, and was sustained by produce from its own lands, provided by its founder or other donors.

missal   The liturgical book containing the texts needed to celebrate the Mass throughout the year.

monk   A man who lives apart from the world, usually as a member of a settled community (monastery) affiliated to a particular religious order (e.g. Benedictine, Carthusian); vowed to poverty, chastity and obedience, he is committed to a daily routine of religious worship, interspersed with periods of prayer and study. Cf. FRIAR.

narthex   A vestibule extending across the west end of a church, sometimes with its own nave and aisles several bays long.

nave   The main body of a church building, extending from the west door to the chancel; it is usually separated from the chancel by a screen, and from aisles on either side by an arcade.

Nicodemite   A term (originally of abuse) coined in the Reformation by John Calvin to describe those who hid their true religious beliefs and conformed outwardly to the established religion; it derives from Nicodemus (John 3:2), who dared to visit Jesus only by night. Usually applied to Protestants in Catholic territories, it was also used in the opposite circumstances and came to mean Christians with radical beliefs in either context.

nonconformist   Originally, one who adhered to the doctrines but not the practices of the Church of England; later, a member of a Church that is independent of the Church of England (such as the Presbyterian Church, Congregational Union and Methodist Church).

nonjuror   One who refuses to take an oath; specifically, a clergyman who, after 1688, refused to take the Oaths of Supremacy and Allegiance to William and Mary and their heirs, and to disavow the Stuart claim to the monarchy.

novice   In religion, a person who is a candidate for admission to a religious order, before taking the required vows and becoming a full member.

oblate   Originally, a boy presented by his parents to a monastery to be brought up there; later, one dedicated to monastic or religious life, often a lay person, attached to a religious house and observing its rule but remaining in the secular world. At Westminster Abbey, the name is now given to special lay members of the abbey community formally committed to prayer and worship.

offices   In the Church, the services said at the seven times of day appointed for worship (such as Matins, Vespers and Compline), consisting of psalms, readings from scripture, and prayers.

ordinary   In Church governance, an ecclesiastic having jurisdiction, as of right, over a diocese or a particular church or community.

orphrey   A decorated band applied to a liturgical vestment, such as a cope, or to an altar frontal.

parclose screen   A partition or railing enclosing a space in a church, or separating one area from another.

perambulation   The act of ceremonially walking round a parish to confirm its boundaries and rights, and to confer a blessing on it.

Perpendicular [Rectilinear]   The third and latest style of English Gothic architecture, current between *c.*1375 and *c.*1640; simpler and more austere than the preceding 'Decorated' Gothic style, it is characterized generally by panel-like decoration created by pronounced vertical and horizontal elements, flattened arches and fan vaulting. Henry VII's chapel in Westminster Abbey is a spectacular example of Perpendicular architecture.

pier   In church architecture, a free-standing solid stone pillar supporting an arch, as in an arcade.

pluralist   A member of the clergy who holds multiple livings simultaneously.

polyphony   Music in multiple (usually four or more) voice-parts, notably where all or several of the parts move to some extent independently.

portal   A doorway of monumental character, elaborated with architectural elements and often extensive sculptural decoration to make it a prominent feature or the main focus of a façade.

praemunire   The offence of asserting or resorting to foreign jurisdiction, especially that of the pope, in England.

prebendary   The holder of a cathedral or collegiate 'prebend' – a benefice that provided an income from an estate or parish. After the Reformation, the collegiate body at Westminster Abbey consisted of the dean and twelve prebendaries; as a result of Section I of the Ecclesiastical Commission Act of 1840, the abbey's use of the term 'prebendary' was changed to 'canon'.

precentor   Generally, one who leads or directs the singing in church; specifically, a member of the clergy responsible for choral services in a cathedral or other major church. At Westminster Abbey, the precentor is a minor canon, responsible to the dean for daily worship and special services.

prelate   A high-ranking cleric, such as an archbishop, bishop, abbot or prior.

Presbyterian   A system of Church governance within the Protestant tradition, particularly in Scotland and Ireland, in which no authority higher than that of 'presbyter' or elder is recognized. Congregations are governed by their minister and elders, and are answerable, through local bodies called presbyteries, to the synod and (in most Presbyterian Churches) to the General Assembly of the Church.

priest   In episcopal Churches, an ordained person authorized to administer the sacraments.

prior   In monastic communities: (i) The deputy head of an abbey, responsible under the abbot for the routine management of the community. (ii) The head of a priory, a subordinate monastery under the authority of the abbey that had founded it, or an independent monastery, often of modest size.

Protestant   One who, either individually or as a member of a particular Christian Church or body, does not adhere to the beliefs and doctrines of the Roman Catholic Church; Protestantism was instituted by the Reformation of the 16th century, though the term was not understood in the modern sense until the reign of Mary I (r. 1553–8).

province   In the Church of England, the area of jurisdiction of an archbishop; there are two provinces in England – Canterbury and York.

Puritan   The name given to English Protestants of the late 16th and 17th centuries, who believed the reformation of the Church in England to be incomplete, and sought further reforms of liturgy, ceremonies and, in some cases, Church governance.

quire   The proper name, at Westminster Abbey, for the CHOIR.

Rayonnant (Fr. lit.: 'radiant', 'radiating')   A style of Gothic architecture, prevalent in France from *c.*1230 to the mid-14th century, characterized by the radiating tracery of rose windows, and vault-ribs spreading out from the piers.

rector   In the Church, a priest who held a parish living and received all the income derived from its tithes and lands; the title survives in parishes where this was once the case. Corporate bodies such as monasteries or colleges could be given rectories and thus gain the rights corporately for themselves. Cf. VICAR.

refectory   In monastic communities, the dining-hall. At Westminster Abbey, the refectory (no longer in existence) was entered from the south cloister.

Reformation Although earlier figures had sought to reform the doctrines and practices of the Roman Catholic Church, the religious movement known as 'the Reformation' is usually considered to have originated in Germany with Martin Luther's publication of his Ninety-Five Theses in 1517. In England, the separation of the Church from papal authority was marked by the Act of Supremacy (1534), which made Henry VIII (r. 1509–47) the supreme head on earth of the Church of England. The English Reformation was briefly suppressed under Mary I (r. 1553–8) but permanently reinstated under Elizabeth I (r. 1558–1603).

reredos An ornamental screen or facing of stone or wood that covers the wall behind an altar; it is usually free-standing.

retable A screen set on or behind an altar, often richly decorated or carved. The Westminster Retable, a 13th-century panel painting, originally stood on three legs behind the high altar; it is now displayed in The Queen's Diamond Jubilee Galleries.

retrochoir In a large church, the parts beyond (i.e. east of) the reredos or retable, behind the high altar. At Westminster Abbey, St Edward the Confessor's Chapel, the radial chapels around the ambulatory and Henry VII's chapel form the retrochoir.

rib A moulded length of stone that helps to support the panels or 'webs' that make up a vault, and also conceals the intersections between them.

Romanesque An architectural style heavily influenced by late Roman and Byzantine buildings, which developed in Western Europe from c.800 and came to maturity in the 11th and 12th centuries. It is characterized by small windows, round-headed arches and the survival of the Roman basilican structure – that is, a central nave, flanked by aisles, with a clerestory and an apsidal end.

rood A cross, specifically the cross on which Jesus died, and hence a three-dimensional representation of Jesus hanging on the cross – a crucifix. In large churches, a rood, in wood or metal, was erected on a beam or in the centre of the screen dividing the nave from the chancel ('rood screen').

rose window A circular Gothic window, with tracery radiating from the centre to form a flower-like design. The north and south transepts of Westminster Abbey have rose windows.

royal peculiar In the Church of England, a church exempt from episcopal jurisdiction and subject only to the monarch. Westminster Abbey is one of the two best-known royal peculiars (the other is St George's Chapel, Windsor).

sacrarium In Westminster Abbey, the space in front of the high altar to the east of the crossing.

sacrist An official in charge of the sacred vessels, vestments, relics and other material treasures and possessions of a church.

sanctuary (i) The area around and in front of the high altar in the chancel of a church. At Westminster Abbey, this space is properly called the 'sacrarium'. (ii) The immunity from arrest (finally abolished only in 1624), within the precincts of a church or other sacred place, afforded to a fugitive from justice or a debtor. At Westminster, the term 'Sanctuary' is reserved for the area outside and to the west of the abbey, adjoining Broad Sanctuary.

screen A permanent partition of decorated wood, stone or metal, separating one area of a church from another (such as the screen between the nave and chancel, or between a chapel and an aisle), and having one or more openings to allow access.

scriptorium A room or area in a monastery dedicated to the writing and copying of manuscript texts.

see The seat (Latin *cathedra* – hence 'cathedral') of a bishop or archbishop, situated in or comprising the town or city after which his office is named; by extension, the area of jurisdiction of a bishop or archbishop, and in this sense synonymous with DIOCESE.

Solemn League and Covenant Primarily, an agreement, made in 1643, that pledged to 'bring the Churches of God in the three kingdoms [England, Scotland and Ireland] to the nearest conjunction and uniformity in religion'; it was both a military league and a religious covenant.

sub-dean In a collegiate church, a member of the clergy who acts as deputy to the dean.

Test Act An act passed in 1673 that enforced on any person filling a public office the obligations of swearing allegiance to the monarch as Supreme Governor of the Church of England, subscribing to a declaration against the Roman Catholic doctrine of transubstantiation, and receiving the sacrament of Holy Communion in the Church of England after taking office.

thegn In Anglo-Saxon England, one who held lands directly from a king or nobleman in return for service (usually military service); a king's thegn was roughly equivalent to a baron in the post-Conquest period and a thegn to a knight.

tithe A tenth of annual produce or income, which by King Edgar's command was from the late 10th century paid by the residents of a parish as a tax for the support of its church and clergy.

tracery Interlaced patterns of stone bars or ribs in the upper part of a Gothic window, where they link the stone members ('mullions') that divide up the opening vertically. The spaces between the mullions and within the tracery are glazed.

Tractarian An adherent of a movement named after a series of pamphlets on theological topics, known as 'Tracts for the Times', published at Oxford from 1833 to 1841. Also known as the Oxford Movement, the Tractarians sought to combat liberalism by reasserting the authority of the Church. For many, this meant a return to medieval practice; for some – including John Henry Newman – it resulted in conversion to Roman Catholicism. An increasingly powerful tendency within the Church of England, the Tractarians were highly controversial and often opposed by Evangelicals and liberals alike.

transept In a cruciform (cross-shaped) church, the arms of the cross, at right angles to the main body of the church; the transept has the nave to the west and the choir to the east. The two main axes of the building intersect at the crossing.

trefoil An ornamental motif, resembling a clover leaf, consisting of three lobes (or 'foils'), separated by pointed projections ('cusps'); a trefoil arch is a pointed arch containing such a three-lobed figure.

tribune In church architecture, a gallery, usually intended for seating, constructed over the aisles of the nave.

triforium In larger Romanesque and Gothic churches, an aisle with its own arcade, above the nave arcade and below the clerestory – that is, the second of the three tiers of the interior elevation of the nave; some churches have a triforium in other parts as well. Westminster Abbey has a triforium above the nave, transepts, choir and chancel; The Queen's Diamond Jubilee Galleries now occupy the eastern triforium, over the transept and chancel arcades.

trumeau A stone pier that supports the middle of the tympanum above a wide doorway, dividing the doorway in half.

tympanum An area of stonework over an opening (usually a doorway) and contained by an arch above; this face is often enriched with relief sculpture.

undercroft An underground vault or chamber.

Use of Salisbury [Sarum Rite] The distinctive form of service and ritual, a variant of the liturgy of the Western Latin Church, developed at Salisbury in the 11th century. Originally used in the cathedral and diocese of Salisbury, it was widely adopted in England and Scotland, and continued in use until the Reformation.

vault A stone or brick arch, taller than it is wide (or multiple such arches intersecting), covering a space so as to create its ceiling; the arches of the vault spring from piers and may be articulated with ribs. Any space covered in this way is said to be 'vaulted'; any vaulted chamber, especially a CRYPT, may be called a 'vault'. In the nave of a church, the bays of the vault continue those of the elevation, so that the building is divided laterally into units of repeating design.

vicar (from Latin *vicarius*: 'substitute') A priest appointed to a parish living appropriated to a corporate religious body (such as a monastery or a college), where most of the tithes were retained by the corporate holder of the rectory of the living or its revenues; the title survives in parishes where this was once the case, and in some more recent parishes. Where monastic possessions devolved to the crown at the Dissolution, the tithes were retained by the crown or sold off, often to local landowners. Cf. RECTOR.

vigil In a liturgical sense, the eve of a saint's feast day or a festival of the Church, marked by devotional watching, prayer and other religious observance.

west end The westernmost part of the body of the church, including the main door; the term refers particularly to the external façade, which, in Romanesque and Gothic buildings (including Westminster Abbey) usually has towers to either side and is embellished with sculpture.

Abbreviations

ACC	Alcuin Club Collections	*CSPD*	*Calendar of State Papers, Domestic Series*, ed. R. Lemon, M. A. E. Green, W. J. Hardy *et al.* (1856–)
ADC	*Acts of the Dean and Chapter of Westminster, 1543–1609, and 1609–62*, ed. C. S. Knighton, Westminster Abbey Record Series 1–2, 4 (1997–9, 2006)	*CSPSpan*	*Calendar of Letters, Despatches, and State Papers, relating to the Negotiations between England and Spain, Preserved in the Archives of Simancas and elsewhere*, ed. G. A. Bergenroth, P. De Gayangos *et al.* (1862–1954)
AH	*Architectural History*		
AJ	*Archaeological Journal*		
ANS	*Anglo-Norman Studies*		
APC	*Acts of the Privy Council of England*, new series, ed. J. R. Dasent (1890–1907)	*CSPVen*	*Calendar of State Papers and Manuscripts, relating to English Affairs, existing in the Archives and Collections of Venice and in other Libraries of Northern Italy*, ed. R. Brown, H. F. Brown and A. B. Hinds (1864–1940)
Arch.	*Archaeologia*		
ASE	*Anglo-Saxon England*		
BAACT	British Archaeological Association Conference Transactions	CUL	Cambridge University Library
BAR	British Archaeological Reports	*EHR*	*English Historical Review*
BIHR	*Bulletin of the Institute of Historical Research*	*ESTC*	*English Short Title Catalogue* <estc.bl.uk/>
BJRL	*Bulletin of the John Rylands Library*	GHL	Guildhall Library, London
BL	British Library	*Hansard*	*Hansard's Parliamentary Debates*, series 1–5 (1803–)
CCR	*Calendar of the Close Rolls Preserved in the Public Record Office*, 47 vols (1892–1963)	HBS	Henry Bradshaw Society
		HJ	*Historical Journal*
CH	*Court Historian*	HLRO	House of Lords Record Office
CJ	*Journals of the House of Commons*	HMC	Historical Manuscripts Commission
CLR	*Calendar of the Liberate Rolls . . . : Henry III* (1916–64)	HMC, 'Statutes'	'Statutes of the Collegiate Church of St. Peter in Westminster', in HMC, *Appendix to the First Report* (1854), 80–108
CM	*Church Monuments*		
CPR	*Calendar of the Patent Rolls Preserved in the Public Record Office* (1891–)	*HR*	*Historical Research*
CS	Camden Society	*JBAA*	*Journal of the British Archaeological Association*

JBS	*Journal of British Studies*	RHS	Royal Historical Society
JEH	*Journal of Ecclesiastical History*	*ROW*	*The Record of Old Westminsters:*
JSAH	*Journal of the Society of Architectural Historians*		*A Biographical List of All Those who are Known to have been Educated*
LC	WAL, Langley Collection		*at Westminster School,* comp. G. F.
LJ	*Journals of the House of Lords*		Russell Barker *et al.* (1928–)
LMA	London Metropolitan Archives	RS	Rolls Series
LP	*Letters and Papers, Foreign and Domestic, of the Reign of Henry VIII,* ed. J. S. Brewer, J. Gairdner and R. H. Brodie (1862–1932)	S	P. Sawyer, *Anglo-Saxon Charters: An Annotated List and Bibliography,* RHS Guides and Handbooks 8; rev. and updated online edn at <www.esawyer.org.uk>
LPL	Lambeth Palace Library, London		
LRS	London Record Society	*SR*	*Sociological Review*
NC	*Nineteenth Century*	TNA	The National Archives
NDWA	Notes and Documents relating to Westminster Abbey	*VCH*	*Victoria History of the Counties of England*
NRS	Northamptonshire Record Society	WAC	Westminster Archives Centre
ODNB	*Oxford Dictionary of National Biography* <oxforddnb.com>	WA Commission	Westminster Abbey Commission
		WAL	Westminster Abbey Library
PH	*Parliamentary History*	WAM	Westminster Abbey Muniments
PP	*Parliamentary Papers*	WAOP	Westminster Abbey Occasional Papers
PRO	Public Record Office		
r.	*rex* ('king') / *regina* ('queen'), indicating regnal dates	*WAR*	*Westminster Abbey Review*
		WCA	Westminster City Archives

Notes

INTRODUCTION

1 Pearson 1957, 128.
2 K. Clark 1972, 258.

CHAPTER 1: c.604–c.1100

This chapter draws heavily on material prepared by Professor Simon Keynes, and I am greatly obliged to him for allowing me to make use of it. I am also very grateful to Professor Paul Binski for giving me access to a draft of his own contribution to this volume, and for allowing me to transfer and adopt material from it relating to Edward the Confessor's church. I am indebted, too, to Dr Tony Trowles and Matthew Payne, respectively the Librarian and the Keeper of the Muniments at Westminster Abbey, who read this chapter in draft and made invaluable suggestions for its improvement, and to Dr Warwick Rodwell for information on archaeological excavations in and around the abbey. Errors of fact and interpretation that remain are my sole responsibility.

1 Whitelock *et al.* (eds) 1961, 138–9 (citing text C of the Anglo-Saxon Chronicle; the account of the consecration occurs in texts C and D).
2 Edward was called 'the Confessor' – a title given to men and women who had led holy lives – to distinguish him from his father's half-brother, King Edward 'the Martyr', who was regarded as a saint because of the violence of his death.
3 J.A. Robinson (ed.) 1909, 34–5.
4 Scholz 1964, 82–5.
5 Colgrave and Mynors (eds) 1969, 142–3.
6 Naismith 2019 provides a comprehensive review of the evidence relating to Anglo-Saxon London. For Westminster see Rosser 1989.
7 Sawyer 1968 [hereafter S] 124.
8 Cf. Genesis 28:17 (Vulgate): 'Quam terribilis est […] locus iste.' The phrase, which Jacob uses to describe the place where he dreams of a ladder from earth to heaven, is translated in the Authorized Version of the Bible as 'How dreadful is this place!'.
9 Blair 1996.
10 Dunning and Evison 1961; Cowie and Blackmore 2008, 90–100 ('U3' is the name assigned to the wooden hall). The Westminster Sword is displayed in the Jewel Tower.
11 For forgery see Clanchy 1993, 318–27; Crick 2003.
12 S 670.
13 Scholz 1964.
14 Authoritatively discussed in Blair 2005.
15 Bloch (ed.) 1923, 83–4.
16 S 670.
17 Winterbottom and Thomson (eds) 2007, I, 280–81.
18 S 753, S 1451, S 1450, S 1447, S 702.
19 British Library, London, Add. MS 37517, available through the 'Digitised Manuscripts' section of the British Library website. See also Breay and Story (eds) 2018, no. 92.
20 For Dunstan's involvement in the monastic reform movement, and his other activities, see Winterbottom and Lapidge (eds) 2012, pp. xli–li, esp. pp. xlvii–xlviii.
21 S 876; Keynes 2013, 108–16.
22 S 894, in WAM, Muniment book XI, f. 77r–v, which includes a witness list omitted from the printed edition; B.F. Harvey 1977, 22–3.
23 S 903.
24 S 1487 (Ælfhelm), S 1522 (Leofwine).
25 Williams and Martin (eds) 1992, 378.
26 J.A. Robinson (ed.) 1909, 70.
27 Mason 1996, 11–12.
28 For a full account of Edward's life see Barlow 1997.
29 Wilson 1985 provides an excellent reproduction of the Bayeux Tapestry, with commentary.
30 Barlow (ed.) 1992; Licence 2016.
31 Keynes and Love 2010, 196.
32 Pratt forthcoming; Breay and Story (eds) 2018, no. 118 (Anderson Pontifical).

33 Breay and Story (eds) 2018, cat. no. 119 (Old English coronation oath); Clayton 2008.

34 Whitelock *et al.* (eds) 1961, 107 (texts C and E).

35 Barlow (ed.) 1992, 66–9.

36 Scholz 1964, 90–91.

37 S 1031; Keynes (ed.) 1991, no. 22.

38 B. F. Harvey 1977, 24.

39 Ibid., 27, 335–64, 471–4 (maps).

40 D. Knowles 1963, 702–3; Mason 1996, 16–17, suggests a net yearly income for Westminster of £511.

41 E. H. Pearce 1916, 41.

42 Henig 2015.

43 Rodwell 2015, 49–53. Dr Rodwell has been generous in supplying information about recent excavations.

44 Gem 1980, 38–9, lists the monastic buildings attributed to the Confessor in the mid-thirteenth-century *Estoire de Seint Aeduuard le rei* ('Life of St Edward the king').

45 Rodwell *et al.* 2006; Miles and Bridge 2010.

46 Barlow (ed.) 1992, 70–3.

47 Ibid., 68–71.

48 Mynors *et al.* (eds) 1998–9, I, 418–19, II, 214; Winterbottom and Thomson (eds) 2007, I, 224–5, II, 89.

49 Fernie 1983, 154–7, 161; Musset 1985, 61–125.

50 The west towers, which preceded the present ones, appear to have been constructed in the early twelfth century, Tatton-Brown 1995, 173–5.

51 S 1131; Harmer (ed.) 1952, no. 87; Gem 2009, 169–70.

52 For Edward's church see esp. Gem 1980; see also Binski 1995, 12 (a plan of Edward's church superimposed on one of Henry III's); Fernie 2000, 96–8; Rodwell 2009.

53 Madden (ed.) 1866–9, III, 294–5.

54 Luard (ed.) 1858, 90, line 2293.

55 Gem 1980, 36.

56 E. Carpenter and Gentleman 1987, 24. The drawing shows the nave completed as far as the west end, though in fact it would appear that building works of some kind were still in progress there.

57 Gem 1980, 44–6.

58 Page 1923, 128–9, 279–80.

59 Barlow (ed.) 1992, 70; Gem 1980, 35–6.

60 Summerson 2010, 177.

61 S 1041, S 1043.

62 Summerson 2010, 177.

63 Barlow (ed.) 1992, 112–15.

64 Ibid., 124–5.

65 Ibid., 126–7.

66 Naismith 2017, 276–7; Whitelock *et al.* (eds) 1961, 140 (texts C and D).

67 Williams and Martin (eds) 1992, 980; S 1043.

68 Whitelock *et al.* (eds) 1961, 144–5. There is some uncertainty as to the identity of the prelate who crowned William. The fact that the version of the Anglo-Saxon Chronicle cited here, known as text D, originated in Ealdred's entourage, suggests that it is likely to be correct on this point.

69 Garnett 1998, 68–71.

70 Bates (ed.) 1998, nos 290–336, pp. 870–973; Harrison and McNeill 2015, 93–4; Bates 2016, 409.

71 Bates (ed.) 1998, no. 292, p. 883. S 1140 contains Edward's original grant.

72 Winterbottom and Thomson (eds) 2007, I, 224–7.

73 Bates 2016, 291–4.

74 Bates (ed.) 1998, no. 181, pp. 594–601.

75 Bates 2016, 383–4.

76 Biddle 1986.

77 Barlow (ed.) 1992, 116–25.

78 Whitelock *et al.* (eds) 1961, 177 (text E); Hollister 2001, 126–30.

79 Hollister 2001, 276–9; Green 2006, 164–7.

80 Mynors *et al.* (eds), I, 414–17, 758–61.

81 Freeland (trans.) 2005, 121–2.

82 Ibid., 200–09, esp. 207–9.

83 Luard (ed.) 1858, 128, 133, 287; D. Carpenter 2007, 885–90.

84 Fernie 1993, 135–6, and table 1, at 138.

85 Greenway 1996, 446–7 (Rufus's comment).

CHAPTER 2: 1100–1307

1 J. A. Robinson (ed.) 1909, 63.

2 *Annales de Waverleia*, for the year 1099, in Luard (ed.) 1865, 208; *Annales Londonienses*, in Stubbs (ed.) 1882, 22.

3 J. A. Robinson (ed.) 1909, 82, 88.

4 Mason (ed.) 1988, nos 4–38, esp. 22.

5 Ibid., nos. 58–71.

6 Ibid., nos 57, 123, 154.

7 Chaplais 1962; Brooke 1971.

8 The greatest social history of the monastery is B. F. Harvey 1993, at 2–3 for the early size of the community; see also E. H. Pearce 1916. For the numbers of monks in other communities at the turn of the 12th to the 13th centuries see Knowles and Hadcock 1971, pp. 61, 64–6, 72, 74–5, 80–81.

9 For the stalls and their 13th-century textile decorations see Binski 1991.

10 Kemp 1947 is the usual starting point.

11 Barlow 1970, 254, 263–4, 267–9; Scholz 1961, 46; Gem 1980, 36.

12 Scholz 1961.

13　. . . *et specialis sancta Romanae ecclesiae filia*, ibid., 44.

14　Ibid., 53; for an English rendition of Ailred's Life see Bertram (trans.) 1990.

15　These reforms were the subject of the Third and Fourth Lateran Councils (1179 and 1215).

16　Lehmann-Brockhaus 1955–60, no. 2522; Barlow 1970, 262–6; Draper 1984.

17　Cheney 1951–2.

18　Lehmann-Brockhaus 1955–60, no. 2588.

19　Woodman 2015.

20　Smalley 1973; Binski 2004.

21　Cheney 1967, 135–57; Tatton-Brown 2000, 19–28; Binski 2004, 35–6.

22　Mason (ed.) 1988, nos. 173–84.

23　Luard (ed.) 1872–83, III, 75.

24　For the larger history of Westminster at this time see Rosser 1989.

25　Colvin (ed.) 1963, 131; Lehmann-Brockhaus 1955–60, nos 2668–9; Binski 1995, 10–13; Binski 2004, 62–4.

26　D. A. Carpenter 2007.

27　CUL, MS Ee.3.59: see Luard (ed.) 1858; for a new textual edition see Fenster and Wogan Browne (trans.) 2008; for a discussion in context see Binski 1995, 52–63; and for its authorship see Binski 1991. An interactive digital facsimile of the manuscript is available at <https://cudl.lib.cam.ac.uk/view/MS-EE-00003-00059/1>.

28　Lehmann-Brockhaus 1955–60, no. 2504 (Edward and St Peter), no. 2728 (Henry and St Edward).

29　Luard (ed.) 1858, 90, at line 2301.

30　Lehmann-Brockhaus 1955–60, nos 2713–14; *CCR 1237–42*, 305; *CLR 1240–45*, 83–4, 134. The standard documentary survey remains Colvin (ed.) 1963, 130–57; see also Binski 1995; C. Wilson 2008.

31　Colvin (ed.) 1963, 133–6.

32　Stubbs (ed.) 1879, 5–6.

33　*CCR 1242–7*, 279; *1247–51*, 409.

34　*CCR 1242–7*, 344.

35　Binski 1995; C. Wilson 2008.

36　Branner 1964; Branner 1965; Binski 1995, 33–43.

37　Binski 1995, 35–6.

38　Wilson in C. Wilson *et al.* 1986, 37–9; Binski 1995.

39　Binski 1995, 45–6.

40　Ibid., 27–8.

41　Rodwell and Mortimer (eds) 2010.

42　D. Carpenter 2010.

43　C. Wilson 2010.

44　Binski 1995, 76–7; D. Carpenter 2010.

45　Colvin (ed.) 1963, 494–500; Binski 1986.

46　For a full account see Binski and Massing (eds) 2009.

47　*CCR 1247–51*, 343.

48　N. Vincent 2002.

49　J. A. Robinson (ed.) 1909, 18–21, 68–73, 74–5.

50　For a comprehensive study see N. Vincent 2001; see also Bynum 2007.

51　Ibid., 9.

52　Ibid.; see also Binski 1995, 141–5.

53　N. Vincent 2001, 86–117.

54　Binski and Guerry 2015, 185–95.

55　The relics were given by St Edward and Henry III (as reported by Flete, see J. A. Robinson (ed.) 1909, 70–71) and thus had special eminence. For further reflections on the relics see Milner 2016. St Thomas's arm is included in the 1469 shrine-keeper's inventory in WAM 9477, as Julian Luxford has kindly pointed out to us.

56　Colvin (ed.) 1971, 196.

57　D. Carpenter 2002, 42–4.

58　Scott *et al.* 1863, 114.

59　Lehmann-Brockhaus 1955–60, nos 2810–14.

60　*CPR 1266–72*, 50, 52, 61, 64–5, 69, 133, 241, 252, 280, 288, 324, 340, 347, 362.

61　*CCR 1268–72*, 66.

62　Lehmann-Brockhaus 1955–60, nos. 2819–21; WAM Book 11, ff. 390, 394r–v.

63　For the painted *capse* or coffin see Colvin (ed.) 1971, 428–9.

64　Barlow 1970, 283.

65　Lehmann-Brockhaus 1955–60, no. 2821.

66　D. Carpenter 2002, 45–6.

67　Lehmann-Brockhaus 1955–60, no. 2819; for the dedication and indulgences see WAM Book 11, ff. 390, 394r–v.

68　Lehmann-Brockhaus 1955–60, no. 2866.

69　N. Vincent 2002, 28; for Henry's burial see D. A. Carpenter 1996, 427–59.

70　Lehmann-Brockhaus 1955–60, nos 2523, 2564–7; for Sæberht see ibid., no. 2986.

71　For the charter effecting Henry III's decision, made six years after the dedication of the Temple church, see WAM 6318A. For the mausoleum see Binski 1995, 90–118; see also Palliser 2004; W. C. Jordan 2009, 100–18.

72　The most accessible general guide to royal tombs and monuments from 1066 to 1485 remains Colvin (ed.) 1963, 477–86.

73　For what follows see Binski 1990; Gardner 1990; Binski 1995, 95–104; Binski 2002. For an alternative opinion on the chronology of the Cosmati see D. A. Carpenter 1996, 409–25.

74　Colvin (ed.) 1963, 479–85.

75 Binski 1995, 107–20.
76 The standard survey is Claussen 1987; see also Binski 1990; Gardner 1990; Binski 1995, 95–104; Binski 2002.
77 Glass 1980, pls. 20, 24, 49, and commentaries at 87, 92, 138; Gardner 1990, 202 n. 7.
78 Richard of Ware did not achieve high office until 1280, three years before his death. He was appointed royal treasurer and was almost immediately caught in a protracted dispute with the Archbishop of Canterbury; see W. C. Jordan, 2009, 180, 185–99.
79 Thompson (ed.) 1902–4.
80 Powicke 1962, 180, 195, 199, 681.
81 CPR 1266–72, 2; Colvin (ed.) 1971, 420–21; for the circumstances see Bolgia 2017, 252–4.
82 Colvin (ed.) 1971, 422–3, 426–7.
83 See the ingenious account by David Howlett of the inscription's numerology in Howlett 2002.
84 The literature is considerable but see principally J. W. Legg (ed.) 1900; L. G. Legg 1901; H. G. Richardson 1960. See also Binski 1995, 126–140; Binski 1997.
85 Wilson 2008, 63.
86 Lehmann-Brockhaus 1955–60, nos 2860–63.
87 Colvin (ed.) 1963, 370–71; Binski 1995, 104–7.
88 For the documentary and stylistic background see Binski 2003. For a general account see Rodwell et al. 2013.
89 On which see D. A. Carpenter 1996, 448–56.
90 For internationalist overviews see Bony 1979; Binski 2014.
91 Scholz 1964, 80–91.
92 Gransden 1974, 420, 453–6, 460.
93 For an extended comparison of the two monasteries see W. C. Jordan 2009.
94 Annales Londonienses, in Stubbs (ed.) 1882, 58; J. A. Robinson (ed.) 1909, 117; B. F. Harvey 1977, 51; Colvin (ed.) 1963, 498, 513.
95 Rosser 1989, 229–30 at 230.
96 Robertson (ed.) 1877, 261–4.
97 Winston Churchill, House of Commons (meeting in the House of Lords), 28 October 1943, Hansard, 5th ser. (1909–), vol. 393, cc. 403–73.
98 Rigold 1976, 6.

CHAPTER 3: 1307–1534

1 Prestwich 1997, 558, 566.
2 Luard (ed.) 1890, 140; E. H. Pearce 1916, 61.
3 WAM 12854; E. H. Pearce 1916, 51.
4 WAM 6318B.
5 WAM 12201.
6 CPR 1301–7, pp. 194–5.
7 Luard (ed.) 1872–83, v, 228, 230, 238, 611; W. C. Jordan 2009, 36–7.
8 B. F. Harvey (ed.) 1965, 8.
9 CPR 1307–13, p. 34; WAM 5460.
10 WAM 4495; E. H. Pearce 1916, 74–5.
11 WAM 22533; E. H. Pearce 1916, 74.
12 Stubbs (ed.) 1882, 255–370 at 261
13 Riley (ed.) 1867–9, II, 119, 123–4; Haines 2003, 242; Andrews 2006, 29–30, 53; Gransden 2015, 83–4.
14 WAM 5460; E. H. Pearce 1916, 61, 73–4.
15 Page (ed.) 1909, 433–57 at 442.
16 Ibid.; CPR 1343–5, p. 502.
17 WAM 5430, 12192; E. H. Pearce, 1916, 75.
18 Rodwell et al. 2013, 21.
19 B. F. Harvey 1977, 133.
20 In particular, Kelvedon, Essex; Paddington, Middlesex; Sawbridgeworth, Hertfordshire; Morden, Surrey; and Longdon, Worcestershire. Ibid., 407–12.
21 CPR 1343–5, p. 281; E. H. Pearce 1916, 84.
22 J. A. Robinson (ed.) 1909, 125.
23 For Hurley see Page (ed.) 1909, 442. For Abbot Henley's and monastic reform see J. A. Robinson (ed.) 1909, 126; Pantin (ed.) 1931–7, II, 5–18; III, 259.
24 Thompson (ed.) 1902–4, II, pp. vi–vii.
25 Ibid., 246.
26 Ibid., 241–3.
27 Ibid., 239–43.
28 Ibid., 187.
29 J. A. Robinson (ed.) 1909, 126.
30 die noctuque, Thompson (ed.) 1902–4, II, 46.
31 Ibid., 232.
32 Bowers 2003, 36.
33 Music à la mode was an interest that Edward II and Isabella shared, and it was passed on to their son, Edward III; J. S. Hamilton 2006, 8–9; Ormrod 2012, 70.
34 Bowers 2003, 16.
35 Ibid., 50.
36 Allmand 1992, 411. It has been suggested that there was greater momentum in the cultivation of music at the abbey from the moment of his accession; Bowers, 2003, 43.
37 Bowers 2003, 52.
38 Ormrod 2012, 56–7.
39 WAM 6300**; E. H. Pearce 1916, 84.
40 Tait (ed.) 1914, 120.
41 Ibid., 153.

42 Edward III kept two 'closets' – enclosures that provided him with private accommodation at the high altar: Monnas 2004, 195; Ormrod 2012, 99–102, 465–6, 628–31 (itinerary in the decade 1367–77).

43 Ormrod, 2012, 582

44 Colvin (ed.) 1963, 486–7; Binski 1995, 195–9.

45 In his will, Edward the Black Prince expressed a special devotion to the Trinity – the dedication of Canterbury cathedral – and the cult of Thomas Becket; Palliser 2004, 10.

46 Maddicott 1970, 53–4.

47 Page (ed.) 1909, 566–71; Colvin (ed.) 1963, 510–25; Goodall 2015, 111–19.

48 J. A. Robinson (ed.) 1909, 101–2.

49 Page (ed.) 1909, 566–7; B. F. Harvey 1977, 92.

50 E. H. Pearce 1916, 83–4.

51 *ut forte sibi nomen acquireret ac beneficia pinguiora, plus omnibus et frequentius laboravit*, Tait (ed.) 1914, 127.

52 W. C. Jordon 2009, 183–4, 219.

53 E. H. Pearce 1916, 92–3; 'Langham, Simon (d. 1376)', *ODNB*.

54 E. H. Pearce 1916, 84–5.

55 WAM 5446.

56 Howgrave-Graham 1948; Wilson in C. Wilson *et al.* 1986, 82–5; Binski 1995, 205–6.

57 B. F. Harvey 1977, 133.

58 WAM 9470–9471; WAM, Memorandum book I, *Liber niger*, f. 85v; E. H. Pearce 1916, 86.

59 E. H. Pearce 1916, 95; Pantin (ed.) 1931–7, III, 76.

60 Pantin (ed.) 1931–7, III, 76–7 at 77.

61 Colchester presided at provincial chapters in 1393, 1411 and 1420, and at general chapters in 1396, 1412 and 1414–17; Ibid., III, 259–61 at 260–61.

62 WAM, Memorandum book I, *Liber niger*, f. 330.

63 In 1392 William Colchester purchased a suite of rooms at Oxford that had been cast off by the monks of Canterbury; Sheppard 1887–9, III. 14.

64 B. F. Harvey 1971, 108–30 at 112–13.

65 E. H. Pearce 1916, 92

66 Ibid., 100.

67 For the text of Richard's *Speculum* see Mayor (ed.) 1863–9. For the Westminster chronicle see Gransden 1982, 157 and n.; Hector and Harvey (eds), 1982, pp. xxxi–xxxiv.

68 R. Sharpe *et al.* (eds), 1996, B105, 613–25 at 615–25.

69 E. H. Pearce 1916, 113; B. F. Harvey 1971, 125. William Sudbury's text survives uniquely in a late fifteenth-century copy commissioned by Abbot John Eastney (1474–98), now Longleat House, Marquess of Bath MS 38, ff. 256v–308r; N. Vincent 2001, 124.

70 E. H. Pearce 2016, 116.

71 J. W. Legg (ed.) 1891–7.

72 Pantin (ed.) 1931–7, III. 76–7 at 77.

73 The incident was described by an unnamed monk of St Albans abbey in attendance as proxy for his own abbot; Riley (ed.) 1870–71, I, 414–17.

74 Saul 1997, 24–6; Hector and Harvey (eds), 1982, 414–17.

75 Hector and Harvey (eds), 1982, 450–51, 454–5, 509–11.

76 Gordon *et al.* (eds) 1997.

77 Hector and Harvey (eds), 1982, 154–7.

78 Ibid., 22–5.

79 Ibid., 378–9, 380–81.

80 Ibid., 176–7.

81 Mayor (ed.), 1863–9, II, 26–39 at 26–7; Eberle 1999, 239.

82 Saul 1997, 412, 414.

83 Saul 1996, 201–2; Saul 1997, 312–13, 461.

84 Saul 1996, 200–04.

85 Howgrave-Graham 1948, 60–78; C. Wilson *et al.* 1986, 82–5; Binski 1995, 205–6.

86 Colvin (ed.) 1963, 487–8; Binski 1995, 199–202.

87 Colvin (ed.) 1963, 527–33; C. Wilson 1997.

88 Saul, 1997, 306–9.

89 Binski 1995, 202–4; Alexander 1997, 197–206.

90 Thompson (ed.), 1902–4, II, 227.

91 For example, WAM, Memorandum book I, *Liber niger*, §388, where he is named as John Murymuth. See also Barron 2014, 39.

92 Rosser 1989, 276.

93 Henry VII's prescription for the clergy required to conduct his commemoration was very precise: a graduate clerk was to preach the weekly sermon; university-educated monks were to serve in the chantry; and a *conversus* or lay brother of the monastery was to join the observance in the Lady Chapel. Copycat commemorations across the country were to be carried out by representatives of every order of religious – monks, canons and friars; Condon 2003a, 64, 86, 95.

94 Harvey 1993, 149–53 at 153, 164; Rosser 1989, 204–6.

95 The monks claimed that the right of sanctuary had been granted to them by the Saxon monarchy, but in reality it was a customary claim that carried a much more powerful charge when the church came to be crowded by public affairs; McSheffrey 2017, 27–35.

96 *dum evangelium a diacono legeretur*, J. A. Robinson (ed.) 1909, 136–7. The claim that Tresilian was in sanctuary at the point of capture was disputed; Hector and Harvey (eds) 1982, 310–13; McSheffey 2017, 30–32.

97 WAM 23455; J. H. Harvey 1956, 82–101 at 86.

98 WAM 9485.

99 For example, John Murymuth (*c.*1349–1393/4) presented an image for the altar of St Benedict; Roger Kirton (*c.*1385–1434) set up and furnished an altar for St Michael, St Martin and All Saints; Thomas Penhall furnished the altar of St Thomas Becket; WAM, Memorandum book 1, *Liber niger*, f. 92v; E. H. Pearce 1916, 95, 120–21.

100 Binski and Howard 2010.

101 Saul 1997, 412–18.

102 Given-Wilson 2016, 147–51 at 150–51; C. Wilson 1990, 186.

103 Given-Wilson 2016, 515–17.

104 Strohm, 1996.

105 Allmand 1992, 180–81; Palliser 2004, 14.

106 Strong and Strong 1981, 90–91.

107 P. Lindley 2007, 165, 171.

108 Allmand 1992, 272–8.

109 Taylor and Roskell (eds) 1975, 44–5 and n. 4; Wylie and Waugh 1914–29, II, 42–3; Palliser 2004, 14.

110 The settlement of matters concerning Courtenay appears to have been on the king's mind in drafting his final will in 1421, which includes a now partially illegible reference to debts incurred in this regard; Strong and Strong 1981, 100.

111 Palliser 2004, 14.

112 P. Lindley 2007, 170.

113 The sacrist's inventory for 1479 recorded a sceptre and an antelope, which had been 'stolen away' in the time of Richard Teddington, who had held the sacrist's office a decade before; WAM 9478.

114 P. Lindley 2007, 167.

115 Griffiths 1981, 190; Wolfe 1981, 48–51.

116 E. H. Pearce 1916, 126–7, 129–30, 141–2; Page (ed.) 1909, 446; 'Millyng, Thomas (d. 1492)', *ODNB*.

117 Page (ed.), 1907, II, 103–5; E. H. Pearce 2016, 152.

118 Ross 1997, 73.

119 'The most plausible explanation for [Edward V's] undoubted disappearance is that [he was] murdered on the orders of Richard III, late in the summer of 1483, to try to pre-empt a rising in [his] favour'; R. Horrox, 'Edward V (1470–1483)', *ODNB*.

120 A. F. Sutton and Visser-Fuchs 1990, 80.

121 Ebesham wrote at least four manuscripts, which passed into the abbey library; they contained copies of John Flete's history of the abbey and William Sudbury's treatise on the relic of the Holy Blood; Doyle 1957, 313–21.

122 Goodall 2011, 262–3. For late medieval worshippers, the legend of St Erasmus vividly characterized the power of martyrdom – not only forbearance in the face of torture but also the divine hand that guided their fate; Duffy 1992, 163, 170.

123 WAM, 9485.

124 Goodall, 2011.

125 Condon 2003a, 64.

126 WAM 19659.

127 Geoffrey Chaucer, *The Monk's Tale*, lines 170–71; *The Nun's Priest's Tale*, line 2851.

128 Rosser 1989, 276, 285–93.

129 Anglo 1960, 8.

130 Ibid.

131 Craig 2003.

132 Condon 2003a, 60–61; P. Lindley 2003, 259–64.

133 M. K. Jones and Underwood 1992, 236–7.

134 C. Wilson 1995, 133.

135 P. Lindley, 2003, 268.

136 Condon 2003b, 133.

137 Condon 2003a, 88–9.

138 Ibid., 64, 68.

139 Ibid., 78–82, 95–7.

140 Ibid., 62, 65–6.

141 Together with the dissolved Benedictine priory at Luffield (Buckinghamshire), the value of the endowment was £400; ibid., 61, 83, 89.

142 Ibid., 95.

143 WAM 19837.

144 Hunt, 2008, 28–9.

145 Pearce, 1916, 175; Smyly, 1922.

146 *LP*, II/1, 1153.

147 Hay (ed.) 1950, 258–9.

148 *LP*, III/2, 2030; IV/1, 1244.

149 Widmore 1751, Appendix x, 206–10; St John Hope 1906, 8–9.

150 For example, Humfrey Charity and William Faith, who signed the deed of surrender of the abbey in 1540; John Grace, William Hope and T. Verity, all of whom died after 1535; R. Chrysostom and William Gregory, both of whom died after 1535; and Richard Jerome, who died in the accounting year 1529/30; E. H. Pearce 1916, 185, 187–8, 190.

151 Bowker 1981, 18.

152 *LP*, XIII/2, 905.

153 TNA, SP 1/18, f. 10 (*LP*, III/1, no. 19).

154 Wolsey's advance on the abbey's territory was incremental and initially indirect. In 1520 he purchased from a third party a lease granted by Abbot Islip for five tenements in King Street. Finally, in Islip's lifetime, property on the east side of King Street and on the west as far as Charing Cross was exchanged with the king for the site of Poughley Priory (Berkshire); *LP*, III/1, no. 652; V, no. 404.

CHAPTER 4: 1530–1603

In preparing this account, I acknowledge with gratitude much preliminary scholarly work undertaken by Charles Knighton.

1   Colvin (ed.) 1982, II, 501n.
2   Kisby 1995, 224, 231.
3   Wyatt 2005, 50.
4   MacCulloch 2018, ch. 3.
5   Cobb 1999; Hawkyard 2016, 189–93.
6   Hawkyard 2016, 337–8.
7   MacCulloch 2016, 24.
8   Lehmberg 1970, 43, 45, 174–5, 184; on Benson's promotions see D. M. Smith (ed.) 2008, 43, 80.
9   MacCulloch 2016, 94–5.
10 TNA, SP 1/98, f. 61 (*LP*, IX, no. 683); undated, but probably autumn 1535.
11 TNA, PROB 11/35/520; will made 10 Sept. 1549, proved 23 Sept. 1549.
12 Bourbon 1540, 360 (Book 6, no. 41); 90 (letter from Lyons of 22 Sept. 1536, appended to Book 1, 84–93).
13 Benson to Cromwell, 30 Dec. [1535], TNA, SP 1/99, f. 164 (*LP*, IX, no. 1041).
14 Byrne (ed.) 1981, I, 49; and see the beginning of the dispute, II, no. 994.
15 For Cromwell's efforts at Walsingham see Richard Vowell, Prior of Walsingham, to Cromwell, 12 Aug. [1538], TNA, SP 1/135, f. 78 (*LP*, XIII/2, no. 86); see also MacCulloch 2018, ch. 21.
16 TNA, SP 1/143, f. 202r–v (*LP*, XIV/1, no. 402).
17 Lehmberg 1988, ch. 3; Scarisbrick 1988. The New Foundation cathedrals were Bristol, Canterbury (former cathedral priory), Carlisle (former cathedral priory), Chester, Durham (former cathedral priory), Ely (former cathedral priory), Gloucester, Norwich (former cathedral priory), Osney then Christ Church, Oxford, Peterborough, Rochester (former cathedral priory), Westminster, Winchester (former cathedral priory) and Worcester (former cathedral priory). In Ireland, Christ Church, Dublin (former cathedral priory) was also remodelled.
18 M. de Marillac to Anne de Montmorency, 27 Dec. [1539], Kaulek (ed.) 1885, 148 (*LP*, XIV/ii, no. 744). There is an excellent summary account of this initiative in J. Edwards 2011, 61–2.
19 William Benson, 'Abbot quondam of Westminster', to [Cromwell], undated, TNA, SP 1/157, f. 50 (*LP*, XV, no. 70).
20 Marillac to Montmorency, 1 June 1540, Kaulek (ed.) 1885, 187–9 (*LP*, XV, no. 737).
21 Bourbon 1540, 91: *tuarum virtutum admiratori summo*. Thirlby's surrender of his canonry is noted in the grant to his successor, Richard Cox (also a future Dean of Westminster), 16 Nov. 1540; Cox also succeeded Thirlby as Archdeacon of Ely on the same day, *LP*, XVI, no. 305/48, 49.
22 Marillac to Montmorency, 3 March 1541, Kaulek (ed.) 1885, 274 (*LP*, XVI, no. 590); and see MacCulloch 2018, ch. 23.
23 Lambeth Palace, Cranmer's Register, ff. 141r–146v; *LP*, XV, no. 860; TNA, E 30/1470, ff. 3, 4v (*LP*, XV, no. 861).
24 E. Hall 1904, II, 310. Hall is likely to be more accurate than the French ambassador, who thought that it was a Carthusian who died in his habit: Marillac to the King of France, 6 Aug. 1540, Kaulek (ed.) 1885, 210 (*LP*, XV, no. 953). The Carthusian and the monk of Westminster did die together, as is witnessed in Kingsford (ed.) 1910, 16, though the punctuation there needs to be emended as it runs together the monk and Giles Heron, another victim.
25 Charles Knighton has meticulously reconstructed it from WAM 6478, ff. 1–5.
26 Gorton was dead by 12 July (*LP*, XV, no. 942/73), having only just become parson of Staines, where he was succeeded by Humphrey Perkins, ex-monk and new canon. See Latimer's recommendations to Cromwell, 8 Nov. [1538], BL, MS Cotton Cleopatra E/IV, f. 174 (*LP*, XII/2, no. 1043); mid-Nov. 1538, TNA, SP 1/126, f. 79 (*LP*, XII/2, no. 1044); and Cranmer's (noting Gorton to be of Burton), 15 Aug. [1535], TNA, SP 1/95, f. 81 (*LP*, IX, no. 98).
27 The Cromwellians among the new canons were Simon Haynes, Edward Leighton, Anthony Bellasis and William Bretton.
28 Null 2003.
29 Bindoff (ed.) 1982, I, 143–5.
30 GHL, MS 9531/12, ff. 243–76.
31 TNA, SC 6/Hen.VIII/2421, m. 5; TNA, E 315/104, ff. 77v–81; Tatton-Brown 2007, 3.
32 This was first pointed out long ago by Widmore 1751, 131; see also Field 1987.
33 Memorandum by an unknown author, probably close to the court, TNA, SP 12/107, f. 98 (*CSPD 1547–80*, 517, no. 42); Elton 1986, 279.
34 WAM LXXXIII (*LP*, XVII, no. 714/5); see also Knighton 1981.
35 WAM LXXXIII (*LP*, XVII, no. 714/5); see also Knighton 1981.
36 Rodwell 2010b, 17–25; for the report, *ADC 1543–1609*, no. 10.
37 *ADC 1543–1609*, no. 54.
38 Ibid., no. 26.
39 Hawkyard 2016, 191–5.
40 *ADC 1543–1609*, nos 85, 296, 397, 430, 504; WAM 39037–8, 41000; J.W. Clark 1896, 50–53; J.A. Robinson and James 1909, 13–17; Tanner 1923, 37.
41 Hallam Smith 2010, 124–7.

42 WAM 51119. The liturgical arrangements, with some modifications on account of the king's youth and 'also for that many poinctes of the same were suche as by the lawes of the realme att this present were nat allowable', are carefully specified in *APC 1547–50*, 29–33. See also Hoak 2003, 136, 146–9.

43 MacCulloch 2011, esp. 329–30, 342–3.

44 Walker 2010, 732.

45 *CSPSpan 1547–9*, 48.

46 *ADC 1543–1609*, no. 85.

47 Hughes 1952–3, 85.

48 W. D. Hamilton (ed.) 1875–7, I, 187; II, 2.

49 Frere and Kennedy (eds) 1910, II, 133.

50 TNA, PROB 11/35/520; for his licensed absence and frequent residence in Peterborough in his last years see *CPR 1547–8*, 86; Mellows (ed.) 1939, p. xxvii; Mellows (ed.) 1940, 78, 88.

51 *LP*, XVI, no. 305/49.

52 MacCulloch 1999, 96.

53 *LJ* I, 23, 27 Feb. 1552, 3 March 1552, 12–14 April 1552, and p. 429; *CJ* I, 3–4, 19, 23 March 1552, 9, 12 April 1552; HLRO, Original Act 5 & 6 Edw. VI c. 36; WAM 6490; WAM, Register book III, ff. 228–30 (copies).

54 WCA, Registrum Bracy, f. 71. For the continuing exercise of jurisdiction into the Jacobean period see *ADC 1543–1609*, no. 88; WCA, Registrum Wyks, ff. 163–70; Loades 2003.

55 *ADC 1543–1609*, no. 186.

56 MacCulloch (ed.) 1984, 223, 272; MacCulloch 2016, 546–7.

57 *ADC 1543–1609*, no. 138.

58 MacCulloch 2016, 538, 563–8, 570.

59 *CPR 1553–4*, 261–2; WAM 37451; Williamson 2016, 254, 268 n. 30.

60 WAM 37412–37413, 37416–37418, 37426, 37432, 37445–37447, 37564, 37569, 37571, 37573, 37727.

61 Comparisons can be made between the accounting years to Michaelmas 1553 and 1554: WAM 37387, 33604.

62 WAM 37646B; Nichols (ed.) 1852, 94; 'skrynne' in the Greyfriars Chronicler's text is ambiguous, but in context seems more likely to refer to the shrine than to the abbey rood screen.

63 Strype 1822, III/1, 320, 329, 341–2; Merritt 2005, 56–7.

64 *ADC 1543–1609*, no. 166; WAM 37452, 37709; Foxe 1570, 1746–9; Nichols (ed.) 1848, 84–5; Tellechea Idígoras 2005, 25.

65 *CSPVen 1555–58*, I, no. 32, at p. 27.

66 Foxe 1570, 1841.

67 D. Knowles 1948–59, III, 421–43, is a fine overall survey; see also Mayer 2000, 283–4. For Westminster, in particular, see Knighton 2006.

68 D. Knowles 1948–59, III, 431.

69 WAM 6485, 37788A; J. A. Robinson 1911, 13–14.

70 Nichols (ed.) 1848, 130, 132; O'Neilly and Tanner 1966; Knighton 2006, 95–6.

71 *The pomander of prayer*, dedicated to her with appropriate godly praise in 1553 by the indefatigable popular Protestant author Thomas Becon, had to wait till the reign of Elizabeth for publication. Anne's conformity under Mary is likely to have been of little more significance than that of Princess Elizabeth.

72 Weston 1554 and Weston 1555; the text of the latter is printed in M. Williamson 2016, Appendix II, from CUL, Pet. w. 9 (printed by John Cawood, n.d.; single printed copy bound into a volume from Peterborough cathedral).

73 Loades 1989, 372.

74 W. D. Hamilton (ed.) 1875–7, II, 142.

75 For details see Bayne 1907; Haugaard 1968; Hoak 2003, 137–8, 149–50; Hunt 2008, 151–9.

76 D. Knowles 1948–59, III, 433.

77 *CSPVen 1558–80*, no. 15.

78 Ellis (ed.) 1807–8, IV, 180–83; N. L. Jones 1982, 122–9.

79 *CJ* I, 24–5, 28–9 April 1559, 6 May 1559; *LJ* I, 579; 1 Eliz. I c. 24.

80 Knighton 2006, 115–16.

81 WAM 33198E, m. 6d, 37849, 37859–37861, 37863, 37923, ff. 2–3.

82 'Goodman, Gabriel (1528–1601)', *ODNB*.

83 Merritt 2002.

84 *LJ* 2, 16, 20, 25 Feb. 1585, 11 Mar. 1585; 27 Eliz. I c. 31; *ADC 1543–1609*, no. 376; Merritt 2003, 171–3; Merritt 2005, 228–34.

85 Croft (ed.) 2002, 293–8.

86 Evenden 2004.

87 Collinson 1980, 267.

88 Merritt 2001, esp. 627–8.

89 'Goodman, Gabriel (1528–1601)', *ODNB*.

90 For his presence at Westminster see *ADC 1543–1609*, nos 215, 435, 521, 523; for his wider activities see Collinson 1967, 141–4; Knighton 1996, 64, 66, 70, 72.

91 BL, Add. MS 40061, f. 4; TNA, LR 2/11, f. 57v; *ADC 1543–1609*, no. 185; Camden 1600, sig. K4r.

92 M. Williamson 2016, 252–4.

93 Ibid., 254, 268; see also Lehmberg 2003.

94 Lehmberg 2003, 108–9.

95 Merritt 2001, 641; Merritt 2005, ch. 9; see also Kisby 1995; 'Ludford, Nicholas (c.1490–1557)', *ODNB*.

96 Croft 1991.

97 Tanner 1934, 7–9.

98 Lehmberg 1996, 93–4.

99 Worden 1994; cf. Camden 1605/1870, 58.

100 Camden 1600, sig. K4v.

101 WAM, Register book v, f. 33; *ADC 1543–1609*, no. 541; A. E. Harvey and Mortimer (eds) 2003, 23.

102 Llewellyn 2000, 151.

103 Camden 1600, sig. 11r.

104 HMC, *Calendar of the Manuscripts of . . . the Marquis of Salisbury* (1883–1976), XII, 142–3.

CHAPTER 5: 1603–1714

1 Woodward 1997, 87–100.

2 Courtney 2014.

3 Larkin and Hughes 1973–83, I, no. 1; Woodward 1997, 138.

4 Guy 2004, 503–5.

5 Stow 1615, 913; TNA, SP 14/71/16; Sherlock 2007, 285; Woodward 1997, 129–38; Sharpe 1979, 89–95; Collinson 2011, 258–60.

6 WAM 33659, ff. 5v, 6v; A. E. Harvey and Mortimer (eds) 2003, 4–11, 21–3.

7 Stow 1615, 886.

8 Kruse 2003.

9 Nichols (ed.) 1828, II, 493–512; Woodward 1997, 148–65.

10 Woodward 1997, 177; Litten 2003, 9.

11 Gittings 1984, 223; Woodward 1997, 190.

12 J. Williams 1625.

13 Nichols (ed.) 1828, IV, 1038; *CSPVen 1625–26*, XIX, 4, 30; Woodward 1997, 194, 197; McClure (ed.) 1939, II, no. 473.

14 Woodward 1997, 177–8.

15 WAM 6612; 33659, f. 6.

16 Foster 1978, 28; Saunders 1997, 51, 58–9; WAM, Muniment book VII.

17 WAM 33679, f. 5v; 33681, f. 5; 33682, f. 43v; Saunders 1997, 59; Hacket 1693, pt 1, 46–7.

18 Hacket 1693, pt 1, 45–6.

19 Camden 1610, 428–31; Weever 1631, 450–92.

20 Hacket 1693, pt 1, 201–12.

21 Tanner 1973, 8–11.

22 Norton 2011, 54–60.

23 Bray (ed.) 2005–6, *passim*.

24 Warmstry 1641.

25 Hampton 2015; Van Dixhoorn (ed.) 2012, I, 39–45; *LJ*, VIII, 18–20.

26 Merritt 2005, 140–79.

27 Hampshire Record Office, Winchester, MS 44M69/F6; Meads (ed.) 1930, 151, 154.

28 Featley 1636, 276–7.

29 McClure (ed.) 1939, I, 392; II, 294.

30 LMA, WJ/SR NS 41/3, 4, 4a.

31 HMC, *Report on the Manuscripts of . . . Reginald Rawdon Hastings* (1928–47), I, 368; LMA, WJ/SR NS 41/9; CUL, MS SSS.44.10; Durham Cathedral Archives, MS Hunter 44, p. 217v.

32 White 1989, 19, 29, 40.

33 White 1985, 23–5.

34 Tite 2003; Merritt 2005, 140–73, 314–16, 338–42; WAC, F6036, ff. 1–2.

35 'Andrewes, Lancelot (1555–1626)', 'Mountain, George (1569–1628)', 'Neile, Richard (1562–1640)', 'Townson, Robert (bap. 1576, d. 1621)', 'Williams, John (1582–1650)', *ODNB*.

36 Croft 2003, 180.

37 Hacket 1693, pt 1, 144.

38 Merritt 2001.

39 McClure (ed.) 1939, I, 392.

40 Jansson (ed.) 1988, 37, 42, 74, 99.

41 Hacket 1693, pt 1, 207; pt 2, 97–8; TNA, C115/M35, no. 8387.

42 Merritt 2001, 625–31.

43 Ibid., 631–7.

44 Surrey History Centre, Woking, LM/1989.

45 LPL, Shrewsbury Papers, MS 709, f. 149; WAM 6586.

46 Merritt 2005, 96–8; Patterson 2000.

47 Hampton 2011.

48 WAM 6561.

49 WAM, Chapter Act book II, f. 64v; WAM 25109; TNA, PC 2/50, p. 232, 3 April 1639.

50 Crankshaw 2004, 57–60; Higgott 2004, 175–82.

51 Spottiswood 1655, sig. a3v.

52 Cressy 2006, 110–29; K. Lindley 1997, 36–61.

53 *CSPD 1641–3*, 217; Cressy 2006, 390; *Diurnall Occurrences*, 27 Dec. 1641–2 Jan. 1642 [1641/2], 3–4.

54 Gardiner (ed.) 1906, 167–70.

55 *CJ*, 29 April 1643, 22 April 1644; WAM 43160.

56 *CJ*, 13 Jan. 1644.

57 E.g. WAM 42488A, 42488B; *CJ*, 28 Feb. 1644, 25 March 1648; *LJ*, 15 March 1644, 26 Dec. 1644, 25 April 1645, 7 Dec. 1646, 7 Feb. 1648.

58 Firth and Rait (eds) 1911, I, 803–5.

59 BL, Add. MS 70005, unfoliated; Spraggon 2003, 88–93.

60 WAM 24850, 24852, 24855, 42268, 42506–42507; BL, Add. MS 70005.

61 Vicars 1645, 184.

62 *LJ*, 25 April 1645. See also WAC, E157–166; WAM 42417–42421.

63 T. Hill 1648, sig. A2v.

64 J. F. Wilson 1969; Webster 2011, 405–9.

65 *CJ*, 28 Feb. 1644; Coates *et al.* (eds) 1982–92, II, 86–7.

66 Crankshaw 2004, 63–4; Evelyn 1659, 11–12; Morrissey 2011, 223–7.

67   Merritt 2013, 110–13; WAC, E30.

68   Merritt 2005, 11–13, 324–7.

69   Merritt 2013, 171–84.

70   WAM 33422.

71   Firth and Rait (eds) 1911, II, 256–77.

72   WAM 42750–42764, 43014.

73   WAM 24851.

74   WAM 3922, and see WAM 43166; Farquhar 1936.

75   *CSPD 1656–7*, 147.

76   *CJ*, 30 April 1649.

77   Shaw 1900, II, 590–1; 'Rowe, John (1626/7–1677)', *ODNB*.

78   WAM 6567.

79   Calamy 1713, II, 41; Boseley 1907.

80   WAM 9357.

81   WAM 24851.

82   *CJ*, 2 Sept. 1652, 173.

83   *Mercurius Politicus*, no. 221, 31 Aug.–7 Sept. 1654, 3743; ibid., no. 327, 11–16 Sept 1656, 7254.

84   Ibid., no. 380, 3–10 Sept. 1657, 1606.

85   Contrast Sherwood 1977; Kelsey 1997; K. Sharpe 2010.

86   Rodwell *et al.* 2013.

87   *CSPVen 1643–47*, 58; Laing (ed.) 1841–2, II, 118.

88   *CSPVen 1653–54*, 96; *Mercurius Pragmaticus*, no. 6, 22–30 June 1653, 48; *Moderate Intelligencer*, no. 8, 20–27 June 1653, 64; *Moderate Publisher*, no. 139, 24 June–1 July 1653; *A Perfect Account*, no. 129, 22–29 June 1653, 1027.

89   *CSPVen 1657–59*, 106–13; *CSPD 1657–8*, 60, 87, 179.

90   *Kingdoms Weekly Intelligencer*, no. 316, 12–19 June 1649, 1397; *CSPD 1649–50*, 135, 164, 165, 183; *CJ*, 11 June 1649.

91   Norbrook 1999, 235.

92   Sachse (ed.) 1961, 17.

93   Phillips 1656, 96; Anon. 1646, sig. A2v; *LJ*, 8 Jan. 1647.

94   *Man in the Moone*, no. 16, 13–20 June 1649, 83–5; Bachrach and Collmer (eds) 1982, 45–6. Cf. Anon. 1649, 3.

95   *Mercurius Politicus*, no. 237, 21–8 Dec. 1654, 5018.

96   Fletcher 1660, 346; Temple and Anstey (eds) 1936, 103–4; Knoppers 2000, 139–46; K. Sharpe 2010, 519–22; Sherwood 1977, 126–32, 164–5.

97   *Mercurius Politicus*, no. 428, 5–12 Aug. 1658, 752.

98   Kurpershoek and Vrieze 1999; Schölvinck 1999.

99   Merritt 2013, 65–132.

100 South 1727, V, 45.

101 Merritt 2013, 75–9, 150–53, 204–7.

102 WAC, E163–166.

103 Goodman 1653, sig. A4v. Cf. WAC, E30.

104 Warmstry 1658, 19, 138–9; *CJ*, 23 June 1657.

105 Chester 1876, 152–6.

106 Ibid., 521–3; Dart 1723, II, 143–6; *Fourth Report*, HMC (1874), appendix, 180.

107 Fincham and Taylor 2013, 197–232.

108 Stubbs 1858, 100–21.

109 Ibid., 114, 121–3.

110 Latham and Matthews (eds) 1970–83, I, 283, 324.

111 WAM, Chapter Act book III, 11 Oct. 1660.

112 Range 2012, 46; Keay 2008, 56–9; K. Sharpe 2010, 233–4.

113 Ogilby 1662; Jenkinson 2010, 66–69; K. Sharpe 2013, 160–62; Latham and Matthews (eds) 1970–83, II, 83–4.

114 'Dolben, John (1625–1686)', *ODNB*.

115 WAM, Chapter Act book V, f. 47v.

116 WAM, Chapter Act book IV, 3 Dec. 1662; 'Dolben, John (1625–1686)', *ODNB*; Latham and Matthews (eds) 1970–83, IX, 89.

117 'Dolben, John (1625–1686)', *ODNB*.

118 *LJ*, 10 July 1644; *CJ*, 10 July 1644; Rosser 1989, 263–7.

119 'Dolben, John (1625–1686)', *ODNB*.

120 Pelling 1685; 'Sprat, Thomas (bap. 1635, d. 1713)', *ODNB*.

121 Edie 1990, 318; Range 2012, 61.

122 Sandford 1687; Range 2012, 61–5, 91–3.

123 Routh (ed.) 1833, III, 218.

124 K. Sharpe 2013, 452.

125 Doebner (ed.) 1886, 12.

126 Claydon 1996, 61–2.

127 Range 2012, 106.

128 Anon. 1689, 3.

129 Range 2012, 28; Monod 1999, 311; Schwoerer 1992, 109; Claydon 1996, 62.

130 *CJ*, 9 April 1689, p. 85.

131 K. Sharpe 2013, 469.

132 Claydon 2002, 99–105; Doebner (ed.) 1886, 12; 'Mary II (1662–1694)', *ODNB*.

133 Doebner (ed.), 1886, 12; 'Mary II (1662–1694)', *ODNB*; K. Sharpe 2013, 468–9.

134 Claydon 1996, 78–9; Range 2016, 88–9, 92–3, 97–8; Anon. 1695.

135 WAM 6431; Barclay 2007, 257.

136 K. Sharpe 2013, 455–69, 479–80.

137 Range 2016, 112–15; K. Sharpe 2013, 617.

138 'Patrick, Simon (1626–1707)', 'South, Robert (1634–1716)', *ODNB*; A. Taylor (ed.) 1858, VIII, 443–64, 521–43; IX, 524–7; Claydon 2002, 101–2; Claydon 1996, 68–9.

139 'South, Robert (1634–1716)', *ODNB*; WAM, Chapter Act book V, ff. 194v, 200, 212.

140 J. Rose 2012, 34–7; Bennett 1975, 44–62.

141 Bray (ed.) 2005–6, IX–X, *passim*.

142 Range 2012, 117, 119, 121; *LJ*, XVII, 68.

143 K. Sharpe 2013, 617–18.

144 Ibid., 625–6.

145 *CJ*, 2 Feb. 1697, 686.

146 WAM 34521; Cocke 1995, 39.

147 WAM, Chapter Act book v, f. 112r.

148 For St Paul's see K. Sharpe 2013, 536–43, 620–21.

149 Luders (eds) 1810–28, vii, 205–7.

150 Boulton 2000, 315.

CHAPTER 6: 1714–1837

For their kindness in reading and commenting on various versions of this chapter, I am most grateful to Brian Young and, as always, Zoë Waxman.

1   Links 1994, 173–7; Links 1977, 68–70.

2   Perkins 1938–52, iii, 141.

3   See, for example, Z. Pearce 1760.

4   See Crook in this volume.

5   Ackermann 1812, 317–19, gives a near complete list of names.

6   Walpole 1985, iii, 14.

7   'Drummond, Robert Hay (1711–1776)', *ODNB*.

8   S. Taylor 1992; 'Bell, William (1731–1816)', *ODNB*.

9   WAM 64459. The archbishop who appointed him to York was none other than his fellow prebendary Robert Hay Drummond. See Thomas (ed.) 1796, i, p. lxxi.

10 Sykes 1959, 214–15.

11 WAM 64607. See also WAM 64602.

12 WAM 49804–48974 gives a useful account of attendance at abbey services. See also WAM, Chapter Act book xiii, f. 179.

13 Jebb 1843, 131.

14 Until 1745 the statutes required that four prebendaries should reside together every four months, each one taking a month's duty. This was changed to require each prebendary to nominate a month a year, with the dean residing for two. See WAM, Chapter Act book ix, unfoliated, 24 April 1745.

15 WAM, Chapter Act book xiii, f. 133. De Quincey described Cleaver as 'a splendid pluralist, armed with diocesan thunder and lightning'; see Crook 2008, 162.

16 WAM, Chapter Act book xiii, f. 240.

17 Sherburn (ed.) 1956, ii, 84; W. St A. Vincent (ed.) 1817, p. xix; S. Taylor 1989, 138–9; H. Smith 2006, 215.

18 Hartshorne (ed.) 1905, 340.

19 Dart 1723, i, p. ix; ii, 23.

20 Hartshorne (ed.) 1905, 340.

21 Moore (ed.) 1761, iii, p. iv; Chamberlain 1997, 25; F. Williams (ed.) 1869, i, 314; Bennett 1975, 191.

22 Bennett 1975, 90, 170; Curthoys 2012, 147–54; E. Carpenter 1948, 186.

23 S. Abbott 2003, 332; Newton 1782, i, 9–10; J. Gibson 2001, 153; Atterbury, quoted in Sherburn (ed.) 1956, ii, 114; Colvin 1979; Port (ed.) 1986.

24 Bennett 1975, 103; Sherburn (ed.) 1956, ii, 55, 84; Moore (ed.) 1761, iv, 301; F. Williams (ed.) 1869, i, 184; WAM, Chapter Act book vi, ff. 9, 16, 18, 55v, 59v, 87v–89v; C. Jones 1999.

25 E. Carpenter 1948, 44; Langford 1988.

26 E. Carpenter 1948, 44; Langford 1988; Bennett 1975, 255–305; Cruickshanks 1988, 100; Stanley 1911, 459, notes the discovery of a secret chamber behind the library chimney in the deanery, uncovered in 1867, which was large enough to hold eight or ten people.

27 F. Williams (ed.) 1869, i, 394; Bennett 1975, 274.

28 W. Gibson 1989, 71.

29 J. Gibson 2001, 242.

30 Moore (ed.) 1761, iv, 2–34; Bradford 1719, 23–4.

31 Brayley 1818–23, i. 185; Lamb 1831, 215.

32 Whiston 1748, 10, 17, 55; Duffy 1976; Lamb 1831, 223.

33 WAM, Chapter Act book vii, note affixed to front, ff. 30, 31v, 43, 73v–74; Hartshorne (ed.) 1905, 340; Whiston 1749–50, i, 182–7.

34 WAM, Chapter Act book ix, unfoliated, 14 Nov. 1745.

35 Wilcocks 1722, 10; WAM, Chapter Act book viii, unfoliated, 2 March 1732, 1 May 1735; Chapter Act book ix, unfoliated, 14 Nov. 1745, 24 April 1745, 20 March 1746; Chapter Act book x, unfoliated, 27 Feb. 1755; Wilcocks 1797, ii, p. x.

36 W. S. Andrews 1952; Z. Pearce 1722a; Z. Pearce 1722b; Z. Pearce 1777, i, pp. vii, xi, xvi; Churton (ed.) 1868, p. xvi; S. Taylor 1998, 96–7; WAM 64665–66666, 64678; 'Pearce, Zachary (1690–1774)', *ODNB*.

37 Z. Pearce 1777, p. xxiv; Hartshorne (ed.) 1905, 174; WAM 64474, 64457, 64723, 64897.

38 WAM 64724; Z. Pearce 1760; Linnell (ed.) 1964, 17–18;

39 WAM 64317, 64543, 64536, 64474.

40 Ackermann 1812, i, 283–4; Gibbon 1994, iii, 576; WAM, Chapter Act book xiii, 45–6; WAM 64459; WAM, Chapter Act book xii, unfoliated, 19 Jan., 28 Jan., 6 May 1774, 3 June 1785; WAM 64472, 64476, 64468, 66476, 64459; Thomas (ed.) 1796, i, p. xcviii.

41 'Pearce, Zachary (1690–1774)', *ODNB*; Pearman 1897, 310; Mather 1992, 168; WAM, Chapter Act book xiii, ff. 55, 66, 71, 72, 91, 101.

42 Horsley (ed.) 1813; WAM, Chapter Act book xiii, f. 60; WAM 60920; Mather 1992, 190; WAM Chapter Act book xiv, f. 10.

43 W. St A. Vincent (ed.) 1817, pp. xv, xlvii–xlviii; 'Vincent, William (1739–1815)', *ODNB*; W. Vincent 1792; W. Vincent 1802; WAM, Chapter Act book xiv, ff. 307, 310, 313.

44 E. Carpenter (ed.) 1966, 214; Ireland 1830, p. iv; Ireland 1797; E. Hawkins 1848, 46; 'Ireland, John (1761–1842)', *ODNB*; WAM, Chapter Act book xv, ff. 2,

147, 400, 407; WAM, Chapter Act book XVI, ff. 55, 131, 170, 349–51.

45 Gibson 2001. See also S. Taylor 1992; S. Taylor 2007.

46 Stanley 1911, 477; Cruickshanks 1988, 102; Rogers 1973, 74–5; Rogers 1989, 171, 184.

47 WAM 34508D; see also Rodwell and Mortimer (eds) 2010.

48 Pearman 1897, 310.

49 C. Jones and Holmes (eds) 1985, 192; Caudle 2000.

50 H. Smith 2006, 234.

51 Risk 1972, 1.

52 Hanham 2016, 276, 289; Malcolm 1803, I, 250; Perkins 1920, 84.

53 Hanham 2016, 276; Cocke 2001; Malcolm 1803, I, 128.

54 WAM, Chapter Act book X, unfoliated, 26 Jan. 1758.

55 Cocke 2003, 319; Burrows 2005, 380; J. Addison, *Spectator* 26, 30 March 1711, 113.

56 H. Smith 2006, 96–7, 104, 116.

57 E. A. Smith 1999, 187.

58 Cannadine 1983, 118.

59 Girouard 1981, 26–7.

60 Stanley 1911, 81; WAM 51168B.

61 Burrows 2005, 256, 524; H. Smith 2006, 100; Range 2012, 155.

62 Chrisman-Campbell 2013, 151.

63 Reeve (ed.) 1896–9, II, 167, 196.

64 Burrows 2005, 256; WAM, Chapter Act book X, unfoliated, 13 May, 24 Sept. 1761, 26 Oct. 1762; Chapter Act book VII, ff. 130, 131v; Chapter Act book XV, ff. 72, 80, 123, 127; WAM 51147; WAM, Chapter Act book VII, f. 132v; Chapter Act book XVI, ff. 78–9, 86–9, 92.

65 Stanley 1911, 94.

66 Perkins 1937a, 31–4; Ackermann 1812, II, 16.

67 J. T. Smith 1828, I, 175; Mortimer 2003.

68 Litten 2003, 17; Malcolm 1803, I, 122; WAM, Chapter Act book X, unfoliated, 3 June 1760; J. T. Smith 1828, I, 175.

69 *House of Commons Proceedings* 10, 16 Feb. 1738, 137–9.

70 'Clayton [née Dyve], Charlotte, Lady Sundon (c.1679–1742), *ODNB*; 'Clayton, William', in Sedgwick (ed.) 1970.

71 Craske 2004, 60, 67.

72 Ogborn 1998.

73 Keepe 1682, 22–3.

74 Wren (ed.) 1750, 295–303.

75 Cocke 1995, 39.

76 Wren (ed.) 1750, 299–300.

77 Dart 1723, I, 58; see also WAM 24660, 34549, 65614.

78 WAM 34517.

79 Friedman 2011, 202–9.

80 Cocke 1995, 57–8.

81 Evelyn 1706, 9.

82 Ralph 1783, 91; Cocke 1995, 43.

83 Colvin 2008, 603; Mowl 1985; Cox 2012.

84 Tatton-Brown and Mortimer (eds) 2003.

85 Wren (ed.) 1750, 300–02.

86 WAM CN56; Worsley 1993. On Beverley Minster see Friedman 2011, 304–6.

87 Du Prey 2000; Jeffery 1996.

88 Tracy 2003.

89 WAM, LC II.8.1; WAM 34517, f. 13; WAM 34893–34896.

90 WAM 64472.

91 Aspin 2011, 222.

92 WAM, Chapter Act book XI, unfoliated, 8 Dec. 1773, 19 Jan., 28 Jan., 25 April, 6 May 1774; Ralph 1783, 91.

93 WAM, Chapter Act book XV, f. 85; Ackermann 1812, 276.

94 WAM, Chapter Act book XII, unfoliated, 12 May, 3 June 1778, 13 Aug. 1779; Chapter Act book XII, ff. 302–3, 305; WAM 52538.

95 J. M. Robinson 2012, 225–6; Cocke 1995, 57; Hunting 1981, 99–102; Malcolm 1803, II, 404–6; George 1951, 99–100.

96 WAM 51672; WAM, Chapter Act book X, unfoliated, 13 March 1764, 23 April 1762; Chapter Act book XI, unfoliated, 17 July 1777; see also Mowl 1985, 84; Field 1987, 47.

97 Ogborn 1998, 91–203.

98 O'Byrne 2008, 295.

99 Coutu 2006, 116.

100 Craske 2004, 61.

101 Coutu 2006, 116.

102 Irving (ed.) 1825, III, 48.

103 J. T. Smith 1828, I, 176.

104 Bindman and Baker 1995, 11.

105 Grosley 1772, I, 218.

106 Ralph 1783,

107 Connell 2005, 559.

108 Bindman and Baker 1995, 6.

109 Craske 2004, 56; Walcot 2010.

110 Coutu 2006, 111, 140.

111 Craske 2007, 91.

112 Grosley 1772, I, 102.

113 Craske 2004, 68; Craske 2007, 17; Bindman and Baker 1995, 16, 6.

114 Bennett 1975, 307; Craske 2007, 238–9.

115 WAM, Chapter Act book VII, f. 119.

116 Fordham 2007, 101; Fordham 2010, 109–11; Coutu 2006, 114.

117 Craske 2007, 28–9.

118 Bindman and Baker 1995, 68.

119 Irving (ed.) 1825, III, 426.

120 Coutu 2006, 117–200; Coltman 2007, 96; Baker 2000, 64; P. Connell 2005, 570–71; Craske 2007, 29.

121 Bindman and Baker 1995, 22.

122   WAM, Chapter Act book XI, f. 51.

123   WAM, Chapter Act book XI, unfoliated, 14 Jan. 1745/6.

124   Ralph 1783, 91.

125   Malcolm 1803, I, 110, 169.

126   Brayley 1818–23, I, p. i.

127   J. Addison, *Spectator* 26, 30 March 1711, 110. See, for example, Henry 1770, 14.

128   Craske 2004, 75.

129   Irving (ed.) 1825, III, 46.

130   WAM 65628.

131   Brownell 1978, 350.

132   Craske 2007, 437.

133   WAM, Chapter Act book VII, ff. 108, 122, 126v.

134   WAM, Chapter Act book XIII, f. 242.

135   WAM, Chapter Act book XVI, f. 125. The memorial to Charles James Fox in 1811 was similarly priced: see WAM, Chapter Act book XIV, f. 172.

136   Perkins 1938–52, III, 20, 148; *Gentleman's Magazine* 46 (1776), 570; 69 (1799), 859; *Annual Register* 19 (1776), 96–7.

137   Crook 1995, 66; WAM 64897, f. 71.

138   WAM 61228B, ff. 11–12; WAM 65627–65628, 34911, 6347B.

139   WAM, Chapter Act book XV, f. 337.

140   WAM 60918A, 60948 B, 60949D; WAM, Chapter Act book XV, fol. 138.

141   Irving (ed.) 1825, III, 48.

142   Roscoe *et al.* (eds) 2009, 256, 1003, 1098, 1175; Baker 2000, 74–7; Baker 1995, 94; Craske 2000, 96; Rogers 1989, 191.

143   WAM 60918D.

144   Bumpus [1908], I, 213; II, 310, 330.

145   Burrows 2005, 463–4, 576–97; WAM 61228B, 31.

146   'Bayly, Anselm (1718/19–1794)', *ODNB*.

147   *Gentleman's Magazine* 137 (1825), 467–8; WAM 60927. WAM 60913 gives a good flavour of his complaints.

148   WAM, Chapter Act book VII, ff. 49, 104v; Chapter Act book IX, unfoliated, 23 Nov. 1744; Chapter Act book x, unfoliated, 12 July 1764; Chapter Act book XIII, 223–4, 293.

149   WAM, Chapter Act book XIV, f. 272; Crook 1995, 40.

150   WAM, Chapter Act book x, unfoliated, 11 Feb. 1766.

151   Linnell (ed.) 1964, 255; Hunting 1981, 104; B. Harris 2002, 256, 266.

152   WAM, Chapter Act book x, unfoliated, 13 June 1750, 10 March, 6 Oct. 1751, 26 Nov. 1765; Chapter Act book XII, unfoliated, 14 Feb. 1781, 19 June 1787; Chapter Act book XIII, ff. 246, 28, 223; WAM 49795.

153   WAM 53012–53094, 49756B, 53156–53203; WAM, Chapter Act book VIII, unfoliated, 28 Jan. 1735; Chapter Act book XII, unfoliated, 2 March 1786.

154   Wren Society 1934, 35–7.

155   J. Harris 1994, 90–91.

156   WAM, Chapter Act book VI, f. 4v.

157   WAM, Chapter Act book VI, f. 50.

158   WAM, Chapter Act book XVI, f. 267.

159   C. Jones 1999.

160   Cocke 1995, ch. 3.

161   H. Smith 2006, 178.

162   S. Smith 1998.

163   Carleton 1965, 44–5; Field 1987, 49, 56.

164   Malcolm 1803, I, 163; Perkins 1938–52, I, 38.

165   WAM, Chapter Act book XII, unfoliated, 3 May 1788.

166   Brayley 1818–23, I, 211; Burney 1785; Weber 1989, 43.

167   Brewer 1997, 404.

CHAPTER 7: 1837–1901

I am extremely grateful to Professor William Whyte for his help in checking a number of these references.

1   *The Examiner*, 19 Oct. 1834, 659; T. Taylor (ed.) 1853, II, 355, 362–3; Shenton 2012, 186.

2   'Ireland, John (1761–1842)'; 'Turton, Thomas (1780–1864)'; 'Wilberforce, Samuel (1805–1873)'; 'Buckland, William (1784–1856)'; 'Trench, Richard Chenevix (1807–1896)', *ODNB*; Stanley 1911, 483; *The Times*, 1 Nov. 2017, 25; 7 Nov. 2017, 25. For Ireland's will, see WAM DE/21/01/003, DE/21/09/001.

3   R. Peel to J. W. Croker, 2 Feb. 1835, Jennings (ed.) 1884, II, 264. For financial arrangements and administrative details see *Companion to the Almanac* (1837), 137–8; WA Commission, 'Final Report', 1891, 29; E. Carpenter (ed.) 1966, 321–30, 342, 463.

4   For context see Mathieson 1923, 152–3; Best 1964, 296ff. For contemporary critiques of the commissioners' work see [W. Sewell], *Quarterly Review* 58 (1837), 196–254; [E. B. Pusey], *British Critic* (April 1838), 455–62.

5   *Hansard*, 30 July 1840; Best 1964, 453ff.

6   Sargeaunt 1898, 241; see also Forshall 1884, 116ff.

7   B. Connell (ed.) 1962, 180–81. For a detailed map of the school precincts in 1881 see *ROW* 3 (1963), 423.

8   Tanner 1934, 48; E. Carpenter (ed.) 1966, 324–8.

9   Perkins 1938–52, I, 158–9.

10   Blore's arrangement was reordered in 1884 by Sir Frederick Bridge, and again in 1895 and 1899 by J. L. Pearson; ibid., 178.

11   *The Ecclesiologist* 7 (1847), 22–4; Venables 1883, 201.

12   *The Guardian* (1847), 425: 'What right have the Dean and Chapter to block up the nave and drive a congregation into the transepts?' Ibid. (1848), 607.

13   Wordsworth, unpublished protest, WCA, 1848.

14   WAM 66416. J. Thynne to E. Blore, April 1848, Reynolds (ed.) 2011, 27 n. 1; Buckland 1848.

15   Perkins 1938–52, ill.

16   *The Ecclesiologist* 9 (1849), 334; ibid. 13 (1852), 140.

17   Scott 1995, 112.

18   Stanley 1882, 270, 273. Thynne may have been prompted by one Westminster prebendary, H. V. Bayley (evidence of Thomas Wright, the abbey's clerk of works, WA Commission, 'First Report', 1890, 14). It was Thynne who arranged for some tapestry from Longleat to be hung in the Jerusalem Chamber; Stanley, 1882, 269. The painted ceiling and cedar panelling were installed by Scott in 1871; Reynolds (ed.) 2011, 278.

19   Hill 2007, 128.

20   G. G. Scott to J. Thynne, 21 Jan., 29 March 1854, TNA, Work 6/111, copy in Gladstone Papers, BL, Add. MS 44379. Selective transcriptions of Scott's reports, from which all these quotations are taken, may be found in WA Commission, 'First Report', 1890, 43–4; W. J. Jordan 1980, 80ff.

21   WA Commission, 'First Report', 1890, 80.

22   *Building News* 83 (1902), 240.

23   W. E. Gladstone to A. P. Stanley, quoted in WA Commission, 'First Report', 1890, 14.

24   *The Times*, 12 Feb. 1855, 8; *The Builder* 13 (1855), 198–9.

25   Scott et al. 1863, 42; Scott 1995, 285.

26   Minute by Canon Edward Repton, quoted by Brindle 2010, 140.

27   Scott et al. 1863, 39; Thornbury 1873–8, III, 451.

28   W. E. Gladstone to A. P. Stanley, 8 Jan. 1866, quoted in WA Commission, 'First Report', 1890, 14.

29   Details cited in Brindle 2010, 143–6.

30   One window was paid for by Stanley's estate, one by Queen Victoria herself, others from later American contributions. Several windows were damaged in the Second World War, then restored and rearranged in 1961. Details in Rodwell and Mortimer (eds) 2010, 12ff.

31   WAM 66344; Reynolds (ed.) 2011, 18, no. 9N.

32   *The Builder* 18 (1860), 119–20.

33   WA Commission, 'First Report', 1890, 80.

34   *The Ecclesiologist* 20 (1859), 139.

35   WAM OS/03/09/001B, G. G. Scott to A. P. Stanley, 30 Nov. 1861, Reynolds (ed.) 2011, 50.

36   WAM OS/03/09/001A, G. G. Scott to J. Thynne, 25 Jan. 1873, Reynolds (ed.) 2011, 92.

37   Crook 2013, 38 n. 65.

38   See, generally, *The Builder* 14 (1856), 471–2; ibid. 19 (1861), 105. Most of the shellac had to be removed later with wire brushes; this was undertaken by S. Dykes-Bower from 1951.

39   WAM OS/03/09/001A, G. G. Scott to A. P. Stanley, 4 July 1876, Reynolds (ed.) 2011, 104.

40   Scott 1861–2, 70–71, 75.

41   Scott 1995, 285.

42   [J. Carter], *Gentleman's Magazine* 69/2 (1799), 578.

43   Lethaby 1925, 104.

44   G. G. Scott to Office of Works, 16 Aug. 1870, quoted in Brindle 2010, 147.

45   J. Thorne, *British Almanac and Companion* (1873), 173.

46   *The Ecclesiologist* 29 (1867), 340.

47   *The Builder* 30 (1872), 98; Scott 1995, 285. Building contractors, Poole and Sons; tiling repairs, Minton and Hollins; sculpture, Farmer and Brindley.

48   *Sessional Papers Read at the Royal Institute of British Architects* (1876–7), 261.

49   S. Bradley and Pevsner 2003, 189.

50   *The Builder* 25 (1867), 823, ill. Antonio Salviati charged £550 for his 'enamel mosaic', WAM, Chapter Act book CH/02/01/021, 1861–8, 29 March 1865, f. 291.

51   Stanley 1882, 54.

52   Hare 1895, 84. For Stanley's response see Stanley 1882, 57–63.

53   *The Ecclesiologist* 26 (1865), 340–44.

54   Psilanthropism was the heresy that Christ was merely human: 'the assertion of the mere humanity of Christ' (S. T. Coleridge, *Aids to Reflection*, 1848, I, 163). Stanley accepted the term 'altar' only as part of the coronation ritual: 'the only Sacrifices acknowledged in the English Prayer Book are those of praise and thanksgiving, and still more emphatically of human hearts and lives'. Thus he conceived of Scott's 'High Altar' as combining 'the ancient forms of the fifteenth century with the simpler and loftier faith of the nineteenth century'. See Stanley 1911, 494–5.

55   Scott 1995, 284; Lethaby 1925, 73.

56   Scott to Thynne, 15 Feb. 1871, WAM RCO5.

57   Scott 1995, 287.

58   WAM RCO5.

59   WAM OA/02/02/001. G. G. Scott [to A. P. Stanley], 8 Feb. 1875, Reynolds (ed.) 2011, 97.

60   For Scott's sources of inspiration, see W. J. Jordan 1980, 75–8.

61   *The Builder* 60 (1891), 386.

62   *The Builder* 48 (1885), 331; ibid. 50 (1886), 938.

63   *The Builder* 59 (1890), 400.

64   Lethaby 1906, 76.

65   To secure a 'variety of inclination' in tool marking. Arthur Cawston believed the result was 'imbued with the spirit of the ancients'; *The Builder* 60 (1891), 386.

66   Quiney 1979, 192–3.

67   A. P. Stanley to C. J. Vaughan, 4 July 1838, Prothero, 1893, I, 199–200.

68   *Quarterly Review* 78 (1846), 267, correcting *Quarterly Review* 77 (1846), 526; E. Carpenter (ed.) 1966, 288.

69   A. P. Stanley, 'Recollections', WAL, 18B.

70   *The Builder* 14 (1856), 597–8, 625–6.

71   *The Ecclesiologist* 2 (1843), 85, 101. See also *Christian Remembrancer* (Jan., Feb. 1843).

72   Stanley 1850, 266.

73   Prothero 1893, II, 541; see also Stanley 1882, 138–52, 198–211.

74   Prothero 1893, II, 61–3, 121. Bunsen's rationalizing views in *The Constitution of the Church of the Future* (1847) were defended by Rowland Williams in *Essays and Reviews* (1860) and in some ways anticipate Stanley's opinions; Bunsen (ed.) 1869, II, 143–4.

75   Benson *et al.* (eds) 1907–32, 2nd ser., II, 302, 20 Jan. 1874; 308, 22 Jan. 1874.

76   Gunn and Wiebe (eds) 1982–, no. 5089, B. Disraeli to Queen Victoria, 10 Sept. 1868, 'Private'. Victoria certainly played a part in Broad Church appointments: for example, A. P. Stanley and George Bradley as deans of Westminster; A. C. Tait as Bishop of London and Archbishop of Canterbury.

77   Stanley 1882, 295; Stanley *et al.* 1863, 126; Stanley 1877, 62.

78   Stanley 1870, 22.

79   Stanley (ed.) 1845, 274.

80   T. Arnold to A. P. Stanley, 21 Oct. 1856, Stanley 1844, II, 52; Prothero 1893, I, 129, 142. See also Stanley (ed.) 1845, 16, 20–21; Arnold 1845, p. lxix, 434.

81   Stanley 1870, p. xix.

82   Wordsworth 1863.

83   Stanley, 'Recollections', WAL, 18B, ff. 102–5; WAM, Chapter Act book CH/02/01/021, f. 241.

84   Prothero 1893, II, 297.

85   E. B. Pusey to A. P. Stanley, 28 Feb. 1864, Liddon 1893–7, IV, 65.

86   E. B. Pusey to A. P. Stanley, 23 Feb. 1864, Prothero 1893, II, 160.

87   H. P. Liddon to A. P. Stanley, 10 March 1864, ibid., 168–9.

88   H. P. Liddon to A. P. Stanley, March 1866, ibid., 168, 171.

89   Stanley 1884, p. [5].

90   Sermon, 1864, Prothero 1893, II, 178.

91   Stanley 1884, 138.

92   Sermon, 18 March 1877, Stanley 1877, 133, 135, 152.

93   Stanley 1884, p. [6].

94   C. C. Abbott (ed.) 1938, 73.

95   A. P. Stanley to Mary Stanley, 1835, Prothero 1893, I, 154.

96   A. P. Stanley to J. C. Shairp, 1841, ibid., 287; 1852, ibid., 437.

97   Quinn and Prest (eds) 1987, 86, 111.

98   Stanley, 'Recollections', WAL, 18B, f. 96; Stanley 1911, 484–5; Prothero 1893, II, 302–3.

99   Stanley 1870, p. xvii, 491–501; Stanley 1884, 307–33.

100 A. Trollope, *The Warden* (1855/1995), 133.

101 [J. Sutton] 1847, quoted in E. Carpenter (ed.) 1966, 423.

102 Bridge 1918, 72–82, 129–32, 139–40, 148, 200.

103 For Scott's altar table in Henry VII's chapel see Perkins 1938–52, II, 199, ill.

104 Stanley, 'Recollections', WAL, 18B, f. 115.

105 WA Commission, 'First Report', 1890, and 'Final Report', 1891, *passim*.

106 Stanley 1911, 315, 493.

107 Witheridge 2013, 263. Stanley was reluctant to accept Hill (WA Commission, 'First Report', 1890, 656), and perhaps unenthusiastic about Palmerston.

108 Prothero 1893, II, 568.

109 Martin 1980, 48, 439, 522, 582–3.

110 Hyland 1962; Bremner 2004, 256.

111 Bremner 2004, 256–7. The Westminster Improvement Commission was set up in 1861 and dissolved in 1891.

112 'Report of Commissioners Appointed to Consider Plans', *PP* (1863), XXIV, 33 (plan); WA Commission, 'First Report', 1890, 44–5; Bremner 2004, 257, plan, fig. 4. For Prince Albert's 'great interest' see Dean and Chapter to the Treasury, 1 March 1889, WA 0A/02/02/001. See also *Building News* 10 (1863), 293; Scott 1995, 287. There was no room for a seated statue of Macaulay in 1864; *British Almanac and Companion* (1864), 130. Instead a bust was installed: a fee of £177 9s. 9d. was charged to Sir Charles Trevelyan, WAM, Chapter Act book CH/02/01/021, 16 Dec. 1865, f. 345.

113 Fisher *et al.* 1981, 61 (8), fig. 14 (Scott plans, watermark 1873). See also *The Architect* 11 (1874), 22; Scott 1995, 207.

114 WA Commission, 'First Report', 1890, 81

115 Stanley 1911, 321.

116 [B. Hope], *The Ecclesiologist* 29 (1868), 278–81.

117 [Barwell] 1839; Barry 1870, 209, 293–5, 406 (plans).

118 'Report of Select Committee on the Thames Embankment', *PP* (1840), XII, 271, no. 354, 271; 'Plans of the Architect of the New Palace of Westminster . . . to Extend the Buildings . . . Westwards', *PP* (1854–5), LIII, no. 333; *British Almanac and Companion* (1868), 142; *British Almanac and Companion* (1869), 214–19; WA Commission, 'First Report', 1890, 45.

119 Like Scott, E. A. Freeman (*Morning Chronicle*, 13 Oct. 1853) denounced Barry's plan to demolish St Margaret's; see *The Ecclesiologist* 14 (1853), 460; ibid. 16 (1855), 326.

120 *British Almanac and Companion* (1878), 130; Brier 2016.

121 *The Builder* 36 (1878), 977–80 (plan). Statham was still arguing for a *campo santo* in Embankment Gardens ten years later: 'A great temple of the honoured dead overlooking the ancient Thames', in gardens currently visited only by 'a lounger or two, or a stray nursemaid'; *The Builder* 56 (1889), 139.

122 *The Builder* 25 (1867), 285–6; Prothero 1893, II 281; Baillie and Bolitho (eds) 1930, 236.

123 Stanley 1911, 175–7.

124 Ibid., 493.

125 'Lefevre, George John Shaw-, Baron Eversley (1831–1928)', *ODNB*. For a bibliography of his writings see Willson 1993, Appendix 2, 351–5.

126 WA Commission, 'First Report', 1890, 28–30 (Shaw-Lefevre's evidence). The Dean and Chapter gave only 'general assent' to Shaw-Lefevre's scheme, since demolition of houses would materially affect the abbey's revenue, WAM, Chapter Act book CH/02/01/023, 17 Dec. 1889.

127 Shaw-Lefevre 1882, 681–2; Shaw-Lefevre 1884, 46–8.

128 *Pall Mall Gazette*, 29 Jan. 1885, 11 (ill.); Bremner 2004, fig. 6.

129 *The Builder* 46 (1884), 227 (plan); Bremner 2004, fig. 5.

130 *The Builder* 46 (1884), 224, 284–5, 320, 354; *The Builder* 56 (1889), 138; *Building News* 63 (1884), 326. To complicate matters, the lease of one of the houses in line for demolition – no. 5 Old Palace Yard – had been bought by an opponent of Shaw-Lefevre's scheme, Henry Labouchere, MP; WA Commission, 'First Report', 1890, 58. It was eventually purchased by parliamentary order in 1902, and still stands.

131 Victoria and Albert Museum, London, 94. J. S., D.1260–1896, Darby 1983, 37 (1–5) [Ran. 15/c/1.1]; Bremner 2004, figs 8–9.

132 Physick and Darby 1973, cat. no. 15 (ill.). Barker and Hyde 1982, 151, pl. 116.

133 *The Builder* 86 (1904), 341.

134 WA Commission, 'First Report', 1890, 30.

135 'That scheme fell through', ibid.; for context see Bremner 2004, 50–73.

136 *The Times*, 25 Jan. 1889, p. 10.

137 J. Knowles 1889; J. Knowles 1890. Knowles suggested that there was room for at least fifty statues, and twice that number of busts and tablets, besides brasses and recumbent effigies.

138 'That scheme became hopeless', WA Commission, 'First Report', 1890, 30.

139 *The Builder* 56 (1889), 137–9; *The Times*, 19 Feb. 1889, 8.

140 Petition of the Dean and Chapter against the Westminster Abbey (Monumental Chapel) Bill, WAM OA/02/03/001; E. Carpenter (ed.) 1966, 323–4.

141 WA Commission, 'First Report', 1890, and 'Final Report', 1891.

142 'Pearson, J. L.', in Lever (ed.) 1976, 41 (1–7).

143 *The Times*, 16 March 1881, 5; ibid., 19 Nov. 1881, 12.

144 *The Architect* 41 (1889), 202.

145 WA Commission, 'First Report', 1890, 41.

146 The conclusion of the 'Final Report' was reprinted in *The Times*, 5 July 1891, 13. For a general plan (1893), see *The Builder* 66 (1894), 13.

147 William Morris, *The Times*, 11 Feb. 1891, 4; Morris 1893; William Morris, *News from Nowhere* (1891), ch. 5 (repr. from *The Commonweal*, 1890); Morris 1889.

148 *The Builder* 67 (1894), 53. E. Carpenter (ed.) 1966, 336.

149 'Thompson, Henry Yates (1838–1928)', *ODNB*. He was proprietor of the *Pall Mall Gazette* and a collector of illuminated manuscripts.

150 In effect a scaled-down version of Pearson's south-east scheme.

151 *The Builder* 66 (1894), 439, 450; *Hansard*, 3 May 1894.

152 Stanley 1882, 230.

CHAPTER 8: 1901–2002

I am enormously grateful to Dr Martin Spychal for his essential research assistance, as well as for his guidance and advice, to all of my fellow contributors to this volume, and especially to Dr John Hall, Sir Stephen Lamport and Dr Tony Trowles for their helpful and incisive comments on earlier drafts.

1 E. Carpenter (ed.) 1972, 338.

2 Baedeker 1898, 242; Barker and Hyde 1982, 150–51; Bremner 2004, 252, 261–3; E. Carpenter (ed.) 1972, 398.

3 McKibbin 2000, 272–4, 276–81; S. J. D. Green 2011, 3–91; G. C. Brown 2001.

4 Jenkyns 2004, 8.

5 Bremner 2004, 271–2; Welldon 1915, 304–7.

6 R. Strong 2005, 421–94.

7 E. Carpenter (ed.) 1972, 454; Longford 1966, 99–104, 224, 627–8; Cannadine 1983, 118, 133–4.

8 WAM DF 58300–58489, coronation of Edward VII, 1902; WAM, Chapter Act book CH/02/01/023, 26 June 1902, 395–7; Brett and Esher (eds) 1934–8, I, 280–81, 284–5, 295–6, 299–300, 304–11, 316–18, 324, 331–6; Longford 1966, 692; Ridley 2012, 307, 351–3, 364–5; Battiscombe 1972, 243–8; Cannadine 1983, 134–7; Roberts 2017.

9 Jenkyns 2004, 168; Bremner 2004, 271–3; Magnus 1975, 367–70; Battiscombe 1972, 249–50.

10 Brett and Esher (eds) 1934–8, I, 339–41, 347–8; Strasdin 2012; Kinsey 2009; Dalrymple and Anand 2017, 269–70; Ridley 2012, 367–9; Bodley 1903, 201.

11 E. Carpenter (ed.) 1972, 334–5, 420, 430; Range 2012, 225–35; Cannadine 1983, 130–31.

12 E. Carpenter (ed.) 1972, 350–52, 449; Perkins 1938–52, II, III; Perkins 1902, 336–7.

13 Bodley 1903, 201; Perkins 1902, 329; Olechnowicz 2007, 25–6; Kuhn 1996, 4, 72, 151; Hinchliff 1997; Readman 2005.

14 B. Edwards 2010; Gunning 2010; R. Brown 2003.

15 E. Carpenter (ed.) 1972, 414; Jenkyns 2004, 169; Beeson 2001, pp. viii–ix.

16 *The Times*, 9 May 1933; E. Carpenter (ed.) 1972, 343; T. F. Taylor 1991, 31–56, 125–35; Beeson 2004, 116–25.

17 WAM, Chapter Act book CH/02/01/023, 11 May 1903, 428; CH/02/01/023, 24 July 1905, 475.

18 WAM, Chapter Act book CH/02/01/024, 2 March 1908, 18.

19 Barker and Hyde 1982, 152–3; Hyland 1962, 136–8; Bremner 2004, 251–5, 270, 275–7.

20 Bremner 2004, 275; Welldon 1915, 328.

21 Ridley 2012, 464–6; Wolffe 2003.

22 WAM DF 58490–58521, coronation of George V, 1911; *The Times*, 13 May 1911; Nicolson 1967, 201–5; Pope-Hennessy 1959, 440–43; A. Edwards 1984, 237–42; K. Rose 1983, 102–4; Range 2012, 239–42.

23 Brett and Esher (eds) 1934–8, III, 53–4; Lunt 2015, 31; Milne 1914, p. viii; *The Times*, 30 Dec. 1911.

24 Lunt 2015, 32; *Illustrated London News*, 24 June 1911 ['Pre-Coronation Number']; 'The Coronation and the Constitutional Question', *Edinburgh Review*, 1 July 1911.

25 Nicolson 1967, 228–37; K. Rose 1983, 131–6.

26 Bremner 2004, 269; Galloway 2000, 289–323; Burman 2004, 259–60; Saint 2004, 459–60; Wolffe 2004, 391.

27 WAM OC/12/01/005, historical notes on the Order of the Bath for the re-inauguration ceremony, 1913; WAM DF 18, Anzac Day file; Perkins 1937b, 107; *The Times*, 18 April 1916.

28 WAM, Chapter Act book CH/02/01/024, 6 Oct. 1914, 177; CH/02/01/024, 5 July 1915, 200; CH/02/01/024, 2 Nov. 1915, 206; CH/02/01/024, 1 Feb. 1916, 210; CH/02/01/024, 4 April 1916, 216; CH/02/01/024, 9 Oct. 1917, 256; CH/02/01/024, 4 Feb. 1919, 295; E. Carpenter (ed.) 1972, 263.

29 WAM, Chapter Act book CH/02/01/024, 3 March 1914; CH/02/01/024, 4 March 1919; WAM 58677–58722, Dean Ryle appeal; *The Times*, 29 June 1920 ['Westminster Abbey Appeal Number']; E. Carpenter (ed.) 1972, 356–7, 364, 378–9.

30 *The Times*, 21 Aug. 1925.

31 Ibid., 29 June 1920; E. Carpenter (ed.) 1972, 356–7.

32 Cannadine 2003, 161–71; P. Williamson 1993; Schwartz 1984; Nicholas 1996.

33 Hyland 1962, 139; Norris 1933, 224–5, 233–4.

34 E. Carpenter (ed.) 1972, 294, 305, 455.

35 WAM OC/05/01/003, funeral of Marquess Curzon of Kedleston, 25 March 1925; Blake 1955, 530–31; Gilmour 1994, 599.

36 E. Carpenter (ed.) 1972, 370; Jenkyns 2004, 171; Gavaghan 1995.

37 WAM 58667–58676, burial of the Unknown Warrior, 1920, correspondence; *The Times*, 15 Nov. 1920; Fitzgerald 1928, 311; Cannadine 1981, 223–4; Cannadine 1995, 103–5.

38 *The Times*, 12 Nov. 1920; Fitzgerald 1928, 311–12; Cannadine 1981, 226.

39 WAM DF 97, Field of Remembrance file; Cannadine 1981, 225; Jenkyns 2004, 172.

40 WAM, Chapter Act book CH/02/01/025, 10 March 1927, 42; CH/02/01/025, 5 April 1927, 45; CH/02/01/025, 6 June 1927, 54; CH/02/01/025, 11 July 1927, 54; CH/02/01/025, 11 Oct. 1927, 56; CH/02/01/025, 12 March 1929, 119; CH/02/01/026, 9 Nov. 1937, 164; Hobsbawm 1983, 302–3; Jenkyns 2004, 173; Beeson 2001, 8.

41 Wheeler-Bennett 1965, 159–60.

42 WAM, Chapter Act book CH/02/01/024, 6 Feb. 1922, 387; WAM DF 58725–58728, wedding of Princess Mary to Viscount Lascelles, 1921–2; WAM, Chapter Act book CH/02/01/024, 5 March 1923, 420; WAM DF 58857–58858, wedding of the Duke of York to Lady Elizabeth Bowes-Lyon, 26 April 1923; Shawcross 2009, 135–6, 168–79; Shawcross (ed.) 2012, 119; Wheeler-Bennett 1965, 150–54.

43 Lunt 2015, 68; *Daily Mail*, 20 Jan. 1922.

44 Owens 2015, 42, 76; Cannadine 1983, 151.

45 Bagehot 2001, 41; Cannadine 1983, 142; Owens 2015, 75–80.

46 Lunt 2015, 82; Jenkyns 2004, 123, 174; Beeson 2001, 150–51; Shawcross 2009, 177.

47 *The Times*, 29 Sept. 1937; E. Carpenter (ed.) 1972, 345; Norris 1933.

48 WAM, Chapter Act book CH/02/01/025, 8 July 1930, 180; CH/02/01/025, 9 Dec. 1930, 201; CH/02/01/025, 29 Nov. 1932, 324; CH/02/01/025, 20 Dec. 1932, 326–7; CH/02/01/025, 18 May 1933, 353; Cosmo Lang to Dean of Westminster, 10 July 1926, WAM DF 58734 A–C; WAM DF 67132, interment of Rudyard Kipling, 23 Jan. 1936; E. Carpenter (ed.) 1972, 359; Jenkins 1967, 589.

49 WAM DF 58836–58853, wedding of Prince George to Princess Marina, 29 Nov. 1934; E. Carpenter (ed.) 1972, 353; Owens 2015, 37–94; *Daily Mirror*, 30 Aug. 1934; Warwick 1988, 81–5.

50 WAM, Chapter Act book CH/02/01/025, 9 Oct. 1934; WAM DF 58855–58856, wedding of the Duke of Gloucester to Lady Alice Montagu-Douglas-Scott, 1935; Frankland 1980, 124–5; Alice, Duchess of Gloucester, 1983, 106–8.

51 E. Carpenter (ed.) 1972, 361; Wheeler-Bennett 1965, 236; Prochaska 1995, 209.

52 WAM, Chapter Act book CH/02/01/026, 26 May 1936, 75; CH/02/01/026, 8 Dec. 1936, 111; WAM DF 58522–58655, coronation of George VI, 1937; Beaken 2012, 132–5; Cannadine 1983, 143–4; Range 2012, 242–7.

53 Owens 2015, 128–76; Wheeler-Bennett 1965, 301–14; Bradford 1989, 210–16; Rhodes James (ed.) 1967, 123–6; Pimlott 1996, 45.

54 Wheeler-Bennett 1965, 208–9, 301–4; Jenkyns 2004, 175.

55 Cannadine 1983, 149; The Times 1937, 184; Perkins 1937b, 104–8, 299–307; Murphy 2013, 16–33.

56 *The Times*, 29 April 1946; E. Carpenter (ed.) 1972, 345–6.

57 WAM, Chapter Act book CH/02/01/026, 10 May 1938, 213; CH/02/01/026, 11 Oct. 1938, 235; CH/02/01/026, 27 March 1939, 262; CH/02/01/026, 18 July 1939, 293; CH/02/01/026, 10 Oct. 1940, 363–4; CH/02/01/026, 10 March 1942, 323; CH/02/01/026, 14 Dec. 1943, 779; E. Carpenter (ed.) 1972, 364–8; Jenkyns 2004, 123; Shawcross (ed.) 2012, 312.

58 WAM 61578–61580, VE Day preparations, 1944–5; 62153–62235, 62314–62324, Battle of Britain memorial chapel and annual service, 1943–7.

59 E. Carpenter (ed.) 1972, 368–9.

60 *The Times*, 4 May 1966.

61 WAM DF 62236–62313, 62449, 62457–62458, wedding of Princess Elizabeth to the Duke of Edinburgh, 1947; Owens 2015, 178–230; Wheeler-Bennett 1965, 752–4; Bradford 1996, 123–5; Pimlott 1996, 125–8, 139–43.

62 *The Times*, 21 Nov. 1947; Owens 2015, 224.

63 Hyland 1962, 139; M. Richardson 1994, 102; Amery *et al.* (eds) 1981, 147.

64 WAM 63090–63098, memorial tablet for Cecil Rhodes, 1951–3.

65 E. Carpenter (ed.) 1972, 359.

66 WAM OC/05/01/015, Roosevelt memorial, 12 Nov. 1948.

67 Jenkyns 2004, 159.

68 WAM OC/05/01/017, funeral of Field Marshal Earl Wavell, 7 June 1950; Rhodes James (ed.) 1967, 445.

69 WAM OC/05/01/018, intercession service for Commonwealth prime ministers, 3 Jan. 1951.

70 WAM DF 63189–63501, coronation of Queen Elizabeth II, 1952–3; Wheeler-Bennett 1965, 691; Bradford 1996, 120; Pimlott 1996, 115–19; J. Hall 2012, 6–19.

71 Owens 2015, 232–66; Shils and Young 1953; Richards 2004.

72 WAM William McKie Collection, 1953 Coronation Correspondence, File 2, Composers; Dimbleby 1975, 234–50.

73 Cannadine 1983, 149–50, 153–4, 158; Pimlott 1996, 202–14; Bradford 1996, 180–92; Rhodes James (ed.) 1967, 475–7; Wilkinson and Knighton 2010, 69–75; Range 2012, 247–59.

74 Birnbaum 1955; Örnebring 2004, 175–95.

75 Cannadine 1983, 157; E. Carpenter (ed.) 1972, 439; Murphy, 2013, 34–65.

76 English 2006, 274.

77 *The Times*, 7 June 1983; E. Carpenter (ed.) 1972, 415; Beeson 2001, 202–3.

78 WAM OC/05/01/015, intercession service for the peoples of India, 17 Feb. 1948; WAM DF 18, Anzac Day services, 1954–74.

79 WAM OC/05/01/025, Nigeria independence, 1 Oct. 1960; Cannadine 2008.

80 WAM OC/05/01/028, Uganda independence, 9 Oct. 1962; OC/05/01/36, Nyasaland independence, 6 July 1964; OC/05/01/37, Zambia independence, 24 Oct. 1964; WAM, Chapter Act book CH/02/01/029, 10 March 1964, 823; CH/02/01/029, 24 March 1964, 835; CH/02/01/035, 22 April 1980, 485.

81 WAM OC/05/01/028, Jamaica independence, 7 Aug. 1962; WAM, Chapter Act book CH/02/01/029, 26 June 1962, 238; CH/02/01/032, 26 April 1971; E. Carpenter (ed.) 1972, 359.

82 WAM OC/05/01/053, memorial service for Sir Frank Worrell, 7 April 1967; OC /05/01/063, memorial service for Lord Constantine, 23 July 1971; *Daily Mail*, 1 April 1967.

83 Matthew 20:27. WAM 63867–63887, Indian Civil Service memorial, 1958; 64254–64262, dedication of the Sudan memorial, March 1960; WAM OC/05/01/044, Colonial Services memorial, 23 March 1966.

84 WAM DF 15, memorial stone for Sir Winston Churchill, 19 Sept. 1965; E. Carpenter (ed.) 1972, 397; Churchill 1956, 132.

85 WAM DF 7, wedding of Princess Margaret to Antony Armstrong-Jones, 1960; WAM OC/02/01/007, wedding of Princess Alexandra to the Hon. Angus Ogilvy, 24 April 1963; WAM DF 97, wedding of Princess Anne to Captain Mark Phillips, 1973; Dimbleby 1975, 255–7.

86 WAM DF 33, funeral of Earl Mountbatten, 1973–9; Beeson 2001, 100–3; Ziegler 1985, 691–3, 700.

87 WAM, Chapter Act book CH/02/01/031, 11 June 1968, 727; Beeson 2001, 100–3.

88 WAM DF 3, Commonwealth Day observance file; Beeson 2001, 11–12, 58.

89 Binder, Hamlyn, Fry & Co., 'Report on the Impact of Tourists on Westminster Abbey', 18 Sept. 1970, WAM OV/02/02/002, esp. 1–9; E. Carpenter (ed.) 1972, 358.

90 Beeson 2001, 8–9, 16–18, 21, 23, 40.

91 Chapman 2015; P. Williamson 2013, 323–66; S. J. D. Green 2011, 273–316.

92 WAM 65048–65051, 'A Million Pounds for a Million People' appeal, 1953–4; E. Carpenter (ed.) 1972, 378–81, 400; Beeson 2001, 3.

93 Beeson 2001, 9–10, 78, 122, 220.

94 *The Times*, 27 Aug. 1998; Beeson 2001, 273, 283–4.

95 Beeson 2001, 51, 82–3, 90–91, 284; De-la-Noy 2016, 108–11.

96 WAM DF 45, One People file; E. Carpenter (ed.) 1972, 361–2; Beeson 2001, 44.

97 WAM, Chapter Act book CH/02/01/035, 9 Oct. 1979, 365; WAM DF 61, the pope's visit to Britain, 1982; Beeson 2001, 68, 135–6, 145, 148, 283–4; J. Hall 2012, 73–4, 109.

98 WAM DF 15, funeral of Earl Attlee and burial of his ashes, 1967; WAM DF 15, Ramsay MacDonald memorial, 1968; WAM DF 15, Lloyd George memorial, 1970; WAM DF 18, service of thanksgiving for the silver wedding of Queen Elizabeth II and the Duke of Edinburgh, 20 Nov. 1972; WAM DF 25, memorial service for the Earl of Avon, 15 Feb. 1977; Beeson 2001, 170–71, 213–14.

99 WAM DF 60, First World War poets' memorial, 11 Nov. 1985; Beeson 2001, 266–7, 279.

100 Beeson 2001, 132–3, 140.

101 WAM DF 64, wedding of Prince Andrew and Sarah Ferguson, 23 July 1986; Beeson 2001, 292, 297, 299, 301.

102 J. Hall 2012, 143–7.

103 WAM DF 68, memorial service for the Earl of Stockton, 10 Feb. 1987; WAM DF 89, memorial service for Lord Wilson of Rievaulx, 12 July 1995; WAM DF 93, memorial service for Lord Home of the Hirsel, 22 Jan. 1996; Horne 1986, 630–31.

104 R. Strong 2017, 14–16; WAM DF 82, memorial service for Lord Olivier, 20 Oct. 1989; WAM DF 85, memorial service for Bobby Moore, 28 June 1993; The Times, 26 April 1990.

105 WAM 67233, 1994; The Times, 12 Nov. 1990; J. Hall 2012, 71.

106 WAM DF 142, inter-faith file, 1988–2005; WAM DF 80, World Aids Day service, 30 Nov. 1990; WAM DF 81a, CARA–HIV Aids service, 13 Sept. 1991; Jenkyns 2004, 177; J. Hall 2012, 41; The Times, 31 July 1998.

107 The Times, 21 May 1987.

108 The Times, 9 Sept. 1980, 14 Oct. 1980, 18 Aug. 1986; J. Hall, 2017–18, 3.

109 Beeson 2001, 86–7, 132, 257, 286, 314–15

110 WAM OV/02/02/001, 1981–3; WAM OV /04/02/001, 1993.

111 WAM 63100–63188, 63188**, Stone of Scone file; Wilkinson 2006.

112 The Times, 15 Nov. 1996; E. Carpenter (ed.) 1972, 371–3; Jenkyns 2004, 182–5.

113 WAM DF 108, Dean Wesley Carr's thoughts on the funeral of Diana, Princess of Wales, 2 Sept. 1997, 5; WAM DF 107, funeral of Diana, Princess of Wales, 1997–9; Dacre 2003; Dayan 2005; Davie and Martin 1999.

114 Jenkyns 2004, 185–6; Frazer 2000; McGuignan 2001; Marriot 2007, 93–100; R. Strong 2017, 235.

115 J. Hall 2012, 142.

116 WAM DF 106, memorial stone for Lord Baldwin, 1986–97; WAM DF 105, memorial service for Denis Compton, 1 July 1997; WAM DF 107, memorial service for Lord Cowdrey, 30 March 2001; Campbell 2014, 748–9; Ziegler 2010, 591; R. Strong 2017, 337–9.

117 R. Strong 2017, 338; J. Hall 2012, 109.

118 R. Strong 2017, 316–18, 351, 381, 414–15.

119 The Times, 19 July 2017; Church Times, 24 July 2017.

120 WAM OV/04/03/001, 1996; WAM OV /04/03/002, 1996–8; Morrin 2004, 342; Jenkyns 2004, 189.

121 The Times, 24 April 1998, 19 Dec. 1998, 19 July 2017.

122 New Statesman, 18 Dec. 1998; The Guardian, 6 March 2001; Daily Telegraph, 10 Feb. 2004; Cameron 2001, 12–17, 25–46, 75–104.

123 WAM DF 105, service of thanksgiving for the golden wedding of Queen Elizabeth II and the Duke of Edinburgh, 20 Nov. 1997; Kirk-Greene 1999, 90–91; Luce 2007, 54, 182–5.

124 WAM DF 119, funeral of the Queen Mother, 1973–2002; R. Strong 2017, 383–8.

125 Jenkyns 2004, 187–8; Shawcross 2009, 933–7; Dalrymple and Anand 2017, 271, 277.

126 Knight 2017; R. Strong 2005, 497–501; Jenkyns 2004, 181; I. Bradley 2012, 230–31, 258–75; Wolffe 2010, 67–71.

CONCLUSION

1 Binski 1995, 82–3.
2 D. A. Carpenter 2007.
3 MacCulloch 2018, 464–5.
4 MacCulloch 2003, 19.
5 Boesch (ed.) 1947, 450–53.
6 Alford 2017, 88.
7 HMC, 'Statutes', 85; Middleton 1604, sig. C4r.
8 Tatton-Brown, 2015–16. On the tomb generally see Higgins 1894, 164–90; Sicca and Waldman (eds) 2012.
9 Cooper 1560, f. 375v.
10 . . . et nobile marmor: / Quod pulcram ad Tamesim deposcit Scotobrittanum, McGinnis and Williamson (eds) 1995, 284–5 (appendices of poems by Melville). This was composed between 1594 and 1603, so anticipating James's arrival.
11 Lehmberg 1996, pp. xxviii–xxix.
12 Wayment 1981.
13 J. A. Robinson 1911, pp. v–vi.
14 Cramer 2001, 183–4.

Bibliography

Books published in London unless otherwise indicated. Titles of works published to 1800 are styled following *ESTC*.

Abbott, C. C. (ed.), 1938, *Further Letters of Gerard Manley Hopkins*

Abbott, S., 2003, 'Clerical Responses to the Jacobite Rebellion in 1715', *HR* 76: 332–46

Ackermann, R., 1812, *The History of the Abbey Church of St. Peter's Westminster: Its Antiquities and Monuments*

'A Clergyman of the Church of England' [Christopher Wordsworth], 1844, *A Letter to the Rev. the Dean and Chapter of Westminster, on the Intended Alterations in the Interior of Westminster Abbey*

Alexander, J. J. G., 1997, 'The Portrait of Richard II in Westminster Abbey', in Gordon, Monnas and Elam (eds), 1997, 197–206

Alford, S., 2017, *London's Triumph: Merchant Adventurers and the Tudors*

Alice, Duchess of Gloucester, 1983, *The Memoirs of Princess Alice, Duchess of Gloucester*

Allmand, C., 1992, *Henry V*

Amery, C., M. Richardson and G. Stamp (eds), 1981, *Lutyens: The Work of the English Architect Sir Edwin Lutyens (1869–1944)*

Andrews, F., 2006, *The Other Friars: The Carmelite, Augustinian, Sack and Pied Friars in the Middle Ages*, Woodbridge

Andrews, W. S., 1952, 'The Life and Work of Bishop Zachary Pearce, 1690–1724', PhD diss., King's College, London

Anglo, S., 1960, 'The Foundation of the Tudor Dynasty: The Coronation and Marriage of Henry VII', *Guildhall Miscellany* 2: 3–11

Anon. 1646, *A perfect relation of the memorable funerall of Robert . . . Earle of Essex*

Anon. [attrib. R. Brandon] 1649, *The last will and testament of Richard Brandon*

Anon. 1689, *An exact account of the ceremonial, at the coronation of Their most excellent Majesties King William and Queen Mary*

Anon. 1695, *The form of the proceeding to the funeral of Her late Majesty Queen Mary II*

Arnold, T., 1845, *Christian Life: . . . Sermons, Preached . . . in the Chapel of Rugby School*, 4th edn

Aspin, P., 2011, '"Our Ancient Architecture": Contesting Cathedrals in Late Georgian England', *AH* 54: 213–32

Bachrach, A. G. H., and R. G. Collmer (eds), 1982, *Lodewijk Huygens: The English Journal, 1651–1652*, Leiden

Baedeker, K., 1898, *London and its Environs*, Leipzig

Bagehot, W., 2001, *The English Constitution*, ed. M. Taylor, Oxford

Baillie, A. V., and H. Bolitho (eds), 1930, *A Victorian Dean: A Memoir of Arthur Stanley*

Baker, M., 1995, 'Roubiliac and Cheere in the 1730s and 40s: Collaboration and Sub-Contracting in Eighteenth-Century English Sculptors' Workshops', *CM* 10: 90–108

Baker, M., 2000, *Figured in Marble: The Making and Viewing of Eighteenth-Century Sculpture*, Los Angeles and London

Barclay, A., 2007, 'William's Court as King', in E. Mijers and D. Onnekink (eds), *Redefining William III: The Impact of the King–Stadholder in International Context*, Aldershot, 241–61

Barker, F., and R. Hyde, 1982, *London as it Might have Been*

Barlow, F., 1970, *Edward the Confessor*

Barlow, F. (ed.), 1992, *The Life of King Edward who Rests at Westminster, Attributed to a Monk of Saint-Bertin*, 2nd edn, Oxford [text and trans.]

Barlow, F., 1997, *Edward the Confessor*, 2nd edn, New Haven, Conn., and London

Barron, C.M., 2014, 'Chaucer the Poet and Chaucer the Pilgrim', in S. H. Rigby and A. J. Minnis (eds), *Historians on Chaucer: The General Prologue to the Canterbury Tales*, Oxford, 24–41

Barry, A., 1870, *Memoir of the Life and Works of Sir Charles Barry*, 2nd edn

[Barwell, W.] 1839, *Westminster Improvements*

Bates, D. (ed.), 1998, *Regesta regum Anglo-Normannorum: The Acta of William I (1066–1087)*, Oxford

Bates, D., 2016, *William the Conqueror*, New Haven, Conn., and London

Battiscombe, G., 1972, *Queen Alexandra*

Bayne, C. G., 1907, 'The Coronation of Queen Elizabeth', *EHR* 22: 650–73

Beaken, R., 2012, *Cosmo Lang: Archbishop in War and Crisis*

Beeson, T., 2001, *Window on Westminster: A Canon's Diary, 1976–1987*

Beeson, T., 2004, *The Deans*

Bennett, G.V., 1975, *The Tory Crisis in Church and State, 1688–1730: The Career of Francis Atterbury, Bishop of Rochester*, Oxford

Benson, A. C., Lord Esher [R. B. Brett] and G. E. Buckle (eds), 1907–32, *The Letters of Queen Victoria*

Bertram, J. (trans.), 1990, *The Life of Saint Edward, King and Confessor, by Blessed Aelred, Abbot of Rievaulx*, Guildford

Best, G. F. A., 1964, *Temporal Pillars: Queen Anne's Bounty, the Ecclesiastical Commissioners, and the Church of England*, Cambridge

Biddle, M., 1986, 'Seasonal Festivals and Residence: Winchester, Westminster and Gloucester in the Tenth to Twelfth Centuries', *ANS* 8: 51–72

Bindman, D., and M. Baker, 1995, *Roubiliac and the Eighteenth-Century Monument: Sculpture as Theatre*, New Haven, Conn., and London

Bindoff, S.T. (ed.), 1982, *History of Parliament: The House of Commons, 1509–1558*

Binski, P., 1986, *The Painted Chamber at Westminster*, Society of Antiquaries of London, Occasional Papers new series 9

Binski, P., 1990, 'The Cosmati at Westminster and the English Court Style', *Art Bulletin* 72: 6–34

Binski, P., 1991, 'Abbot Berkyng's Tapestries and Matthew Paris's Life of St Edward the Confessor', *Arch.* 109: 85–100

Binski, P., 1995, *Westminster Abbey and the Plantagenets: Kingship and the Representation of Power, 1200–1400*, New Haven, Conn., and London

Binski, P., 1997, 'The Liber regalis: Its Date and European Context', in Gordon, Monnas and Elam (eds), 1997, 233–43

Binski, P., 2002, 'The Cosmati and *romanitas* at Westminster: An Overview', in Grant and Mortimer (eds), 2002, 116–34

Binski, P., 2003, 'A "Sign of Victory": The Coronation Chair, its Manufacture, Setting and Symbolism', in R. Welander, D. J. Breeze and T. O. Clancy (eds), *The Stone of Destiny: Artefact and Icon*, Society of Antiquaries of Scotland, Monograph Series 22, Edinburgh, 207–22

Binski, P., 2004, *Becket's Crown: Art and Imagination in Gothic England, 1170–1300*, New Haven, Conn., and London

Binski, P., 2014, *Gothic Wonder: Art, Artifice and the Decorated Style, 1290–1350*, New Haven, Conn., and London

Binski, P., and E. Guerry, 2015, 'Seats, Relics and the Rationale of Images in Westminster Abbey, Henry III to Edward I', in Rodwell and Tatton-Brown (eds), 2015, I, 180–204

Binski, P., and H. Howard, 2010, 'Wall Paintings in the Chapter House', in Rodwell and Mortimer (eds), 2010, 184–208

Binski, P., and A. Massing (eds), 2009, *The Westminster Retable: History, Technique, Conservation*, Cambridge and London

Birnbaum, N., 1955, 'Monarchy and Sociologists: A Reply to Professor Shils and Mr Young', *SR* 3: 5–23

Blair, J., 1996, 'The Minsters of the Thames', in Blair and Golding (eds), 1996, 5–28

Blair, J., 2005, *The Church in Anglo-Saxon Society*, Oxford

Blair, J., and B. Golding (eds), 1996, *The Cloister and the World: Essays in Medieval History in Honour of Barbara Harvey*, Oxford

Blake, R., 1955, *The Unknown Prime Minister: The Life and Times of Andrew Bonar Law, 1858–1923*

Bloch, M. (ed.), 1923, 'La Vie de S. Édouard le Confesseur par Osbert de Clare', *Analecta Bollandiana* 41: 5–131

Bodley, J. E. C., 1903, *The Coronation of King Edward the Seventh: A Chapter in European and Imperial History*

Boesch, P. (ed.), 1947, 'Rudolph Gwalthers Reise nach England im Jahr 1537', *Zwingliana* 8: 433–71

Bolgia, C., 2017, *Reclaiming the Roman Capitol: Santa Maria in Aracoeli from the Altar of Augustus to the Franciscans, c.500–1450*, London and New York

Bony, J., 1979, *The English Decorated Style: Gothic Architecture Transformed, 1250–1350*, Oxford

Boseley, I., 1907, *The Independent Church of Westminster Abbey (1650–1826)*

Boulton, J., 2000, 'London, 1540–1700', in P. Clark (ed.), *The Cambridge Urban History of Britain*, II: *1540–1840*, Cambridge, 315–46

Bourbon, N., 1540, *Nicolai Borbonii Vandoperani Lingonensis, Nugarum libri octo*, 2nd edn, Basel

Bowers, R., 2003, 'The Musicians and Liturgy of the Lady Chapel of the Monastery Church, c.1235–1540', in Tatton-Brown and Mortimer (eds), 2003, 33–57

Bowker, M., 1981, *The Henrician Reformation: The Diocese of Lincoln under John Longland, 1521–47*, Cambridge

Bradford, S., 1719, *A sermon preach'd before the House of Lords: in the Abbey Church of Westminst. On the 30th of January, 1718/9. Being the Anniversary of the Martyrdom of King Charles the First*

Bradford, S., 1989, *The Reluctant King: The Life and Reign of George VI, 1895–1952*, New York

Bradford, S., 1996, *Elizabeth: A Biography of Her Majesty the Queen*

Bradley, I., 2012, *God Save the Queen: The Spiritual Heart of the Monarchy*

Bradley, S., and N. Pevsner, 2003, *London, VI: Westminster*, The Buildings of England

Branner, R., 1964, 'Westminster Abbey and the French Court Style', *JSAH* 32: 3–18

Branner, R., 1965, *St. Louis and the Court Style in Gothic Architecture*

Bray, G. (ed.), 2005–6, *Records of Convocation*, Woodbridge

Brayley, E.W., 1818–23, *The History and Antiquities of the Abbey Church of St. Peter, Westminster*

Breay, C., and J. Story (eds), 2018, *Anglo-Saxon Kingdoms: Art, Word, War*, exh. cat., British Library

Bremner, G.A., 2004, '"Imperial Monumental Halls and Tower": Westminster Abbey and the Commemoration of Empire, 1854–1904', *AH* 47: 251–82

Brett, M.V., and Oliver, Viscount Esher (eds), 1934–8, *Journals and Letters of Reginald, Viscount Esher*

Brewer, J., 1997, *The Pleasures of the Imagination: English Culture in the Eighteenth Century*

Bridge, F., 1918, *A Westminster Pilgrim*

Brier, B., 2016, *Cleopatra's Needles: The Lost Obelisks of Egypt*, London, Oxford and New York

Brindle, S., 2010, 'Sir George Gilbert Scott and the Restoration of the Chapter House, 1849–72', in Rodwell and Mortimer (eds), 2010, ch. 9

Brooke, C. N. L., 1971, 'Approaches to Medieval Forgery', in *Medieval Church and Society: Collected Essays*, 100–20

Brown, G. C., 2001, *The Death of Christian Britain*

Brown, R., 2003, '"It's a very wonderful process …": Film and British Royalty, 1896–1902', *CH* 8: 1–22

Brownell, M. R., 1978, *Alexander Pope and the Arts of Georgian England*, Oxford

Buckland, W., 1848, *A Sermon Preached in Westminster Abbey on . . . the Re-opening of the Choir, and the Application of the Transepts to the Reception of the Congregation*

Bumpus, J. S., n.d. [1908], *A History of English Cathedral Music, 1549–1889*

Bunsen, F. von (ed.), 1869, *A Memoir of Baron Bunsen*, 2nd edn

Burman, P., 2004, 'Decorations, Furnishings and Art since 1900', in Keene, Burns and Saint (eds), 2004, 258–68

Burney, C., 1785, *An account of the musical performances in Westminster-Abbey and the Pantheon: May 26th, 27th, 29th; and June the 3d, and 5th, 1784. In Commemoration of Handel*

Burrows, D., 2005, *Handel and the English Chapel Royal*, Oxford

Bynum, C.W., 2007, *Wonderful Blood: Theology and Practice in Late Medieval Northern Germany and Beyond*, Philadelphia

Byrne, M. St. C. (ed.), 1981, *The Lisle Letters*, London and Chicago

Calamy, E., 1713, *An abridgement of Mr. Baxter's History of his life and times*, 2nd edn

Camden, W., 1600, *Reges, reginæ, nobiles, & alij in ecclesia collegiata B. Petri Westmonasterij sepulti, vsque annum reparatæ salutis 1600*

Camden, W., 1605/1870, *Remains concerning Britain*

Camden, W., 1610, *Britannia, or A chorographicall description of the most flourishing kingdomes, England, Scotland, and Ireland, and the ilands adioyning, out of the depth of antiquitie*

Cameron, A., 2001, *Report of the Review Group on the Royal Peculiars*

Campbell, J., 2014, *Roy Jenkins: A Well-Rounded Life*

Cannadine, D., 1981, 'War and Death, Grief and Mourning in Modern Britain', in J. Whaley (ed.), *Mirrors of Mortality: Studies in the Social History of Death*, 187–242

Cannadine, D., 1983, 'The Context, Performance and Meaning of Ritual: The British Monarchy and the "Invention of Tradition", *c*.1820–1977', in Hobsbawm and Ranger (eds), 1983, 101–64

Cannadine, D., 1995, 'Lord Curzon as Ceremonial Impresario', in D. Cannadine, *Aspects of Aristocracy: Grandeur and Decline in Modern Britain*, Harmondsworth, 77–108

Cannadine, D., 2003, *In Churchill's Shadow: Confronting the Past in Modern Britain*

Cannadine, D., 2008, 'Introduction: Independence Day Ceremonials in Historical Perspective', *Round Table* 97: 649–65

Carleton, J. D., 1965, *Westminster School: A History*, rev. edn

Carpenter, D. A., 1996, *The Reign of Henry III*

Carpenter, D., 2002, 'Westminster Abbey and the Cosmati Pavements in Politics, 1258–1269', in Grant and Mortimer (eds), 2002, 37–48

Carpenter, D. A., 2007, 'King Henry III and Saint Edward the Confessor: The Origins of the Cult', *EHR* 122: 865–91

Carpenter, D., 2010, 'King Henry III and the Chapter House of Westminster Abbey', in Rodwell and Mortimer (eds), 2010, 32–9

Carpenter, E., 1948, *Thomas Tenison, Archbishop of Canterbury: His Life and Times*

Carpenter, E. (ed.), 1966, *A House of Kings: The Official History of Westminster Abbey*

Carpenter, E. (ed.), 1972, *A House of Kings: The Official History of Westminster Abbey*, rev. edn

Carpenter, E., and D. Gentleman, 1987, *Westminster Abbey*

Caudle, J., 2000, 'Preaching in Parliament: Patronage, Publicity and Politics in Britain, 1701–60', in L. A. Ferrell and P. McCullough (eds), *The English Sermon Revised: Religion, Literature and History, 1600–1750*, Manchester, 235–64

Chamberlain, J. S., 1997, *Accommodating High Churchmen: The Clergy of Sussex, 1700–1745*, Urbana, Ill.

Chaplais, P., 1962, 'The Original Charters of Herbert and Gervaise, Abbots of Westminster (1121–1157)', in P. M. Barnes and C. F. Slade (eds), *A Medieval Miscellany for Doris Mary Stenton*, 89–110

Chapman, A., 2015, 'The International Context of Secularization in England: The End of Empire, Immigration, and the Decline of Christian National Identity, 1945–1970', *JBS* 54: 163–89

Cheney, C. R., 1951–2, 'Church-Building in the Middle Ages', *BJRL* 34: 20–36

Cheney, C. R., 1967, *Hubert Walter*

Chester, J. L. (ed.), 1876, *The Marriage, Baptismal, and Burial Registers of the Collegiate Church or Abbey of St. Peter, Westminster*, Harleian Society 10

Chrisman-Campbell, K., 2013, 'Diagnosing the Dress of the Queen's Train-Bearers at the Coronation of George III', *Costume* 47: 145–60

Churchill, W. S., 1956, *A History of the English-Speaking Peoples*, III: *The Age of Revolution*

Churton, E. (ed.), 1868, *Fourteen Letters from Daniel Waterland to Zachary Pearce*, Oxford and London

Clanchy, M. T., 1993, *From Memory to Written Record: England, 1066–1307*, 2nd edn, Oxford

Clark, J. W., 1896, 'On Ancient Libraries: (1) Lincoln Cathedral; (2) Westminster Abbey; (3) S. Paul's Cathedral', *Proceedings of the Cambridge Antiquarian Society* 9/1: 37–60

Clark, K., 1972, 'Epilogue', in E. Abbott *et al.*, *Westminster Abbey*, Wallop, Hants.

Claussen, P. C., 1987, *Magistri doctissimi Romani: Die römischen Marmorkünstler des Mittelalters*, Corpus Cosmatorum 1, Stuttgart

Claydon, T., 1996, *William III and the Godly Revolution*, Cambridge

Claydon, T., 2002, *William III*, Harlow

Clayton, M., 2008, 'The Old English *Promissio regis*', *ASE* 37: 91–150

Coates, W. H., A. S. Young and V. F. Snow (eds), 1982–92, *The Private Journals of the Long Parliament*, New Haven, Conn., and London

Cobb, H. S., 1999, 'Descriptions of the State Opening of Parliament, 1485–1601: A Survey', *PH* 18: 303–15

Cocke, T., 1995, *900 Years: The Restorations of Westminster Abbey*

Cocke, T., 2001, 'The Repository of our English Kings"': The Henry VII Chapel as Royal Mausoleum', *AH* 44: 212–20

Cocke, T., 2003, 'Henry VII Chapel: The Royal Connection', in Tatton-Brown and Mortimer (eds), 2003, 315–26

Colgrave, B., and R. A. B. Mynors (eds), 1969, *Bede's Ecclesiastical History of the English People*, Oxford [text and trans.]

Collinson, P., 1967, *The Elizabethan Puritan Movement*

Collinson, P., 1980, 'Sir Nicholas Bacon and the Elizabethan *Via media*', *HJ* 23: 255–73

Collinson, P., 2011, 'William Camden and the Anti-Myth of Elizabeth: Setting the Mould?' in Collinson, *This England: Essays on the English Nation and Commonwealth in the Sixteenth Century*, Manchester, 270–86

Coltman, V., 2007, 'Commission by Correspondence: John Flaxman's Monument to William Murray, 1st Earl of Mansfield', *CM* 22: 96–110

Colvin, H. M. (ed.), 1963, *The History of the King's Works*, I: *The Middle Ages*, pt 1

Colvin, H. M. (ed.), 1971, *Building Accounts of King Henry III*, Oxford

Colvin, H. M., 1979, 'Introduction', in E. G. W. Bill (ed.), *The Queen Anne Churches: A Catalogue of the Papers in Lambeth Palace Library of the Commission for Building Fifty New Churches in London and Westminster, 1711–1759*, pp. ix–xxi

Colvin, H. M. (ed.), 1982, *The History of the King's Works*, IV: *1485–1660*

Colvin, H., 2008, *A Biographical Dictionary of British Architects, 1600–1840*, 4th edn

Condon, M., 2003a, 'God Save the King! Piety, Propaganda and the Perpetual Memorial', in Tatton-Brown and Mortimer (eds), 2003, 59–99

Condon, M., 2003b, 'The Last Will of Henry VII: Document and Text', in Tatton-Brown and Mortimer (eds), 2003, 99–140

Connell, B. (ed.), 1962, *Regina v. Palmerston: The Correspondence between Queen Victoria and her Foreign and Prime Minister, 1837–1865*

Connell, P., 2005, 'Death and the Author: Westminster Abbey and the Meanings of the Literary Monument', *Eighteenth-Century Studies* 38: 557–85

Cooper, T., 1560, *Coopers Chronicle*

Courtney, A., 2014, 'The Scottish King and the English Court', in S. Doran and P. Kewes (eds), *Doubtful and Dangerous*, Manchester, 134–51

Coutu, J., 2006, *Persuasion and Propaganda: Monuments and the Eighteenth-Century British Empire*, Montreal, and Ithaca, NY

Cowie, R., and L. Blackmore, 2008, *Early and Middle Saxon Rural Settlement in the London Region*, Museum of London Archaeology Service Monograph 41

Cox, O., 2012, 'An Oxford College and the Eighteenth-Century Gothic Revival', *Oxoniensia* 77: 117–36

Craig, L., 2003, 'Royalty, Virtue and Adversity: The Cult of Henry VI', *Albion* 35: 187–209

Cramer, A., 2001, *Ampleforth: The Story of St Laurence's Abbey and College*, St Laurence Papers 5, Ampleforth

Crankshaw, D. J., 2004, 'Community, City and Nation, 1540–1714' in Keene, Burns and Saint (eds.), 2004, 45–70

Craske, M., 2000, 'Contacts and Contracts: Sir Henry Cheere and the Formation of a New Commercial World of Sculpture in Mid-Eighteenth-Century London', in C. Sicca and A. Yarrington (eds), *The Lustrous Trade: Material Culture and the History of Sculpture in England and Italy, c. 1700–c. 1860*, London and New York, 94–113

Craske, M., 2004, 'Westminster Abbey, 1720–70: A Public Pantheon Built upon Private Interest', in R. Wrigley and M. Craske (eds), *Pantheons: Transformations of a Monumental Idea*, Aldershot, 57–80

Craske, M., 2007, *The Silent Rhetoric of the Body: A History of Monumental Sculpture and Commemorative Art, 1720–1770*, New Haven, Conn., and London

Cressy, D., 2006, *England on Edge: Crisis and Revolution, 1640–1642*, Oxford

Crick, J., 2003, 'St Albans, Westminster and some Twelfth-Century Views of the Anglo-Saxon Past', *ANS* 25: 65–83

Croft, P., 1991, 'The Religion of Robert Cecil', *HJ* 34: 773–96

Croft, P. (ed.), 2002, *Patronage, Culture and Power: The Early Cecils*, New Haven, Conn., and London; esp. P. Croft, 'Mildred, Lady Burghley: The Matriarch', 283–99

Croft, P., 2003, *King James*, Basingstoke

Crook, J. M., 1995, *John Carter and the Mind of the Gothic Revival*

Crook, J. M., 2008, *Brasenose: The Biography of an Oxford College*, Oxford

Crook, J. M., 2013, *William Burges and the High Victorian Dream* (1981), rev. and enlarged edn

Cruickshanks, E., 1988, 'Lord North, Christopher Layer and the Atterbury Plot: 1720–33', in Cruickshanks and Black (eds), 1988, 92–106

Cruickshanks, E., and J. Black (eds), 1988, *The Jacobite Challenge*, Edinburgh

Curthoys, J., 2012, *The Cardinal's College: Christ Church, Chapter and Verse*

Dacre, N., 2003, 'The Funeral of Diana, Princess of Wales', *CH* 8: 85–90

Dalrymple, W., and A. Anand, 2017, *Koh-i-Noor: The History of the World's Most Infamous Diamond*

Darby, M., 1983, *John Pollard Seddon*, Catalogues of Architectural Drawings in the Victoria and Albert Museum

Dart, J., 1723, *Westmonasterium, or The history and antiquities of the Abbey Church of St. Peters Westminster*

Davie, G., and D. Martin, 1999, 'Liturgy and Music', in T. Walter (ed.), *The Mourning for Diana*, Oxford, 187–98

Dawson, J. E. A., 1984, 'The Foundation of Christ Church, Oxford, and Trinity College, Cambridge, in 1546', *BIHR* 57: 208–15

Dayan, D., 2005, 'Rituels populistes: Public et télévision aux funérailles de Lady Diana', *Bulletin d'Histoire Politique* 14: 89–107

De-la-Noy, M., 2016, *A Liberal and Godly Dean: The Life of Edward Carpenter*, privately printed

Dimbleby, J., 1975, *Richard Dimbleby: A Biography*

Doebner, R. (ed.), 1886, *Memoirs of Mary, Queen of England (1689–1693)*, Leipzig

Doyle, A. I., 1957, 'The Work of a Late Fifteenth-Century English Scribe, William Ebesham', *BJRL* 39: 298–325

Draper, P., 1984, 'King John and St Wulfstan', *Journal of Medieval History* 10: 41–50

Duffy, E., 1976, '"Whiston's Affair": The Trials of a Primitive Christian, 1709–1714', *JEH* 27: 129–50

Dunning, G. C., and V. I. Evison, 1961, 'The Palace of Westminster Sword', *Arch.* 98: 123–58

Du Prey, P. de La Ruffinière, 2000, *Hawksmoor's London Churches: Architecture and Theology*, Chicago and London

Eberle, P. J., 1999, 'Richard II and the Literary Arts', in A. Goodman and J. L. Gillespie (eds), *Richard II: The Art of Kingship*, Oxford, 231–53

Edie, C. A., 1990, 'The Public Face of Royal Ritual: Sermons, Medals, and Civic Ceremony in Later Stuart Coronations', *Huntington Library Quarterly* 53: 311–36

Edwards, A., 1984, *Matriarch: Queen Mary and the House of Windsor*, New York

Edwards, B., 2010, 'Edward VII Becomes King', in O'Neill and Hatt (eds), 2010, 23–31

Edwards, J., 2011, *Mary I: England's Catholic Queen*, New Haven, Conn., and London

Ellis, H. (ed.), 1807–8, *Holinshed's Chronicles of England, Scotland and Ireland*

Elton, G. R., 1986, *The Parliament of England, 1559–1581*, Cambridge

English, J., 2006, 'Empire Day in Britain, 1904–1958', *HJ* 49: 247–76

Evelyn, J., 1659, *A character of England*, 3rd edn

Evelyn, J., 1706, *An account of architects and architecture: together with an historical, etymological explanation of certain terms, particularly affected by architects. Much inlarg'd and improv'd, since the former impression*

Evenden, E., 2004, 'The Michael Wood Mystery: William Cecil and the Lincolnshire Printing of John Day', *Sixteenth Century Journal* 35: 383–94

Farquhar, H., 1936, 'New Light on Thomas Simon', *Numismatic Chronicle* 5th series 16: 210–34

Featley, D., 1636, *Clavis mystica*

Fenster, T. S., and J. Wogan Browne (trans.), 2008, *The History of Saint Edward the King by Matthew Paris*, Tempe, Ariz.

Fernie, E., 1983, *The Architecture of the Anglo-Saxons*

Fernie, E., 1987, 'Reconstructing Edward's Abbey at Westminster', in Neil Stratford (ed.), *Romanesque and Gothic: Essays for George Zarnecki*, Woodbridge, 1, 63–7

Fernie, E., 1993, *An Architectural History of Norwich Cathedral*, Oxford

Fernie, E., 2000, *The Architecture of Norman England*, Oxford

Field, J., 1987, *The King's Nurseries: The Story of Westminster School*

Fincham, K., and S. Taylor, 2013, 'The Restoration of the Church of England, 1660–62: Ordination, Re-Ordination and Conformity', in S. Taylor and G. Tapsell (eds), *The Nature of the English Revolution Revisited: Essays in Honour of John Morrill*, Woodbridge, 197–232

Firth, C. H., and R. S. Rait (eds), 1911, *Acts and Ordinances of the Interregnum, 1642–1660*

Fisher, G., G. Stamp *et al.*, 1981, *Catalogue of the Drawings Collection of the Royal Institute of British Architects: The Scott Family*, ed. J. Heseltine, Farnborough

Fitzgerald, M. H., 1928, *A Memoir of Herbert Edward Ryle KCVO, DD, sometime Bishop of Winchester and Dean of Westminster*

Fletcher, H., 1660, *The perfect politician: or A full view of the life and actions (military and civil) of O. Cromwel*

Fordham, D., 2007, 'Scalping: Social Rites in Westminster Abbey', in T. Barringer, G. Quilley and D. Fordham (eds), *Art and the British Empire*, Manchester, 99–119

Fordham, D., 2010, *British Art and the Seven Years' War: Allegiance and Autonomy*, Philadelphia and Oxford

Forshall, F. H., 1884, *Westminster School, Past and Present*

Foster, A., 1978, 'A Biography of Archbishop Richard Neile, 1562–1640', DPhil. diss., University of Oxford

Foxe, J., 1570, *The first volume of the ecclesiasticall history contaynyng the actes and monumentes of thynges passed*

Frankland, N., 1980, *Prince Henry, Duke of Gloucester*

Frazer, E., 2000, '"Probably the most public occasion the world has ever known": "Public" and "Private" in Press Coverage of the Death and Funeral of Diana, Princess of Wales', *Journal of Political Ideologies* 5: 201–23

Freeland, J. P. (trans.), 2005, *Aelred of Rievaulx: The Historical Works*, Kalamazoo, Mich.

Frere, W. H., and W. M. Kennedy (eds), 1910, *Visitation Articles and Injunctions*, I: *Introduction*, II: *1536–1558*, ACC 14, 15

Friedman, T., 2011, *The Eighteenth Century Church in Britain*, New Haven, Conn., and London

Galloway, P., 2000, *The Order of St Michael and St George*

Gardiner, S. R. (ed.), 1906, *The Constitutional Documents of the Puritan Revolution, 1625–1660*, 3rd, rev., edn, Oxford

Gardner, J., 1990, 'The Cosmati at Westminster: Some Anglo-Italian Reflexions', in J. Gärms and A. M. Romanini (eds), *Skulptur und Grabmal des Spätmittelalters in Rom und Italien*, Vienna, 201–16

Garnett, G., 1998, 'The Third Recension of the English Coronation *Ordo*: The Manuscripts', *Haskins Society Journal* 11: 43–71

Gavaghan, M., 1995, *The Story of the Unknown Warrior, 11 November 1920*, Wigan

Gem, R. D. H., 1980, 'The Romanesque Rebuilding of Westminster Abbey', *ANS* 3: 33–60

Gem, R. D. H., 2009, 'Craftsmen and Administrators in the Building of the Confessor's Abbey', in Mortimer (ed.), 2009, 168–72

George, M. D., 1951, *London Life in the Eighteenth Century*, 3rd edn

Gibbon, E., 1994, *The History of the Decline and Fall of the Roman Empire*, ed. D. Womersley

Gibson, J., 2001, *The Church of England, 1688–1832: Unity and Accord*

Gibson, W., 1989, 'An Eighteenth-Century Paradox: The Career of the Decipherer–Bishop, Edward Willes', *Journal for Eighteenth-Century Studies* 12: 69–76

Gilmour, D., 1994, *Curzon*

Girouard, M., 1981, *The Return to Camelot: Chivalry and the English Gentleman*, New Haven, Conn., and London

Gittings, C., 1984, *Death, Burial and the Individual in Early Modern England*

Given-Wilson, C., 2016, *Henry IV*, New Haven, Conn., and London

Glass, D. F., 1980, *Studies on Cosmatesque Pavements*, BAR International Series 82, Oxford

Goodall, J. S., 2011, 'The Jesus Chapel or Islip's Chantry at Westminster Abbey', *JBAA* 164: 260–76

Goodall, J. S., 2015, 'St Stephen's Chapel', in Rodwell and Tatton-Brown (eds), 2015, II, 111–19

Goodman, G., 1653, *The two great mysteries of Christian religion*

Gordon, D., L. Monnas and C. Elam (eds), 1997, *The Regal Image of Richard II and the Wilton Diptych*

Gransden, A., 1974, *Historical Writing in England*, I: *c.500 to c.1307*

Gransden, A., 1982, *Historical Writing in England*, II: *c.1307 to the Early Sixteenth Century*

Gransden, A., 2015, *A History of the Abbey of Bury St Edmund's, 1257–1301: Simon of Luton and John of Northwold*, Woodbridge

Grant, L., and R. Mortimer (eds), 2002, *Westminster Abbey: the Cosmati Pavements*, Courtauld Research Papers 3, Aldershot

Green, J. A., 2006, *Henry I, King of England and Duke of Normandy*, Cambridge

Green, S. J. D., 2011, *The Passing of Protestant England: Secularisation and Social Change, c.1920–1960*, Cambridge

Greenway, D. (ed.), 1998, *Henry, Archdeacon of Huntingdon, Historia Anglorum: The History of the English People*, Oxford [text and trans.]

Griffiths, R. A., 1981, *The Reign of King Henry VI: The Exercise of Royal Authority, 1422–1461*

Grimley, M., 2007, 'The Religion of Englishness: Puritanism, Providentialism, and "National Character"', *JBS* 46: 884–906

Grosley, P.-J., 1772, *A tour to London: or New observations on England, and its inhabitants*, trans. T. Nugent

Gunn, J. A. W., and M. G. Wiebe (eds), 1982–, *Benjamin Disraeli Letters*, Toronto

Gunning, T., 2010, 'Reproducing Royalty: Filming the Coronation of Edward VII', in O'Neill and Hatt (eds), 2010, 15–22

Guy, J., 2004, *My Heart is my Own: The Life of Mary Queen of Scots*

Hacket, J., 1693, *Scrinia reserata: a memorial offer'd to the great deservings of John Williams, D.D.*

Haines, R. M., 2003, *Edward II: Edward of Caernarfon, his Life, his Reign, and its Aftermath, 1284–1330*, Montreal and London

Hall, E., 1904, *The triumphant reigne of Kyng Henry the VIII*, ed. C. Whibley as *Henry VIII*

Hall, J., 2012, *Queen Elizabeth and her Church: Royal Service at Westminster Abbey*

Hall, J., 2017–18, 'In Memoriam', *WAR*, Winter: 2–4

Hallam Smith, E., 2010, 'The Chapter House as a Record Office', in Rodwell and Mortimer (eds), 2010, 124–38

Hallett, M., 1993, 'Framing the Modern City: Canaletto's Images of London', in M. Liversedge and J. Farrington (eds), *Canaletto and England*, 46–54

Hamilton, J. S., 2006, 'The Character of Edward II: The Letters of Edward of Caernarfon Reconsidered', in G. Dodd and A. Musson (eds), *Edward II: New Perspectives*, 5–21

Hamilton, W. D. (ed.), 1875–7, *A Chronicle of England during the Reigns of the Tudors, from A.D. 1485 to 1559, by Charles Wriothesley, Windsor Herald*, CS new series 11, 20

Hampton, S., 2011, 'The Manuscript Sermons of Archbishop John Williams', *JEH* 62: 707–25

Hampton, S., 2015, 'A "Theological Junto": The 1641 Lords' Subcommittee on Religious Innovation', *Seventeenth Century* 30: 433–54

Hanham, A., 2016, 'The Politics of Chivalry: Sir Robert Walpole, the Duke of Montagu, and the Order of the Bath', *PH* 35: 262–97

Hare, A. J. C., 1895, *Biographical Sketches, being Memorials of A. P. Stanley, H. Alford . . .*

Harmer, F. E. (ed.), 1952, *Anglo-Saxon Writs*, Manchester

Harris, B., 2002, *Politics and the Nation: Britain in the Mid-Eighteenth Century*, Oxford

Harris, J., 1994, *The Palladian Revival: Lord Burlington, his Villa and Garden at Chiswick*, Montreal and London

Harrison, S., and J. McNeill, 2015, 'The Romanesque Monastic Buildings at Westminster Abbey', in Rodwell and Tatton-Brown (eds), 2015, I, 69–103

Hartshorne, A. (ed.), 1905, *Memoirs of a Royal Chaplain, 1729–1763: The Correspondence of Edmund Pyle . . . with Samuel Kerrich*

Harvey, A. E., and R. Mortimer (eds), 2003, *The Funeral Effigies of Westminster Abbey* (1994), rev. repr. edn, Woodbridge

Harvey, B. F. (ed.), 1965, *Documents Illustrating the Rule of Walter de Wenlock, Abbot of Westminster, 1283–1307*, CS 4th series 2

Harvey, B. F., 1971, 'The Monks of Westminster and the University of Oxford', in F. R. H. Du Boulay and

C. M. Barron (eds), *The Reign of Richard II: Essays in Honour of May McKisack*, 108–30

Harvey, B. F., 1977, *Westminster Abbey and its Estates in the Middle Ages*, Oxford

Harvey, B. F., 1993, *Living and Dying in England: The Monastic Experience, 1100–1540*, Oxford

Harvey, B. F., 2003, 'The Monks of Westminster and the Old Lady Chapel', in Tatton-Brown and Mortimer (eds), 2003, 5–32

Harvey, J. H., 1956, 'The Masons of Westminster Abbey', *AJ* 113: 82–101

Haugaard, W. P., 1968, 'The Coronation of Elizabeth I', *JEH* 19: 161–70

Hawkins, E., 1848, *Inaugural Lecture upon the Foundation of Dean Ireland's Professorship*

Hawkins, J., 1776, *A general history of the science and practice of music*

Hawkyard, A., 2016, *The House of Commons, 1509–1558: Personnel, Procedure, Precedent and Change*, Parliamentary History: Texts and Studies 12

Hay, D. (ed.), 1950, *The Anglica historia of Polydore Vergil, A.D. 1485–1537*, CS 3rd series 74 [text and trans.]

Hector, L. C., and B. F. Harvey (eds), 1982, *The Westminster Chronicle, 1381–94*, Oxford [text and trans.]

Henig, M., 2015, '"A fine and private place": The Sarcophagus of Valerius Amandinus and the Origins of Westminster', in Rodwell and Tatton-Brown (eds), 2015, I, 23–33

Henry, D., 1770, *An historical description of Westminster-Abbey, its monuments and curiosities*

Higgins, A., 1894, 'On the Work of Florentine Sculptors in England in the Early Part of the Sixteenth Century: With Special Reference to the Tombs of Cardinal Wolsey and King Henry VIII', *AJ* 51: 129–220, 367–70

Higgott, G., 2004, 'The Fabric to 1670', in Keene, Burns and Saint (eds.), 2004, 171–89

Hill, R., 2007, *God's Architect: Pugin and the Building of Romantic Britain*

Hill, T., 1648, *The strength of the saints to make Jesus Christ their strength . . . commended . . . in a morning exercise in Westminster Abbey, the 19th of April 1648*

Hinchliff, P., 1997, 'Frederick Temple, Randall Davidson and the Coronation of Edward VII', *JEH* 48: 71–99

Hoak, D. E., 2003, 'The Coronations of Edward VI, Mary I, and Elizabeth I, and the Transformation of the Tudor

Monarchy', in Knighton and Mortimer (eds), 2003, 114–51

Hobsbawm, E., 1983, 'Mass-Producing Traditions: Europe, 1870–1914', in Hobsbawm and Ranger (eds), 1983, 263–307

Hobsbawm, E., and T. Ranger (eds), 1983, *The Invention of Tradition*, Cambridge

Hollister, C.W., 2001, *Henry I*, New Haven, Conn., and London

Horne, A., *Harold Macmillan*, II: *1957–1986*, New York, 1986

Horsley, H. (ed.), 1813, *The Speeches in Parliament of Samuel Horsley, . . . Late Lord Bishop of St Asaph*, Dundee

Horsley, H. (ed.), 1816, *Sermons by Samuel Horsley*

Howgrave-Graham, R. P., 1948, 'Westminster Abbey: The Sequence and Dates of the Transepts and Nave', *JBAA* 11: 60–78

Howlett, D., 2002, 'The Inscriptions in the Sanctuary Pavement at Westminster', in Grant and Mortimer (eds), 2002, 100–10

Hughes, A., 1952–3, 'Music of the Coronation over a Thousand Years', *Proceedings of the Royal Musical Association* 79: 81–100

Hunt, A., 2008, *The Drama of Coronation: Medieval Ceremony in Early Modern England*, Cambridge

Hunting, P., 1981, *Royal Westminster: A History of Westminster through its Royal Connections*

Hyland, A. D. C., 1962, 'Imperial Valhalla', *JSAH* 21: 129–39

Ireland, J., 1797, *Vindiciæ regiæ: or, A defence of the kingly office. In two letters to Earl Stanhope*

Ireland, J., 1830, *Nuptiæ sacræ, or An inquiry into the Scriptural Doctrine of Marriage and Divorce, Addressed to the Two Houses of Parliament*

Irving, W. (ed.), 1825, *The Miscellaneous Works of Oliver Goldsmith, with an Account of his Life and Writings*, new edn, Paris

Jansson, M. (ed.), 1988, *Proceedings in Parliament, 1614 (House of Commons)*, Philadelphia

Jebb, J., 1843, *The Choral Service of the United Church of England and Ireland*

Jeffery, P., 1996, *The City Churches of Sir Christopher Wren*

Jenkins, R., 1967, *Asquith*

Jenkinson, M., 2010, *Culture and Politics at the Court of Charles II, 1660–1685*, Woodbridge

Jenkyns, R., 2004, *Westminster Abbey*

Jennings, L. J. (ed.), 1884, *The Croker Papers*

Jones, C., 1999, '"Jacobites under the beds": Bishop Francis Atterbury, the Earl of Sunderland and the Westminster Dormitory Case of 1721', *British Library Journal* 25: 35–54

Jones, C., and G. Holmes (eds), 1985, *The London Diaries of William Nicolson, Bishop of Carlisle, 1702–1718*, Oxford

Jones, M. K., and M. G. Underwood, 1992, *The King's Mother: Lady Margaret Beaufort, Countess of Richmond and Derby*, Cambridge

Jones, N. L., 1982, *Faith by Statute: Parliament and the Settlement of Religion, 1559*, RHS Studies in History 32

Jordan, W. C., 2009, *A Tale of Two Monasteries: Westminster Abbey and Saint-Denis in the Thirteenth Century*, Princeton

Jordan, W. J., 1980, 'Sir Gilbert Scott', *AH* 23: 60–85

Kaulek, J. (ed.), 1885, *Correspondance politique de MM. de Castillon et de Marillac, ambassadeurs de France en Angleterre (1537–1542)*, Paris

Keay, A., 2008, *The Magnificent Monarch: Charles II and the Ceremonies of Power*, London and New York

Keene, D., A. Burns and A. Saint (eds), 2004, *St Paul's: The Cathedral Church of London, 604–2004*

Keepe, H., 1682, *Monumenta Westmonasteriensia: or An historical account of the original, increase, and present state of St. Peter's, or the Abby Church of Westminster*

Kelsey, S., 1997, *Inventing a Republic: The Political Culture of the English Commonwealth*, Manchester

Kemp, E. W., 1947, *Canonization and Authority in the Western Church*, Oxford

Keynes, S. (ed.), 1991, *Facsimiles of Anglo-Saxon Charters*, Oxford

Keynes, S., 2005, 'Wulfsige, Monk of Glastonbury, Abbot of Westminster (c. 990–3), and Bishop of Sherborne (c. 993–1002)', in K. Barker, D. A. Hinton and A. Hunt (eds), *St Wulfsige and Sherborne: Essays to Commemorate the Millennium of the Benedictine Abbey, 998–1998*, Oxford, 53–94

Keynes, S., 2013, 'Church Councils, Royal Assemblies, and Anglo-Saxon Royal Diplomas', in G. R. Owen-Crocker and B. W. Schneider (eds), *Kingship, Legislation and Power in Anglo-Saxon England*, Woodbridge, 2013, 17–182

Keynes, S., and R. Love, 2010, 'Earl Godwine's Ship', *ASE* 38: 185–223

Kingsford, C. L. (ed.), 1910, 'Two London Chronicles from the Collections of John Stow (1523–1564)', *Camden Miscellany* 12, CS 3rd series 18, pp. iii–59

Kinsey, D. C., 2009, 'Koh-i-Noor: Empire, Diamonds and the Performance of British Material Culture', *JBS* 48: 391–419

Kirk-Greene, A. H., 1999, *On Crown Service: A History of HM Colonial and Overseas Services, 1837–1997*

Kisby, F., 1995, 'Music and Musicians of Early Tudor Westminster', *Early Music* 23: 223–49

Knight, S., 2017, 'Ten Days that will Shake Britain: Life after Queen Elizabeth II', *The Guardian*, 17 March

Knighton, C. S., 1981, 'Economics and Economies of a Royal Peculiar: Westminster Abbey, 1540–1640', in M. R. O'Day and F. M. Heal (eds), *Princes and Paupers in the English Church, 1500–1800*, Leicester, 45–64

Knighton, C. S., 1991, 'The Provision of Education in the New Cathedral Foundations of Henry VIII', in D. Marcombe and C. S. Knighton (eds), 1991, *Close Encounters: English Cathedrals and Society since 1540*, Nottingham, 18–24

Knighton, C. S., 1996, 'The Reformed Chapter, 1540–1660', in W. N. Yates with P. A. Welsby (eds), *Faith and Fabric: A History of Rochester Cathedral, 604–1994*, Woodbridge, 57–76

Knighton, C. S., 2006, 'Westminster Abbey Restored', in E. Duffy and D. M. Loades (eds), *Marian Catholicism*, Aldershot, 77–123

Knighton, C. S., and Mortimer, R. (eds), 2003, *Westminster Abbey Reformed, 1540–1640*, Aldershot

Knoppers, L. L., 2000, *Constructing Cromwell: Ceremony, Portrait, and Print*, Cambridge

Knowles, D., 1948–59, *The Religious Orders in England*, Cambridge

Knowles, D., 1963, *The Monastic Order in England, 940–1216*, 2nd edn, Cambridge

Knowles, J., 1889, 'The Cloisters', *NC* 25: 415–17 [with plan]

Knowles, J., 1890, 'The Threatened Disfigurement of Westminster Abbey', *NC* 28: 54–8 [with plans]

Kruse, A., 2003, *Roskilde Domkirke*, Roskilde

Kuhn, W. M., 1996, *Democratic Royalism: The Transformation of the British Monarchy, 1861–1914*, Basingstoke

Kurpershoek, E., and J. Vrieze, 1999, *The Nieuwe Kerk, Amsterdam*, Amsterdam

Laing, D. (ed.), 1841–2, *The Letters and Journals of Robert Baillie . . . 1637–62*, Edinburgh

Lamb, J., 1831, *Masters' History of the College of Corpus Christi and the Blessed Virgin Mary in the University of Cambridge, with Additional Matter and a Continuation to the Present Time by John Lamb D.D.*

Langford, P., 1988, 'Convocation and the Tory Clergy, 1717–61', in Cruickshanks and Black (eds), 1988, 107–22

Larkin, J. F., and P. L. Hughes (eds), 1973–83, *Stuart Royal Proclamations*, Oxford

Latham, R., and W. Matthews (eds), 1970–83, *The Diary of Samuel Pepys*

Legg, J. W. (ed.), 1891–7, *Missale ad usum Ecclesie Westmonasteriensis, with a Commentary on the Music of the Missal*, HBS 1, 5, 12

Legg, J. W. (ed.), 1900, *Three Coronation Orders*, HBS 19

Legg, L. G. W. (ed.), 1901, *English Coronation Records*

Lehmann-Brockhaus, O., 1955–60, *Lateinische Schriftquellen zur Kunst in England, Wales und Schottland vom Jahre 901 bis zum Jahre 1307*, Munich

Lehmberg, S. E., 1970, *The Reformation Parliament, 1529–1536*, Cambridge

Lehmberg, S. E., 1988, *The Reformation of Cathedrals: Cathedrals in English Society, 1485–1603*, Princeton

Lehmberg, S. E., 1996, *Cathedrals under Siege: Cathedrals in English Society, 1600–1700*, Exeter

Lehmberg, S. E., 2003, 'The Musicians of Westminster Abbey, 1540–1640', in Knighton and Mortimer (eds), 2003, 94–113

Lethaby, W. R., 1906, *Westminster Abbey and the King's Craftsmen*

Lethaby, W. R., 1925, *Westminster Abbey Re-Examined*

Lever, J. (ed.), 1976, *Catalogue of the Drawings Collection of the Royal Institute of British Architects, O–R*

Licence, T., 2016, 'The Date and Authorship of the *Vita Ædwardi Regis*', *ASE* 44: 259–85

Liddon, H. T., 1893–7, *Life of Edward Bouverie Pusey*, ed. J. O. Johnston and R. J. Wilson

Lindley, K., 1997, *Popular Politics and Religion in Civil War London*, Aldershot

Lindley, P., 2003, '"The singuler mediacion and praiers of al the holie companie of Heven": Structural Functions and Forms in the Chapel', in Tatton-Brown and Mortimer (eds), 2003, 259–94

Lindley, P., 2007, 'The Funeral and Tomb Effigies of Queen Catherine de Valois and Henry V', *JBAA* 160: 165–77

Links, J. G., 1977, *Canaletto and his Patrons*

Links, J. G., 1994, *Canaletto*, rev. and enlarged edn

Linnell, C. L. S. (ed.), 1964, *The Diaries of Thomas Wilson DD, 1731–37 and 1750, Son of Bishop Wilson of Sodor and Man*

Litten, J., 2003, 'The Funeral Effigy: Its Function and Purpose', in Harvey and Mortimer (eds), 2003, 3–19

Llewellyn, N., 2000, *Funeral Monuments in Post-Reformation England*, Cambridge

Loades, D. M., 1989, *Mary Tudor: A Life*, Oxford

Loades, D. M., 2003, 'The Sanctuary', in Knighton and Mortimer (eds), 2003, 75–93

Logan, F. D., 1977, 'The Origins of the so-called Regius Professorships: An Aspect of the Renaissance in Oxford and Cambridge', in D. Baker (ed.), *Renaissance and Renewal in Christian History*, Studies in Church History 14, Oxford, 271–8

Longford, E., 1966, *Victoria RI*

Luard, H. R. (ed.), 1858, *Lives of Edward the Confessor*, RS 3

Luard, H. R. (ed.), 1865, *Annales monastici*, II: *Annales monasterii de Wintonia (AD 519–1277). Annales monasterii de Waverleia (AD 1–1291)*, RS 36/2

Luard, H. R. (ed.), 1872–83, *Matthaei Parisiensis monachi Sancti Albani Chronica majora*, RS 57

Luard, H. R. (ed.), 1890, *Flores historiarum*, III: *AD 1265–AD 1326*, RS 95

Luce, R., 2007, *Ringing the Changes: A Memoir*, Norwich

Luders, A., *et al.* (eds), 1810–28, *Statutes of the Realm*, Record Commission

Lunt, A., 2015, 'From Operatic Grandeur to Domestic Pageantry: The Evolution of Ceremonial during the Reign of King George V', BA diss., Princeton University

MacArthur, W. P., 1928, 'The Cause of the Death of William, Duke of Gloucester, Son of Queen Anne, in 1700', *British Medical Journal* 24 March: 502–3

McClure, N. E. (ed.), 1939, *The Letters of John Chamberlain*, Philadelphia

MacCulloch, D. (ed.), 1984, 'The *Vitae Mariae Angliae reginae* of Robert Wingfield of Brantham', *Camden Miscellany* 28, CS 4th series 29, 181–301

MacCulloch, D., 1999, *Tudor Church Militant: Edward VI and the Protestant Reformation*

MacCulloch, D., 2003, *Reformation: Europe's House Divided, 1490–1700*

MacCulloch, D., 2011, 'Foxes, Firebrands, and Forgery: Robert Ware's Pollution of Reformation History', *HJ* 54: 307–46

MacCulloch, D., 2016, *Thomas Cranmer: A Life*, rev. edn, New Haven, Conn., and London

MacCulloch, D., 2018, *Thomas Cromwell: A Revolutionary Life*

McGinnis, P. J., and A. H. Williamson (eds), 1995, *George Buchanan: The Political Poetry*, Edinburgh

McGuignan, J., 2001, 'British Identity and the People's Princess', *SR* 48: 1–18

McKibbin, R., 2000, *Classes and Cultures: England, 1918–1951*, Oxford

McSheffrey, S., 2017, *Seeking Sanctuary: Crime, Mercy and Politics in English Courts, 1400–1550*, Oxford

Madden, F. (ed.), 1866–9, *Matthaei Parisiensis, monachi Sancti Albani, Historia Anglorum*, RS 44

Maddicott, J. R., 1970, *Thomas of Lancaster, 1307–1322: A Study in the Reign of Edward II*, Oxford

Magnus, P., 1975, *King Edward the Seventh*, Harmondsworth

Malcolm, T. P., 1803, *Londinium redivivum, or An Ancient History and Modern Description of London*

Marriot, S., 2007, 'The BBC, ITN and the Funeral of Princess Diana', *Media History* 13: 93–110

Martin, R. B., 1980, *Tennyson: The Unquiet Heart*, Oxford

Mason, E., 1984, 'St Wulfstan's Staff: A Legend and its Uses', *Medium Aevum* 53: 157–79

Mason, E. (ed.), 1988, *Westminster Abbey Charters, 1066–c. 1214*, LRS 25

Mason, E., 1996, *Westminster Abbey and its People, c. 1050–c. 1216*, Woodbridge

Mather, F. C., 1992, *High Church Prophet: Bishop Samuel Horsley (1733–1806) and the Caroline Tradition in the Late Georgian Church*, Oxford and New York

Mathieson, W. L., 1923, *English Church Reform, 1815–1840*

Mayer, T. F., 2000, *Reginald Pole: Prince & Prophet*, Cambridge

Mayor, J. E. B. (ed.), 1863–9, *Ricardi de Cirencestria Speculum historiale de gestis regum Angliae*, RS 30

Meads, D. M. (ed.), 1930, *The Diary of Lady Margaret Hoby*

Mellows, W. T. (ed.), 1939, *Peterborough Local Administration: The Foundation of Peterborough Cathedral, A.D. 1541*, NRS 13 [dated 1941 for 1939]

Mellows, W. T. (ed.), 1940, *Peterborough Local Administration: The Last Days of Peterborough Monastery*, NRS 12 [dated 1947 for 1940]

Merritt, J. F., 2001, 'The Cradle of Laudianism? Westminster Abbey, 1558–1630', *JEH* 52: 623–46

Merritt, J. F., 2002, 'The Cecils and Westminster, 1558–1612: The Development of an Urban Power Base', in Croft (ed.), 2002, 231–46

Merritt, J. F., 2003, '"Under the shadowe of the Church"? The Abbey and the Town of Westminster, 1530–1640', in Knighton and Mortimer (eds), 2003, 152–82

Merritt, J. F., 2005, *The Social World of Early Modern Westminster: Abbey, Court and Community, 1525–1640*, Manchester

Merritt, J. F., 2013, *Westminster, 1640–1660: A Royal City in a Time of Revolution*, Manchester

Merritt, J. F., 2016, 'Reinventing Westminster Abbey, 1642–1660: A House of Kings from Revolution to Restoration', *JEH* 67: 122–38

Middleton, T., 1604, *The Ant, and the Nightingale, or Father Hubburds Tales*

Miles, D., and M. Bridge, 2010, 'The Chapter House Doors and their Dating', in Rodwell and Mortimer (eds), 2010, 251–60

Milne, J. H., 1914, *Great Britain in the Coronation Year, being a Historical Record of the Crowning of their Imperial Majesties King George the Fifth and Queen Mary*

Milner, L., 2016, 'St Faith's Chapel at Westminster Abbey: The Significance of its Design, Decoration and Location', *JBAA* 169: 71–94

Monnas, L., 2004, 'The Furnishing of Royal Closets and the Use of Small Devotional Images in the Reign of Richard II: The Setting of the Wilton Diptych Reconsidered', in W. M. Ormrod (ed.), *Fourteenth-Century England*, III, Woodbridge, 185–206

Monod, P. K., 1999, *The Power of Kings: Monarchy and Religion in Europe, 1589–1715*, New Haven, Conn.

Moore, T. (ed.), 1761, *Sermons and discourses on several subjects and occasions: By Francis Atterbury D.D. late lord bishop of Rochester, and dean of Westminster*

Morrin, J., 2004, 'Estates and Income, 1714–2004', in Keene, Burns and Saint (eds), 2004, 335–42

Morris, W., 1889, 'Westminster Abbey and its Monuments', *NC* 25: 409–14

Morris, W., 1893, *Concerning Westminster Abbey*

Morrissey, M., 2011, *Politics and the Paul's Cross Sermons, 1558–1642*, Oxford

Mortimer, R., 2003, 'The History of the Collection', in Harvey and Mortimer (eds), 2003, 21–8

Mortimer, R. (ed.), 2009, *Edward the Confessor: The Man and the Legend*, Woodbridge

Mowl, T., 1985, 'Henry Keene, 1726–1776: A Goth in Spite of Himself', in R. Brown (ed.), *The Architectural Outsiders*, 82–97

Munro, K., 2001, 'Canada as Reflected in her Participation in the Coronation of her Monarchs in the Twentieth Century', *Journal of Historical Sociology*, 14: 21–46

Murphy, P., 2013, *Monarchy and the End of Empire: The House of Windsor, the British Government, and the Post-War Commonwealth*, Oxford

Musset, L., 1985, *Normandie romane*, II: *La Haute-Normandie*, 2nd edn, La Pierre-qui-Vire

Mynors, R. A. B., with R. M. Thomson and M. Winterbottom (eds), 1998–9, *William of Malmesbury, 'Gesta regum Anglorum' / The History of the English Kings*, Oxford [I: text and trans.; II: commentary]

Naismith, R. N., 2017, *Medieval European Coinage*, VIII: *Britain and Ireland, c.400–1066*, Cambridge

Naismith, R. N., *Citadel of the Saxons: The Rise of Early London*, London and New York, 2019

Newton, T., 1782, *The works of the Right Reverend Thomas Newton, D.D. Late Lord Bishop of Bristol and Dean of St. Paul's, London. With some account of his life . . . written by himself*

Nicholas, S., 1996, 'The Construction of a National Identity: Stanley Baldwin, "Englishness" and the Mass-Media in Inter-War Britain', in M. Francis and I. Zweiniger-Barrielowska (eds), *The Conservatives and British Society*, Cardiff, 127–46

Nichols, J. (ed.), 1828, *The Progresses, Processions, and Magnificent Festivities of King James the First*

Nichols, J. G. (ed.), 1848, *The Diary of Henry Machyn, Citizen and Merchant-Taylor of London from A.D. 1550 to A.D. 1563*, CS 42

Nichols, J. G. (ed.), 1852, *The Chronicle of the Grey Friars of London*, CS 53

Nicolson, H., 1967, *King George the Fifth: His Life and Reign*

Norbrook, D., 1999, *Writing the English Republic: Poetry, Rhetoric and Politics, 1627–1660*, Cambridge

Norris, W. F., 1933, 'Should the Monuments be Removed from Westminster Abbey?', *Architectural Association Journal* 48: 224–34

Norton, D., 2011, *The King James Bible: A Short History from Tyndale to Today,* Cambridge

Null, A., 2003, 'John Redman, The Gentle Ambler', in Knighton and Mortimer (eds), 2003, 38–74

O'Byrne, A. F., 2008, 'Composing Westminster Bridge: Public Improvement and National Identity in Eighteenth-

Century London', in M. E. Novak (ed.), *The Age of Projects*, Toronto, 243–70

Ogborn, M., 1998, *Spaces of Modernity: London's Geographies, 1680–1780*, New York and London

Ogilby, J., 1662, *The entertainment of His most excellent Majestie Charles II, in his passage through the city of London to his coronation*

Olechnowicz, A., 2007, 'Historians and the Modern British Monarchy', in Olechnowicz (ed.), 2007, 6–44

Olechnowicz, A. (ed.), 2007, *The Monarchy and the British Nation, 1780 to the Present*, Cambridge

O'Neill, M., and M. Hatt (eds), 2010, *The Edwardian Sense: Art, Design, and Performance in Britain, 1901–1910*, New Haven, Conn., and London

O'Neilly, J. G., and L. E. Tanner, 1966, 'The Shrine of St Edward the Confessor', *Arch.* 100: 129–54

Ormrod, W. M., 2012, *Edward III*, New Haven, Conn., and London

Örnebring, H., 2004, 'Revisiting the Coronation: A Critical Perspective on the Coronation of Queen Elizabeth in 1953', *Nordicom Review* 25: 170–83

Owens, E., 2015, 'The Media and the Transformation of the British Monarchy, 1932–53', PhD diss., University of Manchester

Page, W. (ed.), 1907, *VCH: Gloucester*

Page, W. (ed.), 1909, *VCH: London*, 1: *London within the Bars, Westminster and Southwark*

Page, W., 1923, *London, its Origin and Early Development*

Palliser, D. M., 2004, 'Royal Mausolea in the Long Fourteenth Century (1272–1422)', *Fourteenth Century England* 3: 1–16

Pantin, W. A. (ed.), 1931–7, *Documents Illustrating the Activities of the General and Provincial Chapters of the English Black Monks, 1215–1540*, CS 45, 47, 54

Patterson, C. F., 2000, 'Corporations, Cathedrals and the Crown: Local Dispute and Royal Interest in Early Stuart England', *History* 85: 546–71

Pearce, E. H., 1916, *The Monks of Westminster, being a Register of the Brethren of the Convent from the Time of the Confessor to the Dissolution, with Lists of Obedientiaries and an Introduction*, NDWA 5, Cambridge

Pearce, Z., 1722a, *A letter to the clergy of the Church of England: On occasion of the commitment of the Right Reverend the Lord Bishop of Rochester to the Tower of London*

Pearce, Z., 1722b, *A second letter to the clergy of the Church of England: On occasion of the commitment of the Right Reverend the Lord Bishop of Rochester to the Tower of London*

Pearce, Z., 1760, *A sermon preached at the abby-church, Westminster, on Tuesday June 3. 1760: at a jubilee then kept by the Members of the Collegiate Church, on Account of its being the 200th year since the Date of their Charter of Foundation*

Pearce, Z., 1777, *A commentary with notes on the four Evangelists and the Acts of the Apostles*, ed. J. Derby

Pearman, A. J., 1897, *Rochester*, Diocesan Histories

Pearson, H., 1957, *Gilbert: His Life of Strife*

Pelling, E., 1685, *A sermon preached at Westminster-Abbey on the 26th of July, 1685: Being the thanksgiving-day for His Majesties victory over the rebels*

Perkins, J., 1902, *The Coronation Book*

Perkins, J., 1920, *The Most Honourable Order of the Bath: A Descriptive and Historical Account*, 2nd, enlarged, edn

Perkins, J., 1937a, *The Organs and Bells of Westminster Abbey*.

Perkins, J., 1937b, *Westminster Abbey: The Empire's Crown*

Perkins, J., 1938–52, *Westminster Abbey: Its Worship and Ornaments*, ACC 33, 34, 38

Phillips, J., 1656, *Sportive wit*

Physick, J., and M. Darby, 1973, *Marble Halls: Drawings and Models for Victorian Secular Buildings*, exh. cat., Victoria and Albert Museum, London

Pimlott, B., 1996, *The Queen: A Biography of Queen Elizabeth II*

Pope-Hennessy, J., 1959, *Queen Mary, 1867–1953*

Port, M. H. (ed.), 1986, *The Commissions for Building Fifty New Churches: The Minute Books, 1711–27, A Calendar*, LRS 23

Powicke, F. M., 1962, *The Thirteenth Century, 1216–1307*, 2nd edn, Oxford

Pratt, D., forthcoming, 'The Second Anglo-Saxon Coronation ordo', *ASE* 46

Prestwich, M., 1997, *Edward I*, New Haven, Conn., and London

Prochaska, F., 1995, *Royal Bounty: The Making of a Welfare Monarchy*

Prothero, R. E., 1893, *Life and Correspondence of Arthur Penrhyn Stanley*

Quiney, A., 1979, *John Loughborough Pearson*, New Haven, Conn., and London

Quinn, E. V., and J. M. Prest (eds), 1987, *Dear Miss Nightingale: A Selection of Benjamin Jowett's Letters, 1860–93*, Oxford

Ralph, J., 1783, *A critical review of the public buildings, statues, and ornaments: in and about London and Westminster*

Range, M., 2012, *Music and Ceremonial at British Coronations, from James I to Elizabeth II*, Cambridge

Range, M., 2016, *British Royal and State Funerals: Music and Ceremonial since Elizabeth I*, Woodbridge

Readman, P., 2005, 'The Place of the Past in English Culture, c.1890–1914', *Past & Present* 186: 147–99

Reeve, H. (ed.), 1896–9, *The Greville Memoirs: A Journal of the Reigns of King George IV, King William IV, and Queen Victoria*, new edn, London and New York

Reynolds, C. (ed.), 2011, *Surveyors of the Fabric of Westminster Abbey, 1827–1906: Reports and Letters*, Westminster Abbey Record Series 5, Woodbridge

Rhodes James, R. (ed.), 1967, *'Chips': The Diaries of Sir Henry Channon*

Richards, J., 2004, 'The Coronation of Queen Elizabeth II and Film', *CH* 9: 69–79

Richards, J., 2007, 'The Monarchy and Film, 1900–2006', in Olechnowicz (ed.), 2007, 358–79

Richardson, H. G., 1960, 'The Coronation in Medieval England: The Evolution of the Office and the Oath', *Traditio* 16: 111–202

Richardson, M., 1994, *Sketches by Edwin Lutyens*

Ridley, J., 2012, *Bertie: A Life of Edward VII*

Rigold, S., 1976, *The Chapter House and the Pyx Chamber, Westminster Abbey*

Riley, H.T. (ed.), 1867–9, *Gesta abbatum monasterii Sancti Albani, a Thoma Walsingham*

Riley, H.T. (ed.), 1870–71, *Annales monasterii S. Albani a Johanne Amundesham, monacho, ut videtur conscripti (A.D. 1420–1440)*, RS 28/5

Risk, J.C., 1972, *The History of the Order of the Bath and its Insignia*

Roberts, B., 2017, 'The Complex Holiday Calendar of 1902: Responses to the Coronation of Edward VII and the Growth of Edwardian Event Fatigue', *Twentieth-Century British History* 28: 489–515

Robertson, J.C. (ed.), 1877, *Materials for the History of Thomas Becket*, III, RS 67

Robinson, J.A. (ed.), 1909, *The History of Westminster Abbey by John Flete*, NDWA 2, Cambridge

Robinson, J.A., 1911, *The Abbot's House at Westminster*, NDWA 4, Cambridge

Robinson, J. A., and M. R. James, 1909, *The Manuscripts of Westminster Abbey*, NDWA 1, Cambridge

Robinson, J.M., 2012, *James Wyatt (1746–1813): Architect to George III*, New Haven, Conn., and London

Rodwell, W., 2009, 'New Glimpses of Edward the Confessor's Abbey at Westminster', in Mortimer (ed.), 2009, 151–67

Rodwell, W., 2010a, 'The Chapter House Complex: Morphology and Construction', in Rodwell and Mortimer (eds), 2010, 1–31

Rodwell, W., 2010b, *The Lantern Tower of Westminster Abbey, 1060–2010: Reconstructing its History and Architecture*, WAOP 3rd series 1, Oxford

Rodwell, W., 2015, 'The Archaeology of Westminster Abbey: An Historiographical Overview', in Rodwell and Tatton-Brown (eds), 2015, I, 34–60

Rodwell, W., D. Miles, D. Hamilton and M. Bridge, 2006, 'The Dating of the Pyx Door', *English Heritage Historical Review* 1: 24–7

Rodwell, W., and R. Mortimer (eds), 2010, *Westminster Abbey Chapter House: The History, Art and Architecture of 'a chapter house beyond compare'*

Rodwell, W., and T. Tatton-Brown (eds), 2015, *Westminster: The Art, Architecture and Archaeology of the Royal Abbey and Palace*, BAACT 39, Leeds

Rodwell, W., et al., 2013, *The Coronation Chair and Stone of Scone: History, Archaeology and Conservation*, WAOP 3rd series 2, Oxford

Rogers, N., 1973, 'Aristocratic Clientage, Trade and Independency: Popular Politics in Pre-Radical Westminster', *Past & Present* 61: 70–106

Rogers, N., 1989, *Whigs and Cities: Popular Politics in the Age of Walpole and Pitt*, Oxford

Roscoe, I., E. Hardy and M. G. Sullivan (eds), 2009, *A Biographical Dictionary of Sculptors in Britain, 1660–1851*, New Haven, Conn., and London

Rose, J., 2012, 'By Law Established: The Church of England and the Royal Supremacy', in G. Tapsell (ed.), *The Later Stuart Church, 1660–1714*, Manchester, 21–45

Rose, K., 1983, *King George V*

Ross, C., 1997, *Edward IV*, new edn, New Haven, Conn., and London

Rosser, G., 1989, *Medieval Westminster, 1200–1450*, Oxford

Routh, M.J. (ed.), 1833, *Bishop Burnet's History of his Own Time*, 2nd edn, Oxford

Sachse, W.L. (ed.), 1961, *The Diurnal of Thomas Rugg, 1659–1661*, CS 3rd series 91

Saint, A., 2004, 'The Reputation of St Paul's', in Keene, Burns and Saint (eds), 2004, 451–63

St John Hope, W. H., 1906, *The Obituary Roll of John Islip, Abbot of Westminster, 1500–1532, with Notes on Other English Obituary Rolls*, Society of Antiquaries, Vetusta Monumenta 7/4

Sandford, F., 1687, *The history of the coronation of the most high, most mighty, and most excellent monarch, James II*

Sargeaunt, J., 1898, *Annals of Westminster School*

Saul, N., 1996, 'Richard II and Westminster Abbey', in Blair and Golding (eds), 1996, 196–218

Saul, N., 1997, *Richard II*, New Haven, Conn., and London

Saunders, J., 1997, 'English Cathedral Choirs and Churchmen 1558 to the Civil War: An Occupational Study', PhD diss., University of Cambridge

Sawyer, P., 1968, *Anglo-Saxon Charters: An Annotated List and Bibliography*, RHS Guides and Handbooks 8; rev. and updated online edn at <www.esawyer.org.uk>

Scarisbrick, J.J., 1988, 'Henry VIII and the Dissolution of the Secular Colleges', in C. Cross, D. Loades and J. J. Scarisbrick (eds), *Law and Government under the Tudors: Essays Presented to Sir Geoffrey Elton . . . on his Retirement*, Cambridge, 51–66

Schölvinck, H., 1999, *Graven in de Nieuwe Kerk Amsterdam*, Amsterdam

Scholz, B.W., 1961, 'The Canonization of Edward the Confessor', *Speculum* 26: 38–60

Scholz, B.W., 1964, 'Sulcard of Westminster: "Prologus de construccione Wesmonasterii"', *Traditio* 20: 59–91

Schwartz, B., 1984, 'The Language of Constitutionalism: Baldwinite Conservatism', in B. Schwartz *et al.* (eds), *Formations of Nations and People*, 1–18

Schwoerer, L., 1992, 'The Coronation of William and Mary, April 11 1689', in L. L. Schwoerer (ed.), *The Revolution of 1688–89: Changing Perspectives*, Cambridge, 107–30

Scott, G.G., 1861–2, 'On the Conservation of Ancient Monuments', *R.I.B.A Trans. 2 Sessional Papers of the Royal Institute of British Architects*

Scott, G. G., 1995, *Personal and Professional Recollections* (1879), ed. G. Stamp, Stamford

Scott, G. G. *et al.*, 1863, *Gleanings from Westminster Abbey*, 2nd edn, enlarged

Sedgwick, R. (ed.), 1970, *The History of Parliament: The House of Commons, 1715–1754*

Sharpe, K., 1979, *Sir Robert Cotton, 1586–1631*, Oxford

Sharpe, K., 2010, *Image Wars: Promoting Kings and Commonwealths in England, 1603–1660*, New Haven, Conn. and London

Sharpe, K., 2013, *Rebranding Rule: The Restoration and Revolution Monarchy, 1660–1714*, New Haven, Conn., and London

Sharpe, R., *et al.* (eds), 1996, *English Benedictine Libraries: The Shorter Catalogues*, Corpus of British Medieval Library Catalogues 4

Shaw, W.A., 1900, *History of the English Church during the Civil Wars and under the Commonwealth, 1640–1660*

Shawcross, W., 2009, *Queen Elizabeth the Queen Mother: The Official Biography*

Shawcross, W. (ed.), 2012, *Counting One's Blessings: The Selected Letters of Queen Elizabeth the Queen Mother*

Shaw-Lefevre, G., 1882, 'Public Works in London', *NC* 12: 667–86

Shaw-Lefevre, G., 1884, 'Statues and Monuments of London', *NC* 15:28–48

Shenton, C., 2012, *The Day Parliament Burned Down*, Oxford

Sheppard, J. B. (ed.), 1887–9, *Literae Cantuarienses: The Letter Books of the Monastery of Christ Church, Canterbury*, RS 85

Sherburn, G. (ed.), 1956, *The Correspondence of Alexander Pope*, Oxford

Sherlock, P., 2007, 'The Monuments of Elizabeth Tudor and Mary Stuart', *JBS* 46: 263–89

Sherwood, R., 1977, *The Court of Oliver Cromwell*

Shils, E., and M. Young, 1953, 'The Meaning of the Coronation', *SR* 1: 63–81

Sicca, C.M., and L.A. Waldman (eds), 2012, *The Anglo-Florentine Renaissance: Art for the Early Tudors*, New Haven, Conn., and London

Smalley, B., 1973, *The Becket Conflict and the Schools: A Study of Intellectuals in Politics*, Oxford

Smith, D. M. (ed.), 2008, *Heads of Religious Houses: England and Wales*, III: *1377–1540*, Cambridge

Smith, E.A., 1999, *George IV*, New Haven, Conn.

Smith, H., 2006, *Georgian Monarchy: Politics and Culture, 1714–1760*, Cambridge

Smith, J.T., 1828, *Nollekens and his Times*

Smith, S., 1998, 'The Westminster Dormitory', in E. Corp (ed.), *Lord Burlington, the Man and his Politics: Questions of Loyalty*, Lewiston, NY, 51–71

Smyly, J. G., 1922, 'Thomas Gardiner's History of England', *Hermathena* 19: 235–48

South, R., 1727, *Twelve sermons and discourses on several subjects and occasions*, 6th edn

Spottiswood, J., 1655, *The history of the Church of Scotland: beginning the year of our Lord 203, and continued to the end of the reign of King James the VI.*

Spraggon, J., 2003, *Puritan Iconoclasm during the English Civil War*, Woodbridge

Stamp, G. (ed.), 1995, *Personal and Professional Recollections of George Gilbert Scott (1879)*, Stamford

Stanley, A. P., 1844, *Life and Correspondence of Thomas Arnold*

Stanley, A. P. (ed.), 1845, *The Miscellaneous Works of Thomas Arnold*

Stanley, A. P., 1850, 'The Gorham Case', *Edinburgh Review*, July: 263–92

Stanley, A. P., 1861, 'Essays and Reviews', *Edinburgh Review*, April: 461–500

Stanley, A. P., 1863, *Sermons Preached before . . . the Prince of Wales during his Tour in the East in . . . 1862*

Stanley, A. P., 1865, 'Theology of the Nineteenth Century', *Fraser's Magazine*, February: 252–68

Stanley, A. P., 1867, 'Ritualism', *Edinburgh Review*, April: 439–69

Stanley, A. P., 1870, *Essays Chiefly on Questions of Church and State from 1850 to 1870*

Stanley, A. P., 1877, *Addresses and Sermons Delivered at St. Andrew's in 1872, 1875 and 1877*

Stanley, A. P., 1879, *Addresses and Sermons Delivered during a Visit to the United States and Canada in 1878*, New York

Stanley, A. P., 1881, 'The Oxford School', *Edinburgh Review*, April: 304–50

Stanley, A. P., 1882, *Sermons on Special Occasions, Preached in Westminster Abbey*

Stanley, A. P., 1884, *Christian Institutions: Essays on Ecclesiastical Subjects*, 4th edn

Stanley, A. P., 1911, *Historical Memorials of Westminster Abbey (1868)*, rev. edn

Stevenson, J. (ed.), 1875, *Radulphi de Coggeshall Chronicon Anglicanum*, RS 66

Stow, J., 1615, *The annales, or A generall chronicle of England*

Strasdin, K., 2012, 'Empire Dressing: The Design and Realization of Queen Alexandra's Coronation Gown', *Journal of Design History* 25: 155–70

Strohm, P., 1996, 'The Trouble with Richard: The Reburial of Richard II and the Lancastrian Symbolic Strategy', *Speculum* 71: 87–111

Strong, P., and F. Strong, 1981, 'Last Will and Codicils of Henry V', *EHR* 96: 79–102

Strong, R., 2005, *Coronation: A History of Kingship and the British Monarchy*

Strong, R., 2017, *Scenes and Apparitions: The Roy Strong Diaries, 1988–2003*

Strype, J., 1822, *Ecclesiastical Memorials, relating chiefly to Religion, and the Reformation of it, the Emergencies of the Church of England, under King Henry VIII, King Edward VI, and Queen Mary the First*, Oxford

Stubbs, W., 1858, *Registrum sacrum Anglicanum: An Attempt to Exhibit the Course of Episcopal Succession in England from the Records and Chronicles of the Church*, Oxford

Stubbs, W. (ed.), 1876, *Radulfi de Diceto decani Lundoniensis Opera historica / The Historical Works of Master Ralph de Diceto, Dean of London*, RS 68

Stubbs, W. (ed.), 1879, *Historical Works of Gervase of Canterbury*, I, RS 73

Stubbs, W. (ed.), 1882, *Chronicles of the Reigns of Edward I and Edward II*, I, RS 76

Sullivan, D., 1994, *The Westminster Corridor: An Exploration of the Anglo-Saxon History of Westminster Abbey and its Nearby Lands and People*

Sullivan, D., 2006, *The Westminster Circle: The People who Lived and Worked in the Early Town of Westminster, 1066–1307*

Summerson, H., 2010, 'Tudor Antiquaries and the *Vita Ædwardi Regis*', *ASE* 38: 157–84

Sutton, A. F., and L. Visser-Fuchs, 1990, *The Hours of Richard III*, Stroud

[Sutton. J.], 1847, *A Short Account of Organs . . . from . . . King Charles the Second to the Present Time*

Sykes, N., 1959, *From Sheldon to Secker: Aspects of English Church History, 1660–1768*, Cambridge

Tait, J. A. (ed.), 1914, *Chronica Johannis de Reading et anonymi Cantuariensis, 1346–1367*, Manchester

Tanner, L. E., 1923, *Westminster School: Its Buildings and their Associations*

Tanner, L. E., 1934, *Westminster School: A History*

Tanner, L., 1973, 'The Jerusalem Chamber', *WAOP* 30: 8–11

Tatton-Brown, T., 1995, 'Westminster Abbey: Archaeological Recording at the West End of the Church', *Antiquaries Journal* 75: 171–88

Tatton-Brown, T., 2000, *Lambeth Palace: A History of the Archbishops of Canterbury and their Houses*

Tatton-Brown, T., 2007, 'The Former Head Master's House, 19 Dean's Yard, Westminster School', unpublished internal report, WAL

Tatton-Brown, T., 2015, 'The Medieval and Early Tudor Topography of Westminster', in Rodwell and Tatton-Brown (eds), 2015, I, 1–22

Tatton-Brown, T., 2015–16, 'Dean's Yard Angels', *Westminster Abbey Chorister* 61: 23–4

Tatton-Brown, T., and R. Mortimer (eds), 2003, *Westminster Abbey: The Lady Chapel of Henry VII*, Woodbridge

Taylor, A. (ed.), 1858, *The Works of Symon Patrick*, Oxford

Taylor, F., and J. S. Roskell (eds), 1975, *Gesta Henrici Quinti / The Deeds of Henry V*, Oxford [text and trans.]

Taylor, S., 1989, 'The Bishops at Westminster in the Mid-Eighteenth Century', in C. Jones (ed.), *A Pillar of the Constitution: the House of Lords in British Politics, 1640–1784*, 137–64

Taylor, S., 1992, '"The Fac Totum in Ecclesiastic Affairs"? The Duke of Newcastle and the Crown's Ecclesiastical Patronage', *Albion* 24: 409–33

Taylor, S., 1998, 'Queen Caroline and the Church of England', in S. Taylor, R. Connors and C. Jones (eds), *Hanoverian Britain and Empire: Essays in Memory of Philip Lawson*, Woodbridge, 82–101

Taylor, S., 2007, 'The Clergy at the Courts of George I and George II', in M. Schaich (ed.), *Monarchy and Religion: The Transformation of Royal Culture in Eighteenth-Century Europe*, Oxford, 129–51

Taylor, T. (ed.), 1853, *The Life of Benjamin Robert Haydon, Historical Painter, from his Autobiography and Journals*

Taylor, T. F., 1991, *J. Armitage Robinson: Eccentric, Scholar and Churchman*, Cambridge

Tellechea Idígoras, J. I., 2005, 'Bartolomé Carranza: A Spanish Dominican in the England of Mary Tudor', in J. Edwards and R. Truman (eds), *Reforming Catholicism in the England of Mary Tudor: The Achievement of Friar Bartolomé Carranza*, Aldershot, 21–32

Temple, R. C., and L. M. Anstey (eds), 1936, *The Travels of Peter Mundy in Europe and Asia*, v Hakluyt Society 2nd series 78

The Times, 1937, *Crown and Empire: The Coronation of King George VI, May 12, 1937*

Thomas, G. A. (ed.), 1796, *The sermons and charges of the Right Reverend John Thomas . . . LL.D. Late Lord Bishop of Rochester, and Dean of Westminster*

Thompson, E. M. (ed.), 1902–4, *Customary of the Benedictine Monasteries of Saint Augustine, Canterbury, and Saint Peter, Westminster*, HBS 23, 28

Thornbury, W., 1873–8, *Old and New London: A Narrative of its History, its People, and its Places*

Tite, C. G. C., 2003, *The Early Records of Sir Robert Cotton's Library: Formation, Cataloguing, Use*

Tracy, C., 2003, 'The Henry VII Chapel Stalls and their Eighteenth-Century Remodelling', in Tatton-Brown and Mortimer (eds), 2003, 227–52

Van Dixhoorn, C. (ed.), 2012, *The Minutes and Papers of the Westminster Assembly, 1643–1652*, Oxford

Venables, E., 1883, 'The Choir of Westminster Abbey', *Notes and Queries* 6th series 7, 17 March, 201–3

Vicars, J., 1645, *Gods arke overtopping the worlds waves, or The third part of the Parliamentary chronicle*

Vincent, N., 2001, *The Holy Blood: King Henry III and the Westminster Blood Relic*, Cambridge

Vincent, N., 2002, 'The Pilgrimages of the Angevin Kings of England, 1154–1272', in C. Morris and P. Roberts (eds), *Pilgrimage: The English Experience from Becket to Bunyan*, Cambridge, 12–45

Vincent, W., 1792, *A discourse, addressed to the people of Great-Britain, May 13th, 1792*

Vincent, W., 1802, *A Defence of Public Education addressed to the Most Reverend the Lord Bishop of Meath*, 2nd edn

Vincent, W. St A. (ed.), 1817, *Sermons on Faith, Doctrines, and Public Duties by the Very Reverend William Vincent, D.D. Late Dean of Westminster*

WA Commission, 1890–91, 'First [Final] Report of the Royal Commission . . . [on] the Present Want of Space for Monuments in Westminster Abbey', *PP* 44: 575–731

Walcot, C., 2010, '"Time enobles, or degrades each line": Monuments to James Craggs, Father and Son, c.1721–27', *Church Times* 25: 133–47

Walker, G., 2010, 'When did "the Medieval" End? Retrospection, Foresight and the End(s) of the English Middle Ages', in E. Treharne and G. Walker, with W. Green (eds), *The Oxford Handbook of Medieval Literature in English*, Oxford, 725–38

Walpole, H., 1985, *Memoirs of King George II*, ed. J. Brooke, New Haven, Conn., and London

Warmstry, T., 1641, *A convocation speech . . . against images, altars, crosses, the new Canons, and the Oath, &c.*

Warmstry, T., 1658, *The baptized Turk*

Warwick, C., 1988, *George and Marina: The Duke and Duchess of Kent*

Wayment, H., 1981, 'The East Window of St Margaret's Westminster', *AJ* 61: 292–301

Weber, W., 1989, 'The 1784 Handel Commemoration as a Political Ritual', *JBS* 28: 43–69

Webster, T., 2011, 'Preaching and Parliament, 1640–1659' in P. McCullough, H. Adlington and E. Rhatigan (eds), *The Oxford Handbook of the Early Modern Sermon*, Oxford, 404–20

Weever, J., 1631, *Ancient funerall monuments within the vnited monarchie of Great Britaine, Ireland, and the islands adiacent*

Welldon, J. E. C., 1915, *Recollections and Reflections*

Weston, H., 1554, *Oratio pia, & erudita pro statu illustrissimorum principum Philippi & Mariæ, regis & reginæ Angliæ Franciæ &c. ut deus eos in multos annos conseruet, & illustrissimam reginam faciat pulchra prole letam matrem*

Weston, H., 1555, *A prayer made by the deane of Westminster, and delyuered to the chyldren of ye Queenes Maiesties gramer scole there, and sayd by them dayly, morninge, and euenyng, for her Maiestye*

Wheeler-Bennett, J.W., 1965, *King George VI: His Life and Reign*

Whiston, W., 1748, *Historical memoirs of the life and writings of Dr. Samuel Clarke*, 3rd edn

Whiston, W., 1749–50, *Memoirs of the life and writings of Mr. William Whiston . . . written by himself*

White, A., 1985, 'Classical Learning and the Early Stuart Renaissance', *CM* 1: 20–33

White, A., 1989, 'Westminster Abbey in the Early Seventeenth Century: A Powerhouse of Ideas', *CM* 4: 16–53

Whitelock, D., with D. C. Douglas and S. I. Tucker (eds), 1961, *The Anglo-Saxon Chronicle: A Revised Translation*

Widmore, R., 1751, *An history of the church of St. Peter, Westminster, commonly called Westminster Abbey. Chiefly from manuscript authorities*

Wilcocks, J., 1722, *A sermon preach'd before the lords spiritual and temporal in parliament assembled, at the Collegiate Church of St. Peter's Westminster, on Monday November 5. 1722*

Wilcocks, J., 1797, *Roman conversations; or A short description of the antiquities of Rome*, 2nd edn

Wilkinson, J., 2006, *The Coronation Chair and the Stone of Destiny*

Wilkinson, J., and C. S. Knighton, 2010, *Crown and Cloister: The Royal Story of Westminster Abbey*

Williams, A., and G. H. Martin (eds), 1992, *Domesday Book: A Complete Translation*

Williams, F. (ed.), 1869, *Memoirs and Correspondence of Francis Atterbury, D.D., Bishop of Rochester*

Williams, J., 1625, *Great Britains Salomon: A sermon preached at the magnificent funerall, of the most high and might king, Iames*

Williamson, M., 2016, 'Queen Mary I, Tallis's *O sacrum convivium* and a Latin Litany', *Early Music* 44: 251–70

Williamson, P., 1993, 'The Doctrinal Politics of Stanley Baldwin', in M. Bentley (ed.), *Public and Private Doctrine: Essays in British History Presented to Maurice Cowling*, Cambridge, 181–208

Williamson, P., 2007, 'The Monarchy and Public Values, 1900–1953', in Olechnowicz (ed.), 2007, 223–57

Williamson, P., 2013, 'National Days of Prayer: The Churches, the State and Public Worship in Britain, 1899–1957', *EHR* 128: 323–66

Willson, F. M. G., 1993, *A Strong Supporting Cast: The Shaw Lefevres, 1789–1936*, London, and Atlantic Highlands, NJ

Wilson, C., 1990, 'The Tomb of Henry IV and the Holy Oil of St Thomas of Canterbury', in E. Fernie and P. Crossley (eds), *Medieval Architecture and its Intellectual Context: Studies in Honor of Peter Kidson*, London and Ronceverte, 181–90

Wilson, C., 1995, 'The Designer of Henry VII's Chapel, Westminster Abbey', in B. J. Thompson (ed.), *The Reign of Henry VII. Proceedings of the 1993 Harlaxton Conference*, Harlaxton Medieval Studies 5, Stamford, 133–56

Wilson, C., 1997, 'Rulers, Artificers and Shoppers: Richard II's Remodelling of Westminster Hall, 1393–99', in Gordon, Monnas and Elam (eds), 1997, 33–59

Wilson, C., 2002, 'The Royal Lodgings of Edward III at Windsor Castle: Form, Function, Representation', in *Windsor: Medieval Archaeology, Art and Architecture of the Thames Valley*, BAACT 25, Leeds, 15–94

Wilson, C., 2008, 'Calling the Tune? The Involvement of Henry III in the Design of the Abbey Church at Westminster', *JBAA* 161: 59–93

Wilson, C., 2010, 'The Chapter-House of Westminster Abbey: Harbinger of a New Dispensation in English Architecture?', in Rodwell and Mortimer (eds), 2010, 40–65

Wilson, C., et al. 1986, *Westminster Abbey*, New Bell's Cathedral Guides

Wilson, D. M., 1985, *The Bayeux Tapestry*

Wilson, J. F., 1969, *Pulpit in Parliament: Puritanism during the English Civil Wars, 1640–1648*, Princeton

Winterbottom, M., and M. Lapidge (eds), 2012, *The Early Lives of St Dunstan*, Oxford [text and trans.]

Winterbottom, M., and R. M. Thomson (eds), 2007, *William of Malmesbury, 'Gesta pontificum Anglorum' / The History of the English Bishops*, Oxford [I: text and trans.; II: commentary]

Witheridge, J., 2013, *Excellent Dr Stanley: The Life of Dean Stanley of Westminster*, Wilby, Norwich

Wolfe, B., 1981, *Henry VI*

Wolffe, J., 2003, 'The People's King: The Crowd and the Media at the Funeral of Edward VII, May 1910', *CH* 8: 123–30

Wolffe, J., 2004, 'National Occasions at St Paul's since 1800', in Keene, Burns and Saint (eds), 2004, 381–91

Wolffe, J., 2010, 'Protestantism, Monarchy and the Defence of Christian Britain, 1887–2005', in C. G. Brown and M. Snape (eds), *Secularisation in the Christian World: Essays in Honour of Hugh McLeod*, Farnham, 57–74

Woodman, F., 2015, 'Edward the Confessor's Church at Westminster: An Alternative View' in Rodwell and Tatton-Brown (eds), 2015, I, 61–8

Woodward, J., 1997, *The Theatre of Death: The Ritual Management of Royal Funerals in Renaissance England, 1570–1625*, Woodbridge

Worden, B., 1994, 'Ben Jonson among the Historians', in K. Sharpe and P. Lake (eds), *Culture and Politics in Early Stuart England*, Basingstoke, 67–90

Wordsworth, C., 1863, *Remarks on the Proposed Admission of the Rev. Dr. Stanley to the Place of Dean in the Collegiate Church of St. Peter, Westminster*

Worsley, G., 1993, 'Drawn to a Find', *Country Life* 197: 100–01

Wren, C. (ed.), 1750, *Parentalia: or, Memoirs of the family of the Wrens; viz. of Mathew Bishop of Ely, Christopher Dean of Windsor, &c. but chiefly of Sir Christopher Wren, late Surveyor-General of the Royal Buildings*

Wren Society, 1934, *Designs . . . for Westminster Abbey, the New Dormitory . . .*, Wren Society 11, Oxford

Wyatt, M., 2005, *The Italian Encounter with England: A Cultural Politics of Translation*, Cambridge

Wylie, J. H., and W. T. Waugh, 1914–29, *The Reign of Henry V*, Cambridge

Ziegler, P., 1985, *Mountbatten: The Official Biography*

Ziegler, P., 2010, *Edward Heath: The Authorized Biography*

Illustrations and Photograph Acknowledgements

Illustrations have been provided by the owners or custodians of works unless otherwise indicated. Additional credit lines are likewise listed below.

Endpapers see **43** below.

page i see **35** below.

page ii The west front of Westminster Abbey. Photo: © Dean and Chapter of Westminster.

page iii see **36** below.

pages viii–ix Floor plan of Westminster Abbey by Andrew Barker.

pages x–xi Ground plan of Westminster Abbey and its precinct by Andrew Barker.

1 (*page xii*) Aerial view of central London. Photo: Getty Images.

2 (*page xvi*) Commonwealth Day service in Westminster Abbey, 2018. Photo: © Dean and Chapter of Westminster.

3 (*page xvii*) Battle of Britain service in Westminster Abbey, 2017. Photo: © Dean and Chapter of Westminster.

4 (*page xviii*) Burial of the ashes of Stephen Hawking in Westminster Abbey, 2018. Photo: © Dean and Chapter of Westminster.

5 (*page xx*) The Queen's Diamond Jubilee Galleries, Westminster Abbey. Photo: © Dean and Chapter of Westminster.

6 (*page xxi*) The Weston Tower, Westminster Abbey. Photo: © Dean and Chapter of Westminster.

7 (*page xxiv*) St Peter, detail from the Westminster Retable, 13th century, Westminster Abbey, The Queen's Diamond Jubilee Galleries, WA 0881. Photo: © Dean and Chapter of Westminster.

8 (*page 3*) Wedding of Prince William and Catherine Middleton in Westminster Abbey, 2011. Photo: Getty Images.

9 (*page 5*) William the Conqueror, miniature from Matthew Paris, *Flores historiarum*, 13th century. Chetham's Library, Manchester, MS 6712 (A.6.89), f. 123v. Photo: Bridgeman Images.

10 (*page 8*) Vigil at the grave of the Unknown Warrior in Westminster Abbey, 2016. Photo: © Dean and Chapter of Westminster.

11 (*page 10*) Westminster Abbey church, detail from the Bayeux Tapestry, 11th century. Musée de la Tapisserie, Bayeux. Photo: Bridgeman Images.

12 (*page 12*) Map of Westminster and London in the Anglo-Saxon period by Jeff Edwards. Based on Tracy Wellman, 'London, *c*.800', in Derek Keene, Arthur Burns and Andrew Saint (eds), *St Paul's: The Cathedral Church of London, 604–2004*, Yale University Press, 2004, p. 6, fig. 3.

13 (*page 13*) The 'Palace of Westminster Sword', late 8th century. Jewel Tower, Westminster. Photo: Cecilia Mackay.

14 (*page 15*) King Edgar's purported charter of 951, returning to Westminster lands originally granted by King Offa, 10th century. Westminster Abbey Muniments, WAM V. Photo: © Dean and Chapter of Westminster.

15 (*page 18*) St Dunstan, drawing possibly by Dunstan himself in St Dunstan's Classbook, 10th century. Bodleian Library, Oxford, 20 Auct. F.4.32, f. 1. Photo: The Bodleian Library, University of Oxford.

16 (*page 19*) Opening of the book of Psalms, from the Bosworth Psalter, fourth quarter of the 10th century. British Library, London, Add. MS 37517, f. 4r. Photo: © British Library Board. All Rights Reserved. Bridgeman Images.

17 (*page 21*) Silver penny of Aethelred II, London mint, early 11th century. Fitzwilliam Museum, Cambridge. Photo: By permission of the Syndics of the Fitzwilliam Museum, University of Cambridge. Bridgeman Images.

18 (*page 23*) Edward the Confessor, detail from the Bayeux Tapestry, 11th century. Musée de la Tapisserie, Bayeux. Photo: Bridgeman Images.

19 (*page 26*) Charter diploma of Edward the Confessor, granting land at Wheathampstead to the abbey, 1060. Hertfordshire Record Office, D/Elw Z 22/4, BAFacs., no. 14.

20 (*page 28*) Anglo-Saxon door, mid-11th century, Westminster Abbey, chapter house vestibule. Photo: © Dean and Chapter of Westminster.

21 (*page 29*) Map of England showing the estates of Westminster Abbey, 1086, by Jeff Edwards. Based on Barbara F. Harvey, 'The Demesne Manors of Westminster Abbey in 1086', in *Westminster Abbey and its Estates in the Middle Ages*, Clarendon Press, 1977.

22 (*page 31*) The abbey church of Jumièges, Normandy, France. Photo: Hemis / Alamy.

23 (*page 33*)   David Gentleman, *The Construction of Westminster Abbey*, 1987. Photo: © Dean and Chapter of Westminster.

24 (*page 36*)   The death of Edward the Confessor, detail from the Bayeux Tapestry, 11th century. Musée de la Tapisserie, Bayeux. Photo: Bridgeman Images.

25 (*page 37*)   The coronation of Harold II, detail from the Bayeux Tapestry, 11th century. Musée de la Tapisserie, Bayeux. Photo: Bridgeman Images.

26 (*page 40*)   Westminster Hall, interior. Photo: Shutterstock.

27 (*page 42*)   Reconstruction of Westminster Abbey and its environs, *c.*1100, by Terry Ball and Richard Gem, Westminster Abbey Library. Photo: © Dean and Chapter of Westminster.

28 (*page 44*)   Henry III, miniature from *Historia Anglorum*, 1250–59. British Library, London, Royal MS 14 C VII, f. 9. Photo: © British Library Board. All Rights Reserved. Bridgeman Images.

29 (*page 47*)   Charter of Henry I, taking the abbey into his protection, 1100. British Library, London, Cotton Charter VII 8. Photo © British Library Board. All Rights Reserved. Bridgeman Images.

30 (*page 49*)   The translation of the body of Edward, miniature from Matthew Paris, *La Estoire de Seint Aedward le rei*, *c.*1250–60. Cambridge University Library, MS Ee.3.59, f. 36r. Photo: © Cambridge University Library.

31 (*page 53*)   Pilgrims at the tomb of St Edward, miniature from Matthew Paris, *La Estoire de Seint Aedward le rei*, *c.*1250–60. Cambridge University Library, MS Ee.3.59, f. 30r. Photo: © Cambridge University Library.

32 (*page 57*)   View of the east end of Westminster Abbey, from the choir. Photo: © Dean and Chapter of Westminster.

33 (*page 59*)   The chapter house, Westminster Abbey. Photo: © Dean and Chapter of Westminster.

34–6 (*pages 60–61*)   Medieval tiles from the pavement of the chapter house, Westminster Abbey. Photo: © Dean and Chapter of Westminster.

37 (*pages 62–3*)   The Westminster Retable, 13th century, Westminster Abbey, The Queen's Diamond Jubilee Galleries, WA 0881. Photo: © Dean and Chapter of Westminster.

38 (*page 65*)   Henry III carrying the Holy Blood relic to Westminster, miniature from Matthew Paris, *Chronica majora*, mid-13th century. Corpus Christi College, Cambridge, MS 16 II, f. 216r. Photo: The Parker Library, Corpus Christi College, Cambridge.

39 (*page 66*)   Wall-paintings on the south wall of the south transept, Westminster Abbey, depicting Christ with St Thomas the Apostle, and St Christopher carrying the Christ Child, late 1260s(?). Photo: © Dean and Chapter of Westminster.

40 (*page 69*)   The shrine of St Edward the Confessor, Westminster Abbey. Photo: © Dean and Chapter of Westminster.

41 (*page 71*)   Effigy of Eleanor of Castile, 1291, Westminster Abbey. Photo: © Dean and Chapter of Westminster.

42 (*page 73*)   Tomb of Prince Edmund Crouchback, 1st Earl of Lancaster, *c.*1296–1301, Westminster Abbey. Photo: © Dean and Chapter of Westminster.

43 (*page 75*)   The Cosmati mosaic pavement, 1268, Westminster Abbey. Photo: © Dean and Chapter of Westminster.

44 (*page 78*)   The coronation of a king, miniature from the Litlyngton Missal, 1383–4. Westminster Abbey Library, MS 37, f. 206r. Photo: © Dean and Chapter of Westminster.

45 (*page 80*)   The coronation chair, 1300, Westminster Abbey . Photo: © Dean and Chapter of Westminster.

46 (*pages 84–5*)   Map of Westminster Abbey and its environs, *c.*1300, by Giles Darkes.

47 (*page 88*)   The Lady Chapel, interior, Westminster Abbey. Photo: © Dean and Chapter of Westminster.

48 (*page 95*)   Benedictines and their choirboys, miniature from John Lydgate, Lives of St Edmund and Fremund, 1434–9(?). British Library, London, Harley MS 2278, f. 6r. Photo: © British Library Board. All Rights Reserved. Bridgeman Images.

49 (*page 98*)   Tomb of Edward III, before 1395, Westminster Abbey. Photo: © Dean and Chapter of Westminster.

50 (*page 99*)   Modern digital reconstruction of the high altar of St Stephen's Chapel, Palace of Westminster, as it would have appeared *c.*1520. Photo: By kind permission of Virtual St Stephens, www.virtualststephens.org.uk. © University of York, St Stephen's Chapel Westminster Project, 2017.

51 (*page 101*)   Tomb of Simon Langham, 1389–95, Westminster Abbey. Photo: © Dean and Chapter of Westminster.

52 (*page 102*)   Armorial bearing of Abbot Nicholas Litlyngton, decoration in the margin of the Litlyngton Missal, 1383–4. Westminster Abbey Library, MS 37, f. 289r. Photo: © Dean and Chapter of Westminster.

53 (*page 103*)   The Jerusalem Chamber, Westminster Abbey. Photo: © Dean and Chapter of Westminster.

54 (*page 105*)   Opening folio of William Sudbury's defence of the Holy Blood relic, 1380s or 1390s. Longleat House, Warminster, MS 38, f. 256v. Photo: © Longleat House, Warminster. Reproduced by Permission of the Marquess of Bath.

55 (*page 107*)   Historiated initial depicting a scene of mourners and monks, from the Litlyngton Missal, 1383–4. Westminster Abbey Library, MS 37, f. 326r. Photo: © Dean and Chapter of Westminster.

56 (*page 109*)   Miniature of a king and queen enthroned, from the *Liber regalis*, late 14th century. Westminster Abbey Library, MS 38, f. 47r. Photo: © Dean and Chapter of Westminster.

57 (*page 112*)   Anon., portrait of Richard II, later 1390s, Westminster Abbey. Photo: © Dean and Chapter of Westminster.

58 (*page 115*)   William Caxton, advertisement for the Sarum Ordinal (or Sarum Pye), *c.*1477, Bodleian Library, Oxford, G e.37, recto. Photo: The Bodleian Library, University of Oxford.

59 (*page 118*)   The coronation of Edward I, miniature from *Flores historiarum*, 13th century. Chetham's Library, Manchester, MS 6712 (A.6.89), f. 247v. Photo: Bridgeman Images.

60 (*page 119*)   Effigy of Catherine of Valois, 1437, Westminster Abbey, The Queen's Diamond Jubilee Galleries, WA 0888. Photo: © Dean and Chapter of Westminster.

94 (*page 191*) Anon., after Wenceslas Hollar, *Tootehill fields*, *c.*1643–50. Photo: AQL / Alamy.

95 (*page 193*) Robert White, portrait of Peter Heylyn, 1681. Photo: © National Portrait Gallery, London.

96 (*page 194*) *The rising of the prentices and seamen on Southwark side to assault the Archbishop of Canterbury's house at Lambeth*, illustration from John Vicars, *A sight of ye trans-actions of these latter yeares* (1646). British Library, London, G.4092, p. 5. Photo: © British Library Board. All Rights Reserved. Bridgeman Images.

97 (*page 197*) Wenceslas Hollar, *Ciuitatis Westmonasteriensis pars (The City of Westminster)* (detail), 1647. Photo: AQL / Alamy.

98 (*page 199*) Thomas Simon, seal of the Governors of the School and Almshouses, 1649. Westminster Abbey Muniments, WAM 3922. Photo: © Dean and Chapter of Westminster.

99 (*page 201*) Robert Walker, portrait of General Richard Deane, *c.*1653. National Maritime Museum, London. Photo: © Royal Museums Greenwich.

100 (*page 204*) Detail of the map of the parish of St Margaret, from John Strype's *A Survey of the Cities of London and Westminster* (1720), Book 6, p. 63. Photo: Antiqua Print Gallery / Alamy.

101 (*page 205*) John Riley, *Richard Busby and a Pupil*, after 1660. Christ Church, Oxford. Photo: By permission of the Governing Body of Christ Church, Oxford.

102 (*pages 208–9*) Dirck Stoop, *Coronation Procession of Charles II to Westminster from the Tower of London, 22 April 1661* (detail), 1662. Museum of London. Photo: Bridgeman Images.

103 (*page 210*) Sir Peter Lely, portrait of John Fell, John Dolben and Richard Allestree, after 1660. Christ Church, Oxford. Photo: By permission of the Governing Body of Christ Church, Oxford.

104 (*page 213*) The coronation of James II in 1685, illustration from Francis Sandford, *The history of the coronation of the most high, most mighty, and most excellent monarch, James II* (1687). Photo: © Dean and Chapter of Westminster.

105 (*page 214*) The vestments and regalia used at the coronation of James II, illustration from Francis Sandford, *The history of the coronation of the most high, most mighty, and most excellent monarch, James II* (1687). Photo: © Dean and Chapter of Westminster.

106 (*page 215*) Anointing spoon, 12th century(?), and ampulla, 1661. Royal Collection Trust. © Her Majesty Queen Elizabeth II 2019. Photo: reproduced by permission of the Crown.

107 (*page 217*) Romeyn de Hooghe, *The Coronation of King William and Queen Mary of England in Westminster Abbey*, 1689. Royal Collection Trust. Photo: © Her Majesty Queen Elizabeth II, 2019. Bridgeman Images.

108 (*page 219*) Henry Purcell, 'In the midst of life we are in death', autograph manuscript of the Second Funeral Sentence for Queen Mary, 1695, in a book of anthems collected by William Flackton. British Library, London, Add. MS 30931, f. 81v. Photo: © British Library Board. All Rights Reserved. Bridgeman Images.

109 (*page 222*) F. Mackenzie, *The choir of Westminster Abbey* (detail), from R. Ackermann's *The History of the Abbey Church of St. Peter's Westminster* (1812). Photo: © Dean and Chapter of Westminster.

110 (*page 224*) Canaletto (Giovanni Antonio Canal), *Westminster Abbey with a Procession of the Knights of the Bath* (detail), 1749. Westminster Abbey (not on public display). Photo: © Dean and Chapter of Westminster.

111 (*page 226*) John Dart, view of the nave, illustration from *Westmonasterium, or The history and antiquities of the Abbey Church of St. Peters Westminster* (1723). Photo: © Dean and Chapter of Westminster.

112 (*page 229*) Entry in a Chapter Act book recording fines levied against nine of the abbey's prebendaries, 1797. Westminster Abbey Muniments, Chapter Act book XIII, f. 133. Photo: © Dean and Chapter of Westminster.

113 (*page 230*) Anon., after Godfrey Kneller, portrait of Dean Francis Atterbury, 1713, Westminster Abbey (not on public display). Photo: © Dean and Chapter of Westminster.

114 (*page 236*) Joshua Reynolds, portrait of Dean John Thomas wearing the robes of the Dean of the Most Honourable Order of the Bath, *c.*1780. Photo: Courtesy of Sotheby's, Inc. © 2015.

115 (*page 237*) Dutch school, *The Choir of Westminster Abbey*, *c.*1700. Photo: © Dean and Chapter of Westminster.

116 (*page 239*) Pages from a Chapter Act book detailing the decay of the Lady Chapel and expenditure on the fabric, and petitioning for restoration funds, 1807. Westminster Abbey Muniments, Chapter Act book XIII, ff. 456–7. Photo: © Dean and Chapter of Westminster.

117 (*page 242*) George Lewis, engraving after Frederick Nash, *Procession of the Knights of the Most Honorable Order of the Bath in Westminster Abbey in 1812* (detail), 1814. British Library, London, Maps K.Top.24.4, ff. 1–3. Photo: © British Library Board. All Rights Reserved. Bridgeman Images.

118 (*page 243*) James Watts, wooden model for the Hanoverian burial vault under the Lady Chapel, 1818, Westminster Abbey, The Queen's Diamond Jubilee Galleries, WA 1037. Photo: © Dean and Chapter of Westminster.

119 (*page 245*) George Frideric Handel, 'Zadok the Priest', autograph manuscript of a coronation anthem for George II, 1727. British Library, London, MS R.M.20.h.5, ff. 2v–3r. Photo: © British Library Board. All Rights Reserved. Bridgeman Images.

120 (*page 246*) Frederick Christian Lewis, *The Coronation of George IV in 1821*, 1824. London Metropolitan Archives, City of London. Photo: Bridgeman Images.

121 (*page 247*) Richard Newton, *Frontispiece to the Wax Work and Monumental Records in Westminster Abbey*, 1792. British Museum, London, 1868,0808.6159. Photo: © The Trustees of the British Museum.

122 (*page 251*) Pietro Fabris, *Proposal for Westminster Abbey by Nicholas Hawksmoor*, *c.*1734–40. Westminster Abbey (not on public display). Photo: © Dean and Chapter of Westminster.

123 (*page 252*) Ravenhill, *The Gatehouse, Westminster, looking towards Tothill Street*, 1836. Illustration from the *Gentleman's Magazine* 5 (March 1836). Photo: © Dean and Chapter of Westminster.

124 (*page 253*) Samuel Scott, *The Building of Westminster Bridge* (detail), *c.*1742. Metropolitan Museum of Art, New York. Purchase, Charles B. Curtis Fund and Joseph Pulitzer Bequest, 1944. Image © The Metropolitan Museum of Art.

125 (*page 254*) Frontispiece and title-page to Thomas Boreman, *Westminster Abbey*, II (1742). Photo: courtesy of Sotheby's, Inc. © 2014.

126 (*page 255*) Poets' Corner, Westminster Abbey. Photo: © Dean and Chapter of Westminster.

127 (*page 256*) Louis-François Roubiliac, monument to Lieutenant General William Hargrave, 1757, Westminster Abbey. Photo: © Dean and Chapter of Westminster.

128 (*page 257*) Thomas Rowlandson, *Death and the Antiquaries*, 1816, illustration from *The English Dance of Death* (1814–16), vol. 2. Society of Antiquaries of London. Photo: Bridgeman Images.

129 (*page 258*) Adrien Carpentiers, portrait of Louis-François Roubiliac, 1762. Photo: © National Portrait Gallery, London.

130 (*page 262*) Ticket for the coronation of George III, 1761. Private collection. Photo: Christie's Images / Bridgeman Images.

131 (*page 262*) Ticket for the coronation of George IV, 1821. Photo: © Museum of London.

132 (*page 264*) Charles Walter Radclyffe, *Westminster School: Interior of the Dormitory*, 1845. London Metropolitan Archives, Metropolitan Prints Collection, Westminster HC 41.1 10465.

133 (*pages 266–7*) Map of Westminster Abbey and its environs, from William Faden, *Horwood's Plan of the Cities of London and Westminster* [. . .] *Shewing Every House* (detail), 4th edn (1819). British Library, London, Cartographic Items, Maps, 33.e.24. Photo: © British Library Board. All Rights Reserved. Bridgeman Images.

134 (*page 268*) Edward Edwards, *An Interior View of Westminster Abbey on the Commemoration of Handel, Taken from the Manager's Box* (detail), *c.*1790. Yale Center for British Art, Paul Mellon Collection.

135 (*page 270*) Thomas Picken, *The Destruction of Both Houses of Parliament as seen from the Surrey Side* (detail), 1834. Private collection. Photo: Peter Jackson / Bridgeman Images.

136 (*page 272*) Lord John Thynne, canon of Westminster and sub-dean, mid-19th century. Photo: © Dean and Chapter of Westminster.

137 (*page 276*) John Bluck after Frederick Mackenzie, *The Choir of Westminster Abbey* (detail), 1812. Private collection. Photo: The Stapleton Collection / Bridgeman Images.

138 (*page 277*) Leighton Bros., *The Choir of Westminster Abbey* (detail), illustration from *Old England: A Pictorial Museum of Regal, Ecclesiastical, Baronial, Municipal and Popular Antiquities* (first published 1845–6). Photo: Lebrecht Music & Arts / Alamy.

139 (*page 278*) George Koberwein, portrait of Edward Blore, 1868. Photo: © National Portrait Gallery, London.

140 (*page 280*) George Gilbert Scott, carte-de-visite, 1860s. Photo: © National Portait Gallery, London.

141 (*page 283*) Thomas Cooke, *Map of the City and Liberty of Westminster* (1847), detail. British Library, London, Cartographic Items, Maps, 3495.(56.). Photo: © British Library Board. All Rights Reserved. Bridgeman Images.

142 (*page 285*) Richard Norman Shaw (with figure drawings by Henry Holiday), memorial window to Isambard Kingdom Brunel, manufactured by Heaton, Butler and Bayne, 1868, Westminster Abbey. Photo: © Dean and Chapter of Westminster.

143 (*page 287*) William Burges, *Proposed Reconstruction of the Shrine of Edward the Confessor*, 1852. Photo: © RIBA Collections.

144 (*page 288*) The vault of the chapter house, Westminster Abbey. Photo: © Dean and Chapter of Westminster.

145 (*page 291*) The high altar and the Cosmati pavement, Westminster Abbey. Photo: © Dean and Chapter of Westminster.

146 (*page 292*) The tympanum of the north door, Westminster Abbey. Photo: © Dean and Chapter of Westminster.

147 (*page 294*) George Hayter, *The Coronation of Queen Victoria, 28 June 1838*, 1839. Royal Collection Trust. © Her Majesty Queen Elizabeth II, 2019. Photo: Bridgeman Images.

148 (*page 298*) Heinrich von Angeli (attrib.), portrait of Dean Arthur Penrhyn Stanley, 1877. Westminster Abbey (not on public display). Photo: © Dean and Chapter of Westminster.

149 (*page 302*) The abbey choirboys with Sir Frederick Bridge, *c.*1908–9. Westminster Abbey Library. Photo: © Dean and Chapter of Westminster.

150 (*page 305*) Joseph Edgar Boehm, tomb effigy of Dean Stanley, 1884, Westminster Abbey. Photo: © Dean and Chapter of Westminster.

151 (*page 306*) George Gilbert Scott, *Scheme for a Cloister Adjacent to the Chapter House*, *c.*1873, published in *American Architect and Building News*, 29 February 1884. Photo: © RIBA Collections.

152 (*page 307*) Anon., engraving depicting the proposed site of Cleopatra's Needle in Parliament Square, 1878. Photo: World History Archive / TopFoto.

153 (*page 310*) William Wyllie and Henry Brewer, *A Bird's-Eye View of London as seen from a Balloon*, illustration from *The Graphic* (1884). Private collection. Photo: Christie's Images / Bridgeman Images.

154 (*page 314*) Coffin prepared for the Unknown Warrior in Westminster Abbey, 1920. Photo: © Imperial War Museum, London, Q 31514.

155 (*page 319*) Edwin Austin Abbey, *The Coronation of Edward VII*, *c.*1902–7. Royal Collection Trust. © Her Majesty Queen Elizabeth II, 2019. Photo: Bridgeman Images.

156 (*page 320*) Thomas Brock, statue of William Ewart Gladstone, 1903, Westminster Abbey. Photo: © Dean and Chapter of Westminster.

157 (*page 321*) Floral tributes laid in Westminster Abbey for the actor Sir Henry Irving, 1905. Photo: © Dean and Chapter of Westminster.

158 (*page 322*)   John Gaye, *Perspective View looking South West of the Proposal for the Imperial Monumental Halls and Tower at Westminster by John Pollard Seddon and Edward Beckitt Lamb* (detail), 1904. Photo: RIBA Collections.

159 (*page 324*)   John Henry Frederick Bacon, *View from the Presbytery of Westminster Abbey looking into the South Transept*, 1911. Photo: © Museum of London.

160 (*page 325*)   George V and Queen Mary progress through London on the day after their coronation, 23 June 1911. Photo: Popperfoto / Getty Images.

161 (*page 327*)   The tomb of Elizabeth I in Westminster Abbey, protected by sandbags, *c.*1916. Photo: © Dean and Chapter of Westminster.

162 (*page 331*)   The gravestone of the Unknown Warrior in Westminster Abbey, laid in 1921. Photo: © Dean and Chapter of Westminster.

163 (*page 333*)   Public viewing of the grave of the Unknown Warrior in Westminster Abbey, 1920. Photo: © Dean and Chapter of Westminster.

164 (*page 337*)   Dean Paul de Labilliere viewing bomb damage in the cloister of Westminster Abbey on 12 May 1941. Photo: Hulton Archive / Getty Images.

165 (*page 338*)   RAF march past outside Westminster Abbey after the Battle of Britain remembrance service, 16 September 1945. Photo: S&G Barratts / Empics / PA Images.

166 (*page 339*)   Hugh Easton, memorial window for those who died in the Battle of Britain, in Westminster Abbey, 1947. Photo: © Dean and Chapter of Westminster.

167 (*page 342*)   Elizabeth II arrives at Westminster Abbey on coronation day, 2 June 1953. Photo: TopFoto.

168 (*page 343*)   Elizabeth II seated, with the coronation regalia, 2 June 1953. Photo: TopFoto.

169 (*page 344*)   Map of the coronation route, issued on coronation day, 2 June 1953. Photo: Topical Press / Getty Images.

170 (*page 347*)   Plaque honouring the Indian Civil Service, 1958, Westminster Abbey, cloister. Photo: © Dean and Chapter of Westminster.

171 (*page 347*)   Dean Eric Abbott and Elizabeth II stand before a memorial stone honouring Sir Winston Churchill in Westminster Abbey, 1965. Photo: TopFoto.

172 (*page 349*)   The funeral of Earl Mountbatten of Burma in Westminster Abbey, 1979. Photo: PA Photos / TopFoto.

173 (*page 354*)   Tim Crawley, Neil Simmons, John Roberts and Andrew Tanser, statues of ten 20th-century martyrs on the west front of Westminster Abbey, 1998. Photo: © Dean and Chapter of Westminster.

174 (*page 356*)   The return of the Stone of Destiny to Scotland, 1996. Photo: PA Photos.

175 (*page 357*)   Elton John performing at the funeral of Diana, Princess of Wales, in Westminster Abbey, 1997. Photo: TopFoto.

176 (*page 362*)   Pietro Torrigiano, tomb of Henry VII and Elizabeth of York, 1518, Westminster Abbey. Photo: © Dean and Chapter of Westminster.

177 (*page 365*)   Barack Obama laying a wreath on the grave of the Unknown Warrior in Westminster Abbey, 2011. Photo: © Dean and Chapter of Westminster.

178 (*page 371*)   Benedetto da Rovezzano, angel made for the tomb of Cardinal Thomas Wolsey, 1524–9. Photo: © Victoria and Albert Museum, London.

179 (*page 375*)   Copes worn at the coronation of Charles II, 1661, and at his funeral, 1685. Westminster Abbey, The Queen's Diamond Jubilee Galleries, WA 3324 and 3327. Photo: © Dean and Chapter of Westminster.

180 (*page 376*)   The east window, St Margaret's Church, Westminster. Photo: © Dean and Chapter of Westminster.

181 (*page 379*)   The funeral of Queen Elizabeth, the Queen Mother in Westminster Abbey, 2002. Photo: © Dean and Chapter of Westminster.

182 (*page 380*)   Service at Westminster Abbey, 2016. Photo: © Dean and Chapter of Westminster.

183 (*page 382*)   The flying buttresses of the Lady Chapel, Westminster Abbey. Photo: © Dean and Chapter of Westminster.

Index

Page numbers in italics refer to illustrations and/or information in a caption; the caption to an illustration may appear on the facing, preceding or following page.

Contributors

SIR DAVID CANNADINE is Dodge Professor of History Emeritus at Princeton University, former President of the British Academy, Editor of the *Oxford Dictionary of National Biography* and Visiting Professor at the University of Oxford. His most recent book is *Victorious Century: The United Kingdom, 1800–1906* (2017).

PAUL BINSKI FBA is Professor Emeritus of the History of Medieval Art at the University of Cambridge and was Slade Professor of Art at the University of Oxford, 2006–7. His many books on English art include *Westminster Abbey and the Plantagenets* (1995), *Becket's Crown: Art and Imagination in Gothic England, 1170–1300* (2004), *Gothic Wonder: Art, Artifice and the Decorated Style, 1290–1350* (2014) and *Gothic Sculpture* (2019).

JAMES G. CLARK is Professor of History at the University of Exeter. He has written widely on the history of medieval monasteries and their contribution to religious, social and cultural life in England down to the Dissolution. His books include *A Monastic Renaissance* (2004), *The Culture of Medieval English Monasticism* (2007) and *The Benedictines in the Middle Ages* (2011).

JOE MORDAUNT CROOK CBE FBA is Emeritus Professor of Architectural History at the University of London and an Honorary Fellow of Brasenose College, Oxford. His many writings include *The Dilemma of Style* (1987), *The Rise of the Nouveaux Riches* (1999), *The Architect's Secret* (2003), *Brasenose: The Biography of an Oxford College* (2008) and *William Burges and the High Victorian Dream* (2013).

THE VERY REVEREND DR JOHN HALL KCVO was Dean of Westminster from 2006 to 2019. He taught in Hull and was then ordained in 1975 to serve in parishes in Southwark diocese before becoming director of education for the Diocese of Blackburn and a Residentiary Canon, and thereafter the Church of England's Chief Education Officer.

SIR DIARMAID MACCULLOCH is Professor Emeritus of the History of the Church at the University of Oxford. His *History of Christianity: The First Three Thousand Years* won the 2010 Cundill Prize; his latest television series was *Sex and the Church* (first shown in 2015). His biography of Thomas Cromwell appeared in 2018.

JULIA F. MERRITT is Associate Professor of History at the University of Nottingham. She has written extensively on early modern religious culture and politics. Her publications include *Imagining Early Modern London* (2001), *The Social World of Early Modern Westminster, 1525–1640* (2005) and *Westminster, 1640–1660: A Royal City in a Time of Revolution* (2013).

HENRY SUMMERSON has published extensively on crime and law enforcement in thirteenth-century England, and his two-volume history of medieval Carlisle appeared in 1993. Between 1993 and 2018 he was a Medieval Research Editor for the *Oxford Dictionary of National Biography*, latterly responsible for the entire history of Britain before 1600.

WILLIAM WHYTE is Professor of Social and Architectural History at the University of Oxford and a Fellow of St John's College. His publications include *Oxford Jackson: Architecture, Education, Status, and Style, 1835–1924* (2006), *Redbrick: A Social and Architectural History of Britain's Civic Universities* (2015) and *Unlocking the Church: The Lost Secrets of Victorian Sacred Space* (2017).